MANAGERIAL LIVES IN TRANSITION

Adult Development and Aging
K. Warner Schaie, Editor

Managerial Lives in Transition: Advancing Age and Changing Times
ANN HOWARD AND DOUGLAS W. BRAY

Longitudinal Studies of Adult Psychological Development
K. WARNER SCHAIE, EDITOR

Aging and Life Course Transitions: An Interdisciplinary Perspective
TAMARA K. HAREVEN AND KATHLEEN J. ADAMS, EDITORS

MANAGERIAL LIVES IN TRANSITION

ADVANCING AGE
AND CHANGING TIMES

Ann Howard
Douglas W. Bray

THE GUILFORD PRESS
New York   London

© 1988 The Guilford Press
A Division of Guilford Publications, Inc.
72 Spring Street, New York, N.Y. 10012

Printed in the United States of America

Last digit is print number: 9 8 7 6 5 4 3 2 1

Library of Congress Cataloging in Publication Data

Howard, Ann, 1939—
    Managerial lives in transition.

    (Adult Development and Aging)
    Bibliography: p.
    Includes index.
    1. American Telephone and Telegraph Company—
Management. 2. Executives—United States—Case
studies. 3. Organizational effectiveness—Case
studies. I. Bray, Douglas Weston. II. Title. III. Series
HE8846.A55H68   1988   658.4'09   86-18441
ISBN 0-89862-126-7

To our parents, steadfast and loving supporters
through our own advancing age and changing times
Marguerite and Lawrence Howard
Lena and Marvin Bray

ACKNOWLEDGMENT

Collection of the data on which this volume is based consumed 30 years of continuous work and the labors of hundreds of people. Several contributors devoted 5 or more years of their professional lives to the studies. As assessment center followed assessment center, interview followed interview, and the mass of qualitative material was painstakingly quantified, our efforts were sustained by a belief: This was that someday, somehow, the work would culminate in a truly important and worthy product.

This belief occasionally weakened as it seemed less and less likely that the growing mountain of data could ever be ordered and presented in a way that would do it justice. Just keeping track of the steady flow of new material was challenging, not to mention digging into the myriad interrelationships and presenting them in a single volume.

Managerial Lives in Transition is nearly entirely the achievement of Dr. Ann Howard. In addition to directing all the data analyses, she immersed herself in the social history of the times in which our participants grew up and developed. She laboriously constructed case studies combining elements of similar individuals to preserve anonymity while staying close to actual lives. Finally, she wrote nearly all of the book. Had Ann not done all this, I doubt whether anyone else would have or could have.

All of us who have put much of ourselves into this research are greatly in debt to Ann. She has proved that it was all indeed worthwhile.

Douglas W. Bray

PREFACE

Prior to the divestiture of January 1, 1984, the Bell System was the nation's largest business enterprise. All of the components of this giant of the communications industry still exist, even though many of them are now legally separate. The research described in this volume started in the Bell System through its parent, the American Telephone and Telegraph Company (AT&T), and now pertains to AT&T and the Bell regional operating companies. Since all the data reported here were collected prior to divestiture, however, we will continue to refer to the business that provided all the support and all the participants for the research as the Bell System.

The success of the Bell System's efforts to provide top-quality communications service and to operate efficiently and profitably depended heavily on the quality of its managers, of whom there were several hundred thousand. Attention, therefore, had long been paid to attracting and employing those with good potential for managerial work.

As long ago as the 1920s, researchers at AT&T had studied the relationship between performance in college, extracurricular as well as scholastic, and performance in management (Bridgman, 1930). Recruiting teams representing various segments of the Bell System visited, and still visit, colleges and universities with the goal of selecting the best available talent as management recruits. Many other persons found their way into lower-level management by promotion from the vocational ranks. Again, there was an effort to select the very best, but this was done considerably less systematically than in the case of college graduates.

Not only did AT&T make a strong effort to select the best candidates for managerial positions, but in the 1950s, the period in which the research underlying this book was begun, extensive efforts were already being devoted to management development. One aspect of this was job rotation: The individual moved from assignment to assignment, or even from department to department, every few years, particularly if that person was thought of as having a bright future.

Formal training also played a large part. Some was technical, but, in addition, much of it was intended to develop general managerial skills. Week-long courses that ran more or less continuously at off-premises locations attempted to improve managerial performance in such functions as planning and organizing and face-to-face leadership. Summer programs at institutions like Dartmouth and Williams Colleges were devoted to broadening managerial horizons, and a select group of middle managers attended 9-month programs at the University of Pennsylvania.

All of this activity rested on many untested assumptions. Those who stressed selection believed that individual characteristics present in early adulthood were the essential ingredient of later excellence in management. Those who believed in development, whether by job rotation or formal training, held that managerial characteristics could be changed or enhanced by deliberate effort. The possibility that managerial characteristics might change with age, independently of any intervention, was rarely considered. One exception was that the vague word "maturing" was frequently heard. Unfortunately, the concept was often put forward by a college recruiter when offering employment to an unimpressive applicant. The hope was that the person might come closer to the ideal when maturity arrived.

One person in a position to observe and ponder all these activities and assumptions was Robert K. Greenleaf, AT&T's director of personnel research in the 1950s. Although not himself a behavioral scientist, Greenleaf was knowledgeable in the field and often brought in top psychologists and other professionals to give seminars to and interact with senior Bell System managers. Exposure to such experts convinced Greenleaf that management developers were not alone in their ignorance. He discovered that there were remarkably few studies of adult lives, and certainly none that focused on managers. Fortunately, he had enough influence to convince the chairman of the board, Cleo Craig, that AT&T should begin an extensive study of managerial lives. Dr. Douglas W. Bray was hired to design and carry out the research.

It was decided early that the initial evaluation of managers would take place in the context of an assessment center. This method had first reached public attention 8 years before the start of the AT&T research with the publication of *Assessment of Men* (OSS, 1948), a book that detailed the use of an assessment center during World War II to select intelligence agents for the Office of Strategic Services (OSS). Bray had been much impressed by this report and found no difficulty in persuading his boss to let him use the method. Greenleaf had carefully saved a copy of a *Fortune* magazine article, "A Good Man Is Hard to Find" (1946), reviewing the OSS experience and suggesting that business would do well to give assessment centers a try.

The original plan for the research, entitled the Management Progress Study (MPS), although ambitious, was far less so that what actually developed over the next two decades. It called for assessing young managers at the beginning of their careers in management and then following them through the next few years, 8 at the most. The follow-up would be accomplished by annual interviews with both the young managers and their supervisors. At the time, no one ever imagined that the participants would be reassessed twice and followed into retirement!

By the time 8 years had elapsed, however, it became clear that questions about changes and stabilities in the MPS participants could not be answered without reassessing them. Results of a second assessment center, parallel to the original one, were needed. By this time approximately 25% of the original group had left the Bell System. Those who remained, however, were reassessed in the years 1964 to 1968, referred to as "MPS:8" since each part of the group was assessed almost exactly 8 years after the assessment in 1956 to 1960 (now referred to as "MPS:0"). Follow-up interviewing continued, although less frequently than earlier.

As the years rolled on, it became apparent that a truly unique piece of research was in progress. MPS was not merely an effort to help a large corporation do a better job of developing managers; it was an intensive, in-process study in developmental psychology, a study of almost the whole of the adult lives of its subjects. A conviction grew that MPS should go on. There was an inside joke that the researchers were working on a schedule for deathbed interviews with the participants!

In 1975, after Dr. Ann Howard had joined AT&T, we began thinking of another assessment center at the 20-year mark for the first group of managers who had entered MPS in 1956. At first it was thought that this third assessment center would be a replica of the two that had gone before. On second thought, however, this did not seem the most desirable course. The first centers had emphasized managerial abilities and motivations, but after 20 years of following each participant's career and two assessment centers, it seemed that there was little left to learn about the men as managers.

Fortunately, initial planning for the 20-year assessment began at a time when interest in the middle years of life was greatly intensifying in both the scientific and popular literature. The investigations underlying most of these publications relied of necessity on retrospective interviewing. Since the men in MPS were now in their 40s, it appeared that the study might be in a unique position to contribute to the understanding of middle life. Reliance on retrospection would be at a minimum, since the men had been interviewed often as their lives had taken shape.

The new assessment center, labeled "MPS:20," included many new dimensions and techniques relevant to the middle years. About a third of the assessment time, however, was devoted to repeating the tests, inventories, and projective instruments administered 20 and 12 years previously. Thus a considerable amount of continuity was preserved.

The confidentiality of information from and about the participants at all stages of MPS has always been scrupulously preserved. The men were promised at the outset that nothing about them as individuals would ever be revealed; other managers interviewed about the participants were guaranteed that their remarks would not get back to the participants. Men in the study are identified by code number, and study records are kept in a locked library.

During the first 20 years of the study, the participants received no feedback. This was true even though many were anxious to learn their personal strengths and weaknesses as revealed at the assessment centers. The researchers feared, of course, that such self-knowledge might influence the individual and so contaminate the study. It was not until the 20-year assessment that the participants were given the information that had been so long withheld. This was done as part of one of the MPS:20 assessment exercises, the Feedback Interview, in which each participant was shown his percentile scores on the motivational and attitudinal inventories he had completed at MPS:0, MPS:8, and MPS:20, and was asked to comment on them.

In the spring of 1977, we presented the design of the MPS:20 assessment to a conference of personnel officers from the Bell System companies. The reaction was enthusiastic, but an important question was immediately raised. This was whether managers currently beginning their careers were not possibly different in their abilities and motivations from their counterparts two decades earlier. MPS had led to improvements in management selection and development in the 1950s and 1960s, including the use of assessment centers (especially for promotion from the nonmanagement to managerial ranks) and the development of high-risk, high-reward career development programs to provide early challenge for new college graduates. Would not parallel research on a sample of the young managers of the late 1970s provide additional valuable information for these and other programs?

The desirability of such a study had, in fact, been discussed from time to time by us and others. Not only would it serve the purposes just outlined, but it would be an invaluable complement to MPS. It would provide another cohort of participants widely separated in time, which is necessary in longitudinal research to help distinguish individual developmental from societal changes.

Although such a new study was extremely attractive, it had never been formally proposed, since it was believed that a chronically tight budget would certainly rule it out. Fortunately, the new head of our division, Richard D. McCormick, who was attending the conference during his second week on his new assignment, saw the contribution the study could make. He proposed it formally to top management, and we began the second longitudinal study a few months later.

The new research, called the Management Continuity Study (MCS), began like MPS with a 3-day assessment center, but approximately 20 years later (1977 to 1982). Although the assessment processes were identical or highly similar to those in MPS, the participants were quite different, even though the criteria for selecting them remained the same. In MPS all the managers were white males. Now nearly half of the participants were women, and about one-third were members of minority groups. Follow-up interviewing of those assessed has now been going on for several years, and a reassessment is planned.

The AT&T research thus consists of two parallel longitudinal studies separated by about 20 years. Bray was their director until his retirement from AT&T in 1983. At that time Howard, who had served as associate director, assumed the position as director of MPS and MCS.

At any point in time there are always more data at hand than can be analyzed, with more rolling in every month. This book, therefore, is not a final report, even of MPS. With the initial round of MCS assessments completed, however, this seemed an appropriate time to carry the MPS story forward and to make initial comparisons with MCS.

The multiple assessment centers, the extensive follow-up interviews, the content analyses and coding of many written documents, the complicated data analyses, and the essential secretarial support involved in our research have consumed the labors of many people. No exact count is practicable, but certainly no fewer than 500 individuals have contributed. Many of these have been from academe, employed on a temporary or part-time basis. Graduate student interns have been a valuable resource, to say nothing of faculty members. It would be impossible to list all of these by name, but two who have been long-term partners making indispensable contributions must be cited.

In addition to serving as an assessor and interviewer, Dr. Walter Katkovsky of Northern Illinois University interpreted the responses to projective exercises in all the assessment centers for both studies and supervised the coding of the resulting reports for later quantitative analyses. Dr. Joseph F. Rychlak of Loyola University of Chicago, also an invaluable assessor, read the lengthy reports of every interview conducted with the participants over the time period reported in this volume. He applied to them his method of life theme coding, which played a critical role in our explorations of the data and which he used in a logical learning theory analysis in *Personality and Life-Styles of Young Male Managers* (Rychlak, 1982). Both these men have contributed their labors and their creativity to this research for 30 years.

Many managers at all levels in the telephone companies not only have facilitated the conduct of the studies, but have served as assessors and interviewers from time to time. At AT&T itself, our efforts have been encouraged and supported by the series of assistant vice presidents and corporate vice presidents who supervised the division in which the work was situated. For 13 years, the department that included this division was headed by Dr. H. Weston Clarke, Jr., senior vice president of personnel at AT&T. His interest and support, always of value, were particularly critical during the divestiture when continuance of the research, like other staff functions, was in question.

The prodigious amount of statistical analyses needed for this volume could not have been accomplished without a creative and dedicated staff, most recently under the supervision of Mrs. Catherine E. Brunson. A fine precedent had been set by Dr. Donald L. Grant, later a professor at the University of Georgia, who directed the quantitative analyses for the first 8 years of the MPS study. The ongoing process of data collection — including keeping track of the participants, scheduling the multitude of interviews of participants and their supervisors with our cadre of interviewers, and various record-keeping tasks — was most recently coordinated by Mrs. Sharon A. Solomita. Secretarial support during final drafting of this lengthy manuscript was provided by Mrs. Cheryl Butterman.

Several AT&T managers provided helpful comments and suggestions on an earlier draft of this manuscript, all of which we gratefully acknowledge. They include Mr. Richard A. Dennis, Mr. Christopher H. Mills, Dr. William S. Taylor, Dr. Leslie A. Klein, Dr. Richard J. Campbell, and Mr. Robert L. Shaughnessy.

Most of all, however, we must thank the 813 participants in these studies, Bell System managers at all levels, who have undergone multiple assessments, cooperated in many interviews, and opened their lives to us. They have embodied the commitment to research, a hallmark of AT&T, of which this book is just one testimony.

Ann Howard
Douglas W. Bray

CONTENTS

MANAGERIAL LIVES IN TRANSITION

CHAPTER 1

Introduction

This is a book about the lives and careers of two generations of American business managers. One group, in the Management Progress Study (MPS), entered telephone company management in the late 1950s. Their careers were launched in times of peace, order, and prosperity, but they were destined to unfold against a backdrop of race riots, Vietnam, Watergate, women's liberation, the drug counterculture, and a revolution in sexual behavior. The second group, in the Management Continuity Study (MCS), entering management jobs in the 1970s and early 1980s, had grown up during these same years. In spite of this social turbulence, all were young managers in a vast enterprise that held steadfastly to an image of stability in the 20 years that separated the two groups — the Bell System.

UNIQUENESS OF THE RESEARCH

There are several qualities that make this research unique among studies of ·adult development. Its setting within one organization provides relative environmental constancy against which individual changes can be evaluated. When we look at the characteristics of those who achieved lesser and greater success as managers, for example, we have the same criterion of success — namely, advancement into specific levels in the same hierarchy. In contrast to other studies, it is unnecessary to try to equate relative success in a variety of different walks of life.

A second way in which this research stands out is the use of a longitudinal-sequences study design — that is, the following of two groups of similar people through time. Longitudinal studies of 20 or more years' duration, like the first of those presented in this book, are rare, and the combination of such a study with a second cohort treated in parallel fashion is quite rare indeed. A third characteristic of the research is the extensiveness of its data collection, drawing substantially from the assessment center method as well as from traditional follow-up interviews and questionnaires. Both of these latter points warrant further exploration.

The Longitudinal-Sequences Design

When the American Telephone and Telegraph Company (AT&T) decision to launch the first research project was made in 1955, it was also decided that the study would be longitudinal. Such a study design was indeed ambitious, but it had the distinct advantage of being able to track changes within individuals (Schaie, 1983). A much more common approach would have been to test incumbents at various levels of management, hoping that comparisons between them would reveal individual characteristics important in management success. This cross-sectional or concurrent approach yields quick results, since there is no need to wait for time to elapse as in longitudinal studies.

One danger of cross-sectional research is that of confusing effects due to cultural change with those due to aging. For years students were taught, for example, that mental ability not only did not improve with age, but even declined from the teenage years on. This finding was based on cross-sectional research in which people of all ages were tested. Longitudinal research proved the conclusion to be false. When the same individuals were followed through the years, mental ability, at least of certain types, gradually increased into later life. The discredited result was associated with social change, since the older people in the original studies had grown up in an environment far less rich than that of the younger people, and therefore tested less well (Bayley, 1955; Eichorn, Hunt, & Honzik, 1981).

Concurrent studies may also impute causal relationships when there are none. Had higher-level managers and new college recruits been tested with a scale measuring hostile impulses, for example, senior managers would have earned higher scores. Concurrent researchers might have concluded that hostility aids advancement. The longitudinal MPS data show that this result is traceable to the fact that higher-level managers are older than college recruits. Hostile impulses were found to increase with age, and not particularly with management rank.

Another strategy could have been to conduct retrospective interviews with present managers, asking them to think back on their careers. They could be asked for critical incidents which had helped or hindered their development of success. This approach has been used by such researchers as Levinson (Levinson, with Darrow, Klein, Levinson, & McKee, 1978) and Lindsey and colleagues (Lindsey, Holmes, & McCall, 1986). Retrospective interviewing also has its perils, however. The importance of past events for good or bad may easily be distorted by one's eventual fate. A vice president may recall a demanding boss of 20 years ago as a positive, if somewhat unpleasant, developmental influence, while a second-level supervisor of the same age as the vice president may remember a similar boss as the basic reason for his or her lack of further advancement. In a longitudinal design, periodic interviewing would record possibly significant events soon after they take place and thus eliminate later misinterpretations of them.

Although longitudinal studies offer clear advantages over the above design, they also face many more hazards. One of these is the danger of loss of financial support. In the present case, AT&T did not guarantee long-term funding for either MPS, begun in the 1950s, or MCS, initiated in the 1970s. Financing was handled in the same way as for other corporate activities: An annual budget for the research was proposed and acted upon sometimes with modifications. That the original study has continued far past the period originally planned (at this writing, it is in its 31st year) is a tribute to AT&T's commitment to research and to the vitality of the study itself. Both studies have continually produced findings of organizational value, as well as contributing to basic behavioral science knowledge.

Loss of financial support is only one of the hazards of launching long-term longitudinal studies such as MPS and MCS. Participants, particularly if they are adults, are subject to gradual geographical disperion, making them difficult to retest or interview. They are also prone to lose interest and may prove uncooperative. If career success is to be a criterion, many will change employers, and equating degress of success may be well-nigh impossible. The original researchers may themselves move on or tire of the same study. If new investigators take over, they are likely to bring in quite different ideas of how the research should be conducted, making comparability across time a real problem. Research methods may be changed over time, a problem acutely faced by Block (1971).

Fortunately, none of these major problems of carrying out longitudinal research materialized and overwhelmed the AT&T research. Enough of the original MPS sample stayed with the Bell System for 20 years or more to make the data reliable. Nearly all were willing to continue to participate, since it was something their management deemed important, and research activities took place on company time. The designer and director of the study, Dr. Douglas W. Bray, continued to direct the research for 28 years until his retirement and still plays a key role in it, assuring continuity in approach and perspective.

Perhaps the greatest threat to the studies was the consent decree mandating the divestiture of the operating telephone companies by AT&T on January 1, 1984. This placed the continuation of data collection entirely on a basis of cooperation among unrelated organizations. This was fortunately not a legal problem, since the group results become part of the public domain. As of this writing cooperation prevails.

A problem with the interpretation of results from longitudinal studies is that when changes in characteristics are found, it is impossible to differentiate whether they should be attributed to maturation and development or to changes in the external culture. To aid in this interpretation, various sequential designs have been proposed (Schaie, 1965; Schaie & Baltes, 1975), which involve testing more than one cohort at different ages and different times. For the AT&T research, the addition of MCS provided a necessary second cohort.

This study, too, is longitudinal in design and attempts to parallel MPS as closely as possible.

The Assessment Center Method

The decision to pursue a longitudinal-sequences design was not the only factor that assured the comprehensiveness of MPS and its later companion, MCS. Another was to seek a complete picture of each research participant though the assessment center method. In 1956 a standard way of conducting a study like MPS, once the decision to make the research longitudinal was made, would have been to collect exhaustive biographical data on the participants and to give them a battery of paper-and-pencil tests. After the passage of time, these data would be related to measures of job performance or advancement. Tests might be readministered to discover changes over time. Methods such as projective tests would have been deliberately excluded as "unscientific." The whole approach would have been highly psychometric and elementalistic.

Instead of this traditional approach, the method used to evaluate the characteristics of the participants was the assessment center. This method uses a wide variety of instruments in arriving at an overall understanding of the person being evaluated. It may include paper-and-pencil methods that yield quantitative scores, such as tests, questionnaires, and inventories — devices dear to the psychometric approach. To these, however, it adds interviews and the hallmark of the method, behavioral simulations. These simulations may be individual or may evaluate the participant in a group setting. The length of the assessment center depends on the instruments used. (The MPS and MCS assessments took 3 days for each group of participants, usually 12 at a time.)

The material produced on each individual assessed is combined judgmentally by a group of assessors in a staff meeting, known as the integration session. Here again is a marked contrast to traditional approaches, which strive to combine observations mathematically. The assessor judgments take the form of ratings on the assessment center dimensions (those characteristics on which the center is focused), as well as such overall ratings as degree of management potential.

The participants in MPS underwent three assessment centers: one close to the time they entered management (MPS:0), another 8 years later (MPS:8), and a third 20 years from the start (MPS:20). The dimensions evaluated were the same on all three occasions, except that a number were added at MPS:20 to reflect attention to midlife and midcareer issues. The MCS group has, to date, been through only an initial assessment. The exercises used have been identical or parallel to those in MPS, with a few instruments added for updating. The dimensions consisted of the original MPS dimensions plus a selection of 10 from those added at MPS:20. A complete description of assessment center dimensions and techniques can be found in the Appendix to this volume.

Each assessment center produced a large number of measures, all of which figure in the chapters to follow. These measures, also described in the Appendix, ranged from overall ratings made on the basis of the 3 days of assessment to answers to single items on the questionnaires. Between these extremes were ratings on the assessment dimensions and combinations of these ratings in assessment factors defined by factor analysis.

For research purposes, assessor interview and simulation reports were coded on various dimensions some time after assessment. The assessment interviews and those conducted with the participants between assessments were also coded on nine life themes and on reactions to a variety of sociocultural issues. Finally, there were test and inventory scores, personality factor scores based on them, and ability factor scores derived from test scores and performance in the simulations as coded postassessment.

Although the material described above is highly quantitative, it must be emphasized that the assessors made their dimension ratings and overall ratings mainly on the basis of narrative reports of performance in simulations, interviews, and projective tests. Although they included the scores on the paper-and-pencil tests and inventories in their deliberations, they did not have access to any factor scores or exercise codings. Such data were generated long after assessment.

The Research Participants

The aim in the selection of participants for both studies was to draw a sample of beginning managers representative of those from whom future middle and upper managers would come. Since the Bell System was an almost completely up-from-within organization, all but a very few higher managers would have once been in first-level management jobs. First-level jobs, in turn, were occupied by individuals from two sources. The majority were those promoted from nonmanagement vocational jobs in which they had performed well and had been appraised as having supervisory ability. Few of this group had any education beyond high school, and very few had college degrees. In addition, college graduates were hired directly into the first level of management — not to be permanent lower-level supervisors, but (it was hoped) to rise to at least the third of seven levels of management (the entry to middle management) and perhaps higher.

Because of the goal that the participants be those with a reasonable chance of reaching middle management, the MPS sample, selected in the 1950s, was made up entirely of men. Although there were many women in first-level management, very few reached middle management. The sample was also made up entirely of whites. In those days blacks in management were rare, even in first-level jobs.

Since telephone company experience suggested that attrition would be much more likely in the college than in the noncollege management group, more of the former were included in the sample. In all, 274 college recruits into management and 148 noncollege men entered the study, for a total of 422.

Although it might have been desirable to draw participants in MPS from all 23 Bell System telephone companies, they actually came from only 6. These were the companies interested in being a part of the research. The college and noncollege groups were not drawn equally from the participating companies, since the interests of particular organizations influenced the category of participant included.

Table 1.1 shows the participating telephone companies and the number and type of participants from each. There was some geographical spread, although the Deep South and the Far West were not represented. The college graduates were 100% samples; that is, all of the college graduates taken on in the recruiting year were included. The noncollege men were random selections from lists of those who had reached first-level management by promotion from the ranks and were no older than 32. The age standard was introduced so that the noncollege group would not be too far from the college graduates in age. In addition, it seemed reasonable that those promoted while still young would be those with the greatest potential.

Table 1.2 presents the design of MPS as it took shape over its first 20 years and the number of participants at each major stage. As noted above, there were three points at which assessment centers were conducted. In between, the participants were interviewed a total of 11 times about events in their careers and lives off the job. They also filled out a questionnaire or two at those times. In addition, someone knowledgeable about the participant, most often the boss, was also interviewed.

Table 1.2 shows that half of the college graduates were not assessed at the 20-year point. This was due almost entirely to attrition, although two or three of those still employed were not present at the assessment for one reason or another. The great majority of the noncollege men were assessed 20 years

Table 1.1   Participants in MPS

Year	Telephone company	College	Noncollege	Total
1956	Michigan	67	—	67
1957	Chesapeake & Potomac	79	—	79
1958	New York	—	84	84
1959	Pennsylvania	56	40	96
1960	Northwestern	36	24	60
	Mountain	36	—	36
Total		274	148	422

Table 1.2   MPS Design and Sample

| Year | Activities | Sample size | | |
		College	Noncollege	Total
0	MPS:0 assessment	274	148	422
1—7	Annual interviews with participants, company representatives; annual expectations and attitude questionnaires			
8	MPS:8 assessment	167	142	309
10—19	Triannual interviews with participants, bosses, terminators; triannual biographical questionnaires			
20	MPS:20 assessment	137	129	266

from the start, and attrition among them was even lower than the table would suggest. A dozen or more decided that they no longer wished to participate.

All of these assessment centers and interviews involved in collecting the data for MPS required the work of scores of people over the years. In general, the assessment centers were staffed mostly by psychologists, either AT&T staff members or individuals hired temporarily (during academic summer vacations), supplemented by a few middle managers from the telephone companies (never the particular telephone company whose managers were being assessed). The follow-up interviews with the participants were also conducted by psychologists. The interviews with bosses or other company personnel about the participants were usually handled by middle managers from telephone companies other than the one in which the interviewing was being conducted.

The sample of participants making up MCS differed in several significant ways from that of MPS. Geographical coverage was much wider. All but one of the operating telephone companies (Ohio Bell), as well as the Long Lines department of AT&T, agreed to take part in the research, so all areas of the United States were well represented. Indicative of the social change that had taken place since the late 1950s was the fact that many of the college recruits of the late 1970s and beyond were women or members of minority groups. Since the MCS sample was designed to be representative of college intake into general management, just about half of the participants were women and nearly one-third were members of minority groups.

All of the MCS participants had at least a bachelor's degree; there was no noncollege sample. As time goes by, fewer and fewer employees without a college degree rise to high places in large corporations. Only a handful of such men in MPS reached more than the lowest level of middle management, and the typical noncollege participant did not get to middle management at all. In addition, the presence of new subgroups, women and minorities, meant that the MCS data would have to be subdivided for analysis, leaving only small numbers of cases in some comparison groups. A further educational sub-classification would have been impossible without doubling the size of the sample.

In all, 344 college graduates from the operating telephone companies and 47 from AT&T Long Lines became subjects of the new research. The MCS data analyzed in this volume generally do not include the sample from the AT&T Long Lines department, since this group was not represented in MPS. The Long Lines participants differed in important respects from those in the telephone companies; these differences are discussed in Chapter 9. Table 1.3 presents the breakdown of the MCS telephone company sample by sex and race.

The initial assessments of those in MCS took place in the years 1977 to 1982, with 1980 being omitted due to budgetary problems. As with MPS, nearly all of the assessment centers were conducted during the summer months, when academically based psychologists could be hired to serve as members of assessment staffs. Follow-up interviews with participants and, independently, with their bosses, are now under way at 2-year intervals; these interviews are not covered in this volume.

MAJOR ISSUES ADDRESSED

MPS was originally conceived of as a study of the natural progression of managerial careers — how the qualities brought to the job would change or not change as the managers aged and gained experience in a business environ-ment. This seemed to be a simple prescription, but it proved to be more complex than it at first appeared.

Table 1.3   Participants in MCS

Ethnic group	Males	Females	Total
Whites	129	108	237
Blacks	44	35	79
Hispanics	11	11	22
Others	2	4	6
Total	186	158	344

There was, first, the question of the areas of possible change. Certainly of interest were abilities, such as general intelligence, administrative skills, and interpersonal effectiveness. Another important class of variables was motivation, of which the drive for advancement and high standards for quality of work are key examples. Personality traits such as assertiveness and independence were hypothesized both to underlie certain abilities or motives and to be important in their own right. Finally, attitudes and values made up another significant area.

Continuity-Discontinuity

One issue receiving much attention in the psychological literature is the extent to which characteristics, especially personality, represent relatively stable traits within individuals or are subject to great fluctuation and change (cf. Costa & McCrae, 1986; Mischel, 1968). On the side of change, it can be said that there was almost no individual characteristic measured in MPS in which some change was not observed among a substantial number of people. On the other hand, the standing of the participants at MPS:20 on nearly all characteristics was significantly related to their standing at the beginning of the study. Discussion of change should not suggest that individuals lack a solid core and are completely at the mercy of life events.

Without gainsaying change, there was enough stability in the participants to permit us to make predictions of their futures in management from the very beginning at a level very much better than chance. This was in the face of assignments to different departments, experiences with a great variety of bosses, crises in personal lives, and all the other circumstances that might upset prediction.

More specifically, of the college graduates predicated at the original assessment to reach fourth-level management or higher (among seven levels of management in the telephone company hierarchy), 60% did so as compared to 24% of the others. Of the noncollege men predicted to reach at least the third level, 58% did so as compared to 22% of those not so predicted. (Different level standards were used for the two groups, since the college graduates progressed further than the noncollege participants.) The reader is reminded that assessment results were available to no one and did not influence advancement.

Correlations between initial status on a number of measures and later personal adjustment were also substantial, although personality characteristics were more important here, while abilities were critical in predicting advancement. Inventory scores indicative of self-confidence and emotional stability, for example, correlated .29 and .33, respectively, with adjustment as evaluated by the assessment staff 20 years later. Once again, here is evidence for a stable core of personality that persists over the years.

In spite of a basic stable core, there was evidence of a great deal of change over the 20 years of the study. The best example of orderly change in a variable of interest was mental ability. The average score on the Verbal scale of the School and College Ability Test (SCAT) increased over the period of study from the 34th percentile on Bell System college-hire norms to the 56th. Yet the participants maintained their relative positions: The test-retest correlation of scores over 20 years was .89. This almost perfect relationship is about what would be expected had the test been given on two successive days! This means, of course, that everyone changed by just about the same amount; they were on an escalator and very few changed steps, so to speak.

Unfortunately for orderly science, this same pattern of change to this degree was found in no other characteristic. Still, changes over time for the total group were often found to a statistically significant degree, while test-retest correlations were typically in the .40s and .50s. For example, the MPS men increased substantially on Autonomy and Aggression, while they decreased on Affiliation.

Causal Attributions for Change

Where measured change was substantial, particularly for the total group of participants, the question can be raised as to the cause of the change. Was it developmental in the sense of relating to experiences concomitant with age, or did variations in the external culture prompt the change? Such attributions of causality are important, in that they facilitate prediction of the ways in which a new group will or will not change.

Inventory scores showed, for example, that the MPS participants were less willing to defer to authority at age 45 than at age 25. Was this just a matter of maturity — of taking one's place as the leader rather than the subordinate, the father rather than the son? Or was it related to the fact that all institutions were challenged and devalued during the 1960s and 1970s, commanding less respect from society in general according to opinion polls?

Were there no other data available than those from MPS, separating changes due to age from those for which cultural change was more responsible would be difficult if not impossible. Fortunately, comparable data from another cohort became available from the second AT&T longitudinal study, MCS.

When the MCS group was tested on Deference, they scored similarly to the MPS men as tested in the 1970s, which was significantly higher than the MPS participants scored when they joined the company as young managers in the 1950s. The results, then, pointed to a change in the culture as the hypothesized source of lower Deference, rather than to experiences related to aging. Causality is still only hypothetical, however, even with this kind of comparison. More data to support the hypothesis can be garnered when the MCS group is reassessed and their new scores evaluated against their previous ones.

As will be seen, changes observed in the MPS participants were much more often attributed to individual development than to global culture changes. The increases in verbal ability and in aggressive impulses, already mentioned, are good examples of this. In these instances, the MCS group scored much as the MPS men had scored in their youth. If the developmental hypothesis is correct, it should be verified by subsequent increases in those scores on the part of the MCS group.

As research goes, however, many changes observed in the MPS participants did not fit neatly into a category of changes attributable to aging or changes attributable to societal influences. An example is that of advancement motivation. On a paper-and-pencil measure of this motivation, the college recruits in MPS dropped from an average score (50th percentile) when they joined the company and the study, to well below average (8th percentile) 20 years later. A reasonable explanation was that the urge to rise in the organizational hierarchy had lost its potency with the attainment of advancements and/or the realization that they were not forthcoming — a developmental change.

However, the MCS group scored at only the 17th percentile in their initial assessment, considerably below where the MPS group had begun but significantly above their scores in midcareer. Apparently something was also at work in the larger culture, diminishing the value of promotions in a large organization. Our hypotheses of causality in a case like this are mixed — a combination of developmental changes and cultural changes.

As it happened, at MPS:20, the correlation between management level attained and life satisfactions other than career was insignificant. Reaching higher management may, and does, make for greater career satisfaction, but it does not appear to make for any more off-the-job happiness. In the 1950s people might have believed otherwise. Now many, such as the average participant in MCS, believe just the opposite. They voice the fear that too much advancement will lead to unhappiness, although the insignificant correlation of .10 between MPS:20 level and rated happiness shows this belief also to be unfounded. As becomes clearly evident in this volume, one can be just as unhappy as an occupational "failure" as one can be as vice president.

Where changes in the MPS group reflected both age-related changes and cultural changes, there were signs that the new generation characterized by MCS represented a new breed of manager. In addition to lesser needs for advancement, they had lower expectations about what life as a manager would be like. Some other data pointed to additional differences.

On some measures, the total group of MPS participants showed no meaningful changes over time, but the MCS group was clearly different. For example, the MPS college men's average score on Nurturance, or being helpful and supportive to others, was at the 49th percentile both at MPS:0 and MPS:20. By contrast, the MCS group scored at the 71st percentile, significantly higher. This was not due to a sex difference; the white males in MCS scored at the 69th percentile. Changes in the external culture are again the hypothesized source of the difference, but the culture change was apparently one that affected young people but not older people. Thus is born the concept of a generation gap, where the younger generation appears very different from its elders, regardless of the time at which the elders were evaluated.

Criterion Subgroup Changes

In addition to the issue of changes over time for the total group, characteristics of subgroups defined by specific criteria were also of concern. One area of particular interest in launching MPS was how the characteristics of the participants would fit with career demands, leading to greater or lesser success as managers. In this case, success was primarily defined as being advanced into higher levels of management. Another area of concern developed when the MPS:20 assessment approached and attention turned to midlife issues. Interest became focused on the degree of psychological adjustment manifested by the participants and how this related to their patterns of development and their relative success as managers.

The absence of change for the total group often masked some important developments or declines among subgroups. For example, for the college recruits there was no change in level of administrative skills from MPS:0 to MPS:8. This fact was important to management, since it appeared that 8 years of experience mattered little. This group result, however, concealed a great deal of individual change. Those who were on their way to higher management were notably better administrators at MPS:8 than they had been at the start. Those whose futures were not to turn out well had, on the average, become poorer administrators, apparently practicing the wrong thing for 8 years.

Another type of change occurred when there was both a total group change and individual changes within that general trend. An example is a measure of Achievement, where the total group rose significantly over the 20 years between the first and final assessments. The correlation of individual scores between these two points was .43, indicating that individual differences in Achievement were moderately persistent but that individuals did not change in lockstep. Many of the participants showed increases, but some rose more than others. The greatest increases, once again, were found among those who reached the higher management levels. In a similar fashion, the total group declined in ambition over the 20-year period, but those who advanced the least as well as those most poorly adjusted declined more than the others.

Demographic Group Differences

In addition to subgroups defined according to preselected criteria — namely, managerial advancement and personal adjustment — there were also some naturally formed subgroups based on demographic characteristics for whom relative characteristics were of interest. In MPS, educational level was the major subgroup classification. At the original assessment, major differences between the two groups related to greater ambition and cognitive ability on the part of the college-educated men. At the same time, they had the disadvantages of less experience on the average (the noncollege men had considerable exposure to the company in nonmanagement jobs) and less maturity (the noncollege men were nearly 6 years older and much more likely to be settled into married life). Over time, the differences between these two subgroups increased, as much because the noncollege men declined in important characteristics as because the college men improved. The weaker motivation of the noncollege men is hypothesized to have had a strong effect on their results.

Within MCS, though all were college graduates, differences were (and continue to be) explored between the sex, race, and ethnic groups. It is somewhat startling to note that white males were decidedly in the minority among current college-educated management recruits when they represented almost 100% of the candidates in the past.

When sex differences were considered, it was clear that the women had no disadvantages compared to the men in the ability to perform management jobs. In some ways, in fact, they were more promising, such as in greater creativity, interpersonal sensitivity, and written communication skills. Traditional masculinity-femininity scales easily differentiated the two groups, although masculinity had declined among men in both studies compared to the 1950s. More women than men were expected to leave the organization voluntarily because of anticipated family-career conflicts.

Blacks and whites showed sharp differences on many variables, with Hispanics often falling halfway in between. In the ability realm, the closer the measures tapped behaviors learned in a school environment, the more difficulty the blacks were likely to have. Family backgrounds for many blacks, especially males, showed significant deprivation, in spite of the fact that these participants were comparable to the other race and ethnic groups in level of education. Self-esteem was lower for the blacks than the other groups, while the Hispanics exceeded both blacks and whites in poise.

These and other findings point to some of the complexities involved in evaluating the characteristics of two generations of managers. A key finding was the great increase in heterogeneity across time, not only because the new managers came from different sex, race, and ethnic groups, but because the MCS white males were more disparate from each other than those of the 1950s. Combined with the increased heterogeneity observed in the MPS men as they aged, the results present a significant challenge not just to business organizations but to other social institutions attempting to meet the needs of such a diverse group of people.

THE PLAN OF THIS BOOK

The issues raised in this chapter, and many others, are addressed in the remainder of this volume. Three sources of information comprise the presentation of the book. The first type of information is sociocultural history. Since we were investigating adult development over a particular period of time, and since an important goal was to try to differentiate cultural changes from age-related changes, it seemed important to review events in the external environment.

The American culture of the 1950s, the 1960s, the 1970s, and the beginning of the 1980s is summarized, along with world events impinging on the country. Significant events for the Bell System over the same period of time are also brought in. As part of the follow-up interviews, the participants were asked to comment on what they saw as the most important challenges to the country and to the company. These responses, summarized in interview protocols, were later coded for sociocultural attitudes. Consequently, the reactions of the study participants to events from the mid-1950s to the early 1980s are also provided.

A second type of information is biographical. Since arrays of statistics can often be dry and lifeless, we have attempted to bring the research findings to life by illustrating them with case histories. A major concern in presenting the histories was our promise of confidentiality to our participants. To maintain our commitment, each prototype has been based on six different individuals who shared similar characteristics. Since 25 prototypes are presented, 150 different cases have been reviewed in detail and combined in ways that would illustrate the points made but would obscure any individual's identity.

The method of selecting the typologies for each of the 25 composite characters is shown in Figure 1.1. The selection of cases was determined by ratings on the two criteria of interest in the book, managerial advancement and personal adjustment. For MPS, advancement was considered average if the individual was promoted to the modal level for his educational group by the 20th year of the study. For the college men this was the third level of management, while for the noncollege men it was the second level. Advancement was considered high if the individual was promoted beyond the mode for his educational group and low if he had fewer promotions than the average for his educational group.

In MCS, management potential was used as the criterion of future success. This was based on the overall judgments of the assessors at the initial assessment in rating the maximum management level for which each individual was thought to be qualified. Average potential was estimated to be for the third level. Those considered to have more than third-level potential were rated high, while those thought to be marginal or poor possibilities for third level were rated low in potential for advancement.

For both studies, the assessors' ratings on the dimension of Adjustment were used as the criteria for this area of interest. On a 5-point scale, those with ratings of 4—5 were considered well adjusted, those rated 2.5—3.5 moderately adjusted, and those rated 1—2 poorly adjusted. As with the advancement criterion, measures were taken from MPS:20 but from the initial assessment of MCS.

Management Progress Study

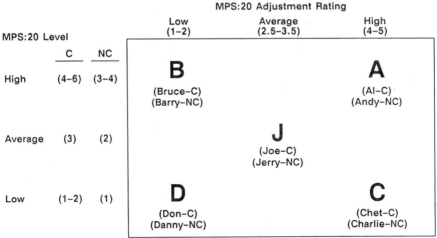

C = College (one-syllable names)
NC = Noncollege (two-syllable names)

Management Continuity Study

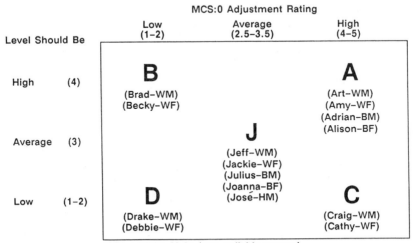

WM = White Male (one-syllable names)
WF = White Female (two-syllable names)
BM & BF = Black Male and Black Female (three-syllable names)
HM = Hispanic Male

Figure 1.1.   Typologies for composite characters.

Examples of average participants in the different demographic subgroups are called "type J," and their names begin with the letter *j*. They experienced management success or had management potential to an average degree for their subgroup and were rated moderate in adjustment. The number of syllables in the name helps to distinguish those from the different subgroups. In MPS, all the college men have one-syllable names, while the noncollege men have two-syllable names. Thus the example of an average college man in MPS is called Joe, while the example of an average MPS noncollege man is named Jerry. In MCS, the white men have one-syllable names to match the MPS college men; the example of an average white male in MCS is called Jeff. The MCS white women have two-syllable names, so the example of an average white female is named Jackie. Joanna and Julius are examples of average black participants, since the MCS blacks have been given three-syllable names. José provides an example of an average Hispanic male.

The A, B, C, and D types represent different combinations of advancement or management potential and rated adjustment. In MPS Al, Andy, Bruce, and Barry were all promoted to high levels for their subgroup, but Al and Andy were well adjusted and Bruce and Barry were poorly adjusted. Chet, Charlie, Don, and Danny remained in the lower rungs of management, but Chet and Charlie accepted their fate in a well-adjusted manner, while Don and Danny responded in a poorly adjusted manner.

In MCS, both white males and white females represent each of the A, B, C, and D quadrants — Art, Amy, Brad, Becky, Craig, Cathy, Drake, and Debbie. To illustrate race and sex within race differences, two well-adjusted, high-potential blacks, Adrian and Alison, are also included.

The last and most important type of information is psychological. An abundance of statistical tables and figures and their interpretations are offered to present data addressing the major issues covered in this volume. In presenting the data in the chapters, figures have been substituted for tables where appropriate to give a better picture of the relative magnitude of changes and differences presented. Our original plan was to include detailed data and statistical test information in an additional appendix, but we changed that plan when we realized that it would add 100 pages or more to the text! We will do our best to meet the individual requests of scholars interested in such detail. Meanwhile readers should be assured that when we speak of changes or differences, we are basing them on two-tailed statistical tests that proved significant with a probability of less than .05. Strongly significant findings had a probability of less than .005, while data reported as "trends" or "not quite statistically significant" had a probability of more than .05 but less than .10. Multivariate tests were typically conducted on independent blocks of data prior to univariate explorations.

The forthcoming chapters are organized as follows. Chapter 2 reviews the American culture in the 1950s and considers the characteristics of the MPS participants as young men during the first round of assessment centers in

1956-1960. College graduate recruits are compared with the noncollege group on backgrounds, lifestyles, work interests, personality and motivation, and abilities. Supplementing the quantitative data are the case studies of Joe and Jerry, examples of average members of each of the two groups.

Chapters 3 and 4 address the question of prediction — that is, how well the characteristics evaluated at the beginning assessment centers foretold the status of the participants 20 years later in terms of advancement and adjustment. In Chapter 3, a discussion of the characteristics of those who left the Bell System precedes the data detailing the prediction of management level attained for those who stayed. Case studies of the well-adjusted men who later arrived at widely different levels of management (Al and Andy vs. Chet and Charlie) are introduced as they appeared at MPS:0.

Chapter 4 addresses the prediction of personal adjustment, illustrated with the cases of the poorly adjusted men with high career advancement, Bruce and Barry, and the poorly adjusted men with low career advancement, Don and Danny. Again, the characteristics of these prototypes are presented as they appeared as young men in the 1950s.

The next four chapters are concerned with changes over time and continue the 10 illustrative MPS case studies begun in the previous chapters. Chapter 5 reviews the social and political history of the 1960s and 1970s and examines the responses of the MPS participants to major aspects of this history. Changes in lifestyles over this period are also analyzed. Chapter 6 presents changes in work interests and attitudes, personality and motivation, and abilities; the careers of Joe and Jerry, who exemplify the average college and noncollege men, are presented against the backdrop of changes in the telephone business.

Chapter 7 examines differential changes among those reaching various levels of management, while Chapter 8 discusses the changes experienced by those who manifested differing degrees of personal adjustment at MPS:20. Thus Al, Andy, Chet, Charlie, Bruce, Barry, Don, and Danny are followed as they moved toward their midlife destinies.

In Chapter 9, attention is turned to the young managers in MCS. Similarities and differences between them and the beginning college graduates in MPS 20 years earlier are examined. The case of Jeff, an example of an average white male manager in MCS, is presented in contrast to Joe, who represents the average MPS college graduate.

Gender, race, and ethnic group comparisons are the subjects of Chapters 10 and 11. In Chapter 10 Jackie, who exemplifies an average white female management recruit, illustrates the statistical data. Case studies of Joanna and Julius, both black, and José, a Hispanic, illustrate the material in Chapter 11, which contrasts whites with minority group managers.

Chapter 12 completes the consideration of the MCS group by projecting the implications of their beginning characteristics for future managerial performance and personal adjustment. Comparisons are made with the kinds of data used to estimate these criteria in the MPS college group. Here are brought in the A, B, C, and D types for MCS: Art, Amy, Adrian, Alison, Brad, Becky, Craig, Cathy, Drake, and Debbie.

The final chapter reviews the wide range of findings presented and their implications for behavioral science and for organizations. Here we consider the extent to which people change and yet remain the same as they grow older, confronted with common and unique experiences in an evolving culture. The MPS and MCS data are pulled together, and hypotheses are drawn for the sources of these changes and differences — whether primarily aging, the changing culture affecting most people or just the young, or some combination of these. The practical problems of the selection and development of managers, which gave rise to the AT&T studies, are considered in light of the research results.

CHAPTER 2

The First Assessment

Most of the men in MPS began their careers in the telephone companies in the 1950s. Early in that decade, the noncollege men entered as craftsmen and were trained for such jobs as installing and repairing telephones. They would do well and by mid-decade would be promoted to foremen or other management positions. From the mid- to late 1950s the college men entered the Bell System, beginning immediately in management. Thus the college and noncollege forces joined ranks at the bottom of the Bell System management pyramid.

From among these young men of the 1950s would come the leaders of the 1970s and 1980s. The future character of the company would be determined in part by their genetic inheritance, family influences, and educational experiences. But the organization and its managers would also be molded by the nature of the times during which these men were maturing and entering adulthood. It is thus instructive to remember those times.

THE 1950s

As the 1950s dawned, America was recovering from the shortages, inflation, and unemployment that characterized the period immediately following World War II. From an era of scarcities and sacrifice was emerging one of unprecedented prosperity. Disengagement from the war was a welcome relief, but the Allied victory was shadowed by the growth of a new enemy.

> The Soviet Union, with what seemed like sheer barbarian malice, had torn up its wartime agreement with the Allies and gobbled down half of Europe. . . . By 1950 Russia had three times as many combat airplanes as the United States, four times as many troops, 30 tank divisions to America's one. Communism, obviously, was out to conquer the world. The only thing that prevented it was America's monopoly of the atomic bomb. . . . (Time-Life, 1970, p. 25).

But by late 1949, there was no such monopoly; the Soviet Union exploded its first atomic bomb.

The Truman administration was stunned by the discovery and did not even announce the Russian explosion for several weeks. Up until that time, the aim of the Truman Doctrine had been to "contain" Communism behind its existing borders and to support, economically and militarily, free peoples resisting attempted subjugation. The Marshall Plan, which allotted huge sums of money to bolster the economies of Europe, had successfully brought together the Western European nations and resulted in 1949 in the formation of the North Atlantic Treaty Organization. But the Russians' possession of the atomic bomb signaled a frightening tilt toward a new imbalance of power.

The United States responded with the construction of a hydrogen bomb with a force 1,000 times more potent than the atomic device dropped on Hiroshima, but by 1953 the Russians broke that monopoly as well. And so the spectre of nuclear war would haunt the minds of Americans in the 1950s. Atomic shelters went on sale, and homeowners dug up their backyards and bought stocks of canned goods. Schoolchildren were taught to cover their eyes and necks and huddle beneath their desks.

The shock of the Russian atomic bomb was not the only event to provoke fear in 1949. Mao Zedong forced Chiang Kai-shek's Nationalist government to Formosa, and China fell to Communism. The first trial was held for Alger Hiss, a handsome American of the privileged class, accused of spying for Russia. The Hiss trials pitted a political left against a political right: the New Dealers, allegedly soft on Communism, and the anti-New Dealers, to be christened "conservatives" (Goldman, 1960).

The combination of the Communist threat abroad, the Russian bomb, the Hiss trials, and the sympathy of some New Dealers for Hiss spawned a theory of a great conspiracy to undermine the traditional American institutions of democracy and free enterpise. There was the suspicion that the Rooseveltians had stunted business by increasing bureaucracy and controls, pursued a wartime foreign policy which gave advantage to the Communists, and, under Truman, helped bring about the loss of Eastern Europe and China to the Communists (Goldman, 1960).

The invasion of South Korea by North Korea in 1950 might have added support to this theory had not Truman responded quickly by pledging U.S. arms to defend the South. The president, fearing Russia and China, favored limited warfare, while his general in charge of the war, Douglas MacArthur, preferred the quick, total solution. Truman fired MacArthur in 1951, enraging many. "Old soldiers never die, they just fade away," sighed MacArthur, in a sentimental speech before the House of Representatives.

Anti-Communist sentiments spread further, spearheaded by Senator Joseph McCarthy and his condemnation of liberals. Communist hunting began in Congress, and McCarthy's "witch hunts" in the early 1950s threatened Hollywood stars and writers as well as others with blacklists, ruining the careers and lives of many innocent people. McCarthy continued unchecked until 1954, when the words of a soft-mannered attorney representing the U.S. Army became a turning point. "Have you no sense of decency, sir, at long last?" inquired Joseph Welch, voicing the question that triggered the disgrace and demise of McCarthy.

Out of the darkness of threatening bombs and carnivorous encroaching Communism came a smiling hero by the name of Dwight Eisenhower. In spite of accusations of vague, nonideological politics, the famous general easily defeated two intellectuals in the 1952 presidential race: Robert Taft on the right for the nomination, and Adlai Stevenson on the left in the election. His opponents found his familiar, homespun manner and hero-worship popularity unmatchable and his ambiguous politics unassailable. Said a Taft man, "It looks like he's pretty much for home, mother, and heaven" (Time-Life, 1970, p. 34). But that was exactly what people wanted in the 1950s.

As the Eisenhower era was ushered in, there was some relaxation of anxiety about nuclear war. Eisenhower ended the Korean War within 6 months, China didn't invade Formosa after all, and World War III didn't begin. With McCarthy finally in disgrace and no strong bellowing for change by liberals, the country began to pursue a moderate couse. Even Secretary of State John Foster Dulles began to move away from the belligerence accompanying Communist containment and toward a position of coexistence.

The liberal press was highly critical of Eisenhower, denigrating him as lacking energy, leadership, and political skills. Yet recently released archives reveal a keen and incisive analytical mind with an extraordinary capacity for detached, orderly examinations of problems and personalities. Greenstein (1982) notes Eisenhower's "hidden-hand" leadership, operating behind the scenes, and his instrumental use of language (criticized as tangled, rambling rhetoric) to reveal only what he wanted to.

In retrospect, Eisenhower's accomplishments were commendable. After quickly ending the Korean War, he held down military expenses (to the strong criticism of the liberals, who accused him of creating a missile gap) and did not let the Cold War reheat into military confrontations. On the domestic front he also avoided conflicts and expanded welfare programs slowly, while keeping a tight reign on public spending. Thus Eisenhower presided over 8 years of peace and prosperity with a balanced budget and negligible inflation.

Eisenhower's cabinet was very probusiness. Perhaps most renowned was his secretary of defense, former General Motors president Charles Wilson, whose comment, "What was good for our country was good for General Motors and vice versa" was reversed by the press to "What's good for General Motors is good for the country and vice versa." In spite of such teasing, the 1950s saw American business develop greater technology and increasingly gigantic corporations. The Bell Laboratories invented the transistor in 1948, and the computer was first marketed in 1950. Transatlantic telephone service began in 1956, and color television and stereo recording evolved during the decade.

Corporations made extensive use of their research and development capabilities to expand the consumer culture, especially in electronics, chemicals, and plastics.

The opening of the 1950s saw the beginning of years of abundance in America; in fact, John Kenneth Galbraith (1958) argued in *The Affluent Society* that the problems of economic production were solved and shortages were over. When production doubled, advertising was called upon to get consumption to double (Lewis, 1978). There seemed no end to the creative ways to get people to buy, buy, buy. Beginning in 1955, each new model of automobile was longer, lower, and fancier than the last, in every color of the rainbow with tail fins and extra lamps. Color, too, hit telephones and appliances, and every 2 years a new wave of electric dryers or stoves appeared with more dials and gadgets until they began to resemble the cockpits of the new jet airplanes. A "throwaway" philosophy developed, with cans, baking tins, and TV dinners designed for immediate obsolescence. Soon everyone seemed to have a television or hi-fi set, and what you didn't own you could rent, from silverware to a Kelly Girl.

Critics began to fear that this continuous raising of the standard of living, along with a philosophy of coexistence with the enemy, would turn the American culture into an overly contented, numb civilization, oblivious to the individualistic spirit that had made America great in the first place. In *The Organization Man* (1956), W. H. Whyte lamented that the American dream had changed. The ideal of individual salvation through competition, hard work, and thrift (the Protestant work ethic) was, he believed, being replaced by an organization ethic, emphasizing a sense of belonging as the ultimate need of the individual and organizational loyalty as a high-priority concern. Corporations were no longer accused of being the robber barons of the late 19th century but of the opposite — being too benign, imprisoning employees in brotherhood and belonging. Similarly David Riesman, in *The Lonely Crowd* (1950), complained that the psychology of abundance had taught children to adapt not by internalizing traditional values but by sensitizing themselves to the expectations of others. To be popular was the ultimate value.

Conformity did, in fact, seem to characterize much of 1950s life. There was a mass exodus to the suburbs, populated with ranch houses and Levittowns complete with at least two cars in the garage and all the appliances, gadgets, and material goods one could possibly buy. Concurrently, there was a sweeping propaganda campaign to establish woman's place in the home. There was pressure for women to marry young and chaste, to drop out of college to support their husbands, and to avoid having careers at all costs. The role of women was to breed children. This propaganda was highly successful, for it produced a gigantic baby boom, the consequences of which would be felt for decades.

There were actually two models of femininity in the 1950s. One was the lady of high style — feminine and dignified, with white gloves and neatly tailored clothes. This proper lady was exemplified by such actresses as Deborah Kerr and Joan Fontaine, but the ultimate role model was Grace Kelly, who reached the pinnacle of feminine dreams by marrying a prince in 1956. The other model for women was the sex object, usually blonde and large-breasted. Marilyn Monroe, Jayne Mansfield, and Brigitte Bardot were favorite examples of this prototype. Though to some extent irreconcilable, both models circumscribed women's role to the home or the bed (Lewis, 1978).

The suburbs were saturated with housewives and children during these times, but their homes welcomed a new source of companionship: television. Friends abounded, like Milton Berle, Phil Silvers, and George Burns and Gracie Allen. The top program from 1952 through 1957 was *I Love Lucy*, and star Lucille Ball even managed to have her real baby the same day her television baby was born in 1953. Since videotape was not perfected, television was live, and quiz shows cast with personalities attracted the biggest audiences.

Television had a devastating effect on radio drama and also caused the demise of several magazines (*Colliers, Saturday Evening Post, Look*). The film industry also felt the competition and began to respond by creating bigger and bigger screens, including Cinerama, 3-D, Cinemascope, Vistavision, and Todd-A0. The big screens had to be filled with something, and Hollywood met the challenge by producing big Westerns (*Shane, High Noon*), building films around well-known stars (Marlon Brando, Judy Garland), and creating religious epics (*Quo Vadis, Ben-Hur*) (Lewis, 1978).

Religious themes were prevalent elsewhere in the 1950s, for the Cold War was, in a way, a religious war. Pope Pius XII denounced atheistic Communism and all cooperation with it, and anti-Communist sentiment fed on its affront to organized religion. In this spirit it was perhaps unsurprising to find a revival of religion, with Billy Graham leading a crusade to appeal for a personal encounter with Jesus Christ. In 3 of the 10 years comprising the 1950s, the top nonfiction best seller was the Holy Bible, and top fiction bestsellers included *The Cardinal, The Silver Chalice*, and *The Robe*. On the popular song hit parade were "I Believe" and "Vaya con Dios" (Time-Life, 1970). Norman Vincent Peale published *The Power of Positive Thinking*, and Dial-A-Prayer began in 1956.

Much of religious enthusiasm was artificial, "compounded of social aspirations and fervid desire to avoid thinking" (Goldman, 1960, p. 305). But religious themes helped sell books, such as *The Power of Prayer on Plants* and *Pray Your Weight Away*. Popular magazines also had their share: As Jane Russell said in *Modern Screen*, "I Love God. And when you get to know Him, you find He's a Livin' Doll" (quoted in Goldman, 1960, p. 305).

A more convincing form of religious inspiration came from Martin Luther King, the Baptist minister who represented the hope to American blacks that their rightful place in society could be won by nonviolent means. The crusade began slowly, and the 1950s were a decade of black awakening but not much progress (Lewis, 1978). Although the separate but equal system of education was struck down by the 1954 Supreme Court decision in *Brown v. Board of Education of Topeka*, 10 years later only 1% of the blacks in the South went to school with white children (Leuchtenberg, 1973).

King came to prominence in 1955 by leading a boycott of buses in Montgomery, Alabama after Mrs. Rosa Parks, a tired black seamstress, refused to give up her seat near the front of a bus for a white passenger. Her refusal sparked a revolution. King's boycott took a year to bring about its desired results, but it began a series of sit-ins and nonviolent demonstrations that were the first steps on the road to black equality. It cannot be said that there was no social progress during the Eisenhower years, but it was attributed more to the decisions of the Supreme Court under Chief Justice Earl Warren than to the President himself (Leuchtenberg, 1973).

The popular culture in the 1950s has been resoundingly denounced as banal, a "worship of the material, the gaudy, the violent, and the mediocre" (Goldman, 1960, p. 291). With affluence came fads and frivolities to appeal to mass tastes. Children of all ages rushed to twirl hula hoops around their bodies or paint by numbers, while youngsters sported Davy Crockett coonskin hats and devoured comic books. College boys tried to see how many of them would fit into a telephone booth or a Volkswagen Beetle. Men adorned themselves with pink shirts, ties, hankies, and undergarments, while women paraded in poodle skirts, cinch belts, and pop-it beads.

The 1950s culture was accused of fostering a docile nation of standardized one-class suburbs, sleepy college campuses, and phlegmatic and routinized citizens. Yet there was more diversity than was often typified. Television, for example, brought not only quiz and variety shows, but Edward R. Murrow and dramatic showcases for new playwrights such as Gore Vidal and Paddy Chayevsky. Some of the criticism may have been part of the warfare of intellectuals against a prospering middle class (Leuchtenberg, 1973).

The intellectuals saw Eisenhower as the representative figure of the quiescent, homogenized society, if not its leader; the "bland leading the bland." Yet this impression was contradicted by firsthand observers, who commented on his "electric" presence, "magnetic appeal," vibrant personality, and energetic, restless temperament. His smile beamed pleasantly from "I Like Ike" campaign buttons, but it concealed a fiery temper that he consciously withheld. Eisenhower's reputation seemed deliberately self-contrived out of a deep conviction that a proper leader must keep his impulses in check and subordinate his personal feelings in order to act rationally and present an image of dignity (Greenstein, 1982).

It was not only the intellectual critics who found dissatisfactions with the 1950s' conformity and sentimentality. Throughout the decade, distrust of elders, adult values, and the conspiracy of silence over sex were repeated themes of the younger generation. Holden Caulfield, the young protagonist of

J. D. Salinger's 1951 novel *The Catcher in the Rye*, lamented the "crumby" and "phony" adult world, and on film James Dean portrayed a *Rebel without a Cause*. Delinquency became a special form of protest, especially from the motorcycle gangs with black leather jackets and longish greasy hair with sideburns and a "D.A." in back.

Accompanying the antiadult and antibourgeois feelings was the new music of the times — rock and roll. The starting point for the new music is usually credited to the Bill Haley band's soundtrack for the 1955 movie *Blackboard Jungle*, when the exuberant sound of "Rock around the Clock" burst into movie theatres. Rock and roll made such sentimental ballad singers as Frankie Lane, Perry Como, Doris Day, and Rosemary Clooney sound middle-aged by comparison, yet the two musical styles managed to exist side by side.

The most prominent rock-and-roll star was Elvis Presley. Groaning his lyrics and making other undefinable sounds while sensuously moving his torso, he was described as the first white to sing about naked lust (Lewis, 1978). The teenage response to Elvis and the other rock-and-roll stars began to set them apart as a new breed. Yet being a rebel in the 1950s demanded no violent sacrifices, and even Elvis was a hero of the consumer culture with his gold lamé suits and pastel Cadillacs.

Another musical strain was the new cool jazz and sophisticated rhythms of such performers as Stan Getz, Miles Davis, and the Modern Jazz Quartet. This was the preferred music of the first American dropouts, the "beats" or "beatniks," who sought freedom by wandering across the country in their quest for "beatitude," depicted in Kerouac's *On the Road* (1957). They rejected canons of respectability such as organized religion, striving for material success, and homage to the state, and they helped popularize marijuana, a habit they picked up from jazz musicians. Their other entertainments included poetry readings and the routines of social protest comedians, such as Mort Sahl and Lenny Bruce, who said what had heretofore been unsayable. The beats were the successors to the existentialists on the Left Bank in Paris; they, in turn, would be succeeded by the hippies of the 1960s (Lewis, 1978).

Soaring across the soundtracks of rock and roll and cool jazz was the shrill voice of Nikita Khrushchev in 1956, saying, "We will bury you!" (Time-Life, 1970, p. 31). Less than a year later, America was shocked to find the Russians in space with the launching of the first globe-circling satellite, Sputnik. When Washington tried to launch its own satellite orbiter 2 months later, it crashed. (Explorer finally made it in January 1958.) There was suddenly a criticism of school standards, especially science, as Americans tried to understand how they could have fallen so far behind. In 1959 Fidel Castro ousted the Batista government in Cuba, and before much time had passed it became apparent that he was not only Communist but anti-American — just a few miles from American soil.

Then in 1960, the pilot of a U-2 spy plane, Francis Gary Power, was shot down over Russia. Eisenhower stopped the flights but refused to apologize for them. At a summit meeting with DeGaulle of France, Macmillan of England, Eisenhower, and Khrushchev, the Russian refused a visit by the American president to Russia (reciprocal to his in the United States), and the summit meeting ended before it began. Khrushchev called a press conference, pounded the table, and shouted that American "aggressors" should be treated the way he as a boy handled cats that stole cream or broke into pigeon lofts. "We would catch such a cat by the tail and bang its head against the wall, and that was the only way it could be taught some sense" (Goldman, 1960, p. 338).

Thus it became clear that American complacency could lead quickly to disaster, especially if combined with bungling. Eisenhower's peaceful decade was but a calm before the storm.

BACKGROUNDS OF THE MPS MEN

During the summers of 1956 through 1960, 422 young men traveled to their first MPS assessment center. The first group, from Michigan Bell, journeyed to the banks of the St. Clair River in eastern Michigan and the Barlum House, a separate building of the St. Clair Inn rented just for the assessment center. Following this elegant beginning, quarters were obtained in the ensuing years in metropolitan hotels.

The assessees were typically met by a staff of 10, which included the director, a graduate student test administrator, and a group of assessors to observe and evaluate the various exercises. Though assured that the results of the center would be strictly confidential and would have no effect on their future careers, most participants did not realize that the study would involve their cooperation up to and perhaps including retirement. Neither, of course, did the planners of the study!

The young men who filed into the assessment center typically wore the uniform of the day — business suits with white shirts and narrow ties. Argyle socks frequently topped dark shoes, and hair was cropped short or crewcut. The men came in all shapes and sizes and varied in personality from friendly to hostile and from exhibitionistic to painfully shy. It seemed clear that Bell System selection methods had followed no particular stereotype.

On some characteristics, the college graduates were readily distinguishable from the vocational men who had advanced into management. This chapter describes these differences. First of all, the noncollege men (more precisely, men who had not graduated from college at the time of employment) were 5 or 6 years older than the college men. Most ranged from 26 to 31 years of age (full range 23—33), and their median age was 29.7. The college men were primarily 22 to 27 (full range 21—31), with a median age of 24.3. With age often went maturity, so that the typical college man was likely to be naive and ungraceful, compared to the more stable and settled noncollege man.

The bulk of information about the family and educational backgrounds of each participant came from an in-depth interview with a psychologist/assessor, a personal history questionnaire, and essay questions. Social class and status differences distinguished the college and noncollege men, as summarized in Table 2.1. The college men's families had deeper roots in America: Two-thirds of them had been in the United States four generations or more, while only one-third of the noncollege men came from such backgrounds. The vocational men were likely to have had grandparents or great-grandparents emigrate to this country, usually from European countries. The noncollege men's families tended to be slightly larger than those of the college men.

The parents of the noncollege men had not progressed as far either educationally or occupationally as those of the college graduates. The majority of their fathers had completed only grade school, and only 4% had completed college. By contrast, less than one-third of the college men's fathers had not completed high school, and more than one-quarter had college degrees. In both groups, however, the sons had done considerably better educationally than their fathers.

The mothers of the noncollege men had done slightly better than the fathers in school, though nearly half had not completed high school. The

Table 2.1   Family and Educational Background Variables Differentiating MPS College and Noncollege Groups

Variable	College	Noncollege
Fourth or more generation in United States	66%	31%
No. of siblings, average (mean)	1.9	2.3
Father's education		
College graduate	26%	4%
High school	44%	37%
Grade school	30%	59%
Mother's education		
College graduate	18%	5%
High school	61%	46%
Grade school	21%	49%
Father's occupation		
Business, professional	48%	27%
Skilled or unskilled	33%	50%
Mother's occupation		
Housewife	51%	63%
Professional	18%	7%
High school grades		
Excellent	24%	9%
Good	44%	32%
Fair or poor	32%	59%

college men's mothers were typically high school graduates; less than one-fifth had completed college.

Skilled and unskilled occupations were more typical of the noncollege men's fathers than the college men's fathers, who were more likely to be businessmen or professionals. At least partly because of the difference in fathers' occupations, the college men were more likely to have lived in more than one community before they were 16 years of age.

The occupations of the mothers of the assessees were not as markedly different, since the majority of mothers for both groups tended to be house-wives. More college men's mothers were apt to be in some kind of professional work, but this was true for less than one-fifth of them. Mothers from both groups were equally likely to have skilled or unskilled jobs or to be in business or white-collar occupations.

The differences in parental background no doubt led to many other dis-similarities in the childhoods of the college and noncollege men. Although the assessment interviewers did not probe deeply into early life as a psychodynamic therapist would, the habits, likes and dislikes, and attitudes of the men, discussed later, pointed to variations in the values they were taught and experiences they had had in the early years. Questionnaire responses hinted at a somewhat rougher childhood for the noncollege men: They were more likely as children to fight with others, play practical jokes, and take things that didn't belong to them. On the other hand, the college men reported that they were more likely to suck their thumbs!

Scholastic achievement was, of course, a major factor distinguishing the men at the time of the first assessment. Of the 148 noncollege men, 126 had ended their schooling with high school graduation; only 3 had not completed high school. Another 15 had earned some college credits, and 4 had com-pleted a college degree at night following employment in the Bell system. In addition to earlier termination of schooling, their grades in high school were not as good as the college men's. The majority of the noncollege men reported their high school grades as fair or poor, compared to only one-third of the college group. Nearly three times as many college as noncollege men claimed to have achieved excellent grades in high school.

Among the 274 college men, 259 had stopped with the college degree. Twelve had postgraduate credits, and three had a master's or professional degree. The undergraduate majors of the college men were fairly evenly divided among business, technical fields (engineering, math, or science), and the humanities and social sciences, with only 2% in education or other fields. They reported that their grades in college were not as good as they had been in high school (only 3% rated them as excellent), but external verification of college grades revealed that 31% were in the top quarter of their graduating class and 61% in the top half.

To illustrate the differences between the two groups of men, the composite character of Joe captures the substance of the typical college man, while Jerry illustrates the noncollege participant.

The first thing one noticed about Joe was his pleasant smile and friendly manner. He was trim, and looked no more than his age of 22. His short, curly, blond hair surrounded an attractive youthful face with blue eyes and a fair complexion. He was nattily dressed in a dark brown suit with narrow stripes, a white oxford button-down shirt, a small-pattern wool tie, argyle socks, and brown shoes. Joe easily carried the conversation in his first interview, often bubbling with the pleasure of having someone earnestly interested in him and his life.

Joe acknowledged "home" as a small town in the Midwest. He described his father, an insurance company salesman, as "an extrovert. He's always been very well liked. Mother was trained as a practical nurse, but she stopped practicing soon after she got married. She was active in clubs and the like, but she spent most of her time being wife and mother. Both my parents expected me to go to college and had the same aspirations for my two sisters."

Joe moved several times during his childhood as his father changed positions, but the family settled in their current town for his last 3 years of high school. He had a circle of close friends there as in previous places. He said, "I think the moves helped me to relate to many sorts of people. Overall I feel I benefited from them a good deal and really didn't suffer that much."

Joe's college years were spent in the state university, where he majored in business. He had to work harder in college than in high school, earning mostly B's, some A's, and a few C's. In spite of putting in a lot of time on academic work, he still participated in many extracurricular activities, including a fraternity and student government.

Jerry was a quiet and reserved person who won the affections of his interviewer by being straightforward and sincere. He was an athletic-looking man of 30 years, with closely cropped dark brown hair. He was clean and neat but not stylish in a Brooks Brothers way.

Jerry was raised in a small town with two brothers and one sister. His father had completed 10 grades of education and was a foreman with an electric company. His paternal grandparents had emigrated from Germany, and Jerry's father had done quite well by their standards. His electrical company job kept the family in a middle-income category, even during the Depression.

Jerry's mother was a high school graduate. She had had a clerical job before her marriage, but she had resigned a few months later to become a housewife.

As a child, Jerry got into occasional fights with other children but he remembered his childhood as a happy time. His grades were average or above average in elementary school.

In high school Jerry became interested in sports and other activities and let his grades slip below average. He said, "I didn't study much. But I earned letters in baseball and football and I was proud of that."

Joe and Jerry will appear several times later in this chapter to illustrate other aspects of the comparison of the college and noncollege groups.

LIFESTYLES

The assessment center interviews with the MPS men delved into their many diverse avenues of interest and concern. Summaries of these initial interviews were scored on nine orientations or life themes (Rychlak, 1982). Each theme, described below, was rated on a 7-point scale according to how much psychological investment the participant manifested in that area of life. Four ratings were given for each theme: current involvement; current satisfaction; retrospective developments, or attentions to the theme in the past; and projected developments, or prospective future involvements in the area. Averages across the four ratings represented total involvement in each category. The themes were as follows:

- *Marital-Familial*: Spouse, children, in-laws; premarital relationships such as dating and engagement.
- *Parental-Familial*: Parents, siblings, relatives on the parents' side, activities deriving from parents' home.
- *Locale-Residential*: Kind of housing and its location.
- *Financial-Acquisitive*: Wealth and material possessions, including savings, investments, conspicuous consumption; concern with making ends meet.
- *Ego-Functional*: Conditioning and development of the mind and body, including reading, educational pursuits, exercise, self-help efforts, therapeutic activities; concern with disease or disability.
- *Recreational-Social*: Leisure-time pursuits, including hobbies, sports, partying, and socializing.
- *Religious-Humanism*: Ethical and humanistic involvement, not necessarily part of an organized religion; concern with a philosophy of life acting as an ethic.
- *Service*: Community activities such as the Chamber of Commerce, Boy Scouts, and political parties, excluding church activities (scored under Religious-Humanism).
- *Occupational*: Work life, including job content, supervisors, promotions, raises, attitudes toward the company and so on.

Average ratings for current involvement in each life theme are illustrated in Figure 2.1. It is clear that for both groups, there was still intensive involvement in the parental family. For the noncollege men, however, the marital family had begun to assume slightly greater importance. At the time of the assessment 94% of the noncollege men were married, compared to only 56% of the college men. The college men were rated somewhat higher on the Locale-Residential life theme, which probably represents their transitional state from their parental families and single lives to new jobs and creating their own families.

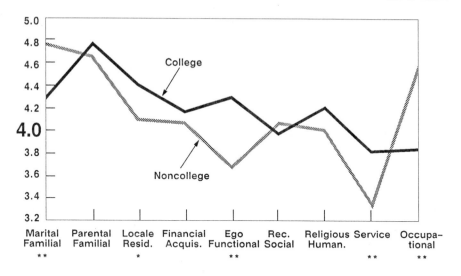

Figure 2.1.   Current involvement in life themes at MPS:0, college and noncollege groups.

The married college men, being younger and more newly married, also had fewer children. Nearly half (45%) had no children, and 37% had only one. The most typical situation for the married noncollege men was a two-child family (39%), and only 9% had no children.

Only one-third of the married college men had wives with college degrees, showing the tendency for women in the 1950s to give up their educations for marriage. About one-quarter of the wives had professional jobs, such as nursing or teaching, but almost as many were white-collar workers. The largest number (42%) were housewives. Nearly all the noncollege men's wives were high school graduates. Most were housewives, but 29% were in white-collar jobs.

Joe was not married, but he claimed to have his wife all picked out. He was first smitten when he found her sitting next to him in a college English class. She had completed 2 years of college but was not sure she wanted to go on.

Joe's girl was now back home in a nearby town for the summer, and he expected he would be popping the question soon. In his bubbly way he confessed, "She's really pretty, and so easy to talk to. She's very feminine and likes to wear skirts with those crinolines underneath that make them stick out and her waist cinched in with a wide elastic belt. She's a good dancer too. We watch Dick Clark's *American Bandstand* on television. We were the first couple to do the Stroll at my fraternity party. I'm really ready to settle down now. I've got a steady job, and now I want a wife, a house in the suburbs, and a family."

Jerry had long been married by the time of assessment and was the father of two daughters and one son. He had met his wife in high school. They began to date then but didn't get serious until after he was discharged from the Navy. She resigned from her job as a bank teller to become a housewife 4 months after their marriage.

Asked to describe his wife, Jerry said, "She's a hard worker who keeps a clean house. She makes sure the kids are properly groomed and well behaved. She's religious and goes to church regularly. She belongs to a women's organization in the church and teaches Sunday School." She seemed to be a reserved woman with simple tastes, much like Jerry's mother.

Another life theme involvement distinguishing the college and noncollege groups was Ego-Functional, where the college men were more inclined to focus on improving their minds and bodies. They were more positive about the state of their health on the personal history questionnaire, with 58% describing it as "excellent," compared to only 32% of the vocational men. The college men spent more time off the job reading than did the noncollege men. They claimed to have read more books and more technical journals in the 2 months prior to assessment, but not more magazines. The types of magazines usually read differed, however, with more college men preferring current events and more noncollege men preferring pure entertainment.

Joe enjoyed the *Saturday Evening Post*, *U.S. News and World Report*, and *Business Week*, as well as the daily newspaper. He read several books a year, either histories and biographies (such as a recent one about Churchill and World War II) or crime and adventure fiction.

Jerry skimmed the newspaper daily and enjoyed reading magazines like *Life* and *Reader's Digest*. On the few occasions when he read a book, he preferred action fiction, especially involving the military. Favorites of his were *Mr. Roberts* and *From Here to Eternity*.

The college men were more involved in the Service life theme, and they projected even more involvement in the future, when their lives would assume a traditional course in the community.

Said Joe, "After we're married and settled down, I'd like to join the Junior Chamber of Commerce and maybe the Rotary Club. I have several reasons for this. I want to be of help in community affairs, I want to represent the company in public service, and I want to be looked up to."

Jerry's only community involvement was attending Parent-Teachers Association (PTA) meetings.

Few of the men in either group were actively concerned with politics, and most seemed poorly informed about current issues. About one-quarter of each sample professed to belong to no political party, but 56% of the noncollege and 44% of the college men identified with the Republican party. The Democrats claimed only 14% of the noncollege and 19% of the college men.

Coding of sociocultural attitudes from the assessment interviews showed no overall difference between the college and noncollege men. They were rated on the conservative side in political philosophy (3.9 on a 5-point scale, where 5 was the conservative pole), though their position on social issues (3.1) was more liberal than their position on economic issues (4.6). Their level of understanding was rated at 2.1 on a scale of 5, where 5 showed high understanding.

In line with their conservative stand on economic issues, the men were generally negative toward a big federal government. The inefficiency of the government bureaucracy was often mentioned as a reason for their opposition.

Joe was a Republican who supported Eisenhower. He said, "I respect him because he worked up from a lowly position and achieved so much in spite of poor grades at West Point. I envision government as one big business. Why take inept politicians and give them positions of responsibility in the government? The Republicans take people with leadership ability in business, like Wilson. I'm also concerned about the right of the individual to chart his own course free of government interferences. The individual is capable of availing himself of a decent income and social climate; it shouldn't be dictated by the government."

Jerry also identified with the Republicans. He said, "I don't know much about politics, but the Republicans have the reputation of having business at heart. I suppose indirectly this should be a greater help to a man like me. I guess I think of Democrats as fast giveaway program people."

Though both the college and noncollege men were probusiness, they had different positions about unions. The noncollege men had been union members before their promotions into management, and their position was more favorable (3.5 on a 5-point scale) than that of the college men (2.5).

Joe said, "I have reservations about unions. My theory is that when something is based on conflict, it is bound to be troublesome. And the union is based on conflict. There are lots of things this labor movement does that cause us headaches. They're often unfair, and some even make threats of physical violence. It doesn't do the country any good."

Jerry thought unions were a good thing. "They give the workers a chance to express their feelings. They provide a representative group of some sort for all workers so that management can deal with someone. Unions help companies like Bell; they have good suggestions to make. People like [Teamsters head James] Hoffa frighten me, though. The only thing unions are guilty of is the caliber of leaders they sometimes have."

The life theme showing the greatest differences between the two samples was Occupational, where the noncollege men showed significantly greater involvement as well as satisfaction. The noncollege men had on the average 9

years of experience in the telephone companies when they came to the assessment center, while the college men had a median time of only 4 months. For
some of the college men, in fact, the assessment center was their first job
experience! It is not surprising, then, that work had not yet captured their
spirits in the same way it had those of the noncollege men. The next section
describes the work experiences of the two groups, the nature of the company
they joined, and their expectations and preferences for the future.

WORK INTERESTS

The attraction of the MPS participants to the telephone companies was a
function not only of the general appeal of large corporations to young men in
the 1950s, but also of the reputation and image of AT&T and the Bell
System. The then-prevailing culture of the company can best be appreciated by
a brief look at its evolution and organization.

The Bell System in the 1950s

Had the MPS men joined the company at the turn of the 20th century rather
than in the middle of it, their fortunes would have looked considerably less
promising. As has been well documented by Brooks (1975), the Bell System
was then plagued by ineffective and uninspired leadership, frequent accidents
and fatalities in plant work, and noise and delays in long-distance service. The
work force was generally demoralized, and the company's public image was
soured by questionable competitive practices, such as refusing to connect rival
companies. A major turnaround began in 1907 with the installation as AT&T
president of the man revered as the savior of the Bell System, Theodore Vail.

Vail realized that profits were necessary to provide the capital needed for
renovation and innovation of facilities, and he created the research and
development units that would later become the Bell Laboratories to further
this end. He clearly laid the groundwork for a policy of subordinating profits
to service for the customer. He felt there should be universal service and
connection provided by a national network. At the time, however, dissociated
companies were competing within the same jurisdictions with a duplication
even of telephone lines. There was grave public inconvenience, since sub-
scribers to one telephone system couldn't talk to those on another. To best
serve the public interest, Vail thought that telephone service should be a
natural monopoly, but that the privilege of acting as a monopoly should be
controlled with regulation by state and federal authorities.

Vail's dream eventually was realized, although not without a history of
government investigations and interventions, including a year under complete
government ownership during World War I (an experiment that failed, returning the Bell System to private hands). By the mid-1950s the telephone system
was regulated by state authorities and the Federal Communications Commis-

sion (FCC), created in 1934 as part of the New Deal legislation. There were still more than 1,500 independent telephone companies that operated in their own circumscribed territories as parallel monopolies, interconnected to the much larger Bell System network.

The Bell System was controlled by an owner, AT&T, with central headquarters at 195 Broadway in New York City. The chief executive officer was the president of AT&T until 1961, when the chairman of the board assumed that role. Twenty-two Bell operating companies, which provided basic telephone service, were substantially owned by the parent company; they paid a certain proportion of their gross revenues to AT&T for specialized services under what was known as the license contract. Another operating unit, Long Lines, was considered a department of AT&T; it provided telephone circuits between the states and across international boundaries. The manufacturing arm of the company was Western Electric, with plants scattered across the country. Finally, the research and development organization, Bell Laboratories, was owned half by AT&T and half by Western Electric. AT&T was thus vertically integrated.

The Justice Department filed an antitrust suit against AT&T in 1949, concerned that the states couldn't set rates properly if they had no way of knowing whether Western Electric's equipment prices charged to the operating companies were fair. The government wanted to separate Western Electric from AT&T and split it into three companies competing with other manufacturers for the Bell business. In the early 1950s, however, the Bell System was making a large contribution to the Cold War effort, especially since it operated at government request the Sandia Corporation, which manufactured atomic bombs. The Defense Department was accordingly not too sympathetic toward breaking up the Bell System, and the suit was settled in 1956 with a consent decree.

The decree left standing the vertically integrated Bell System but specified that Western Electric would seek no external markets other than government defense work. AT&T also agreed not to engage in any business other than common-carrier communications and incidental operations, and to grant nonexclusive licenses and related technical information to any applicant on fair terms.

With its structure and mandate clarified, the Bell System in the 1950s must have looked like a stable but progressive giant. Business boomed after World War II, and more phones were installed in the 7 years following the war than in all the years before it. During the Eisenhower administration, the number of telephone calls per day was nearly 500 million. AT&T had more than $1\frac{1}{2}$ million stockholders in the mid-1950s and nearly 750,000 employees by the end of the decade.

Labor was well represented in the Bell System workforce, primarily by the Communication Workers of America. There were no major labor problems in the decade of the 1950s, and the adversarial relationship seemed to function cordially. For managers, there was the strong influence in the early 1950s of AT&T President Cleo Craig, who sought to break away from the narrow technical orientation of the past and expose managers to broadening courses, sometimes a year long, in the humanities. MPS itself was one product of the Craig emphasis on the quality of the managerial workforce.

Company earnings were up in the 1950s, partly because of general national prosperity and partly because the regulatory bodies had allowed the company better rates. As a result, equity financing was possible for the huge capital outlays required to expand communications service. Company productivity was also increased considerably by the numerous innovations of the Bell Laboratories. The transistor alone, which vastly improved on the speed and efficiency of vacuum tubes, made possible an endless array of advances not just in telephony but in numerous achievements appreciated throughout the world, from the computer to later explorations in space. Another high note was basic development of the laser, with a first paper published in 1958.

The company also had a rather heroic image. Battalions of Bell System employees had carried the major responsibility for U.S. Army communications in France in World War I. Western Electric had basically been a war plant in World War II, implementing many innovative designs of Bell Laboratories scientists, as in the use of radar. Moreover, in times of domestic emergencies such as floods, hurricanes, or snowstorms, Bell System people, from installers to operators, could usually be counted on to show exceptional speed and resoluteness in restoring calm and efficient service.

Thus young men looking optimistically toward a career in business in the 1950s might easily have been impressed with a company that was financially sound, growing rapidly, technologically very advanced, beneficent toward its employees, and providing an important public service, often in a rather heroic fashion. But critics could point to the paradox of an efficient giant serving the public interest that was also a privately owned monopoly in a stridently competitive economy and culture.

The middle managers of the organization had the 1950s urge to conform and to fit into the organization and its procedures, according to two consultants to the company at the time (Williams & Peterfreund, 1958). Managers became very absorbed in the Bell System and the technology of the business. Compared to managers in other organizations, they were more emotionally stable but less daring and more bound by rules. As managers of a government-controlled monopoly, they were less "dollar"-conscious in a proprietorship sense, but assumed social responsibility for the service the telephone business provided and had a real sense of obligation to the community.

The consultants also noted that there seemed to be less political maneuvering in the Bell System than in other organizations and more acceptance of fate in individual career achievements. Managers were usually quite busy. They were oriented toward line jobs rather than staff, seeing themselves as "doers" with an eye on performance indices rather than intellectual or artistic pursuits.

They led family-centered lives of moderation with no unusual or bizarre habits.

Work History of the MPS Participants

Although the noncollege men were more likely to have had a previous job before joining the Bell System, neither group was widely experienced. Among the vocational men, 39% had begun with the Bell System right out of high school and 31% had held only one earlier regular job. Most of the college group (70%) had had no previous jobs, and another 21% had held only one previous regular job.

The noncollege men were much more likely to have served in the military by the time of assessment. Some 74% of the noncollege men were veterans, and only 11% had yet to serve. Among the college men, 44% were veterans and 36% had still to serve, with the remainder in the active reserves or permanently deferred. More than one-third of the college men who had served were officers, but almost none of the noncollege men were discharged with a commission.

In spite of more experience on other jobs and in the military, the majority of the noncollege men were under the age of 21 when employed by the telephone company. Most were employed initially for assignments in the Plant Department, which was responsible for the installation and maintenance of equipment. Based on their performance in these positions, they were promoted to management, usually within the same department, while they were still quite young. By the time of assessment, the average noncollege man had been with the telephone company 9.4 years and had spent the last 2 in management.

Two-thirds of the vocational men were still in the Plant Department at assessment, and another 18% were in the Commercial Department, which handled business relationships with telephone company customers. The remainder were spread across various other Bell System departments. Three-quarters of these men were still at the first level of the telephone company's seven-level hierarchy, but another 21% had been promoted again to the second level, and one man was at the third level.

Jerry enlisted in the Navy for 3 years after high school and became a third-class petty officer. He said, "I enjoyed those years, especially since I got to travel abroad, but I decided I didn't want a military career. After I was discharged, I took a job as a tool grinder. I wasn't there even a year, though, when a friend of mine lured me into the telephone company. I liked the idea of being able to work with my hands and still be outdoors as an installer."

Jerry served as in installer for 3 years and then moved on to the position of central office repairman for 2 years. The next job change put him in the position of switchman, but within one year he had been made a chief switchman at the first level of management. For the last 2 years he had been a service foreman, supervising eight installers, which he enjoyed. "I really like going out on the job with my men since I don't care much for paperwork. I feel like I'm making a greater contribution to the company now that I'm a boss."

As mentioned above the college men had only 4 months of Bell System experience on the average when they arrived at the assessment cventer. Nearly half had been on the job less than 1 month, and only 5% had been employed more than 1 year. Only one man was at the second level of management; the rest were still at the first level.

The college graduates were spread much more widely across the Bell System departments than were the noncollege men. The Plant and Commercial Departments each claimed about one-fifth of the group. Almost the same number were in the Traffic Department, which planned and administered operator services, and in the Engineering Department, which planned and made arrangements for the construction of the telephone "plant," including buildings as well as telephone equipment. Another 12% were in the Accounting Department, which recorded and collected all revenues earned by the company and paid out monies owed to the company's suppliers and employees. The remainder were in sales or various staff departments. Although the organization of the Bell System changed dramatically in later years due to deregulation and other factors, these were the traditional departments that characterized the company in the 1950s and 1960s.

Joe began his career with Michigan Bell right out of college. He had yet to serve in the military but was anticipating being drafted into 6 months of active duty fairly soon. He discussed this with the personnel representative during his employment interview and was told that he could take a military leave of absence and return to his job in the Bell System. He would then be expected to serve $7\frac{1}{2}$ years in the reserves.

Joe had only been on the job for 5 weeks by the time he came to the assessment center. His first position was in the Commercial Department, where he thought his ease in meeting people was a great help to him. He supervised seven female service representatives keeping customer records in the business office.

Expectations and Work Preferences

There were a number of ways in which the participants in the MPS:0 assessment center revealed their aspirations and expectations for the future. Interviewers specifically probed in this area, and additional information was revealed in projective tests, essay questions, and questionnaires. (Descriptions of all exercises are given in the Appendix to this volume.)

One particularly revealing questionnaire was the Expectations Inventory, where the assessees gave their preferences for and expectations of what would be true 5 years hence. The 56 items on the questionnaire ranged across a wide variety of areas, from promotions and salary to geographical location and intellectual stimulation by peers. Average scores for the two groups of men were surprisingly optimistic. On a 4-point scale from +2 ("fairly certain to be true") to −2 ("fairly certain to be false"), the average rating on each of the 28 most positive items was +0.95 for the college group and +0.86 for the noncollege group. Thus both groups generally thought the positive outcomes were more likely to be true than false.

Responses to the items the men designated as most desirable or most undesirable are illustrated in Table 2.2. There was general agreement about the items that were most positive, although the noncollege men put greater emphasis on living in a desirable community close to the job, while the college men placed greater importance on social and community activities and a challenging job.

The right-hand columns of Table 2.2 show the proportions answering each question with the most favorable expectation, which for the positive items was "fairly certain to be true." It should be noted that on almost every item, those not giving this most favorable response at least rated it "more likely to be true than not." The college men were not quite so sure as the noncollege about making more than $8,000 a year. Both groups gave their most conservative estimates to reaching the district or third level of responsibility (the entrance to middle management) within 5 years, although the college group was generally more confident of this outcome.

On the undesirable items, the college men were considerably more concerned than the noncollege men with the possibility of not being promoted at the same rate as their initial peers in the company. The noncollege men worried more about having to travel and being away from home a lot or finding themselves making less than $7,000 a year. The noncollege men's greater family responsibilities were no doubt instrumental in these responses. As with the desirable items, both groups were overwhelmingly optimistic about the future; that is, most rated the undesirable items either fairly certain or more than likely to be false.

Many more college men indicated that they would hate to find they had gone to work for the wrong company. Although almost all of both groups thought such an outcome unlikely, more of the noncollege men were "fairly certain" of their favorable answer.

In summary, the Expectations Inventory revealed that large proportions of both groups of participants felt it was important to have challenging work they enjoyed, advancement, and a good salary. They also wanted their spouses to be happy that they worked for the Bell System, and they did not want to experience conflicts between job and family. For the most part, they expected these ideals to be realized. In true 1950s style, they believed that only the best

Table 2.2 Responses to Most Important Items in Expectations Inventory at MPS:0, College and Noncollege Groups

Most desired items	% citing most desirable		% fairly certain of favorable outcome	
	C	NC	C	NC
I have a real chance to follow my basic interests and work at the things I like to do.	39	48	42	39
I have reached the district level of responsibility.[a]	54	45	25 *	17
I am earning $8,000 a year or more	41	33	51 **	85
My job is challenging with many opportunities to to learn and do new things.	61 **	40	69	65
My spouse is happy that I work for the Bell system.	36	34	69	80
I have discovered that working for the Bell System has helped me to meet the kind of people I like and to engage in desirable social and community activities.	46 **	24	76	69
I am advanced about as rapidly as my interest and ability warrant.	41	30	37	38
I live in a desirable community with relatively easy access to my job.	14 **	42	47	52
I feel an increasing amount of conflict between obligations of my job and my family.	55	55	65	48
I regret not having gone to work for another company.	46 **	26	63 **	83
I have fewer opportunities for promotion than if I had gone to work for a different company.	38	32	62	63
I am earning less than $7,000 a year.	25 *	38	63 **	93
I have not reached as high a level of responsibility as most of the people who started in the company when I did.	45 **	15	55	57
The company doesn't provide sufficient opportunity for me to learn new things.	34	24	65 *	57
I have to travel and be away from home a lot of the time.	20 **	43	24	28

Note. Group differences in desirability computed from chi-square tests on proportions; expectations from t-tests on means. Abbreviations: C, college; NC, noncollege.
[a] The district level is the third of seven levels of management running from foreman to president.
* $p < .05$.
** $p < .005$.

lay ahead. Depressions, wars, and shortages were forgotten; prosperity and security beckoned.

The noncollege men had higher expectations about salaries, and salaries were more important to them; the college men had higher expectations about advancement, a matter of greater significance to them. The college men also placed greater emphasis on challenging work and the opportunity for social and community activities. The noncollege men responded more like home-bodies; they wanted to live close to work and not have to travel too much. These findings are consistent with other survey results showing that college-educated workers place more emphasis on affiliative and achievement satis-factions and less emphasis on financial rewards than those less educated (Veroff, Douvan, & Kulka, 1981).

Another questionnaire measure, the Work Conditions Survey, asked the men to rate 30 statements about types of work situations on a 6-point scale from "highly desirable" (1) to "would make the job impossible" (6). Among the items generally rated on the positive side of the scale, the college men gave more desirable ratings to jobs requiring much initiative, a lot of respon-sibility, and dependence on one's own decisions. The noncollege men, on the negative side of the scale, found it less objectionable to be always under supervision or to do very routine or monotonous work.

Another Work Conditions Survey preference that differentiated the two groups was relative desirability of jobs with interpersonal contacts. The college men gave more desirable ratings to jobs requiring selection of personnel, a lot of social contact, intimate personal interviews, and advising people on personal difficulties. Among work settings generally rated as negative, the noncollege men had fewer objections to having little social contact or no one to talk to. The noncollege men were more positive about a job working only with men and the college men more positive about a job working only with women, although both groups, given the choice, would prefer working only with men. Thus in two separate exercises, the Expectations Inventory and the Work Conditions Survey, the college men revealed greated interest in challeng-ing work and in having social contacts.

Jerry was attracted to the Bell System because he thought it would offer him a secure future. "The wages were good and the fringe benefits looked very generous," he said.

Joe had actively sought a big company that offered good chances for advancement. He, too, appreciated the security and liked the idea of working for a service organiza-tion.

When asked about the ideal job for him, Joe said, "One where I would have a lot of responsibility and make decisions. I am people-centered, and I'd like to work closely with people rather than administer technical aspects of a job. I see the telephone company manager as akin to an independent business man rather than a cog in a wheel. I'd like to be in a position like that and have people working for me."

Work Attitudes

A measure of the men's attitudes toward their work and the company was not taken at the original assessment, since some had only been on the job a few days. Along with the interviews conducted over the next 7 years, the men were administered the Management Questionnaire. This questionnaire, described more fully in the Appendix, was scored on nine specific scales and one more general scale. The scales were as follows:

- *Supervision*: Attitudes toward one's immediate boss, including fairness and appreciation of and interest in the participant.
- *Personal Satisfaction*: Satisfaction with various aspects of the job, including responsibility, freedom, variety, challenge, and promotional opportunities.
- *Job Satisfaction*: Global measure of satisfaction with working at the telephone company.
- *Pride*: Pride in working for the company as shown in relating to outsiders.
- *Impersonal Communications*: Satisfaction with information about company policies and the workings of the business.
- *Personal Communications*: Information and freedom of expression between participant and his supervisor.
- *Identification*: Feeling of being consulted and appreciated as a member of management.
- *Authority*: Satisfaction with freedom to make own decisions.
- *Salary*: Satisfaction with fairness of salary treatment.
- *General Management Attitude*: Selected items from the nine other scales, somewhat weighted toward attitudes toward supervision; one additional item on confidence in higher management.

A comparison of the college and noncollege groups on the Management Questionnaire scales as administered 1 year after the original assessment is shown in Figure 2.2. The largest difference between the two groups was on the Salary scale, where the college men indicated much more pleasure with their salaries than the noncollege men. Part of the reason may be the non-college men's greater interest in making money, as shown on the Expectations Inventory, but their dissatisfaction was also tied to reality. The college men's salaries were more than 25% higher than the noncollege men's at the original assessment, in spite of the fact that more than one-fifth of the noncollege group was already at the second level of management. Apparently higher salaries had been used as a lure to bring the college men into the business.

Two other scales showing a difference between the educational groups in Figure 2.2 were General Management Attitude and Supervision. The college men were more positive about their bosses than the noncollege men and had a generally more favorable view of the company and its management. Although the educational groups were mostly in different departments of the company during the early years that may have differed in the quality of supervision offered, it is likely that the noncollege men's greater work experience may have exposed them to more supervisory weaknesses than the college men.

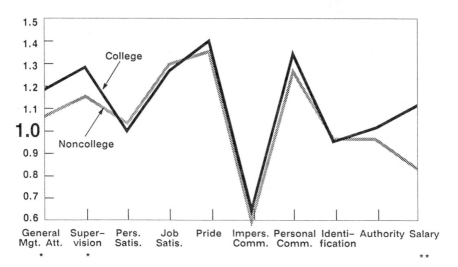

*p < .05. **p < .005.

Figure 2.2.   Management Questionnaire scales in year 1, MPS college and noncollege groups.

More is said on this subject in Chapter 6, as these men are followed through the next 20 years of their careers.

PERSONALITY AND MOTIVATION

Personality and motivational characteristics were revealed by a total of 37 different scores, each described in the Appendix. Most of these were from paper-and-pencil tests: the 15 scales of the Edwards Personal Preference Schedule, 5 from the Guilford-Martin Inventory (GAMIN), 3 derived from the Sarnoff Survey of Attitudes Toward Life, and a measure of Authoritarianism from the Bass (1955) version of the California F Scale. In addition, summaries of responses to the projective exercises, which included stories written to Thematic Apperception Test (TAT) pictures and responses to two incomplete-sentences exercises (the Rotter Incomplete Sentences Blank and the Business Incomplete Sentences Test), were coded on nine characteristics. Four motivational characteristics were coded from interview protocols, including Need for Advancement, Primacy of Work, Inner Work Standards, and Need for Security.

These 37 scores were subjected to a factor analysis to bring together related scales and to reduce the many measures to an underlying structure. Six personality and motivation factors were produced by this analysis, with 30 of the 37 scales meaningfully circumscribed by a factor. The scales making up each factor and the interpretation of each are given below.

Self-Esteem: High scores on GAMIN Ascendance, Masculinity, Lack of Inferiority Feelings, and Lack of Nervousness; low scores on Edwards Succorance. Those scoring high on this factor show self-confidence and emotional stability without dependence on others for emotional support. They report relatively less fear of speaking up in social situations and have traditionally masculine attitudes and interests.

Leadership Motivation: High projective ratings on Leadership Role and Achievement/Advancement Motivation; low projective ratings on Subordinate Role, Dependence, and Affiliation. High scorers on this factor have positive reactions to a leadership role and a desire for career accomplishments. They dislike a subordinate role or being dependent on others.

Positiveness: High projective ratings on General Adjustment, Optimism, and Self-Confidence. High scorers show an optimistic and positive approach to life and good overall coping and adjustment. They have confidence about being able to handle their work and other matters.

Impulsivity: High scores on Edwards Exhibition and Heterosexuality; low scores on Edwards Abasement, Order, Endurance, and Deference, and low interview ratings on Need for Security. High scorers on this factor like to stand out in a crowd, have a tendency to show off, and enjoy interactions with the opposite sex and jokes about sex. They are less likely to be orderly, deferent to those in higher authority, concerned with job security, or persistent in work or other tasks. They tend not to feel guilty or to punish themselves when something goes wrong.

Affability: High scores on Edwards Nurturance and Affiliation; low scores on Edwards Autonomy and Aggression. Those scoring high on this factor take pleasure in doing things with and for friends, and show sympathetic and supportive tendencies toward others. They are less likely to feel hostile to others or to be concerned with independence and autonomy.

Ambition: High scores on Edwards Dominance, on Sarnoff Motivation for Advancement and Forward Striving, and on interview ratings of Primacy of Work, Inner Work Standards, and Need for Advancement. Those scoring high put much store in personal advancement, generally looking forward to the future and striving for something better. They enjoy leading and directing others, are very involved in their work, and have high work standards.

For each MPS participant, a score was derived for each personality and motivation factor by averaging his standardized scores on each scale in the factor and translating the result into a scale with an average of 50 and standard deviation of 10. A comparison of the average personality and motivation factor scores for the two educational groups is shown in Figure 2.3. Two factors showed a clear difference between the college and noncollege groups: the college men scored higher on Ambition and Impulsivity.

In light of the differences in wanting and expecting advancement shown by the two groups on the Expectations Inventory, it is not surprising that the college group scored higher on Ambition. Many scales in the Ambition factor

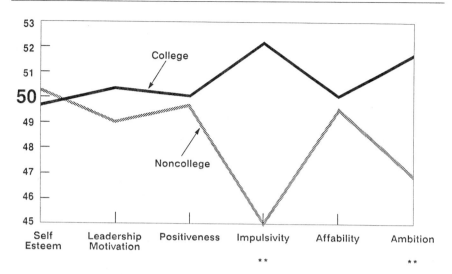

**p < .005.

Figure 2.3.   Personality and motivation factors at MPS:0, college and noncollege groups.

pointed to this difference. On the Sarnoff questionnaire, the college men scored higher on the subscale measuring Motivation for Advancement; using MPS college norms, the college men were at the 50th percentile and the noncollege men at the 39th. The college men also showed more interest in Forward Striving (55th percentile vs. 49th for the noncollege men). They were also somewhat higher on the Edwards Dominance scale, which is a measure of liking to lead and direct others. Interview ratings pegged the college men as more interested in advancement and more likely to consider work one of the most important things in their lives. Related data from the Leadership Motivation factor showed them rated higher on the projective tests in Motivation for Achievement/Advancement and lower in preference for a Subordinate Role.

This is not to say that the noncollege men were lacking in motivation. On the Motivation for Money scale of the Sarnoff, their average score at the 69th percentile exceeded that for the college men, which was at the 57th percentile. Recall that the vocational men also showed more interest in financial rewards on the Expectations Inventory. Thus the college men were more interested in the status and leadership opportunities of advancement, while the noncollege men's ambitions were grounded in the desire for a high income.

The college men also scored higher on the Edwards Achievement scale, indicating greater motivation toward having a difficult, challenging job, as compared to the noncollege men. This confirmed their greater interest in challenging work revealed in the Expectations Inventory and the Work Conditions Survey. But the noncollege men were motivated to perform well on the jobs they had. Their interview ratings were higher than those of the college men on Inner Work Standards, indicating that they had their own high standards for quality of work, regardless of external criteria.

When asked in the interview about his future career goals, Joe said, "I have an intense desire to be in a top executive position. Whenever I see a chance to try for a higher job, I'll always attempt it, both for the service I can render and personal recognition. In 10 years I hope I'll be at the third or even the fourth level. I really think that my motivation and desire will take me to top levels."

Joe's projective responses also indicated his interest in taking on additional responsibilities. To the incomplete-sentences stem "*In 20 years from now . . . ,*" he responded, "I hope to be in a position of authority." Another reply was "*The best job is one that offers a constant challenge.*"

Jerry did not seem to have strong needs to advance. In fact, on an incomplete-sentences response he wrote, "*What I need most is more ambition.*" In the interview he put it this way: "I don't have those dreams of going to the top like some of the guys here. Once the vocational people break into management at the first level, they begin to look at second or even third. But I'd rather not go all the way to third if it were questionable that I deserved it and I was just hanging by a string. I'd be really happy if I made it to second level in 8 to 10 years. I just want to make sure I have enough money to support my family. I can't imagine going beyond third since I'm a poor public speaker. Anyway, the college men will probably be promoted over me. The vocational men don't get many promotions."

The college men scored higher in Impulsivity on every scale making up that factor. This meant that they were more likely to want to stand out in a crowd or be the center of attention (higher on Exhibition) and were more attuned to activities with the opposite sex (higher on Heterosexuality), perhaps because they were more likely to be single and courting. The noncollege men were more orderly and more inclined to persist at a task once they had begun it (higher Order and Endurance). "I *hate* to see people give up on a problem," responded Jerry.

Job security (coded from the interviews) was of greater importance to the noncollege men; this may have been a very realistic concern, since they were more likely to have families to support and fewer opportunities than the college graduates for jobs outside AT&T at a comparable salary.

Jerry had responded on the incomplete-sentence test, "*The worst that could happen is that you would be fired.*" To the stem, "*A secure job . . .* " Jerry had replied "is very desirable," while Joe wrote "is usually one that precludes promotion."

The noncollege men tended to defer to those in higher authority and to feel guilty when they did something wrong (higher on Deference and Abasement).

"*Taking orders never bothered me,*" replied Jerry, and "*If a supervisor criticizes me he is usually right.*"

One final aspect of personality differentiated the college from the noncollege participants. Although the Affability factor in total revealed no difference, the college men showed more interest in relating to people in terms of friendship (with a higher score on Edwards Affiliation) and wanting emotional support and understanding (shown by a higher score on Edwards Succorance). This is consistent with their preferences for working with people on the Work Conditions Survey and desires for social contacts expressed on the Expectations Inventory.

"*Making close friends at work* is an important thing," said Joe, while Jerry responded, "*When I first meet someone* I am cautious about committing myself to friendship." Similarly, "*Listening to other people's troubles* is an art," according to Joe, but "is annoying" to Jerry.

In summary, on motivation and personality measures, the college men were more impulsive, exhibitionistic, and people-oriented and more motivated toward challenging jobs and leadership positions than their noncollege counterparts. The vocational men were more enduring and restrained in their self-perceptions. They were oriented toward job and financial security, with less emphasis on advancing in the management hierarchy.

ABILITIES

Managerial abilities were measured in a number of different ways at the assessment center, including paper-and-pencil tests, the interview, and several simulations, all described in the Appendix. The paper-and-pencil tests included the SCAT, the Critical Thinking in Social Science Test, and a Contemporary Affairs Test developed each calendar year. Simulations included one for individuals (the In-Basket), a group business game (the Manufacturing Problem), and an assigned-role group discussion (the Promotion Problem). These exercises yielded some immediately quantifiable results, such as scores on the paper-and-pencil tests and overall ratings by assessors observing the participants in the group exercises. In addition, the interview and simulation summary reports also provided the opportunity for postassessment coding on relevant dimensions.

The most important of these scores (14 in all, described in the Appendix) were subjected to a factor analysis, as with the personality and motivation scales. The analysis indicated that three critical types of ability were being measured:

- *Administrative Ability*: Stresses Organizing and Planning, and Decision Making, both as assessed by the In-Basket.
- *Interpersonal Ability*: Emphasizes Leadership Skills, Forcefulness, and Oral Communication Skills from the two group exercises and the interview.
- *Cognitive Ability*: Based on paper-and-pencil measures of verbal and quantitative ability, logical reasoning, and knowledge of current affairs.

As with the personality and motivation factors, a score was derived for each participant on each ability factor by averaging his standardized scores on each scale in the factor and translating the result into a scale with an average of 50 and a standard deviation of 10. A comparison of the average ability factor scores for the educational groups is shown in Figure 2.4.

Although there were no overall differences between the two educational groups in the Administrative or Interpersonal Ability factors, their performances on the simulations varied somewhat because of their respective personalities. For example, in the Manufacturing Problem the men were required as a group to buy Tinker Toy parts and to manufacture and sell toys as market conditions changed. Joe, the more affiliative one, was talkative and sociable in this exercise. He proved a good team member whose frequent lapses into humor increased his popularity and called attention to his point of view. Jerry assumed the role of order maker and parts figurer. He worked industriously and became the leader's right-hand man. He had several good ideas about the product to be manufactured, but offered them deferentially, never making a final decision. Both Joe and Jerry were given average ratings on effectiveness in this exercise.

The only significant college-noncollege difference in the ability factors was in the Cognitive Ability factor, but this difference was rather large. Four test scores made up the Cognitive Ability factor. Two came from the SCAT and indicated verbal and quantitative abilities. As shown in Figure 2.5, the college men outpaced the noncollege group on both the Verbal and the Quantitative

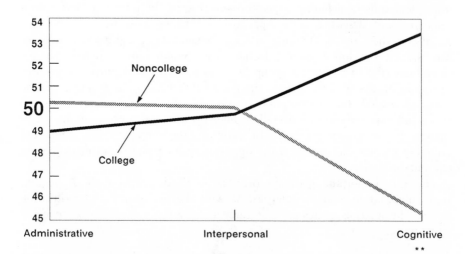

**p < .005.

Figure 2.4.   Ability factors at MPS:0, college and noncollege groups.

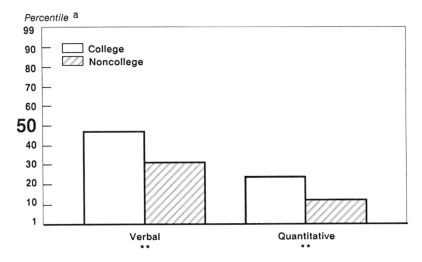

Figure 2.5.   Scores on SCAT scales at MPS:0, college and noncollege groups.

scales. Verbal scores for both groups exceeded Quantitative, as measured against a norm group of 585 college hires brought into the Bell System in 1958. However, there is reason to believe that those norms were somewhat high, especially on the Quantitative scale.

When compared to a norm group of 1,419 college seniors reported by the Educational Testing Service in 1963, 48% of the MPS college graduates were above the median of the college seniors on the Verbal subtest and 67% were above the median on the Quantitative subtest. Using this standard, the MPS men were better on the average on Quantitative items than Verbal items. Apparently the Bell System hired graduates with particularly well-developed quantitative skills in 1958, the year its norms were compiled. The MPS non-college men did not fare that badly compared to the college senior norms on the Quantitative test; 42% were above the median. However, only 25% of them scored above the college senior median on the Verbal subtest, showing particular weaknesses there.

The remaining two tests in the Cognitive Ability factor were the Critical Thinking in Social Science Test, measuring the ability to make inferences from verbal, tabular, and graphic materials, and the Contemporary Affairs Test, measuring knowlege of recent events in a variety of fields. The norms for these tests were based on a sample of Bell System middle managers, most of whom were middle-aged. Compared to these men, both the college and noncollege groups did poorly, although the college men were the better of the two.

Almost half the college graduates scored in the lowest quarter on each test, as did nearly three-quarters of the noncollege group.

It was particularly disturbing that the men seemed both uninformed and unconcerned about many events of the decade of the 1950s. On a 5-point scale of political understanding rated from the interviews, both groups had an average rating of 2, showing that they were inconsistent, vague, or ambiguous in their thoughts or statements and only casually followed politics. For example, Joe did not know which political party controlled the two houses of Congress after the 1956 election. Nor were their tastes or knowledge very well developed in such cultural areas as art or music. They were either part of the Eisenhower era's bland and complacent masses or still too young to have a sense of perspective or world view. It could only be hoped that with maturity would come greater knowledge and wisdom.

OVERALL ASSESSMENT EVALUATIONS

When all the data about each participant accumulated in the assessment center were digested, final reports were read aloud in an integration session and ratings made on the 26 assessment dimensions. The ratings of the dimensions, defined in the Appendix, were the culmination of the assessment process. Here the assessors attempted to capture and integrate all the relevant information about managerial abilities and motivations, which would in turn lead them to predictions about each man's future with the company.

The dimensions were also factor-analyzed to reveal their underlying structure, as reported elsewhere (Bray & Grant, 1966). Factor scores were constructed by averaging the ratings on each dimension that characterized that factor (listed in the Appendix). Since the dimensions were rated on 5-point scales, the factors also were represented as 5-point scales. Differences between the two educational groups on average factor scores are shown in Figure 2.6.

The differences shown in the figure are consistent with the exercise data reported so far, as would be expected. The college men had a strong edge over the noncollege men in Intellectual Ability, which was evident from the various paper-and-pencil tests previously reported. Statistically significant differences favoring the college group were shown on the General Mental Ability and Written Communication Skills dimensions.

Another factor favoring the college men was Advancement Motivation, which includes dimensions relating to wanting to move ahead in the organization. The college men had higher average ratings on the Need for Advancement dimension and lower average ratings on Ability to Delay Gratification (of promotions) and Realism of Expectations (about promotions). Actually, they aspired higher than their abilities would probably take them, but the impossible dream can be highly motivating to a young manager.

The noncollege men scored in the more favorable direction on the Independence factor, meaning that they were freer of the influence of other people

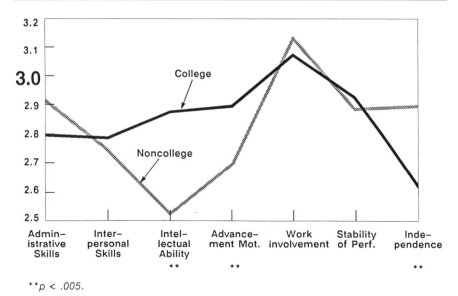

Figure 2.6.   Dimension factors at MPS:0, college and noncollege groups.

and more able to stand on their own. Their lower dimension rating on Need for Peer Approval was no doubt related to their lesser affiliative needs, but could also be accounted for by greater maturity. The noncollege group also was rated lower in Goal Flexibility, indicating that they were more sure that a career in the telephone company was their destiny, while the college men were thought more likely to be swayed by other opportunities that might come their way.

The noncollege men were rated somewhat better than the college men on Decision Making and Inner Work Standards. The differences were rather small and may be accounted for by the greater work experience of the vocational men.

At the end of the assessment process, three types of predictions were made (fully described in the Appendix): Will this person be advanced to the entry level of middle management (third level) within 10 years; should he be; and will he stay with the Bell System for the rest of his career? On all of these predictions, there were highly significant college-noncollege differences. Nearly all (98%) of the noncollege men were expected to stay with the Bell System because of their already long tenure with the company and fewer opportunities open to them in management elsewhere. Only 70% of the less settled college graduates were expected to remain.

The overall predictions of each participant's future in management were made in the form of "Will" and "Should" ratings. The "Will" rating was a straight prediction of reaching third level in 10 years. At least a few individuals among those receiving this positive rating were expected to achieve advancement because of personal impact, likability, or some other characteristic more than because of their general managerial ability. Conversely, it was expected that some who possessed good ability might be held back by lack of social presence, blatant nonconformity, or some other factor. The "Should" rating, on the other hand, meant that the assessors were convinced that the participant had the ability and motivation to do well at a third level job, even though some so rated might be overlooked by management. The "Should" prediction was the truer measure of potential and is shown in Table 2.3.

In light of the differences in Intellectual Ability and Advancement Motivation, it is not surprising that more of the college men were rated as having third-level potential and above. It was disappointing that nearly half the college men and more than two-thirds of the noncollege men were seen as lacking potential for middle management.

Joe entered readily into the various assessment center activities. He talked a great deal and was affable and gregarious. In informal activities he was usually prominent but not obtrusive. He seemed eager to make a favorable impression and sometimes tried to do this by reaching for words beyond his vocabulary and pronunciation. With his unrealistically high goals, he seemed youthful and immature, but his friendly and outgoing manner made him very likeable.

Joe impressed the staff with his determination to be a good member of the community, but in some ways he seemed almost too responsive to social pressures. His concern was always with doing what was proper and accepted. He showed no spark of creativity, nor particularly wide interests. Perhaps he was a 1950s conformist who would become an organization man or, in telephone company terminology, "develop a Bell-shaped head."

In the final evaluation sessions, the staff thought that Joe would stay with the Bell

Table 2.3   Predictions of Management Potential at MPS:0, College and Noncollege Groups

Prediction	College n	College %	Noncollege n	Noncollege %
Should be above third level	35	13	6	4
Should be at third level	58	21	28	19
Questionable for third level	52	19	11	8
Should not be at third level	129	47	102	69
Total	274	100	147	100

Note. Group differences were all significant at $p < .001$.

System and that he would and should reach the third level of management within 10 years. They did not think he would go further. His strengths were his ability to get along with people, his sound intellectual abilities, and his eagerness to succeed. On the negative side, they noted some superficiality and questionable motivation to stick with individual task accomplishment.

Jerry was cooperative in the various assessment exercises, although reserved and polite. He related to his peers in an easy-going but somewhat unpolished manner, primarily due to his use of language. He had difficulty expressing himself and often seemed to grope for words. He was not very forceful.

Jerry impressed the assessors as a sincere fellow who strove to make a decent living. He was relatively uncomplicated, a man concerned with the immediate situation and little involved with long-range planning. He seemed to just work along, hoping to get what he could and taking each encounter in stride. He appeared fairly satisfied with his own life to date.

The staff thought that Jerry would be a fine, loyal employee, but that his lack of forcefulness and drive and mediocre scholastic ability made him a poor bet for higher levels of management. They predicted that Jerry would stay with the Bell System, but would not and should not be advanced into middle management.

Joe and Jerry were typical young Bell managers at that first MPS assessment center, reflections of the corporate world of the 1950s and representative of the difference a college education can make. But in spite of the accusations of conformity in that era, not all young managers were alike. The typical were joined by the atypical — the potential stars and future failures, the complacent and the disturbed. We will become accquainted with some of the others in the next two chapters.

CHAPTER 3

Harbingers of Career Advancement

Like most companies, the Bell System was keenly interested in which of its young employees would develop into successful leaders and advance to high places in the business. Yet no matter what a young manager's potential, it was clear that he would not become a future telephone company executive unless he stayed on the company's payroll. Before turning to the indicators of management success among the MPS men, then, we address the issue of turnover — what difference it made, and whether it could have been predicted.

THE TERMINATORS

In the 1950s, males joining large organizations typically expected that they were entering into a relationship that would be ended only upon their retirement. This was particularly true of those joining the Bell System, which had a strongly established reputation for providing job security. Many of the participants in MPS had heard from older relatives that Bell had bent over backward to keep layoffs at an absolute minimum, even during the Great Depression. It will be recalled from Chapter 2 that at MPS:0 only 1% of the group thought it likely that they would regret not having gone to work for a different company.

In spite of this optimism, nearly half of the college graduates, 128 of 274, had departed from the Bell System by the MPS:20 assessment. Such a loss rate was typical for Bell System recruits, though below that of many other businesses. The bulk of the terminations occurred in the first few years of employment; one-fourth were gone within 4 years and more than 40% within 10. Partly because of the early termination phenomenon, the loss rate for the study among the MPS noncollege men was negligible; they had been on the company payroll more than 9 years on the average before coming to the assessment center. This examination of terminations, then, focuses on the college men.

Effect of Termination on the Management Pool

Termination is often an unpleasant life experience for the terminators, especially those asked to leave because of poor or unimpressive performance. It also represents an economic loss to business. Campus recruiting is expensive, with many interviews needed to produce one hire. Much more costly are the salaries and other expenses of those put on the payroll and given training and job rotation experience, only to have them leave before making any significant contribution to the organization. There are other costs as well, since the organization must bear the administrative burden of termination and replacement as well as losses of productivity and supervisory time as the work group readjusts.

In addition to the expense, terminations are of concern to an organization because of the possibility that high-potential employees may be lost. In order to judge the quality of terminators versus stayers in MPS, information was gleaned from the lengthy reports of interviews conducted in the company about each man. These interviews were with personnel department staff for the first 4 years, then with ex-bosses in year 5, and with bosses in the years that followed.

These "in-company" interviews, as they were called, allowed a classification of the terminators as "promising" or "unpromising." Some criteria for classification were automatic. If a terminator had reached the third level of management before leaving, he was considered promising, since this was the minimum goal for college recruiting. At the other extreme, those fired or induced to resign were classified as unpromising.

Use of these automatic criteria allowed the classification of most of the terminators but left about 40 unclassified. We then read independently all of the in-company interviews for each of these men and judged whether they would have arrived at the third level of management had they stayed. In the few instances where we disagreed, we dug deeper and discussed the evidence until a mutually agreeable decision was reached. This process and the objective criteria resulted in the classification of 108 of the 128 terminators (84%).

There was clearly no need for Bell System personnel managers of the 1950s to lose any sleep because terminators might be draining the pool of competent managers. Only 15% (19 men) of the classifiable leavers were judged as promising. The remainder either were let go by management for inadequate performance or potential (52%), or were judged unlikely to be successful on the basis of interviews with their management representatives (31%). The evidence that termination did not cost the telephone companies very much in good managerial talent is strong indeed.

Prediction of Termination

The likelihood that some of the newly employed management recruits would not make a career with the Bell System was apparent from the start. One of

the predictive ratings made by the assessors at the conclusion of each integration session was whether or not the candidate would stay with the Bell
System. The staff predicted that 70% of the MPS college men would stay,
which was an overestimate of the actual retention rate of 53%. As far as
individual predictions were concerned, however, the staff judgments were
considerably better than chance. As shown in Figure 3.1, two-thirds of those
predicted to leave actually left, while only two-fifths of those predicted not to
leave did so.

Although the number of leavers classified as promising was too small for
separate comparisons, a differentiation between types of terminations was
made by comparing those who were fired or induced to leave (forced terminators) with those who left voluntarily, regardless of their ultimate true potential
(voluntary terminators). Of the 128 participants who terminated, 72 (56%)
had done so of their own accord, and 56 (44%) were discharged or led to
resign. As shown in Figure 3.1, the assessors were able to predict terminations
with better-than-chance accuracy within each category, although they did
somewhat better for the voluntary terminators.

Various assessment exercise ratings and scores were examined to determine
the types of variables that supported prediction of terminations. For the most
part, the forced terminators were distinguished by a different set of variables
from that for the voluntary terminators. One exception was the Edwards scale
of Intraception, or interest in understanding the motives and feelings of others,
where both types of terminators scored significantly higher than those who
stayed (stayers were at the 35th percentile of 1958 Bell college-hire norms,
compared to the 55th and 53rd percentiles for the forced and voluntary

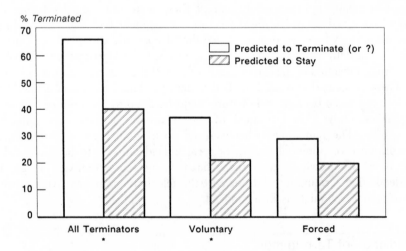

*p < .01.

Figure 3.1.   MPS:0 predictions and terminations, college sample.

terminators, respectively). Perhaps the terminators were more sensitive to the reactions of others toward them and their performance or were overconcerned with such reactions, prompting them to seek better alternatives elsewhere.

Assessment exercise scores that differentiated the forced terminators from the voluntary terminators and stayers are shown in Table 3.1. The first set of variables consisted of deficiencies in administrative and intellectual abilities that are critical to success in management. Ratings on the In-Basket, the assessment simulation focused on administrative skills, showed the forced terminators to be significantly weaker both in Decision Making and in Organizing and Planning, as well as being rated substantially below average on the overall exercise. They also scored lower on the SCAT, especially the Quantitative subtest. At the conclusion of the assessment center, only 20% of the forced terminators were rated as having potential for middle management, compared to 35% of the stayers.

In spite of lesser abilities, the forced terminators had aspirations in line with the typical MPS college graduate, thus warranting a lower rating on the dimension of Realism of Expectations. This rating was part of a trio of variables categorized in Table 3.1 as a lack of resilience. On the other two, the forced terminators were rated lower in Resistance to Stress and scored lower on the Edwards scale of Endurance, which measures motivation to persist at a task until it is completed. Thus the forced terminators were not only less capable than those who stayed or left voluntarily, but lacked the resources that would help them cope with a difficult situation.

The voluntary terminators were quite different from those asked to leave. They were equal to the stayers on such important characteristics as Administrative Skills and General Mental Ability, and 43% were judged to have middle-management potential, slightly more than the stayers. Yet only about

Table 3.1   Variables Distinguishing MPS Forced Terminators

Variable	Source	Stayers	Voluntary terminators	Forced terminators[b]
Abilities				
Organizing and Planning	In-Basket	2.9	2.9	2.4
Decision Making	In-Basket	2.8	2.8	2.4
Overall In-Basket	In-Basket	2.7	2.7	2.1
General Mental Ability	SCAT total[a]	40 %ile	44 %ile	29 %ile
Resilience				
Endurance	Edwards[a]	46 %ile	50 %ile	34 %ile
Resistance to Stress	Dimension	3.0	3.0	2.7
Realism of Expectations	Dimension	3.3	3.1	2.9

[a] 1958 Bell System norms.
[b] Forced terminators were different at $p < .05$.

one-fourth of them had shown clear signs of eventual success up to the point when they resigned.

The key to the terminations of the voluntary group lay in the area of motivation. As shown in Table 3.2, several types of motivational characteristics differentiated the voluntary terminators. They were more ambitious than the stayers or forced terminators, being rated higher on Need for Advancement. But this ambition was also of a rather insistent and rigid kind, for they were less willing to delay the gratification a promotion would bring and less able or willing to modify their own actions or style to achieve better results (low Behavior Flexibility). Their loyalty to the organization was more questionable, since having a secure job meant less to them and they were not as closely identified with the Bell System and its values. For such persons, leaving the organization may have been a viable alternative if movement up the organization seemed slow.

A problem with the voluntary terminators was that their high ambitions for status were not matched by an intrinsic interest in the work itself. From the interviews with them, it was apparent that they did not consider work to be of as high priority as others in the sample, and their standards for the quality of their work were lower. Presumably they were not doing well in their jobs, in spite of adequate abilities, because they were uninvolved and just didn't care enough.

The voluntary terminators, then, had as much ability as the stayers to do their jobs in a satisfactory fashion, but most were not motivated for superior performance. No one asked them to leave, but their records with the company

Table 3.2   Variables Distinguishing MPS Voluntary Terminators

		Average score		
Variable	Source	Stayers	Voluntary terminators[a]	Forced terminators
Insistent ambition				
Need for Advancement	Dimension	3.2	3.5	3.1
Ability to Delay Gratification	Dimension	3.4	3.1	3.2
Behavior Flexibility	Dimension	3.1	2.8	3.0
Organizational loyalty				
Need for Security	Interview	3.6	3.1	3.4
Bell System Value Orientation	Interview	3.8	3.4	3.7
Work involvement				
Primacy of Work	Interview	3.3	3.0	3.2
Occupational life theme	Interview	3.3	2.9	3.2
Inner Work Standards	Interview	3.7	3.3	3.6

[a] Voluntary terminators were different at $p < .05$.

were for the most part mediocre. Yet they expected rapid advancement and were impatient to get it. When it didn't materialize, they departed, being relatively uninterested in security and having developed no allegiance to the Bell System.

BACKGROUNDS

By the time of the MPS:20 assessment, there were 281 men remaining on the company's payroll. Since 15 of them declined or were unable to participate in some or all of the MPS:20 activities, data are available for a total of 266 men. This group is the focus of the analyses in the remaining chapters on MPS.

In a sense, all of the men who remained with the company should be considered successful, for they had long-term careers in which they were compensated for satisfactorily performing the jobs in which they found themselves. Yet their level of work and their compensation varied greatly at MPS:20, since some had received several or more promotions while others had never advanced. Level attained represents the sum total of the organization's evaluation of a manager. Those who go far have been judged favorably by a number of supervisors while performing many different jobs under various conditions. Although the promotion process is not perfect and not everyone at a particular level is a better performer than those below, management level is the best single index of success in a managerial career.

During the time preceding the MPS:20 assessment, most of the men who remained with the company had received at least one promotion and some as many as five. In a seven-level telephone company hierarchy, this meant that three of the men had achieved the status of vice president (sixth level). The distribution of college and noncollege participants by management level attained by MPS:20 is shown in Table 3.3.

There was an obvious difference in the relative achievements of the college and noncollege groups. One-fifth of the noncollege men were still at the first level of management after 20 years, and only four had gone beyond the third level. By contrast, only four college men remained at the first level, and about one-third had gone beyond the third level. The most typical or modal level for the college men was third, while that for the noncollege men was second.

The reasons for the discrepancy in advancement rates for the two educational groups are twofold. First, the college men, on the average, had better abilities and stronger motivation for advancement, as demonstrated in Chapter 2. A second reason was that an expectation was generated within the companies that college graduates would be promoted, while no such expectation prevailed for the noncollege men.

To a great extent, the men who would go on to higher levels of success in the organization and those who would remain in the lower rungs of the hierarchy were already distinguishable at the MPS:0 assessment center. A description of what these men with different destinies were like at the

Table 3.3   Management Levels at MPS:20, College and Noncollege Groups

Level	College		Noncollege		Total	
	n	%	n	%	n	%
6	3	2	0	0	3	1
5	12	9	0	0	12	5
4	27	20	4	3	31	12
3	64	46	37	29	101	38
2	27	20	61	47	88	33
1	4	3	27	21	31	12
Total	137	100	129	100	266	100

beginning can be structured from significant correlations between variables measured at the original assessment and progress in management 20 years later.

Since the college men were generally more successful in the business than the noncollege men, many of the biographical characteristics that distinguished the two groups (as discussed in Chapter 2) were also related to success in management. Those that seem to have been artifacts of sample selection are not discussed here (such as advancement related to being younger at assessment, having fewer children, or being employed a shorter length of time). Variables that predicted success for each educational group separately as well as the combined group are, of course, the most convincing, but variables that showed relationships with success for the combined group alone may also be important if the content seems to have been more logical than artifactual.

To illustrate the differences between the men who were to experience many promotions and those who were not, the composite characters Al, Andy, Chet, and Charlie have been developed from related MPS case histories. All were well adjusted at the MPS:20 assessment. Yet their very appearance at the initial assessment gave clues to their future destinies.

Among the college men, Al showed great promise, and by MPS:20 he had advanced to the fifth level.

Al was an attractive young man, with bright dark eyes that sparkled against fair skin and a broad round face that stood out imposingly beneath his crew-cut brown hair. His face typically wore an open, easy smile that conveyed a relaxed and self-assured manner. Al arrived at the assessment center neatly groomed and stylishly dressed in a dark blue summer suit, white broadcloth shirt, and oxblood shoes topped with dark blue socks. A dark red tie with thin blue stripes wove his ensemble together into a conservative but fashionable harmony.

Al related comfortably to his interviewer, but he seemed sensitive to the impression he was creating and tried to influence it in a positive direction. His answers to questions were forthright, yet he picked up subtle cues as to when to continue a point and when to defer it. He was both reflective and alert, suggesting a bright and active mind at work.

Chet was a college graduate with considerably less potential than Al, and initial impressions of him were not as favorable.

Chet had attractive features, but his facial expression was often bland, reflecting his lack of spontaneity. He was passive and sluggish — slow in words, thought, and movement. Verbal fluency was a problem for him; his speech was hesitant, his ideas fuzzy, and his expressions muddled.

Chet's reaction to the assessment was a combination of friendliness and confusion. He seemed eager to relate to others in an agreeable way and tried to make interpersonal relationships as pleasant as possible by being a good listener. He was cooperative in the assessment exercises but often seemed puzzled by the process. In the interview he expressed concern about the impression he created on others and revealed some feelings of inadequacy.

Among the noncollege men, Andy represents a high-potential participant. He had reached middle management by MPS:20, which was a mark of achievement for one without a college degree.

Andy's conservative, dark suit and frequently serious expression intimated that he found neither life nor the assessment center a laughing matter. The staff usually found him congenial and good-humored, but it was clear that he was concerned about creating a good impression. He tried hard to give appropriate answers and often impressed others by doing so.

Charlie, a noncollege man who advanced no further than the first level, also took the assessment seriously, but his nature was more sweet than striving.

No sooner had he entered the air-conditioned interview room than Charlie promptly removed his jacket, pulled off his clip-on shiny red bow tie, and unbuttoned the collar of his white shirt without one spoken word. The interviewer at first suspected arrogance, but it soon became clear that this burly, ruddy-faced participant was simply an outdoor man temporarily confined in an indoor suit. The clothing so readily discarded was an inexpensive non-Ivy League cut of dark blue gabardine, which was worn with gray and green pseudo-argyle socks and brown shoes — not a fashionable mix.

Charlie's speech was colloquial and matter-of-fact, but he had a poor vocabulary and weak verbal skills. To compensate, he would often punctuate his remarks with somewhat extravagant gestures. He was a simple, nonintellectual man whose sincerity and good intentions were so clear and compelling that the interviewer strained to understand the points he was trying to make so as not to disappoint him.

A few aspects of family and childhood background related to later success in management. The educational level of parents was related to advancement only for the group as a whole, suggesting that if a man achieved a baccalaureate, it did not really matter for his future whether his parents went to college or not. The father's occupation did have a relationship to success among the noncollege men, however, with the least successful much less likely to have fathers in business or professional activities.

Andy was born in Philadelphia, but his family gradually moved into the suburbs and then into more rural Allentown. His father, who had an eighth-grade education, worked for a number of years as a driver-salesman for a baking company. He eventually moved into real estate, often dealing with farms in the rural areas of Pennsylvania. Andy described his father as a hard-working, honest man who was strict with his children.

Andy's mother was much more outgoing than his father. Having a high school education, she worked as a secretary before her marriage but became a housewife when the couple started a family. There were two children besides Andy: a sister 2 years older and a brother 8 years younger.

Charlie was born and raised in a small town in Minnesota. His father, educated through the eighth grade, had once owned his own grocery but lost it during the Depression. He steadfastly weathered those hard times, relying on welfare and picking up odd jobs until he eventually found work as a butcher. Charlie's major recollection of those times was "Our family was real poor. Me and my brother and two sisters didn't have much in the way of toys. But we still had fun." Charlie's mother scrimped and saved to do the best she could to provide for her children.

One finding of interest possibly related to the father's occupation was the tendency for household movement to be positively correlated with later business success. The number of communities lived in before age 16 showed a significant relationship with level attained at MPS:20, as did just living in more dwellings before age 16. It may be that the men who were subjected to more moves learned to adapt and adjust to new situations in a way that their more stable peers did not.

The frequency of childhood problems listed on the biographical questionnaires yielded no consistent relationship with advancement for the noncollege group. The more successful college men reported that they were less likely to have nightmares or to be left to bring up the rear. They may have exhibited some early dominant and aggressive tendencies, since they reported being more likely to fight with others.

Academic success was also a good predictor of success for the college men. The more successful had better grades in high school, although grades for the noncollege participants were not related to their advancement. The more successful college men had also attained better grades in college, had more scholarships, and had attended colleges of better quality. College major also showed a relationship to success, with the higher-level men more likely to have been humanities or social science majors than business or technical majors (for a full discussion of college experiences and managerial success, see Howard, 1986).

Al grew up in various suburbs of a large Western city, and he felt that his early educational experiences were rich ones. He enjoyed school, received all A's and B's, and was an honor student in high school. In his spare time he read books from the school library and found that his interests were increasingly diverse. He acted in the school play, was a member of the Student Council for 2 years, served as president of the junior class, and was the commencement speaker. At no sacrifice to his grades, he also enjoyed athletics and held several part-time jobs, including those of gas station attendant and florist's helper.

Al went to the state university, where he majored in economics. He said he chose that subject "because it encouraged thinking, not just a passive acceptance of facts. I was president of the economics club and a member of the honor society. I wish I could have afforded to go on to graduate school, but I'm now working on my MBA at night."

Chet had a series of academic difficulties, beginning in grammar school where he failed the second grade. He had little academic interest and put forth only minimal effort in high school, attaining below-average grades. At his mother's insistence he enrolled in a state teacher's college after his high-school graduation, but he dropped out after one year to join the Air Force.

The GI bill allowed Chet the opportunity to continue his college education. He took his education somewhat more seriously after his military interlude, and he was able to achieve average grades. He graduated from a state university with a general business degree.

LIFESTYLES

Current lifestyles at MPS:0, as reflected in the life themes codes from the assessment interviews, showed some relationships to future success, but a stronger correlation was often obtained by using the codes for projected developments rather than current involvement, as shown in Table 3.4. In other words, future planned involvements in certain areas of life were frequently more indicative of future advancement than involvements at the time of the original assessment.

One of the implications from the life themes correlations is that being too much of a homebody was related to less advancement in the company. For the noncollege men, projections of Marital-Familial involvement related negatively to later success, while among the college men projected Locale-Residential concerns were a negative indicator. Perhaps the men who were most oriented to home and family were unwilling to make the sacrifices of time and relocation that a successful career was likely to involve. Nevertheless, the relationship of the Financial-Acquisitive life theme to success for the

Table 3.4   Correlations of Projected Developments in Life Themes at MPS:0 with
Level at MPS:20, College and Noncollege Groups

Life theme	College ($n = 137$)	Noncollege ($n = 129$)	Total ($n = 266$)
Marital-Familial	.03	−.16*	−.11*
Parental-Familial	−.09	−.12	−.11*
Locale-Residential	−.20*	−.09	−.06
Financial-Acquisitive	.15*	.08	.16**
Ego-Functional	.32**	.16*	.26**
Recreational-Social	.08	.00	.06
Religious-Humanism	−.12	−.06	−.06
Service	.03	.23*	.26**
Occupational	.26**	.38**	.21**

* $p < .05$.
** $p < .005$.

college and combined groups suggests that acquiring such possessions as houses and cars was important to those who would later advance in the company, and may have been a reflection of their ambition.

Andy was married soon after high school, and by the time of the initial assessment was the father of two sons and a daughter. He described his wife as "A real doer. She just has to be active and working at something, and she'll take on any job. During the war, while I was in the Army, she joined me on the West Coast and got a job as a riveter. She's a good athlete and likes to do things outdoors, like garden or fish."

It was also apparent that Andy's wife was prepared to be married to an executive. She seemed to be always behind him, supporting and even pushing him. Added Andy, "She doesn't mind moving around for my job assignments and training."

Charlie met his wife when she was a telephone operator at the company, and he claimed it was "love at first sight." She resigned from her job after their marriage, and by the time of the MPS:0 assessment they had two daughters, aged 5 and 3. Charlie admired his wife's housekeeping skills, claiming that "she always has the best of meals prepared and on time."

Charlie and his family lived in an older home they bought for $12,000 with $3,000 down. It was a three-bedroom ranch-style house and quite ample in size for the family. An important but unpretentious acquisition for Charlie was a small cabin at a camp site near a fishing stream, 20 miles away. He clearly had roots, and the thought of pulling them up would have been very threatening to him.

Charlie claimed he would only leave the telephone company under two conditions: if he were fired, or if he were transferred to Omaha (Northwestern Bell headquarters) or some other big city. He reasoned, "Life isn't worth all the effort of commuting. My family is more important than my job." He wanted enough income to give his children an education or a start in life, but he didn't want too much pressure from business, since he preferred to spend time with his family or puttering around his house or camp. He said, "I'm happy now, and if the future stays this way, I'll be happy." He added optimistically, "I have all the faith in the world that the little I ask for will be granted."

For both educational groups, projected Ego-Functional life theme developments constituted a strong indicator of later success. Those destined for later advancement were clearly concerned about developing and improving themselves, both mentally and physically. Biographical data already showed that those destined for greater advancement had better health: 61% of those who eventually attained the fourth level or higher rated their health as excellent, compared to 44% of those who made third level and 35% of those who remained at the first or second level. More frequent opportunities for public speaking at the time of assessment and self-reports of effectiveness as a speaker were significantly correlated with promotions.

In the noncollege and combined groups, the Service life theme, pointing to interest in the community and public affairs, related to later advancement. Political affiliation did not separate the more from the less successful, although the men who were to gain more promotions did have somewhat more positive feelings toward Eisenhower.

Al was working on his MBA at nights, but he still found time for other reading. He enjoyed popular books that commented on life in the 1950s, such as *The Organization Man*, *The Affluent Society*, and *The Man in the Gray Flannel Suit*. He also enjoyed reading speculations about the future of capitalism and democracy, such as *1984* and *Main Street USSR*. He tried to keep abreast of current events by reading the local newspapers as well as skimming *Newsweek*, *Life*, the *Wall Street Journal*, and *Fortune*.

Although Al wasn't yet involved in community activities, he hoped to join the Kiwanis Club and the Junior Chamber of Commerce. He had begun meeting people in the community through weekly participation in Lutheran church services. This was an important tie to his youth, where he had been church youth group president and had done a fair amount of public speaking in this connection. He had a positive attitude toward public service, saying, "I want a morally sound life where I can feel I'm doing something for society, giving it something rather than always taking from it. In my small way, I'd like to make this country a fine and decent place to live."

Al identified with the Republican party, not just because he thought Republicans were more favorable to the views of business but because he felt they were better for the country. He opposed too much government spending and intervention, stating, "Everyone wants their hand held. People should accept responsibility and work for themselves." He praised Eisenhower with "I'm a stout Ike man and compare everyone with him; there's just no comparison. Anyone that can tell me that the past 8 years with Ike have not been good is crazy. The Republican party is good for me — why should I change? U.S. prestige is tops."

By contrast, Chet had little interest in community activities or politics. Confessing his immaturity, he commented, "I'm still pretty young in this man's world."

Chet's recreational time was spent with his wife and young daughter, often watching television. He was not a book reader but did enjoy some popular magazines. He also liked parties and sports, and played on a company softball team.

WORK INTERESTS

A final life theme that differentiated the men in terms of their later advancements was projected Occupational involvement. Being oriented to job and career at a young age was clearly a strong sign that one's career would be successful. As shown in Table 3.4, the relationship was stronger within each educational group than for the combined group. This was because the more experienced noncollege men were more involved in work at the time of assessment but would attain fewer advancements later on.

For the noncollege men and the total group, having a positive attitude toward one's anticipated experiences as a Bell System manager over the next 5 years was a positive indicator of later success. Scores on the MPS:0 Expectations Inventory correlated significantly with later management level, although this same relationship did not hold for the college group alone. Within both educational groups, though, having high expectations about salaries related to later management success.

A total of 21 of the 56 items on the Expectations Inventory showed a positive relationship with later advancement, but only a few of these held for one of the educational subgroups alone, suggesting that college—noncollege differences accounted for many of the total group correlations. Among the noncollege group as well as the total group, those who would be most successful later were more positive about having challenging work and a chance to use their imaginations. They expected to take work home from the office for evenings and weekends and thought they would be given full responsibility for decisions if promoted. The most successful in the college and combined groups did not think they would experience increasing conflicts between job and family as they looked toward the future.

The college and noncollege men scored differently on a number of items on the Work Conditions Survey, which influenced the relationship of those items with later success for the combined group. Yet many items were related to later advancements for one or both of the educational subgroups as well as for the combined group.

Within both subgroups and for the total group, those who were to become more successful had stronger preferences at MPS:0 for jobs that had a lot of responsibility and that required initiative. The most successful college men wanted a job that would depend on their own decisions, while the most successful noncollege men preferred work that would require practical intelligence. In addition, the most successful from the noncollege and the combined groups showed greater antagonism toward routine work.

The more successful noncollege men had some additional work preferences that remained influential when the two subgroups were combined. Those promoted most often by MPS:20 were more antagonistic toward well-defined jobs and toward jobs with little social contact. In line with this rejection of social isolation on their part was a more positive attitude toward work in personnel selection.

The overall impression from these results is that those who were to advance furthest had early yearnings for work conditions that higher-level jobs would provide — responsibility and opportunities to use one's initiative and intellect. They were rejecting of jobs that were too routine or structured or that resulted in social isolation.

After 3 rather disappointing years working under an autocratic boss as a salesman for a manufacturer of soap and home products, Al began to look for another job that would offer a management training program. By chance, a neighbor was a division manager (fourth level) in the Bell System and offered strong praise of the telephone company. Al became interested in the company as one that was respected in the community, interested in its people, and offered a good opportunity for advancement. He also liked the fact that it met a service need. He settled comfortably into Mountain Bell in a position in Revenue Accounting, supervising 20 women handling customer complaints.

Al wanted to provide well for his family, but he was also idealistic about working to his capacities and being useful to the company, especially as a leader. He commented, "It's easy to get lost in this work of ours and become a cog in a wheel. I don't ever want this to happen; I wouldn't be happy that way. I want to feel I'm contributing something to the company where I work in a creative sense, in a human relations sense, and in a productive sense."

Andy also made a couple of false starts before finding the telephone company as the place for his future career. After his military experience, he and his wife moved to New York State to be nearer her family. He worked $1\frac{1}{2}$ years as a warehouseman for Sears but found it far beneath his abilities, commenting, "I was the only one there who could count!" A year at a gas company was not much of an improvement, for he grew weary of routine paperwork. He applied to New York Telephone in hopes that a large, technical organization would offer him more opportunities.

After $3\frac{1}{2}$ years as a switchman, Andy was offered the opportunity for a 9-month training program, which led to his promotion to management as a chief switchman. By the time he appeared at the assessment center, he was a toll wire chief.

Andy was pleased that he had moved to the telephone company, saying, "You can progress here if you apply yourself — that's what I like about it." He felt well suited to management work, saying, "I get a kick out of supervising. I especially like working with personnel — overcoming personnel problems and the like." He also responded enthusiastically to the technical aspects of his position and enjoyed "licking an equipment problem." He added, "My job is challenging and interesting, because I'm always learning new things. It's almost impossible for a person to go fast enough to keep up with developments in the telephone business. There is new equipment all the time."

Chet and Charlie, the MPS participants who would not advance far in the organization, were much more likely to be satisfied with more routine and well-defined tasks.

Chet was motivated to come to the telephone company by the dean at his university, who had a very favorable view of utilities. In addition, he liked the campus interviewer and was impressed by his sincerity. Since Chet's wife didn't want to move out of the state, Michigan Bell seemed to be a good choice.

When asked what aspects of the telephone company were particularly appealing to him for his future, Chet said, "This company is steady, safe, and secure. I thought I'd have a sense of belonging here. I like the idea of a company offering a service, and any company interested in the long-term welfare of its employees must be progressive. The benefits and pension plan are good, and the pay isn't bad. I've made up my mind that this is where I want to spend my career."

After high school graduation, Charlie looked for a job that would primarily offer him security. Smarting from his father's loss of his small business, he especially liked the idea of a large organization. The telephone company seemed ideal to him since it had a reputation, in Charlie's words, as "a good place with wonderful benefits. The telephone company never lays you off. And you get automatic raises."

He began his career as a lineman, an appealing job to him since he had always enjoyed outside work and mechanical things. A year before he came to the assessment center, Charlie's work was acknowledged by making him first an acting foreman and then a full foreman with two two-man crews reporting to him. He and his crew covered the downtown district in their small Midwestern town location, where they placed poles, laid aerial and underground cable, and did building work.

Charlie sincerely liked his job, saying "It's a dull day without a laugh, and on our job we have lots of laughs." Placing cable and poles was fun to him, but he disliked paperwork and going to meetings.

Many of the scales on the Management Questionnaire administered in year 1 of MPS were related to later advancement. These tended to be statistically significant only for the combined group, as shown in Table 3.5.

One interesting finding was that the noncollege men who were most negative toward supervisors in year 1 were the ones who advanced the furthest. Many of the most negative men must have been already at the second level of management at the time of the assessment and had had greater opportunity to experience many bosses. Within the combined group, later advancement was related to having a more positive general attitude toward higher management, the company, and information about company policies and procedures; more satisfaction with and pride in having a job in the telephone company; and more satisfaction with their own level of authority and salary.

Table 3.5 Correlations of Management Questionnaire Scales at Year 1 with Level at MPS:20, College and Noncollege Groups

Scale	College ($n = 108$)	Noncollege ($n = 127$)	Total ($n = 235$)
General Management Attitude	.16	.06	.18**
Supervision	.07	−.19*	−.04
Personal Satisfaction	.01	.08	.04
Job Satisfaction	.10	.06	.16*
Pride	.10	.13	.13*
Impersonal Communications	.14	.14	.16*
Personal Communications	.07	.05	.12
Identification	.14	.06	.09
Authority	.22*	.01	.15*
Salary	.04	.15	.21**

* $p < .05$.
** $p < .005$.

PERSONALITY AND MOTIVATION

Several of the personality and motivation factors described in Chapter 2 were significantly related to success 20 years later. The Ambition factor, as shown in Table 3.6, was most closely related to career advancement for the total group, with significant relationships in each of the educational subgroups as well. For the noncollege group, this desire to rise in the organizational hierarchy among those to be most successful was also reflected in the Leadership Motivation factor (derived from the projective exercises), where they rejected a subordinate role.

Table 3.6 Correlations of Personality and Motivation Factors at MPS:0 with Level at MPS:20, College and Noncollege Groups

Factor	College ($n = 137$)	Noncollege ($n = 129$)	Total ($n = 266$)
Self-Esteem	.20*	.09	.12*
Leadership Motivation	.05	.18*	.10
Positiveness	.16	.20*	.15*
Impulsivity	.06	.16	.25**
Affability	−.02	−.09	.00
Ambition	.18*	.41**	.37**

* $p < .05$.
** $p < .005$.

Within the Ambition factor, all the exercise scores except the Sarnoff scale of Forward Striving were significantly related to later advancement in the noncollege and combined groups. This meant that those rising highest in the organization scored higher than the others at the original assessment on the Edwards Dominance scale, measuring desire to lead and influence others, on the Sarnoff Motivation for Advancement scale, and on the interview ratings of Primacy of Work, Inner Work Standards, and Need for Advancement. For the college group, however, only the interview rating of Need for Advancement was significantly related to later advancement. Actually, the Need for Advancement rating from the interview showed the strongest relationship with later promotions for both groups and proved one of the most potent predictors of later success in the entire assessment center ($r = .46$ for the combined group).

One related variable outside the Ambition factor is of interest. For both educational groups and the total group, a low Need for Security rating based on the interview was characteristic of the success-oriented. It will be remembered that Al and Andy had been attracted to the Bell System for its advancement opportunities, while Chet and Charlie wanted an organizations that was safe and secure. These men had more to say about their specific ambitions.

"I want to be able to demonstrate the things I learned in college and get to the top," said Al, "maybe even be president. I expect to work hard and be at the third level within 5 years, and to rise to much higher levels in the years beyond that. I am specifically working on my MBA to aid in my advancement. If I'm thwarted on advancement, or find the challenge is lacking, I'll leave the company. Job security doesn't particularly interest me because I have my own security. You see, I'll do a good job wherever I am. I don't want to just ease through a job."

The sentence-completion responses also illustrated Al's ambitions and work orientation. He said, "*I secretly* long to be a good executive," and "*In 20 years from now* I'll be a V.P." He was excited by the responsibility and authority inherent in jobs involving supervision, replying, "*I wish* I could make more important decisions."

Andy was also interested in advancement, although he felt that division manager, or fourth level, was the highest to which he could reasonably aspire. He said, "My technical knowledge is good, and I believe I can supervise and develop people. I realize the college boys will be brought along fairly quickly, but I think I'll eventually get my chance. I feel I'm equal to them in most respects, although I don't have knowledge of the finer arts. Beyond fourth level, I might have difficulty handling the social aspects of the job."

Even though Chet had the benefits of a college degree, his below-average scholastic performance did not fill him with confidence in his capabilities. He hedged a bit with his interviewer when asked about his specific aspirations, saying he wasn't sure what the management levels were. When pressed further, he replied, "I'd like to feel no job is out of my reach, but I'm not really possessed of a lot of ambition. There are times when I just want to say, 'To hell with everything.' "

The peak of Charlie's career aspirations was to be a half step above his present status at the first level of management, although he would not be discontented to stay exactly where he was. He did not expect to leave the Plant Department or the general type of work he was doing. He said, "I don't have an education so I can't go too high. Some are eager and push for it, but I'm not that way. Advancement isn't anything I'll ever worry about. I'm doing okay."

His projective responses also showed no specific aspirations for climbing the corporate ladder. "*My ambition* is to be a good father," responded Charlie.

There are also indications from Table 3.6 that positive mental health was related to later career advancements. The most successful college men and the combined group had higher scores on the Self-Esteem factor. This result derived from the GAMIN scale of Ascendance in social situations (significant for both groups and the total group) and from the GAMIN scale showing self-confidence or Lack of Inferiority Feelings (significant for the college and combined groups). General Adjustment ratings from the Positiveness factor were related to career progress in both educational subgroups and the combined group.

It was clear from the projective responses that Al's standards were high, and he avoided thinking about possible failures and inadequacies. "*I regret* very little because I've benefited from experiences," he wrote. He took a businesslike, matter-of-fact attitude toward the future that was self-accepting and positive. "*When I compare myself with others* I'm happy with what I see," he replied.

There were many indications in the assessment that Chet was insecure. He tended to be self-critical, belittling his accomplishments and unsure of his future. He regretted not putting forth greater effort in the past and doubted his ability to attain his goals. He thus kept his aspirations low for fear of not attaining them. He was particularly apprehensive about not doing his work properly or appearing foolish in social situations.

Chet had a strong need for acceptance and a sense of belonging. He identified closely with groups and adhered to the attitudes that were common and acceptable to those around him. By thinking and speaking in accepted generalities, he could protect himself from being shown up as incorrect or stupid. One result, however, was that his comments were often trite and platitudinous.

ABILITIES

Although only some of the personality and motivation factors were predictive of later management success, all three of the ability factors were, as shown in Table 3.7. Most important for the combined group was the Cognitive Ability factor. It will be recalled that this was the only ability factor showing a significant difference between the college and noncollege groups, and that it favored the college men. Since they also advanced further, the relationship of Cognitive tests and later advancement is not surprising.

Table 3.7   Correlations of Ability Factors at MPS:0 with Level at MPS:20, College and Non-college Groups

Factor	College		Noncollege		Total	
	n	r	n	r	n	r
Administrative Ability	135	.05	126	.36**	261	.16*
Interpersonal Ability	103	.21*	128	.36**	231	.20**
Cognitive Ability	106	.20*	128	.28**	234	.38**

* $p < .05$.
** $p < .005$.

The predictive power of the Cognitive tests was not, however, merely a function of sample selection. As shown in Table 3.8, three of the four exercises composing the Cognitive factor also related to later advancement within one or both educational subgroups. The only exercise not doing so was the Contemporary Affairs Test, which measured knowledge of current events across a variety of fields. This was significantly related to advancement for the combined group, even though it was not meaningful within the educational subgroups. Similarly, analyses of sociopolitical attitudes from the interviews showed significant correlations of both political understanding and political conviction with advancement after 20 years, even though the educational subgroups had not differed in these ratings at the time of the MPS:0 assessment.

The Administrative Ability factor was a powerful predictor of success for the noncollege group but failed to demonstrate a relationship with advancement for the college group. As indicated in Table 3.8, this was true for the two major areas of In-Basket performance as well as the total rating. Chapter 2 showed that the college group did no better than the noncollege group on these skills (even slightly worse), which may be attributed to their lack of business experience. Within the noncollege group, the rating of Decision Making in the In-Basket task turned out to be very highly related to later success, although Organizing and Planning was also a meaningful predictor.

Andy organized the contents of his In-Basket carefully. He was noticeably perceptive of due dates and spotted many inconsistencies. He had a good grasp of the district and laid insightful plans to rectify situations that were out of hand. His written communications were brief but to the point.

Andy's decisions were excellent, and he had good reasons for the actions he took. He acted in a fashion consistent with his management philosophy of being firm but just with subordinates. He expressed concern for those who worked for him and was always careful to look out for their interests.

Table 3.8   Correlations of Components of Ability Factors at MPS:0 with Level at MPS:20, College and Noncollege Groups

Factor	College		Noncollege		Total	
	n	r	n	r	n	r
Administrative Ability						
Overall rating (IB)	106	.05	129	.31*	235	.11
Organizing and Planning (IB)	135	.04	126	.30**	261	.18**
Decision Making (IB)	128	.08	125	.40**	253	.17*
Interpersonal Ability						
Oral rating (CGD)	106	.11	129	.21*	235	.13*
Oral Communication Skills (CGD)	97	.19	125	.24*	222	.16*
Oral Communication Skills (Int.)	113	.29**	84	.39**	197	.33**
Forcefulness (BG)	102	−.01	121	.29**	223	.10
Leadership Skills (CGD)	94	.31**	120	.15	214	.18*
Overall rating (CGD)	106	.19*	129	.20*	235	.10
Overall rating (BG)	106	.00	129	.34**	235	.07
Cognitive Ability						
SCAT Verbal	137	.16	129	.20*	266	.31**
SCAT Quantitative	137	.17	129	.31**	266	.36**
Critical Thinking	137	.15	128	.31*	265	.33**
Contemporary Affairs	137	.09	128	.04	265	.17**

Note. Abbreviations. IB, In-Basket; CGD, competitive group discussion (Promotion Problem); Int., interview; BG, business game (Manufacturing Problem). SCAT not administered in one company; scores estimated from year 8. Competitive group discussion not administered in one company.
* $p < .05$.
** $p < .005$.

Charlie had great difficulty handling his In-Basket. He approached the task with no clear plan of action and paid minimum attention to details. He seemed to lack understanding of the problems depicted in the exercise and took an oversimplified approach to solving them. He worked slowly and seemed confused and incapable of decisions on many items. His written communications were poorly worded and contained many spelling and punctuation errors. This kind of task was definitely not Charlie's forte, and his distaste for paperwork on his own job was probably a reflection of his inadequacy in administrative skills.

Interpersonal skills were related to later success for both educational subgroups. Table 3.8 indicates that the interview was a particularly good measure of Oral Communication Skills, which related to success within both subgroups and the combined group. Al's interviewer found his speech clear and expressive, while Charlie had difficulty communicating with his interviewer because of his poor vocabulary and slow manner of talking.

The competitive exercise with assigned roles (the Promotion Problem) was more revealing for the college men than the business game (the Manufacturing Problem), although the most successful noncollege men were readily identified in both exercises. Leadership Skills as well as Oral Communication Skills from the Promotion Problem related meaningfully to later advancements.

When it was his turn to present his candidate in the Promotion Problem, Al's voice, manner, and appearance all contributed to a good impression. He had organized his material well, had solid knowledge of his candidate, and made a clear and convincing case while maintaining good eye contact with his audience. His vocabulary seemed well developed though not esoteric, and he was easily understood. He appeared sincere and good-natured, although he needed some polish.

In the group discussion that followed, Al's relaxed air of confidence and assurance, along with extensive planning and organizing efforts, soon led to his acceptance as the leader of the group. As such, he exerted considerable influence on the group without appearing to force himself on them.

Al was active both in promoting the evaluation of the various candidates and in trying to sell his own man. Adroitly clever, he was able to question others in such a fashion as to detract subtly from their candidates' qualifications, which led, of course, to bettering the position of his own candidate. Though goal-oriented, Al could shift his plans in response to the group interactions, to which he was sensitive. By remaining calm and in control, he was also able to handle the aggressions of others without becoming ruffled. It was no surprise to find him rated the most effective member of the group by his peers.

Chet had some difficulty with his oral presentation, since his speech was tense and halting. His presentation was not well organized, and he failed to cite the chief points about the man he was representing.

He was moderately active during the group discussion and was friendly and sociable. He did not attempt to assume leadership of the group, however, and he made few suggestions. He was frequently conciliatory and sought compromises when group members disagreed. Thus he served as a harmonizer, rescuing group members who were being attacked too strongly by others.

For the noncollege men, the Manufacturing Problem was related to later success, based on ratings of both forcefulness and overall performance.

Andy played an important role in getting the group organized for the business game and assigned roles to the various members. He was consistently forceful in pushing his ideas, which were reasonably good ones. He was highly identified with the problem and worked efficiently at his task. His hard work and good suggestions gained him the respect of his peers, who rated him highly on their evaluation questionnaires.

Charlie tended to watch others and follow directions as his group proceeded with the Manufacturing Problem. One of the group leaders assigned him the task of toy assembler, and he worked diligently and effectively in this role. He was especially helpful in spotting some errors in construction and realizing parts shortages. He maintained a pleasant smile, made an occasional joke, and was friendly to the other participants. Charlie was thus a fine team player, although he showed no inclinations toward a leadership role.

It is apparent from the discussion so far that a major predictor of success for these Bell System men was whether or not they had graduated from college. The college men advanced much further in management on the average because their skills were somewhat better, they were more highly motivated to advance, and the company was more oriented to their advancement. It is important to know, then, to what extent personality, motivation, and ability factors contributed to success even beyond their relationship to educational level. To explore this question, educational level was included with the personality and motivation factors and the ability factors in a multiple-regression analysis, shown in Table 3.9.

The educational variable was indeed potent, correlating alone with MPS:20 level at .54. Yet two ability factors, Interpersonal Ability and Cognitive Ability, and one personality and motivation factor, Ambition, made independent contributions to the prediction of advancement beyond the influence of education. Taken together, these variables accounted for 40% of the variation in MPS:20 level. Without the educational variable, shown in the second equation of Table 3.8, the Ambition and Cognitive Ability factors acccounted for 25% of the variation in MPS:20 level. Thus education meant a lot in Bell System management, but certainly not everything, and the assessment center

Table 3.9   Multiple Correlations of Educational Level, Ability Factors, and Personality and Motivation Factors at MPS:0 with Level at MPS:20

Variable	R	Beta
Including education variable		
Educational level	.54	.54
Interpersonal Ability factor	.60	.26
Ambition factor	.62	.20
Cognitive Ability factor	.64	.14
Excluding education variable		
Ambition factor	.41	.41
Cognitive Ability factor	.51	.31
Impulsivity factor	.52	.13

Note. $n = 226$.

was able to identify additional characteristics that went far toward predicting later advancements.

OVERALL ASSESSMENT EVALUATIONS

Summarized characteristics of the assessees are represented by the dimensions, and summaries of the dimensions are represented by the dimension factors. The relationships of these factors to MPS:20 level are shown in Table 3.10. For the combined group, five of the seven dimension factors related to advancement after 20 years.

The factors showing significant relationships with later promotions within each educational group as well as the total group were both motivational, with Advancement Motivation carrying more weight than Work Involvement. All three ability factors were important for the combined group and for the noncollege men. When the individual dimensions were examined, nearly all the ability and motivation dimensions were related to later success for the noncollege and combined groups if not the college group. Key variables related to success for both subgroups were Oral Communication Skills, Need for Advancement, Inner Work Standards, and Energy.

The last two factors in Table 3.10 are personality factors, and these had very little relationship to advancement 20 years later. Within the Stability of Performance factor, Resistance to Stress was unrelated to advancement in either subgroup or the total. Tolerance of Uncertainty had a low but significant correlation with MPS:20 for the combined group only. The Independence factor showed a significant correlation with MPS:20 level only for the college group, derived from dimension ratings of Need for Superior Approval and Goal Flexibility.

A few additional dimensions showed no relationship to later success. Bell

Table 3.10   Correlations of Dimension Factors at MPS:0 with Level at MPS:20, College and Noncollege Groups

Dimension factor	College ($n = 137$)	Noncollege ($n = 129$)	Total ($n = 266$)
Administrative Skills	.15	.39**	.19**
Interpersonal Skills	.13	.33**	.22**
Intellectual Ability	.14	.22**	.25**
Advancement Motivation	.22**	.30**	.28**
Work Involvement	.19*	.21*	.15*
Stability of Performance	.13	.13	.12
Independence	.18*	.05	.00

* $p < .05.$
** $p < .005.$

System Value Orientation, or identification with the organization, had no influence on later advancements for either subgroup or the total. Apparently being a conforming "organization man" did nothing to assure later success in the telephone companies. Social Objectivity, or lack of prejudice, neither helped nor hindered the path to advancement, and Realism of Expectations at the first assessment also had no effect. Advancement, then, was mostly related to early signs of the three basic types of ability (Administrative, Interpersonal, and Cognitive) and to motivation, especially the drive to succeed. Other variations in personality and attitudes, including love of the company, were mostly irrelevant.

Throughout the discussion of this chapter, it has become clear that predictions of later advancement from variables and factors measured at MPS:0 were much more successful for the noncollege group than the college group. The reasons for this are complex and have been partially documented elsewhere (Howard, 1985). Suffice it to say here that the MPS:0 data had much stronger relationships to early advancement than to a goal as far in the future as 20 years. Also, the college men had more maturing to do, and their performance at the MPS:8 reassessment was much more strongly related to their advancement at MPS:20 than was their original MPS:0 performance. Since the purpose of this chapter is to describe how the more successful looked at the start of their management careers, additional later data are not provided.

In spite of the vicissitudes of the college group's data, overall predictions of success from MPS:0 were still quite strongly related to management level achieved 20 years later. Figure 3.2 shows the percentage of men in each educational subgroup predicted at MPS:0 to do well in Bell System management and their progress at MPS:20. Although the prediction was couched in terms of who would attain the third level within 10 years, qualitatively it represents those who appeared to have the characteristics that would lead to advancement versus those who did not.

The promotion figures in Figure 3.2 are based on attainment of more than the modal or typical level for each educational subgroup after 20 years. Table 3.1, presented earlier in this chapter, shows that the modal level for the college men was third after 20 years and for the noncollege men was second. Thus the most successful men are defined for Figure 3.2 as those reaching fourth level and above among the college men, and third and above among the noncollege men.

In terms of reaching their criterion of success (fourth level), the college men thought by the assessors to be good bets for promotions outnumbered those not so predicted by a ratio of more than 2:1. Among the noncollege men, the ratio was nearly 3:1 for reaching their criterion of third level. These differences in progress for those with high and low final MPS:0 assessment evaluations illustrate the power of the assessment center procedure for predicting success in management, even for such a distant time as 20 years hence.

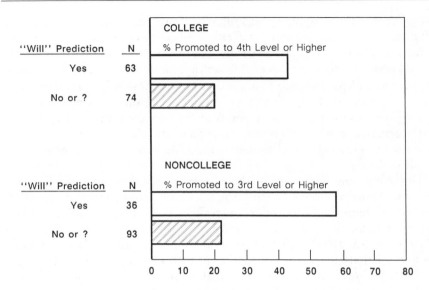

p < .005 both samples.

Figure 3.2.   MPS:0 predictions and attainment of more than modal level at MPS:20.

The assessment staff predicted that both Al and Andy would be successful in advancing in the company.

Throughout most of the assessment exercises, Al maintained a forward, self-confident air. Though composed and self-contained, he was very active in all the exercises and seemed both energetic and highly involved. There were noticeably deliberate efforts to make a good impression, but he wasn't overly controlled. He approached each task as if accustomed to doing his best at everything he undertook. Yet he managed to relate easily to others at the same time as he was often outperforming them.

Al's well-developed mental abilities, persuasiveness, interest, and motivation to get ahead were certainly above average, even though his administrative skills could have used some improvement. Moreover, his mature, realistic, accepting approach to others and likeable manner would probably earn him the respect of co-workers and supervisors. The staff predicted rapid advancement to a fairly high level, certainly above third.

Andy was also seen as having a most promising future, easily advancing into middle management. While he was not as interpersonally skillful as Al, his strong drive to succeed and his well-developed administrative skills would serve him well. His hard work and dedication to the company would bring attention to the managerial skills he could apply to the tasks he was assigned.

The various kinds of data about Chet and Charlie indicated that their talents for management were not nearly as strong.

Chet had misgivings about the likelihood of his success in management and so did the staff. His lack of self-confidence, problems with authority figures, and questionable motivation were seen as diminishing his possible contributions to the company. His communications ability was also weak, although his friendly manner and team approach could be definite assets. It was thought improbable that he would contribute any new ideas or suggestions of his own given his concern with not deviating from the group.

Although some of the staff members felt his advancement in management would be quite limited, others felt that maturity and job familiarity would increase his confidence over time. It was speculated that Chet's developmental course might depend on the type of supervision he had. He was searching for a warm, personal relationship with an authority figure, and a boss of this type might draw out the best of his abilities. However, a hostile supervisor could divert his energies into dealing with the relationship, and his job performance thus suffer the consequences.

Charlie seemed to accept the fact that his assessment performance would fall below that of the group as a whole. He appeared unperturbed by his failures on various exercises and continued to be easy-going, friendly, and compliant, and to smile in a boyish fashion.

Charlie was, above all, cooperative. If he didn't seem particularly interested in one of the techniques, it was more a function of his failure to see the significance of the project than a lack of motivation to comply. In spite of his desires, his approach was often slow and confused, and he didn't seem to understand what some of the exercises were about. His verbal skills were quite poor, and it appeared that he would be seriously disadvantaged in work that was cognitively complex.

The assessment staff concluded that Charlie would probably remain in a job similar to the one he now had and would continue to do a conscientious, satisfactory job supervising a small group of men placing cables and poles. But his limited administrative ability, motivation, and social skills would stand in the way of his taking on additional supervisory responsibility, in spite of his liability. It was felt that his abilities were probably restricted to manual and mechanical skills, which might be quite good, but that greater supervisory responsibility, especially outside the range of his construction experience, would probably overwhelm him. The staff believed that Charlie would be content to stay with the company at his same management level as long as his salary was adequate to meet his familial responsibilities.

By the time of the original assessment, the die had been cast for the participants in many respects. Those who would succeed in the organization and receive numerous advancement opportunities were in many ways already groomed for the part. What they lacked primarily was maturity and experience. It was also fairly clear who were not likely to be moved along to higher-level positions. Although some would develop with time, many seemed to lack the ability and motivation to progress much further, and advancement would not be forthcoming.

But career success is certainly not the only criterion of interest in human development. Another important construct evaluated in the study was personal adjustment, or the ability to cope with the problems and challenges of life and to bring oneself a measure of comfort and satisfaction unrelated to the achievement of organizational markers of success. Early characteristics of those who would turn out to be more and less adjusted after 20 years in the company constitute the subject of the next chapter.

CHAPTER 4

Seeds of Personal Adjustment

The dimension called "Adjustment" was one of 21 new dimensions added for the MPS:20 assessment, when the MPS men were in middle age. This assessment began in the mid-1970s, when much popular attention was directed to the concept of the midlife crisis. As the MPS men sized up their accomplishments and disappointments in life, relative success in climbing the corporate ladder would be only one yardstick of personal development. How well they had coped with their destinies was another matter, complex and highly important.

Adjustment was defined as the extent to which each man had changed or adapted to his life situation in an emotionally healthy way — that is, had coped with life's inevitable problems in a relatively conflict-free and realistic manner. The well-adjusted men were defined as those who managed to work constructively toward their own goals, rather than becoming their own worst enemies, as neurotic behavior may involve. Lofty goals were not required to earn a positive Adjustment rating, however, and those who set their sights modestly compared to their potential were rated no lower than those with higher aims as long as they were achieving those goals to their own satisfaction and contentment.

In defining Adjustment, there was deliberate avoidance of the value judgment inherent in the term "self-actualization" (Maslow, 1954), which suggests that persons are obligated to fulfill their own potential in a maximal way. If the individual cared nothing about such things as managerial success or contributions to the community or philosophical enlightenment and did not suffer for it, his rating on Adjustment was not diminished, as long as he was successfully pursuing what was important to him. If a happy home life and comfortable living were the only important things to a man, and he was successful and satisfied on those fronts with no evidence of inner turmoil or guilt feelings, he was judged well-adjusted, even though idealists might have wanted more from such a man if he had other talents.

At the other end of the scale, those rated low on Adjustment were not ready for a mental hospital. This was, after all, a group of men able to cope well enough with life to hold down a job in the management of a large corporation for a span of 20 or more years. There were no psychotics; in fact, relatively few men had even undergone psychotherapy over the years. The poorly adjusted were those who in various ways were made significantly uncomfortable by emotional problems. They might suffer from anxieties and depression, drink heavily, have pathological relationships with wives or other family members, experience difficulty getting along with others at work, be totally unrealistic in their aspirations or interpretations of events or self-concepts, or remain torn by conflicting desires and feelings. Their problems were not serious enough to get them fired (although some were demoted or given low performance ratings), and none were involved in crimes or prosecutable acts of violence. Yet all were in one way or another rather miserable inside.

The distribution of the MPS men at the MPS:20 assessment on the dimension of Adjustment is shown in Table 4.1. Not quite a third of the men were rated high on this dimension (i.e., given a modal rating of 4, 4.5, or 5 on a 5-point scale), and about the same number were rated low (1, 1.5, or 2), with a little more than a third rated moderate (2.5, 3, or 3.5). More of the noncollege men were rated moderate in Adjustment, and more of the college men were rated low. Nevertheless, the overall difference between the educational groups on this dimension was not statistically significant.

As was the case with the more and less successful in management level achieved, described in Chapter 3, a description of those young men who would be more and less adjusted by MPS:20 can be structured by considering the correlations of the original assessment variables with ratings on Adjustment 20 years later.

In Chapter 3, descriptions have been given of Al, Andy, Chet, and Charlie, contrasting the A and C characters on potential for management success. Against this difference, these characters had something in common: All were very well adjusted at the time of the MPS:20 assessment. Four additional characters are now considered — the B and D types defined in Chapter 1. They also had contrasting potential for management (B high and D low), but

Table 4.1   Adjustment Ratings at MPS:20, College and Noncollege Groups

	College		Noncollege		Total	
Rating	n	%	n	%	n	%
High	42	31	40	31	82	31
Moderate	46	34	59	46	105	39
Low	49	36	30	23	79	30
Total	137	100	129	100	266	100

they were alike in being *poorly* adjusted in middle age. These characters are called Bruce and Don (college) and Barry and Danny (noncollege). In this chapter, illustrations will focus on the B and D types, so that the correlations will suggest what predicted later adjustment, but the case studies will primarily illustrate the antithesis — the characteristics of those who would end up maladjusted.

When Bruce, the high-potential college graduate, arrived at the MPS:0 assessment center, he had the trim look of the professional businessman. Yet he lacked the relaxed self-confidence that had been exhibited by his well-adjusted counterpart, Al.

With fine features and freshly cut short brown hair, Bruce appeared neatly packaged in a handsomely tailored gray flannel suit and a serious demeanor. His approach to the interviewer was somewhat formal, revealing an awareness of himself as an intellectual person. He spoke well during the interview, with an excellent vocabulary and interesting, thoughtful conversation. Yet he was also guarded, deliberate, intellectualized, and sometimes pedantic. Though poised for a man of 24 years, he often seemed ruminative and self-punishing.

Don, the low-potential college graduate, had his own distinctive manifestation of looming adjustment problems.

Don was extremely frank in his interview. He spoke spontaneously and openly about himself with a minimum of defensiveness. His conversation was somewhat difficult to follow, however, for he often jumped from one topic to another, babbling out his immaturity like rock and roll erupting from a college fraternity house.

Don was restive and rebellious during various parts of the assessment process. For example, he often showed up late for his appointments, and he had to be chastised for reading magazines instead of taking his tests. Don was in some ways the antithesis of the sober Bruce; it was as if he were a careening carnival Dodgem car, a collision awaiting the sound of the crash.

Among the noncollege men, Barry proved to have a good future in management, but his exterior demeanor could be off-putting.

Barry impressed the assessment staff as somewhat of a "wise guy." His manner was straightforward to the point of being curt and even gruff. He was aggressive and outspoken — at various times critical of the hotel, the food, and the nature of the study. He resisted some questions in the interview, for example, complaining that he had already given his answers in the Personal History Questionnaire. He even became argumentative with an upper-management guest at the cocktail party given for the assessees, although he did not seem to lose the executive's respect. Barry paraded sharp edges, but the staff suspected they were concealing deep feelings of inferiority.

Danny, who represents a noncollege, low-potential participant, seemed depressed and devoid of verbal energy.

Passivity and lethargy seemed to envelop Danny like a low-hanging fog. He was cooperative during the assessment process, but spontaneity was wanting. During his interview he was quiet, serious, and soft-spoken — his large, long face yielding only an occasional wistful smile. He appeared pressured by life and had frequent complaints about it.

BACKGROUNDS

An examination of the biographical items available for analysis in relation to later Adjustment ratings was indeed disappointing. Among nearly 70 items on the biographical questionnaire, only a handful were statistically significant predictors of ratings on the Adjustment dimension at MPS:20. It might even be argued that some or all of these relationships occurred simply by chance.

Among the noncollege and combined groups, those later in birth order among their siblings were better adjusted in middle age. The better-adjusted among the noncollege and combined groups reported biting their nails less frequently as children, while the better-adjusted college men reported they were picked on less frequently. Such data give no more than whiffs of childhood comfort and security, and certainly do not tell the whole story of the early backgrounds of those would would later become the best adjusted.

Coded inteview ratings provided little additional information, since this was not the primary focus of the MPS:0 assessment interview research. However, casual inspection of the interview data concerning early childhood and the characteristics of the parental family suggests that more meaningful information may be available. Interview summaries from MPS composite case histories illustrate this potential.

The family backgrounds of those who turned out well adjusted had seemed pleasant and supportive. For example, Charlie's mother was an outgoing, friendly, and good-natured woman, full of humor and outwardly expressive in showing her affection. And even though his father had little time for his children, he was considerate, kind, even-tempered, and undemanding. However, the backgrounds of the B and D types suggest considerably more early turmoil for the poorly adjusted men.

Barry's father was on relief during the Depression and turned in soda and milk bottles to keep the family going. He railed at the poor way he was treated by these circumstances, and bitterness now saturated his taste of the world. He chronically looked for injustices toward himself — new fodder from which to spew out his complaints. Yet he was also a very dependent man who too readily sought advice from others.

Although Barry saved his most negative remarks for his father, Danny had more complaints about his mother.

Danny claimed his mother was "the root cause of many arguments in the family.

She was bossy and quick-tempered — high-strung, they call it — and excitable. Even the slightest disruption of her ways would send her into a frenzy. She was smart enough but had trouble making decisions; she'd buy things and then turn around and send them back." Perhaps as a reaction to his mother's instabilities, Danny's early years were characterized by frequent temper tantrums, and he often bit his nails, a habit that continued noticeably into the present.

LIFESTYLES

The various life themes at the time of the MPS:0 assessment had only negligible relationships to later Adjustment ratings. Table 4.2 shows the correlations of current satisfaction and current involvement on each life theme at MPS:0 with Adjustment at MPS:20. The overall impression given by the table is that most of the correlations lacked statistical significance, and even the ones that were significant were quite low in magnitude.

The life theme relating most strongly to later Adjustment ratings was Marital-Familial satisfaction in the early years. This relationship held for both educational subgroups and the combined group. The case examples of the later maladjusted college men illustrate some early marital disenchantments.

At the time of the MPS:0 assessment, Bruce's wife was expecting their first child. She had earned her bachelor's degree in education, but had not begun a teaching career due to marriage and the anticipated child. Bruce said, "She's a very intelligent woman and more interesting than most. She is subject to some emotional ups and downs and can be headstrong, but I surmise this is due to her being an only child."

Bruce's intellectualizations about his marriage were somewhat surprising to the interviewer. He said, "In 5 years I expect that romantic love will have changed to conjugal love. I suppose that's good — one can't remain on an immature basis in marriage forever." He hoped his marriage would bring him "three bright kids."

While in his junior year, Don married a young woman he had met at college. They had no children, but she had dropped her academic studies for financial reasons and was a housewife. His ardor had already begun to cool, and he was chafed by the bonds of matrimony. One source of friction with his wife was his propensity to have rowdy "nights with the boys," which usually led to an argument when he returned. She also nagged him to go to church on Sunday, while he found things to do that he considered more important, such as mowing the lawn or making repairs around the house.

For the noncollege men, who were 5 years older at the original assessment, Marital-Familial involvement related to later Adjustment, as did Locale-Residential involvement. Concomitantly, those best adjusted later showed less Parental-Familial involvement at MPS:0. These data lend themselves to the interpretation that the noncollege men best adjusted later in life had established their independence from their parents and settled down early to a

Table 4.2 Correlations of Current Satisfaction with and Involvement in Life Themes at MPS:0 with Adjustment at MPS:20, College and Noncollege Groups

	College		Noncollege		Total	
Life theme	Satisfaction	Involvement	Satisfaction	Involvement	Satisfaction	Involvement
Marital-Familial	.15*	.05	.15*	.15*	.15*	.10
Parental-Familial	.02	−.02	.11	−.17*	.05	−.09
Locale-Residential	.05	−.05	.08	.23**	.05	.06
Financial-Acquisitive	.08	.03	.10	.07	.08	.04
Ego-Functional	.10	−.11	.05	−.10	.09	.11*
Recreational-Social	.04	.06	−.06	−.01	−.01	.03
Religious-Humanism	.09	−.02	−.06	.01	.03	−.01
Service	.08	.01	.05	.03	.08	.00
Occupational	.11	−.10	.12	.14	.13*	.03

* $p < .05$.
** $p < .005$.

pleasing home and family life. Those on the path to maladjustment, such as Barry and Danny, were less likely to have achieved such stability.

Barry's life was complicated by a dominating mother-in-law who lived with him and his wife. She had objected to their marriage in the first place, and he found her hypercritical and irritating. She shared expenses on the apartment and they used her furniture, a situation not very conducive to establishing Barry and his wife as an independent couple.

Danny acknowledged his wife as an attentive mother who took good care of their home, although she was too money-conscious for him. She disliked entertaining, which supported her frugality but restricted their social life. This wasn't a source of great discontent for Danny, however; he complained more that she was preoccupied and often unresponsive to his needs.

Another life theme related to later Adjustment ratings, albeit weakly, was less involvement in Ego-Functional or self-development concerns. There was no less satisfaction with themselves in such activities on the part of the well-adjusted, only less interest in developing their talents and physical capabilities. The more poorly adjusted often seemed to be exploring their personalities and potentials, striving toward a self-satisfaction that the better-adjusted took for granted. Bruce and Don, having the broader interests of college-educated men, serve as good examples.

Bruce regretted that his job was restricting his leisure time and feared that children would be even more of an imposition, even though he wanted them. He was still pursuing photography as a hobby, an interest he developed in college, and was involved in both still and motion pictures. Refinishing antique furniture was another activity that had taken his interest. He disliked popular music, claiming instead to be a jazz enthusiast as well as an aficionado of classical compositions, especially by Beethoven and Saint-Saens.

Reading was his great love, but he feared his literary pursuits were waning. "I'm afraid I'll know less in the future than I know now," he lamented. "I really love to learn all I can about everything." Some time was spent on newspapers and magazines, such as *Time, Life, National Geographic*, the *New Yorker*, and *Harper's*. He still had a stong affection for books, and he could have generated an almost endless list of his favorites. Of particular interest were the Greek classics (Homer's *The Odyssey*, Plato's *Dialogues*, and the tragedies of Sophocles) and books about world War II (e.g., Montgomery's memoirs and Heinrich's books from the German point of view). He had a keen appreciation for a good novel as well as nonfiction, naming as favorites *The Sun Also Rises, Lord Jim, All Quiet on the Western Front*, and *Northwest Passage*. His favorite poet was Emerson, but he also enjoyed the work of Edgar Allan Poe.

Don was a man of multiple interests. Music was one of his passions, and he played piano occasionally with a small group and also sang in a barbershop quartet. At different stages of his life he had collected stamps, guns, and model railroad cars and repaired radios and cars. Athletic interests included golf, tennis, water and snow skiing, ice skating, and speedboat racing. He was not one to indulge his interests idly. He said, "I go hog-raving wild about an activity and I just can't see anything else. I pursue it madly and constantly, and then just give it up."

In matters of physical and mental health, global judgments made by two researchers (based on a review of medical reports as well as the assessment exercises) indicated that the more poorly adjusted in both educational subgroups and the combined group were more likely to have health problems and nervousness. More detailed analyses of the medical data will be reported in a future volume, but the initial summaries of medical findings for Barry and Danny illustrate the types of problems they were having.

Barry's chief complaint was frequent headaches. They were particularly likely to emerge when his job brought frustrations and when he was tense. He chain smoked during his interview, and his typical rate of consumption was a pack and a half of cigarettes daily.

Danny admitted to the physician examining him his increasing feelings of concern about his family and job responsibilities. Under periods of high tension he had cramps in the lower abdomen and gastrointestinal disturbances, suggesting an irritable colon. Both his mother and his wife were sources of irritability, the latter often because of nagging about money. Job pressures were becoming a burden, and he usually experienced a pronounced tiredness at the end of the day.

Interest in community or public service (the Service life theme) had no relationship to later Adjustment ratings, and there were no differences by Adjustment in political understanding or position on political or sociocultural issues. There were some indications of greater conviction on the part of the poorly adjusted about such issues as the implementation of integration. That is, though their positions on the issue might be the same, the well-adjusted were more likely to equivocate while the poorly adjusted were more likely to be opinionated and to stand firm in their beliefs.

WORK ATTITUDES

One other life theme that was related significantly to Adjustment ratings at MPS:20 was Occupational satisfaction. The relationship was again small, but it suggested that the men who would be maladjusted in middle age were already showing some signs of discontent with their work at the original assessment. Their preferences for certain work conditions did not differ from those of the better-adjusted men.

Overall expectations about what the job would be like in 5 years, as expressed on the Expectations Inventory, did not differentiate those who would be more or less adjusted later in life. However, several items did show such a difference. For the combined group, those who ended up well adjusted more often anticipated that others in the company would share similar backgrounds and interests to theirs. They felt that loyalty to the company would be important for fast promotions, and they were less likely to believe the company cared more about the public than the feelings of its own employees.

Two of the scales from the Management Questionnaire, administered at year 1 of MPS, also related to later adjustment. The well-adjusted men showed more pride in the early years in being a member of the Bell System. They also had more positive attitudes toward their supervisors than those who turned out poorly adjusted. There is some evidence, then, that those who would be well adjusted had some early attitudes toward work and company that were more positive than those of the individuals who would end up poorly adjusted.

Al, Andy, Chet, and Charlie had all indicated great pleasure in the work assignments they had at the beginning of their management careers. For example, Al enjoyed the challenge of his supervisory role in Revenue Accounting, and Charlie was pleased to have a job where he could get outside with his men and place cables and poles. Bruce was less sanguine about what the company had to offer him.

After his discharge from the Army, Bruce thought seriously about becoming a journalist. With English as his college major, he felt he could have had a whirlwind career in the newspaper business, but he wasn't sure he could take the pressure. "I'm probably the ulcer type," he said. "I thought the pace and pressure at Bell would be more moderate and less sustained. There should also be good opportunities for promotions, especially since they were looking for general rather than specific skills among managers."

Bruce accepted an offer from Chesapeake & Potomac Telephone and had been in a training program for about 2 months at the time of MPS:0. "Of course, I'm living with the notion that this is not really my first choice of a profession. Moreover, this training program is certainly teaching me some things that are an incredible bore. I'm hoping I'll be assigned to a department that requires some creativity and is an intellectual challenge, maybe a staff job requiring research and analysis. I suppose I could be a plant manager if I had to, but it would be sort of like asking Dostoevski to write comedy — completely out of character."

Danny had begun to register complaints about his job at MPS:0, which led to his feelings of tension.

Danny's most recent assignment for New York Telephone was as an Installations Foreman, working a district in lower Manhattan aided by ten subordinates. He put in long hours, from 7:00 a.m. to 5:00 p.m. — required, he said, "to get the trouble tickets out to the fellows early." He enjoyed handling technical problems and the variety of the work, but he grumbled about the paperwork. "I can't spend as much time with the men in the field because of the paperwork, and it's increasing. Higher-ups pressure us to be on the job more, but at the same time they pile on more forms and documentation. They use these graphs and indices to measure everything, and that keeps up the pressure. There's also pressure from so many rush orders, and we have to push to keep appointments."

PERSONALITY AND MOTIVATION

The best predictors of later Adjustment ratings among the MPS:0 assessment exercises were measures of personality and motivation, particularly the paper-and-pencil questionnaires. Among the factors reflecting personality and motivation, only the Ambition factor was uncorrelated with later Adjustment. Relationships between the other personality and motivation factors and Adjustment ratings at MPS:20 are illustrated in Figure 4.1.

Two of the factors showed strong correlations with Adjustment in middle age. Both the Self-Esteem and Affability factors were significantly related to Adjustment for the combined group (correlations were .25 and .27, respectively). The relationships held for both educational subgroups at this same general level.

Within the Self-Esteem factor, three of the five exercise scores, all from the GAMIN, showed a meaningful relationship to later Adjustment. The well-adjusted men had scored higher at the original assessment on the Lack of Inferiority Feelings scale, indicating that they were sure of themselves, and on

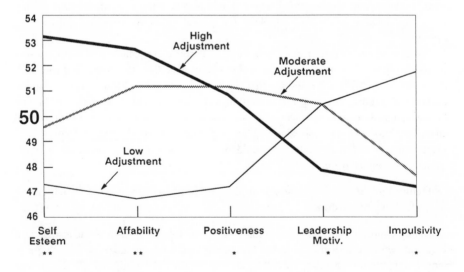

*p < .05.   **p < .005.

Figure 4.1.   Personality and motivation factors at MPS:0 by Adjustment at MPS:20.

the Lack of Nervousness scale, showing control over their moods and feelings. The better adjusted had also scored higher on the Ascendance scale, indicating that they were unafraid to step forward in social situations.

It may seem unusual that someone like Bruce, an obviously bright college graduate with high potential for management, would lack self-esteem, but this was part of his pathology.

Like Al, Bruce wanted to be prominent in the company and gain respect from others, but he steeled himself for possible failure by suggesting that he would settle for less than high goals. Though Al projected self-assurance, Bruce lacked such confidence and was very aware of his shortcomings. "*When I compare myself with others* I often underestimate myself," he replied with awareness of his own self-critical nature. "*I need* more self-assurance, I think, as much as anything," he wrote, and "*I secretly* wish I were more grand than I am in reality."

There were other indications that Bruce was a worrier and inclined to get upset. "*Sometimes* I worry," he wrote, and "*I suffer* from anxiety often." Striving for control, he responded, "*My nerves* are something I have to watch very, very closely."

Related to the Self-Esteem factor was the Positiveness factor, which showed a more moderate relationship to Adjustment in middle age. The ratings of both General Adjustment and Optimism from the projective summaries were correlated with Adjustment at MPS:20 for the combined group, though the generally positive correlations did not always reach statistical significance for the subgroups. As Figure 4.1 shows, those who were poorly adjusted at MPS:20 were already distinguished as poorly adjusted pessimists in their early years, although those who would be moderately adjusted were not differentiated from those who would be well adjusted. Danny provides a good example of early pessimism among the poorly adjusted.

Danny agonized over life and was pessimistic about external events. "*The worst that can happen* is almost here," he responded. He was attracted to a peaceful, pastoral form of existence free of strife and competition. "*I regret* to find the world constantly upset," he replied with dismay.

The Affability factor contained four scales from the Edwards, each equally related to later Adjustment. Thus the better-adjusted men were, in their youth, more interested in making and keeping friends (high Affiliation) and in being sympathetic and supportive toward others (high Nurturance). They were less motivated toward freedom and independence (low Autonomy) and showed fewer tendencies to express hostility (low Aggression).

Another factor in Figure 4.1 is related to Affability. The Leadership Motivation factor showed a mild negative correlation with later Adjustment, with the well-adjusted group rated lower on the factor at MPS:0. This was due entirely to the rating of Affiliation on the projective exercises, which was negatively related to Leadership Motivation but correlated positively with Adjustment 20 years later. Thus the relationship of Adjustment to a lack of

Leadership Motivation is only a reconfirmation of the greater Affability of the well-adjusted group. The lack of relationship between later Adjustment ratings and the other scores in the Leadership Motivation factor (e.g., liking a leadership role, rejecting a subordinate role, having high motivation to achieve and advance), as well as the Ambition factor, indicates that the drive to advance to higher levels of advancement did not affect later Adjustment either positively or negatively.

A good example of the lack of Affability in a poorly adjusted manager is provided by Barry.

It was clear from the projective exercises that Barry did not relate closely to others. He was envious of superiors, competitive with peers, and critical of subordinates. He had little need to relate to people as people, though he craved their attention and admiration. He lacked confidence in himself underneath, and as a result he tried to adopt a more determined, forceful manner. He seemed uncertain of how aggressive he wanted to be — disturbed by friction, but afraid of being an easy mark.

"I will give people the shaft if I think I can get away with it and it will benefit me," Barry confided to his interviewer. "I am not very happy with myself the way I am, but good guys don't win."

One final factor related to Adjustment in Figure 4.1 is that of Impulsivity. For the college and combined groups, but not the noncollege, high Endurance (persistence at a task) and low Heterosexuality (interest in erotic relationships with the opposite sex) were both predictive of later Adjustment. That interest in sex could be a predictor of later poor Adjustment ratings came as a surprise, but our interpretation is that high scores on this scale may indicate an overdependency on the opposite sex, or need for an emotional prop. Marital status at assessment was unrelated to later Adjustment. The combined and noncollege groups with better later Adjustment also indicated greater interest in job security at the original assessment, although this was not true for the college men.

Don illustrates well the impulsive qualities of a poorly adjusted college recruit.

Don seemed ready to burst into new and unstructured situations that might bring excitement. The stories he created in response to the TAT pictures were creative and displayed a rich fantasy life. They also indicated he had difficulty organizing his thoughts. Exhibitionism was to be expected from Don, for he thrived on being the center of attention.

Don also liked to have his own way and could be very stubborn. He regarded himself as spoiled and unfocused, saying to his interviewer, "I probably have not completely grown up. I'm still very self-centered. I'm a bit brash and outspoken, and I like to throw lines to impress people. I'm certainly not as cautious as many telephone company people are, and I may not say the right thing at the right time."

When the personality and motivation factors were put in a multiple-regression equation to determine their combined prediction of later Adjustment, all five factors shown in Figure 4.1 entered the equation as making independent, significant contributions. The final equation $(R = .41)$ was clearly significant in predicting Adjustment ratings made at MPS:20.

ABILITIES

Administrative and Interpersonal abilities at the MPS:0 assessment were completely unrelated to later Adjustment ratings. Neither these factors nor any of the individual exercises making up the factors showed a relationship to later Adjustment.

It was somewhat surprising to find that the Cognitive Ability factor at MPS:0 had a negative correlation $(-.14)$ with Adjustment at MPS:20. This was not a strong relationship for the combined group and did not reach statistical significance for either of the educational groups considered separately. However, all of the four exercise scores making up the Cognitive Ability factor showed the same type of relationship, with three reaching statistical significance. This is shown in Table 4.3.

It appears that those who had better verbal skills, were more adept at critical thinking, and were more knowledgeable of the world around them were more apt to be *maladjusted* later in life. Our best explanation for these findings is that the brighter and more aware men simply could more easily find things to worry about. For many of the better-adjusted, it appeared that the saying "ignorance is bliss" was not without some merit.

It appears that intellectual aptitude and accomplishments were running at cross purposes in terms of the attainment of the two desirable criteria studied in this book: advancement in management and high personal adjustment in middle age. The brighter, more intellectually capable men were more likely to succeed in rising in the management hierarchy. Yet the same Cognitive variables were negatively related to Adjustment ratings, such that those less intellectually able had fewer adjustment problems later in life. This phenome-

Table 4.3   Correlations of Components of the Cognitive Ability Factor at MPS:0 with Adjustment at MPS:20, College and Noncollege Groups

Component	College ($n = 137$)	Noncollege ($n = 129$)	Total ($n = 266$)
SCAT Verbal	−.16	−.14	−.16*
SCAT Quantitative	−.11	−.05	−.10
Critical Thinking	−.11	−.12	−.13*
Contemporary Affairs	−.15	−.11	−.14*

* $p < .05.$

non is illustrated by the scores on the Critical Thinking Test shown in Figure 4.2.

At each level of rated Adjustment, those who achieved the highest management levels had, on the average, higher Critical Thinking scores. But within each management level, the downward slope of each line shows that those highest in Adjustment scored lower on Critical thinking. On the average, the most astute thinkers at the fourth to sixth levels were at best only moderate in Adjustment. At the bottom end of the scale, those first-level men highest in Adjustment were the least capable on intellectual measures such as this one.

The letters on Figure 4.2 indicate the placement of the different MPS composite characters. For example, Bruce (B) was more intellectual than Al (A), although Al was certainly superior to those who did not advance nearly as far. The lowest men on the figure are the C types, illustrated by Charlie, who sometimes got confused, struggled with spelling, had difficulty verbalizing, and was limited in his reasoning powers. But thanks to his own ability to adjust, these things really did not seem to bother Charlie that much; he was quite comfortable in his own niche.

OVERALL ASSESSMENT EVALUATIONS

The only MPS:0 dimension factor related to MPS:20 Adjustment was Independence, which had a weak positive correlation for the combined group and did not reach statistically significant levels for the educational subgroups considered separately. The relationship stemmed from the Need for Peer Approval

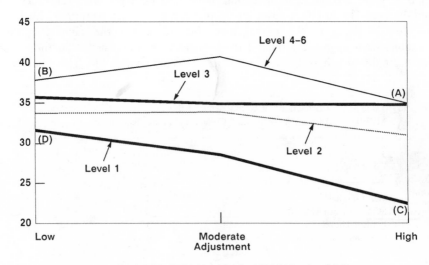

Figure 4.2.   MPS:0 Critical Thinking Test by MPS:20 level and Adjustment.

dimension and is consistent with the tendency toward higher Affability shown for the better-adjusted.

Other dimensions related to later Adjustment were few, and relationships were weak. Still, they were consistent with data already presented. For example, the greater positivism of the well-adjusted men and their greater satisfaction with work were illustrated by their higher ratings on the Bell System Value Orientation dimension.

The General Mental Ability dimension showed the same weak negative relationship with Adjustment for the combined group that the Cognitive Ability factor had shown. Perhaps related to the verbal side of such ability, Oral Communication Skills also showed a mildly negative relationship with Adjustment for the combined but not the individual groups.

In summary, the dimensions added little to the prediction of MPS:20 Adjustment, for the original assessment dimensions were designed to reflect managerial motivations and abilities rather than aspects of mental health. It was only later in the study that research interest in emotional stability began to blossom. Fortunately, many of the personality and motivation instruments allowed for some differentiation of the well-adjusted from the poorly adjusted at the time of the original assessment, although even these were not that clinically oriented.

The final evaluations of the B and D types, then, were much more dependent on the abilities they demonstrated in the various exercises than on their potential difficulties in psychological adjustment. Both Bruce and Barry were considered to have promising management careers ahead.

Bruce's performance in the MPS:0 assessment exercises was usually influenced by his skillfully written and spoken communications. He was a shrewd conversationalist who could convey honesty and sincerity without necessarily revealing his motives.

In spite of Bruce's self-criticisms, the assessment staff thought he would certainly make the third level of management within 10 years and could go further. His scholastic aptitude, verbal facility, good organization and decision-making skills, and leadership abilities all pointed to significant potential for management. He would also benefit from his high standards and interest in self-improvement as long as he didn't become too preoccupied with his weaknesses. The staff thought it unlikely that he would leave the Bell Stystem and look for work elsewhere, although some thought he might seek a more intellectualized field with less stress.

Despite Barry's overly aggressive manner, he appeared to possess many of the abilities and characteristics which would enable him to perform effectively in middle management. His strong planning and organizing skills, decisiveness, mental ability, and motivation for advancement were likely to result in his being evaluated positively by others. The consensus of the staff was that Barry's career with the Bell Stystem would be a successful one.

The D types, Don and Danny, were not expected to go far in management.

The assessors concluded that Don's future would depend heavily on the degree to which he matured in the next few years. It was thought that his forthcoming military experience might result in more effective behavior in dealing with others. Don was bright, certainly unafraid to assert himself, and had good oral communication skills. But his disorganization, impulsivity, and lack of smooth human relations skills were problems that, if unaltered, could result in his leaving the company or being asked to leave.

Danny approached most of the assessment exercises in a concrete, unimaginative fashion. He was compliant with what was requested of him, but showed little enthusiasm and seemed to find little intrinsic interest in the techniques or the purposes of the program. Some activities were stressful to him, and he generally looked uncomfortable and lacking in self-confidence. Most of the time his drive, energy, and inner work standards were below average.

In making their final evaluations, the staff predicted that Danny would stay with the Bell System but that he would not and should not be promoted into middle management. It was clear that he lacked the drive and motivation for higher levels of management, preferring technical work. Moreover, his abilities for managerial work were deficient, and he would probably experience pressure and feel threatened when expected to act persuasively.

INTERPLAY OF MANAGERIAL SUCCESS AND ADJUSTMENT

The two criteria we have examined in middle age, advancement in management and personal adjustment, are not completely independent phenomena. For the total group at MPS:20, management level showed a modest positive relationship with Adjustment ratings ($r = .15$, $p < .05$). A clearer picture of the relationship between management level and Adjustment ratings is shown in Table 4.4. For those at the third and second levels of management, there was no particular tendency to be more or less adjusted. But at the highest

Table 4.4   Distribution of MPS:20 Sample by Management Level and Adjustment

| | MPS:20 Adjustment ratings | | | | | | | |
| | Low | | Moderate | | High | | Total | |
MPS:20 level	n	%	n	%	n	%	n	%
4—6	11	24	16	35	19	41	46	100
3	34	34	32	32	35	35	101	100
2	22	25	43	49	23	26	88	100
1	12	39	14	45	5	16	31	100

management levels, considerably more men were high in Adjustment than low, and at the lowest management levels, considerably more men were low in Adjustment than high. Thus Adjustment ratings at MPS:20 and management success tended to go together only at the extremes of the distribution of management level.

A comparison of predictors of advancement and Adjustment ratings gives some clues as to why the relationship between these two criteria may not have been higher. These are summarized in Table 4.5. The predictors related to the criteria in differing ways, although there were no significant interactions. The relationships of predictors with Adjustment were essentially the same for all management levels, and the relationships of predictors with management level were essentially the same for all levels of Adjustment.

Some variables predicted the two criteria separately, which would suggest that advancement and Adjustment ratings should have been unrelated. Those receiving the most promotions had better Administrative and Interpersonal Skills and stronger Ambition, while those achieving high levels of Adjustment had greater Affability at MPS:0 and had better physical and mental health. Other variables predicted both criteria in the same direction, which might have led to a positive relationship between advancement and Adjustment. These included high Self-Esteem, high Positiveness of outlook, and positive attitudes to work.

Finally, some other variables predicted the two criteria in opposite directions, which might have been expected to lead to a negative relationship

Table 4.5   Predictors of Advancement and Adjustment at MPS:20 from MPS:0

	MPS:20 advancement	MPS:20 Adjustment
Predictive of one criterion	Good Administrative Skills Good Interpersonal Skills Strong Ambition	
		High Affability Good mental and physical health
Predictive of both criteria	High Self-Esteem High Positiveness Strong Work Involvement	
Predictive of criteria oppositely	High Ego-Functional involvement High Cognitive Ability High Impulsivity Low Need for Security Low Marital-Familial involvement	Low Ego-Functional involvement Low Cognitive Ability Low Impulsivity High Need for Security High Marital-Familial satisfaction

between advancement and Adjustment. The Cognitive Ability factor has been mentioned earlier: High intellectual ability related to advancement and lower ability to Adjustment. Similarly, those promoted higher were more oriented to self-development (according to the Ego-functional life theme), were more impulsive and less security-oriented, and expected less future Marital-Familial involvement. Contrarily, the better-adjusted had lower interests in self-development as young men, were less impulsive and more security-oriented, and were experiencing greater Marital-Familial satisfaction. A message from these data may be that as much as one might like to be both well adjusted and a high achiever, there are some contrary forces that may make it difficult.

The last three chapters have described what the MPS men were like in the 1950s when they were just beginning their managerial careers. In Chapters 3 and 4, we have described where they were headed in terms of professional advancement and personal adjustment. But the characteristics the men brought with them to that first assessement center are only part of the story of their career trajectories and personal development. Much happened along the way, both in the external environment and within the men themselves.

The next three chapters look at the years between the first assessment in 1956—1960 and the last in 1976—1980. There would be much change, and the men would not all change in the same ways.

CHAPTER 5

Changing Times and Lifestyles

In the two decades following their initial assessment, the MPS men would be assessed two more times, at years 8 and 20, and be interviewed 11 times, annually during the first 7 years and triannually from years 10 to 19. In addition, their bosses or other company representatives would be interviewed about them on almost the same schedule. These data indicated many changes in the men as they passed from young adulthood into middle age.

The ways in which the MPS men changed were influenced not only by their own processes of maturation, but by events occurring in the outside world. These events were in many ways dramatic, as Americans passed from the relatively tranquil, prosperous 1950s through the turbulent 1960s and soul-searching 1970s.

THE SIZZLING 1960s

The Eisenhower era offered endless opportunities for home and family and material achievements, but everyone was expected to stay in his or her own niche. The wide-ranging fear for national security, pressure toward conformity, and Eisenhower's own crisis-minimizing demeanor all acted to muffle dissent. For many, the lack of change produced a quiet frustration.

Like the first spring day after a long, frigid winter, John F. Kennedy warmed the political scene with new hopes for escape from mediocrity. Installed as president in 1960 after defeating Eisenhower's vice president, Richard Nixon, the young Kennedy and his aristocratic wife, Jacqueline, transformed the White House into a fantasy Camelot. It was the closest thing to royalty America had yet produced, with the habits and liberal social attitudes of the well-heeled upper classes.

America was fascinated with the handsome, articulate President, his alluring French-speaking wife, and their young family, memorialized in photographs of baby John-John crawling among the panels of the Presidential desk. Kennedy promised to "get the country moving again" by stimulating the economy (he later became an enthusiast for Keynesian economics), enacting social reforms, and advancing on the Cold War (Matusow, 1984).

The MPS men who spoke of Kennedy in their interviews were somewhat negative about him (their average rating by interview coders was 2.8 on a 5-point scale of agreement with him and his administration). The major criticisms were directed at his domestic policies, which were seen by some as antibusiness, although he was also criticized for personal characteristics (e.g., inexperience and ineffectiveness) as well as his Catholicism.

Said Joe in 1961, "I still haven't made up my mind on Kennedy. I've been a little bit upset about his seeming antibusiness approach, especially by his surrounding echelon. I think he's sincerely trying to do something for the country, but I don't agree with all his methods. I do admire his patriotism and his enthusiasm."

Kennedy saw the country's problems as technical and administrative rather than ideological. His initial approach to civil rights was to walk a middle ground between black demands and Southern white objections to integration (Matusow, 1984). After a series of rather passive involvements, the administration met its most difficult test in 1962, when James Meredith, a black man, tried to enter the University of Mississippi. Kennedy found he needed to send in the National Guard to guarantee black rights. He repeated this solution in 1963 at the University of Alabama, where Governor George Wallace had pledged in 1958 that he would stand in the doorway to prevent blacks from entering. Following this, Kennedy finally sent to Congress a civil rights bill to meet the movement's most urgent demands.

A spiritual highlight for the black civil rights effort was the march on Washington in August 1963 and the moving speech by Martin Luther King, echoing the phrase, "I have a dream." But only a few months later John Kennedy was assassinated, and the spirit of the nation, so recently awakened, struggled not to accompany him in death.

The black dream did not die, for with the ascent of Vice President Lyndon Johnson came not only a fervid belief in the importance of their cause but a concentration of built-up political power and adroitness that assured his will would be done. The Republicans, who put forth a right-wing conservative, Barry Goldwater, to challenge Johnson in the 1964 election, were unable to penetrate the momentum the liberal Johnson created as he finished Kennedy's term. In 1964 Congress passed and Johnson triumphantly signed the Civil Rights Act, which outlawed segregation against blacks in public accommodations and set up the five-person Equal Employment Opportunity Commission (EEOC) to protect the rights of minorities and women. (Women's rights were added by Southerners trying to squelch the bill with mockery.) But the struggle was not over with this one act.

Six days after Martin Luther King won the Nobel Peace Prize in 1964, he journeyed to Selma, Alabama to dramatize the plight of disenfranchised blacks and was jailed for his efforts. He then organized a march from Selma to

Montgomery, the capital of Alabama, but since Governor George Wallace would offer his group no protection, Johnson again had to federalize the National Guard. In March 1965, Johnson swayed the national conscience with his own famous speech to Congress on the "We Shall Overcome" theme. By August he signed the Voting Rights Act, which forbade obstacles to black enfranchisement, such as literacy tests.

In spite of these legislative triumphs, pent-up black fury erupted into violence and radicalism for the next several years. Five days after the Voting Rights Act, Watts, a suburb of Los Angeles, went up in flames; firemen were unable to reach the fires because they were stoned by blacks (Leuchtenberg, 1973). The next two summers were equally tempestuous, with riots in Chicago, Newark, Detroit, and Cambridge, Maryland. The official count was 43 racial disorders in 1966 and 164 during the first 9 months of 1967 (Matusow, 1984). Liberal politicians, including Johnson, discovered that close identification with black causes was becoming a political liability.

Another swell of race riots followed the assassination in early 1968 of Martin Luther King, as radical groups like the Black Panthers gained power. Some black leaders, such as Stokely Carmichael, Malcolm X, and Rap Brown preached "black power" and hatred of whites; they sought to replace the nonviolence of King with bellicose segregation and identification with their African heritage. White liberals were rejected as part of this process, and civil rights workers, some of whom were killed in their efforts, were at a loss to deal with demands not for equality but for retaliation. But black nationalism offered no solution to American blacks' problems of separation, and the militant movement was doomed.

Racial equality was considered a desirable goal by most of the MPS men; they were given average ratings of 4 on the 5-point scale of agreement. About one-third of those who gave their rationale said that blacks had been repressed and deserved equality, although nearly as many said that the blacks should do more to help themselves and earn their rights. About 20% of those commenting believed that equal educational opportunity would result in racial equality.

Said Joe, "I get boiling red mad when I hear prejudiced comments. They've only been a hundred years or so out of slavery, and they've never had any equality of opportunity. And they should — it's in the Constitution. I don't think we can be very happy if we don't learn to live with everyone, regardless of color."

The MPS men were closer to the neutral point on agreement with the implementation of integration (2.9), many feeling it was moving too quickly. They were generally negative to black activism to achieve civil rights (1.8); they were concerned about violence and pressure tactics, even though they might sympathize with the intent and goals.

"Civil disobedience is disturbing," said Jerry. "Civil rights are moving in the proper direction, but they're moving too fast. You can't legislate morality overnight. Everybody says they're for integration, but when you ask about having blacks move into their neighborhoods, they start to back down, worrying about their property values. I think blacks' rights should be protected, but they shouldn't be permitted to riot. They're not going to get any sympathy that way."

The black protest movement was a model for other groups who felt economically and socially disadvantaged. Puerto Ricans, Mexican Americans, and American Indians began to organize and fight for "brown power" and "red power," although they were primarily attracted to King's way of non-violent marches and demonstrations (Leuchtenberg, 1973). With a climate in the country in the early 1960s among the white majority of both abundance and self-conscious guilt about past denials of equal rights, the path was opened to offer entitlements to those who could proffer a moral claim. This soon extended beyond race and national origin to groups such as the handicapped, old people, gays, environmentalists, students, educators, farmers, and untold others.

According to White (1982), the 89th Congress, which convened after Kennedy's assassination, became the "Grandfather Congress of Programs and Entitlements," led by a Lyndon Johnson who "loved Congress, stroked it, twisted it to his ends" (p. 125). In 1964 and 1965 entitlements were guaranteed in such Great Society programs as (in addition to those mentioned for blacks) mass transit for city dwellers, community action programs, the Job Corps, Head Start, food stamps, legal aid to indigents, Medicare for those over 65, Medicaid for the poor, aid to elementary and secondary schools, college loans and scholarships, housing subsidies for low-income families, and so on, seemingly without end.

The claims and rewards in these programs were clearly compassionate, and some, such as Medicare, Medicaid, and federal aid to education, have become permanent parts of the American system. There were also many failures, and Johnson's "war on poverty" was accused of making the poor dependent on the government for support. A major problem was that the entitlement programs could not be regulated by the annual process of Congressional appropriations. The price was to be paid in the next decades with previously unexperienced levels of inflation and bureaucratization (White, 1982).

The MPS men were somewhat negative toward Johnson and his administration, with average favorability ratings of 2.7 on a 5-point scale. One-third of those who discussed him were opposed to his domestic policies, although one-fourth also referred to negative personal characteristics, such as his being a political opportunist and wheeler-dealer or being dishonest and conniving.

"Johnson seems to think he can buy security and happiness for the entire world," said Joe. "I don't think he can, not even with all my money. I'm pretty much in agreement with his approach to international affairs, but he's pushing too hard for a welfare type of state on the domestic scene. Speaking personally, a man like Kennedy was one I could identify with — he was young, vigorous, attractive, and inspiring.

Johnson isn't. He may be more effective in getting things done, but he doesn't have the same appeal."

Prosperity led not only to Johnson's Great Society programs, but to changes in attitudes toward the fundamentals of life — work and the family. Dating back to the Reformation, Western civilization up until World War II was dominated by what Max Weber called the "Protestant work ethic," which equated religious purity with hard work and self-denial. This value system encouraged such habits as industry, sobriety, moderation, self-discipline, avoidance of debt, postponement of gratification, submission to social discipline, and strong ego mechanisms to control the instincts. Masculinity was equated with being a good provider, while women were expected to devote themselves to housewifery and motherhood.

After World War II ended and the women relinquished their wartime jobs, their role of bearing and rearing children was so overstated that it resulted in the biggest baby boom in U.S. history. An ethic of procreation permeated every race, class, and educational group from 1946 until its peak in 1957 and decline in the early 1960s. The parents, who had known both the war and the Great Depression, determined that their children would never know such hardships and deprivation; they would have all the material possessions that could be obtained. Instead of stressing obedience and compliance in children as previous generations had done, they would focus on the children's potential and desires (Veroff *et al.*, 1981).

Progressive education and permissiveness went hand in hand with this approach to raising children. So did an emphasis on social interaction, encouraging children to get along with all the other baby boom children. The importance placed on permissiveness and facilitative social interaction began to undermine the Protestant work ethic philosophy of self-discipline and hard work. Similarly, the abundance of material goods challenged the deferral of gratification.

Using the theories of economist Richard Easterlin as a basis, Jones (1980) has described how this enormous, pampered cohort of boom babies became competitors for the scarce resources of an unprepared academic community as they advanced through elementary and secondary schools and into college. Record numbers and proportions of them entered college; struggling there in prolonged adolescence, they began to create a culture of their own. Because of their large numbers, they began to dictate to society rather than the other way around (Morris, 1984).

Fueled by a growing disrespect for parental and institutional values, as well as by their draft-proneness in what was (in their opinion) an unjustifiable war in Vietnam, the baby boom generation began to riot on college campuses. What began as a quest for free speech and student power eventually erupted into a massive and violent outbreak at Columbia University in 1968. Occupying administrative offices for 6 days, the students compelled the university to shut down, and for 2 years afterwards they engaged in violent activities such as burning professors' notes and library books, disrupting lectures, and roughing up students and faculty (Leuchtenberg, 1973). Similar outbreaks followed at such places as Cornell and Yale Universities, the University of California at Santa Barbara, and the University of Wisconsin. The "new left" on campus came to believe that a racist, imperialist America played politics with civil rights, fought a phony poverty war, and napalmed innocent Vietnamese (Matusow, 1984). But to many they seemed more intent on destroying the system than revolutionizing it (Schnall, 1981).

The hippies and flower children were the most extreme expression of the new counterculture. They rejected not just hard work as unfulfilling and meaningless activity, but also the other values held by their parents. They condemned the older generation's world as militaristic, corrupt, repressive, materialistic, and joyless. In reaction, they announced their own values as embracing personal freedom, openness, joy, and love.

Hippies roamed the streets of the Haight-Ashbury district of San Francisco, bearing flowers and estranging passers-by with unsolicited "I love you's." Long hair was paraded as the antithesis of the crewcuts of the repressed 1950s, and freedom of expression was extolled. Thus the achievement ethic was replaced by the pleasure principle, which expressed itself in sex, drugs, and communal togetherness.

The counterculture appealed to the nonintellectual, emotional side of the personality, spurning Western rationality for Asian or African creeds or the occult, including astrology and witchcraft. Hallucinogenic drugs, which represented a major departure by the hippies from the previous "beat" culture (Matusow, 1984), were used to expand perceptions and escape from the drabness of a life of hard work. Psychologist Timothy Leary, the "Johnny Appleseed of LSD," encouraged young people to "tune in, turn on, and drop out," while Jerry Rubin of the Yippie radical group pronounced that drugs signified the end of the Protestant work ethic (Leuchtenberg, 1973). Deference was denied to everyone from college administrators and military officers to the clergy. There was so much questioning of the church and religion that people began to ask if God was dead.

Social changes stimulated by the counterculture were reflected in the arts. Novels of the 1960s, such as Joseph Heller's *Catch-22* (1961), expressed a sense of futility and impotence that would live into the next decade and beyond (Dickstein, 1977). Nontraditional journalism, represented by the *Village Voice*, *Rolling Stone*, or the *Berkeley Barb*, went beyond descriptions of facts and engaged in personal feelings and interpretations, advocacy, and obscenity. In contrast to the formalism and control of the 1950s, art, poetry, and theatre became free-form and reverberated with energy and intensity. But the most vivid expression of the 1960s, almost its religion, was rock music.

The early years of the 1960s were best expressed by folk music, where single performers like Joan Baez with acoustic, nonamplified guitars represented purity, simplicity, and sincerity. As the decade darkened into violence, popular music was fused with complexity, surrealism, and volume — the beginnings of acid rock. Psychedelic colors and deafening, amplified sounds enveloped the audience and raised them to a frenzy of intensity. Bob Dylan, a protegé of Joan Baez, led the way in turning hard rock into a cultural statement. Most popular were the Beatles, who began with amiable irreverence and childlike exuberance but later sang of the nirvana of dope. The Rolling Stones were more sneering and negative, projecting an outlaw image.

The climax of the counterculture movement was the music festival held in Woodstock, New York, in August 1969, attended by up to 400,000 young people (Leuchtenberg, 1973). Nudity, promiscuity, drugs, and total Dionysianism prevailed. The young people reveled, but their parents were less amused. By this time some of the dangers of the counterculture began to become apparent; in Freudian terminology, *eros* had to contend with *thanatos* (Matusow, 1984). "Speed" (amphetamines) had moved into the Haight-Ashbury district 2 years earlier, and teenagers went on scary trips or perished from overdoses, like rock idols Janis Joplin and Jimi Hendrix, both only 27. A rock concert at the Altamont Raceway near San Francisco only 4 months after Woodstock led to a fatal stabbing near the stage under the eyes of the performing Rolling Stones.

The values of the counterculture were lauded in a controversial book entitled *The Greening of America* (Reich, 1970). Antagonistic critics, who were legion (cf. Nobile, 1971), were almost as dismayed by the fact that a Yale law professor had written the book and the *New York Times* and *New Yorker* had serialized it as by the message it gave. By this time the counterculture values propagandized in the book were berated for sponsoring a parasitic, self-indulgent, alienated culture that would be incapable of keeping the motors of the economy going on its own.

The MPS men reacted to radical youth and the counterculture values with some dismay. The college men had a better understanding of the issues involved than did the noncollege men and were also less negative; the college men were rated 2.4 on a scale of favorability to the counterculture, while the noncollege men were rated only 1.7. About one quarter of the college men addressing the subject said that they admired the honesty of the radical young people and felt they had a right to dissent. They thought their questioning of institutions created new ideas. About an equal proportion of the noncollege men said that the young people had too much freedom and needed more discipline. The noncollege men were somewhat more inclined than the college men to give negative stereotypes about the antiestablishment protesters (e.g., they were selfish, had no values or direction, avoided reality, or lacked respect for authority).

"These days, what the young men and women are doing on campus should be considered partly our fault," said Joe. "We've educated them better, made them more aware. The trouble is, the kids are a little too smart for their own good. They don't really know the practical implications. There is too much philosophy and no solutions.

"When I came along, my folks had come through a depression. If I wanted material things, I had to work for them, yet my kids have more crap than you can inventory. I wonder if I am doing the right thing.

"One thing about this generation is they're a helluva lot more outspoken than my generation. That's good. You can recognize some good in what they're talking about. They are much more questioning, they have no qualms about challenging authority, and the sex thing is infinitely healthier. However, there also seems to be an extreme lessening of respect for things that ought to be respected. I don't think a little rebelliousness is so bad, short of tearing the campus apart, but I don't think the violence is justified."

Jerry was more disturbed by the young people's demonstrations. He said, "I think a big problem right now is the tendency for young people to do their own thing no matter what it is or what the reactions could be. I am of the opinion that these kids would protest against one thing or another even if the Vietnam war were over tomorrow. Things are getting out of hand on campus. These kids are given too much freedom; there's a lack of discipline.

"The colleges are at fault. They've got some real kooks teaching at the colleges. You know, talking about free love, revolution, and things of that sort. I think the universities should take a dictatorial approach and expel students or faculty if they say things like this. College students have gotten far too much power just because some stupid jerk listens to them.

"The moral code is being destroyed, what with drugs, immoral sexual behavior, and kids doing things just for the kicks of it today. Society is much too permissive with their children and doesn't give enough responsibilities to them at an early age. There should be a firm background in what's right and what's wrong and not what each person thinks he should do."

Perhaps most resistant to the counterculture were the "hardhats," those non-college-educated blue-collar workers who struggled for their financial gains, supported the police and the flag, and resented upper-middle-class youth's careless disregard for the advantage college would give them. In the 1968 presidential campaign, George Wallace set himself up as a third-party candidate, claiming "liberals, intellectuals, and long-hairs have run the country for too long" (Leuchtenberg, 1973). He was against "welfare cheats" and the draft protesters refusing to fight for their country. Wallace stirred up much support from whites and other ethnic groups in the working class who were also resentful of blacks' gains and seeming impunity for the violence they created.

Among the Democrats, the increasingly unpopular Johnson was challenged for the presidential nomination by Eugene McCarthy, the antiwar intellectual favorite of the counterculture, and by Robert Kennedy, who could attract the minorities. Johnson decided not to run, and after Robert Kennedy was murdered, Vice President Hubert Humphrey became the primary winner. However, the Democratic convention in Chicago fostered Humphrey's undoing. Mayor Daley had stocked the city with police in light of so many episodes of violence, and a cadre of young people decided to savage the police with word and deed, such as throwing bags of excrement. The police "lost their cool," and many innocents were beaten with clubs as the country watched on television.

Not only were the promises of the liberal Democrats since the Eisenhower administration — managing the economy, keeping peace, solving the race problem, and reducing poverty — unfulfilled, but efforts to keep them had disintegrated into chaos. The Democratic problems and pitfalls opened the way for Republican Richard Nixon to make a comeback with an appeal for domestic tranquility. "Bring Us Together Again" said an Ohio girl's sign during his campaign. On a platform of moderation, Nixon won the election, though narrowly, with third-party candidate George Wallace taking less than 14% of the popular vote (Matusow, 1984).

Nixon shared the glory of Neil Armstrong's walk on the moon in 1969 with an earth-to-moon phone call. This triumphant culmination of the space race was taken as reassurance that the institutions mocked by the counterculture were still capable of worthy achievements. The nation breathed a momentary sigh of relief.

THE SORRY 1970s AND EMERGENCE
OF THE 1980s

In the 1960s, not only did each successive administration place the American economy under strain, but the national climate grew hostile to business (Johnson, 1983). Kennedy threatened the steel industry in 1962; the stock market ceased its bullish expansion; and writers like Rachel Carson and Ralph Nader spurred an era of environmental and consumer protection. From the mid-1960s on, a mass of regulatory legislation was passed that helped correct many abuses but also carried a huge price tag for both business and taxpayers. Courts aided the government intervention by embracing the principles of affirmative action in employment and promotions, as stipulated in an executive order by President Johnson in 1965, for members of groups found to have been discriminated against in the past. Business resources and executive time went increasingly toward responding to litigation, while the public sector grew by leaps and bounds.

The Nixon administration employed a philosophy of centrism on the economic front. When the economy began to reel with inflation, Nixon first tried gradualism and control of the money supply, but when recession resulted, he tried everything from wage, price, and rent freezes to tax cuts for industry until the situation eased. He also approved some environmental protection legislation, saw 18-year-olds get the right to vote, increased Social

Security benefits, and pushed for détente with China and Russia. Although Nixon may not have brought the country together, he may have kept it from disintegrating by walking a middle, moderate course (Leuchtenberg, 1973).

Vice President Agnew won no points with liberals, however, when he insulted upper-middle-class youth as an "effete corps of impudent snobs." Nixon supported his criticisms of the permissive upbringing of youth (attributed in large part to Dr. Benjamin Spock's book on baby and child care) and his accusations that college faculty were even more permissive than parents. Nixon also irritated liberals with his conservative social policies (opposition to abortion and to child care centers; vetoes of health, education, and welfare legislation) and the invasion of Cambodia in 1970.

A confrontation with youth boiled over at Kent State University in 1970, when students threw bottles at police cars, smashed car windows, and burned the ROTC building. Nixon sent in the National Guard, who were also attacked with rocks; they first responded with tear gas and then, without warning, opened fire. Four students were killed and 11 others wounded as the country recoiled from the horror.

For a while Nixon was conciliatory toward youth, but the hardhats picked up the cudgel and became violent with long-haired protesters. In a culmination of demonstrations, 100,000 building workers and longshoremen paraded for 3 hours in New York City, carrying placards, pledging support to America and to Nixon, and slugging bystanders who wore long hair or peace buttons. The extreme of the hardhat position was represented on television in comedy form in the person of Archie Bunker, an authoritarian hostile to minority groups, nonconformists, and liberals, who was doomed to live with the personification of the new left in the form of his son-in-law (Carroll, 1982).

Nixon was able to claim the support of those on the social right, especially after Wallace was shot and wounded in 1972. The Democratic party seemed to be in the hands of a liberal leadership dedicated to ending the war in Vietnam and eliminating racial and sexual discrimination. Meanwhile, the white working class felt neglected. The 1972 presidential election found Nixon faced with left-wing George McGovern, who said he'd crawl to Hanoi and beg rather than bomb any more in Vietnam. Nixon won by a landslide, especially since 2 weeks before the election Secretary of State Henry Kissinger claimed peace was at hand.

Nixon interpreted his majority in the election as a mandate for conservatism and abandoned his centrist policies, in spite of a Democratic Congress. He gave up on welfare reform and health insurance, vetoed rural antipollution measures and aid to the handicapped, and dismissed the outspoken head of the Civil Rights Commission.

The MPS men generally favored Nixon's policies during this period, with the college men showing greater understanding of the issues.

Said Joe, "I see Nixon as a responsible person. I think he's doing a good job trying to combat inflation, set up a workable welfare program, and see us out of Vietnam. Prior to Nixon's election, the country was going a little too far to the left. I resent people that say Nixon hasn't done anything good. They act as if he's happy that we're still in the war. If Kennedy had done what he did, they'd have statued him all over the world. Nixon just doesn't have the charisma."

One group struggling against Social conservatism was women, whose consciousness of their own second-class status in society had been raised by the appearance of Betty Friedan's book *The Feminine Mystique* in 1963, and whose claim had been legitimized by the Civil Rights Act the same year. Women's groups joined the radical mainstream as the limitations of the roles of housekeeper and mother became more apparent. More and more women opted for jobs and against marriage by living as singles or getting divorced. Women's groups managed to get a plank in the 1972 Democratic platform supporting an Equal Rights Amendment (ERA) for women in the constitution, but Nixon and the Republicans entered a platform paying tribute to women as homemakers and mothers.

In spite of the movement of women into the job market, their income remained less than two-thirds that of men. Discrimination against women proved to be extremely resistant to reform, caught up as it was with definitions of masculinity and femininity and with deeply rooted social and cultural traditions. Sexism was even institutionalized in the radical movement, as women discovered that there, too, they were dominated by men and frequently relegated to making coffee.

Organized women's groups, such as the National Organization for Women formed by Friedan, began to exert pressure on the government for legal reform. Many successes were attained in 1972, including federal legislation guaranteeing equal pay for equal work and prohibitions of sex discrimination in federally funded educational programs. After 50 years of inattention to the matter (since the granting of women's suffrage in 1920), Congress finally approved the ERA, though it still required passage by the states to become law. In the eyes of many women, another political victory was attained in 1973 when the Supreme Court declared abortion legal.

On the military front, Nixon had begun a "Vietnamization" process by pulling out American troops, ending the draft, and working out peace negotiations while still threatening the Vietcong with military offensives and bombing. American support for the war had been overwhelmingly positive until the Tet offensive in 1968, even though the press had begun to harangue Johnson about it a year or two earlier. But by the mid-1970s, most would not admit supporting the war or would protest about having been gulled about it (Morris, 1984).

The MPS men followed the national trends, being rated 3.6 in favorability toward U.S. presence in Vietnam and the Far East in 1964—1966, 3.0 in 1967—1968, and 2.3 in 1969—1972. In the earliest period (1964—1966), many more men favored bombing and going in to win the war if the United States was to be there at all. The earliest period also produced more comments about waging a limited war or support for the "domino" theory that Communism must be defeated lest it spread elsewhere. By the last period (1969-1972), there was more support for the position that the United States had nothing to gain in Vietnam. The war was seen as eroding American prestige, and some began to advocate that the United States pull out gradually with honor.

In 1966, Joe was very much a hawk. He said, "We should honor our commitment to Vietnam. There is a definite threat of Communism, and we must enable the people to choose whether they want freedom and a democratic government. Maybe we shouldn't be in Vietnam to begin with, but now that we are, we should clean it up. We'd lose face if we pulled out now; other countries would lose faith in us and no longer believe in our ability and desire to defend them. We should let the military do whatever they think is necessary to win the war, though I quickly draw the line at nuclear weapons. I would like a negotiated peace, but I'm not too optimistic about the Communists' sticking to one; I think the only way we're going to get peace is through victory."

Two years later, Joe was not so sure of what U.S. policy should be in Vietnam. "I guess I have mixed feelings on this," he said. "I think we have to remain in Vietnam at least until some logical, peaceful conclusion takes place. I wish we had taken a different position initially, a position which would have involved us as part of a U.N. resolution rather than going it alone. As to what to do, I'm not knowledgeable enough to outguess the generals. Perhaps a diplomatic approach would be preferable over either an escalation or a de-escalation."

By the early 1970s, Joe had given up on a victory. He said, "At one time I was a real hawk. Now I'm a tired hawk. I want out. This has been a senseless situation, and I don't think that the world will come to an end if we get out. We will never win this thing. The American public has had foisted on it some bit of fiction that we cannot pull out of Vietnam because we've never lost a war. This is pure baloney. I don't know who nominated us to be the saviors of the world. Every country can't have a democracy, and these people aren't ready for it. We should exit stage left and let the world think what it will. It can't hurt our reputation; we're still the bad guys anyway." When asked what he thought of the domino theory, he said, "I think the dominos done fell."

Nixon finally signed a peace treaty in 1973, 13 hours after Lyndon Johnson died. Congressional action publicly announced its unwillingness to back up the accords with military action (Johnson, 1983), and South Vietnam fell victim to the Communist North. The war came to represent humiliating defeat and a grim reminder of the negation of U.S. omnipotence and superiority.

Nixon was eventually dishonored by the revelations of Watergate. The break-in at the Democratic headquarters was discovered in June 1972, but it took an agonizing 2 years of progressive disclosures — primarily through the efforts of Bob Woodward and Carl Bernstein of the *Washington Post* — to expose the high-level involvement and the moral corruption of the Nixon administration. The Congressional hearings into the affair provided daytime television with enough scandal to compete with soap operas.

Nixon's best hopes for "stonewalling" his way out of the investigation were dashed when it was revealed that the Secret Service had installed a taping system to record White House conversations for history. Confidence in the President was greatly reduced with the revelation of an $18\frac{1}{2}$-minute gap in a tape, thought to be deliberately erased, of a conversation between Nixon and his lieutenant Bob Haldeman. Public faith turned to disgust when the contents of other tapes revealed a president who was profane, devious, vacillating, and generally lacking in dignity. With impeachment proceedings imminent, Nixon resigned in shame in August 1974. He was pardoned by his successor, Gerald Ford, 4 weeks later.

Nixon's favorability rating among the MPS men fell from 3.8 during his first presidential administration to 2.6 between 1973 and 1978, while the conviction with which their attitudes were expressed rose from 2.9 to 3.5. Some thought Watergate was not such a terrible thing — a fairly common happening in politics that Nixon was unfortunate to get caught in. But a more common sentiment was that the affair led to doubt and suspicion of all levels of government that irreparably harmed the country.

Joe said, "It's hard to believe that only a few months ago Nixon had more things going for him than any president in history, and now so many things have happened that turned it the other way. I thought Nixon was great, and I never suspected he would have such a scandal. It makes me wonder if there is anybody who would get in there that would be completely clean.

"At this point I'm so sick about Watergate I refuse to read any more about it. It's made me concerned about the validity of a lot of things in Washington, the way our money is spent. It's hard to trust anybody anymore. Nixon's actions shattered me as to politics. I think it's a shame for the whole system of government and both political parties. I think we'll come out of it, but there will have to be some tough times. There's a lot of credibility that's been lost that will need to be regained. I think the American political system will still work and that it's still the best system. At least I keep telling myself that.

"It annoys me to think that Nixon got off scot-free. It annoys me more that I voted for him. I'm convinced that a symbolic whipping of Nixon will help the country."

Ford never quite recovered from granting the pardon or from his reputation as a bumbler, as he tripped on a runway, fell on a Colorado ski slope, and bumped his head on the presidential limousine. He also appeared somewhat incompetent, such as when he denied Soviet domination of Eastern Europe in his 1976 election debate. But Ford was a calm and trustworthy if uninspiring leader, and he was able to provide reassurance during additional troubled times.

Scandal did not cease with the revelations of Watergate. A 1975 Senate report found numerous intelligence abuses by the CIA and FBI, including involvements in assassination attempts against foreign leaders, interception of private correspondence, programs to discredit political dissent by groups such as the Black Panthers, domestic intelligence files, and wiretappings and buggings. Prominent Democrats, too, came in for their share of scandal, with two congressmen, Wilbur Mills and Wayne Hays, involved in sexual improprieties. Violence would not die, as mobs attacked black children and school buses in the white ethnic neighborhoods of Boston that were being subjected to court-ordered busing to achieve integration. Another crisis was the revelation that New York City was on the edge of bankruptcy. The city's appeal to the federal government for financial assistance was met with scorn by Ford, for New York represented to him the follies of the excesses of liberalism.

Ford also vetoed much legislation, such as federal aid to education, health care, and control of strip mining, but inflation did recede by nearly 50% in the period from 1974 to 1976. This was no mean feat, since the Arab oil cartel, OPEC, had instituted an oil embargo in 1973 in response to U.S. support of Israel in the Yom Kippur war. Long gas lines resulted from the embargo, and the price of gasoline doubled by 1975.

Ford nearly won the 1976 election, but his apple cart was upset by an unknown named Jimmy Carter, who rose from obscurity to primary and election triumphs on a platform of noncorruption by the Washington machine. He managed to straddle many of the important issues in the campaign, offending no one, and also had the advantage as a Southerner of being able to eliminate the ubiquitous threat of George Wallace.

It soon became clear that a major problem for Carter was the economy. As documented by White (1982), the entitlement programs established during the Johnson administration and expanded under Nixon and Ford began to raise the country's deficits. In the 1950s these were $15 billion, in the 1960s they were $63 billion, and by the 1970s they were up to $420 billion. The percentage of the national budget dedicated to the armed forces began to decline from nearly half the budget in 1960 to less than one-quarter by the end of the 1970s. The difference went into income transfer payments from the middle class to help the poor, underprivileged, and old; Social Security was indexed to the cost of living in 1972. By the end of the decade it could be said that more than one-third of U.S. families received direct aid from the government. The government, having made more promises than it could keep, followed a tradition of borrowing; this buried the shortfall in currency that soon began to lose its value, fueling inflation. Family income was less in 1980 than in 1973, with any increases in wages and benefits wiped out by inflation (Lamm, 1982).

Many of the MPS men saw inflation as a critical problem during the middle to late 1970s, and there were frequent cries to balance the budget and reduce deficit spending.

"Inflation is hard to stop," said Joe, "but the government must tighten up on the benefits it gives too freely to people. The government has got to reduce its own labor costs, too. We have to slow the economy down, and increasing interest rates is a necessary step."

Said Jerry, "The government has some fancy ideas about inflation, but ultimately the people will pay. You can't keep taking more and more out of the pot and put nothing back in. The working man will end up giving more and taking a little less."

Accelerating inflation was just one more factor that was causing cynicism to wash into American attitudes. Watergate was the nadir of a series of blows, including Vietnam, the campus riots, and black violence, to American faith in its institutions and its past. More political corruption was later revealed. In 1976 came "Koreagate," the discovery that over 100 congressmen had taken bribes from a South Korean lobbyist to enact legislation favorable to their cause. Another derivation, "Billygate," marked the questionable financial transactions of the President's brother, Billy Carter, as a lobbyist for Libya. In 1980, in an FBI undercover investigation code-named "Abscam," U.S. congressmen were shown on videotape taking bribes from supposed Arab millionaires.

A Harris poll in the mid-1970s showed a marked drop over the past decade in public confidence in not only political leaders, but such groups as doctors, lawyers, and business executives. Patients increasingly sued physicians for malpractice, and major insurance companies tripled physicians' malpractice insurance premiums in 1975 (Carroll, 1982). Corporations were implicated in exposing employees and communities to toxic chemicals, carcinogens, and other hazards. Even science became suspect, and schools declined in discipline and effectiveness. The College Entrance Examination Board reported steady annual decreases in verbal and mathematical aptitude scores since the early 1960s, as did the Scholastic Aptitude Test and Graduate Record Examinations, especially on the verbal portion (Adelman, 1985). Meanwhile, students were more and more involved in unprecedented criminal activities against schools, teachers, and other students.

As established professions and institutions lost the support and faith of common men and women, the American culture was left in a vacuum of values. Some sought solace in writings that a "midlife crisis" was but a normal, predictable course of events and beneficial to growth. Others leapt to varieties of the "human potential movement," seeking both therapy and growth in a wide variety of programs offering the liberation of self from worldly restraints into expanded consciousness, such as transcendental meditation, Zen, Erhard seminar training (est), yoga, and various charismatic and Asian religions. Many were left vulnerable to radical cults, resulting in tragedies such as the mass suicide of over 900 souls belonging to the People's Temple in Jonestown, Guyana, and desperate attempts by parents to kidnap and "deprogram" their children from the treatises of groups like the Reverend Sun Myung Moon's Unification Church and Krishna Consciousness.

The lapse in institutional authority spurred a retreat into the self. As documented by Lasch (1978), it appeared that instead of looking outward for inspiration, people began to look within, until the culture earned the label "narcissistic" and the 1970s became known as the "me decade." The new narcissists had turned away from the past as well as the future and seemed to live only for the moment. If the society had no future, it made no sense to live in anything but the present; if inflation would erode investments and savings, it was foolish to put off until tomorrow the pleasures one could have today. The Protestant work ethic increasingly unraveled as people turned to personal, psychic self-improvement for hope and help. With the collapse of parental and institutional authority, the society seemed to have shifted from dominance by the superego values of self-restraint to those of the self-indulgence of the id.

Within bureaucratic organizations, the complaint was that the loyalty of White's "organization man" was being replaced by the manipulations of Maccoby's (1976) "gamesman." The critics of the 1950s had complained of guiding one's behavior too much by others' expectations, but the critics of the 1970s lamented the opposite: a disregard for social norms and preoccupation with the self (Veroff *et al.*, 1981).

The search for individualism and the "do your own thing" imperative was mirrored in architecture, which changed from the cool and aloof glass box of the 1950s to the more romantic, emotional, and historically eclectic styles of the 1970s. Nowhere was this better exemplified than by AT&T's new corporate headquarters at 550 Madison Avenue in New York City, the "Chippendale skyscraper." Architecture was seen "more as a continuous, unrelated stream . . . a turning inward and even backward — a loss of belief in a utopian future — that seem characteristic of American culture right now" (Goldberger, 1981, p. 90).

The narcissism of the 1970s was described by Kennedy (1979) as a time of exponential individualism: Different groups had begun to demand their rights in the 1960s to the point where their claims were so large and varied that they could not possibly be met or benefit the common good. The combination of assertion of individual claims and the questioning of authority resulted in a displacement of blame from the self to others. The dismantling of guilt, laid on by the Protestant ethic and the Catholic conscience, created a no-fault society, from no-fault insurance to open sexual relationships and a marked increase in litigation.

Jimmy Carter discovered Americans' reluctance to blame themselves when he tried to chastise them for a crisis of confidence in his "malaise" speech on television in 1979. Though his analysis of the public loss of faith and confidence in each other was no doubt correct, the public was mostly aware of its loss of confidence in him.

Carter was a remote and somewhat mysterious leader, quick to change policies in midstream and seemingly tortured by a devout Christianity and concern for human rights across the globe. Although being outside the Washington political mainstream helped him win the election, it was his undoing in getting Congress to cooperate with him to solve the problems of the time. His successes were not insignificant, for he appointed scores of minorities and women to public office, passed the Panama Canal treaty, triumphantly brought together an agreement between Egypt and Israel at the Camp David summit in 1978, and in 1979 restored formal relations between China and the United States. But his triumphs were solitary, executive acts, for Jimmy Carter seemed to trust no one, except one eternally stalwart supporter — his wife, Rosalynn.

Carter's administration was filled with contradictions and embarrassments that made him look foolish and inept. He announced that a Russian brigade was in Cuba, then discovered it had vanished a few weeks later. He overreacted to Russia's invasion of Afghanistan by dubbing it the "gravest threat to world peace since World War II," leading to the need to withdraw the second arms limitations treaty (SALT II) with the Russians from Senate consideration. When Castro released some Cuban refugees, Carter welcomed them with "open heart and open arms," but less than 2 weeks later he had to call out the Coast Guard to protect Florida from the onslaught. He announced an upturn in the economy a day before his Council of Economic Advisers announced a decline that predicted the sharpest recession in years.

Although Carter's motives may have been beyond reproach, his thinking and actions were muddled at best. In the end Carter was a "man caught and gripped, then squeezed and crushed, by those stupendous forces of history rising from a world America had once freed and dominated — where now Jimmy Carter's moralities were irrelevant" (White, 1982, p. 225).

Carter received no more than a 2 in average favorability ratings from the MPS participants, who often spoke negatively of his personal characterisitics, such as being weak, indecisive, a poor manager, and an incompetent leader.

"Carter is an honest person," said Jerry, "but he doesn't know how to get things done. He hasn't provided leadership in meeting the country's needs. Frankly, I'm looking forward to his downfall."

In November 1979, a group of students seized the American Embassy in Teheran, Iran, and took the emissaries hostage. Enraged by the escape of the Shah in the wake of the Islamic revolution and his acceptance into the United States by Carter for medical treatment, the Iranians demanded the Shah's return to certain destruction. Carter refused and tried to negotiate his way out of the crisis. But the Iranians did not follow American rules of reason or organization. They threatened the hostages with death and paraded them blindfolded as American television sets carried scenes of Iranians shouting "Death to America," "Death to Carter," or "Down with the Great Satan." In April, Carter tried a rescue operation by helicopter without the knowledge of his secretary of state, Cyrus Vance, who later resigned over the incident. The attempted rescue resulted in the failure of three of eight helicopters, an aborted raid, and the death of eight Americans. The humiliation of the proudest nation on earth was complete.

With the Iranian crisis, oil was again cut off; world prices rose; and Americans, panicky because of uneven distribution more than real shortfalls, agonized in long gas lines that sometimes erupted into violence. Carter's response to the energy crisis was mostly a bland appeal to conservation. A controversial energy alternative, nuclear power, received a frightening setback when an accident at a facility in Three Mile Island, Pennsylvania threatened a meltdown that could release deadly radiation throughout the surrounding area. To add to domestic problems, the Japanese turned out to have the most fuel-efficient automobiles, and Detroit found itself unable to sell its flashy American gasoline hogs. The Chrysler Corporation finally went on its knees to the government for a loan to save it from bankruptcy. Business productivity elsewhere declined, and inflation nearly doubled between 1977 and 1980. Said *New West* magazine of the 1970s, paraphrasing Dickens, "It was the worst of times, it was the worst of times" (cited in Carroll, 1982).

In the midst of such difficulties, Carter was easy prey in 1980 for conservative Ronald Reagan, no stranger in presidential politics. Along with chiding him about his record on the economy, Reagan bested Carter with a warm personality and easy quips. Too, he appealed to those who despaired of America's future by promising to return the country to greatness, while Carter spoke of the need to recognize limits.

Reagan's victory seemed to be a mandate for budget control, strengthening America's position in the world, and rearmament, for the Soviet Union, Communism, and nuclear war remained constant threats. The liberal philosophy of a freely spending, omnipotent federal government met its demise in 1978 with the death of liberalism's most verbose and steadfast supporter, Hubert Humphrey, and the passing of Proposition 13 in California, limiting property taxes and symbolizing taxpayer revolt.

Reagan was also brought to office by the efforts of social conservatives who railed at the changes in American attitudes and lifestyles. Fundamentalist Christians lashed out at "secular humanism" and "situation ethics," which were, they believed, destroying the fabric of American life. Support for capital punishment began to revive. Conservatives also propounded antihomosexual ordinances and backed reverse discrimination charges, which claimed that affirmative action programs in education and employment discriminated in reverse against white males.

The conservatives also were opposed to the ERA, in spite of (or perhaps because of) the changing role of women. Sonia Johnson was excommunicated by the Mormons just for advocating the ERA. Yet the old norm of a working husband with a dependent homemaker/housewife — the conservative ideal — fit but a small minority of American households by the early 1980s as women of all ages entered the labor force in record numbers. There were growing tendencies for women to delay marriage, postpone childbearing, and have fewer children than women of previous generations; those who did have children were more likely to remain in the labor force or to return to it soon after giving birth.

Pivotal to the antifeminist position of the conservatives was their hostile rejection of legalized abortion. A right-to-life movement, supported by Roman Catholics as well as fundamentalist Protestants, succeeded in passing legislation to forbid the use of Medicare funds for abortion (denying abortions to the poor), to restrict the practice for military and other personnel, and to permit employee health insurance programs to cancel abortion coverage. Other attempts to ban abortions completely were still being propounded, in spite of the fact that public opinion polls showed that the majority of Americans supported women's abortion rights.

Other statistics (White, 1982) showed changing lifestyles. The ratio of marriages to divorces went from 4 to 1 in 1948 to 2 to 1 in 1978. The number of unmarried couples living together doubled between 1970 and 1980. Illegitimacy began escalating, especially among whites, and within the decade of the 1970s the number of families headed by a single parent rose from 11% to 19%. In 1981 for the first time fewer than 60% of American households included a married couple, down from more than 78% in 1950 ("Married Couples," 1981). Clearly the American society had changed, and to most social conservatives it was definitely a change for the worse.

A number of MPS men saw moral decay as one of the major problems facing the United States in the 1970s.

"I think there is a great deal of dishonesty and not much morality in the people in government or the people in society in general," stated Jerry. "The average person wouldn't bat an eye over cheating on his income tax. He would try to get into a movie theatre on a children's pass if he could get by with it. This is small, but when you escalate that with influential positions in Washington, it's a great problem in the country.

"Anything goes today as long as you don't get caught at it. It troubles me that we have deteriorated to the extent we have. Watergate was a big issue, but it's related to other things too, like drug problems. The constant use of sex in advertising is having a detrimental effect on American morals and should be stopped. In the future our children will wake up and want to know why their parents didn't do something about it. I think this is reflected in the increased number of illegitimate births and other statistics which indicate that the moral fiber of the American people is disintegrating. Not that I'm a puritan, but I think the pendulum is swinging too far on one side.

"People generally seem to feel it's okay to do things I would never think of doing or would never allow my children to do. Little things like not showing respect for authority or even to elders. There's destruction for the sake of destruction. Fifty percent of the people know a fence they can buy stolen goods from, but nothing is done about it. If adults have this attitude, why shouldn't the children? Kids today are naive, self-centered, and lazy, but they got this way because parents let them. The only way to correct it is to give kids a lot of responsibility early and bring them up in a religious tradition."

Women, blacks, and other minorities were considerably less enchanted with Reagan and his conservative philosophy than white males, such as those in MPS. Inflation of living costs and government cutbacks of social programs for fiscal austerity exacerbated the poverty that minorities seemed unable to escape. Black unemployment remained twice that of whites, and black women, who headed 40% of black families, were doubly penalized by economic discrimination against both minorities and women. The immigration of ethnic minorities, especially from Southeast Asia and Mexico, added language barriers and difficulties of cultural assimilation to their economic problems.

For women the problems were economic, legal, and social. The gaping male—female wage differential was shown to be due not just to less pay for the same work but to the assumption in pay evaluation systems that traditionally female jobs were worth less in the marketplace. Although many legal decisions supported women's rights, it was clear that it would be difficult to win their cause on a case-by-case, statute-by-statute basis without the over-reaching principle established in a constitutional amendment. Yet local politics continued to thwart passage of the ERA in spite of majority support in public opinion polls. Moreover, traditional stereotypes of women as sex objects began to reappear, as in the "jiggly" television programs, focusing on women's sexual appeal. Feminists claimed, too, that escalating incidences of rape, wife beating, and pornography were reaffirmations of male dominance in its most scurrilous form (Carroll, 1982).

Although minorities and women may have felt crushed by the new conservative tide, others would see it as the natural dialectic, a recycling to the orderly 1950s after the violent excesses of the 1960s and 1970s. A recycling could incorporate progress and reforms, or it could mean a return to darker, more restricted times past. Reagan, like others, believed it was possible to go home again to a place where authority was respected. Some argued for a return to traditional concepts of duty, morality, and a willingness to accept personal guilt "if only because it forces a shape and meaning on our actions which they otherwise do not possess" (Kennedy, 1979 p. 68). There was a call for limits, with claims that freedom was in greater jeopardy without them (Schnall, 1981). Yet such arguments smacked of restriction of freedom to those who had tasted it during the post-1950s years. As the 1980s began, the American culture seemed to be struggling for its identity, its future course unclear.

Overall ratings of the MPS men on political philosophy showed them to be generally conservative across the two decades of the study. Yet, as Figure 5.1 shows, their attitudes were pulled in the more liberal direction in the 1960s and

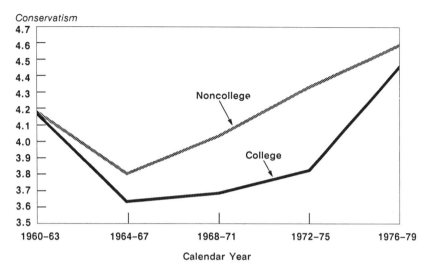

Figure 5.1.   Political philosophy over time, MPS college and noncollege groups.

early 1970s. By the end of the Carter era, however, the MPS participants were more conservative than they had ever been.

On their year 19 questionnaires, one-third of the men responded that they did not identify themselves with either political party but were middle-of-the-road — about the same proportion as at the original assessment. The Democrats now registered 11% of the group (compared to 17% at the MPS:0 assessment) and the Republicans had 55% (compared to 53% at MPS:0). Looking at it another way, of those claiming to be Republicans at MPS:0, 57% remained so, while of those Democrats at MPS:0, only 26% remained so at year 19.

There were no college—noncollege differences in typical political identification; on the 9-point scale used, the average man saw himself as being one step to the right of the political spectrum, which was less conservative than the raters viewed them in coding their interview statements. In spite of general agreement between the college and noncollege men in placing themselves on the questionnaire scale of agreement with political parties, there was more polarization among the college men. Some 18% of them were left of center, compared to 4% of the noncollege men, and 33% agreed with conservatives, compared to 3% of the noncollege men.

On economic issues, ratings of the MPS men's views across time showed a similar pattern to that illustrated in Figure 5.1, but were in all periods strongly conservative. By the late 1970s, the men were concerned that government spending had gotten out of control.

"There has to be a balance in our financial policy in this country," said Joe in 1978.

"The government must control spending and stop trying to give something to everyone. Government is getting bigger and bigger, and more people depend on government for salary, benefits, and aid. It's a snowball. There aren't enough taxpayers to support the programs. Cutting out everything would be great, but I guess it's not realistic. People are afraid to vote 'no' on issues because they're afraid it will take some benefits away from them. I don't know how we're going to get out from under all this government spending."

The pattern for social issues was different, however, as shown in Figure 5.2. Although the college men remained near the neutral point in social attitudes over the two decades, the noncollege men grew considerably more conservative in the 1970s. The ratings are certainly not definitive, especially considering that there was much information missing in various interviews, but the results do suggest that the noncollege men may have had strong negative reactions to the societal changes and upheavals of this time period.

LIFESTYLE CHANGES AMONG THE MPS MEN

As the country aged in the 1960s and 1970s, so did the MPS men. An understanding of how the men's lives and life interests developed over the 20-year period comes from the codings of the life themes from the annual interviews with the participants in the first 7 years and the triannual interviews from years 10 through 19. The similarities between the college and noncollege men in their life interests and satisfactions were greater than their

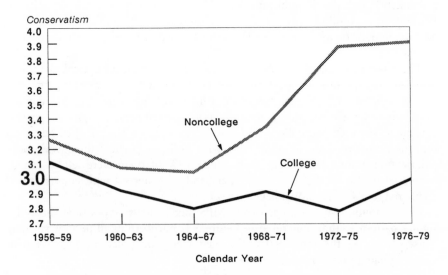

Figure 5.2.   Position on social issues over time, MPS college and noncollege groups.

differences, and in most cases the combined group best represents the trends found.

Family, Home, and Finances

Figure 5.3 shows the average level of involvement over the years in the life themes having to do with family, home, and finances. In spite of increasing divorce rates and threats to married life in the 1960s and 1970s, Marital-Familial involvement for the MPS men showed a steady increase over the first 7 years after the first assessment and remained the area in which the men invested most of their concerns throughout the next decade.

The noncollege men were originally higher on the Marital-Familial theme than the college men, since nearly twice as many were married at the time of the MPS:0 assessment, but the differences between the two groups gradually disappeared. The noncollege men's greatest increase in involvement in their marriages and families occurred during the first year after MPS:0, while for the college men there was increasing involvement for 6 years following MPS:0.

All but one man had married by MPS:20, and marital stability was high. There had been 28 divorces (19 of these men remarried) and 2 separations, so that instability characterized only 11% of the marriages. Seven men had been widowed, but six of these remarried. In all, 86% of the men were still married to their first wives, with no significant differences related to the men's educational status, although the college men were somewhat more likely to be

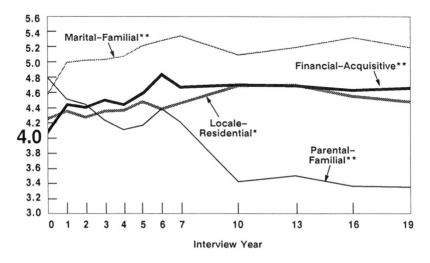

*p < .05, **p < .005 time effects.

Figure 5.3.   Current involvement in family, home, and financial life themes, MPS over time.

separated or divorced and the noncollege men to be widowed. At any rate, the MPS men were clearly among the more traditional in the evolving American culture. The college men had had an average of 3.1 children, of whom the youngest was 12 years old at MPS:20; the noncollege men had produced 3.4 children, with the youngest nearly 17 at MPS:20.

Along with developing concerns for the marital family in the early years went increasing interest in home and residence and in acquiring material things, as shown by the Locale-Residential and Financial-Acquisitive life themes. The college men maintained slightly more involvement in each of these themes than the noncollege men over the years. For both groups, level of satisfaction closely approximated their involvement in the Locale-Residential theme, although they were somewhat more involved than satisfied in the Financial-Acquistitive theme.

As involvement in the marital family and home increased, ties to the parental family began to decrease. The noncollege men maintained those ties longer than the college men, perhaps because they were less likely to move away from their original environments. For both groups the greatest drop in Parental-Familial engagement occurred between years 7 and 10 of the study. By MPS:20 only about half the participants' fathers were still alive (54% of the college men's and 42% of the noncollege). As longevity statistics would have it, their mothers fared better: 78% of the mothers of the college men were still alive, compared to 59% for the noncollege men. The men did not waver in their satisfaction with their parental families in spite of lesser involvement.

Joe and Jerry, representing the college and noncollege men, illustrate the evolution of the life course in the home and family arena.

Joe had indeed married his best girl, as he intended at assessment, and she became pregnant almost immediately. The first child, a boy, was followed by two girls, each about 2 years apart. Joe was now the provider, and his Bell System job became quite important to him.

Joe's wife had been concerned about his working for the telephone company because of the ever-present prospect of moving. And, indeed, their four moves from years 9 through 16 upset both her and the children. The older daughter suffered most, since the moves always seemed to come at a critical period. Still, the promotions brought prosperity: by year 10 Joe was living in a $17,000 home and driving a Rambler. Yet his wife yearned to settle down.

This goal seemed to have been reached when Joe was assigned to Michigan Bell headquarters in year 16. Thanks to an increased salary ($40,000 in the mid-1970's) and some good investments, Joe had raised his standard of living considerably; he now had a brick house in the Detroit suburbs, as well as a vacation place where he could enjoy fishing. But by this time all was not rosy with Joe's family.

The older daughter, influenced by the liberalizing 1960s and 1970s, began to question her parents' whole value structure. By MPS:20 Joe lamented that he might have been too lax with her, but he was resigned to her probably leading a nonachieving, unconventional life. His son, too, disappointed him by leaving college during his freshman year to join the Air Force (though he would later return). As Joe's children became more independent and out of his control as a parent, he began to reflect on his own needs.

Joe saw less and less of his mother. His father had died shortly before MPS:20, and his mother now led her own life. His wife's parents were now in their 70s, and they saw them about twice a year. Both of Joe's sisters had moved to other states, and he saw them only for an occasional holiday get-together.

As the 1970s took hold, Joe began to express doubts about the American dream of the 1950s, where making it was everything. The revolution of the 1960s had disturbed him and opened up thoughts about alternative life goals. He found himself yearning to move to a small town and feeling that big metropolitan areas were "for the birds." He was more comfortable now with his older daughter's quest for a simple way of life, but he admitted it would be hard to give up his present standard of living. Yet with inflation, he wondered if he was really that far ahead.

In year 4 of the study, Jerry and his wife added one more child to their family, giving them two daughters and two sons — their contribution to the baby boom. By this time they were able to stop renting and purchase a $19,000 home, putting $5,000 down. During the next several years the amounts owed on furniture and appliances were paid off. Jerry put in wood paneling in the basement himself and did other remodeling.

Jerry's wife was supportive of his work with the telephone company, although she resented the overtime and was especially annoyed when Jerry forgot to call and tell her he would be late. She had a tendency toward nervousness and was an insomniac when the children were young. Still, the first 8 years of the study were relatively peaceful times for Jerry. He and his wife saw both sets of parents several times a year, and the grandparents were important to the children.

Jerry supported his children's activities by attending PTA meetings and umpiring in the Little League, but his approach to the children tended to be authoritarian. At one point he told the interviewer, "The children know my position in the house. I'm the father and they're the children. Usually what I say goes. I don't like the idea of being pals with my children. I don't think it's my responsibility to entertain them every minute I'm home."

In spite of this authoritarian approach, or perhaps in reaction to it, two of the children posed serious problems in their adolescent years. The older boy smoked marijuana regularly and began to drift, borrowing money heavily. The younger daughter began to indulge in too much partying when she reached high school, letting her studies slip.

Problems were exacerbated in 1976 when Jerry became a business office manager, which required the family to move to Pittsburgh. The work and its expected community involvements left Jerry with less time for the family, and the added strain on his wife increased her nervousness. She was very dependent on Jerry, and her rambunctious teenagers pushed her to require frequent medication. In addition, Jerry's father died of cancer during this period, and Jerry had to help support his mother.

The stress on Jerry and his wife gradually abated as the two troubled children worked their way through their problems. The boy eventually tired of his vagabond life and tried to borrow money from his father to pay off his debts. Jerry refused, telling him to get a job. This the son was able to do, and he had paid off most of his debts by the time of MPS:20. The younger daughter made it through high school, and now worked as a secretary.

To her parents' great relief and appreciation, the other daughter had led an exemplary life. She had done well in school and became a registered nurse. She and her husband, an accountant, lived nearby with their first child. Said Jerry, "You know you're getting older when your grandson calls you Pa-Pa for the first time."

Prosperity added to Jerry's sense of peace in these later years, although he had not done as well financially as Joe. By MPS:20 he was living in a large three-bedroom home only 15 minutes from the office. He was earning $34,000; he had $55,000 equity in his home, $12,000 in the Bell System Savings Plan, and $5,000 in AT&T stock; and he owned two cars, a 1975 Buick and a 1973 Chevrolet.

Involvements External to Work and Family

The men engaged in other activities not necessarily related to their family life or to their jobs. Average ratings over the years on four life themes encompassing these other activities — Recreational-Social, Ego-Functional, Religious-Humanism, and Service — are shown in Figure 5.4.

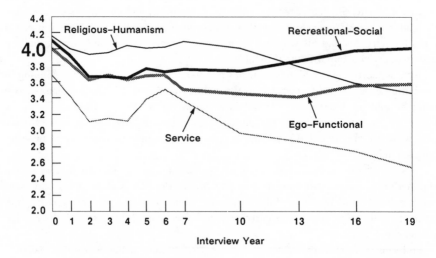

p < .005 time effects, all scales.

Figure 5.4.   Current involvement in life themes external to work and family, MPS over time.

Involvement in the Recreational-Social life theme showed some decline for both samples during the early years, when young children were no doubt significant distractions. Interest in recreational and social activities revived during the second decade of the study.

The Ego-Functional life theme also declined during the early years and did not climb back to its former level. A minority of the men continued to pursue academic credentials following the original assessment. Among the college graduates with no postgraduate records, 42 went on to gain some credits and 17 gained a master's degree. Business administration was by far the most popular graduate course.

Among the noncollege men who had not attained a degree by assessment, 12 attained the baccalaureate, and 3 of these went on to some postgraduate work. None attained a master's degree. There were many indications on various records throughout the study that the noncollege men were much more likely to point to education as something they regretted not getting more of in the past.

The college men remained higher than the noncollege men on both involvement in and satisfaction with the Ego-Functional life theme. They were consistently more avid readers of both magazines and books. In the period covering years 16—19, 88% of the college men indicated that they had read at least one book, compared to only 53% of the noncollege men. The college men also belonged to more clubs (1.8 on the average, compared to 1.4 for the noncollege men).

Joe maintained his interest in fishing over the years, even though he didn't go often when the children were young, and he accumulated some 20-odd fishing rods. He dabbled in golf from time to time but never seemed to gain any proficiency; his athletic involvements eventually became confined to television watching. Joe and his wife tried to help themselves adjust to each new locale by joining various bridge clubs, often with other telephone company people. His interests in music continued, although he "got fed up with pop music" and came to prefer semiclassical, instrumental music, as well as scores from Broadway shows. Disco was not his cup of tea, he emphasized.

Joe's reading interests continued to expand, although he was not an intellectual. He joined the Book of the Month Club and purchased both fiction and history books. He also reported reading *Time*, the *Reader's Digest*, and *National Geographic*. The late 1950s found Joe reading *How to Win Friends and Influence People* and *What We Need to Know about Communism*. By the 1960s it was *Black like Me* and *Vietnam Diary*. His tastes for books in the 1970s often included violence and gore, such as *The Godfather*, *Jaws*, and *The Exorcist*, but also a search for inspiration, as with *Jonathan Livingston Seagull*.

Jerry's family took him away from recreational activities in the early years, though he would go hunting on weekends to get away from the home scene from time to time. On these weekends, some 10 or 12 men would get together and supplement the hunting with poker and drinks. Television held occasional interest for him, and he preferred the Jackie Gleason and Ed Sullivan shows. He also made the effort early in his managerial career to develop his knowledge with a television course in economics. Jerry didn't read many books, especially in the early years, but he kept up with the *Reader's Digest* and *Newsweek*. Hunting magazines could also claim his time, and he did some reading on refinishing and home repairs.

During the second decade of the study, Jerry's social activities with neighbors tapered off as he lost the taste for cocktail parties. He still thrived on outdoor activities and liked to fish and backpack with his sons. The younger son was an athlete, and he and Jerry especially enjoyed the camaraderie of camping and cookouts.

Two life themes showing significant declines in the men's involvement over the years were Religious-Humanism and Service. The decline in religious involvement began after year 10 of the study, in the late 1960s and early 1970s, and has continued to decline since. It is likely that this reflects the general turning away from traditional religions that has been occurring in the larger culture. Both educational groups showed the same declining interest, although satisfaction with religion was not affected.

Joe and his wife were more active in the Presbyterian church in the early years of their marriage and made sure their children attended Sunday School regularly. But as the years went on and moves meant changes in churches and congregations, Joe went to church less and less frequently. He claimed he hadn't lost his faith in God, but just didn't feel the need to express it so often or so openly.

Allegiance to the church declined among Jerry's family after their move to Pittsburgh in the mid-1970s, and he once criticized the church for seeking money from him. Even in the later years, though, he claimed he still enjoyed a good sermon and found in it some solace for his troubles.

The college men had been more involved in the Service life theme at the MPS:0 assessment and remained so during the next two decades. However, both groups declined in interest to about the same degree, so that Service remained the life theme with the least involvement for the college as well as the noncollege men. As with Religious-Humanism, however, satisfaction with the theme remained at an average level over the years. There are various hypotheses to explain the decline in this theme, and the most appropriate explanation is unclear. Interest in community service might have declined because the men tired of such activities, found it more difficult to get involved with successive moves, found it increasingly less important to the company, or responded to the turning away from institutions and inward to the self that occurred in the 1970s.

Joe's activities in the community increased markedly after joining the Bell System. After he was made a district commercial manager in a small town in year 9 of the study, he went all out, as the company wanted him to do. He was on the Junior Chamber of Commerce, belonged to the Kiwanis and Rotary Clubs, and worked for the Community Chest and other community action groups. In support of his son, he also became a Cub Scoutmaster and later was on the board of directors for a boys' club until he lost interest.

In the second decade of his career, Joe began to grumble about his involvement in community activities. While he was in the Commercial Department, he still got pressure from his boss to continue as a community leader; however, in other departments the feeling was that it took time away from work, so he got some relief.

The MPS men's lives and lifestyles seemed to be influenced both by their own aging processes (e.g., decline in involvement in the parental family) and by events in the external culture (e.g., decline in religious participation). In the next chapter, we look at these influences on their work involvement and attitudes, their personalities and motivation, and their capabilities.

CHAPTER 6

Advancing Age and Accumulating Experiences

Many of the lifestyle changes reviewed in Chapter 5 were closely related to the development of the MPS men's careers. In this chapter, we consider the progression of their work lives and attitudes about them before turning to changes in their personalities, motivation, and abilities.

CAREER DEVELOPMENT AND WORK ATTITUDES

One life theme that showed a large difference between the college and noncollege men was the Occupational theme. The noncollege men had shown more current involvement in their work at the original assessment, but, as illustrated in Figure 6.1, they were overtaken in this regard by the college men

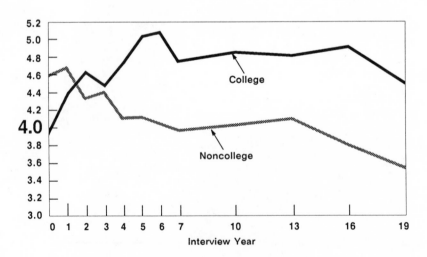

$p < .005$ group x time effect.

Figure 6.1. Current involvement in Occupational life theme over time, MPS college and noncollege groups.

128

as early as year 3 of the study. The college men continued to grow in involvement until year 6, after which they reached a point of stability for over a decade. Some disengagement from work began to show itself in year 19 of the study, when the college men were in their mid-40s.

After year 1, the noncollege men showed a decrease in their involvement in work. Following a rapid decline, their interest plateaued between years 4 and 13, then declined again, hitting a new low in year 19. Both educational groups, then, showed a lessening of interest in work in the 1970s.

As their careers progressed, most of the MPS men stayed neither in the same work location nor the same department of the company. The college men were more mobile than the noncollege, working on the average in 3.3 departments (2.7 for the noncollege) and moving 3 times (1.9 for noncollege). Moves were more likely during their early careers; some of these were made laterally to assume a job at the same level in a different geographical location, and others were for promotions.

Figure 6.2 shows the promotion rates for each educational group by year of the study. The college men were obviously more likely to be promoted than the noncollege, with advancements particularly frequent during years 3 through 6. Promotions had become negligible by MPS:20. By this time the typical college man had reached the third level, while the typical noncollege man was at the second level. The college men had an average of 236 subordinates in the hierarchies below them, compared to 67 for the noncollege men.

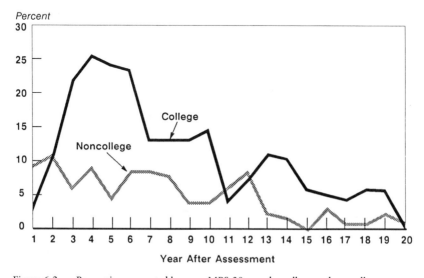

Figure 6.2.   Proportion promoted by year, MPS:20 sample, college and noncollege groups.

When interviewed in year 19, the noncollege men were experiencing quite a bit of stability. They had been on their current jobs an average of 4 years, 8 months, compared to only 2 years, 10 months for their college peers. They had had the same boss for 3 years, 1 month, compared to 2 years, 3 months for the college men. Between years 16 and 19, 36% of the college men made a job-related move, but only 10% of the noncollege men faced such an event.

It may be recalled from Chapter 2 that the men in both educational groups had been quite optimistic about what their careers and lives as managers in the telephone company would be like. The Expectations Inventory, which showed this result, was readministered to the men annually during their first 7 years and again at MPS:20. Instruction varied, in that they had been asked at the original assessment to indicate their expectations that each item would be true or false 5 years hence. One year later they were asked to speculate 4 years ahead, the next year 3 years ahead, and so on. From year 5 onward, they were simply asked how things were currently. Items concerned various aspects of managerial careers, from advancement and salary to relationships with peers and community involvements.

The average scores for the college and noncollege men at each administration are shown in Figure 6.3. As the men moved closer and closer to the 5-year target point of those early expectations, they became less and less favorable. Yet when the reality of the 5-year mark was attained, at about year 4, average scores leveled off. The college and noncollege men showed very similar average scores during the first 7 years, but by MPS:20 the noncollege men had become more negative about their managerial lives, even though the college men remained about the same as at year 7.

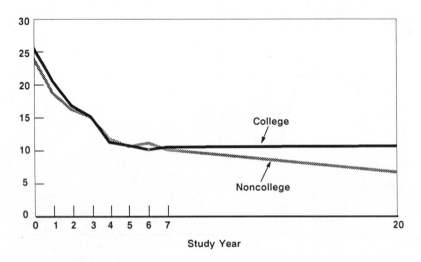

p < .05 group x time effect.

Figure 6.3.   Expectations Inventory scores over time, MPS college and noncollege groups.

SPECIAL RATES
Only for Students and Educators

TIME
- [ ] 25 issues for $14.88
- [ ] 50 issues for $29.95

SPORTS ILLUSTRATED
- [ ] 30 issues for $19.95
- [ ] 54 issues for $35.90

ENTERTAINMENT WEEKLY
- [ ] 26 issues for $12.87
- [ ] 52 issues for $25.74

FORTUNE
- [ ] 14 issues for $13.95
- [ ] 27 issues for $26.50

LIFE
- [ ] 14 issues for $17.50
- [ ] 28 issues for $35.00

MONEY
- [ ] 9 issues for $12.98
- [ ] 13 issues for $18.75

PEOPLE
- [ ] 20 issues for $22.99
- [ ] 35 issues for $39.99

☐ Payment Enclosed. ☐ Bill Me. Check One: ☐ Student ☐ Educator

NAME _____ (Please Print)

ADDRESS _____ APT. NO. _____

CITY _____ STATE _____ ZIP _____

NAME OF SCHOOL _____

SCHOOL ZIP _____   YEAR STUDIES END _____

TIME & ENTERTAINMENT WEEKLY are published weekly, except for two issues combined in one at year-end. SI and PEOPLE are published weekly. SI and PEOPLE also publish occasional special issues. FORTUNE is published biweekly. MONEY and LIFE are published monthly. (For monthlies please allow 60 days for delivery of your first issue.)

7002

A downward trend of attitudes was also shown in the various subscales of the Management Questionnaire, administered in years 1 through 7 of the study and again at MPS:20. One of the scales that had shown a difference between the college and noncollege men in year 1 was the General Management Attitude scale, a composite of items selected from the other scales in the measure but somewhat weighted toward attitudes toward supervision and higher management. Figure 6.4 shows that the difference between the two educational groups on this scale continued until MPS:20, although the gap had narrowed somewhat.

In contrast to the Expectations Inventory results, which were focused on a variety of work conditions, the General Management Attitude scale showed a fairly steady decline in each year of the study. The downward slope of the lines shows that the greatest disillusionment took place over the first 7 years of the college men's careers after the original assessment and the first 4 years of the noncollege men's. Declines after those times were more gradual. A very similar pattern was shown for the Supervision scale; here, too, the noncollege men had originally scored lower, but by MPS:20 the gap between the two educational groups had essentially closed.

Most of the other scales in the Management Questionnaire also showed greater declines in the first 7 years than in the last 13, as shown in Figure 6.5. All of the scales dropped significantly during the period from year 1 to year 7. Even the Impersonal Communications scale, which had been rated most unfavorably at year 1, dropped still further; the men felt even less well informed through formal channels about what was going on in the company after many years of experience than they had at the beginning.

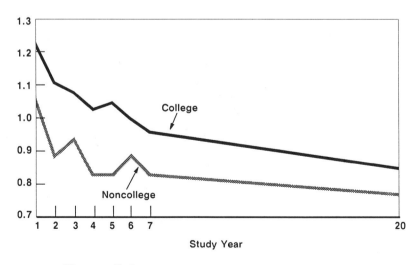

p < .01 group effect.

Figure 6.4.   General Management Attitude scale over time, MPS college and noncollege groups.

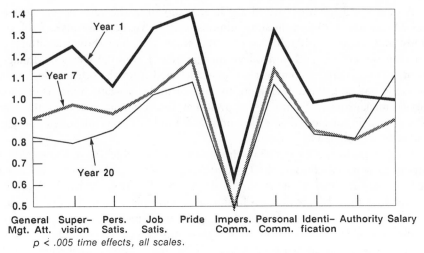

p < .005 time effects, all scales.

Figure 6.5.   Management Questionnaire scales, MPS years 1, 7, and 20.

In addition to General Management Attitude, the only scale with a difference between the educational groups that persisted into year 20 was that of
Identification (with management). Although the two groups had scored the
same in the first year, by year 7 the noncollege men had dropped significantly
lower, while the college men remained the same. Scores at year 20 were about
the same as those at year 7. The Identification scale had questions probing
whether the participant felt he was treated like a real member of management,
privy to important information, and involved in goal setting. The college men
maintained such a feeling of belonging over the years, while the noncollege
men felt more left out. The noncollege men apparently identified more with
day-to-day operations, responding to a greater degree than the college men on
a questionnaire given at year 19 that their jobs were of importance to the
continued functioning and future growth of the telephone business. On the
same instrument, the college men were more likely to praise their jobs as
contributing to their individual growth.

    The only Management Questionnaire scale that showed a revival after year
7 was that of Salary, which rose to become the area of greatest satisfaction for
the men by year 20. The noncollege men had been more dissatisfied than the
college men with their salaries at year 1, and their pay had indeed been lower.
The college men's satisfaction declined by year 7, but by year 20 both groups
had grown more favorable and there was no longer a disparity between them.
Although the college men were still making higher salaries on the average
because of their higher levels, they held no advantage within the levels the two
groups shared (namely, second and third). In fact, at the third level the
noncollege men had larger salaries than the college men, perhaps because of
regional differences in wage rates.

Four of the 10 attitude scales showed significant declines between years 7 and 20: General Management Attitude, Supervision, Personal Satisfaction, and Pride. The Supervision scale showed the greatest overall decline for the 20-year period. Clearly the men had been disappointed in the fairness and appreciation shown by their bosses over the years. The Personal Satisfaction scale reflected continuing disenchantment with such aspects of the job as promotional opportunities, performance feedback, responsibility, freedom to use one's own judgment, and variety. The declines in the Pride scale indicated that the men were less inclined to boast about being an employee of the telephone company as time went on. This could certainly be related to the negative attitudes toward business and other institutions that developed during the 1960s and 1970s.

The message from the Expectations Inventory and the scales of the Management Questionnaire is clear: the men grew less idealistic, optimistic, and satisfied as time wore on. Their supervisors' frailties became more obvious, and their jobs in reality were not as rosy as they had once seemed. However, this decline in positiveness should not be interpreted as negativism; average scores were still far from dipping below the neutral (zero) point. The men were still generally favorable toward their jobs and the company by midcareer — just less favorable than they had been in their youth.

True to his expectations, Joe was drafted into the Army during year 1 of the study. Fortunately, from his point of view, his active duty lasted only 6 months, and he was able to return to the same job in the Commercial Department of Michigan Bell. Joe had a variety of assignments in this department during the early years and a number of different bosses. He had great admiration for his first district manager, finding him very sincere and compassionate. Although his more immediate bosses wore less of a halo, Joe's feelings were nearly always positive. He seemed rather small-townish at first, calling others "Mr." or "Miss" when it wasn't necessary, and was almost overly deferent.

Joe was pleased to reach second level in year 3 of the study. By this time his bosses thought well of his ability to analyze problems and his interpersonal skills, but they also found weaknesses. They reported that he tended to talk a better game than he played and sometimes seemed more interested in making a good impression than in effective performance. He also seemed overly dependent on superiors.

Joe ran into trouble during year 5 of the study, when the district in which he worked suffered high turnover, low morale, and poor indices. The district-level boss felt Joe wasn't tough enough with his subordinates. All this happened while Joe himself was finding it harder and harder to get motivated. Since salary increases were in jeopardy, he decided to take a data-processing test for a possible transfer into the Accounting Department. He succeeded in getting the transfer, and the change provided a needed stimulus to his motivation and his career.

Joe's hard work led to his promotion to district level in year 8. He returned to the Commercial Department in a staff job doing efficiency studies of the department. He enjoyed the challenge of the job and his status at the third level, but he looked forward to being a line manager — "Mr. Telephone" in a small community. He got his wish after only a year, much to his family's consternation, since it involved a relocation.

Joe thrived in this job. He worked long hours as needed, and he was developing a fine leadership style, combining firmness with a sense of humor. He motivated his people to achieve good results while remaining flexible and willing to take on additional responsibilities. His growing knowledge of the company enabled him to represent it well to his subordinates and outside the business. His early small-town image faded as his knowledge and fine speaking voice began to create an aura of sophistication.

In spite of all this, Joe began to express some growing dissatisfactions and disillu-sionments to the study interviewers. He squirmed under the constant pressure to "make the numbers," and he felt that his recent bosses exercised too tight control and gave too little recognition. He had discovered that top management was mortal and even described some of their decisions as "gutless." He didn't like being so far removed from policy making.

Nevertheless, Joe's performance impressed his superiors, and, in year 10 of the study, he was given a rotational assignment at AT&T for further development. He welcomed the chance to "find out how the organization was run from the top," although his family was fearful of a move to "crowded, crime-ridden New York." On balance, Joe turned out not to enjoy the job. He reported, "I was initially challenged by the measurement study we were doing, but after a couple of years it got to be a bore. I was itching to be back in a line operation. I told my boss what I thought of the project and of New York and got myself returned to Michigan Bell 6 months early." As usual, Joe's attitudes didn't interfere with a creditable performance.

Back in Michigan, Joe was assigned to Customer Services and enjoyed being back in the field. He worked hard, but had some run-ins with his bosses, who complained he argued with them too long before getting into action.

One more move was in the cards for Joe, and he was relocated to company head-quarters in Detroit in year 16 of the study. After a brief stint in the Personnel Depart-ment, he returned to Customer Services, still at the third level. As Bell began to move gradually from its traditional monopoly status, phone center stores were added to his responsibilities. He also oversaw residence service centers, customer problems, and public relations in his district. He had a spell of poor results, but he was still well thought of. He was a high-energy manager who put in long days. He learned to size up situations quickly and take appropriate action.

In Jerry's early years as a first-level service foreman, he had a model he admired and imitated in the person of his immediate supervisor. Still, he had difficulty adjusting to management, and his boss complained that he seemed more union than company-oriented. This may have been one reason he was moved to a staff assistant job, still in the Plant Department, in year 3 of the study. He did well enough here to move up half a level before returning to the field as a splicing foreman. There the new boss liked the way he brought subordinates along and commented that everybody liked Jerry. He was made an "acting" second-level foreman for a while and then promoted to that level.

Jerry's move to being a second-level supervising service foreman marked the beginning of 8 years in essentially the same job. He supervised first-level foremen who bossed installation crews, scheduling jobs and going into the field to troubleshoot. His bosses commented that he was a self-starter who needed little prodding or supervision. In fact, he came to know his job so well that he needed no supervision, and he sometimes didn't tell the boss all he needed to know. Bosses commented that he often seemed uncooperative, but this may have been due simply to his quietness. He didn't seem very flexible, and he was slow to change to new methods.

Jerry's independence was at least partially a reaction to his feelings of needless pressure from above and not having a chance to run his own show. He got some relief when he was moved to an outlying office, but he inherited a barrelful of other problems. He entered a tough metropolitan district where management had been weak, the union ruled, and results were abysmal. Jerry gained the respect of his people and the union by working long hours and by being firm but scrupulously honest. He reigned by being quietly strong-willed, knowledgeable, and an effective organizer. He gained a reputation as a respected though not charismatic leader.

As results improved, Jerry began to complain about his lack of progress. "I haven't been promoted because nobody goes to bat for me when openings appear. I'm getting stale; after several years on the same job, you've solved most of the problems." He also found himself getting more critical of the company, which bothered him. "Maybe I can allow myself to be critical now that my job is more secure," he said.

Jerry gained a reprieve from the sameness of his job when he was made a sales manager for public telephones in year 14 of the study. His job was to figure out profitable locations for phone booths and try to get them installed. This was no soft job, since his group had to persuade people to commit prime space in return for a very small commission. Jerry, however, made his dollar objectives and was well respected.

Jerry made his last department change prior to MPS:20, which required his second change of residence. He became a business officer manager in Pittsburgh, responsible for service orders and business collections, working through first-level people. Much of his time was spent on customer complaints and overdue collections. For the first 2 years, Jerry reported to a woman. This was a shock, since he had always felt that women in management were "taking men's roles." His boss considered him generally congenial with peers and subordinates but said that criticism from her provoked a vehement reaction until he settled down. "Perhaps supervisors bring out the worst in him," she said.

The MPS men's declining scores on scales such as General Management Attitude and Pride could be related to the fortunes and misfortunes of the company, as well as to individual experiences and general cultural changes. The history of the organization during this 20-year period (cf. Brooks, 1975) illustrates some reasons for discontent, and the men often responded to the company's various difficulties in their interviews.

THE BELL SYSTEM DURING
THE 1960s AND 1970s

It seems unlikely that the company's fate was a negative influence on the attitudes of the MPS men during the late 1950s and early 1960s, when the company advanced and prospered. As the national economy grew without inflation, so AT&T seemed to be able to score record profits just by improving production efficiency; in fact, Western Electric's prices in 1965 were 16% below those of 1950. Long-distance rates continued a downward trend, and AT&T found it necessary to make very few requests for rate increases.

Advancing technology was no small part of the company's financial triumphs as well as of its positive image. The operator's job was to a great extent automated by the Traffic Service Position System, and electronic switching systems began to be installed in the early 1960s. About the same time, the company produced Telstar I, the first communications satellite; nondial Touch Tone service and Trimline, with the dial built into the handset; Centrex switching exchanges for business offices, offering the opportunity to dial internal numbers directly; and the Data Phone, which enabled computers to communicate with each other via telephone wires. AT&T stock split twice, in 1959 and 1964, and investors began to view the company as one of high growth as well as high technology.

Later in the 1960s, weakening social norms and general upheavals took their toll on the telephone company as well as on other institutions. By 1966 there were 375,000 complaints of obscene phone calls. As race relations deteriorated in the large cities, there were attacks in black urban areas on Bell System equipment and threats to installers and repairmen (who were usually white, as were most of the company's employees). Public phones were increasingly vandalized, so that by the late 1960s the company was losing $5 million per year in repairs and stolen coins.

The vandalism and disruptions of pay telephone service were part of even more serious service crises that came to a head in 1969 and 1970, especially in New York City. Circuits became overloaded, so that customers often had to wait 2 or 3 minutes for a dial tone; calls failed to get through; and there were cross-talk, false rings, and incorrect bills. The immediate cause was the unprecedented and unpredicted demand for service. Yet there were also claims that the switching network had become degraded by policy decisions to take profits from service costs rather than rates. Personnel problems also abounded, with astronomical turnover due at least partly to the company's salary rates being below market level. Although the company spared no effort or expense in correcting the problems, virtually rebuilding the physical plant in New York City in a very short time, the company's reputation suffered.

There were also financial problems to cope with, and AT&T's earnings dropped markedly in the later 1960s. In 1965 the FCC began a full-scale on-the-record investigation of interstate rates to determine what constituted a fair return for the Bell System and precisely how the rate base should be calculated. This increased militancy of the FCC caused the stock price to drop, and the company found itself facing increased costs of material and labor and a stock lagging so badly that equity financing became impossible. At the same time demands for service skyrocketed; in 1967 the chairman of AT&T presented President Johnson with the 100 millionth telephone in the United States (Boettinger, 1977). The only recourse was to borrow, but a national money crunch had pushed interest rates high. The company appealed to the FCC for an increased rate of return in 1969; it got some relief, but soon found itself with the same problem again.

Government control and regulation became a subject of some complaint by the MPS participants, with the lower-level men even more negative than the higher-level men.

"The FCC is beginning to tell us what to do too much," commented Jerry. "They're telling us what rates we should have and what profits we should have, and this is bad. Whenever we get a rate increase, someone complains and they usually end up cutting it down. We are forced to readjust to these cutdowns, and it's hurting our construction program a great deal. By the time you get a rate settled, you're already saddled with other expenses. We seem to be running behind the average company in the country."

The company appealed to the FCC again in 1970 to increase the rate of return and this time found itself with an additional problem. The EEOC intervened in the case, requesting that the company be denied further rate increases until it ended its alleged discrimination in employment practices against both racial minorities and women. Although the threat to the rate increase was allayed, the civil rights case and the consent decree that settled it had far-reaching consequences.

AT&T had begun a series of steps toward greater opportunities for minorities during the late 1960s, and it was no worse and often better than most U.S. corporations in its treatment of minorities and women. Yet it was certainly not difficult to find evidence of underrepresentation of the protected groups in the highest ranked jobs in the company. Moreover, the Bell System was big — the world's largest corporation in employee population — and 5—6% of the EEOC backlog involved complaints against AT&T. In addition, it was regulated and thus a ready target for government action.

The government claimed that jobs were sex-segregated and stereotyped, with low-paying jobs primarily "female." Recruiting, hiring, and promotion practices were alleged to restrict opportunities for women. According to the EEOC, Hispanics were underrepresented; most blacks in the company were women and suffered a dual handicap; most black males were in the bottom craft jobs; and few blacks were in management jobs.

The case culminated in two consent decrees (one for nonmanagement and a later one for management employees) signed by AT&T, EEOC, and the Department of Labor in 1973 and 1974. AT&T committed to facilitate the movement of women and minorities into better jobs and to adopt a new promotion and pay policy for those put in higher rated jobs. The company also agreed to implement a special program (an assessment center, thanks to the precedent set by MPS) to evaluate the interests and qualifications of female college graduates who had been hired into management and to identify those with potential for upward movement. The company was also obligated to make compensatory payments of $15 million, with additional agreements in 1974 and 1975 for nearly $10 million more.

The impact of the consent decree on Bell System operations and culture was well documented in an independent study by scholars at the Wharton School of the University of Pennsylvania (Northrup & Larson, 1979). The objective of the decree was to achieve "statistical parity" in the labor force, so that the race and sex profile of employees in each job category approximated that of the labor pool. To accomplish this, numerical goals were derived by complicated formulas. Also, principles were adopted that (1) where necessary to meet the employment targets, nonmanagement assignments would go to those "basically qualified" rather than "most qualified" and (2) the company could override seniority provisions to attain these goals.

Numerical gains were impressive in the 1973—1979 period when the decree was in effect. (After the consent decree's expiration, AT&T's affirmative action efforts were in comformity with Executive Order 11246.) Minority representation grew from 14.5% to 17.3% of the total work force, with increases in every category of jobs; their representation in management went from 4.2% to 8.7%. Men increased their proportions in administrative, clerical, and operator positions, while women increased their representation in management, sales, craft, and service positions.

Problems developed in trying to reduce the sex segregation of jobs, especially those with heavy physical demands, such as outside craft work. Even with special training and newly designed equipment, women had twice the accident rate of men in such jobs, and turnover was high (as it was also for men in clerical jobs). Women often had difficulty in building maintenance jobs, since many lacked the training and skills for operating steam equipment or doing plumbing, carpentry, or electrical work.

On balance, the consent decree had the effect of increasing the heterogeneity and representativeness of the Bell work force, but not without some difficulty. On the positive side, the pool of workers considered for promotions increased, so that many of the most able and ambitious of the protected groups advanced. However, they often suffered from lack of experience and training. Use of the "basically qualified" rather than "most qualified" criterion reduced average quality somewhat. Accidents and higher turnover also resulted in lower productivity.

The implementation of the consent decree curtailed the authority of supervisors and higher management, with attendant morale problems. Hiring and promotional authority was centralized in the personnel office, and veto powers were available to override seniority or assessment center results. Equal employment opportunity (EEO) counselors were established as respites where protected groups could seek redress for their complaints, further subverting supervisory authority. Supervisors often found themselves shorthanded, since if EEO targets couldn't be met, succeeding promotions were held up until candidates of the proper race and gender mix could be found. Most of these difficulties occurred in management, where one unfilled opening could hold up 20 promotions.

The positive response of minorities and women to the consent decree was a major benefit to the company, and to those most concerned with equal opportunity, both inside and outside the company, it was a major triumph. It is unlikely that such an enormous number of opportunities for the employment and advancement of protected groups could have gone forth with such speed without the concerted effort and sometimes drastic measures required by the consent decree. But many white males in the company, especially older ones, regarded it as an unfair burden. The major Bell System unions — the Communications Workers of America and the International Brotherhood of Electrical Workers — fought the decree, especially the seniority override, with grievances, arbitration, and court cases. They failed to change either the decree or the override, although this latter aspect expired with the end of the consent decree in 1979.

The higher-level MPS men were definitely more favorable toward affirmative action in the Bell System than were those at lower levels (based on ratings from their interviews), and the college men were more favorable than the noncollege men. There was also a shift in favorability over time, with an average rating of 3.5 (on a 5-point scale) before the consent decree but 2.2 during its implementation. Major reasons given for disapproval were the difficulty of finding qualified minorities and opposition to reverse discrimination. On the positive side was the ethical and practical need to help minorities progress.

"We're losing millions of dollars of the shareholders' money implementing these affirmative action programs," said Joe. "You spend more time trying to find minorities than doing the regular job. The need to fill racial and female quotas makes it sometimes necessary to advance those who are not the best-qualified. I think it's good that the company is trying to bring in people who have been discriminated against, but it would be better if we could be more selective.

"It's difficult to explain why there hasn't been a single female at the third level for so long. We've always had a large pool of women working for the company, and we have a lot of talent available in this pool. For some reason the opportunity for advancement wasn't made available to women. We've obviously done something wrong. Now the pendulum swings the other way for a while, and we have to give them special consideration. It's tough placing them in the craft jobs, but the company is doing the right thing by testing their aptitudes and seeing if they have the physical requirements for jobs."

Jerry was negative about what he called "social experimenting." "Unqualified people are being promoted," he said, "and this makes for bad morale among the high producers in the company, because they can't move up. There's only so many poor performers we can carry, and I think we've reached the saturation point. We're being forced to take the hard-core unemployed, and some of them don't want to work. Our foremen aren't equipped to rehabilitate and mother them. They should go to a rehabilitation center first and then be sent to us for training and a job. Hiring people just to make a quota is stupid."

The EEOC action was not the end of major government intervention into the conduct of Bell System business in the late 1960s and 1970s. The FCC began a gradual reversal of policy by encouraging competition in various areas of the telephone business. In the Carterfone decision of 1968, the FCC decided another company could interconnect private two-way radios with the Bell System. As a result, the "interconnect" industry grew in the 1970s, supplying customer-owned telephone equipment that could be connected to Bell and independent networks. In 1970, the FCC also reversed policy by letting independent companies known as "specialized common carriers" set up intercity microwave relay systems for business telephone usage, in direct competition with the Bell System. The company accused the FCC of encouraging competitors to grab the "cream" of the business, since Bell, in accordance with federal policy, charged higher rates for such business customers to subsidize local telephone service. Although the FCC barred one specialized common carrier, MCI, from providing private line service, this decision was reversed by a federal court of appeals, opening the entire long-distance market to competition.

The MPS men saw both positive and negative aspects to competition. They saw a need for the company to sharpen up, but also felt that the government should allow the Bell System to compete on an equal footing with other companies, free of restrictive regulation.

When asked in an interview in the mid-1970s about major problems facing the telephone company, Joe got up, walked over to the telephone in the interviewer's room in the Holiday Inn, and showed him that the instrument was made by Stromberg Carlson. He said, "There are very few places left in town that still use Bell System equipment. Our company can no longer be a fat and happy monopoly, but has to compete, which makes things more difficult but also more exciting and complex. Competition is keen in station equipment, PBXs [private branch exchanges], data sets, telephones, private lines, and so on. Because of cream skimming, our competitors give us fits in the cost picture. They have lots of good salesmen who are trained and aggressive and are getting old Ma Bell off her dead butt. We're beginning to look more like IBM every day. Soon I think we'll have 80% of the market instead of 100% with lots of others handling the 20%. But we're changing our image and becoming a sales company.

"I just hope the government doesn't destroy something we were once best at," Joe continued. "They are throwing every type of communications open to the market without any controls or regulations. This will end up in lots of quantity, as with the automobiles we have, but a lack of quality. It just goes to show what can happen without careful planning. Instead of long-range planning, the government is going for the immediate future."

"Competition per se isn't bad," said Jerry, "but the inevitable cost to the consumer is a reality that must be reckoned with. Competition is probably responsible for the rapid technological development of various services that are now available to the public. It helped bring out these new features, and Bell's business is higher than ever as a result. The competition has an advantage, since we're governed by the PSC [Public Service Commission] and they're not; they ought to be governed by the same things we're governed by. But they also have a disadvantage, in that there's a heavy initial investment that they probably can't get a fast return on."

As a culmination of investigations, the FCC in 1980 released a final order on what was known as Computer Inquiry II, detariffing enhanced network services and terminal equipment. AT&T was permitted to provide such untariffed services through a fully separated subsidiary later named American Bell.

The major blow to the company was set into motion in 1974 with the federal government's second antitrust suit, which charged anticompetitive behavior and sought to break up the Bell System. The lawsuit proceeded through discovery and trial preparation while the MPS men were undergoing their 20th-year assessment (1976—1980). They were not favorably disposed to the government's goals, but again the higher-level men and the college graduates did not have as negative a view as the lower-level and noncollege men.

Joe thought the company was doing well in fighting the antitrust suit. "We're doing all we can without being accused of trying to overpower the opposition. It's hard to take such a complex problem to the public. But I think we're fighting a losing battle if we expect to stand firm in our demands for no changes. Rather than risking alienation and losing the entire ball game, we should try to accommodate and compromise with those who want to break up the conglomerate."

Jerry was not persuaded the company would have to change at all. "The suit against AT&T by the Justice Department is a big bunch of crap," he said. "It was a bureaucratic move to save jobs in the government. I wonder if some of them are sorry they ever got into it. I don't think they'll get the support to get AT&T to divest itself of Western Electric. If the company were accused of making great profits, I could see it, but they're not. They're just trying to break it up because it's big. You don't create change by breaking up the Bell System. That's going to cost everybody money. It will cost millions to fight it, and the customers and taxpayers will pay through the nose for it."

"One Bell System, It Works," said the ads as the suit waged on. It is safe to say that almost none of the MPS participants anticipated the 1982 outcome

— the consent decree mandating the divestiture by AT&T of the 22 operating companies on January 1, 1984.

PERSONALITY AND MOTIVATION

Average scores on all six personality and motivation factors showed significant changes across MPS:0, MPS:8, and MPS:20. These scores are plotted for the combined MPS:20 sample in Figure 6.6. Some college-noncollege differences remained and are described in turn, but for the most part the same types of changes affected both educational groups.

Ambition and Leadership Roles

The most dramatic change in personality and motivation occurred in the Ambition factor, which dropped steeply in the first 8 years and again by the 20th year. The college group was considerably more ambitious than the noncollege at the original assessment, but the college men declined even more over the years so that the gap between the groups' average factor scores narrowed from 6 points to 4.

Three of the six scores or ratings in the Ambition factor contributed to the dramatic decrease — the Sarnoff Motivation for Advancement and Forward Striving scales, and the rating of Need for Advancement from the interview. The Sarnoff Motivation for Advancement scale is illustrative of the effects and is shown in Figure 6.7. Although the noncollege group was somewhat below the college group at the MPS:0 assessment, by MPS:20 they had fallen to the

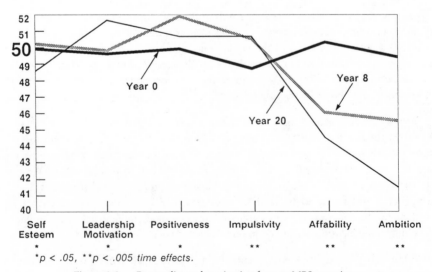

Figure 6.6.   Personality and motivation factors, MPS over time.

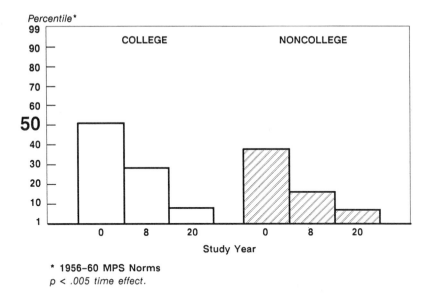

Figure 6.7.   Sarnoff Motivation for Advancement scale over time, MPS college and noncollege groups.

7th percentile of the original college norms, while the college men were at the 8th percentile. Interview data coded for Need for Advancement showed a drop in ratings for the college men from 3.5 on a 5-point scale at MPS:0 to 2.2 at MPS:20. The noncollege men dropped from 2.7 to 1.5, showing them to be still less ambitious than the college men.

It was clear from the biographical questionnaire administered during year 19 of the study that many felt they had plateaued at their current level of management. This was especially true for the noncollege men, who, when asked when their next promotion would occur, typically responded either "6 years or more" or "never." They indicated that promotion to the next level was only "slightly important" and promotion two more levels was "not important." The college men were more optimistic and more interested in promotions on the average, though not much more so. Their response to expectations of when the next promotion would occur was typically "6 years or more" or "4 or 5 years." The next level was considered "slightly" or "moderately" important, while two more levels were "slightly important" to "not important."

One of the MPS:20 exercises was a feedback interview in which the men were shown their scores on the personality and motivation questionnaires at all three assessments and asked to comment on whether they agreed with the changes they saw and, if so, what factors they believed accounted for the changes. These responses were transcribed and later coded for rationales. In explaining the declines in their Sarnoff scores, 119 men mentioned being resigned to a lack of advancement in the future. More specifically, 37 said they were discouraged by their own lack of promotions; 24 saw limited opportunities in general; and 22 mentioned EEO targets. Aging and age discrimination were mentioned by 18; 17 thought past or present bosses had ruined their chances; 15 thought their abilities were too limited; and 10 mentioned their educational backgrounds as being a liability.

Another category of rationales for the declining Sarnoff scores involved the rejection of advancement as a goal, mentioned by 110 men. Contentment with current achievements, position, status, and general work satisfaction was mentioned by 43, and changes in values, priorities, and perspectives were mentioned by 37 men. Other frequently given reasons were concern about business demands as one moved higher up (mentioned by 28); unwillingness to relocate or change lifestyle (mentioned by 21); and a distaste for business politics at higher levels (mentioned by 13).

Not only were both samples less concerned with their personal advancement by the 20th year, but they were less inclined to believe in always looking to the future and planning for future goals. The college and noncollege men had scored at about the 50th percentile on the Sarnoff Forward Striving scale at the MPS:0 assessment, but their scores had dropped to the 23rd percentile by MPS:20. However, their Motivation for Money scores on the same questionnaire did not change: the noncollege men had responded with more interest in financial gains at the original assessment, and they did so again at MPS:20. Both groups changed imperceptibly on this scale over time.

Although motivation for advancement declined over time, this did not mean that the men were no longer interested in what jobs at their current management levels had to offer. As shown in Figure 6.8, their interest in having a challenging job or a difficult assignment, as measured by the Achievement scale of the Edwards, increased with time, especially during the first 8 years. Greater interest by the college group, established at the MPS:0 assessment, remained. For both groups, careers that were plateaued in terms of promotions did not mean the end of motivation to tackle the job at hand; they still enjoyed investing their energies in task accomplishment.

When asked about reasons for the increase in this scale at MPS:20, 35 men mentioned positive job-related factors as responsible for the change, primarily the work itself. Their job assignments were seen as interesting, challenging, or tough but satisfying. Only two men mentioned their bosses as inspiring their motivations to achieve. Other rationales for the increase in scores did not refer to work per se, but attributed it to greater self-assurance that came with experience and maturity (mentioned by 35 men) or development of individual values and standards for one's own fulfillment (mentioned by 26).

Furthermore, the decline in advancement motivation did not mean that the men had no interest in leadership positions. In fact, one contradiction in the general decline in the Ambition factor was an increase in the average score on

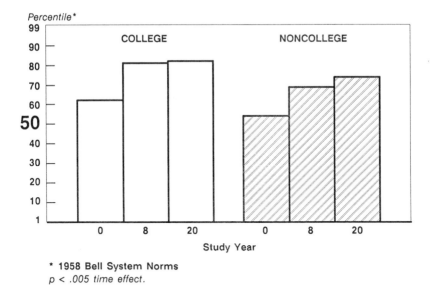

* 1958 Bell System Norms
p < .005 time effect.

Figure 6.8.   Edwards Achievement scale over time, MPS college and noncollege groups.

the Edwards Dominance scale from the 45th percentile to the 52nd. Development of a leadership style with changes in position was mentioned by 26 men
as an explanation for a higher Dominance score, while 25 attributed it to
rising self-confidence gained through maturity and experience. The Leadership
Motivation factor, derived from five projective ratings, also increased during
the last 12 years of the study, as shown in Figure 6.6. This was especially true
for the college men, although the noncollege men showed a slight gain as
well.

A higher rating was shown for both educational groups on the specific
projective rating of Leadership Role, indicating they were better able to
identify with this role as they gained experience in the company. The manner
in which the college and noncollege men took charge may have differed. Their
scores on the measure of Authoritarianism (the California F Scale) showed the
college men generally remaining the same with time (55th percentile at MPS:0
and 51st at MPS:20 on the original MPS college norms). The scores of the
noncollege men increased over this same period from the 57th to the 70th
percentile. Although the California F Scale is a measure of repressive, power-
oriented political attitudes, it might be interpreted to indicate that the noncollege men approached their supervisory positions in a more heavy-handed,
by-the-rules style as time went by.

As late as year 4 of the study Joe was still talking about aspiring to an executive
level position at AT&T. Upon his promotion to the third level at year 8, he still referred

to himself as "burning with ambition," although his goal was modified to reaching a fifth-level department head position, a target he felt was within his grasp. The MPS:8 projective exercises also indicated his ambitious, competitive nature and eagerness to demonstrate leadership, although he still exhibited considerable immaturity with carelessness, impulsivity, and a variety of poorly formulated but strong opinions.

Within a couple of years after the MPS:8 reassessment he had changed his mind about advancement, now saying a department head's job would require him to give up too much of himself and he would be happy with fourth (division) level. By the middle of the second decade of his career, Joe no longer felt fourth level was in the cards for him. "I don't have the breadth to assume my boss's job when he retires. I admit it would be nice to have another promotion before retirement, but I'm not hung up on it."

By MPS:20 Joe seemed to be adjusting to third as his terminal level. He claimed his material needs were satisfied, and he no longer cared that much about achieving fourth level. Still, he remained achievement-oriented and competitive, according to the projective exercises, and eager to prove he had the ability to be successful. He also indicated being an influential leader was important to him. For example, on the incomplete sentence "When I am in charge of others...," he wrote, "I find my greatest satisfactions," and "The job I am best fit for is one which requires leadership ability."

Jerry had not aspired high in his earlier years, and he felt he had done quite well when he reached second level. At the MPS:8 reassessment he expressed some concern that the additional responsibility and uncertainty of a higher position might be difficult for him. Since he placed a premium on quality, with a high Inner Work Standards rating, he felt he would rather stay where he was and do well at it. He appeared to be a methodical problem solver who, though not coming across as a leader among peers, had a common-sense influence on decisions and events. His approach tended to be authoritarian, as if he didn't know how to be flexible without appearing to be weak.

In year 11 of the study, after 5 years at the second level and some feelings of being in a rut in the same job, Jerry confessed to his interviewer that he was "getting itchy to make third." He thought the challenge of a higher-level job would be revitalizing, and he would also appreciate the financial advantages.

It appeared that this was not to be, especially after his lateral move in year 14. By year 16 he was somewhat resigned to a second-level career, saying, "The problem is there are enough fellows around with college degres who will fill those third-level jobs."

His Sarnoff Motivation for Advancement score was quite low at MPS:20, but his Edwards Achievement score had risen over the years, which he attributed to "being determined to do as well as people with a college degree." He showed some disappointment with his career progress, stating on the incomplete sentences, "I regret not having gone one level further in the company." He clearly liked his work with the Bell System, stating, "I am secretly happy in my present job." The fact that he thought of his reaction as secret indicated ambivalence about advancement; that is, in spite of his grumblings about promotions, he was not unhappy to remain where he was.

Affability, Impulsivity, and Self-Esteem

A fondness for leadership roles may have also derived from an increasing dislike for a role that was dependent on others. The Affiliation ratings from the projective exercises, scored negatively in the Leadership Motivation factor, showed a decline, while the ratings for Leadership Role increased. Correspondingly, there was a dramatic decrease in the Affability factor, as shown in Figure 6.6. Three of the four Edwards scales in this factor contributed to the decline over time.

The college group had initially been higher on the Edwards Affiliation scale, which measures liking to do things with friends and enjoying friends, as shown in Figure 6.9. By MPS:20 they had dropped to the level of the noncollege group, near the 35th percentile of the 1958 Bell System norms. As time wore on, these college men seemed to turn away from fraternity, military, and bachelor life and toward home and family and career. The noncollege men had already had these orientations at the time of the original assessment, due to their greater age and longer time in marriages and careers.

In the feedback interviews, the largest number of men (32) explaining the decrease on this scale mentioned job-related factors as contributing to their loss of interest in friends, with 12 also referring to investments in their career advancement. In addition, 30 men mentioned they had come to value time spent with family over that spent with friends. Apparently involvements with work and family left little time for strong ties with friends that had been important in the past. Between 15 and 20 men mentioned each of four other

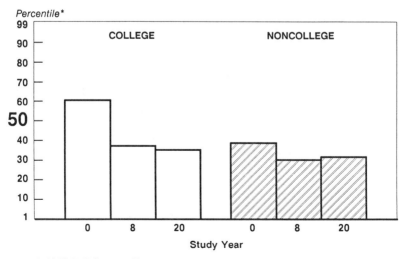

* 1958 Bell System Norms
p < .005 time effect, p < .05 group x time effect.

Figure 6.9.   Edwards Affiliation scale over time, MPS college and noncollege groups.

rationales: that they had come to value a few close relationships over too many superficial ones; that they did not believe in making friends out of coworkers; that there was a decline in association with fraternities, clubs, and the military; and that relocations and transfers had interfered with friendships.

Another Edwards scale, though not in the Affability factor, reaffirmed the lessened interest in people for both the college and noncollege samples. Both groups declined significantly on the Intraception scale, which measures interest in analyzing the motives and feelings of others, as shown in Figure 6.10. Sixteen men explaining the drop in Intraception said they had come to feel that sensitivity to others was not worth the time and energy, either because it was none of their business, because it didn't work, or because they just weren't interested. Thirteen said they had become more results-oriented and less people-oriented, and nine said they had come to accept people at face value without probing beneath the surface.

At the same time that the MPS men became less sensitive to others' feelings, they became more aggressive, as also shown in Figure 6.10. The Edwards Aggression scale does not measure mere assertiveness, but is made up of items indicating angry and hostile feelings. Both educational groups rose 12 or 13 percentile points on this scale between MPS:0 and MPS:20.

Many responded in job-related terms in giving rationales for increasing hostility in their feedback interviews. Twenty-five men said that the rise reflected frustration with their jobs, though only six pointed to plateauing careers. Nineteen thought that aggression was necessary to accomplish their

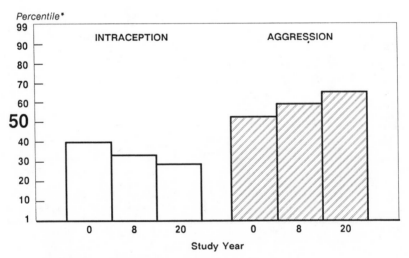

* 1958 Bell System Norms
p < .005 time effect, both scales.

Figure 6.10. Edwards Intraception and Aggression scales, MPS over time.

tasks or to survive on the job. Twenty-three men mentioned that they viewed themselves as more self-confident and found it easier to express aggression. Becoming more critical, less tolerant, and less patient with age was offered as an explanation by nine.

The most dramatic change in the Affability factor was the increase on the Edwards Autonomy scale, shown in Figure 6.11. Both the college and non-college groups increased steadily on this scale from MPS:0 to MPS:8 and again between MPS:8 and MPS:20, until they were at the 85th and 87th percentile of the 1958 Bell System college-hire norms, respectively. As time wore on, they seemed increasingly motivated to throw off the shackles of dependency and become their own men.

Forty men gave positive, job-related rationales for the increase in Autonomy, including having challenging jobs (mentioned by 20), having good bosses who were supportive and respected (mentioned by 10), and having career paths that led to promotions and more decisions (mentioned by 10). But 18 men also mentioned negative job-related factors, suggesting rebellion against controls or procedures in the company (mentioned by 9), bosses whom they didn't respect or who played favorites (mentioned by 6), or other factors. Fifteen men felt an increased need to separate or detach themselves from the company.

Among other rationales, 34 men claimed they had increased in their needs for independence since they were more secure and sure of themselves. Twenty-five men perceived the increase as a natural developmental process, indicating

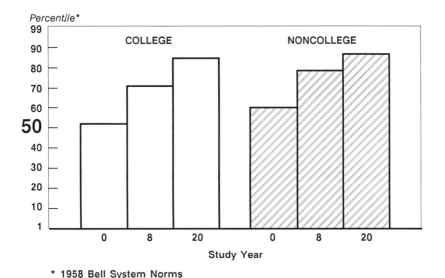

Figure 6.11.   Edwards Autonomy scale over time, MPS college and noncollege groups.

that they "flowered" or "broke out of a mold." Outside interests, second careers, or family influences were cited by 26 men.

In sum, many sources of data identified the MPS men as less affable over time, with strong upsurges of autonomy desires accompanied by increased feelings of hostility and decreased needs for friendships or for understanding others. It was as if their years of living from youth to middle age had propped them up for the assumption of individual responsibilities, but at the same time had hardened them into willful independence.

The personality and motivation factor called Impulsivity showed a significant increase between the MPS:0 and MPS:8 adminstrations, as depicted in Figure 6.6. For the college men, the general trend toward Impulsivity was offset by decreasing exhibitionistic tendencies and greater needs for security. But both samples showed increased Impulsivity with the decline in three Edwards scales — Deference, Abasement, and Endurance — all shown in Figure 6.12.

The lower Deference scores showed a disinclination with time in the motivation to defer to those in higher authority. In the feedback interviews, the most frequent explanation for this change, given by 38 respondents, was that they were increasingly self-reliant and resourceful and had become their own bosses. Twenty-nine men gave negative job-related replies, including disrespect for their bosses (by 17). Twelve said low deference was necessary to complete the job; 17 said they had come to dislike rules and authority; and

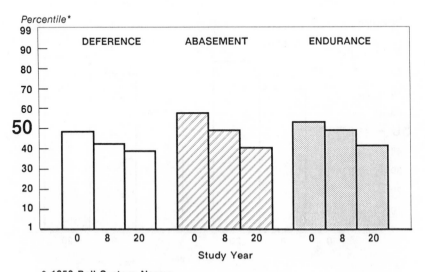

* 1958 Bell System Norms
p < .005 time effect, all scales.

Figure 6.12.   Edwards Deference, Abasement, and Endurance scales, MPS over time.

12 viewed themselves more as leaders than as followers. These rationales in many ways confirmed the findings of higher scores on the Autonomy and Aggression scales.

The noncollege men had originally been higher than the college group on the Edwards Abasement and Endurance scales, but over time both groups declined. By MPS:20 the two groups had become indistinguishable in average level of Endurance, though the noncollege men were still higher on Abasement. The message in the declining Abasement scores was that the men were no longer so inclined to take the blame on their own shoulders when something went wrong. In the feedback interviews, 16 men attributed this to breaking away from their backgrounds and upbringing, while 10 thought it was more realistic to lower their standards in this way.

The lower Endurance scores meant that the men were less content to continue persisting at the same task for long periods of time. The most frequent explanations given for this by the men were that a broader scope of activities reduced their ability to complete one task at a time (mentioned by 14), or that they had adopted a principle of not taking work home or putting in overtime hours (mentioned by 19).

This lack of stick-to-it-iveness did not necessarily mean that the men longed to move away from established habits and preferences, for both groups declined significantly on the Edwards Change scale, indicating less interest in doing new and different things, such as trying out new restaurants or traveling to new places. A desire for security and settling in was cited by 23 men to explain the decline, while another 23 pointed to job-related factors, such as relocation.

One final personality and motivation factor from Figure 6.6 deserves comment, since it seems to fly in the face of the other evidence presented here. The Self-Esteem factor showed a decrease between MPS:8 and MPS:20, even though the men repeatedly said that they felt more confident and self-assured with age. The decline was shown in the Lack of Inferiority Feelings scale from the GAMIN, although in the feedback interviews the men often claimed they did not identify with such a drop. Some (11 men) speculated that they must have been more cocky than self-assured when they filled in the questionnaire in earlier years, although 29 pointed to work-related factors as negatively affecting their level of self-confidence.

There was also a decline in the Masculinity scale of the GAMIN (the college men dropped from the 52nd percentile to the 42nd, while the noncollege men dropped from the 54th to the 46th). Fifteen men said they had broadened their experiences to include more artistic areas; 8 pointed to family influences; and 14 said that with maturity they had less need to prove themselves in a masculine way than they had had in their youth.

The changes in motivation and personality over the 20 years of the study were for the most part consistent across both samples. Both the college and noncollege men declined in ambition, although they clearly enjoyed leadership positions and thrived on individual task accomplishment and job challenge. Some restlessness seemed to characterize their maturity, as they sought more independent roles and were less content to persist at the same old tasks, although they were not anxious to stray from the paths they had carved for themselves. Accompanying their demands for autonomy was an assertion of self, often with feelings of irritation and hostility toward others. They were less motivated to defer to those in higher authority, less likely to take the blame themselves when something went wrong, and less interested in preserving friendships. In short, the path to middle age seemed to toughen these men, not to soften them.

Even though the men were asked for their causal interpretations of the changes in their personalities and motivations, their rationales should not necessarily be taken as definitive. Many were unable to conceptualize or verbalize the changes that were presented, and the interviewers' tape recorders often turned up long stretches of silence as the men wrestled with the challenge of explaining something that seemed inexplicable.

When the men did try to explain their changing personalities and motivations, they tended to point to their jobs for rationales (although the fact that the assessments were performed in a work-related setting may have influenced such thoughts) or to point to maturational forces from within. Seldom did they refer to events in the outside world, perhaps because such connections are more abstract and remote and less conscious. Yet many inferences could be made from the external environment to the changes shown in personality and motivation. For example, the "do your own thing" imperative might have influenced the rise in their motivations for autonomy as well as their growing internal self-confidence. The impudence and rebelliousness of youth or the demands of protected groups in the 1960s and 1970s could have prompted the MPS men's increased aggressiveness, and the decline of the Protestant work ethic could have fostered lessening feelings of guilt and abasement. Certainly generally declining trust in America's institutions may have brought about the decrease in the need to show deference, and the "me decade" was consistent with the turning away from others illustrated in lower needs for affiliation and intraception. The declining economy might also have taken the edge off forward striving and produced discouragement about further advancements.

One way to help differentiate the viability of developmental or experiential explanations as opposed to cultural explanations for change is to take new measures of another cohort, especially one experiencing the same culture in a different phase of its own developmental cycle. Such a cohort was readily at hand with the MCS sample, who experienced their young adulthood in 1970s America rather than 1950s America. Further comments on the explanation of the personality and motivation and other changes in the MPS men await the introduction of the MCS group in Chapter 9 and the final summation in Chapter 13.

In the MPS:20 feedback interview, Joe discovered that his Aggression scores had increased substantially over time. He said, "I do more often find myself arguing about things I don't agree with. If you don't speak up, you don't get the service and quality you need." His desire to be in control was also evident in his increased Autonomy score. He said, "I inwardly rebelled against the discipline and regimentation the organization calls for. It's too structured."

Joe's Deference score also declined sharply, and his explanation further exposed his desire to be his own man. "I don't want to have to do anything. Nobody knows my job better than I do, and I wouldn't take directions on it from anybody." His lower Endurance score prompted the remark, "I want results quicker now."

Accompanying his struggles for individuation and self-assertion were decreased scores on both Affiliation (needing friends) and Intraception (analyzing motives and feelings). Joe wasn't surprised at these scores, since he noted that after his marriage his life quickly became confined mostly to family and job responsibilities. Also, he lost friends with each relocation. In later years he commented in his interviews that he had become more cynical, less tolerant of others, and more irritated at thoughtless and inconsiderate people.

Joe's projective responses also showed his lack of interest in interpersonal relationships or making friends at work. He wrote, "*Getting others to like you* is not important to me." He obviously liked getting his own way, making his own decisions, and being free to do what he wanted. He said, "*I need* more freedom on the job."

He presented himself as a forceful person, indicating, "*When working with others* I sometimes ruffle feathers," and "*When I disagree with others* I tend to get louder." His reaction to authority showed hostility coming through, as he spoke of "getting his hackles up." He saw his own weakness as a tendency to lose his temper, and indeed his responses indicated a quick, spontaneous person who reacted inconsistently and superficially to his own experiences.

The highly masculine image Jerry had projected remained in effect at the MPS:8 reassessment but declined somewhat at MPS:20. He noted that he may have followed his son's interests, from backpacking to music. He agreed with the increase in his Aggression score when he saw it in the feedback interview, noting, "I have no trouble telling off those in the organization who aren't doing their part." He was lower on both Affiliation and Nurturance at MPS:20 than he had been at MPS:0. He said, "I expect more of others now and am not too sympathetic with their failure to perform." He added rhetorically, "Do I really need friends?"

The MPS:20 projective exercises painted a picture of Jerry as a matter-of-fact, controlled individual who was uneasy with emotions. There were indications of an accepting, appropriate, and conscientious approach to his experience, but an underlying sense of rigidity and stubbornness was also inferred. For example, he firmly rejected using his imagination to write a story to the blank card of the TAT, writing, "Nothing! I see nothing and see no reason to state otherwise."

Jerry wanted to be appreciated by superiors, but his own reluctance to acknowledge weakness promoted defensiveness and annoyance if he was criticized. He felt cautious and uneasy with authority figures, but responded critically if he believed their positions were unjustified. He stated, "*I hate it* when goals are set for me," and "*What annoys me* is when I am told what my objectives are."

ABILITIES

As described earlier, the MPS:20 assessment made a radical departure from the goals and procedures of the MPS:0 and MPS:8 assessments, with a focus away from managerial abilities and motivations and toward midlife and midcareer concerns and satisfactions. As a result, some managerial abilities were not well measured at MPS:20. In particular, there was no In-Basket task to measure administrative skills, and although group discussions could get at leadership abilities, there was neither an explicit set to compete in these discussions nor an opportunity to make a formal oral presentation. Consequently, considerations of how managerial abilities changed over time must rest primarily on analyses of data from the first two assessment centers, which covered an 8-year time span.

The changes in the ability factors between MPS:0 and MPS:8 are shown in Figure 6.13. Although it might be expected that managerial skills and abilities would increase with 8 years of experience, the results do not confirm this in any but the Cognitive area. The Interpersonal Ability results are particularly distressing, with declines by both groups and a particularly dramatic decline by the noncollege men. This group also showed a small decline in the Administrative area.

The slightly higher score on Administrative Ability for the college men

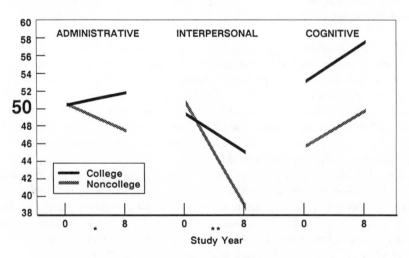

*p < .05, **p < .005 group x time effect.

Figure 6.13.   Ability factors, MPS:0 to MPS:8, college and noncollege groups.

at MPS:8 came from a higher rating in the In-Basket on Organizing and Planning rather than on Decision Making. It is likely, of course, that their decision making relative to the actual technicalities of their jobs improved, but the decisions about managerial problems measured in the In-Basket showed no gain with experience.

The noncollege men slipped only slightly on Organizing and Planning, according to codes made from In-Basket reports from the two assessments, but they declined on Decision Making from an average rating (on a 5-point scale) of 2.9 at MPS:0 to 2.3 at MPS:8. Perhaps they found problems in the In-Basket more difficult than they had at MPS:0, since the task at MPS:8 was somewhat more complex. At any rate, there is little encouragement for thinking that Administrative Ability improved over time for this group.

Joe performed somewhat better on the In-Basket at MPS:8 than he had at MPS:0. He handled the items in a workmanlike though somewhat unimaginative fashion with good organization. Although his making of decisions was marred by missing several subtleties and complexities, he generally had a good grasp of the problems and executed his plans with dispatch.

Jerry seemed to need an overabundance of facts before making a decision in his In-Basket, and he often stalled and sought more structure. There were few indications of using the reference material effectively, and he failed to interrelate most items. He did make some plans, but they lacked depth and long-range thinking. Many items were delegated with no guidance and direction for his subordinates. The overall outcome made Jerry look like an information gatherer rather than a decision maker.

The sharp decline in Interpersonal Ability for both groups was observed in both the business game and the competitive group discussion. More deterioration across time was apparent to those actually observing the exercises at the assessment centers than to those making ratings later from reports, but the evidence was clear from both kinds of data. Oral Communication Skills were rated lower at MPS:8, especially for the noncollege men, in the formal activities of the group discussion. In the one-on-one situation of the interview, Oral Communication Skills were not described that differently across the 8-year period for either group. Leadership Skills were definitely less in evidence at MPS:8 for both educational groups in both group exercises, even though forcefulness was rated the same.

It is difficult to accept that the *ability* to be interpersonally effective declined over an 8-year period. A better interpretation is that there was a loss in *motivation* to relate interpersonally. This was most apparent when the men were observed in group situations, especially the noncollege men. Such a motivational change toward less interest in others has been well documented in the discussion of personality and motivation, above.

In the Investment Problem (the business game conducted at MPS:8), Joe's impressive voice helped him to be a dominant force in policy and decision making. He seemed to share the leadership with the designated chairman and sold many of his ideas through him. He was action-oriented to a fault, though, and the other group members had to check him several times for impulsiveness.

In the Organization Problem (the competitive group discussion at MPS:8), where the group was to decide among competing plans for reorganization, Joe's strong voice helped maintain the interest of the group. Yet the content of his oral presentation only scratched the surface of the problem of reorganization, and he seemed unprepared to go beyond the most rudimentary level. In the discussion that followed he played devil's advocate to some extent, refusing to defer automatically to the chosen leader. Although he was influential in the group, his ideas weren't up to his personal impact, which was considerable when he chose to use it. He tended to talk too much at times and was superficial, excitable, and easily distracted.

At MPS:8, Jerry was dogmatically assertive in the Investment Problem business game and used little tact in making his points. He got into a battle early on with another man making assignments and ended up with no effective role for himself. He tried to keep to the rules of the problem, but he lacked new ideas for analyzing stock trends. Most of his comments were either to insist on certain interpretations of the rules or to argue about details, in which he seemed to bog down.

His oral presentation in the Organization Problem took less than 4 minutes of the 10 allotted. He remained seated, made no introductions, made little eye contact with his audience, and appeared uninterested. His talk was given in a humdrum fashion with many long pauses and overreliance on his notes. Although he presented his case with good volume and enunciation, he delivered it in a dry and mechanical fashion. He had few innovative ideas, and his plan seemed as though it would create an inverted organization with more chiefs than Indians.

He performed better in the group discussion that followed; although often quiet, he did ask some good questions that exposed weaknesses in the plans of others. Still, he looked annoyed much of the time and showed little flexibility. In fact, he was so skeptical and negative about a number of ideas raised by others that his impact turned out not to be constructive for the group's goals.

The cognitive data presented a more encouraging picture of the men's development, since both groups improved with time. Figure 6.14 shows the gains in scores for both the college and noncollege groups on the Critical Thinking and Contemporary Affairs Tests. Both groups showed strong gains on the Critical Thinking Test, but the college men outpaced the noncollege men on the Contemporary Affairs Test. The college men's average on this test moved to the midpoint of the norm set by third-level Bell System managers, while the noncollege men advanced only from the 20th to the 26th percentile. Hence the college men appeared to enhance strongly their general knowledge of current events in the world over the 8-year period, while the noncollege men showed more negligible advances.

Another measure of understanding of newsworthy events comes from the rating of political understanding, based on reactions to sociocultural events

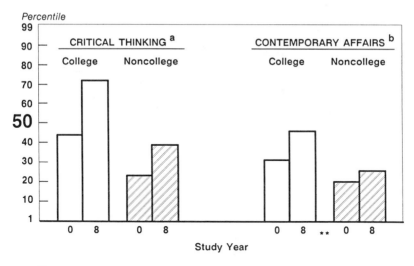

Figure 6.14.   Critical Thinking and Contemporary Affairs Tests, MPS:0 to MPS:8, college and noncollege groups.

discussed in the interviews. Figure 6.15 shows the average ratings of the college and noncollege men in 4-year periods corresponding to presidential terms, beginning with each election year. Both groups received increasingly higher ratings into the first Nixon administration, with the college men better informed than the noncollege. The declines since the first Nixon term may be related to the greater inconsistencies of administration policies during the 1970s and to the general disenchantment with political and other institutions.

The SCAT was repeated at MPS:20 as well as at MPS:8, and the results are shown for the three time periods in Figure 6.16. Changes over time were about the same for the college and noncollege groups, so the combined results are graphed in the figure. A significant rise in Verbal scores was registered over time, most pronounced in the first 8 years but increasing still further in the next 12.

The story was different for the Quantitative scores. There were gains in the first 8 years, but these gains were completely undone by year 20. The Quantitative scale contains mostly simple arithmetic, and it is possible that over time the men either got out of practice on such exercises or became addicted to pocket calculators. At any rate, the decline in Quantitative scores offset the increase in Verbal scores at MPS:20, giving the impression from the total SCAT score that no further gains were made in the last 12 years. Taking this result at face value would unfairly obscure the real gains in vocabulary

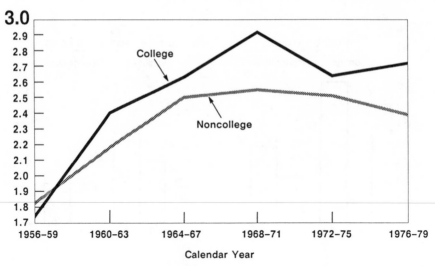

Figure 6.15.   Political understanding over time, MPS college and noncollege groups.

and use of language that other longitudinal studies have demonstrated to accumulate with age.

OVERALL ASSESSMENT EVALUATIONS

The many changes in personality and motivation and in abilities that occurred in the MPS men over time were reflected in the ratings of the various dimensions and the factors that summarized those dimensions. Figure 6.17 shows the average scores on the seven dimension factors for the two educational groups at the three assessment centers. There were marked changes in the men's standing on the factors over the three time periods.

The college men gained most dramatically in the Independence factor, dropping to particularly low levels on the Need for Peer Approval dimension. Their declines in people-oriented needs as well as their increased needs for autonomy played important roles in these changes. The increase in the Work Involvement factor was due not so much to an increase in Primacy of Work as to the development of higher Inner Work Standards over time.

Another gain for the college men was on the Intellectual Ability factor, which was primarily a function of increased General Mental Ability. Range of Interests did not change much for these men on the average. An increase in the Administrative Skills factor was a function of better Organizing and Planning rather than better Decision Making, although it should be remembered that Decision Making was not as well measured at the MPS:20 assessment as it had been in the previous two, when an In-Basket had been included.

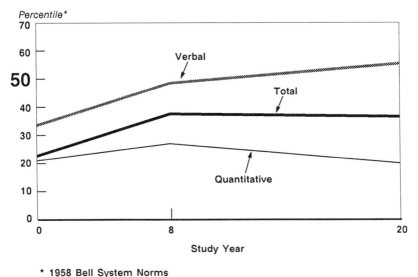

Figure 6.16.   SCAT scores, MPS over time.

The college men dropped on the Stability of Performance factor at MPS:8, due to lower ratings on both Tolerance of Uncertainty and Resistance to Stress. It may be that the men were still struggling to prove their mettle in this stage of their careers as they initially approached the challenges of middle management. By MPS:20, as maturity and experience became advantages, they were again rated much as they had been at MPS:0 on being able to cope with uncertain conditions. They had moved ahead on Resistance to Stress from an average rating of 3.0 to 3.3.

The college men declined sharply on both the Advancement Motivation and Interpersonal Skills factors. They had lost their ambitions by MPS:20, either because they could see that advancement was not forthcoming or because they had set new goals for themselves. Their level of energy was rated the same, but they declined on the Need for Advancement dimension and were rated notably higher in Ability to Delay Gratification and Realism of Expectations, indicating that they had a clearer view of the limits of their potential and were more patient about being passed by for promotions. Their Need for Security rating increased somewhat, also taking the edge off the drive for advancement.

The college men's increasing lack of interest in others and seeming obsessions with their own autonomy reduced their effectiveness in dealing with others, as the Interpersonal Skills factor showed. Although they were rated just as high on forcefulness, and their face-to-face Leadership Skills showed

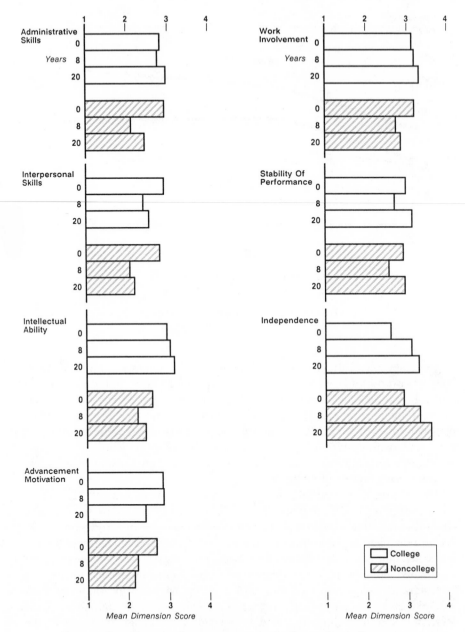

Figure 6.17.   Dimension factors over time, MPS college and noncollege groups.

only a modest decline, they were rated much lower in Behavior Flexibility and Perception of Threshold Social Cues.

The noncollege men showed declines on all the ability and motivation factors between the first two assessments, although they rallied somewhat between MPS:8 and MPS:20. On the Administrative Skills factor, they lost the most on Decision Making, while the decline in the Intellectual Ability factor reflected a narrower Range of Interests rather than mental ability per se, which had shown an increase on the SCAT and the Critical Thinking Test. All of the dimensions related to Interpersonal Skills showed strong declines among the noncollege men; again, it is assumed that they became less motivated to relate to others. A decline in Social Objectivity reflected their increasing authoritarianism.

The noncollege men were rated lower in the Work Involvement factor, primarily because they lost points on the Primacy of Work dimension. As the Occupational life theme showed, their involvement in work was tapering off over time. Their rating on Inner Work Standards also declined, but only about a third as much as their rating on Primacy of Work. The Advancement Motivation factor did not rally between MPS:8 and MPS:20 but continued its decline. All of the dimensions in the factor contributed to the decrease.

Like the college men, the noncollege group showed vulnerability to stress and uncertainty at MPS:8, but they rallied by MPS:20 on both dimensions. They did not, however, show the increase in Resistance to Stress demonstrated by the college men at MPS:20. They continued their quest for independence between MPS:8 and MPS:20 even more concertedly than the college men.

In addition to the seven dimension factors that were produced from factoring the assessment dimensions, there was a higher-order factor that appeared for both the college and noncollege groups called "General Effectiveness" (Bray & Grant, 1966). Most of the assessment dimensions were averaged to form scores on this factor for each man.

The college men stayed at the same overall level on General Effectiveness (2.9 on a 5-point scale) across the three assessments. The losses they suffered in Advancement Motivation and Interpersonal Skills were compensated for by gains in the other factors. Among the noncollege men, however, there was an overall loss. Their average rating on the General Effectiveness factor of 2.8 at MPS:0 dropped to 2.4 at MPS:8 and went back up to only 2.6 by MPS:20.

The lowered level of assessment performance by the noncollege men is worrisome and suggests several possible explanations. One thought was that their performance was tempered by about 40% of the group's being assessed along with the college men at MPS:8, whereas the two groups had been treated separately at MPS:0. But a comparison at MPS:8 of those noncollege men assessed with the college men versus those assessed only with other noncollege men showed negligible differences in their performances.

Another explanation for the phenomenon, as discussed elsewhere (Howard, 1986), rests on the argument that individuals adopt qualities appropriate to the roles and expectations assigned by their educational status. The noncollege men often put forth the conviction that their own chances for promotion were reduced by the fact that the college men were much more likely to be advanced in the company. They may have tried less hard as they took on characteristics appropriate to the lower levels of management that they assumed would be their place.

The changing characteristics of both groups of MPS men have some strong implications for those who supervise them. On the one hand, it should be easier to entrust middle-aged managers with responsibility than young managers. In spite of declining attitudes, the MPS participants still identified strongly with the Bell System (their ratings on Bell System Value Orientation remained at the same level at MPS:20 as at MPS:0) and were very positive toward the challenges of their work, thriving on their own achievements. Their mental abilities had increased, and, at least among the college men, they had developed greater planning and organizing skills and could better tolerate stressful conditions. Perhaps most of all, they wanted to be their own bosses and handle their jobs independently.

On the other hand, the men were no doubt more difficult to control in middle age than they had been as young managers. They were less deferent to superiors and less satisfied with them, and they grumbled more about how things were done in the company. They were more likely to be aggressive when things didn't please them and less likely to feel guilty about it. They had lost much motivation to please others and were more interested in pleasing themselves. They were unlikely to respond to the "carrot" of promotion as a motivator, since they had either given up on more promotions or were not interested in them. These men had not lost their values of hard work and responsibility and would handle a work assignment they were given, but they were determined to handle it their own way.

One issue not heretofore discussed is the extent to which the men became more different from one another versus more alike as they went from youth to middle age. Social criticism of the 1950s, such as in *The Organization Man* and *The Lonely Crowd*, warned of individualism's being lost in corporate norms and conformity. In Bell System parlance, old-timers were thought to develop Bell-shaped heads. If these prognostications were true, it would be expected that the measures taken of the MPS men at the beginning of their careers and again 20 years later would show that they had become more alike in their opinions and characteristics. The data showed that this was far from the case.

The heterogeneity of the MPS men at MPS:0 was compared to that at MPS:20 by examining the ratio of variances on the major variables. In almost no cases did variability decrease significantly over time, according to statistical tests (F ratios). More typically, on about half the scales or more in a given measure, there was *greater* variability with time. For example, more variability was shown at MPS:20 compared to MPS:0 on all 9 life theme summation scores, all 5 GAMIN scores, 2 of the 3 Sarnoff scales, 13 of the 25 dimensions, 4 of the 7 dimension factors, 3 of the 6 personality and motivation factors, and 4 of the 10 scales in the Management Questionnaire. Only the Edwards scales did not show this increase in variability over time, and the forced-choice nature of that instrument could be responsible for the difference. Clearly, with few exceptions, the men became more different from each other with age, more their own men. Their development edged not toward conformity but toward individuation.

One factor related to the differentiation of the men from one another was their relative success in being advanced up the organization. Differential development by management level achieved is the subject of the next chapter.

CHAPTER 7

The Experience of Career Advancement

There were great disparities in the career paths of the MPS men in terms of advancement into higher levels of management. Some rose as high as the sixth level (i.e., vice president) in the 20 years following their first assessment, and others remained at the first level; two were even demoted back into nonmanagement positions. In Chapter 3, we have presented data indicating the extent to which these relative rates of advancement were predictable from the men's performance at the first assessment center. Often those initial differentiating characteristics persisted throughout the next 20 years. Yet the characteristics of those who advanced the furthest were not all determined at the entry point; to some extent, those who would be more successful changed and developed over time in ways different, in degree and/or kind, from those of the men who were ultimately less successful in the business. Such changes are the subject of this chapter.

LIFESTYLES

Because the college men advanced higher in the company on the average than did the noncollege men, some of the traits that distinguished the college graduates from the noncollege men by virtue of the sample selection process also characterized the more successful groups in middle age. For example, the men receiving the most promotions were younger on the average (and their wives were also younger) than those who remained in the lower rungs of management (and their wives). Aside from these artifactual considerations, there were substantive differences in the lifestyles of the men that were related to the degree of career advancement they experienced. A summary of differences between the men in higher and lower management levels at MPS:20 in involvement in the nine life themes coded from the interviews through the years is given in Table 7.1.

164

Table 7.1   Summary of Changes over Time in Current Involvement in Life
Themes by MPS:20 Level

Life theme	Involvement over time
Marital-Familial	Lower levels consistently higher
Parental-Familial	Lower levels consistently higher
Locale-Residential	Lower levels consistently higher
Financial-Acquisitive	—
Ego-Functional	Higher levels consistently higher
Recreational-Social	—
Religious-Humanism	—
Service	Changes varied by level (higher levels higher)
Occupational	Changes varied by level (higher levels higher)

Home and Family

A trio of themes surrounding home and family were consistently related to
advancement over the 20-year period — Marital-Familial, Parental-Familial,
and Locale-Residential. The lower-level men always had a little more invested
in these home and family themes than those who went on to higher levels.
The differences were not wide, and only the first two at the original assessment had shown a significant correlation with MPS:20 level, but the cumulative effect was still there. Satisfaction with these three themes did not differ by
management level, however — only the amount of involvement the men had
in those pursuits.

Andy, a noncollege man who had been quite successful in the company, always
acknowledged that his family was an important aspect of his life, even though he was
almost married to the job. By MPS:8 he was working 9 hours a day as well as 10 hours
a week in overtime. On the projective exercises he made it clear that he enjoyed and
was proud of his family, but that this area of life was not as important to him as one in
which he could achieve. Interestingly, he introduced an achievement theme into family
interactions with the statement, "*The average person* is not going to be my son."

By MPS:20, Andy's children were grown; his two sons had graduated from college
and his daughter was married. His parents were aging, and although they did not live
that far away, he saw them rarely. His mother was having serious vision problems,
which worried him, but he was still an infrequent visitor.

By contrast, Charlie, our noncollege man who remained at the first level of management, was always intensely involved with his family. Charlie's third child and only son
was born a year after the original assessment, to his great delight. His girls were then 4
and 6 years old. He said, "It keeps us home, although we go out occasionally. Home

life is enjoyable. I'll come home on a weekday and play with the kids until supper and help around, and then after supper I play more with the kids and in nice weather I'll take them out for a walk. Then I bathe them and put them to bed." Charlie was very oriented toward home and family, and he saw his parents and in-laws at least once a week during those early years.

Charlie was handy around the house, and he was frequently involved in painting or making repairs. Social life was also centered around the home. He said, "For visiting and social stuff, we have people in more than we go out. We only go out maybe to a telephone [employees'] party. People come in a couple of times a week or so. Mostly they're relations."

By the time of MPS:8 Charlie's life had changed mostly as a result of the fact that his children were growing older; his two girls were 13 and 11 and his boy 7. He said, "My children are just great. I try to spend as much time as possible with them. We go to the cabin together and we're always in contact."

Charlie's father passed away in year 18 of the study at age 80. Charlie's visits with his parents had fallen off to only a couple of times a month, but after his father's death he saw his mother once a week to be sure everything was all right. By MPS:20 the children were all grown, aged 25, 23, and 19, but the two younger ones still lived at home. The older daughter had married, and Charlie was now a grandfather. His second daughter worked in a bank, and his son was seeking employment, hoping that a job in the telephone company would open up so he could follow in his father's footsteps.

There was no evidence of greater or lesser marital stability by managerial level attained. Yet the role of the wives tended to vary according to the management level of their husbands. Of the wives of the fifth- and sixth-level men, 70% were college graduates compared to only 15% of the wives of the men at the first level of management at MPS:20. In spite of this educational difference, the higher the level of the man, the more likely it was that his wife was a housewife; among the first-level men, 50% were housewives, but among the fifth- and sixth-level men, 93% were.

It is difficult to speak of Al's personal life over the years without referring to his business life, for four promotions and five relocations of his home had a significant effect on his lifestyle. Al and his wife had a second son in 1963. This gave them three children under school age and was for several years confining, for Al's wife at least.

The 1970s were extremely busy years for Al, who had heavy responsibilities in the Plant Department. He was concerned that the job took him away from home so much. He thought the children particularly needed parental help and guidance as they confronted teenage crises, and his wife had to bear most of the burden.

As Al plunged into yet another new assignment in yet another city in 1979, his wife took up many community ventures. Al was well aware what an asset she was and had been to him. She was an outgoing person, and she had "moved well," adjusting fairly easily to the many relocations. He described her as "a very intelligent, sensitive, and sensible person. She's artistic as well as social and energetic. I admit I'm glad she's been content to be a homemaker, in spite of the women's liberation movement, since not being tied down to a regular job has given her so much flexibility. She's a fine companion, partner, and household manager."

Similarly, Andy's wife had been very supportive of his career, adjusting well to their many moves and devoting herself to raising the children. After 25 years of this, she seemed to have difficulty in reconnecting with the outside world. He tried to find ways for her to develop interests and to do community work. They took a stained glass workshop together at the high school, but this turned out to be a bad experience for her since it had come much easier to Andy than to her. She seemed to be happier after they joined a historical society, and she was developing into something of an expert in state history.

Those wives who worked tended to be in clerical or professional positions, although few made major contributions to family income. For example, among the first-level men, whose wives were most likely to work, the average wife's salary was about one-third that of her husband's.

Chet's wife had originally been more attracted to working than rearing a family. Even when she had three youngsters at home, she made plans to get a teacher's certificate and to become a teacher in the future. By the second decade of the study, she accomplished her goal and had a full-time job teaching in a local elementary school.

Several interviewers noted that his wife was more ambitious than Chet and a strong influence in his life. They participated in a number of activities together, including bowling in the company league and boating and swimming in the summer. They traveled often with their children, and family relationships seemed to be close. An example of this was the fact that for a number of years the children took care of the lawn without being asked.

By year 13 of the study, Charlie's older daughter had graduated from high school and was taking nursing courses; the other two children had also become much more self-sufficient. Charlie's wife began to work 1 or 2 days a week cleaning houses, which provided income for "extras" and also kept her occupied. When she told Charlie of her interest in returning to work, he agreed on two conditions: that his meals would be ready when he came home, and that "I wouldn't hear no garbage about her being tired." Charlie didn't really believe in the women's movement, but he was willing to go along with his wife's plans as long as they didn't disrupt his life to any perceptible degree.

Projected developments on the Financial-Acquisitive life theme at the original assessment had been a predictor of MPS:20 level, and it was specu-lated that this was part of the most successful men's initial drive and ambi-tion. A greater concern with finances did not continue to characterize them over time, however, although their satisfaction on the Financial-Acquisitive life theme became greater as their promotions brought them additional financial rewards. There were no differences between the more and less advanced men in terms of their involvement in or satisfaction with the Recreational-Social or Religious-Humanism themes of life.

In the early years of the study, Al and his family were relocated to a small city, still in Mountain Bell territory, and they had to sell their first home, buying another much like it. When another child was born, they decided they needed a larger house. Higher expenses made Al somewhat dissatisfied with his salary, but his promotion to the third level in 1966 eased the financial situation.

The last 2 years of the 1960s brought a radical change, for Al was relocated to New York City to put in a stint at AT&T. Al and his wife took advantage of the change of locale to see plays, visit art exhibits, and partake of the other cultural activities that New York provided. In 1970, however, they were back in a small town in the West. Here they rented a house, since Al's boss predicted he would not be there long. This time it was a four-bedroom home on one-third of an acre. The boss's prediction was quite correct, and Al and his family moved to a city that would be their home for most of the 1970s.

As Al's salary rose, he built a five-bedroom Cape Cod home, accumulated considerable funds in the Bell System Savings Plan, and, by 1978, owned a BMW, a Jeep, and a new Mercury. Al was moved to another city in 1979. By this time his two oldest children were away at college, but he still bought a large home as well as a vacation retreat in the mountains.

Charlie's salary had grown by the time of MPS:8 to over $10,000. He commented, "Of course, you can always use more money, but I'm not unhappy with what I earn. We're able to do a few more things and buy a few more extras than we could a few years ago." Charlie had difficulty recalling specific figures about his finances, admitting, "I never pay much attention to it because Ma [Charlie's wife] handles the money in the house."

Self-Development

As Table 7.1 shows, the higher-level men were consistently more involved in the Ego-Functional life theme, meaning that they focused more on self-development of mind and body. Some of the biographical data from questionnaires in year 19 of the study reflected the disparity in self-development interests by level. When the men were asked at year 19 whether they had read any books since their interview 3 years previously, the higher a man's level, the more likely it was that the answer would be "yes." Among the fifth and sixth levels, 100% responded affirmatively, compared to 90% of those at fourth, 80% of those at third, 65% of those at second, and only 40% of those at the first level. There was a similar sliding pattern of results when the men were asked how many newspapers they read regularly, ranging from 2.8 per day for the fifth- and sixth-level men to 1.7 for the first-level men.

During the 1960s, Al maintained an interest in nonfiction that was unrelated to business (*Brave New World Revisited, Russia and the West under Lenin and Stalin*) and an occasional novel (*The Brothers Karamazov*). He managed to keep fairly well informed on national and world affairs by reading newspapers and magazines such as *Newsweek, Life, Changing Times, Nation's Business*, and *Sports Illustrated*.

The 1970s found Al pursuing a home course in economics as well as reading such books as *The Greening of America, Management by Objectives, All the President's Men*, and *Ragtime*. Al was also interested in popular black literature, reading books such as *Soul on Ice* and *The Autobiography of Malcolm X*.

Chet had also had the benefit of the intellectual stimulation of college, but he was not a self-developer. His life centered on his house, where he liked to cook and putter, and on the television set, where he was likely to spend as much as 20 hours a week. Gardening and sailing also occupied him in the summer, but he tended not to be a reader. He did read the local newspaper and subscribed to *U.S. News and World Report*.

The noncollege men were not as likely to enjoy reading as the college men, but those of higher potential still had a bent toward self-development.

Andy tried to keep up with business events through newspapers and magazines and was quite conscientious about reading company practices in his early years in management. He clearly spent time thinking about things and making adjustments to his work style. From time to time he also forced himself to do things of a self-cultivating nature, such as visiting museums, often with his wife.

Charlie was not a book reader, although he would occasionally look at the magazines *Popular Mechanics* or *Life*. He got the local paper, saying in the 1960s, "I just look at the headlines to see what missiles they shot out and then I look at the sports page." By the time of MPS:20, Charlie's reading was still sparse, though he tried to read a little out of the Bible during the week.

All the men who had reached the fifth and sixth levels of management by MPS:20 were college graduates, and two-thirds of them had gone on to graduate courses. Half of the postgraduate group (one-third of the total group) had obtained master's degrees. Among the fourth levels, 16% had received master's degrees and another 29% had postgraduate credits. Business administration was the postgraduate major for 60% of the total who attended and more than three-quarters of the fifth- and sixth-level men who attended. At the other end of the scale, only four (13%) of the first-level men had undergraduate degrees.

During the early years of his career, Al completed his MBA degree at night. He attended school three nights a week, received mostly A's and B's, and graduated with a special commendation on his thesis.

Not content with his MBA as the finale of his education, Al took a correspondence course to improve his written skills. A couple of years with the Toastmasters brought his oral communication skills more in line with where he wanted them.

The higher-level men were more likely to exercise, although they also reported being more likely to drink alcohol. The health of the higher-level men was better; a questionnaire at year 19 found 93% of the fifth- and sixth-level men reporting their health as excellent, compared to 50% of the first-level men. Contrary to some popular notions, there were no significant differences in height or weight among those in the different management levels.

Al's busy schedule did not preclude recreational activities, and in the early years of his career he enjoyed coaching the church softball team and playing tennis. At one point in the 1970s, when Al's work schedule was particularly heavy, he let himself get run down, got the flu, and spent 1 week out of the office and 3 additional weeks trying to get himself back up to par. He began a regular exercise program after this experience, resuming tennis and taking up jogging. In addition to improving his physical condition, he developed a striking tan, and with graying temples softening his moon-shaped face, he began to take on the appearance of a distinguished gentleman.

By MPS:20, Al's life was consumed by working long hours, doing his duty to the community and the church, attending the symphony and art galleries, and going out socially about once a week. He still read voraciously, jogged, and kept his weight down. In his last interview, clad in an olive-gray plaid suit with pale yellow shirt and black, olive-gray, and yellow striped necktie, he looked like a fashion ad for Hart, Schaffner, and Marx. He personified business success.

Charlie had a hernia operation shortly after MPS:8 but recovered with no complications. He had a tendency toward being overweight, especially as his physical activities began to decrease. He noted that during a strike, when he worked on the line gang, he was able to lose 15 pounds and felt in far better physical shape. Unfortunately, he regained the weight.

This tendency toward being overweight was implicated in the discovery of Charlie's high blood pressure at about the year 13 of the study. Charlie tried to diet, but he found that increasing his physical activity was an easier way to maintain control. To the delight of his son, he began to participate in the Little League 3 nights a week, but he grew lax again as his son outgrew the team. Charlie led a virtuous life and did not drink or smoke.

Even as he entered middle age, Charlie's tall, muscular build was rather Paul Bunyanesque. At his last interview he was dressed in a red sports shirt and sweater and corduroy trousers, which complimented his ruddy complexion and thick brown hair. He looked like the line foreman he was; in fact, he seemed as if he might be able to pick up a pole all by himself.

Community and Political Interests

Interest in the Service life theme (community activities) had varied at the original assessment among those who were to advance to different levels by MPS:20, as described in Chapter 3. By year 19 these differences had become considerably more pronounced, as shown in Figure 7.1. Since the effect of level pertained equally to life theme ratings of retrospective developments, current involvement, current satisfaction, and projected developments, an average of these four codes is plotted in the figure. The lowest three levels of managers dropped considerably on the Service life theme over time. The fourth-level men dropped slightly, while the fifth- and sixth-level men actually increased on the theme by year 19. It is likely that the greater visibility of the top executives had brought forth more invitations to serve in community leadership roles.

Biographical questionnaires at year 19 showed greater civic membership with increased management level. Among the fifth and sixth levels, 79% belonged to civic groups, compared to 57% of those at the fourth level, 42% of those at third, 37% of those at second, and 26% of those at first. The higher-level men also indicated greater activity in such groups. The company certainly encouraged managers to participate in community activities, but it is not clear whether such participation aided managerial success or was a consequence of it. At any rate, the notion that those not promoted to high levels would seek outside community groups in which to exercise leadership denied them by the company is not borne out in these data. The typical lower-level man quickly retreated from participating in such activities.

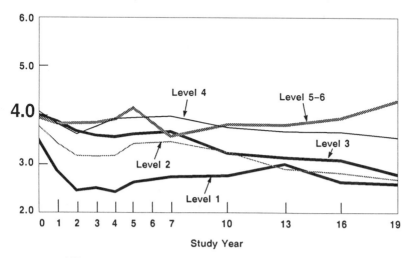

p < .005 group x time effect.

Figure 7.1.   Service life theme over time by MPS:20 level.

Andy seemed to be constantly active in community organizations and a strong community leader. Over the years he mentioned involvements in the Chamber of Commerce, the Rotary, the Red Cross, the PTA, and the Salvation Army advisory board. He became involved in or helped establish numerous civic projects, such as urban renewal, a service devoted to blind people, and a sheltered workshop for unemployed ex-offenders of the law.

In his later years Andy confessed that his membership in the Rotary and Chamber of Commerce were a result of his position in the corporation and didn't necessarily reflect his real interests. However, he found other activities intrinsically enjoyable, especially being on the board of directors for a bank. At one point he considered becoming politically active and running for the town council, but he decided it would take too much time away from his work.

Charlie did not neglect his community, but his involvement was considerably less than Andy's and took a different form. Because of the pleasure he took in his children, he served for many years as an assistant scoutmaster. He transferred his attention to the Little League as his son grew older and Charlie wanted more exercise. Charlie had little interest in community activities that did not involve children.

The fifth- and sixth-level men indicated stronger interest in politics than the other groups did in their year 19 questionnaires. When asked with what political parties or positions they were more inclined to agree (liberals, Democrats, sometimes Democrats and sometimes Republicans, Republicans, or conservatives), there was no consistent pattern by level. More than half of the first-level men claimed a middle-of-the road position, compared to about a third of those at the other levels, suggesting that a lack of conviction on the part of the first-level men may have accompanied their lack of interest. When political conviction was rated independently of sociocultural attitudes expressed in the interviews, the higher-level men were, in fact, rated as having stronger convictions than the lower-level participants.

Ratings of overall political philosophy from the interviews showed the men at all levels to be less conservative in the 1960s and early 1970s than in the late 1970s. On the year 19 questionnaire, less than 15% of the men at either level described themselves as generally agreeing with Democrats or liberals. Across time, the men at fourth through sixth levels were rated similarly in political philosophy (3.7 on a 5-point scale, where 5 was the conservative pole) and less conservative than the men in the first through third levels (about 4.1 for each of these levels). For example, the fourth through sixth levels were generally negative toward Barry Goldwater in the 1964 election, finding him too radically conservative, while the men in the first through third levels were on the positive side of neutral.

The interview ratings showed no differences by level in position on economic issues. The higher-level men were, however, more liberal on social issues, with average ratings in the 1960s of 2.7 (on a 5-point scale with 5 the conservative pole) for the fourth through sixth levels and 3.1 for the first through third levels. Since differences between the men on general political philosophy and stance on social issues were not stepwise by level, it appears that such attitudes were determined more by whether or not the men were college graduates than by their particular managerial level.

Al's political interests remained on the conservative side of the spectrum, although in the early 1960s he had predicted, "In 10 years I'll be a Democrat. We're going toward socialism and this may be the way all the people are marching." Barry Goldwater was too far right for him in 1964, and he voted for Lyndon Johnson. He said, "I read *Conscience of a Conservative* twice because I couldn't believe it the first time. I think the Negro should certainly enjoy all public accommodations; Goldwater shouldn't have voted against civil rights." Al also believed it would be broadening for his children to associate with blacks, and he was against segregation. "They can't get the education they need because of the pull of their environment — the ghetto," he said.

Chet was not very interested in politics, and sometimes did not vote because he had not bothered to register. He considered himself a Conservative and favored Goldwater in 1964. However, in 1965, he said he thought Johnson was doing a good job.

The various changes in involvements in the life themes over time for the men attaining different management levels altered the priorities the men gave to different aspects of their lives when they reached middle age. Ratings of current involvement in each life theme relative to the other themes at year 19 are shown in Figure 7.2, comparing those at the first level with those at the fifth and sixth levels for maximum contrast.

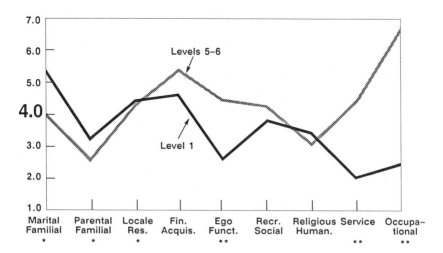

*p < .05, **p < .005 group effects over time across 5 levels.*

Figure 7.2.   Current involvement in life themes at year 19, MPS:20 first and fifth + sixth levels.

At the highest levels, the Occupational life theme was clearly the dominant factor, with Financial-Acquisitive, Ego-Functional, and Service also running high in importance. Their satisfactions with these themes likewise exceeded those of the men who had less involvement. Both the Marital-Familial and the Parental-Familial themes carried less importance to the highest-level men, although they had no less satisfaction in these areas. For the men at the first level, the Marital-Familial, Financial-Acquisitive, and Locale-Residential themes dominated their interests, while the Occupational, Service, and Ego-Functional themes were given short shrift. The high-level men seemed to live for accomplishments, while the low-level men seemed to live for their families.

The great disparity between management levels in the Occupational life theme warrants further exploration, which is undertaken in the following section.

CAREER DEVELOPMENT AND WORK ATTITUDES

Although the progress of the men up the managerial ladder was to a meaningful extent predestined by their own abilities, as shown by their original assessment performances, the men also had different experiences on the job that influenced both their careers and their reactions to them.

Environmental Variables

The men who advanced the furthest tended not to be promoted in a straight line through the same type of function. Movement between departments was common, as was movement to different geographical locations. By MPS:20, the men at the fifth and sixth levels had worked in an average of 4.9 departments. By comparison, the men at the fourth level had been in 3.3, third level 3.0, second level 2.9, and first level 2.2. Relocations for work were also highly linearly related to level attained. Two-thirds of the first-level men had never relocated for their work, compared to 58% of the men at the second level, 31% at the third, 19% at the fourth, and none at the fifth and sixth levels. The average number of job-related moves for the top executives was 5.5, compared to about 3 for those at the third and fourth levels and 1 for those at the first and second levels.

Aside from the stimulation and stress of changing jobs and territories, other factors within the job environment had some influence on the men's careers. A series of potential factors were coded from interviews with the men's bosses or other company representatives, as well as from the men's personal interviews during the first 8 years. These codes were then correlated with MPS:20 level to see whether any had direct relationships with advancement. The men's levels at MPS:8 were partialed out of these correlations to extract the influence of their progress by year 8.

The results, shown in Table 7.2, identified several environmental variables that appeared to enhance advancement. Job stimulation affected the promotion rates of both the college and noncollege men, although the other variables indicated some subtle differences between the two groups. For the college men, being challenged by the total job as well as its supervisory aspects loomed as important for success. The noncollege men seemed to thrive best with freedom, either in unstructured assignments or in not having close supervision. For the combined group, it helped to work in groups with good morale.

When these environmental codes were combined into a multiple-regression equation for predicting MPS:20 level, they were able to account for variance beyond that determined by MPS:8 level alone. It had been important, then, regardless of the men's level in the early years, to provide them with stimulation, challenge, and enough freedom to develop their own resourcefulness.

By year 19, according to questionnaire responses, the higher-level men continued to see their jobs as more challenging and stimulating and less structured by company policies and procedures than did the lower-level men. The higher-level managers also felt they had more control in directing events on the job than did the lower-level men, and this was no doubt true.

When asked to rate their bosses, the higher the man's level, the higher his rating of his supervisor's job experience, quality of decisions, and dedication. Supervisors' leadership skills and organizational ability were, however, not perceived that differently by the men in various levels.

The lower the man's level, the more likely he was to work alone; the executive's job requires dealing with other people. Also, the higher the man's level, the more likely it was that his subordinates participated in decision

Table 7.2   Correlations of Environmental Variables during the First 8 years with Level at MPS:20 (Level at MPS:8 Partialed Out), College and Noncollege Groups

Environmental variable	College ($n = 128$)	Noncollege ($n = 128$)	Total ($n = 256$)
Achievement models of bosses	.06	−.00	−.00
Job stimulation	.24*	.18*	.19**
Given supervisory responsibilities	.25**	−.15	.02
Unstructured assignments	.13	.31**	.15*
Stress and pressure of assignments	.09	.01	.03
Working in groups (vs. alone)	−.08	−.13	−.09
Morale of groups worked with	.13	.14	.16*
Little supervision from bosses	.07	.19*	.06
Overall job challenge	.21*	.10	.14*

* $p < .05.$
** $p < .005.$

making. Although direct span of control did not differ by level (the average manager had four or five direct subordinates), the average fifth- or sixth-level man had over 2,400 people under his authority, while the typical first-level man had only 6.

Even though the noncollege men did not extend over as wide a range of management levels at MPS:20 as did the college graduates, differences in the work environment between the men who were the most successful, such as Andy, and those who did not progress higher in management, such as Charlie, were quite well delineated. It was clear from Andy's bosses over the years that there had been great challenge and stimulation in his various assignments.

Andy had been a toll wire chief at the time of the MPS:0 assessment. He quickly became the right-hand man for the District Manager, who was impressed with Andy's talent and sponsored his promotion to a second-level wire chief position within a year. Andy responded well to the extra responsibility of his second-level position, and within 2 years he was moved into a completely new assignment to enrich his experience.

Andy became the manager of a centralized business order negotiating unit. He was responsible for 71 people, which was larger than comparable units. His subordinate group was experienced, unionized, and by no means timid, but Andy handled the assignment effectively and with ease. He was willing to stick to his guns, yet came across as reasonable and approachable. Mastering the technical aspects of the job earned him the respect of others, and he not only met his objectives but exceeded them. According to his boss, he virtually held up the district and the western area of the state.

Andy's success was rewarded by a promotion to District Traffic Manager in year 6 of the study. He was responsible for managing the flow of calls in the district, both automatic and operator-monitored. He had to deal with multiple changes and troubles with traffic procedures, but he handled these challenges quite well.

Andy was moved into a staff job as Traffic Methods Supervisor in year 8 of the study. This was a busy and complicated job, requiring him to maintain high efficiency measures, make frequent field visits to suggest more effective methods and ideas for force management and training, and to provide detailed forecasts of costs and production. His boss complimented Andy for the exceptional energy, initiative, and creativity he brought to the job, though noting that his intense enthusiasm about a project could lead to its being oversold. Andy was extremely well organized and made excellent decisions.

In year 10 of the study, Andy became a District Manager for Outside Plant. He was in charge of a special services group that provided equipment for things like football games, golf tournaments, airline ticket services, and traffic control systems. Andy soon became a specialist in video, PBX, and teletype installations. His technical knowledge and expertise became universally admired, and he developed a reputation as a tough but compassionate boss.

Five years later, Andy was brought in to handle the central office and regional switching center, including central office maintenance and dial administration. He had

300 people in his group and managed the largest and most demanding of the four districts reporting to his boss. Andy needed little supervision and proved himself an excellent administrator and independent thinker. He was innovative, as when he developed a machine that diagnosed trouble and kept management informed. He worked overtime regularly and brought energy and zeal to his work.

Charlie's assignments had been much more structured than Andy's but this was the kind of situation in which he could thrive and benefit the company most.

Charlie's job during year 1 of the study was that of construction foreman in charge of a four-man truck. The group's responsibilities included placing poles, aerial wire, and underground cable. Charlie was on the job at 7:00 a.m., even though things really didn't get started until 7:30. He got the materials on the truck, went out on the job, and assigned the work to his men. He would often "pull the line or help them pull on blocks, but I ain't paid for no climbing or digging." Charlie held a safety meeting once a week, which he felt was very important. His day ended at 4:30 p.m.

Charlie's boss commented on his warm, friendly personality and the liking his men had for him. His dealings with customers were equally fine, and he worked hard and was thoroughly dependable. Both bosses felt, however, that he might be too easy-going to be a really good supervisor. Also, his paperwork was poor and he had weak communications skills.

Charlie's boss was replaced in year 3 of the study, with somewhat disastrous results. Charlie complained that the new boss was a worrier who was "so afraid things won't get done he has to do everything by himself." Charlie was very unhappy about being checked on every detail. "Like last month, me and another foreman always took the pole inventories; you find out the length of the pole and the class and the type. I counted with this foreman 18 40-foot treated pines, and I reported that to the boss. He called me in and questioned me. Did we really count them and know they were there? I got kind of angry and told him we didn't make it up out of thin air, and if he didn't believe us, he could go down and count them himself, which he did. I'm not smart, but I can count to 18!"

Charlie finished up his 6-year stint as a construction foreman working with three men on one truck and two men on a digger. He reported, "My job is to be sure everything is done correct and as close to Bell System practices as possible. Also, I got to make sure it's done safely and there's no property damage. Like if you step on the flowers while you're doing a job, you'll get a complaint, and you got to have a report on it. I'm also responsible for the truck to make sure it don't get wrecked or nothing like that."

Charlie's loyalty to the company was put to the test during several years when he was rotated out of the Construction Department. After a brief assignment as an investigator in the Security Department, Charlie was moved into a control foreman's position in year 10 of the study. In this staff job without subordinates, Charlie received all work orders pertaining to construction and routed these orders to the field. He corrected time sheets, made out work loads, and figured results. Such clerical and administrative work was definitely not Charlie's cup of tea. Although the boss knew Charlie would never stop trying, even under these circumstances, he realized Charlie was out of place. In less than a year he was transferred to the job of service foreman.

This new job brought its own problems, for Charlie had never installed a telephone in his life. "I don't know where the black wire goes; I don't know where the red wire goes," he lamented. Charlie's immediate boss told the interviewer that he was very weak technically and that he used poor judgment in assigning people to tasks, especially new ones. "But," the boss added, "he's a big-hearted guy who tries very hard, and things get done even though you wonder how. He's poor in oral and written expression, so he takes a pad and writes down painstakingly what I want him to say. He's so personable, however, that his people like him instead of resenting him."

Much to his delight, an opening as construction foreman appeared after only 6 months on the service foreman's job, and Charlie returned to the work he loved. Although an outside observer might decry its routine nature, the job was exciting to Charlie. He wanted to work with his hands and be in a spot where "not too many people are telling you what to do. Also, I like seeing something built. Each telephone pole is like a different individual; it has its own personality. It has different attachments. Every job you do is a challenge one way or the other. You never get two poles the same way."

Charlie's most astute boss recognized that Charlie could exercise independence but still needed to feel wanted, appreciated, and understood. He did his job gladly and looked for no exceptional stimulation. He would happily leave paperwork and advancement to other more bookish characters while he did some of the company's more rugged work.

Work Involvement and Attitudes

There is no question that the higher-level men became more involved in their work and careers as time went on. At the same time, the lower-level men became less interested. This was clearly illustrated by codes of Work Orientation from the projective protocols and by the Occupational life theme from the interviews with the men over the years. Figure 7.3 plots the average of retrospective developments, current involvement, current satisfaction, and projected involvements in the Occupational life theme, all of which showed similar developmental patterns by management level attained.

Although the level groups were very similar in ratings on the Occupational theme at the original assessment, a differentiating trend began to show itself as early as year 1 and continued to grow each year after that. It cannot be discerned from these data whether becoming involved with one's job helped gain promotions or whether getting promoted increased one's involvement in the job. Most likely both effects occurred, but the fact that a difference began to appear as early as year 1, when few promotions had taken place, suggests that greater Work Involvement was not solely an outcome of being advanced to higher levels.

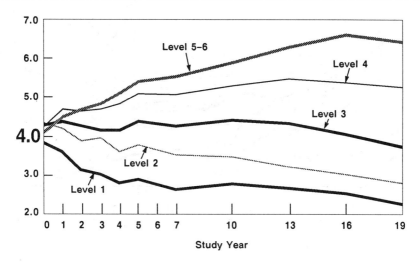

p < .005 group x time effect.

Figure 7.3.   Occupational life theme over time by MPS:20 level.

Along with greater involvement in work, the higher-level men appeared to find greater satisfactions in it. The Expectations Inventory, administered annually in the early years and again at MPS:20, reflected early-year declines for all level groups as reality altered rosy predictions of what life as a manager would be like. But as shown in Figure 7.4, the highest three levels lowered their expectations considerably less during those early years and increased in favorableness during the later years. Those at the first level diminished in their expectations at the fastest rate and ended up below the neutral point on the scale by MPS:20.

A number of scales on the Management Questionnaire showed differences in average score by management level attained. In most cases, as summarized in Table 7.3, the higher-level men were consistently higher on the scales over the years. This was true for General Management Attitude, Pride, Impersonal Communications, Authority, and Salary, all of which had shown significant correlations with MPS:20 level as early as year 1 (discussed in Chapter 3). In addition, Personal Satisfaction was related to MPS:20 level in the majority of later years, even though it was not in year 1. Several of these scales seem to relate naturally to position in the hierarchy; that is, the higher-level men would be expected to have more challenging and varied jobs (reflected in the Personal Satisfaction scale), greater authority, higher salaries, and access to more informative communications. The General Management Attitude and Pride scales relate more to identification with the company and faith in its management.

A questionnaire response at year 19 confirms the differentiation of job

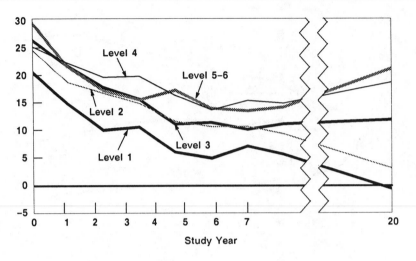

$p < .005$ group x time effect.

Figure 7.4.   Expectations Inventory over time by MPS:20 level.

Table 7.3   Summary of Changes over Time in Management Questionnaire Scales by MPS:20 Level

Scale	Attitudes over time
General Management Attitude	Higher levels consistently higher
Supervision	—
Personal Satisfaction	Higher levels consistently higher
Job Satisfaction	—
Pride	Higher levels consistently higher
Impersonal Communications	Higher levels consistently higher
Personal Communications	—
Identification	Changes varied by level (higher levels higher)
Authority	Higher levels consistently higher
Salary	Higher levels consistently higher

attitudes by level, but also illustrates that job dissatisfaction was hardly rampant, even at the lowest levels. When asked their feelings about their current jobs, 79% of the men at the fifth and sixth levels gave the most favorable response of "very pleased." This compared to 52% at the fourth level, 32% at the third, 31% at the second, and 20% at the first level. None of the men at the fourth through sixth levels checked the response indicating even the mildest degree of dissatisfaction. This was done by 9% at the third level, 13% at the second, and 8% at the first level. The lower-level men were still basically satisfied with their jobs; they just didn't have the overwhelming work enthusiasm expressed by the higher-level men.

One scale of the Management Questionnaire that showed increasing differentiation by management level over time was that of Identification. This scale has items indicating that the person feels accepted as a member of management and feels considered in matters of importance. As shown in Figure 7.5, men at all levels except the fourth declined on this scale over the first 7 years, but the lowest two levels of men declined most sharply. In the period between years 7 and 20, the fifth- and sixth-level men sharply increased in their feelings of identification with management, which would be appropriate to their station, while those at the second and first levels felt even less a part of the management team.

Al's career experiences, as revealed by periodic interviews with him and his bosses, illustrate how the evolving work life of a very successful executive absorbed his interest and inspired his pleasure.

It wasn't until Al completed his rotational training program and settled into supervising 20 women in Revenue Accounting that he began to really understand the operations of the department. During his first year in this job they were converting to computerized operations, which provided good experience in programming but also led to considerable overtime. Al didn't mind this at all, saying, "The Protestant work ethic is still there in the Accounting Department; these new machines really get into your blood!"

Al was pleased to be promoted to second-level management before he had completed 2 years with the company. Again he supervised a group of women, this time in Separations Accounting, which divided revenues, as appropriate, between Mountain

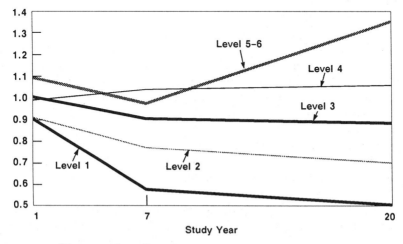

p < .05 group x time effect.

Figure 7.5.   Identification scale over time by MPS:20 level.

Bell and interconnecting independent telephone companies. Al found it challenging to try to forecast monthly expenses accurately and to work at uncovering bugs in the operations. Results were less than acceptable when he arrived, but he aggressively made plans for improvement. The boss found that Al had a quick mind and took charge with a minimum of guidance. Al clearly wanted to do the best job possible, and his group responded with improved performance and high morale.

Al was as enthusiastic about higher management as his boss was about him. He called them "a group of fine executives who get things done without clubbing people over the head." He credited the telephone company with being "one of the reasons the nation has moved ahead as well as it has." Al was clearly developing a strong identification with the business.

After a year as a revenue requirements supervisor, Al was transferred to the position of accounting supervisor. He had about 40 people under him, responsible for the accounting of all long-distance messages originating in the state. He was stimulated by the quick pace and need for quick decisions in the job; his various responses brought performance indices up to high levels.

A significant sign of "making it" appeared in Al's sixth year with Bell. He was promoted to third level, the threshold of middle management. Moved to a different state as district accounting manager in data processing, he had a staff of 175 and was responsible for six computers. Al loved the work and enjoyed knowing more about data processing than others around him, even more than his boss. Computer management was a relatively new field in 1966, and Al was challenged by the need to work things out for himself.

Al's boss found him to be very decisive, even too quick to react at times. Nevertheless, the boss saw him as eventual executive material and attributed any present weaknesses to inexperience. Al, in turn, seemed totally hooked on both the job and the company, describing himself as "a telephone man from head to toe."

After 2 years in this job, Al was rotated into AT&T in New York for a 2-year developmental assignment in Business Information Systems. Upon completion of his AT&T assignment and his return to Mountain Bell, Al was in for some big changes. He was assigned to a department and operation completely new to him, the Plant Department, in a small town. Al realized that this was an opportunity to broaden his knowledge of the total business and that an assignment as district manager in a small town was often a testing assignment for further advancement. He was quite successful and moved on to a larger district.

Al's boss judged him as clearly showing officer potential, even though he once had to slow Al down on attempting too many special projects at the same time. A current weakness, according to the boss, was impatience and occasional offhand negative remarks.

Al was promoted to a division-level position in the Plant Department in year 13 of the study. After 1 year in a staff job, he was moved laterally into a Plant Department line job, which he was to hold for 2 years. He now had 2,500 people working under him with a $26 million operating budget, along with $14 million for maintenance. He was on call at all times, and it was not unusual for a weekend to bring an emergency such as a bomb threat, a serious job injury, or someone accidentally cutting an underground cable. He loved the responsibility and the fact that the organization was depending on him to such a major extent.

In year 16 of the study, Al returned to Accounting in Data and Disbursements. Al's boss told the study interviewer that Al was being groomed for the next level and perhaps beyond. Only 1 year was to elapse before Al was made head of the Accounting Department, a fifth-level assignment.

Al was now moving rapidly. In two more years, at year 19 of the study, he became assistant vice president of customer services and had to relocate to another city. He was now responsible for all staff activities related to the Plant, Test Centers, Outside Plant Engineering, Construction, and Safety Departments. His boss was impressed with his unlimited energy and skill in assigning priorities. He made changes and shored up weak points without damaging morale.

Al thrived on the responsibility and prestige of his position. His now fully developed identification with the company caused him to worry about young people coming into the business. He viewed them as lacking in the dedication of the older generation, an attitude that was difficult for a fully committed man like Al to understand.

Chet, who never went beyond the second level, showed considerably less involvement in his work than Al almost from the start of his career. He also derived less satisfaction from it.

Chet began in the Commercial Department, but he early announced his dislike for sales-oriented work and was transferred to the Revenue Department after 1 year. Here he primarily made estimates for central office additions of equipment. His performance was considered satisfactory but not outstanding in any way.

This job was followed by a tour in the Security Department, where he had to investigate such things as the fraudulent use of credit cards, deliberately incorrect third-number billing, wiretapping, unauthorized equipment, and coin telephone larcenies. He assisted the police in some investigations and looked into thefts of company property and damage to company buildings. Chet was intrigued by the idea of this job at first, but he soon settled into a very relaxed pace.

His next job assignment, in year 4 of the study, was in the Comptroller's Department as a systems analyst. There was little pressure on this job, causing one of the interviewers to describe it as, "a number of coffee breaks tacked together with calls to his stockbroker in between." Chet showed little enthusiasm for his job and simply did his work with little noise or complaint, and no one bothered him.

He was able to develop some expertise as an analyst, however, which led to his promotion to a second-level systems analyst in year 6. In this position he was responsible for updating and maintaining computer programs. Although his performance was considered satisfactory, his boss complained that Chet never went beyond the minimum requirements of the job and would put in extra hours only if paid overtime. He also did not anticipate problems so that he could deal with them before they caused a major interference in the work schedule.

In year 11 of the study, Chet was transferred to the Accounting Department to handle corporate book entries. He supervised two management people and eight clerks in a job that was largely routine except for an occasional conversion to a new system sent by AT&T. He also was responsible for preparing a quarterly report for the Securities Exchange Commission and got involved in taxes and rate cases. His subordinates liked Chet but did not consider him an expert in the work. Although he took some accounting courses on his boss's recommendation, he made little attempt to improve himself on his own.

An additional transfer in year 17 of the study put Chet, still at the second level, in a budget job in the Personnel Department. He kept track of expenses, estimated future costs, maintained the force count, and took care of general equipment requirements. His strengths were in the human interest he took in those around him; he had empathy for others and tried to be helpful. However, he was passive, seemed to lack energy, and was not forceful, even described as a "born follower." He had trouble wrapping up completely the details of an assignment and tended to settle for a superficial job.

In reflecting on his lower than average attitudes toward his job and company in his MPS:20 feedback interview, Chet said, "I thought the company should show me it was worthy of good attitudes." Yet he had never thought of leaving because he enjoyed the security of his job and his work associates. "I haven't done that badly," he reflected. "I just don't want to work more than an 8-hour day."

In spite of the fact that they were less identified with the company's management, outside influences on the Bell System drew more negative reactions from the lower-level men. This was a reflection of both their greater conservatism and often more limited understanding of the issues. For example, the coding of sociocultural attitudes from the interviews pointed out that the higher-level men saw more need for regulation as long as it wasn't overdone, while the lower-level men viewed it primarily with hostility.

In the early 1970s, Al said, "Big business needs the Ralph Nader type to make sure it isn't overstepping its bounds, and the telephone business needs the commission [i.e., the FCC] to keep it in line. Right now controls don't allow us to make enough profit, which we need to get capital to improve the plant, but this doesn't mean we don't need controls.

Chet complained about the FCC, saying, "They're beginning to tell us what to do too much. They tell us what rates we can have and what profits we can have. And that's very bad. Whenever we get a rate increase, someone complains, and they usually end up cutting it down. We went for a rate increase not too long ago, and they prolonged it and finally gave us a quarter of what we were asking for. So we're going to have to go back soon. We are forced to readjust to all of these cutdowns."

With respect to the antitrust case, most of the men were negative, but the higher-level men could see some justifications while the lower-level men tended to see it as an unjustifiable threat.

Al said, "The antitrust suit and what the government is allowing to happen in the way of competition has some very serious connotations for the long haul. A lot of good has come out of the change. It has jarred the telephone industry into greater sensitivity and development, which should have happened before. But as long as competitors are allowed to skim the cream, the cost of telephone service has got to go up. That could lead to government control, and there's no evidence from other countries that that's in the best interest of anyone."

Charlie was less appreciative of any positive benefits of the antitrust suit. He said, "They shouldn't bust up this company because you need a company this big in order to do the job. The company is doing the right thing by fighting it in the courts."

The higher-level men were on the positive side in evaluating affirmative action in the Bell System, but the lower-level men were generally negative.

Al believed the affirmative action program of the company was one of the best. "We have taken in a number of disadvantaged people whom we would not normally hire, based on past practices. By having patience with these people, I think we've been able to help many of them to find themselves and do work they can take pride in doing and become self-sufficient in our society. This is one road that holds real promise. There are costs because your level of efficiency suffers and many people have preconceived assumptions which get trampled on, but I think it's worth the effort. The adjustment may be tough for us, but it's a lot tougher for minorities and for women.

"I'm surprised that we have moved as far and as fast as we have, and I'm delighted. We had no choice but to do this. If anything, we've done it too late. We should have hired blacks and women and more of them earlier."

Charlie was considerably less favorable. He said, "I think our business has bent over backward to help these people with their jobs. They've been given promotions which I question was on their own merit. The company's attitude is to bend over backward to improve their lot to the point that they are discriminating for them instead of against them. The government's demands are unreasonable, and we're getting some unqualified people just to satisfy numbers."

PERSONALITY AND MOTIVATION

Five of the six personality and motivation factors showed some differences by MPS:20 level, as described in Table 7.4. The Self-Esteem factor at the original assessment had shown a small correlation with MPS:20 level, but this group difference did not hold over time. Also predictive of MPS:20 level from the original assessment was the Positiveness factor, which continued to show level differences. Within that factor, which was based on ratings from the projective exercises, greater Optimism and General Adjustment characterized the higher-level men at all three assessments. In addition, the higher-level men were higher in Self-Confidence, and their Self-Confidence increased more than did the other men's between MPS:0 and MPS:8.

Table 7.4   Summary of Changes over Time in Personality and Motivation
Factors by MPS:20 Level

Factor	Changes over time
Self-Esteem	—
Leadership Motivation	Changes varied by level (higher levels higher)
Positiveness	Higher levels consistently higher
Impulsivity	Higher levels consistently higher
Affability	Changes varied by level (lower levels higher)
Ambition	Changes varied by level (higher levels higher)

Ambition

The strongest predictor of MPS:20 level among the personality and motivation
factors measured at the original assessment was the Ambition factor. Contributing to this, of course, was the fact that the noncollege men had lower
levels of Ambition than the college men and did not rise as far in the
organization on the average. Ambition continued to differentiate the men
sharply, with the disparity growing slightly larger over time due to a surge in
Need for Advancement (according to interview ratings) between MPS:0 and
MPS:8 on the part of those who would rise to the fifth and sixth levels. By
MPS:20 all level groups had declined in Ambition, but the higher a man's
level, the more likely he was to cling to the possibility of another promotion.
Al and Andy illustrate the milder tempering of Ambition shown by the higher-
level men.

Al had been promoted to the district level by the time of MPS:8 and certainly
expected to go further. Although he still wouldn't pinpoint wanting to be president (his
wife's dream for him), he certainly had a vice presidency (sixth level) in mind as early
as year 2 in the study, after his first promotion.

By the time Al reached the fifth level, in year 17 of the study, he claimed to be
happy there. He said, "My job is extremely challenging and exciting. I'm able to have
some influence on policy at this level, although within geographical constraints. Sixth
level still looks possible, but that doesn't really drive me as much as the job and the
challenge I face every day."

As a noncollege man, Andy felt that it would probably be more difficult for him to
advance in the company than for a college graduate, but his aspirations did not begin
to dwindle until he had been at the third level for about 5 years. Then he began to
speak of "if" he made fourth level, not "when" he made fourth level.

By MPS:20 Andy had only a mild hope for another promotion before his retirement,
and he showed some conflicting feelings about it. To one TAT picture he wrote a story
portraying the protagonist's ambivalence about accepting a promotion in light of his

wife's antagonism to moving. Furthermore, his status in the company did not seem to give rise to dissatisfaction; he wrote, "*When I compare myself with others*, I feel I have done fairly well in my career."

Chet and Charlie, who remained at the lower tiers of the management pyramid, soon lost any original interest they had had in advancing in the organization.

In spite of being a college graduate, Chet had no high aspirations for his career. When, in the early years, he told his boss he really didn't want to be in middle management, his boss suggested he should consider leaving the company. After Chet's promotion to the second level, he looked more favorably upon middle management, but he still indicated he would not be dissatisfied to stay at the second level. Chet just seemed to take each position as it came; if he ever looked ahead, he didn't appear to look up.

Charlie had thought he might advance beyond first level at the beginning of his management career, perhaps to the jobs half a level above first that were possible then. He heard there were openings for assistant engineers during year 2 of the study and thought a lateral transfer into such a job might put him in a better position to achieve the half promotion. On further study he decided against applying, since, as he put it, "it wasn't a big enough increase in pay and you'd have to buy white shirts and suits."

During years 10 and 11 of the study, when Charlie was experiencing difficulties with the control foreman and service foreman jobs, he stated that he felt extremely fortunate ever to have been made part of management and seemed almost expecting to be demoted to a craft job again. He might even welcome this, since he thought it would require little financial readjustment on his part, and "there's no reason why I shouldn't be a laborer." The most important thing to him was to keep busy with a continued round of useful activity.

Once Charlie had settled back into his more comfortable role as construction foreman, he indicated that he would be very happy to stay where he was. He said, "First level is like chief petty officer in the Navy, not a white-cap or commissioned officer. To go any higher you have to be more educated." By MPS:20, Charlie knew his chances for promotion were nil, but he had no regrets. "After 30 years I ain't going to be promoted. I don't want one anyway. The money at second level, for what they have to put up with, is just peanuts. I'd just be getting into the thing I hate most, which is paperwork."

Leadership Motivation

One personality and motivation factor that varied over time with management level was Leadership Motivation. As shown in Figure 7.6, most of the men increased on this factor except for those at the first level, who decreased slightly. The most dramatic change on the factor was the shift upward by the fifth- and sixth-level men between MPS:0 and MPS:8. The fourth-level men

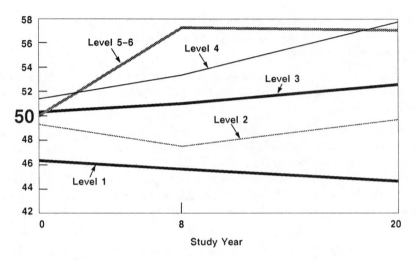

p < .05 group x time effect.

Figure 7.6.   Leadership Motivation factor over time by MPS:20 level.

surged forward somewhat later, between MPS:8 and MPS:20, bringing their
MPS:20 rating up to that of the fifth- and sixth-level men.

Examination of the components of the Leadership Motivation factor, all of
which were from the projective ratings, reveals that the higher-level men were
consistently rated higher on Leadership Role and lower on Subordinate Role
and Dependence. Achievement-Advancement Motivation also clearly distinguished the level groups over time, but the higher-level men increased in these
desires and the lower-level men decreased.

Projective responses at MPS:20 showed that Al was not enthusiastic about being in
the role of a subordinate and clearly preferred being in a leadership position. He also
prided himself on his effectiveness as a manager, responding, "*I have impressed* others
with my managerial abilities," and "*I depend on* others to carry out my plans and
directions."

Andy was also highly attracted to leadership responsiblities and said he usually
ended up the chairman of committees. At MPS:20 he responded to an incomplete
sentence, "*Taking orders* is not as much fun as giving them."

The lower-level men were much more likely to be comfortable in subordinate rather than supervisory positions.

At MPS:8 it seemed clear that Chet's cautiousness and desire to depend on others
was likely to make it difficult for him to fulfill a supervisory role. He was apt to turn to
others for help whenever they were available to him and to depend more on the
judgment of others than on his own thoughts. He replied, "*When working with others* I

tend to follow their ways when they are good." By MPS:20 he was more accepting of a supervisory position but felt most comfortable in a subordinate role. He wrote, "*Taking orders* is easy, for it removes the danger of a bad decison."

Charlie acknowledged the importance of leadership in group efforts in his projective responses at MPS:20, but he was not totally comfortable with supervisory responsibilities, particularly where decisions were involved. He also appeared to be a misfit for administrative work, shuddering at anything to do with writing. He replied, "*My greatest fear* is writing a report."

Related to Achievement/Advancement Motivation on the projectives were scores on the Edwards Personal Preference Schedule scale of Achievement (liking to do a difficult job well), shown in Figure 7.7. All the groups increased on this scale with time, but the men at the fifth and sixth levels (and the third level) made dramatic gains between MPS:0 and MPS:8, much as they had done on the Leadership Motivation factor.

Al rose from the 65th to the 85th percentile on the Edwards Achievement scale between MPS:0 and MPS:20. In his feedback interview he said, "I just love to tackle tough jobs. I must have been young and naive 20 years ago not to appreciate what a challenging job is." On his MPS:20 incomplete sentences he wrote, "*I need* a challenge to be stimulated," "*I am best* when the pressure is on," and "*What I need most* is a challenging environment."

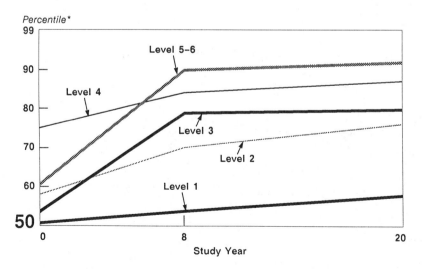

* **1958 Bell System Norms**
p < .05 group x time effect.

Figure 7.7.   Edwards Achievement scale over time by MPS:20 level.

By year 8, Andy had become preoccupied with specific aspects of his responsibilities and was committed to excellence of performance. He responded, "*I am satisfied* with nothing less than the best." His dedication to achieving high standards was sustained into MPS:20. In responding to his high scores on the Edwards Achievement scale in his feedback interview, Andy said, "Doing the best is an ego trip for me."

Although the lower-level men did not reach the extremes of achievement orientation of their higher-level counterparts, interest in doing a good job was present for them as well.

Chet exhibited modest achievement needs at the MPS:8 assessment in the sense that he was conscious of his weaknesses, wanted to improve his skills, and was interested in doing a good job. At MPS:20 he noted that he put a lot of energy into his job when challenged, but he admitted there were other times when he didn't want to bother.

Charlie's approach to work and career was largely compliant with the attitude, "I do my share." He said, "*I believe in* a good day's work for a good day's pay." He believed in persevering to meet the expectations others had for him, but there was little evidence of internalized standards for achievement.

There are some indications that the higher-level men's preferences for leadership roles did not mean they were necessarily heavy-handed in executing them. On the Bass version of the California F Scale, shown in Figure 7.8, it was the lower-level men who gravitated toward greater Authoritarianism as time went by. One might infer that they were more insistent on doing things

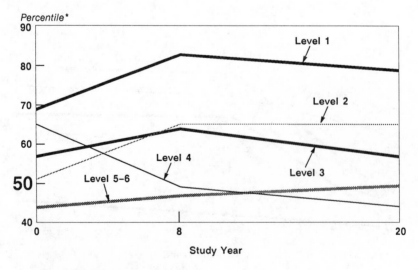

*1956–60 MPS College Norms
$p < .05$ group x time effect.

Figure 7.8.   Authoritarianism over time by MPS:20 level.

by the book with strict enforcement of the rules. The fourth- through sixth-level men ended up the lowest on Authoritarianism by MPS:20. A possible interpretation is that they had developed a broader perspective and had learned to operate with more uncertainty and greater flexibility in higher-level positions. The more liberal stance on social issues on the part of the higher level men also reflected less Authoritarianism.

Affability

The personality and motivation factor with the greatest change by level was Affability, shown in Figure 7.9. Here the first-level group was primarily responsible for the effect. While the other level groups declined markedly in Affability over time, the first-level group actually increased. The externally easy-going manner that this factor score indicated for the first-level men was in sharp contrast to their higher scores on Authoritarianism. Apparently these men were gentle, friendly, and kind on the outside, but they could become rigid if their rules were broken.

The components of the Affability factor (all from the Edwards) leading to this effect were not the ones scored negatively for Affability (Autonomy and Aggression scales), where all groups increased with time. Rather, it was the scales scored positively for Affability-Affiliation (enjoying friends) and Nurturance (liking to be sympathetic and helpful) scales — that showed differing patterns of change by level. On Affiliation, the first-level men ended up at the 50th percentile of the Bell System college-hire norms, while the other level groups declined to average percentile scores in the 30s. On

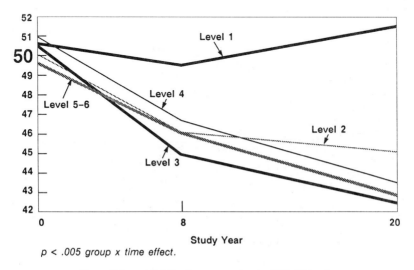

$p < .005$ group x time effect.

Figure 7.9.   Affability factor over time by MPS:20 level.

Nurturance, the results by level were even more startling and are shown in
Figure 7.10. Here the first-level men ended up at the 81st percentile, while the
fifth- and sixth-level men scored on the average at the 34th percentile by
MPS:20. It is clear that by year 20, the lowest-level men were most likely to
offer sympathetic understanding and help to others, while the top executives
were least likely to do so.

Charlie's satisfaction was tied more to interpersonal aspects of the job than to career
success or achievement. The MPS:20 projective exercises indicated that he valued
friendships, believed that friends at work "make working easy," and expected to be
liked and to have harmonious relationships. He believed in being kind, helpful, and
empathic. "*People* are friends," he wrote, and "*My friends* are real and would go all
out to help me out." Yet his outlook was quite narrow, and he adhered closely to rules,
regulations, and established procedures.

Charlie's principles were not always just rigid rules, however, but principles often
wrapped in human kindness and consideration. For 15 years he shoveled the driveway
of a neighbor he had never met personally because it was the neighborly thing to do.
He was the kind of man who took his son hunting and enjoyed sitting with the boy
and talking about the forest, the trees, and the animals. But he never loaded his gun
because he didn't want to kill any of the animals. Charlie had a heart that fully filled
his imposing frame.

The inclination of the top executives to retreat from nurturant behavior has
been described previously (Howard, 1984) as "cool at the top." When com-

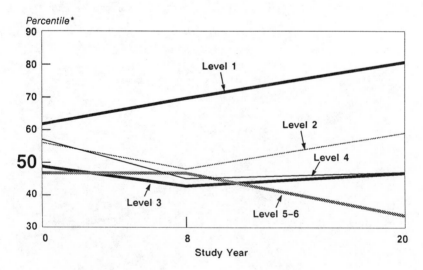

Figure 7.10.   Edwards Nurturance scale over time by MPS:20 level.

bined with their relative lack of Authoritarianism, the highest-level men appeared to strive to be flexible and objective in their leadership style, but without warm, emotional involvement. "They are like steely-eyed Solomons, attempting to size up situations in a rational way without the distractions of emotional entanglements. They achieve grace not through sympathy and compassion but through a determination to be open to all the alternatives and to make decisions that are ultimately objective, practical, and fair" (Howard, 1984, p. 21).

Al's personality tests indicated that with time he had become less involved with people in general and more conscious of his own desires. There was some suspicion on the part of one of the staff psychologists that his previously higher Affiliation and Nurturance scores were predicated on his perception of these as ways of gaining recognition and status, but that this perception had now changed. Al himself admitted in his feedback interview that as he had matured, he had became more self-sufficient and had less need for friends.

At MPS:20 the projective responses painted a picture of Al as matter-of-fact, direct, rational, and realistic. He displayed a low tolerance for troublesome emotional reactions and didn't expect them. He wrote, "*When I disagree with others* I try to keep emotions out of it and talk issues." He avoided serious attachments in his dealings with others and was not interested in becoming involved with other people's problems.

Al reacted to others with an appropriate and friendly manner but carried a certain air of detachment. He wrote, "*A large company* is often impersonal." He was relatively unconcerned with interpersonal relationships, noting, "*Getting others to like you* can be a wasteful effort." He wanted to be independent, self-reliant, and self-directed, saying, "*Taking orders* is agreeable only when they are broad enough to allow latitude."

ABILITIES

Considerations of how managerial abilities changed over time must again rest primarily on data from the first 8 years, since some types of exercises were lacking at MPS:20. Changes in the three ability factors by MPS:20 level are shown in Figure 7.11.

There was a rather startling difference on the Administrative ability factor in type of change by management level. Those at the lowest two levels showed declines in this factor between the first two assessments, while those at the fifth and sixth levels showed a marked increase. This gain was clear whether evaluated by the initial overall rating of the In-Basket or in the later codings of Decision Making and Organizing and Planning from the In-Basket reports. The future executives had developed their administrative capabilities over the first 8 years to a rather extraordinary degree, compared to their cohorts.

Al's work in the MPS:8 In-Basket was truly outstanding. He had an excellent overall grasp of the problem and demonstrated farsighted and precise work. He took a

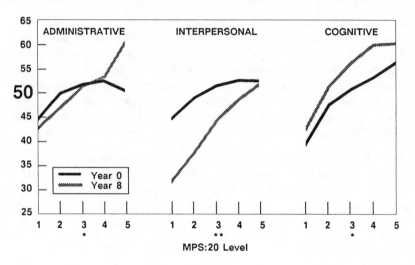

*p < .05, **p < .005 group x time effect.

Figure 7.11.   Ability factors, MPS:0 to MPS:8 by MPS:20 level.

forceful, no-nonsense approach, delegating heavily and demanding action. Although he presented a friendly exterior, he was sometimes given to sardonic comments in his memos, such as "It seems we've had a year to figure out our action." He was forceful and decisive but sometimes could be overly tough with subordinates.

The third- and fourth-level managers showed little change in Administrative Ability between the MPS:0 and MPS:8 assessments, but those at the lowest two levels declined on this factor.

Chet worked extremely slowly on the In-Basket, as was his general nature, and appeared unwilling to speed up. He was indecisive and seemed to want his boss to guide him in nearly every matter and to decide things for him. When Chet did make decisions, he based them on some rather unreasonable assumptions. The In-Basket interviewer felt that Chet could quickly become a stone around his boss's neck.

Charlie's approach to the MPS:8 In-Basket was shallow and perfunctory. He seemed unable to deal with any problem unless he had had exactly the same experience on his own job. He did not comprehend the important details of the various situations presented and tried to get rid of problems by superficial treatment or delegation. On many items he simply wrote at the top, "Forward to Gen. Mgr." or the like. Planning was almost nonexistent, and he was unconcerned with implications for the future. His written work showed a poor choice of words and sentence construction as well as frequent misspellings.

None of the level groups demonstrated better Interpersonal Ability at MPS:8 than they had at the beginning, and most were rated more poorly, as shown in Figure 7.11. Even the fifth and sixth levels showed no improvement in Interpersonal Ability, although they did not decline to any significant degree. Again, one must suspect that motivation was the key to these reduced levels of interpersonal proficiency.

Ratings of assessors who were on the scene observing the group discussions contributed most heavily to the declining scores; later coding of the assessors' written reports showed lesser though still significant declines within each level group. In fact, ratings from the written reports showed gains by those at the fifth and sixth levels on Oral Communication Skills rated from the interview and Forcefulness rated from the business game.

In the group exercises, Al's MPS:8 performance was as strong as it had been at the original assessment. He made a notable contribution to the Investment Problem business game, pushing the group along in an energetic way and having an influence on decisions. When one group member became obstreperous, he handled him firmly but tactfully.

In the Organization Problem, Al was logical and articulate in his oral presentation. His introductory remarks were excellent and got the attention of the group. He spoke in a strong voice, used questions, and emphasized the important points. His oral presentation was diminished only by his running out of time before he was finished. Al was also one of the more effective members of the group discussion, presenting his own ideas clearly and forcefully, questioning others, and pushing for a compromise solution.

The men who ended up at the third level, such as Andy, were not as impressive in the interpersonal exercises at MPS:8 as they had been at MPS:0.

Andy showed a good grasp of the Investment Problem and made his assigned role of banker a very important one. However, his greatest weakness was in the inter-personal area, for he appeared domineering and impatient with the slower group members. His ideas were logical, analytical, and orderly, which helped to get some of them accepted, but he would have had much more success if he had been able or motivated to exhibit better interpersonal skills. He was highly involved in the problem and very task-oriented, but his approach to others was impersonal.

The dramatic losses in Interpersonal Ability shown in Figure 7.11 were suffered most by those at the first and second levels. If motivation was responsible for the general decline, we must conclude that the lower-level men were considerably less motivated at MPS:8 than were the men destined to go on to higher-level positions.

Chet's oral presentation in the Organization Problem was rated poorly. His proposal was too limited, inadequately planned, disorganized, and vague. Moreover, his manner of presenting it was self-conscious and lacked forcefulness. In the group discussion, he was extremely quiet and nonassertive. He demanded little attention and was unwilling to challenge his peers or to present his ideas forcefully.

Charlie had even more difficulty with the MPS:8 group exercises than he had had with those in the original assessment. In the Investment Problem business game he was assigned to fill out sales forms by the leader but bungled this job badly. At one point he made a buy order for stock at another man's suggestion, but when this was passed around for the other participants to initial, one group member noted that he had erroneously subtracted the commission instead of adding it. Charlie seemed embarrassed by this and did not prepare any buy or sell slips for some time. During most of the game he sat with his chin in his hand, nibbling on a pen, and made no comments to the rest of the group.

On Cognitive Ability, in opposition to Interpersonal Ability, all the men gained on the average, with the third- and fourth-level men making the greatest advances. Gains did not vary by level for the SCAT Verbal scale (including through MPS:20) and the Critical Thinking Test, where all groups increased. But the men at the third level and above gained more on the Contemporary Affairs Test between MPS:0 and MPS:8 than did the lower-level men. Continuation of one's self-education in worldly affairs was more a function, then, of whether or not one was a college graduate than of specific management level.

There were specific level effects in political understanding rated from comments on such events in the interviews. As Figure 7.12 shows, all the levels gained in political understanding with time. But the fifth and sixth levels stood out from the others in the late 1960s and 1970s. This is consistent with the differences by level reported earlier in ratings of political conviction and questionnaire responses indicating greater political interest, both of which favored the higher levels.

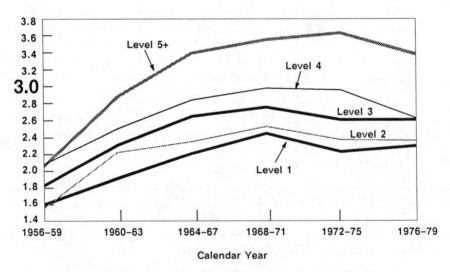

Figure 7.12.   Political understanding over time by MPS:20 level.

OVERALL ASSESSMENT EVALUATIONS

Average ratings by MPS:20 level on the composite General Effectiveness factor at the three assessments are shown in Figure 7.13. The pattern of results shown by this factor illustrates the cliche, "The rich get richer, and the poor get poorer." The fifth- and sixth-level men gained significantly in managerial effectiveness between MPS:0 and MPS:8, and again between MPS:8 and MPS:20. The fourth-level men showed little change, but each succeeding level of men below that showed greater and greater declines. The MPS:20 assessment dimension ratings were somewhat more favorable to the men in general than the MPS:8 ratings had been, but when either later period is compared to the MPS:0 results, the same pattern is evident.

The "rich get richer, poor get poorer" phenomenon applied to five of the seven lower-order dimension factors. One exception was Independence, where all groups gained over time. The other exception was really a modification of the general principle: For Advancement Motivation, all the groups declined, but the higher-level groups declined less than the lower-level groups.

All the dimension factors relating to abilities (Administrative Skills, Interpersonal Skills, and Intellectual Ability), as well as Work Involvement and Stability of Performance, showed the "rich get richer, poor get poorer" phenomenon. Among the Administrative skills, both the Decision Making and Organizing and Planning dimensions showed this pattern. Within the Interpersonal Skills factor, the pattern applied to the Leadership Skills, Oral Communication Skills, and Personal Impact dimensions. Within the Intellec-

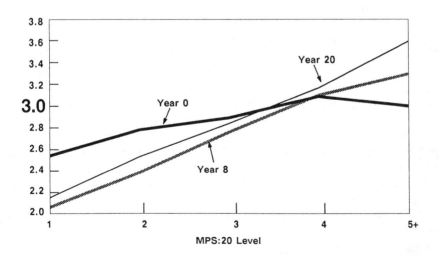

p < .005 group x time effect.

Figure 7.13.   General Effectiveness factor over time by MPS:20 level.

tual Ability factor, the Range of Interests dimension showed an increase for
the highest-level men, while the first-level men showed a considerable decline.

The major contributor to the "rich get richer" pattern in the Work Involvement factor was the Primacy of Work dimension; as the Occupational life
theme showed, the higher-level men became considerably more involved in
their jobs and careers over time, while the lower-level men became less
interested. Inner Work Standards showed a similar pattern, but not to as
great a degree as Primacy of Work.

The two components of the Stability of Performance factor showed slightly
different patterns. Tolerance of Uncertainty showed the typical "rich get
richer, poor get poorer" pattern, with the fifth and sixth levels showing a
marked increase in their ability to cope with ambiguity. The Resistance to
Stress dimension did not show the "poor get poorer" side, since the ratings of
those at the first and second levels changed little with time; however, the
third- and fourth-level men increased in stress tolerance, and the fifth- and
sixth-level men showed marked gains. Thus there was considerable variability
by level at the MPS:20 point on Resistance to Stress.

In Chapter 3 we have reviewed evidence that shows that the educational
level of the men had a strong relationship to later promotions, but that there
were also some key factors contributing to the college men's greater success
over and above their education (e.g., Cognitive Ability, Interpersonal Ability,
and Ambition). Nevertheless, there is still the nagging concern that, all other
things being equal, the noncollege men may not have been advanced as far in
the company as they would have been if they had begun their careers with the
benefit of a baccalaureate.

An additional way of looking at that issue is to compare the average
ratings on the MPS:20 dimensions of men at the same level who had a college
degree with those who did not. For those at the second level, differences were
few, so that it appeared that no injustice had been done. At the third level,
however, the noncollege men showed a definite superiority to the college men.
On the General Effectiveness factor, the 64 college men at third level had an
average rating of 2.8 while the 37 noncollege men had an average rating of
3.0 ($p < .02$).

Searching deeper into the data we find that the noncollege men were rated
higher, at a statistically significant level, on the dimensions of Decision
Making, Leadership Skills, and Tolerance of Uncertainty and were more
independent of the approval of superiors and peers. The college men were
rated higher on General Mental Ability, however, and scored higher on the
SCAT. Interestingly, the noncollege men showed much greater satisfaction
with their work and careers than did the college men, although they were
more likely to have given up on further advancements. The noncollege men at
third level had of course done quite well for their peer group, while the college
men at that level were simply average.

It appears, then, that the most successful noncollege men may have been held back from further advancements because of not having a college degree, even though their demonstrated abilities were superior to those of the college men at the same level. The case studies that have been presented offer some support for that idea, for Andy had much stronger endorsements from his bosses than did Joe, his third-level counterpart who represented the average college participant.

When Andy was the District Manager for Outside Plant, his boss said, "Andy has an exceptional mind; he pays a lot of attention to administrative detail and always backs up his decisions with details and facts. He's also the most motivated individual I've even seen. I have him rated outstanding and promotable. He maintains a good rapport with colleagues, although he lacks some social graces and is not a particularly dynamic, charismatic personality."

On the Central Office job, Andy's boss commented that his subordinates loved him, for he gave them positive direction, involved them in decision making, was helpful in clearing obstacles for them, and was fair. Andy's only weakness was that he didn't have "instant public charm." Nevertheless, the boss had rated him outstanding and was making efforts to get him promoted to the fourth level. There was still time for the company to acknowledge Andy's exceptional contributions.

By the time of MPS:20, the differences between the men relative to their rates of advancement in the company had become quite pronounced. As the men gathered together for the third assessment, it was much easier to pick out the most successful from the least successful in the business than it had been at the original assessment, for their years of maturity and experience had made the men more clearly different from one another in systematic ways.

It was also true that the years generated more distinguishing characteristics among those who would be well adjusted, moderately adjusted, or poorly adjusted by the time they were middle-aged. Such changes are the subject of the next chapter.

CHAPTER 8

Maturation and Personal Adjustment

The men in MPS did not all reach their middle years in a comparable state of psychological adjustment. Data presented in Chapter 4 have indicated to what extent the men's later adjustment was predetermined by the characteristics they brought to the company as young men. Although a number of significant predictions could be made, other things happened along the way in the men's lives and careers to change their course of adjustment. This chapter addresses these kinds of developmental sequences.

For purposes of comparison, the men were divided into groups according to their ratings on the dimension of Adjustment at MPS:20, whether high (modal assessor ratings of 4—5), moderate (2.5—3.5), or low (1—2). There were 82 men rated as high in Adjustment, 105 rated as moderate, and 79 rated as low. Adjustment was defined as the extent to which each man changed or adapted to his life situation in an emotionally healthy way (the dimension is explained more fully in Chapter 4).

The Adjustment ratings were based on MPS:20 data, but there was evidence from questionnaires administered with the interviews in the year prior to MPS:20 that those rated lower were experiencing more stressful self-concerns. The low-rated or poorly adjusted were more prone to worrying; 34% said they worried "sometimes" or "often," compared to 19% of the moderately adjusted and 21% of the high-rated or well-adjusted. They also were more inclined to feel bored: 39% of the poorly adjusted said they were bored "sometimes" or "often," compared to 21% of the moderately adjusted and 22% of the well-adjusted. While two-thirds of the well-adjusted and moderately adjusted said it was "rare" or "very rare" for their feelings to be hurt, only half of the poorly adjusted group felt this secure.

Few of the men in the study had sought psychological counseling or therapy, but the incidence was greater among those less well adjusted. Of those rated as low, 11% had had individual psychotherapy, compared to 2% of those rated as moderate or high. The results were similar for religious counseling, where 12% of the low-rated group sought help, compared to 2% of those rated as moderate or high.

LIFESTYLES

The lifestyles of those in the various Adjustment groups showed different emphases over time, as revealed by coded life themes from the numerous interviews. The most pronounced differences between the Adjustment groups were in the relative amounts of satisfaction they experienced. As summarized in Table 8.1, the better-adjusted men showed more satisfaction on five of the nine life themes than did the more poorly adjusted.

Home and Family

Chapter 4 has indicated that the better-adjusted men already showed greater Marital-Familial satisfaction at the original assessment, and this trend continued throughout the later years. Charlie is a good example of this.

Charlie was exceptionally family-oriented, and he enjoyed many hours of companionship with his children throughout all the stages of their youth. He also spoke very warmly of his wife. He described her as "beautiful, loving, understanding — a wonderful wife and mother. She keeps a neat, clean home and is the best cook in the world. I'd never find another one like her; they don't come any better. Not only is she beautiful to look at, but she is beautiful in the many things she does for me and the family."

The poorly adjusted men indicated on their year 19 questionnaires feelings of both less control over family events and more regrets about what had transpired in that area. When asked how much control they felt they had in directing family events, 15% of the poorly adjusted responded that they had "little" or "very little," compared to 3% of the moderately adjusted and well-adjusted groups. Asked how often they regretted things done in the past concerning the family, 26% of the poorly adjusted answered "sometimes" or

Table 8.1   Summary of Changes over Time in Satisfaction with Life Themes by MPS:20 Adjustment

Scale	Satisfaction over time
Marital-Familial	Well-adjusted consistently higher
Parental-Familial	Well-adjusted slightly higher
Locale-Residential	—
Financial-Acquisitive	—
Ego-Functional	Well-adjusted consistently higher
Recreational-Social	—
Religious-Humanism	Poorly adjusted declined most
Service	—
Occupational	Well-adjusted consistently higher

"often," compared to 15% of the moderately adjusted and 7% of the well-adjusted. Responses were similar to the question asking about regrets over family opportunities missed. The apprehensive and self-critical Bruce provides a good example.

Bruce's children proved somewhat difficult for him, even in the early stages of childhood. His daughter, who was 5 years old when the family moved for his third-level assignment, was defiant, outspoken, and prone to temper tantrums. She would argue with other children and fight long and hard when they didn't do things her way. She refused to go to kindergarten for 3 days after the change of residence.

Her older brother, then aged 7, adjusted to the move but 2 years later became nervous and had frequent stomachaches. This might have been an imitation of his father's style, but the family physician suspected that he might have ulcers. Tranquilizing medication seemed to help, but Bruce wondered "if my wife and I have been pushing him too hard, in Little League as well as in school. He's strong-willed like me, which means we get after each other from time to time." Bruce saw some of his own worst qualities in this older son and felt guilty about it.

This boy may have shared some personality traits with his father, but he did not share Bruce's intellectual propensities. In fact, he was a below-average performer in school; he just wasn't motivated. Bruce said, "Maybe I destroyed his competitive spirit. I'm afraid he sees me as so successful he can't compete with me."

All three children became even more difficult over time, and Bruce spoke of the "grief associated with every school day started, every report card, and every graduation. The headaches of each school year multiplied by three create one big headache! It's become our family tradition to do as badly in school as you possibly can. They know it gets the old man excited, and I haven't let them down. They know I'll explode, and I do. I'm also disappointed in their choices of friends. They're the scum of the world. I think they choose them just to get my attention."

By MPS:20, Bruce was having a major problem with his daughter. He reported, "She went berserk in high school, and now I just can't stand her. I thought she was on drugs, and we argued strenuously until she refused to listen to me and I stopped talking to her. Then she became depressed, and we began to fear suicide. She was hospitalized for a while and had some psychotherapy, which seemed to help. Still she'd sometimes come home in a state that suggested drugs, alcohol, or both. I blame myself for being aloof and too involved in my career and other activities."

The older son had managed to graduate from high school, but still didn't know what kind of work he wanted to do. The younger son, with whom Bruce had tried to spend more time, had above-average grades and a number of friends. Bruce hoped he would go to college, and he desperately tried to keep from pushing him.

Therapeutic experiences were more often undertaken with spouses or families than by individuals alone, and those less well adjusted were more apt to be involved. Among the poorly adjusted, 33% had been in couples therapy and 11% in family therapy. Comparable figures for the moderately adjusted were 10% and 7%; none of the well-adjusted had had these experiences.

Barry's early marriage was complicated by living with his mother-in-law, with whom he had severe conflicts. When she passed away in the third year of the study, he looked forward to a marital life of tranquility. This was not to be, for he discovered that his mother-in-law had to some extent been a buffer between him and his wife. Barry's aggressive nature had been evident at the assessment, but his wife proved not to be one he could easily dominate.

Barry and his wife had four children in quick succession, which brought him a heavy financial burden. Nevertheless, his wife was not very supportive of his career. After her mother died, she nagged him to move to California to be near her sister, but he refused. She seemed very resentful of the time he put in on the job. At one point she even encouraged him to "foul up on the job so they'll quit sending you all over the country to those schools."

Barry and his wife clashed often on how to rear the children. As their offspring greeted adolescence, the oldest son began flirting with delinquency. He was rebellious and conflicted most strongly with his mother. Barry reported, "Her father was a cop and a real authoritarian. She didn't like him very much, but she acts like him. The difficulties with our son are straining our marriage and putting the whole family on edge. We're all in therapy together now. The sessions have been tough so far, and my wife and son don't really want to attend.

"Home is a constant turmoil," Barry confessed. "The children are always fighting with each other. There's endless bickering, petty unkindnesses, and intolerance. I yearn for a little peace and harmony. I think my wife contributes to the home situation, and I wish she could show more affection to the children. She's so different from my mother, who was always full of warmth and kindness."

In the later years, Barry was chagrined to find that his second-oldest daughter eloped with a young man for whom he cared little and who did not seem likely to be able to offer his daughter a good future. Though not quite 18, she was expecting a child. "I don't know how so much can go wrong." he said about his family. "I thought I had done things right. We went to church. My wife didn't work but stayed home with the kids. How could all this happen?"

Failed marriages were few among the group as a whole, but of the 30 men divorced or separated at MPS:20, only 2 were in the well-adjusted group. Whether the wife was a housewife or not bore no relationship to the men's rated Adjustment, though the level of career involvement among the wives in the study was generally too low to have had much of an impact.

An impulsive and immature Don had married in his junior year of college, but by the time of the assessment he was already disenchanted. Over the years his relationship with his wife degenerated to the point where they agreed that they should never had gotten married in the first place. He claimed they simply had too many dissimilarities in interests and personality.

Don related a number of incidents to his interviewers that indicated poor communication on both sides. The outcome of these incidents was usually offended withdrawals with both spouses ending up feeling frustrated and irritated. Don's wife threatened to leave him from time to time, but fears of what a broken family would do to their children held them together. She would avoid him by spending a lot of time alone in bed doing crossword puzzles and watching television; he grumbled that the children were even supposed to make their own school lunches. For his part, Don spent time pursuing his hobbies or having his "nights with the boys." He no longer considered marital fidelity his responsibility, although he did not discuss this with his wife.

Don and his wife were both escapists who avoided each other and their responsibilities. Danny had somewhat the opposite problem, for after he came home exhausted from his daily battles at the telephone company, his wife greeted him with her own restless activities.

At the time of the assessment, Danny's two sons were 7 and 5 and his daughter 2. His wife was a full-time housekeeper and mother, and the children posed no special problems. Nevertheless, she was preoccupied with her own concerns and their home life was often full of tension. She tended toward arty interests; he liked outdoor activities. She liked classical music; he deplored it, preferring to play popular or folk tunes on the accordion. More serious stress was generated by her dislike of his mother, which she seemed unable to control. Danny felt trapped between the two of them.

During some of the early years of the study, Danny worked in a crime-ridden area of New York City, which disturbed his wife. He put in long hours and came home "so beat I had no romantic inclinations." His wife complained about the tension brought home from work, and Danny admitted that he was grouchy, yelled at his kids, and was harsher and stricter than he wanted to be. In spite of this, he did participate to some extent with his sons in the Boy Scouts, getting movies together and joining in hikes and camping trips.

Danny spent most of 1963 commuting to a rotational job with the Bell Laboratories in New Jersey. His wife decided to use the time in seeking a teacher's certificate in order to teach English in high school. Part of her motivation may have come from trying to help the older boy, now 12, with his reading problem. Though in the seventh grade, he read only at third- or fourth-grade level.

Danny decided he didn't want her to teach in the New York City school system for safety reasons. "I don't want her in one of those dens of iniquity, and we don't need the money," he explained. So she spent her time doing a little tutoring instead and also became politically active. She began picketing with anti-Vietnam protesters, and she and Danny often got into arguments about her activities and her beliefs. Several times they appeared on the brink of divorce. The children, fortunately, did not seem to be causing any additional turmoil. They had learned not to bring up these controversial topics at home because, according to Danny, "it's like uncapping a volcano. I try to show them that my rational approach is better than her radical approach."

As the children reached adolescence, they began to be less tractable, and Danny looked forward to the time when they'd support themselves and "get off my back." This happened in the mid-1970s, when the older son left home to join the Navy, the daughter married shortly after graduating from high school, and the younger son graduated from college. Danny's wife became an advocate of environmental issues, which disturbed him a lot less than her anti-war activities. They seemed to communicate more effectively once the children were gone, but still Danny never spoke of his marriage with much enthusiasm.

Parental-familial satisfaction was also related to Adjustment, such that the higher the rated level of Adjustment, the greater the satisfaction. These differences were quite small, however, compared to those on the Marital-Familial life theme.

Self-Development and Recreation

There were also differences among the Adjustment groups in their satisfactions with areas outside work and family life. The well-adjusted rather consistently got more satisfaction from their self-development activities, as illustrated by the Ego-Functional life theme in Table 8.1. They were no more involved in self-development than the others — only more satisfied with their efforts.

There was no difference in satisfaction or involvement with the Recreational-Social life theme for the different Adjustment groups. Yet when the men were asked in the year 19 questionnaires to rank areas of life by importance to them, the more poorly adjusted men gave somewhat higher rankings to hobbies and to rest and relaxation than did the better-adjusted men. An explanation for this difference lies in comparing the absolute level of satisfaction with the different life themes, shown in Figure 8.1. Among the well-adjusted group, the Marital-Familial, Occupational, Financial-Acquisitive, and Religious-Humanism life themes were rated as providing more satisfaction

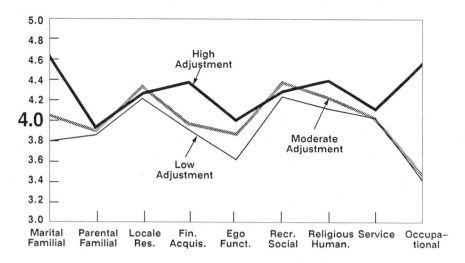

Figure 8.1.   Satisfaction with life themes at year 19 by MPS:20 Adjustment.

than Recreational-Social. Hence, even though satisfaction with the Recreational-Social life theme did not differ systematically among the different Adjustment groups, within the poorly adjusted group it was one of the highest-rated themes, since other themes showed so much more dissatisfaction.

Like other men who advanced to higher levels, Bruce and Barry were involved in self-development activities, but these sometimes took on the quality of an obsession.

Bruce's favorite use of his private time was for reading, which he did avidly. He delved into about 30 books a year from a broad selection of novels, thrillers, and books about art, history, philosophy, religion, and economics. He read relentlessly, sometimes going on "kicks" and attacking a series of books on the same subject, as if no one book was completely satisfying.

After Bruce moved to the toll office, he had one friend he would talk to about religion for hours on end and another with whom he would discuss geology and archeology. Photography also remained an important interest, and he began making home movies. He dabbled in furniture building and refinishing and collected Colonial furniture along with his wife. To aid his self-development, he took a 9-week course in practical politics, sponsored by the Chamber of Commerce and encouraged by the company, but he griped about its low intellectual content.

In the late 1960s, Bruce spoke about a renewed interest in music. He remained faithful to his jazz favorites, like Duke Ellington, but he expanded his classical interests to works by Mendelssohn, Brahms, and Chopin. His book reading slowed somewhat with the advent of third-level responsibilities, but this still meant he read about 20 books a year. He became interested in military strategy during World War II, using one book to gather reference leads to another book and so on, until he was able to make good comparisons of different authors' opinions. Among his choices in fiction were *In Cold Blood, The Group* (which he said nearly made him throw up), and *Candy* (which he saw as a great, humorous book).

Bruce became frustrated that his life was cutting into his reading, which he saw as a threat to his intellectual development. He stopped watching television so he could read more. He said, "I've been trying to talk my wife into having a little ceremony, in which in front of the children we would smash the TV set with hammers and dance around it." The MPS:20 projective exercises indicated that Bruce dealt with his disappointments in life by withdrawing to the solitary activity of reading. This provided perspective to minimize the importance of his personal worries and to dull his pain.

Barry was hardly an intellectual, but he spent 10 years going to school at night, relentlessly pursuing a degree in electrical engineering, which he finally earned. He originally seemed to be attracted to college work in compensation for an underlying sense of inferiority. However, after he began conducting seminars, he seemed to become more genuinely sure of himself.

Barry's recreational pursuits tended to be athletic and offered him some exercise. He played golf, bowled, and worked in his yard. A continuing hobby was raising tropical fish, which offered him treasured moments of peace.

The lower-level men, such as Don and Danny, were less concerned with self-development, but they often used hobbies as an escape from their other concerns.

Don continued to play the piano with a small group, as much, his interviewers suspected, to get away from home as to take pleasure in the activity. He would also go on trips to ski in the winter or to pursue photography in warmer weather. He bought a motorcycle in year 16 of the study; he liked to rev up the motor and zoom away on it, especially after an argument with his wife.

Danny watched television a lot and tended to go to bed early. What time and energy he did have went to working about the house, doing carpentry and the like. He griped that his salary was too small for him to afford the materials to do more. This may have been an excuse, however, given his generally lethargic nature. He slept going to and from work, which meant he was not a newspaper reader. He did occasionally read *Popular Science* and *Popular Mechanics* magazines.

Danny's work around the house was motivated by his dissatisfaction with outside help, since he got upset when others did what he considered slipshod work. He approached his work at home in a perfectionistic manner, sometimes taking months to get something to his satisfaction. He particularly enjoyed woodworking, tracing it to a craving he had had since boyhood. Another hobby, which netted him a few hundred dollars per year, was repairing others' radio and television sets. This was associated with additional reading on microwave or radio topics in books or the *Radio News* magazine.

When his wife began working on her teaching degree in 1963, Danny also got the notion of wanting to go back to school. He preferred an engineering course, but thought he would probably take business courses because they were easier. This turned out to be a pipe dream, since it would have been very difficult at that time to try to combine school with his commute to Bell Laboratories in New Jersey. He said, "If I were starting over, I would stay in school, become a professional engineer, and never come to the telephone company."

Religious and Community Involvement

The Religious-Humanism life theme showed a difference in satisfaction among the Adjustment groups and an even greater difference in involvement that grew with time. Figure 8.2 plots ratings on involvement with the Religious-Humanism life theme for the three Adjustment groups from each participant interview. Although differences were insignificant during the first decade, the second decade found the poorly adjusted men declining rapidly on religious involvement, while the better-adjusted men showed relatively few changes. The interviews from year 13 on took place in the 1970s, when interests in traditional formal religions declined generally in the American culture. The life theme ratings suggest that it was the poorly adjusted men who were most

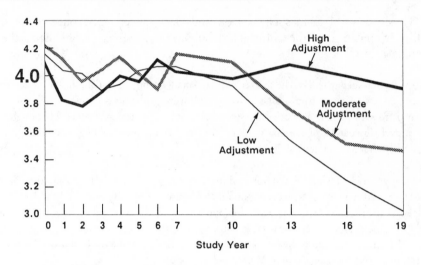

p < .005 group x time effect.

Figure 8.2.   Current involvement in Religious-Humanism life theme over time by MPS:20 Adjustment.

vulnerable to this loss of faith, while the well-adjusted men persisted in their religious beliefs and practices.

Charlie's religious beliefs, of great importance to him, were strict and fundamentalist. He didn't believe in smoking or drinking, and he wouldn't attend movies in the late 1960s and 1970s since he was concerned about pornography and violence. He said, "The movies these days are so filled with murder and sex, I wouldn't want to make a poor example for my children by going to see them when I won't let them go. You can't glorify Christ by doing those things." When his children were young, the whole family attended weekly prayer meetings together. After they grew up, Charlie contented himself with attending regular church services with his wife and reading the Bible.

The year 19 questionnaire responses indicated that among the poorly adjusted, disengagement from religion was reflected both in religious activities and in intellectual involvement with the spiritual aspects of life. By this time only 34% of the poorly adjusted were attending religious services weekly, compared to 46% of the moderately adjusted and 58% of the well-adjusted. When asked for the amount of interest and thinking given to spiritual or religious aspects of life, only 39% of the poorly adjusted indicated they were "moderately interested and concerned" or "very interested and concerned," compared to 50% of the moderately adjusted and 62% of the well-adjusted.

Danny was a regular churchgoer in the early years of the study, attending his Catholic church every Sunday and every day of obligation. He tried to influence his children to do the same. He claimed he was not overzealous about religion but did believe in practicing it.

In the early 1970s, Danny began to complain that the church lacked drive and the sermons were getting stale. He criticized the priests for lacking the ambition to become more involved with people. By the late 1970s, his church attendance had declined considerably. He said, "I've got little motivation or interest in religion now that the children have left home. It's easier to sleep on Sunday."

Bruce, as might be expected, did not relinquish religion without considerable intellectual probing.

Bruce began to go through a religious upheaval in the late 1960s, trying to "figure out what it's all about." He had trouble with concepts like eternal life, saying, "It seems inconceivable that someone would generate so many billions of people and send such a large proportion of them to hell."

With time, Bruce's attitudes toward religion became more and more remote. He felt he had no need for ritual, and he did not believe in a personal God, saying, "I don't take an anthropomorphic view of religion." Still, he considered himself more moral than his friends and believed he carried these standards into business.

Bruce was deeply troubled at MPS:20, but by then there was no solace in religion. He said, "I have beliefs based on my own integrity, but I don't understand any organized viewpoint toward religion. Organized churches tend to be dishonest, and anyway, I don't need an intermediary in dealing with God." Bruce tried some intellectual approaches to understanding his situation through reading psychologically oriented books, such as *Transactional Analysis* and *Winning through Intimidation*, but nothing struck the right chord for him. Religion no longer sustained him, but he found no substitute.

Another life theme that showed a differentiation of the adjustment groups over time was that of Service (i.e., service to the community). Here there were no differences among the groups in satisfaction, but the poorly adjusted declined rapidly in their involvement in the second decade. Figure 8.3 shows the differing involvement in the Service life theme according to Adjustment group. The pattern is similar to that for the Religious-Humanism life theme, with the well-adjusted group changing much less than the others.

At year 19 of the study, 19% of the poorly adjusted described themselves on a questionnaire as "moderately active" or "very active" in civic groups, compared to 26% of the moderately adjusted and 37% of the well-adjusted. Political orientation on the questionnaire was not related to MPS:20 Adjustment, nor were the interview ratings of sociocultural attitudes.

Barry joined in Little League activities to help his sons and became quite active in it — coaching and participating on regional boards. He ceased this activity once the boys outgrew the Little League. Another favorite involvement for Barry during the early years was as a volunteer for the fire department. The Rotary Club was also of some

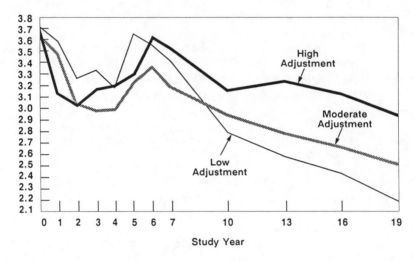

p < .005 group x time effect.

Figure 8.3.   Current involvement in Service life theme over time by MPS:20 Adjustment.

interest. However, once he was asked to relocate from his hometown area, he was unable to generate interest in community activities.

CAREER DEVELOPMENT AND WORK ATTITUDES

Ratings of Adjustment at MPS:20, it will be recalled, showed only a modest relationship to career success as measured by management level attained by year 20. In spite of this relationship, there was no overall difference between the college and noncollege men on rated Adjustment, nor was the dimension related to salary. Some aspects of the job, however, were related to Adjustment.

Career Development

The poorly adjusted men described their jobs on the year 19 questionnaire as more often involving administrative work. In fact, 46% of the poorly adjusted group said that 100% of their time was spent in administrative duties, compared to 32% of the moderately adjusted group and 25% of the well-adjusted group. The poorly adjusted were more likely to work alone, with 32% indicating that this was the case more than half the time. By contrast, 21% of the moderately adjusted group said that more than half their time was spent working alone, and 13% of the well-adjusted described their jobs this way. Apparently the poorly adjusted men were more likely to be in staff than in line jobs. Cause-effect relationships for this phenomenon represent an intriguing question that awaits further analyses.

In spite of working alone more, the poorly adjusted group felt they had less control over events on the job: 16% of the poorly adjusted described such control as "little" or "very little," while only 8% of the well-adjusted group offered this negative a description. This result parallels the poorly adjusted group's feelings of less control in relation to family events and suggests general feelings of inefficacy.

Most men in the study described their jobs as quite challenging, but here, too, results varied by degree of rated Adjustment. Only 6% of the well-adjusted saw their jobs as no more than "mildly challenging," but 15% of the moderately adjusted and 14% of the poorly adjusted described their jobs this way. The well-adjusted also rated their jobs more favorably with respect to contributing to the development of their knowledge and abilities: 28% of them thought their jobs did this to an "outstanding" extent, while only 4% said it did so no more than "slightly." By contrast, 19% of the poorly adjusted and 15% of the moderately adjusted rated their jobs outstanding in this regard, while 15% of both groups found the job made only a slight contribution to their own development.

Bruce managed to make his way through several layers of the management hierarchy into jobs of increasing complexity, but he frequently offered complaints along the way that his job was beneath him.

Bruce had been in a general interdepartmental training program for 2 months prior to his initial assessment, but didn't feel he was doing much worthwhile until he was positioned in the Traffic Department. He worked first as a staff assistant, making studies to become familiar with technical aspects of the business, and then in a local office in Dial Administration, supervising 25 women.

His next assignment, in year 3, was a lateral move into the Accounting Department. Bruce didn't find this appealing, but he took the move at the urging of the division manager as a broadening experience. It did indeed offer a contrast, in which Accounting suffered in Bruce's eyes. He said, "Traffic people have a 'big deal complex'; they feel they're running the company and really doing something. Accounting sounded boring and repetitive to me, and it is. In Revenue Accounting you punch cards and deal with computer equipment. It's hard for me to see it as a service to humanity." He did admit, however, that if a company doesn't bill people, it can't provide service.

In spite of such attitudes, Bruce was complimented by his boss for having a knack for searching out facts and devising new ways to get work done. He noted that he was energetic, conscientious, and worked long hours. He also observed that Bruce was a bit cold and introverted, although people tended to accept him after they got acquainted with him. Still, he worked best on tasks he performed alone.

Bruce's hard work was rewarded with a promotion to second level in the Traffic Department in 1963, year 4 of the study for him. This required a relocation to another town to supervise a toll office. He performed quite satisfactorily during his 2 years on the assignment and was next transferred to Traffic Engineering, still at second level. After 6 weeks at switching school, he was put in charge of step-by-step equipment in the local Dial section, a job he said was boring and dull. He then moved to Trunk Engineering, estimating the proper number of interbuilding trunk lines. He disliked this assignment, saying that it was not a management job and that "85% of the work done by first and second levels could be done by clerks with little or no training. There's absolutely no creativeness or imagination required or allowed; I'm obviously misplaced."

Bruce's final job at second level was a staff assignment in personnel, making salary studies and investigating high attrition among college recruits. After a little over a year in personnel, Bruce returned to Traffic with a promotion to third level. He again had to relocate. He had a force of 350 in his district organization, and he had to do force planning to have just the right number of operators on duty to meet customer demand and maintain the quality of service. He was also involved in forecasting needs for automated equipment and in training operators and their supervisors.

Bruce's next career change involved a new department, Public Relations, and a move to the moderate-sized city of Richmond. He was in charge of internal news and employee information, school relations, and advertising displays. He welcomed the change, since he had been an English major and worked on the college newspaper and yearbook. He felt rewarded when newspapers picked up on any of his material, and he was happy to have a smaller organization — 13 first- and second-level staff members and a clerk. He remained perfectionistic, however, and became irritated if anything went out in less than impeccable shape. He corrected nearly everything his people wrote, which brought complaints to his boss.

The boss noted that Bruce was very well read, which provided a basis for his creative ideas, and he saw Bruce as an informed, innovative, and liberal thinker. He observed, however, that Bruce did not handle subordinates well and could be quite tactless with those of modest ability. This did not deter the boss from backing Bruce's promotion to fourth level in 1975, Bruce's 16th year in the company. He moved to company headquarters in Washington and was put in charge of employee information, closed-circuit television, and speech writing. He supervised three third-level and one second-level staff members, all specialists. The company was intent on keeping employees informed about what was happening in the communications industry and how it affected them, and the Public Relations group was seen to have an important role. The group also provided information about benefit programs and the contributions of the company to the community.

Bruce saw the job as somewhat of an ego trip, since he worked with top management and got perspective and power from knowing what was going on. In fact, the president of the company had complimented Bruce on some of the speeches he had written for him. His boss, however, criticized him for not delegating well and getting bogged down in details. He said, "Bruce works hard and learns quickly, but he strikes people as snooty and not very friendly."

There is evidence that the poorly adjusted offered less to their jobs in the way of performance, as well as receiving less in perceived challenge and opportunity for self-development. According to the men's self-reports on questionnaires, 35% of the well-adjusted men had received outstanding ratings on their performance appraisals, compared to 32% of the moderately adjusted and 21% of the poorly adjusted. Ratings of interviews with the men's bosses showed that at year 20, even with the effect of level statistically removed, the well-adjusted men were rated better in overall job performance and potential as well as on a number of other dimensions.

Don, who never did seem to mature into a responsible adult, had frequent performance problems.

Don's work experience began in the Commercial Department, where he claimed he got off to a bad start. "I had a terrible supervisor who made me read the Bell System practices for 6 months because he was too busy to show me anything else to do. I wasn't given challenging work, interesting assignments, decent instructions, or the opportunity to move from one job to another. I finally asked for a transfer to the Plant Department, where it looked like something was happening."

Don claimed he liked his first job there, doing inventory management. After 2 years in a junior level assignment, he was promoted to the second level, where he was involved in purchasing a variety of equipment. Things seemed to be going well until, as Don put it, "they brought in a dodo of a supervisor who couldn't keep his hands out of my job. He put some negative things on my appraisal that absolutely were not true. I was relieved when they transferred me to the budget job."

His budgeting responsibilities were still in the Plant Department, but Don proved to lack the technical competence to carry out this assignment. He also had trouble with his subordinates — dominating them, not listening to what they had to say, and generally not inspiring their respect. His boss reported several incidences of his using very poor judgment, and it was clear that although Don was bright, he had his mind on other things. He often came to work late, spent too many hours at lunchtime reading about photography in the library, and ran up hundreds of dollars monthly on personal telephone calls. It was not long before Don was again transferred, this time to Internal Auditing.

Don found much to like in auditing. He told his interviewer, "I love the freedom to set my own schedule. I can slack off one day and come back hard the next. Also, I work alone and don't have to deal with subordinates." However, his boss thought that Don was doing much more slacking off than working hard, and he was not completing nearly as much work as expected. He dropped back into his old habit of coming late and leaving early and showed a lack of initiative and energy. He spent inordinate amounts of time talking about non-Bell activities in the office. He was independent in the extreme, showing disinterest in his boss's appraisals, no motivation to improve, and providing lame excuses when his boss grew angry with him for missing deadlines. His boss finally had his job re-evaluated at a lower level and Don was demoted.

Don admitted to some culpability in his demotion. He said, "I know I'm the world's worst organizer. I don't know what to handle first and just shuffle papers around. Then I move too quickly without thinking." He decided to try to get a fresh start and requested a transfer into another area of the company. He was placed in a headquarters staff job rewriting supply practices. Although this was not an exciting job, Don's boss imposed a firm structure and guidelines, which compensated for Don's difficulty in setting priorities. His performance improved, and he moved back into a second-level slot a few years later, preparing management training courses in administrative procedures for plant foremen. Don did enough satisfactory work to get by, but he seemed to be just going through the motions to, as he put it, "play out the string."

The poorly adjusted men were less involved in their careers than those rated higher in Adjustment, evidenced both by ratings of involvement in the Occupational life theme from the personal interviews and by ratings of Work Orientation from the projective reports. Questionnaire data from year 19 confirmed the ratings. When asked to rate the importance of the career compared to other areas of life, only 8% of the well-adjusted rated it less important than some other areas, while 21% of the moderately adjusted and 33% of the poorly adjusted rated it this way.

Perhaps to justify their lesser career involvement, the poorly adjusted were more inclined to think that high involvement with one's career did not pay off in terms of promotions, raises, or other forms of recognition. More than half (58%) of the well-adjusted felt that this payoff was usually true; only 32% of the moderately and poorly adjusted groups agreed. Yet the poorly adjusted also admitted to more regrets about opportunities missed in their careers; 26% said they "sometimes" or "often" had such regrets, compared to 15% of the moderately adjusted and only 7% of the well-adjusted.

Barry had approached his job with interest and zest during the early years, but his involvement waned later in his career.

Barry was an assistant engineer in the Plant Department when he arrived at the assessment center. He was very involved in engineering as a profession, pursuing a degree in electrical engineering at night. Soon after he received his degree he was promoted to a $1\frac{1}{2}$ level engineering specialist, where he figured underground cable loads and routes. He worked hard at the job and frequently took work home. He was sent to a special school to study switching systems in year 3 of the study, and soon developed into an expert on the subject. He was promoted to a second-level position as senior staff engineer in year 5.

Barry was so involved and knowledgeable about his work that he could be relied upon to handle tasks of any complexity involving electronic switching systems. He became recognized as one to go to for advice and soon developed a reputation for being a fine teacher. The company decided to take advantage of this talent and put him in a public contact job in the Marketing Department. As a project engineer, he was involved in the plan for the development and introduction of picturephone service. Since Barry was a showman at heart who loved to be on stage, he thrived on the public relations aspect of this job. His enthusiasm sometimes ran away with him, and his hard-sell approach could be overbearing. But his techniques usually succeeeded, and his success was rewarded with a promotion to the third level in year 11.

Barry was made a seminar leader at AT&T, where he taught and sold Bell System services to businessmen all over the country. He had to present material effectively to a sophisticated audience and field questions that were often loaded and critical. He was not only articulate and engaging but could convey technical information in terms readily comprehensible to the layman. He was seen as bright, ambitious, and hard working, although his boss complained that he often tended to be blunt and tactless in the office. He saw things in black and white terms and complained when situations didn't go his way. He bristled easily, often offending those around him.

Barry was best when he was on stage, presenting the company to business and government leaders. With peers, however, he was at his worst, coming across as pushy, arrogant, and stubborn. A new boss, annoyed with his behavior, got Barry transferred to a position as a marketing supervisor. He was again involved with the Picturephone service, overseeing trial implementation and interpreting regulations. It was a job requiring ingenuity and the ability to work in an unstructured situation, but Barry's boss found him wanting. He did not meet deadlines and made many poor decisions, seeming to have difficulty identifying the major issues in the unstructured environment. His boss felt he had a low energy level and was not very job-oriented. Believing Barry to be a fish out of water, he sought another assignment for him.

Barry was placed in another marketing supervisor job, this time to develop methods for teaching and implementing functional accounting in the operating telephone companies. This staff position had little appeal to Barry, and he was not doing well. He had begun to abuse travel privileges and to take more sick time. Although he could still be counted on to make fine presentations, he was inattentive to the necessary homework and again made poor decisions. His involvement in work was low, and his frictions with others had begun to escalate.

At MPS:20 Barry complained that he never received the proper recognition for his speaking ability and public relations value to the company, and this had left a bitter taste in his mouth. He said he had grown tired of constantly trying to make a good impression on new bosses, and he was now planning to retire early.

Work Attitudes

According to the life theme ratings, even more pronounced than differences in Work Involvement was the tendency of the poorly adjusted to be more dissatisfied with their work lives. As shown in Figure 8.4, the poorly adjusted group showed significantly more dissatisfaction with the Occupational life theme as early as year 1 of the study, while the moderately adjusted began to be rated notably lower than the well-adjusted group (and higher than the poorly adjusted group) by year 3. The figure also shows a new high in work satisfaction on the part of the well-adjusted in year 19, while the moderate- and low-rated groups each reached new lows.

Attitudes in general, toward job, boss, company, or career, were typically more negative among the poorly adjusted. On the year 19 questionnaires, although the majority of men in all groups were pleased with their jobs, 14% of the poorly adjusted group admitted to job dissatisfaction and another 22% said they were only "moderately satisfied." In the well-adjusted category,

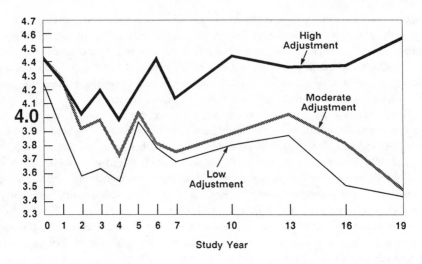

p < .005 group effect.

Figure 8.4.   Current satisfaction with Occupational life theme over time by MPS:20 Adjustment.

only 2% indicated dissatisfaction and 11% gave the "moderately satisfied" response; nearly half said they were "very pleased" with their jobs.

The Expectations Inventory had asked the men in the first few years of the study to speculate about what their lives and careers in the Bell System would be like 5 years from the original assessment; after year 5, they specified current characteristics of their jobs. As noted in Chapter 6, expectations dropped precipitously during the first 4 years but then leveled out when reality set in. This trend varied by level of rated Adjustment, as shown in Figure 8.5.

The well-adjusted dropped no more in positiveness toward their managerial lives after the 4-year point. The lower the level of Adjustment, the more precipitously expectations declined in the early years, and both the moderately and poorly adjusted groups showed additional declines by MPS:20. It is notable that even at year 1 of the study, those who would end up poorly adjusted showed more pessimism and negativism toward the company and their future careers.

The Management Questionnaire offered more evidence of the relationship of attitudes and adjustment. On 8 of the 10 scales — General Management Attitude, Supervision, Personal Satisfaction, Job Satisfaction, Impersonal Communications, Personal Communications, Identification, and Authority — changes over time varied by Adjustment rating, with the poorly adjusted always ending up the least satisfied and the well-adjusted group ending up the most satisfied. Attitudes on the Supervision scale are illustrative of this effect and are shown in Figure 8.6. The well-adjusted group remained quite positive toward their bosses throughout most of the time period, with meaningful

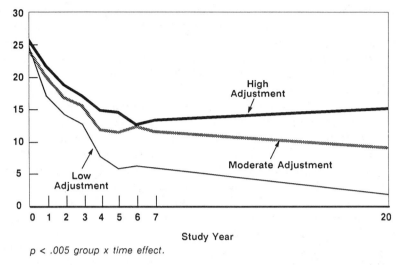

p < .005 group x time effect.

Figure 8.5.   Expectations Inventory scores over time by MPS:20 Adjustment.

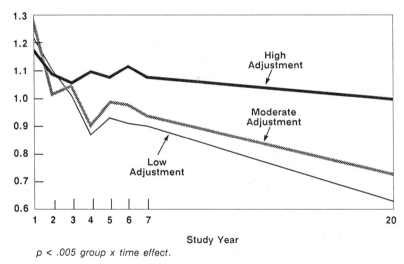

p < .005 group x time effect.

Figure 8.6.   Supervision scale (showing attitudes toward supervisors) over time by MPS:20 Adjustment.

drops in scores only between years 1 and 2 and between years 7 and 20. The moderately and poorly adjusted dropped off steadily in the first 4 years and became much more negative than the well-adjusted group by MPS:20.

A series of questions about the boss in the year 19 questionnaire confirmed these findings on the Supervision scale, with the well-adjusted being significantly more favorable in their replies than the moderately and poorly adjusted (who tended to score similarly). In particular, the well-adjusted rated their bosses as making higher-quality decisions, having more energy, and being more assertive, helpful, and fair. Some 80% of this group thought the boss served as a model for subordinates; only 63% of the moderately adjusted and 53% of the poorly adjusted group felt that way.

As for the two scales on the Management Questionnaire that did not show the change pattern reflected in the Supervision scale, the Pride scale showed a consistent difference among the Adjustment groups (the higher the Adjustment rating, the greater pride in working for the company), with the difference neither growing nor shrinking with time. Only the Salary scale did not show a difference in attitudes among the three Adjustment groups.

Differences among the Adjustment groups by MPS:20 on all the scales of the Management Questionnaire are shown in Figure 8.7. Except for the Salary scale, the differences were large and consistent among the three groups. Regardless of level of adjustment, the men tended to be most positive about Personal Communications, Pride, and Job Satisfaction (having jobs with the Bell System instead of somewhere else); they were least positive about Impersonal Communications. But on every scale, the well-adjusted were most positive and the poorly adjusted least positive, with the moderately adjusted falling somewhere in between.

In the discussion in Chapter 7 about the career development of the well-adjusted men, their loss of naiveté and ability to see the faults of the company were clear after a few years of experience. Yet Al could look at the company's faults as things to be corrected, and he remained a solid company man.

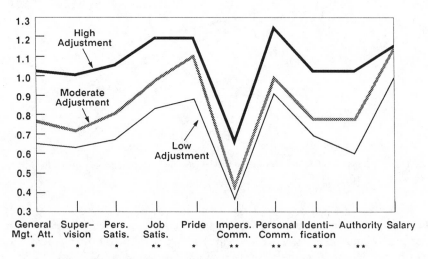

*p < .05, **p < .005 group effects over time.

Figure 8.7.   Management Questionnaire scales at MPS:20 by MPS:20 Adjustment.

Charlie remained ever grateful to the company for a secure job and income, saying of both the company and most of his bosses, "They don't come any better." The poorly adjusted men were considerably more negative than this, and their negativism grew stronger with time. The most notable example of this was Danny, whose chronic complaining eventually began to wear on the interviewers.

After 2 years as an installation foreman on Manhattan's Upper East Side, Danny was transferred to a much poorer, rougher area of New York, going, he stated, from "riches to rags." He complained that the location was "unsanitary and teeming with motley characters. The practice in those neighborhoods is to throw your garbage out the window into the backyard. You have to be on the watch when you walk under windows; children like to hit moving targets. There are certain blocks and addresses that aren't safe for one person, so the installers work in pairs. You have to go into basements and backyards where the people who live in the buildings won't go, and there's often only one way in and out. Dope addicts and drunks congregate in some blocks, and you just hope they don't need any money to buy their heroin or marijuana or whatever."

Following a temporary assignment writing up Bell System practices at the Bell Laboratories, Danny returned to New York in year 6 as an installation foreman on Wall Street. When the stock market was up it was difficult to keep up with customer demand for telephones, and Danny complained bitterly about the pressure of his job. He claimed that top management was only interested in performance indices and the men only in trying to beat the numbers. He said, "The tendency is not to do a picture job; they'll run a wire on a baseboard instead of around the molding so they don't have to spend time getting a ladder."

Danny soon was able to reel off a list of complaints about the company. "First, I'd like to see the production index thrown out the window," he said, "because it's not a true picture of what's happening and it's not saving the company any money. Second, we should have district- and division-level men with hearts, who don't look at people just as machines. Third, craftsmen should get a better break on promotions; they're out of consideration once they're 35. Fourth, upper management falls down in getting the proper rates from the Public Service Commission so they can't meet their earnings goal. Then they try to make us work harder so they can make the earnings anyway. Fifth, top management doesn't know what is going on, because middle management is afraid to tell them. Top management has only one thing on their mind and that's getting ahead personally." Although this was still relatively early in Danny's career, he had already acquired a reputation as one of the sourest participants in the study.

Danny always seemed to feel that, for one reason or another, his burden was the heaviest. He complained that the Installation Department took the brunt of all other departments' failures. "If another department fails to meet its date on an order, they're okay because in the end Installation will catch the blame, since they're the ones in contact with the customer. Everyone knows we're the lowest of the low." He added, "Anything that goes wrong is usually blamed on the foreman. That's not right, because the foreman doesn't have anything to do with the policies that cause the problems. Also, he's afraid to make a decision because it's been reversed too many times. When they're reversed, the men get the feeling the foreman is nothing but a puppet."

Danny didn't always complain about his bosses; he just did so most of the time. In 1965, for example, he described his boss as "ineffective. He certainly can't run a job he doesn't know. He came from the Central Office and is basically an inside man out of his element. He just hopes to keep out of trouble and get transferred somewhere else fast. We might as well not have him." Another was described as "the most useless person to the telephone company I've ever met. He spends most of his time handicapping the horses and listening to the races. When he does make a decision, he vacillates and makes a mess of everything."

Danny had many changes of bosses during his 5 years on Wall Street and may have had some basis for a lack of confidence in those who were just learning the ropes. There was, however, a consistent message from these bosses about Danny. He procrastinated and frequently missed deadlines, then tried to talk himself out of trouble and blame others. Under pressure, he would become antagonistic and negativistic and say that things could not be done, the company was wrong, and so forth. He was quite critical of those above him or on his level, but appeased his subordinates to keep their allegiance. He would keep them happy by not checking on what they were doing or failing to crack down on attendance problems. As a result, jobs would take too long, the index would suffer, and unnecessary overtime would cost the company money.

Some of Danny's bosses had talks with him about his lackluster performance, threatening him and even carrying out threats of low performance ratings and withholding pay increases. But Danny never seemed bad enough to fire, and the boss would move on to leave him with another, who would appreciate his technical ability but bemoan his loose supervisory approach and his negative attitudes.

The company capitalized on Danny's technical skill by assigning him as a repair foreman, including a 2-year stint in Albany as a trainer in installation and repair skills. He admitted he was stimulated by the problem solving needed for repair work, but it didn't reduce his griping. He said, "The telephone company as I knew it died in the 1960s. It's turned shabby from top to bottom. If they'd bring up the salaries, maybe they could hire some decent employees instead of all these refugees. We're not making it, and unless things change radically, the business will go down the tube."

Danny found many reasons to feed his ever more negative attitudes toward the company. One was paperwork. "There are so many of these small nitpicking forms that aren't very complicated, but all together they take a hell of a lot of time and keep you from doing what you should be doing — namely, be out there supervising your men." Here was a good excuse for his usual lax style of supervision.

The EEOC consent decree became a new chant in Danny's litany of gripes. He said, "The EEOC edicts have killed quality, increased management unhappiness, and pushed morale even further down. We did it to ourselves, and the company will continue to deteriorate. All the promotions go to women and minority groups. They make as much as I do with less time on the job. A guy has no incentive. I'm at the end of the road. I'm in semiretirement. My whole attitude toward life has changed. I don't give a damn. I won't do anything to further myself. What's the use?"

PERSONALITY AND MOTIVATION

Five of the six personality and motivation factors were related to Adjustment ratings; only Leadership Motivation showed no systematic difference for the three Adjustment groups. As summarized in Table 8.2, time often had the effect of magnifying group differences that were already there at the original assessment.

Figure 8.8 shows the relative standing of the three Adjustment groups on the personality and motivation factors by MPS:20. Most strongly implicated in Adjustment were Positiveness, Self-Esteem, and Ambition. Affability and Impulsivity showed more modest relationships.

Ambition

The Ambition factor had not been a significant predictor of later Adjustment ratings when measured at the original assessment. This changed with time, however, as shown in Figure 8.9. The MPS men in general decreased in Ambition over time, as described in Chapter 6, but those rated as low in Adjustment suffered the most exaggerated decline. This was true for both the Motivation for Advancement and Forward Striving scales of the Sarnoff and is consistent with declines in the Expectations Inventory.

When asked on year 19 questionnaires how important advancing one more level was, 22% of the well-adjusted responded that it was "very" or "extremely" important, compared to 16% of the moderately adjusted and 10% of the poorly adjusted. Nor were expectations of promotions very high among the poorly adjusted: 74% responded that they thought they would never be promoted, compared to 67% of the moderately adjusted and 44% of the well-adjusted. Apparently the poorly adjusted men gave up readily on career aspirations, while among the well-adjusted, hope sprang more or less eternal.

Related to career aspirations was the Dominance scale of the Edwards, where the poorly adjusted men decreased while the other two Adjustment groups increased. Thus the well-adjusted men grew in preference for leading

Table 8.2   Summary of Changes over Time in Personality and Motivation Factors by MPS:20 Adjustment

Factor	Major changes over time
Self-Esteem	Poorly adjusted declined
Leadership Motivation	—
Positiveness	Well-adjusted increased; poorly adjusted declined
Impulsivity	Well-adjusted consistently lower
Affability	Difference diminished with time (well-adjusted remained higher)
Ambition	Poorly adjusted declined most

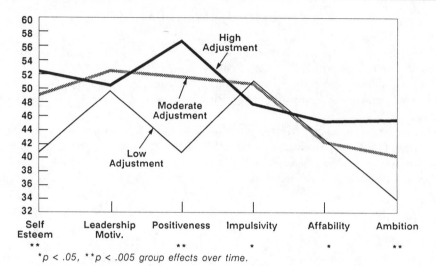

Figure 8.8.   Personality and motivation factors at MPS:20 by MPS:20 Adjustment.

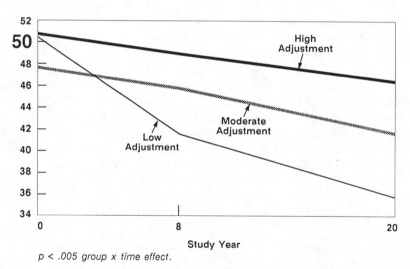

p < .005 group x time effect.

Figure 8.9.   Ambition factor over time by MPS:20 Adjustment.

others while the poorly adjusted men turned away from it, perhaps out of lack of confidence.

As would be expected from the data already presented on the Occupational life theme, the poorly adjusted men declined on Primacy of Work between MPS:0 and MPS:20, as rated from their interviews, while the moderately adjusted group gained and the well-adjusted group gained even more. The moderately adjusted and well-adjusted groups also gained in Inner Work Standards over time, while the poorly adjusted remained at the level of their original assessment. Thus the better-adjusted men became more interested in work over time and raised their own standards of excellence.

In line with these score changes, two indicators of achievement motivation, the Edwards Achievement scale and the projective rating of Achievement/ Advancement Motivation, showed a relationship with Adjustment that grew with time. On the Edwards Achievement scale, all groups increased, but the poorly adjusted group increased only modestly compared to the other two groups. On the projective rating, the poorly adjusted group declined while the well-adjusted group gained in scores over the 20 years. Even on Motivation for Money, from the Sarnoff, the poorly adjusted declined while the well-adjusted increased.

It will be remembered that the college men had originally been more ambitious than the noncollege men, but these ambitions were firmly put aside over the course of the career among the poorly adjusted, such as Bruce and Don.

Bruce had just been promoted to third level at the time of MPS:8 and admitted he would have been disappointed if he hadn't gotten that far. Yet even earlier he had commented that he had no burning ambition for top management. By year 10 he was concerned that "increases in prestige and pay that would go with further promotions may not be worth the higher work demands." He occasionally whiffed the acrid perfume of competitive jealousy, confessing "when weak sisters among my peers are promoted, it still annoys me."

By year 13, Bruce had been at third level for 5 years. He evaluated his chances of reaching his original goal of fourth level at 50%. He said, "If there's anything holding me back, it's my own shortcomings. I'm too critical and argumentative, and sometimes I express myself too openly. This tends, of course, to irritate people. I feel I have the ability for fourth level, but I don't tolerate others' ideas and opinions as much as I should."

Bruce did make the fourth level at year 16 of the study, and never expressed any desire to go further. At MPS:20 he showed some lingering jealousy that some had beaten him out, but he was also quite negative about the competitive process. "A few years ago," he said, "we were all fighting for that piece of red meat they threw in the middle of the floor. Now I don't know why we bothered. I see those officers going 12 to 16 hours a day, projecting the image of the company. They have to maintain community relationships, push fund drives, and cope with endless demands. That stuff is not for me. I don't feel comfortable in the world of the executive suite. The whole thing is fake and phony."

Bruce realized that he probably wasn't on any promotion list. His recent bosses hadn't pushed him with upper management, and he hadn't been sent to management education or on a tour of duty at AT&T. He knew he was rated tops in ability but weak in what he termed "political skills." It irritated him that his intellectual qualities were overlooked because of a lack of "phony" personal qualities, but further promotions had lost their appeal.

At the MPS:20 assessment center, Don's personality exercises reflected his declining career motivation. He wrote to an incomplete sentence, "*I can't* work with the same motivation as I did 20 years ago." Yet he sought no new outlets. "*This place*, the company, sucks you along like a paper game because of its fringes," he replied.

In the feedback interview he blamed the drop in his Dominance score on depression from his demotion. He generally tended to externalize the causes of what happened to him, both at work and home, rather than attribute them to himself. He wrote, "*When I compare myself to others* I feel unlucky."

Positiveness and Self-Esteem

It has been demonstrated in Chapter 4 that the Positiveness factor at the original assessment could predict Adjustment at MPS:20. Over time, the relationship of this factor to Adjustment became even more pronounced. As shown in Figure 8.10, the well-adjusted men rose considerably on this factor over the 20 years, and the moderately adjusted group rose slightly; however, the poorly adjusted group showed a sharp decline between MPS:8 and MPS:20.

The components of this factor (ratings of General Adjustment, Optimism, and Self-Confidence from the projective reports) contributed to these trends to about the same degree. Related to these findings was a drop over time in the General Activity scale of the GAMIN by the poorly adjusted, though the two

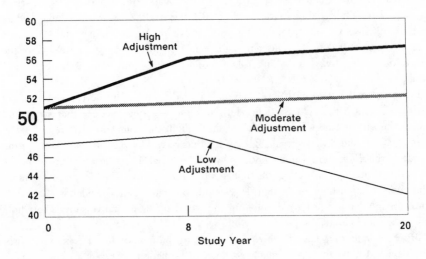

p < .05 group x time effect.

Figure 8.10.   Positiveness factor over time by MPS:20 Adjustment.

better-adjusted groups increased. This suggests that the poorly adjusted may have bogged down in neurotic fatigue. Danny was the most obvious example of such low energy.

In the 1960s, Danny was usually described as looking depressed and lacking energy. He spoke in a rambling fashion and seemed uninspired. His voice was soft, sometimes almost inaudible, but it carried a tone of fatigue and disgust. He gave the impression of someone who was sorely disappointed with life but who felt too tired and hopeless to put up much of a fight.

Danny's appearance did not improve over the years. He usually sat stoop-shouldered and had a flabby and rumpled look. He was restive and unhappy, and he increasingly gave voice to his dissatisfactions.

Both Bruce and Danny tended to see the negative side of life by MPS:20, reflecting their general pessimism.

After year 13 of the study, the interviewers began to find Bruce more difficult to know personally, as if he were fighting the truth and analyzing each interviewer as an enemy. Stomach problems plagued him, suggesting unrelieved tension. He developed an ulcer, for which he took medication and had to watch what he ate.

When he reached his mid-40s at MPS:20, Bruce remained trim, but his hair was thinning and graying. His penetrating eyes were somewhat hidden by tinted glasses, and a moustache expressed his will to differ from the crowd. Bruce was still uptight, perhaps more so than ever, with apprehensions about his work and home life.

Bruce harbored many regrets about missed opportunities in the past and brooded over his experiences. He was a sensitizer who worried about discrepancies between what happened and what he thought should happen. He responded on the incomplete sentences, "*Sometimes* I wish I could live over certain aspects of my life," and "*I failed* in several aspects of raising my children." He even worried about his worrying, with "*I wish* at times I would worry less."

With respect to the future, Bruce focused more on difficulties and uncertainties than on satisfactions and accomplishments. He was very sensitive about possible failures, the press of time, and his inability to accomplish all he thought he should. He expected life to be difficult and thought the best way to cope was to plan ahead, work hard, and keep a firm grip on one's emotions.

Bruce was chronically pricked by the brambles of self-criticism. His searching, analytical mind was his beacon and his undoing. For Bruce, there seemed to be no answers, no resolutions, no satisfactions — only the emptiness of space explored and abandoned.

Danny had a generally cynical and fatalistic view of government, industry, and other people. He thought that the government was corrupt and wasted tax dollars on welfare. Industry was indicted as a polluter of the atmosphere, a contaminator of the food supply, and a destroyer of personal initiative. Other people were variously described as "gullible," "easily misled," or "reckless in their actions," with indications that he found them uncooperative and intrusive. He had regrets about the past, saying *"The things I want* seem to elude me," but he had little hope that the future would be any better.

Danny experienced relatively little contentment in life apart from his few hobbies and recreations. Time had perhaps brought some degree of peace to his conflict-ridden marriage, but his sentiments about his job, his company, his country, and his fellow citizens were swollen with acerbic bile. He lay curled in his bed of insecurity, protecting himself with a blanket of cynical darts aimed at the rest of the universe.

Although the Self-Esteem factor did not show the same kind of increase over time on the part of the well-adjusted, the poorly adjusted group declined on this factor quite steadily between the MPS:0 and MPS:20 assessments. This factor had also been a predictor of MPS:20 Adjustment from the original assessment, but the drop in Self-Esteem by the lowest group meant that the three Adjustment groups were even more dissimilar on this factor at MPS:20 than they had been at MPS:0. Further confirmation comes from the year 19 questionnaire, where 30% of the well-adjusted group described themselves as well above average in Self-Confidence, compared to 19% of the moderately adjusted and 15% of the poorly adjusted.

Four of the five scales in the Self-Esteem factor came from the GAMIN (Ascendance, Masculinity, Lack of Inferiority Feelings, and Emotional Stability), and these all showed a relationship to Adjustment over time. Differences among the Adjustment groups grew larger with time for each scale except Emotional Stability, with the poorly adjusted group declining sharply relative to the other groups. Apparently confidence in themselves deteriorated steadily with time for those who ended up maladjusted in middle age.

The fifth scale of the Self-Esteem factor was the Edwards Succorance scale, measuring need for emotional support from others. There were rather consistent differences among the Adjustment groups on this scale over time, with the poorly adjusted showing more need for attention and sympathy. At MPS:20 the poorly adjusted were at the 73rd percentile on this scale, compared to the 59th and 53rd for the moderately adjusted and well-adjusted groups, respectively.

Barry found it particularly difficult to gain sympathy, for his assertive manner often pushed people away.

Barry lacked a firm sense of purpose apart from meeting family and job responsibilities, and the fact that they were not going well at MPS:20 was very threatening to him. He admitted to his interviewer that others might think him confident because of his aggressive manner, but in truth he always felt he could be doing a better job than he actually did. To the incomplete sentences he wrote, "I *believe* in my abilities less today than I did 20 years ago, and "I *need* some successes to maintain confidence."

In his later years Barry was troubled with high blood pressure. He was on the company cardiovascular exercise program, but it appeared that he would benefit from equal attention to his psychological well-being.

Affability and Impulsivity

The Affability factor from the MPS:0 assessment data was a strong predictor of Adjustment ratings at MPS:20 with each component (Edwards high Nurturance, high Affiliation, low Autonomy, and low Aggression) predicting later Adjustment. These results were somewhat mitigated over time. All the Adjustment groups dropped in Affability, but the poorly adjusted group dropped less than the others, partially evening up the difference in scores originally shown. One scale retaining its ability to differentiate among the Adjustment groups was Aggression; all groups increased on the Aggression scale with time, but the lower the level of Adjustment, the greater the Aggression in each time period.

Although Barry's excellent speaking voice often made him sound like an actor, he communicated a great deal of rage and anger underneath. In his MPS:20 interview, he said, "I've been known as a rabble rouser throughout my life. I've been told I don't know when to lay off."

Part of Barry's problem was a self-centered lack of concern for others and a suspicion of their motives. He said, "I really don't care what other people think and this is becoming more and more true about me. I am becoming increasingly disillusioned with the capabilities of other people." His projective exercises revealed not just a lack of confidence but a lack of trust. "*People* in general cannot be depended upon," he wrote. "*The only trouble* with the world is people."

Authority figures elicited hostile, defensive reactions in Barry, and he could be very outspoken when interacting with them. He envied their power and resented their potential interference and control over him. He wrote, "*I believe* in pushing oneself as most bosses push only their friends." He added, resentfully, "*People in authority* generally do not care what their subordinates think."

The Impulsivity factor at MPS:0 also showed a relationship to later Adjustment, with the poorly adjusted group scoring higher on the Edwards Heterosexuality scale and lower on Endurance. This difference among the groups remained over time. On the Heterosexuality scale, the poorly adjusted men scored at the 72nd percentile of the Bell System norms at MPS:20, compared to the 64th percentile for the moderately adjusted group and the 51st percentile for the well-adjusted group. Again, our interpretation is that the poorly adjusted men were more dependent on women, just as the Succorance scale showed them to be more emotionally dependent on others in general.

At MPS:20, the well-adjusted group scored at the 53rd percentile on the Endurance scale, while the moderately adjusted were at the 41st percentile and the poorly adjusted at the 35th. The tendency for the well-adjusted group to persist in a multitude of characteristics in spite of changes by the other groups has been evident throughout this chapter. They maintained their interests in religion and service to the community more than the others in spite of environmental influences to do otherwise, and they held more steadfastly to their expectations about their careers, satisfaction with their work, and positive attitudes toward their supervisors. Even the cynical 1970s could not jeopardize their persistently positive and optimistic outlooks.

By contrast, the poorly adjusted men, such as Don, had difficulty sticking to one task or interest.

There was a hurried quality conveyed in Don's projective responses, and he tended to shift to new matters without completing his prior thoughts. His approach to life stressed activity and pleasure seeking, and he wanted to maintain a variety of interests. Autonomy remained one of his highest values, and he saw others as intrusive. "*Other people* expect me to fit their desires," he wrote plaintively.

ABILITIES

The three ability factors, Administrative, Interpersonal, and Cognitive, showed no relationship to Adjustment when the MPS:0 and MPS:8 assessments were compared. Nevertheless, two of the components making up the Cognitive Ability factor, the SCAT Verbal scale and the Contemporary Affairs Test, did show a small but statistically significant relationship to Adjustment. It will be recalled that these two tests (as well as the Critical Thinking Test) taken at the original assessment had a small negative correlation with Adjustment 20 years later, with the best-adjusted registering the lowest early scores. This trend persisted over time to about the same degree, as illustrated by the SCAT Verbal results in Figure 8.11.

The findings are somewhat discouraging for those who idealize both

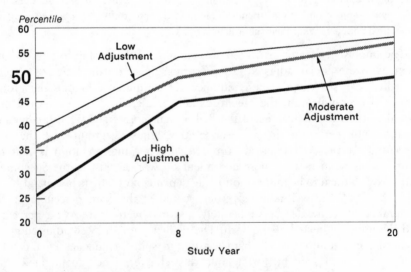

p < .05 group effect.

Figure 8.11.   SCAT Verbal scores over time by MPS:20 Adjustment.

intellectual superiority and personal adjustment, and their interpretation is a matter of speculation. The poorly adjusted men may have been using their somewhat greater verbal abilities to ruminate and worry aloud. Lack of awareness of worldly affairs or lack of understanding of ideas may also relieve people from having to be stressed by them.

OVERALL ASSESSMENT EVALUATIONS

The seven dimension factors, measured over the entire 20-year period, showed a number of relationships to Adjustment, as summarized in Table 8.3. For all except Independence and Intellectual Ability, it was the changes over time that created the differences among the Adjustment groups. In every case, the poorly adjusted men decreased in the characteristics measured.

The changes took three forms. For the General Effectiveness and Administrative Skills factors, the well-adjusted and moderately adjusted did not change dramatically over time, but the poorly adjusted declined. On two other factors, Interpersonal Skills and Advancement Motivation, all three Adjustment groups declined, but the poorly adjusted group declined the most. This is illustrated for the Interpersonal Skills factor in Figure 8.12. Although both the well-adjusted and moderately adjusted groups revived at MPS:20 after their precipitous drop on Interpersonal Skills between the first two assessments, the poorly adjusted group continued to decline even further. This was true for the dimensions of Behavior Flexibility, Leadership Skills, and Oral Communication Skills.

Yet another pattern of change was evidenced on the Work Involvement and Stability of Performance factors. In both cases, the well-adjusted and moderately adjusted men improved in their ratings while the poorly adjusted group declined. This is illustrated in Figure 8.13 for the Stability of Performance factor. This effect was clear for the Tolerance of Uncertainty dimension but was much stronger for the Resistance to Stress dimension. Both the well-

Table 8.3   Summary of Dimension Factors over Time by MPS:20 Adjustment

Dimension factor	Changes over time
General Effectiveness	Poorly adjusted declined
Administrative Skills	Poorly adjusted declined
Interpersonal Skills	Poorly adjusted declined most
Intellectual Ability	—
Advancement Motivation	Poorly adjusted declined most
Work Involvement	Well-adjusted increased; poorly adjusted declined
Stability of Performance	Well-adjusted increased; poorly adjusted declined
Independence	Well-adjusted remained slightly lower

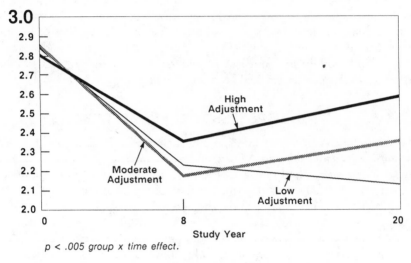

Study Year

p < .005 group x time effect.

Figure 8.12.   Interpersonal Skills dimension factor over time by MPS:20 Adjustment.

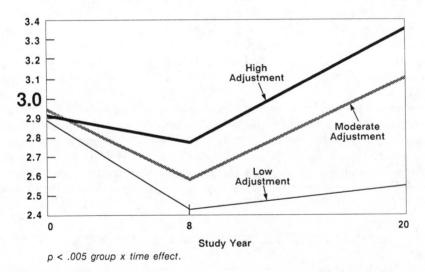

Study Year

p < .005 group x time effect.

Figure 8.13.   Stability of Performance dimension factor over time by MPS:20 Adjustment.

adjusted and moderately adjusted groups improved in their ability to cope with stressful situations over time, while the poorly adjusted group responded even more negatively in middle age than they had when they were young.

Another dimension that followed the pattern of the Stability of Performance factor was Bell System Value Orientation. With time, the well-adjusted men become even more identified with the organization (companies like Bell "don't

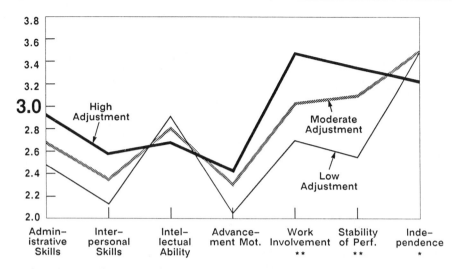

*p < .05, **p < .005 group effects over time.

Figure 8.14.   Dimension factors at MPS:20 by MPS:20 Adjustment.

come any better," according to Charlie) while the poorly adjusted men dropped to a below-average rating (as Danny's many complaints illustrate).

Because of the many changes with time, ratings on the dimensions at MPS:20 showed a number of differences by level of Adjustment. As illustrated in Figure 8.14, the Work Involvement and Stability of Performance factors most strongly differentiated the Adjustment groups, with the poorly adjusted relatively uninterested in their work and having difficulty tolerating stress and uncertainty. Lesser differences were shown on the Independence and Intellectual Ability factors, although it was on these two factors that the well-adjusted group actually scored lower.

Even though the correlation between Adjustment and career advancement was small at MPS:20, it is clear from the dimension ratings that, in the final analysis, poor Adjustment had hurt performance. As mentioned earlier, ratings of the men's performance by those interviewing their bosses showed better overall performance and potential for those in the best-adjusted group. In addition, Adjustment was related to the job performance dimensions of Leadership Skills, Interpersonal Sensitivity, Inner Work Standards, Bell System Value Orientation, Organizing and Planning, and Decision Making. The well-adjusted men had also received more recognition for their work and showed more self-confidence on the job. The evaluations of the assessors, then, were clearly confirmed by evaluations by the men's supervisors: The well-adjusted men were better performers than the poorly adjusted.

CHAPTER 9

The New Generation

A generation went by between the original assessment centers of MPS and MCS. The MCS participants knew nothing of World War II, and they were too young to relate to the culture of the 1950s. Their youth was spent during the turbulent 1960s and 1970s, when values seemed to be turned on their heads and unconventionality sought rather than avoided. It is not surprising that this generation of young business managers was different in important ways from the generation spawned 20 years earlier; these differences are the subject of this chapter.

The same criteria were used to select the MCS sample as had been used for the MPS college sample (i.e., the participants had been hired into low-level general management jobs and were considered to have potential for middle and upper management). But because the late 1970s were a time when affirmative action had clearly taken hold in the Bell System, the MCS sample was far from being all white males like that of MPS. In fact, the later sample was nearly half female and one-third racial and ethnic minorities. This was not due to purposeful oversampling of the women and minorities; they were being hired in these proportions by the telephone companies.

To represent the true generational differences between the two groups of telephone company managers, comparisons are made here between the college sample of MPS and the total MCS group. Yet since some of the differences are no doubt due to the introduction of women and ethnic minorities into the sample, comparisons are also made between the MPS college sample and the MCS white males only. This look at differences between generations of white males should provide somewhat clearer evidence of the impact of cultural changes over the 20-year period.

BACKGROUNDS

On nearly every biographical data item contained in the personal history questionnaire, there were differences between the MPS and MCS samples. In most cases these differences were apparent for the white male sample of MCS as well as the total sample, so it was not just a matter of women and racial/ethnic minorities being different from white males.

The MCS group was more heterogeneous in age, and their average age was slightly older. The median age for the total MCS group was 25, with a range of 21 to 43 but with 80% ranging from 22 to 28. By contrast, MPS had a median age of 24 and a range of 21 to 31. Within MCS, 43 participants were in their 30s (12.5%) and 3 additional persons were in their early 40s. The white male sample was less varied than the total MCS sample, with their ages ranging from 21 to 35. Their median age was even older, at 26.

Differences between the MPS and MCS samples in family and educational backgrounds are summarized in Table 9.1. Size of parental families was noticeably different between the two generations. The MCS participants averaged more than one more sibling than the MPS participants. Some of this difference was due to the racial and ethnic minorities, who came from larger families on the average, but the white males also had larger families than did those in MPS (not quite one more sibling). Another reason accounting for the difference was religion. The MCS sample had notably more Catholics, and the Catholics came from larger families than did the other religions represented.

Table 9.1   Family and Educational Background Variables Differentiating MPS and MCS Samples

Variable	MPS college	MCS total	MCS white males
No. of siblings, average (mean)	1.9	3.0	2.8
Father's education			
College graduate	26%	36%	42%
High school or less	58%	50%	43%
Mother's education			
College graduate	18%	25%	30%
High school or less	65%	57%	52%
Father's occupation			
Business	22%	35%	43%
Skilled craft	30%	14%	16%
Mother's occupation: Housewife	51%	49%	57%
High school grades			
Excellent	24%	65%	57%
Good	44%	26%	29%
Fair or poor	32%	9%	14%
College grades			
Excellent	15%	46%	45%
Good	56%	44%	45%
Fair or poor	29%	10%	10%
Higher education: Master's degree	1%	28%	29%

Note. On all variables MCS total and MCS white males significantly different from MPS college group at $p < .005$.

But even when race, ethnic group, and religion were taken into account, the MCS participants still came from larger families than did the MPS participants. The MCS group was part of the postwar baby boom, and their greater numbers of brothers and sisters were evidence of this phenomenon.

The parents of the MCS participants were better educated than the parents of the MPS men. While 26% of the MPS fathers had been college graduates, this was true of 36% of the MCS fathers and 42% of the MCS white males' fathers. Among the mothers, the percentages of college graduates were 18% for MPS, 25% for MCS, and 30% for MCS white males. Postgraduate study was also more frequent for MCS parents, characterizing 20% of the MCS fathers (26% of white males' fathers) and 13% of the MCS mothers (13% of white males' mothers), compared to 8% and 1% of MPS fathers and mothers, respectively.

These educational differences were reflected in occupational differences for the fathers. More MCS fathers were in business and fewer were in skilled craft positions. Among the mothers, housewife was still the dominant occupation, being typical of about half the MPS and MCS mothers.

Some other data indicated that mothers may have grown in power and influence over the two generations. The indicators might have been expected in the total sample, due to the presence of the female participants, but the data were equally strong in the white-male-only sample. When asked which parent they were closest to, in MPS 27% responded "mother," 41% "father," and 28% "both." Among the MCS white males more said "mother" (35%), fewer said "father" (25%), and more said "both" (37%). When asked about parental discipline, about the same proportion of MCS white males as of MPS participants identified their mothers as the disciplinarians (20% MPS, 18% MPS), but fewer identified their fathers (49% MPS and 31% MCS) and more identified both parents (30% MPS, 51% MCS). Very few of the white males in either sample came from homes where the parents were separated (7% MPS, 11% MCS), so this does not explain the differences. It appears that for the younger generation, mothers had begun to assume positions of greater equality relative to fathers in the hearts and minds of their children.

The differences between the backgrounds and aspirations of the two generational groups can be illustrated by an example of the original assessment interview with an MCS participant. A typical white male, Jeff, is described here, with references harking back to Joe, the typical MPS white male college graduate.

Jeff appeared slightly older than his 26 years because of a full, neatly trimmed beard, but he had the look of one who kept in good physical shape. He was quite well dressed, with a three-piece navy pinstriped wool suit, light blue button-down shirt, and navy and burgundy striped tie. He spoke clearly, with a strong, modulated voice and correct grammar. He seemed relaxed, sitting at the far end of a sofa in the interviewer's room with one leg curled underneath him.

Jeff had spent most of his childhood in a suburban community in Illinois. He described it as having a small-town friendliness, where everyone knew everyone else's business. There were a large number of children in his neighborhood — so many, in fact, that it was dubbed "Incubator Alley." Jeff's father was an architectural engineer and vice president of a consulting firm. Yet he was never too busy to find time to spend with his four children.

Jeff described his father as a hard-working, honest, dedicated, loving, and intelligent man who set high ideals for him and his siblings. Jeff did have some conflicts with his father, since he was very negative to some modern trends, such as "long hair, rock music, fast cars, and loose women." Jeff said, "My school, which was Jesuit, required short haircuts, but my dad required even shorter haircuts. I did make some headway with him on that, though, and by the 10th grade I wore my hair as long as the school would allow."

Jeff's mother completed only 2 years of college, leaving to get married and raise a family. Jeff was very close to her as well and thought she had exerted a great deal of influence on him. He described her as loving, hard-working, dedicated, opinionated, and quite perceptive. She was also a perfectionist and insisted on a very neat, clean, and organized house.

Jeff described his family as close-knit, with the parents very interested in their children and expressing pride in their accomplishments. They were actively involved parents, attending Little League games, PTA nights, and school plays. Jeff was the third child in the family, with one brother and one sister older and one brother 2 years younger. Even though he claimed they were close at one time, they did not seem too involved with one another in adulthood; there were only occasional visits.

Many concerns were expressed about grade inflation in the 1960s and 1970s, and the self-reports of the study participants were testimony to this. In high school, about one-quarter of the MPS participants had described their grades as "excellent," compared to more than half of the MCS participants. In college, only 15% of the MPS men said they had "excellent" grades, compared to 46% of the MCS group. Since the recruiters had consistently looked for those in the top half of their class over the 20-year period, it appears that grade inflation rather than differing standards accounted for the difference.

The MCS participants had gone further in their education than their earlier counterparts. Among the MPS men, 95% had stopped with a bachelor's degree, with 4% getting postgraduate credits and only 1% attaining a master's degree before employment. Within MCS, 28% had a master's degree and another 19% had some postgraduate credits (among white males 29% had a master's degree, 18% had postgraduate credits). Undergraduate majors did not differ that much across the generations among white males; about one-third had business degrees; one-third had degrees in engineering, science, or math; and the final one-third had degrees in humanities, social science, education, and other disciplines.

In high school Jeff got excellent grades and particularly liked math, becoming a member of the Math Society. He participated in many sports activities, especially running and baseball. His social life was casual and group-oriented, with his friends a mixture of males and females.

Jeff's grades gained him entrance into a well-respected Midwestern university. He decided to go into engineering because he had always enjoyed math and science and they were his strongest subjects in high school. He was again a good student and managed a 3.6 grade point average overall.

In his first year at college, Jeff was in a dormitory with other engineering majors. Many shared his love of outdoor activities, although he participated in formal sports or other extracurricular activities less than he had in high school. During his last year he lived in a coed dormitory on a floor with four suites — two for boys and two for girls, six in a suite. This was a purposeful move on the part of 12 friends, including the girl who would become Jeff's wife after graduation.

LIFESTYLES

Important interests and preoccupations in the lives of the participants were revealed in the life themes coded from the personal interviews. Comparisons of the average ratings on current involvement in the life themes for the total and white male groups of MCS and for the MPS college sample are shown in Figure 9.1.

The pattern of differences between the MCS total group and the MPS group suggests that the MCS group had adopted the concerns with self that seemed to predominate in the 1970s culture. They were higher on the

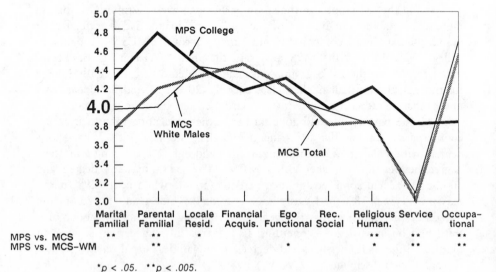

Figure 9.1.   Current involvement in life themes, MPS:0 and MCS:0.

Occupational and Financial-Acquisitive life themes, showing greater concern with working and with making money and acquiring material things. By contrast, the MPS group was higher on themes showing consideration for others, including Marital-Familial, Parental-Familial, Religious-Humanism, and Service.

In spite of being older, the MCS participants were somewhat less likely to be married, which helps explain their lesser involvement in the Marital-Familial life theme. Some 56% of the MPS men had been married at the original assessment, but the figures in MCS were 47% of the white males and 38% of the total group. It had been quite rare for an MPS man to be divorced, separated, or remarried; this was true for less than 0.5%. In MCS, the comparable figure was over 7% for the total group and over 6% for the white males, indicating a great cultural change over the 20-year period.

Among the married participants there was no generational difference in current involvement in the Marital-Familial life theme, although the total MCS group and the MCS white males indicated greater projected involvement in the marital family in the future. The married MCS participants had better-educated spouses than did their MPS counterparts. Among the wives of the MPS men, 32% had college degrees and 1% had done postgraduate work; among the wives of the MCS white males, 34% were college graduates and 23% had gone beyond that level. The numbers were even higher for the total MCS sample, since women are less likely to marry those with less education than are men, at least among whites. Some 27% of the spouses of the total MCS sample were college graduates and 37% had gone on to postgraduate work.

The spouses' occupations also differed across the two generations. The MCS spouses, whether for white males or the total group, were much less likely to be full-time housekeepers or clerical workers than the MPS wives. They were more likely to have jobs in business.

Jeff's family at the time of the assessment consisted of his wife of 19 months. She shared his outdoor interests, especially canoeing, tennis, and running. He described her as "logical and forceful. She's very affectionate, although she can sometimes be quite opinionated." She had majored in psychology as an undergraduate, but through a company training program had learned computer programming. She was now enjoying a career in that capacity with a local firm.

Jeff was very positive toward his wife's career. He said, "I think the traditional woman's role is a waste of assets; if both people can earn money, then they should." Her salary of $22,000 a year was nearly equal to his. He was not convinced, however, that either he or his wife would stick to their present way of life if children came along.

The lesser involvement in the Parental-Familial life theme on the part of MCS could certainly be related to the decline in centrality of the nuclear family that occurred in the 1960s and 1970s. Yet it should be remembered that the MCS participants were also slightly older than those in MPS and had been on their own a little longer. When the MCS assessment data were compared with the MPS data from interviews 1 year after the MPS:0 assessment, the differences in the Parental-Familial life theme were still apparent for both the total sample and the white males. It thus appears that cultural changes rather than artifacts of sample selection were in large part responsible for these MPS—MCS differences.

The higher ratings by the MPS group on the Ego-Functional life theme were somewhat surprising, considering the self-help movement of the 1970s as well as the attention to physical fitness. The MCS participants seemed more attentive to caring for their bodies, and more of them rated their health as excellent on the personal history questionnaire (76% of MCS total and 81% of MCS white males, compared to 58% of MPS).

The difference in the Ego-Functional life theme favoring MPS appeared to be in the area of intellectual development and rooted in the immediate present. The MPS men stated they had read an average of 3.2 books in the 2 months prior to the original assessment, compared to 2.4 for the MCS total group and 2.0 for the MCS white males. Perhaps not just outdoor activities but television was luring the MCS participants away from reading. In retrospective developments on the Ego-Functional life theme, the MCS sample (both the total sample and the white males) was rated higher. This may be because more of the MCS people had been involved in postgraduate education before entering the Bell System. There were no differences between the MPS and MCS groups on projected developments for this theme.

Jeff spent as much of his free time as he could in the outdoors, engaging in whatever sports activity was available. When the weather precluded many of those activities, he busied himself around the house with painting and plumbing. He also enjoyed television, his favorite shows being news or comedies such as M*A*S*H.

He was not much of a reader, preferring the outdoors, although he did keep up with the local and city papers if he had time. He read no publications about business on a regular basis, but occasionally watched *Wall Street Week* on television. There were some magazines that he liked, such as *Handyman*, *Sports Illustrated*, or *Playboy*, but he didn't seem to have time for books.

On the Religious-Humanism theme, the MCS participants had less current involvement as well as fewer projected developments. Apparently the turning away from religion that occurred in the 1970s affected young people as well as older ones. Protestants and Catholics made up 91% of the MPS sample but only 81% of the MCS group, indicating both the greater presence of other religions and the greater absence of any religion within MCS. In the MCS total group, 2% were Jewish (also 2% of white males), 5% were of other religions (3% of white males), and 11% professed no religious faith (15% of white males). This compares to the MPS distribution of 0% Jewish, 2% other religions, and 6% with no religious faith. The increase in number of people with no religious preferences between the 1950s and 1970s has also been shown in survey research (Veroff *et al.*, 1981).

As mentioned previously, there were more Catholics among the MCS group than in MPS. Proportions were 23% Catholic for MPS, 37% for MCS as a whole, and 41% for MCS white males. By contrast, 68% of the MPS college men were Protestant, compared to 44% of the MCS total and 39% of the MCS white males. Comparisons of the Protestants and Catholics on the assessment exercises showed very few differences in their average performance, so this must be considered an irrelevant factor as far as managerial characteristics are concerned.

Although Jeff had been raised a Catholic, he said religion didn't mean that much to him. He went to church only two or three times a year. He said, "I do maintain a personal belief in a higher being, but I don't believe too much in organized religion. I still say I'm a Catholic, though, so I can take my kids to church and to the Catholic school when the time comes. I want them to be sensitive people and have a background which will prepare them for life."

The Service life theme indicated that the MPS men were more involved in community activities at the original assessment than the MCS participants, and they definitely had intentions of being involved in the future. However, there was greater satisfaction with this theme in both the MCS total and white male groups than in MPS.

On the political front, among white males in each sample there were far more Republicans (44% in MPS and MCS) than there were Democrats (19% MPS, 13% MCS). When rated on political philosophy from their interviews, the MCS white males were less conservative (3.5 on the 5-point scale) than the MPS college men had been when they joined the company (3.9). This was true for economic issues (3.7 MPS, 3.3 MCS), and the MCS group was less antagonistic toward big government (rated 1.8) than the MPS group had been (rated 1.2).

The differences did not hold for military stance or social issues. The social issues rated were clearly of a different nature in the 1950s and the 1970s, and it is unlikely that the MPS generation would have been as liberal as MCS if asked about such things as premarital sex, abortion, equal rights for women, or gay rights.

The white males in MCS were also more liberal than the MPS men when the comparison was made for issues in the late 1970s and early 1980s. This was true for general political philosophy and position on economic issues (too few MPS responses were coded on social issues and military stance during this period to permit a sound comparison). The MCS men had more positive feelings about welfare (2.4) than the MPS men (1.5).

Although Joe had had his eyes on the Rotary Club and the Junior Chamber of Commerce back in the 1950s, Jeff had no interest in participating in any community or civic activities. He claimed he had nothing in particular against them but felt most of them were social, and he didn't have time for such activities.

Joe had called himself an Eisenhower Republican at his MPS:0 assessment interview, but Jeff claimed to have no party affiliation, preferring to "take things as they come and decide." He admitted to being on the conservative side, "but not as conservative as my father."

Joe had made some strong statements against welfare. He said, "The less people have to work, the less they will work. This will break the back of the essence of what has made America great — individual initiative. When the immigrants came over, it was their drive to achieve that pushed the country ahead. Just giving money away won't do a thing; you've got to teach people to upgrade themselves. My parents didn't approve of people drawing welfare, and I'm the same way. It takes away man's desire to care for himself."

Jeff was not a strong advocate of welfare either, but his attitudes were more mild than Joe's. He said, "Society should make sure that people in need are taken care of. But we need to get back to the point where the government has control over the spending done by social programs. These programs should be administered at the local level. They have grown out of proportion, and cutting them has become a painful necessity."

Jeff had a more liberal attitude toward sexual conduct than was prevalent in the 1950s. He said, "I think trying out sex before marriage prevents divorce; you have to find out if the shoe fits before you wear it! Needless to say, Jeff did not agree with official Catholic doctrine on premarital sex and birth control. He said, "Even my mother says the Pope must be a fool on those subjects."

Among the total MCS sample, Democrats slightly outnumbered Republicans (32% vs. 26%), representing an even more dramatic change in point of view among the new generation. Ratings of political philosophy highlighted this greater disparity (3.9 MPS vs. 3.0 MCS). The difference was particularly pronounced with respect to economic issues (4.7 MPS vs. 3.3 MCS), but also applied to social issues (3.0 MPS, 2.5 MCS). If 1961—1965 is used as an anchor point for the MPS men, they were more "hawkish" in military stance than the MCS participants (3.7 MPS, 2.7 MCS). This difference in politics is explored more fully in the chapters on women and on race and ethnic minorities.

WORK INTERESTS

The MCS group showed greater involvement in the Occupational life theme, and also greater retrospective developments. One reason for the disparity is that the MCS group was somewhat more experienced in work than the MPS group. The large majority of MPS men had had no previous jobs before joining the telephone company; this was true for less than half of the MCS participants. Some 18% of the MCS group (total and white males alike) had had two jobs before joining the telephone company, compared to only 6% of the MPS participants.

On the other hand, nearly half the MPS men had had military service, compared to less than one-fourth of the white males (and minority males) in MCS and only 12% of the MCS total group. By the time the MCS participants matured, there was no more draft, and the women were excluded even when there was a draft. Among the MCS participants who did join the military, more were discharged as officers compared to the MPS men.

The MCS participants also had somewhat more experience within the telephone companies before coming to the assessment centers — about 6 months more, on the average. Within MPS, nearly half had been employed with the company less than a month before attending the assessment center, and only 5% had been there more than 1 year. In MCS 49% had been there 6 months or less, another 38% had worked there between 7 and 12 months, and the remaining 13% had been there more than 1 year (with few exceptions within 18 months).

Expectations and Work Preferences

Although the Occupational life theme showed the MCS sample to be more involved in their work, it did not show them to be more satisfied with it. The Expectations Inventory revealed that they did not hold out as high hopes about what their managerial careers would be like. On this questionnaire, the assessees gave their preferences for and expectations of what would be true 5 years hence. On a 4-point scale from +2 ("fairly certain to be true") to −2 ("fairly certain to be false"), the average rating on each of the 28 positive items was 0.63 for the MCS total group, compared to 0.95 for the MPS sample. This put the MCS group as a whole at the 17th percentile of the MPS norms, indicating considerably less favorable responses to the various questions, though still on the positive side of neutral. The average score for the white males in MCS was 0.56, putting them at the 13th percentile, so this was certainly not a finding representing only differences created by the women or minorities.

It is true that the MPS men were unrealistically positive about their future careers and that their Expectations Inventory scores dropped over the next few years after MPS:0, as shown in Chapter 6. However, the greater negativism of the MCS group was not due just to the fact that they had been around the company longer, for the MPS group's year 1 scores were also significantly higher than the MCS original assessment scores. It might be hoped that the MCS group was more realistic and would not experience the same level of decline as the MPS men. Yet a preliminary look at later administrations of the questionnaire to the MCS group shows their scores declining just as precipitously over the same period of time. Apparently the MCS group was not as optimistic at the start, and the realities that they faced with experience made them even less so.

Responses to the items designated as most desirable or most undesirable on the Expectations Inventory are illustrated in Table 9.2. There was general agreement between the two generations that it was most desirable to have a challenging job, to be able to follow one's basic interests, to make a sufficient salary, to be advanced as rapidly as one's interests and ability would warrant, and to get broad experience.

Somewhat different emphasis was given to the desirability of other items by the two samples. Two of these items were already suggested by differences in the life themes. The MPS men considered it more desirable to engage in social

Table 9.2   Responses to Most Important Items in Expectations Inventory, MPS:0 and MCS:0

Most desired items	% citing most desirable			% fairly certain of favorable outcome		
	MPS col.	MCS tot.	MCS WM	MPS col.	MCS tot.	MCS WM
I have a real chance to follow my basic interests and work at the things I like to do.	39	47	43	42	46	42
I live in a desirable community with relatively easy access to my job.	14	22	27**	47	51	44
I have reached the district level of responsibility.[a]	54	43*	46	25	39	36
I am earning [MPS, $8,000; MCS, $35,000] a year or more.	41	38	38	51	64	72*
I have gone back to school for additional courses useful in my work.	14	27**	24*	38	56**	50
I have had experience in different types of work and more than one division of the company.	22	28	22	55	41**	34**
My job is challenging with many opportunities to learn and do new things.	61	64	55	69	47**	39**
I have discovered that working for the Bell System has helped me to meet the kind of people I like and to engage in desirable social and community activities.	46	17**	23**	76	24**	22**
I am advanced about as rapidly as my interests and ability warrant.	41	39	40	37	26**	26**
My spouse is happy that I work for the Bell System.	36	24*	29	69	41**	45**

Table 9.2 (Cont'd)

Least desired items	% citing least desirable			% fairly certain of favorable outcome		
	MPS col.	MCS tot.	MCS WM	MPS col.	MCS tot.	MCS WM
I have too much invested in the company — both psychologically and materially — to feel free to move to another job.	16	28**	25	20	21	25
I have fewer opportunities for promotion than if I had gone to work for a different company.	38	31	32	62	42**	36**
I have to travel and be away from home a lot of the time.	20	22	33*	24	16**	16*
I feel an increasing amount of conflict between obligations of my job and my family.	55	49	51	65	24**	16**
The company doesn't provide sufficient opportunity for me to learn new things.	34	26*	21*	65	36**	29**
I feel the company resists new ideas and experimentation.	27	21	18	64	26**	19**
I have found that an open display of ambition or competitive drive is detrimental to a successful career in the company.	26	11**	9**	48	35	34
I am earning less than [MPS $7,000; MCS $30,000] a year.	25	24	31	63	76*	82**
I regret not having gone to work for another company.	46	28**	27**	62	50**	50**
I have not reached as high a level of responsibility as most of the people who started in the company when I did.	45	34*	37	55	49*	50

Note. Group differences in desirability computed from chi-square tests on proportions; expectations from *t* tests on means. Abbreviations: col., college; tot., total; WM, white males.

[a] The district level is the third of seven levels of management running from foreman to president.

* Significantly different from MPS at $p < .05$.

** Significantly different from MPS at $p < .005$.

and community activities (they had a higher Service life theme) and for their spouses to be happy about their employer (higher Marital-Familial life theme). The latter comparision was true for the total MCS sample but not for the white males, just as it had been on the Marital-Familial life theme, since marriage rates were lower in groups other than the white males.

Also more desirable to the MPS men was reaching the third level of the management hierarchy. The MCS group was more interested in taking additional coursework for self-development, and the MCS white males were also more interested in living in a desirable community with easy access to the job.

The certainty of being able to attain the desirable items is shown in the right-hand columns of Table 9.2. The MCS group was more sure of being able to take the outside coursework, perhaps because this was under their control more than the company's, and they were also more sure of attaining a good salary level. This sureness may have been influenced by the fact that the dollar value given in the inventory was not changed over the 1977—1982 assessments, although the rate of inflation suggested that it probably should have been. It is also possible that the MCS generation was more used to having material things and took money somewhat more for granted.

For the undesirable items, there was agreement between the two generations that having job—family conflicts, having fewer opportunities for promotion than at other companies, earning too little, and having the company resist new ideas were especially negative situations to be in. The MCS total group indicated they would find it more undesirable to have too much invested in the company to leave, while the MPS men would find it more objectionable to regret not having gone to work for another company. This suggests that the MPS men were seeking company loyalty while the MCS participants were resisting it.

Two other items relating to advancement confirm the difference found on the desirable item of reaching the district level. That is, the MPS men would find it more undesirable to discover that ambition was detrimental to one's career and not to be promoted as high as one's peers. The evidence begins to mount, then, that promotions were not as important to the MCS participants as they were to the MPS participants at about the same age.

In terms of outcomes on the undesirable items, the MCS group was more optimistic that things would turn out well on only one item — that dealing with salary. Again, this could be attributed to the dollar sum presented or to the fact that they were used to receiving financial rewards. The MPS group was more positive on seven of the remaining nine items, ranging across a wide variety of circumstances. The generally greater pessimism of the MCS group did not seem to relate to any particular area of their careers, then; they were just not as certain as the MPS participants that their work life would provide optimal rewards.

On the Work Conditions Survey, the MPS group was again more positive and tolerant on a wide range of items. They scored in a more favorable direction on 13 of the 30 statements. The MPS group was more positive toward interviewing a variety of individuals, working exclusively with men, advising people, deliberate thinking, and selecting personnel. They were less negative toward idleness, a strict boss, desk work, close supervision, physical danger, physical endurance, working only with women, or frequent foul-ups.

The MCS group indicated more tolerance or positiveness on only two items: They were more favorable toward having excitement and less negative toward having little social contact.

In these two separate questionnaires, the Expectations Inventory and the Work Conditions Survey, the MCS group was shown to be considerably more negative toward things that might happen to them in the work situation. They were not convinced their work lives would be as rosy as the MPS men anticipated, and they indicated that many conditions would be less acceptable to them than had been the case with their predecessors. It appeared that the new group would be both more difficult to inspire and harder to please.

Work Attitudes

The Management Questionnaire, administered not at the original assessment but with the follow-up interviews, provides more information on the feelings of the MCS group about their jobs, their careers, and the telephone company. A comparison of average scores by the MPS men at their year 1 with those by the MCS group are shown in Figure 9.2. The MCS white males had scores almost identical to those of the MCS total group, so they are not presented separately. It should be noted that only one MCS group was administered the questionnaire 1 year after assessment and the rest filled it in at year 2 of MCS, since annual follow-ups were replaced by biannual follow-ups.

There were strong differences on all the scales of the Management Questionnaire, with the MCS group considerably more negative on all but one of them. The difference in timing of the questionnaire administration had little

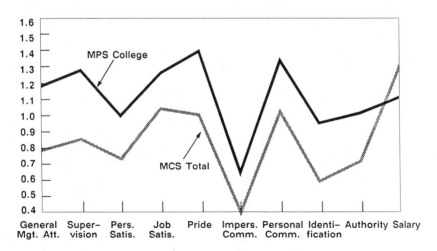

p < .005 all scales.

Figure 9.2.   Management Questionnaire scales, MPS (year 1) and MCS (years 1—2).

influence on the results; the MCS group scored more negatively than the MPS group up until the older group's 20th year. In fact, even at MPS:20, the MCS group was more dissatisfied on the Personal Satisfaction, Authority, and Impersonal Communications scales, although these were no doubt related to the different levels of the two groups.

The pattern of average scores in the early years was very similar across the two samples, indicating that they found the same types of things more or less satisfying. Job Satisfaction, Pride, and Personal Communications were rated among the highest for both groups, while there was more dissatisfaction with Impersonal Communications, Identification (with management), Authority, and Personal Satisfaction. The MCS group showed more discontent with Supervision relative to the other scales than the MPS group had.

The only scale where the MCS group showed greater satisfaction than the MPS group was Salary. It is likely that salaries were indeed better in the telephone companies relative to other industries in the 1970s as opposed to the 1950s.

After graduation Jeff accepted a job with a consulting engineering firm that specialized in transportation and traffic studies. He seemed to be following in his father's footsteps, but he was soon very dissatisfied with his role as "general flunky." His position offered no independent responsibility, but consisted of gathering data for others. Jeff decided he would best advance his career by getting more education, and he completed an MBA at night, majoring in finance.

He then registered with his university's placement service and received an inquiry from Illinois Bell. After several interviews and a couple of tests, he was offered a job and jumped at the chance to leave his "flunky" position. He was told that although he would begin in the engineering department, he would probably move on to other responsibilities and departments after a year or two.

Jeff realized after a few weeks that he had been put on a special accelerated management program for college graduates showing high potential. The program (actually growing out of the MPS findings that early job challenge was especially important for later success) involved rotating among different job assignments, being given supervisory responsibilities, being under close supervision, and receiving a series of performance appraisals at 3-month intervals. Provided that he progressed well, he would be promoted into the second level of management within 3—5 years and to the third level in 5—8 years. Jeff was surprised to learn that his job would entail supervising others, and found himself reading manuals about employment and affirmative action. He seemed unsure that he was right for a manager's role but thought he would try.

Jeff was attracted to Bell because he thought it would offer a different experience and challenge, and because the salary was good. But unlike Joe, he didn't mention opportunities for advancement or the appeal of a service organization as reasons for joining the company. He did indicate that he was interested in telephone technology and also in the finances of the business.

He had worked for Illinois Bell nearly a year by the time he arrived at the assessment center, but he was still reserving judgment about the Bell System as an employer. He was waiting for a position to really "jell" for him, and his attitude was that if he didn't like the company, he could easily leave and go somewhere else. Although he claimed to have no objections to big companies per se, he admitted to being frustrated by some Bell System bureaucratic procedures. He said, "I don't understand why I have to request a maintenance person to change a light bulb when I'm more than capable of doing it myself."

Jeff also spoke somewhat negatively of the company's middle managers, claiming they had been on the job too long and lacked imagination. He was dissatisfied with his current boss, whom he viewed as too dictatorial and unsupportive. Jeff said, "If something goes wrong, my boss is quick to jump on my back. But he has never thanked me for doing a good job." His boss was an up-from-the-ranks craft man who admitted to a resentment toward the accelerated program for college graduates.

PERSONALITY AND MOTIVATION

Many of the personality and motivation exercises administered to the MCS participants were identical to those given to the MPS men. These included the Edwards and Sarnoff questionnaires, interview ratings for the four motivational variables, the incomplete sentences, and the TAT pictures (with a few pictures added to be more appropriate to the women). The MCS group was not administered the GAMIN, however, with the better-constructed and revised Guilford-Zimmerman Temperament Survery (G-Z) taking its place. It was possible to construct some common General Activity, Ascendance, and Masculinity scores for the MPS and MCS groups based on items common to both tests, and these comparisons are presented in this chapter as well. The MCS group was also given the California Psychological Inventory (CPI), which further enriched their personality profiles.

Because of the absence of the GAMIN, the Self-Esteem factor, which included four scales from the GAMIN, could not be calculated for the MCS group. Scores on the other five factors could be calculated and are presented here. (A recomputation of the factor analysis using the same personality and motivation scores, minus the five GAMIN scores, showed great congruence in factor structure between the MCS males and MPS males, though it did not hold up well for the female sample.)

Ambition

A comparison of the average scores on the five personality and motivation factors for the MPS and the MCS groups showed no differences except for the Ambition factor, where the MCS group scored markedly lower (51.8 average score for MPS, compared to 46.0 for the MCS total group and 46.6 for the MCS white males). Differences between the two generations on the test scores contained in the Ambition factor are shown in Figure 9.3. The lower scores by

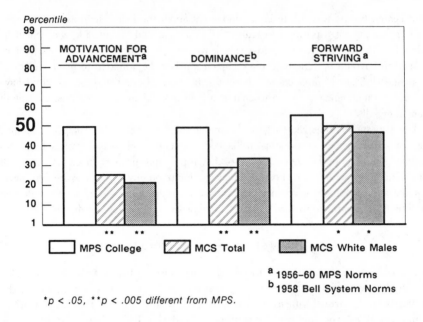

Figure 9.3.   Test scores in Ambition factor, MPS:0 and MCS:0.

the MCS group on two of the scales are rather startling. It was clear on the Sarnoff scale of Motivation for Advancement that the MCS group, whether the total group or just the white males, had a great deal less drive to advance to higher levels in the organization. The MCS white males were only at the 21st percentile of the MPS norms of the Sarnoff Motivation for Advancement scale, scoring lower on each of the five items in the scale. Similarly, when Need for Advancement was rated from interview summaries, the MPS group received an average rating of 3.5 on a 5-point scale, while the MCS group was notably lower — 3.1 for the total group and 3.2 for the white males.

Also dramatically lower for MCS were scores on the Dominance scale of the Edwards, where the MCS group scored at the 29th percentile of the Bell System college-hire norms and the MCS white males at the 34th; the MPS group had been at the 49th percentile. The Dominance scale measures liking for leadership positions, and the MCS group's lower scores here are consistent with their lesser interest in advancement as expressed in the interview and on the Sarnoff. Similarly, the MCS total group and white males were rated higher on acceptance of a subordinate role on the projective exercises than were the MPS men.

The MCS group also scored somewhat lower on the Sarnoff scale of Forward Striving, likewise shown in Figure 9.3. This scale measures general attitudes about reaching into the future, including bettering oneself, setting high goals, and striving for things beyond one's reach. The lower scores by the younger generation are a reflection both of less ambition and of the greater pessimism about the future expressed in the late 1970s and 1980s. Even the Motivation for Money scale of the Sarnoff showed a more positive response by the MPS men, primarily influenced by the item "People should always try to raise their standard of living." The MPS men gave a greater endorsement to that item in the 1950s, when it was assumed to be possible, than the MCS group did in the 1970s, when economic prosperity was showing its limitations.

There were no differences between the MPS and MCS groups on the interview ratings of Primacy of Work or Inner Work Standards, also included in the Ambition factor. This suggests that in spite of less ambition, involvement in work and caring about high-quality work were not problems for the MCS group. It will be remembered that they were rated even higher than the MPS men on the Occupational life theme. On another Edwards scale, Achievement, the overall MCS group scored about the same as the MPS group (MPS 62nd percentile, MCS 68th percentile); the MCS white males were slightly higher, at the 70th percentile.

Lower drive for advancement was not related to a lack of energy, for the MCS total group and white males scored higher than the MPS men had on the General Activity scale items common to the GAMIN and the G-Z, perhaps because of their greater interest in maintaining physical health. On a normative scale based on the MPS college men at their original assessment, the MPS men's average was at the 55th percentile, while the MCS total group scored at the 65th and the MCS white males at the 64th. The lesser ambition of the MCS group, then, was primarily related to moving up in the organization. It did not equate to a lack of energy, nor did it diminish their desire for challenge and a chance to perform work of high quality.

When Joe joined the Bell System in 1956, he aspired to be a top executive, but Jeff showed no interest in anything beyond middle management. He said, "I'm not even that interested in the fourth level; third will be fine with me. Promotions just aren't that important to me; I place my family life first. Of course I haven't conveyed this to my supervisors, because it might stand in the way of my even getting to the third level. I think Bell frowns upon people who don't place their career above all other aspects of their life. But I must have some of my own time. If I can't accomplish what I consider a strong family life and some other things, I just don't want to go that high."

Joe had likewise been interested in a solid family life, but he realized he might have to sacrifice some family time to his career. Jeff was not so willing. He said, "I'd work overtime if there were important jobs that needed to be done, but I certainly won't do it to get a promotion." He also had some misgivings about relocating to advance his career, although he said he was agreeable to that "to a certain extent."

The projective exercises indicated that Jeff's achievement motivation was average or a little above, with greater interest in self-development and deriving a sense of satisfaction from his work than in the external symbols of success that advancement would bring. His only stated career objective was to enjoy his work, and he appeared to have little idea of what might be involved. He said in response to an incomplete-sentence stem, "*The job I am best fit for* could be any number of things I've ever considered."

He was not only ambivalent about what he really wanted in his career but indeed in his life in general. To the stem "*The things I want . . .* ," he responded, "are not sometimes what I really want." He appeared to be defending himself against frustration and the fear of being "trapped" into an unhappy lifestyle by refraining from a commitment to goals. He stated "*My ambition* is to live a comfortable, stress-free life," and he expressed fears about giving success too large a role in his life. He complained, "*I secretly* think about my work too much," adding, "*My greatest worry* is allowing work to dominate my life."

Impulsivity and Affability

Although the overall Impulsivity factor showed no significant MPS-MCS differences, two scores in the factor indicated a generational difference. As shown in Figure 9.4, the younger generation scored significantly lower on the Edwards scale of Deference, indicating that they were less inclined to defer to those in higher authority. Combined with their lesser interest in leading others, as shown by the Dominance scale, and their lesser Motivation for Advancement scores, it appears that there was generally less importance attached to hierarchical positions by the MCS generation. Relative to the MPS group, they did not want to lead and they did not want to follow!

Ratings from the interview on Need for Security showed the MCS group lower; the average rating for MPS was 3.4 on a 5-point scale, compared to

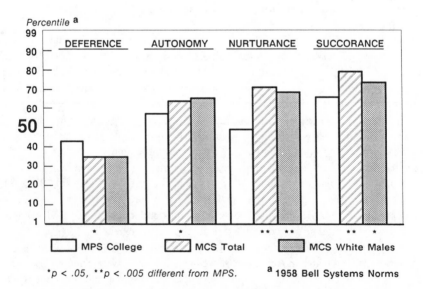

Figure 9.4.   Selected test scores from Impulsivity and Affability factors, MPS:0 and MCS:0.

3.1 for both the MCS total group and the white males. Evidently holding onto the same job was not of as high priority for them. This harks back to some responses to the Expectations Inventory, where the MPS group indicated it would be more serious to them to regret their decision to join the company, while the MCS group indicated it would be more serious to find they could not leave the company because they had too much invested in it. Corporate loyalty and job security are mutually compatible, and the MCS group seemed less interested in both.

Another personality and motivation factor, Affability, showed no overall generation difference but offers some evidence of other distinctions between the two groups. As shown in Figure 9.4, the MCS group scored noticeably higher than the MPS group on the Edwards Nurturance scale (71st percentile for MCS total group, compared to 49th percentile for MPS), indicating an interest in providing emotional support and help to others. This was not due to the influence of the women in the MCS sample, for the MCS white male average was at the 69th percentile, almost as high. Another Edwards scale, Succorance, is somewhat the flip side of the Nurturance scale, indicating that receiving emotional support and help from others is also desired. Here, too, the MCS group scored higher — both the total group (at the 79th percentile, compared to MPS at the 66th percentile) and the white males (at the 75th percentile). The MCS participants scored no higher on Affiliation than the MPS men and even scored somewhat higher on Autonomy, as also shown in Figure 9.4. But when they did interact with others, they hoped for more caring and supportive relationships.

It is perhaps characteristic of the changing times that the traits measured by the Nurturance and Succorance scales, long thought of as more "feminine" than "masculine" qualities, characterized the men in the MCS sample to as great an extent as they did. There is other evidence of a lessening of some aspects of masculinity among the MCS men in a scale comprised of the common items from the GAMIN and G-Z scales of Masculinity. Here the MCS males scored lower than the MPS men had scored; when the MPS college men are used as a norm group, the MPS average was the the 56th percentile, while the MCS males were at the 45th percentile. The MCS men were particularly less interested in rugged outdoor occupations (being a forest ranger or contractor) and activities where animals were killed or injured.

Jeff's high score on the Edwards Autonomy scale (67th percentile) and his low Edwards Deference score (35th percentile) suggested that he might encounter some conflict in accepting directions and orders from others. This tendency was also clear from the projective exercises. He said, "*Taking orders* is hard if I don't believe it's a necessary demand," and "*When I talk with someone in authority* I don't always act with utmost respect." By contrast, Joe had replied, "*Taking orders* is a must," and "*When I talk with someone in authority* I am respectful." Jeff seemed to be an individualistic person whom others might find hard to please and difficult to know.

Yet Jeff wasn't without needs to relate to others. The projective exercises indicated that he was sensitive to the needs and problems of others, and he referred to people as "really hurting inside." His projective responses indicated his above-average dependence and nurturance, in spite of the fact that his need for affiliation was not strong. Dependence appeared to be a problem for him, for he would like advice and help from others but had little faith in it. In a story written to a TAT picture, for example, the character sought and followed the advice of his father but was never sure it was the right solution. He wrote, "*Advice and guidance* are often not sincere."

The combination of higher Nurturance and lower Dominance scores might suggest a rejection of an authoritarian style of leadership. But the Dominance scale makes no references to style; it only questions whether one likes to be the leader in groups to which one belongs. Moreover, the Authoritarianism scale from the Bass (1955) version of the California F Scale showed no significant differences between the MPS and MCS groups (either the total group or the white males).

It seems doubtful, then, that a rejection of authoritarianism or masculinity by the younger generation was primarily responsible for their lesser interests in assuming leadership positions. On many scales and scores, they simply dismissed the climb to the top of the corporate ladder as of much less importance than it had been to their forerunners. Given the strong relationships between ambition in the early years and later advancement of the MPS men, these characteristics of the new generation of managers are a cause of some concern for the future of the organization. Ambition promises to decline even further as careers progress, according to the MPS findings. Will this new generation of managers prepare themselves appropriately for higher-level jobs, or even be willing to accept them, if they are apathetic about advancement when young?

ABILITIES

No postassessment recoding was done for the In-Basket and two group discussions for MCS, as had been the case for MPS, and not all of the Cognitive ability tests were repeated. It was thus not possible to derive comparable ability factor scores for the two groups. Nevertheless, there are some appropriate scores than can be consulted and from which MPS—MCS comparisons can be made in each of the three ability areas. These are shown in Table 9.3.

Administrative skills can be compared only in terms of the overall dimension ratings of Organizing and Planning and Decision Making. The weight of information in rating these dimensions came from the In-Basket, however, so they are not a poor substitute for direct ratings on the In-Basket itself. No significant differences were shown between the two generations on these Administrative abilities.

Table 9.3   Ability Factor Scores and Ratings, MPS:0 and MCS:0

Factor	MPS college	MCS total	MCS white males
Administrative			
Organizing and Planning (dimension)	2.89	2.87	2.98
Decision Making (dimension)	2.70	2.62	2.63
Interpersonal			
Competitive group exercise — oral presentation	3.44	3.06**	3.11**
Competitive group exercise — overall rating	3.32	2.88**	2.99**
Cognitive			
SCAT Verbal	47 %ile	51 %ile	55 %ile**
SCAT Quantitative	31 %ile	32 %ile	48 %ile**
SCAT total	39 %ile	42 %ile	53 %ile**

*   Significantly different from MPS at $p < .05$.
** Significantly different from MPS at $p < .005$.

On Interpersonal abilities, the most comparable scores were those on the competitive group discussion, where assessees were given assigned roles to defend in a competition for limited awards. (In MPS, this exercise was the Promotion Problem; in MCS, it was either the City Council Problem or the School Board Problem.) On the ratings given by the assessors immediately after observing the discussion sessions, the MPS group was higher than both the MCS total group and the MCS white males. This was true for the oral presentation of one's position at the beginning of the discussion, as well as for overall contribution to the functioning of the group in achieving its goals. These data suggest that the MCS group's lesser interest in leadership may also be reflected in performance where leadership is needed to attain a goal.

The lower ratings of the MCS group on the oral presentation part of the exercises are in direct contradiction to their self-ratings of their effectiveness as speakers on the personal history form. Here 53% described their effectiveness as excellent or above average (54% of white males), compared to only 34% of the MPS men. The MCS participants were not aware of their relative weakness in this area, then, or at least were not willing to admit it.

In the competitive group exercise, Jeff's oral presentation was undistinguished. He presented his points in a disorganized way and lacked impact. He did not appear to be very committed to his proposal, and he seemed to lack confidence in his presentation. His voice was powerful, but his memory was weak. There were frequent pauses, often used to consult his notes, and he seemed to be at a loss to recall details.

In the group discussion following the presentations, Jeff exhibited some forcefulness but was not very persuasive. The assessor observing his behavior described him as "not a leader of this group, but a fomenter of trouble." He seemed to enjoy arguing with another group member and was quite obstinate. He did not see himself this way, however; in his written comments after the discussion, Jeff described his contribution as good "because of a willingness to listen to others' arguments and reasonable discussion." He added that his major opponent's arguments were not reasonable. Jeff failed to form coalitions, but instead persisted in a negativistic approach of pointing out deficiencies in the proposals of others, especially his primary opponent. He eventually was unable to stand on his own in the arguments and became quiet.

In the Counseling Center Group Discussion (the other MCS group exercise without assigned roles) Jeff was better able to consider the viewpoints of others, although he still was not easily swayed. He was less active in this discussion and sometimes gave the appearance of lack of interest, but his occasional comments revealed he was actually paying close attention. He made several conciliatory remarks, facilitating the group, though the observers thought he might have taken a more antagonistic role if his views had differed more from those of the others.

In the Cognitive area, the SCAT test showed no overall differences between the MPS and MCS groups, but the MCS white males scored higher than their previous counterparts. This was especially true on the Quantitative scale. After the MPS research had begun, the telephone companies had instituted general ability tests as part of their selection procedures, so it should be expected that the general level of mental ability would be higher. However, concerns about challenges to test fairness, in light of the push for equal employment opportunities, led some of the companies to drop their employment tests, at least temporarily, at the time when the MCS participants were being screened. Thus, the average scores are not as different as they might have been.

The Critical Thinking and Contemporary Affairs Tests were not administered to the MCS group, but a General Information Test was substituted. This test focuses on general knowledge about a variety of fields but does not reflect current events. The MCS group scored at the 58th percentile and the MCS white males at the 71st percentile of a group of 589 Bell System new college recruits into the Bell System tested in 1978. Unfortunately, there is no way to compare these scores to those of the MPS generation who took a different test in the 1950s.

Ratings of understanding of political issues from the interviews did provide a measure of the MCS group's awareness of contemporary national events. Here the total MCS group was rated 2.6 and the MCS white males 2.9 on a 5-point scale, significantly higher than the MPS average of 2.1 at the time of their original assessment. By this criterion, the MCS group seemed notably better informed as young managers in the late 1970s and early 1980s than the MPS group had been when they emerged from the less eventful 1950s.

OVERALL ASSESSMENT EVALUATIONS

The MCS participants were rated on the same 26 dimensions as the MPS participants had been, as well as 10 more dimensions adopted from those added at the MPS:20 assessment. The original dimensions were subjected to a factor analysis in much the same way as the MPS ratings had been, and the results were highly consistent. A comparison of the MPS and MCS groups on the resulting eight factor scores is shown in Figure 9.5. The Nonconformity factor has not been presented in previous chapters, since it did not emerge for the MPS noncollege group. Both the MPS and MCS college sample analyses produced the factor, which consisted of the dimensions Social Objectivity and Range of Interests, scored positively, and the inverse of Need for Security, Bell System Value Orientation, and Need for Superior Approval.

The first three dimension factors in Figure 9.5 directly follow the scores presented in the preceding section on abilities. As noted above, there were no differences on the Administrative Skills factor between the MPS and MCS groups, although on the Creativity dimension the MPS group scored higher than either the MCS total group or the MCS white males (MPS = 2.58, MCS = 2.09, MCS white males = 2.04).

Several dimensions in the Interpersonal Skills area showed relative weaknesses on the part of the MCS participants, which contributed to their lower factor score. There were no differences on Leadership Skills, Forcefulness, or Perception of Threshold Social Cues. The MCS white males and the MCS total group were, however, rated lower than MPS on both Oral Communication Skills (paralleling their competitive group exercise scores) and Behavior Flexibility, showing more entrenchment on the part of the MCS people. The

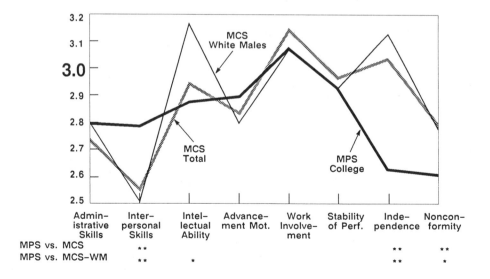

$*p < .05.$ $**p < .005.$

Figure 9.5.   Dimension factors, MPS:0 and MCS:0.

MCS white males were also rated less likeable by the assessors than the MPS men, and their Self-Objectivity was rated lower.

On the Intellectual Ability factor, the MCS group was very similar to the MPS group, but the MCS white males were rated higher both on General Mental Ability (paralleling their SCAT performance) and on Range of Interests. There were no differences in the dimensions of Written Communication Skills between the MPS group and MCS group (either total or white males).

It was surprising that the MCS group did not score lower on the Advancement Motivation factor, given the many indications of their lesser ambition. They were indeed rated lower on the dimension of Need for Advancement, but on several other dimensions in this factor (Energy, Ability to Delay Gratification, and Realism of Expectations), there were no significant differences, and the MCS group showed a trend toward lesser Need for Security. As a consequence, the Need for Advancement difference was swamped by the other scores in the factor.

Not a surprise was the lack of group differences on the Work Involvement factor, with no differences on average dimension ratings of either Primacy of Work or Inner Work Standards. Although the Occupational life theme had pointed to more work involvement on the part of the MCS participants, there were no significant differences between the generations on the interview rating of Primacy of Work or the projective rating of Work Orientation.

Two of the three personality factors did show a difference between the MPS and MCS groups, with the MCS participants oriented toward greater Independence and Nonconformity. All three dimensions in the Independence factor showed sharp differences between the two generations, whether comparisons were with the total MCS group or the white males. The newer generation was notably less concerned with either superior or peer approval and rated less likely to be swayed from their life goals (lower on Goal Flexibility). On the Nonconformity factor, the MCS scores were also raised by their lesser Need for Superior Approval and the trend toward diminished Need for Security. The MCS total group was also rated higher on Social Objectivity, and the MCS white males displayed greater Range of Interests.

In terms of the MCS group's potential as managers, there were both pluses and minuses as compared to the previous generation. Certainly their involvement in work, energy, and resistance to conformity would be beneficial, as would their more advanced education and awareness of the outside world. Yet their lesser advancement motivation, relative lack of interest in leadership, and less developed leadership skills raise questions about their suitability for general management positions, especially at higher-level jobs.

In the final analysis, after the assessors had pooled their judgments in rating the dimensions, they made a number of predictions about the future careers of the MCS participants. These are shown in Table 9.4. In terms of overall potential, the assessors called it a draw between MPS and MCS. That is, the proportion rated "Should make middle management" (within 10 years)

Table 9.4   Assessment Predictions, MPS:0 and MCS:0

Prediction	MPS college (%)	MCS total (%)	MCS white males (%)
Should make middle management			
Yes	34	49	43
Questionable	19	10	12
No	47	42	44
Will make middle management		*	*
Yes	41	52	56
Questionable	12	11	7
No	47	37	37
Will stay with the company		*	
Yes	70	60	68
Questionable	9	11	9
No	22	29	23

* Significantly different from MPS at $p < .05$.

was about the same. Although the "yes" percentage looks larger for MCS, this is because of fewer in the "questionable" category, not any fewer in the "no" category.

In evaluating those who would actually be promoted to middle management, the assessors rated more MCS participants "yes" and fewer "no," showing an overall significant difference between the two generations. This was a function of at least two factors. First, the fast-track programs that many of the MCS participants were on made a commitment to promotion to the third level of management in 10 years or even less. Second, affirmative action policies might boost the promotion rates of women and minorities.

On the predictions of attrition, more of the total MCS group was predicted to leave, although this was not true for the white males. It was surprising that more white males were not rated as likely to leave, given their resistance to attaching themselves too readily to the company and their lower interest in job security. It may be that the troubled economy of the 1970s seemed to offer fewer opportunities for the MCS participants to find new positions readily, in spite of a greater inclination to do so.

After all the assessment data were in and the dimensions rated, the staff voted that Jeff would stay with the company, although he might be swayed by greater income elsewhere. It was thought that he would and should make middle management within 10 years. His strengths were seen as his quantitative ability and technical knowledge, his organizing and planning skills, his energy, and his response to a challenging situation where he could achieve something, especially on his own.

On the negative side, the assessors pointed to his low drive for advancement, his mediocre oral communication skills, and his tendency to be somewhat inflexible. They were concerned that he was stronger in technical skills than management skills and seemed to lack many of the person-oriented, leadership qualities required in management positions. His intelligence suggested that he would probably develop in decision making, but that his leadership skills might remain relatively weak without the motivation to improve them.

Compared to their counterparts in MPS, the overall assessment center picture for the MCS group, especially the white males, is of an intelligent group with advanced levels of education that was clearly as responsive to the challenge of work and as interested in doing a good job. Yet they were considerably less motivated to advance in the organization or to take on a leadership role. Perhaps as a consequence, their own abilities to perform the oral communication and leadership functions associated with management were not on a par with those of the preceding generation.

The MCS participants' expectations about their future as telephone company managers were far less rosy than those of their counterparts of the 1950s, while their views of themselves were overinflated. They desired interpersonal support but had considerably less interest in forming loyalties with their employer. They took a more autonomous stance and were less inclined to defer to higher authority. At the same time, they were less influenced by religion or the opportunity to perform community services and were less involved with their parental families. In short, they seemed more detached from all of society's institutions — business, community, church, and the parental family. Perhaps their need for the exchange of emotional support was a grasp at involvement with something meaningful.

THE VANTAGE POINT OF THE
BABY BOOM GENERATION

How did the MCS generation arrive at this particular pattern of characteristics? In Chapter 5 we have traced the historical events of the 1960s and 1970s, but there they are approached from the point of view of the MPS generation, who watched the world they knew in the 1950s being challenged and attacked from within. The MCS participants, part of the baby boom generation, were infants and young children in the 1950s, while their formative college years were in the 1970s. The culture of the 1970s would have a different meaning and impact for them than for the MPS men, who were well-established adults by that time.

College students in the 1970s, the later wave of baby boomers, were not the same as those in the 1960s. Campus student personnel administrators, when asked for comparisons of students in the late 1970s to those in the late

1960s, described the later crop as career-oriented and practical, concerned with self, motivated for material success, and well groomed (Levine, 1980).

There was evidence, though, that the younger baby boomers looked upon college life in the 1960s with some envy. Even though less than a third of the 1960s college students actually participated in any kind of demonstration, students in the 1970s compared themselves to a "mythical creature who walked our campuses a decade ago" (Levine, 1980, p. 5), a dreamer and hero who tried to change the world. But by the early 1970s, movement veterans were burned out, and students entering college had heard too much too long about racism and imperialism to be shocked by either (Matusow, 1984).

This is not to say that prior happenings had no impact on them; far from it. When asked what historical and political events had most influenced their views, students in the late 1970s most often cited Vietnam and Watergate, followed by civil rights, assassinations, and the 1960s protests. The most common response to Watergate was, in effect, "Politics and politicians are like that; Nixon just got caught" (Levine, 1980, p. 28).

This view represented the epidemic of cynicism that swept the campuses and many other parts of the country. A Harris poll showed that between 1966 and 1979, those expressing a great deal of confidence in leaders of social institutions dropped from 73% to 30% for medicine, 61% to 33% for higher education, 41% to 20% for organized religion, 55% to 18% for major companies, and 22% to 10% for organized labor (Levine, 1980). About the same time, one-third or more of college freshmen surveyed described large corporations, major labor unions, Congress, the U.S. president and his administration, and the national news media as considerably dishonest or immoral (Bachman & Johnston, 1979).

With such pessimistic views, it is not surprising that activities on campus had toned down: "Idealists may become revolutionaries, but cynics never" (Matusow, 1984, p. 343). There was still student activism in the 1970s, but it tended to be concerned with a multiplicity of local issues rather than national ones. Students were more concerned with their rights on campus than with issues like racism. They were also less violent, opting for litigation and lobbying rather than strikes, sit-ins, and building takeovers. The ideological or student groups were replaced by self-interest or me-oriented groups, who wanted to protect or improve the lot of a single group of people (Levine, 1980).

The pessimism of the later baby boom generation led to a heightened importance of money, illustrated by greater involvement in the Financial-Acquisitive life theme for the MCS group. Levine (1980, p. 103) describes this as "going first class on the Titanic." If they were doomed passengers on a sinking ship, they might just as well go out first class. But the meaning of money had changed. It was still valued for the enjoyment of possessions, travel, leisure, and the like, but it had lost much significance as a measure of success or for placing people in social strata (Yankelovich, 1981).

Although the early years for many in the baby boom generation were affluent, the reality of the 1970s was that they were likely to face a lifetime of limited resources, a struggling economy, and competition. They learned to want everything as children, but they found a huge gap between their aspirations and expectations. This was reflected in the generally lower Expectations Inventory scores achieved by the MCS participants compared to the MPS cohort.

The realization on the part of college students in the 1970s that they might not achieve what they set out to do discouraged their willingness to try, and they wound up with an anxiety syndrome of high aspirations and low motivation. Perceiving that they might not be able to get ahead in work, they self-protectively turned away from the external symbols of success and emphasized internal ones (Jones, 1980). Hence the tendency for the MCS group to report lesser desires for advancement or for moving into leadership roles.

There is other evidence of the decline in motivation to advance and become leaders. In a series of studies of business students, Miner has traced a decline in the motivation to manage that began in the 1960s and leveled out in the early 1970s. Decreases were most conspicuous in attitudes toward authority, competitiveness, assertiveness, and the desire to perform routine communication and decision-making functions (Miner & Smith, 1982).

When the Protestant work ethic prevailed, people used to believe that self-denial, sacrifice, obeying the rules, and subordinating the self to the institution made sense. In the cynical 1970s, they began to believe that such an arrangement needlessly restricted the individual while advancing the power of large institutions, especially government and business. Some became convinced that the old value system depersonalized the individual — a theme from the existential critique of modern society and the Marxist critique of capitalist society (Yankelovich, 1979).

Climbing the socioeconomic ladder might be success as others saw it, but it clashed with the philosophy of self-fulfillment. Old-style success required subordinating the self to external goals, not cultivating it (Yankelovich, 1981). The children of those who were dubbed "workaholics" swore that they would not trade life for financial success (Veroff et al., 1981).

Yet people knew what they wanted in the 1950s and 1960s, while in the 1970s they did not. Instead of clear ideas of what constituted success, there was an amorphous, elusive notion of fulfilling one's potential, of having a duty to oneself to grow psychologically and spritually. This self-fulfillment philosophy has also had its share of criticism: "There is no 'real' me. . . . By concentrating day and night on your feelings, potentials, needs, wants and desires, and by learning to assert them more freely, you do not become a freer, more spontaneous, more creative self; you become a narrower, more self-centered, more isolated one. You do not grow, you shrink" (Yankelovich, 1981, p. 242). Enthusiasts for self-fulfillment become not free spirits but conformists in disguise, argued Schnall (1981), locked into a compulsive, self-indulgent and pleasure-seeking value system of their peers. Even sexual freedom was not liberating; in the age of *Looking for Mr. Goodbar* (Rossner, 1975), women didn't gain the right to do as they pleased as much as they lost the right to say "no."

One price of such freedom of choice was anxiety; the level of worry among those 21—39 years of age rose from 30% in 1957 to 50% in 1976 (Veroff *et al.*, 1981). The baby boom generation seemed plagued by uncertainty, unsure what they should be (Jones, 1980), as the interview with Jeff revealed.

The baby boom generation also lost perspective about themselves, in accordance with the lower assessment ratings of Self-Objectivity demonstrated for the MCS group. Grade inflation began in the 1960s and continued into the 1970s, yet three out of five students still felt that their grades underrated the quality of their coursework. They exhibited "a misplaced sense of entitlement, a confusion of aspiration with accomplishment, and a loss of perspective about what constitutes merit" (Levine, 1980, pp., 72—73). In spite of dramatically declining Scholastic Aptitude Test scores, writing ability, and math achievement and problem solving during the 1970s, an increasing number of undergraduates described themselves as intellectuals (Levine, 1980).

Baby boomers also had difficulty making individual commitments, in light of their unsureness above their own identities. Marriages were postponed (also due to the increased freedom of women from economic dependence on men), and baby boomers have played a large role in the divorce epidemic. Childbearing was postponed or avoided, since many in the generation rejected the parental model of sacrificing themselves for their children (Jones, 1980). At the height of the postwar baby boom there were 23.7 babies per 1,000 women of childbearing age, but a baby bust was in evidence by 1978, when the numbers were reduced to 15.3 per 1,000 (White, 1982). "They fear being claimed, this generation. How ridiculous" (Doctorow, 1984).

The thinning of social commitment and investment produced increased sensitivity to interpersonal relations. A desire grew for warm relationships at work and in the family (Veroff *et al.*, 1981). The liberation of sex moved rapidly in the 1970s from the celebration of random promiscuity to a need for enduring emotional bonds. There was a new respect for "webs of relationships that provided collective support and warmth" (Carroll, 1982, p. 296). This trend, too, was reflected in the increased Nurturance and Succorance scores on the part of the MCS group.

The search for individualism also resulted in greater diversity. Students on college campuses were more different as individuals than ever before, and this brought little sense of a shared collegiate culture (Levine, 1980). This greater diversity is clearly seen when comparing the MPS and MCS groups on a variety of measures used in the study, including the dimension ratings, personality questionnaires, projective exercises, the Expectations Inventory, Work Conditions Survey, biographical data, and life themes ratings. The MCS group was more heterogeneous than the last generation, even when a comparison is made of just the white males. This greater variability has been described as follows (Howard & Bray, 1980):

> From the photographs of the assessees of more than 20 years ago, crew cuts and clean shaven faces peer back at us with skinny ties trimly adorning pressed, white shirts. It seemed as if most of these men were political conservatives who wanted a homemaker wife, children, and to be Mr. Telephone in their local communities. Off-the-job they fished and went to church.
>
> By comparison the new generation explodes with diversity. Some are still just like the men of the past, others extremely different. Beards and black faces and long female hair have joined our crew cuts in the photographs of men and women in business suits, sports jackets, pants suits, and dresses ranging from wildly colorful to staunchly traditional. They may be right wingers, or Marxists, or disgusted with the whole idea of politics. There were women who want to be Vice President and men whose hobby is home decorating. They may aspire to running for the state legislature or returning to school for a degree in speech pathology. There are homosexuals and vegetarians, amateur botanists and horse trainers" (p. 13).

The MCS participants are young representatives of an increasingly multi-faceted and complex culture. There will be no simple formulas for managing such a varied group.

THE AT&T LONG LINES PARTICIPANTS

Before leaving this chapter, it is appropriate to consider the group that was generally left out of the MCS analyses, the 47 participants from the AT&T Long Lines department. As mentioned in Chapter 1, this group was treated separately from the other MCS participants in the various data analyses because there was no comparable group in MPS. The Long Lines participants did not differ from those in the telephone companies by demographic subgroup; approximately one-third were minorities (27.7% black, 8.5% Hispanic), and nearly half were women (46.8%). However, the results for this group were notably different.

An overview of these differences is shown in Figure 9.6, which plots average scores on the dimension factors for the telephone company sample and the AT&T Long Lines sample. The AT&T group was rated considerably higher on almost every dimension factor. Very strong differences were shown on the Administrative Skills, Interpersonal Skills, Advancement Motivation, Work Involvement, and Stability of Performance factors, with somewhat smaller differences shown on the Independence and Nonconformity factors. Only on the Intellectual Ability factor were the differences not statistically significant, probably due to the fact that the AT&T Long Lines group was at the time of the assessment not being screened before hire by a mental ability test.

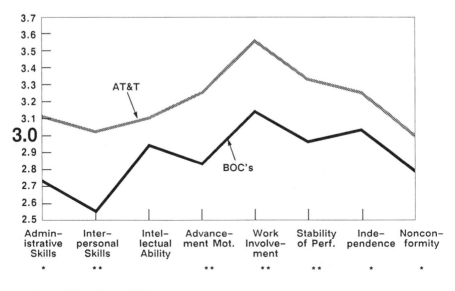

*p < .05.   **p < .005.

Figure 9.6.   MCS:0 Dimension Factors, Bell Operating Companies and AT&T Long Lines.

Many dimensions contributed to the differences in average scores on the dimension factors, supported by various test scores and exercise ratings. Within the Administrative Skills factor, Decision Making was the primary dimension where the Long Lines group was superior to the other MCS participants. None of the dimensions in the Intellectual Ability factor nor related tests showed significant differences between the two groups.

Leadership Skills, Oral Communication Skills, Behavior Flexibility, and Forcefulness contributed to the higher ratings of the Long Lines group on the Interpersonal Skills factor; they were rated no higher than the other MCS participants on Social Objectivity, Perception of Threshold Social Cues, or Likeableness. Thus the Long Lines group succeeded interpersonally more by being dynamic and forward than by being sensitive or agreeable. Several test scores support this idea, since they scored higher on the Edwards scales of Dominance and Autonomy and came close to scoring lower ($p < .06$) on Nurturance. Similarly, on the G-Z they scored higher on the Ascendance scale but lower on the Friendliness scale than the telephone company participants, while on the projective exercises they were rated higher on Leadership Role and lower on Subordinate Role.

On the motivational dimensions, the Long Lines group had considerably higher ratings on Need for Advancement, Primacy of Work, Financial Motivation, and Energy, and much lower ratings on Need for Security and Ability to

Delay Gratification. They were only slightly higher than the other MCS participants on Inner Work Standards, and were no different from the rest on Bell System Value Orientation. Ratings from the projective exercises showed them higher on Achievement/Advancement Motivation and Work Orientation. Thus the Long Lines group was highly committed to work and clearly desirous of the extrinsic rewards that corporate life could bring. This may explain why they were also rated higher on the Selfishness dimension.

Within the Stability of Performance factor, the Long Lines group was rated higher on Resistance to Stress but not on Tolerance of Uncertainty. Contributing to their higher ratings on the Independence factor was lower Need for Peer Approval; they did not differ from the other MCS participants on Need for Superior Approval nor on the Edwards Deference scale.

When the assessors made their final judgments about the Long Lines participants, they rated nearly three-fourths as having potential for middle management or higher, compared to about half of the telephone company sample. Nearly one-third of the Long Lines group was thought to have potential beyond the third level, compared to only 12% of the telephone company sample.

What accounts for these extraordinary differences? One thing that is clear is that the Long Lines college recruiters were being much more selective in terms of whom they invited to the company. The recruiters were known to work carefully with college placement officers to be sure that only the "cream of the crop" were referred to them for interviews. Secondly, the department had a high-risk, high-reward program, which was based on the same model as the one used to recruit Jeff (derived from MPS), but implemented with higher risks and higher rewards than was typical in the telephone company programs. Many of the recruits began their careers acting in second-level jobs, which provided them with considerably more challenge than the usual first-level jobs. It is highly likely that such a program would attract risk takers who valued advancement highly and were confident they could meet the rigorous test of performance in the Long Lines environment.

Various kinds of biographical information point to the standards used to select the Long Lines candidates. The majority of the recruits (63.8%) had master's degrees, primarily MBA's. It is likely that many had been oriented to business positions in their youth, since nearly half had fathers in business management occupations. However, the Long Lines recruits were less likely than the telephone company participants to have been business majors as undergraduates; their undergraduate majors were more often engineering or subjects within the humanities or social sciences. Undergraduate grades for the Long Lines recruits were slightly higher than those of the telephone company group. Nevertheless, the Long Lines candidates participated in more extracurricular activities in college and held more leadership positions in them.

The comparison to the AT&T Long Lines sample with those from the telephone companies underscores the tremendous diversity within this new generation. Another part of their heterogeneity comes, of course, from a significant population of women and minorities in the management ranks. In the next chapter we take up the issue of gender differences, to be followed in Chapter 11 by a consideration of differences among ethnic and racial subgroups.

CHAPTER 10

Men and Women in Management

A major and very visible difference between the college recruits of the 1950s and the 1970s was that being male was no longer a requirement for the kinds of jobs that might lead to advancement to higher levels of management. When the telephone companies were asked to provide a sample for the MCS assessment, they were given no instructions as to how many men or women to include; the only proviso was that the sample should be representative of current intake. When 186 men and 158 women showed up for the assessment, it was clear that times had changed. Women were not merely represented among new management trainees; they constituted 46% of new college graduates hired directly into management. Furthermore, just as many women as men were enlisted in the fast-track programs that promised, if they performed well, to bring them to middle-management positions in a fairly short time.

It was especially true during the 1950s, the era so vividly described in Betty Friedan's *The Feminine Mystique* (1963), that women were not thought to have the necessary skills or temperament to succeed in management jobs. The women's revolution in the 1960s and 1970s succeeded in challenging those assumptions. Yet it remained for women to be put to the test in management to see if they could handle such jobs and stick with them. When the men and women arrived at the MCS assessment center, it was of great interest to see how their talents and dispositions compared, especially in the simulations of the tasks they would be required to perform as middle-level managers.

There were, of course, the expected differences in physical appearance. The male bodies were distributed on frames that were on the average 5′ 11″ tall and 174 pounds, while the females reached only 5 feet 5 inches on the average and weighed in at 126 pounds. The women were about 2 years younger than the men, their ages ranging from 21 to 43 with a median of 24. The men ranged in age from 21 to 37 and had a median age of 26.

BACKGROUNDS

An initial question was whether or not the men and women came from the same types of backgrounds and had the same opportunities in terms of education and personal experiences that would prepare them for managerial positions. There was no overall difference between the sexes in the educational or occupational levels of their parents. The men's families did move around a little more (they lived in 3.7 dwellings on the average before they were 16 years of age compared to 3.1 for the women). The MCS men came from somewhat larger families (they had 3.3 siblings on the average, compared to 2.7 for the women).

Fathers of the MCS participants had more influence over their sons than their daughters; although 45% of both the men and women participants named both parents as having equal influence over them, 21% of the men said their fathers had the most influence compared to 8% of the women. Yet even among the men, mothers were more influential overall than fathers: 31% of the men named their mothers as most influential in their upbringing, compared to 45% of the women.

The situation for parental discipline was slightly different. Again, about half of both gender groups said both parents provided the discipline (52% of the men and 48% of the women). Where one parent was singled out as providing the discipline, the men more often cited their fathers (28% fathers, 18% mothers), while the women more often cited their mothers (18% fathers, 33% mothers).

To illustrate some of the gender differences described in this chapter, we go to the composite character of Jackie, a white female, who is compared to Jeff, the typical MCS white male reviewed in Chapter 9.

Jackie, a trim 23-year-old woman, had a multitude of freckles and short, light brown curly hair that aptly echoed her bubbly personality. She spoke freely and became quite involved during the interview. She went into more detail than needed on a number of occasions and seemed to have difficulty controlling this tendency. Her liveliness and energy were conveyed in facial expressions and arm gestures. She seemed a blithe spirit, given to humor, and eager to participate in the discussion of her life.

Jackie's father was a third-level manager with the Chesapeake & Potomac Telephone Company. She described him as an intelligent man but one who could be somewhat short-tempered. Nevertheless, he was a caring person and one she respected as honest, hard-working, and dedicated to his career and his family.

Of her mother, Jackie said, "She's a great lady — a mom that's really a mom." A model in her younger days, she spent the years when Jackie was growing up as a housewife. Recently she had become a real estate agent, which she did on a part-time basis, primarily for pleasure but also with appreciation for the extra income.

There were four children in Jackie's family, and Jackie was the youngest. Her two older sisters were separated from her by 9 and 11 years, so she felt closest to her brother, who was 5 years older. All the children had gone to college, but the two older sisters had given up their original career plans to raise families. Jackie's brother was an accountant for a medium-sized firm in Washington, D.C.

Jackie had many friends as a child and numerous school accomplishments to her credit. Her parents stressed good grades, and she expected the best performance for herself. The family lived in Baltimore throughout the early years of her childhood in what she described as a close-knit neighborhood. Everybody in the building knew everyone else, and people watched out for each other. This made playing on the streets more acceptable and much more fun than it would have been had the neighborhood been less intimate. Boys and girls played together, rather than separating by sex, and they all enjoyed city games like jumprope, hopscotch, and freeze tag. She attended a Catholic elementary school.

About the time she reached junior high school age, Jackie's father was transferred to Chesapeake & Potomac's central headquarters in Washington, and the family moved to a suburb in Virginia. Jackie was excited about this move, but she soon discovered that "the suburbs are not all they're cracked up to be. My high school was far more wild than anything I had previously experienced in the city. The kids in seventh grade knew all about sex and cursed a lot, which was in sharp contrast to the more protected environment of my Catholic school."

A comparison of educational backgrounds for the two sexes is shown in Table 10.1. In high school, the women were the better students. More than three-quarters characterized their grades as "excellent," compared to about half of the men; only 2% of the women said their grades were "fair" or "poor," compared to 14% of the men. When asked about their best and worst subjects in high school, the men were somewhat more likely to do well in science and the women in the humanities. The women participated in slightly more extracurricular activities than did the men (5.1 on the average for the men, compared to 6.0 for the women), although the men were more likely to be involved in athletic endeavors.

The women also had better grades in college. Some 54% of the women rated their grades as "excellent," compared to 39% of the men, and their overall grade point average was 3.38, compared to 3.24 for the men. This tendency also held up in graduate school, where 69% of the women described their grades as "excellent," compared to 54% of the men.

There were some differences between the sexes in undergraduate majors. Although it might have been expected that more women than men would major in the humanities and social sciences, there were also more women math majors than men (15% of the women, 7% of the men). The reason for the discrepancy is best explained by taking into account the greater proportion of men than women (22% vs. 8%) with engineering majors. Since engineering has not often been a major selected by women, it was difficult for the telephone companies to find women to fill their more technically oriented entry positions. Hence one solution was to hire math majors and provide them with additional technical training on the job. There were no meaningful differences between men and women in number of extracurricular activities or number of leadership activities in college, with the exception of athletic activities (where the men were more involved, as they had been in high school).

Jackie reported positively about her high school experiences. She said "I got into lots of activities, including making scenery for a theatre group, the French Club, the

Table 10.1   Educational Background Variables Differentiating MCS
Males and Females

Variable	Males	Females
High school grades		
Excellent	53%	80%
Good	33%	18%
Fair or poor	14%	2%
College grades		
Excellent	39%	50%
Good	48%	40%
Fair or poor	13%	10%
College grade point average (mean)	3.24	3.38
College major		
Humanities	5%	10%
Social science	16%	22%
Science	7%	5%
Math	7%	15%
Engineering	22%	8%
Business	39%	31%
Education	1%	8%
Graduate school grades		
Excellent	54%	69%
Good	39%	31%
Fair or poor	7%	0%

Note. On all variables differences between groups significant at $p < .05$.

Pompom Girls, the yearbook, and committees for homecoming and the prom. I was also a student senator (a member of the student government) and did some debating on a competitive team. On Saturdays I worked in a shoe store. Still, I managed to be a top student without working too hard at it."

After high school, Jackie decided to leave her family's area and attend a university in Florida. Again she got involved in multiple activities, many of which stemmed from her sorority membership. The yearbook and a debating team attracted her again, and she served one year as a student director of special events, bringing in concerts, lectures, and other public events to the university campus. She began academically as an English major but switched to retailing, feeling it was more practical and something women tended to go into. She discovered that the retailing courses were easy and boring, and she was much more interested in general business courses. She then changed to being a finance major in the business school.

LIFESTYLES

The relative involvement by the two sexes on the nine life themes coded from their interviews is shown in Figure 10.1. Both the Marital-Familial and

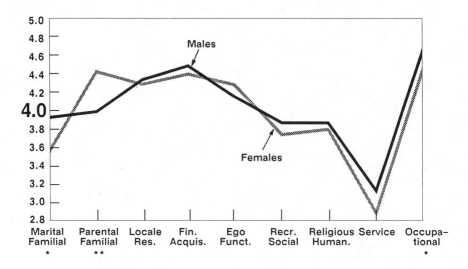

*p < .05.   **p < .005.

Figure 10.1.   Current involvement in life themes at MCS:0, males and females.

Parental-Familial life themes showed meaningful differences, with the men more involved in the marital family and the women more involved in the parental family.

The men's involvement with marriage and family was greater than the women's, both in the past and currently, and they were also more satisfied with their marital lives. A primary reason was that more men were married at the time of assessment, as shown in Table 10.2. Almost two-thirds of the women had never been married, compared to less than half the men. The divorce and separation rate was the same for both sexes, as was the incidence of cohabiting. Nevertheless, when only married participants were compared on the Marital-Familial life theme, the men still showed greater current satisfaction and anticipated more future involvement with their marital families than did the women.

The women tended to marry men of the same or higher educational level; only 20% had spouses with less than a college education, and half of these had at least some college training. More than half the husbands of the MCS women had a graduate degree. By contrast, nearly half the wives of the men in the study had not graduated from college, and only one-quarter had graduate degrees.

Occupations of spouses also differed depending on whether they were male or female. Housework was a primary occupation for none of the husbands but 20% of the wives. Among the wives who worked, 12% were in clerical positions and 17% in business management. Among the husbands who

Involvement in the Ego-Functional or Recreational-Social life themes did not differ by sex, but the biographical data indicated that these activities took a somewhat different form for each gender. The women reported more social activities, amusements, and participation in the arts, while the men were more apt to be involved in outdoor recreation. Consistent with this, more men than women (24% vs. 14%) indicated that they "fairly often" or "often" put themselves through some sort of physical strain. The women's reports of excess were more likely to relate to food. Overeating was claimed to be the case "often" or "fairly often" for 21% of the women but only 8% of the men. The wrong foods were eaten "often" or "fairly often" by 34% of the women and 18% of the men.

The women reported more hours of off-the-job reading than the men. In fact, they reported having read three books on the average in the 2 months prior to assessment, compared to only two for the men. But the men indicated they read more newspapers on a regular basis (1.6 for the men, compared to 1.3 for the women) and were more interested in current events. This was supported by ratings of political understanding in the interviews, where the men surpassed the women with an average rating of 2.9, compared to the women's 2.5. The men were also rated higher on political conviction (3.2 vs. 2.8).

Much of Jackie's free time was spent at the pool in her apartment complex. Other favorite activities were outdoor concerts in the summer and baking or doing needlework in the winter.

Jackie claimed that she also liked to read. She said, "I always have a good novel I'm working on. Right now I'm reading *The Moneychangers*. I also read nonfiction, like *The Joy of Money* and *Against Our Will: Men, Women and Rape*. My favorite magazines are *Ms., Psychology Today, Glamour, Redbook, Working Woman*, and *Newsweek*.

The men's involvement in the Service life theme was not significantly higher than the women's at the time of assessment. They were rated slightly higher in retrospective developments, indicating more past concern for community activities than the women.

The men's political views tended to be more conservative than those of the women, with nearly two-fifths indicating on questionnaires that they agreed with the Republican or conservative points of view, compared to less than one-fourth of the women. One-third of the women identified with Democratic or liberal viewpoints, compared to one-fifth of the men. More than two-fifths of each group indicated they were middle-of-the-roaders, sometimes identifying with the Democrats and sometimes with the Republicans.

Ratings of the interviews on sociocultural attitudes showed a similar tendency for the women to be more liberal than the men. On overall political philosophy the men were rated 3.2 (on a 5-point scale, with high scores more conservative) and the women 2.8. The difference was quite pronounced for

Table 10.2   Marital Background Variables Differentiating MCS
Males and Females

Variable	Males (%)	Females (%)
Marital status		
Never married	46	62
Married to first spouse	44	28
Divorced or separated	7	7
Cohabiting	3	3
Spouse education		
Postgraduate degree	26	57
College graduate	29	24
Less than college graduate	45	20
Spouse occupation		
Housekeeper	20	0
Clerical	12	0
Business	17	55
Professional	31	20

worked, none were in clerical jobs and more than half were in business management. Thus the married MCS women were much more likely than the men to have spouses similar to them in education and occupation.

Jackie was not married, but was involved with a man who had been a friend of her brother in high school. He was a CPA with an undergraduate degree in accounting. His career was important to him, as hers was to her; nevertheless each had indicated a willingness to relocate if the other got a good economic offer.

Jackie thought they would eventually get married, although they had no specific plans then. She added, "I don't expect us to have any children until I'm about 30. Right now I can't picture myself as a mother, but maybe I'll grow into the parenthood role. If I do have children, I wouldn't consider staying at home, although I might consider working part-time for a while. Of course, if I kept working full-time, with both our salaries, we ought to be able to afford a nanny."

The women were more involved with their parental families than the men, whether this involvement was rated for the past, rated for the present, or projected for the future. There was no difference between the sexes in current satisfaction with the parental family. The old adage seemed to be true in MCS that parents don't lose daughters, they just (when their daughters marry) gain sons.

Though Jeff seldom saw his parents or brothers and sister, Jackie visited her parents as often as she could and talked to them weekly by phone. Her brother lived in the city where she worked, and she saw him at least once a week.

social issues (men 2.7, women 2.2) but was not significant for economic issues.

The women were much more favorable than the men toward a woman's right to have an abortion if she so chose (average favorableness rating 3.2 for men, 4.0 for women). More than half the women providing a rationale for their position stated that a woman has a right to decide for herself and that the government should not intervene (over one-third of the men also offered this point of view). But 18% of the men said abortion was acceptable only when there was a physical risk to the mother or in case of rape (5% of the women agreed), and 16% of the men equated abortion with murder (5% of the women agreed).

The women tended to be more favorable toward ERA (men rated it 3.4, women 3.8), although the difference was not quite statistically significant. In presenting rationales for their positions, many more women were inclined to mention equal pay for equal work (15% of the men and 41% of the women who offered rationales).

Jeff equivocated on his support for ERA. He said, "Even though I support the intent of the legislation, the proposed amendment is too broad and general and subject to all sorts of misinterpretations. I think women should be paid equally for the same job as men, but they shouldn't be in the Army. If I were on the front line, I wouldn't want to be placed in a position where I would have to force a woman to fight."

Jackie was more positive. She said, "It's dismaying that this amendment has not yet been passed. It seems that people are afraid to change the status quo. I certainly support equal pay for equal work but also equal jobs. The amendment would entail equality in all areas, including responsibility for national defense. I see nothing wrong with a draft for women, although I think they should be fully combat-qualified. I think the amendment is necessary to overcome the natural tendency to favor the male."

Although neither gender group was favorable to the Moral Majority, the women were more opposed to it than the men (men were rated 2.2, women were rated 1.5 in favorableness on a 5-point scale). About one-third of each sex group citing reasons for their feelings felt that the Moral Majority was too extreme and did not speak for the majority of Americans. But more than half the women opposed the movement's desire to dictate values and control others, compared to only about one-third of the men. Another third of the men mentioned they felt the Moral Majority had a right to express their opinions, but only one of the women mentioned this.

Jeff felt the Moral Majority had been unfairly characterized by the media. "I believe in some of their programs," he said, "but I think they have to be more separated from the church. Religion has too often consisted of money-mongers who try to impose their values in the name of Jesus Christ when they are really in the name of big money. I think they are quite sincere, though, and should be free to have their own beliefs."

Jackie made a shuddering noise when she mentioned the name of the Moral Majority, saying, "I think they're dangerous because they're so narrow-minded. They live in an environment that is totally male-dominated and that has very restrictive views about sexuality and religion. Where do they get off thinking they can tell everyone what to do? They just don't have that right."

The average MCS male favored Ronald Reagan and his administration (rated 3.5 in favorability) while the average MCS female was slightly opposed (rated 2.9). More women than men opposed his economic policies and cuts in social programs as well as his foreign policy, which was considered too aggressive and war-mongering.

Jeff said, "I believe in Reagan's economic policies, although I'm looking over my shoulder for hungry protesters! I think we're giving people too many handouts, though I feel mildly guilty about some elderly people and those in truly desperate straits who actually deserve benefits. I really wasn't particularly happy with the late 1960s political attitudes, and I'm happy the country seems to be entering a new era of conservatism. I'm basically in agreement with Reagan's policy of a military buildup as well and was frustrated with Carter's lack of activity. I didn't like having sand kicked up in our faces; Iran should have been flattened into a desert."

"Reagan bothers me because he is uninformed and short-sighted," said Jackie. "His tax decisions are only favorable for the affluent. The middle-income people don't benefit. He's so intent on putting a stop to the fraud in government and digging so deeply, he's hurting the folks who need help. He's not sufficiently compassionate, probably because he's never been poor. The cuts are in the wrong places; reducing the size of the school lunch is wrong. He's hurting a lot of people who can't fight and don't have lobbyists in Washington. He could cut a lot of other things like defense spending, where they buy obsolete weapons. Anyway, he scares me because his defense policies could lead to a war."

On military stance, the men were more likely to be "hawks" than the women (3.1 vs. 2.1 in interview ratings). In accordance with this position, more of the men favored U.S. support of Israel, though neither group was very positive (men were rated 2.5, women 1.8).

Jeff said, "I think Israel is a spunky little country, and I wouldn't mind seeing the PLO chased out of Lebanon. The Israeli use of U.S. weapons in the Middle East is a wonderful way of showing the Russians that our weapons are far superior to theirs."

"I'm afraid World War III will break out in the Middle East," said Jackie. "They're all out of their minds. I don't see why we're an ally to Israel — they're so aggressive. But their lobbies are strong."

WORK INTERESTS

The men were rated higher on involvement in the Occupational life theme, as shown in Figure 10.1, but the difference was greater in projected developments on that theme. Here the men had an average rating of 4.4 on the 7-point scale, compared to 3.7 for the women. This is consistent with survey research on national samples indicating that men have greater commitment to work than women at various age, educational, and occupational prestige levels (Lacy, Bokemeier, & Shepard, 1983).

The women indicated much greater ambivalence in their interviews about the importance of their jobs and careers in the future, when they would have to face such issues as relocations due to their own or their husbands' careers; the question of whether or not they would have families; and, if so, the integration of child care into a busy work life. Most of the women were unmarried and childless at the time of assessment, so they were not facing these issues then, only anticipating them.

In questionnaire items about possible future relocations due to job changes, the men were consistently more positive than the women. For moves where no promotion was involved, 73% of the married women said they would be "unfavorable" or "very unfavorable" toward such a move, compared to 46% of the married men. Only 11% of the married women would be negative toward a move with a promotion, although 21% said their families would be negative. Comparable figures for the men were 9% and 16%. Only 5% of the married women said their families would be very favorable to such a move compared to 29% of the married men.

The men and women did not vary in their number of previous jobs before coming to the telephone company, although only 1% of the women had served in the military, compared to 22% of the men. When they arrived at the telephone company for initial job placement, their assignments were widespread, and one sex was generally not placed much differently from the other. However, there were notable discrepancies in a few departments. More than one-quarter of the men were placed in the Engineering or Installation Departments, traditionally quite male-dominated in the telephone companies, compared to less than 10% of the women. By contrast, 11% of the women were placed in Marketing, compared to only 6% of the men.

After graduation, Jackie interviewed with a number of organizations, including eight banks. The salary offers from the banks were not particularly good, however, and she narrowed down her choice to the Bell System (inspired by her father) and a popular national magazine. She said, "At first the magazine job looked very promising for advancement, but I finally decided it would make me too specialized and I'd have difficulty moving on to another company. The job at Southern Bell looked like it offered real management experience and a chance to work in a large corporation. I thought I would enjoy being in Atlanta, and it seemed that many of the women were able to balance career with family obligations."

After only a few days on the job, Jackie went to a basic sales training course for 7 weeks. After this she was assigned to the role of market administrator. Although she had no subordinates, she was a coordinator of functions supplied by installers, engineers, the business office, and customer services.

Jackie described her job this way: "If there's a business that needs a new telephone system, my job is to do all the paperwork. I do the orders and make sure the job is engineered. I talk to the customer about the nature of his business and make sure that a system is designed that will meet the customer's needs. Then I coordinate the 'cut' with the foreman. I make sure the orders are given to the right people, set up training with the business office, then make sure the people in the field are aware of what is going on. I check out the site and see that there is sufficient wiring and that all facilities are adequate.

"Then on the day of installation and the next day I'm there to solve problems for the customer and to calm everyone down when they panic! On big cuts I also go over the entire first bill before the customer gets it so that the customer will not have to bother with trying to weed out errors in a bill that he doesn't understand." She actually served as a support person for the account executive, who had total market responsibility.

Expectations

When asked on the Expectations Inventory what they most and least wanted to characterize their managerial careers 5 years hence, the men and women agreed on about two-thirds of the items. These items, as well as the ones where they differed significantly, are shown in Table 10.3.

Among the most desirable items, more men than women wanted to have deep friendships with at least two or three work associates. More women than men indicated the desirability of having a chance to follow their basic interests, having experience in different types of work and more than one division of the company, and having a challenging job with many opportunities to learn and do new things. These preferences are certainly contrary to customary stereotypes, with the women focusing on interesting work experiences and more of the men (though not many) interested in friendships. Women's greater preference for meaningful and challenging work has been found in other recent research (Jurgensen, 1978; Lacy et al., 1983; Siegfried, Macfarlane, Graham, Moore, & Young, 1981), although past research data have generally been inconsistent with respect to male and female job preferences.

The men's and women's expectations about whether their most desired outcomes would be achieved were similar, with statistically significant differences in average ratings on only 3 of the 11 top items. The men were more sure of earning $35,000 or more at the end of the 5 years than were the women, but the women were more sure that they would have gone back to school for additional courses and that they would have a challenging job.

On the most undesired items, the men indicated that they would find it more disturbing to have to travel and be away from home a lot of the time, probably because more of the men were married and resisted leaving their spouses. The men were also more concerned that they might earn less than $30,000 per year. More women were concerned that they would have too

Table 10.3   Responses to Most Important Items in Expectations Inventory at MCS:0, Males and Females

Most desired items	% citing most desirable		% fairly certain of favorable outcome	
	Males	Females	Males	Females
I have deep frientships with at least two or three work associates.	23 *	13	52	48
I have a real chance to follow my basic interests and work at the things I like to do.	42 *	53	43	51
I live in a desirable community with relatively easy access to my job.	24	18	49	54
I have reached the district level of responsibility.[a]	46	41	40	37
I am earning $35,000 a year or more.	40	35	71 *	56
I have gone back to school for additional courses useful in my work.	25	29	55	58
I have had experience in different types of work and more than one division of the company.	22 *	34	41	41
My job is challenging with many opportunities to learn and do new things.	57 *	71	43 *	51
I am advanced about as rapidly as my interest and ability warrant.	37	41	24	28
My spouse is happy that I work for the Bell System.	26	20	44	37
I have a real chance to use my imagination and don't have to be concerned with traditional procedures.	22	19	15	7

Least desired items	% citing least desirable		% fairly certain of favorable outcome	
	Males	Females	Males	Females
I am in the department of the company in which I shall stay for the rest of my career.	21	27	35	36
I have too much invested in the company — both psychologically and materially — to feel free to move to another job.	23 *	34	25	17
I have fewer opportunities for promotion than if I had gone to work for a different company.	30	30	35 **	50

Table 10.3 (Cont'd)

Least desired items	% citing least desirable		% fairly certain of favorable outcome	
	Males	Females	Males	Females
I have to travel and be away from home a lot of the time.	29 *	13	17	14
I don't know what the company thinks of my potentialities.	18	23	38 *	53
I feel an increasing amount of conflict between obligations of my job and family.	50	48	26	22
The company doesn't provide sufficient opportunity for me to learn new things.	23	30	35	36
I am making less money than those in similar jobs in other companies.	18	24	42 *	50
I feel the company resists new ideas and experimentation.	16 *	28	25	29
I am earning less than $30,000 a year.	32 **	15	80 *	71
I regret not having gone to work for another company.	27	29	52	49
I have not reached as high a level of responsibility as most of those who started in the company when I did.	35	35	49	49

Note. Group differences in desirability computed from chi-square tests on proportions; expectations from *t* tests on means.

[a] The district level is the third of seven levels of management running from foreman to president.

* $p < .05$.

** $p < .005$.

much invested in the company, both psychologically and materially, to feel free to move to another job, suggesting that they were somewhat less loyal to the company than were the men. The women also indicated they would consider it more undesirable to find that the company resisted new ideas and experimentation.

In terms of their expectations regarding the undesirable items, the women were more optimistic than the men that their futures would not be blighted on 3 of the 12 most undesirable outcomes. The women were more positive in expecting that they would do better in terms of advancement and salary than those who went to work for other companies, and they felt more sure they would know what the company thought of their potentialities. But when it came to expectations about specific salary amounts, the men were again more sure of a positive outcome than the women, this time that they would not be earning less than $30,000 per year.

Attitudes and Work Preferences

Although average salaries for the men were about $1,000 higher than those of the women at the time of the assessment, the difference did not reach statistical significance. Interestingly, when the Management Questionnaire was administered in years 1—2 after the assessment, there was only one scale showing a sex difference: The women were *more* satisfied than the men with their salaries. Both sexes thought their salaries were adequate for their responsibilities, but the women were more likely to feel that the telephone company paid better than other businesses.

The apparent contradictions about salary, on both the Expectations Inventory and the Management Questionnaire, are best explained by taking into account the fact that in the United States in the late 1970s and early 1980s, women earned on average about three-fifths the salary of men. Within such a perspective, the MCS women would not expect that they would get better salaries at other companies; if other women were their comparison group, they were doing quite well indeed. The men could more easily entertain the idea of earning more money elsewhere, although on the average they, too, felt well paid as compared to those in other companies.

When asked to rate the desirability of more specific aspects of work on the Work Conditions Survey, the men showed more willingness to put up with undesirable situations. They were less negative toward monotonous work or that with lots of idleness, toward working under a strict or harsh boss, or toward work requiring great physical danger or endurance. Other research supports the notion that women care more about the physical environment and convenience factors such as working hours (Siegfried *et al.*, 1981; Walker, Tausky, & Oliver, 1982). The men were also less negative toward working with only one sex than were the women. Among the positive items, the men gave higher desirability ratings to having things depend on their decisions, while the women gave higher desirability ratings to work that was full of excitement.

When the three inventories are viewed together, the women seem more restless, wanting challenge, change, and excitement. They were also less tolerant of situations that would bore or irritate them or tie them down. Yet they were somewhat more optimistic than the men that opportunities for developing themselves would be present in the Bell System as compared to other jobs they might have taken, and they were more satisfied with their salaries. The men were more willing to tolerate undesirable situations at work. Although they were not as enthusiastic as the women about their salaries, they were more confident that their specific monetary expectations would be met. Except for salary, there were no differences in job satisfaction between the sexes, consistent with what has frequently been found elsewhere (Weaver, 1977).

Jackie was mainly concerned about her own development and being challenged on the job. She said, "I just don't want to be bored. This is why I like the fast-track program. They keep you moving so you can't get bored." A negative for her, though, was the long hours that were often required, which she said were "bumming me out."

PERSONALITY AND MOTIVATION

It may be recalled from Chapter 9 that the paper-and-pencil measures of personality and motivation differed somewhat between MPS and MCS. The new managers were administered the Edwards, Bass, and Sarnoff questionnaires as before, but the G-Z was substituted for the GAMIN, and the CPI was added as an additional source of information. The same TAT pictures were given to the males in MCS as in MPS, but a few pictures depicting women rather than men were substituted for the benefit of the MCS females. The same projective ratings were used for both the male and female responses; again, they were applied to reports that synthesized responses to the TAT stories and to the two sets of incomplete sentences. Two additional projective ratings were added to the nine made for the MPS reports: Willingness to Reveal Self and Aggression/Hostility.

Because of the addition of the other scales, a new factor analysis was conducted of the personality and motivation variables used with the MCS sample. In addition to the 15 Edwards scales, 3 from the Sarnoff, and the Bass Authoritarianism score, there were 10 scales of the G-Z, 22 of the CPI, 11 ratings from the projective exercises, and the 4 motivational ratings from the interviews. Five of the new factors were very similar to those found for MPS. The MPS Self-Esteem factor did not appear, since it was based primarily on the GAMIN, which was not used with MCS.

Summaries of the five factors for MCS similar to those for MPS follow. Note that these factor summaries include statements suggesting that certain behaviors, feelings, and motivations are highly related to standing on the factors. This has not, of course, been demonstrated. The statements are intended to convey the essence of the factors, not to imply that behavior is necessarily predictable from them. Some factors are based, in large part, on self-concept.

Submissiveness: Somewhat the flip side of the MPS factor of Leadership Motivation, with the projective ratings of Subordinate Role, Dependence, and Affiliation rated high, plus Aggression/Hostility rated low. High scorers on this factor show dependence on others and liking for a subordinate role, along with a lack of aggressiveness.

Positiveness: High ratings of Adjustment, Optimism, and Self-Confidence from the projective exercises. As with the factor for MPS, high scorers show an optimistic and positive approach to life and better overall coping and adjustment. They have high interest in their work and confidence about being able to handle various tasks.

Impulsivity: Similar to Impulsivity for MPS, including high scores on the

Edwards Exhibition and Heterosexuality scales and low scores on the Endurance and Deference scales. It excluded the low Abasement score from the Edwards, but included low Intraception from the Edwards and low Restraint and Thoughtfulness from the G-Z. High scorers like to stand out in a crowd and tend to show off. They also enjoy interactions with the opposite sex and jokes about sex. They are less likely to be orderly or restrained, or to think before acting. High scorers are also less deferent to authority, unconcerned with job security, and not very persistent with tasks.

Affability: Included three of the four Edwards scales that loaded on this factor for MPS (high Nurturance and Affiliation and low Aggression scores) and two additional ones (high Succorance and low Achievement). Those scoring high take pleasure in doing things with and for friends. They have sympathetic and supportive tendencies toward others and like the same in return. They are less likely to be hostile to others or to seek out challenges and problems to solve.

Ambition: Included the scales for this factor in MPS (high Dominance, Motivation for Advancement, and Forward Striving, plus interview ratings of Primacy of Work, Inner Work Standards, and need for Advancement), with some additions. The projective ratings that went into the Leadership Motivation factor for MPS in a positive way (Leadership Role and Achievement/Advancement Motivation) were in this factor instead for MCS, as was the Work Orientation rating. Those scoring high on this scale put a lot of store in personal advancement and being in a position of leadership over others. They are also very work- and achievement-oriented.

The remaining five personality and motivation factors were derived primarily from the CPI and G-Z questionnaires, with the occasional addition of a related scale from another questionnaire.

Adjusted Conformity: Made up of nine scales from the CPI (Sense of Well-Being, Self-Control, Tolerance, Good Impression, Achievement via Conformance, Intellectual Efficiency, Psychological Mindedness, Socialization, and Responsibility) and four from the G-Z (Emotional Stability, Objectivity, Personal Relations, and Friendliness). High scorers have a high sense of responsibility and self-control. They have internalized social values and are tolerant of social institutions and of others, not resisting dominance or hostilities. They deny major physical or emotional problems or antisocial behavior, are even-tempered, and are relatively "thick-skinned." They find it easy to apply their efforts and abilities, and achieve best in situations that are well structured and organized.

Poise: Made up of five scales from the CPI (Sociability, Dominance, Self-Acceptance, Social Presence, and Capacity for Status) and three from the G-Z (Sociability, Ascendance, and General Activity). Extraversion was a strong component of this factor. High scorers are energetic persons who seek out others and take the initiative in interpersonal situations. They also have a strong sense of their own personal worth and radiate the self-confidence and self-assurance characteristic of successful persons and those of high social status.

Flexibility: Tied together some relevant concepts from the CPI (Flexibility and Achievement via Independence), the Bass (Authoritarianism, scored negatively), and the Edwards (Order, scored negatively). High scorers are adaptable, with high tolerance for uncertainty and ambiguity. They tend to be nonjudgmental and reject the dogmatic assertions that characterize the typical authoritarian. They lack a concern for order and can be messy and disorganized. Their most successful mode of achievement is in settings where independent thinking and creativity are rewarded.

Unconventionality: Combined the Communality scale of the CPI with the Autonomy and Change scales from the Edwards. High scorers seek to escape from traditional behavior and attitudes. They enjoy novelty and experimentation and avoid situations where they would be expected to conform. They like to feel free to do and say what they please without regard for what others might think.

Masculinity: Combined scales from the CPI (Femininity) and the G-Z (Masculinity) that differentiate masculine and feminine interests and attitudes. Those scoring at the masculine end of the factor have fewer fears and disgusts, prefer outdoor to indoor activities, and appreciate math and science more than art, music, and literature. They express a preference for occupational roles traditionally dominated by men, show more interest in politics, and inhibit their emotional expression.

When average scores were calculated for the men and women on each of these 10 personality and motivation factors, gender differences were apparent in half of them, as shown in Figure 10.2. The sharpest differences were on the scales designed to differentiate males and females in the Masculinity factor. The CPI and G-Z scales on this topic are very similar in content, and they were equally able to demonstrate that the men in MCS were much more likely to have traditionally masculine interests and attitudes, while the women were likely to respond to situations classified as feminine. The differences were quite pronounced: On male norms, the women scored on the average at the 5th percentile of the G-Z Masculinity scale and the 97th percentile of the CPI Femininity scale.

Positiveness, Poise, and Affability

Of more interest, perhaps, are the four factors in Figure 10.2 that show aspects of temperament in which the women scored notably higher than the men. Two of the three projective ratings in the Positiveness factor showed the women with somewhat higher scores. The women were more optimistic than the men, confirming their expressed beliefs on the Expectations Inventory that the career outcomes they most desired would come true and those they least

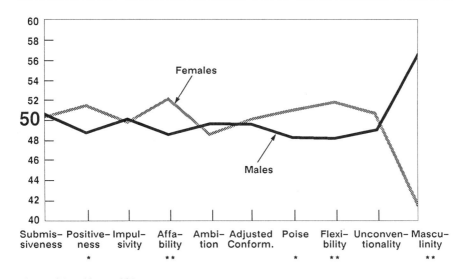

*p < .05.   **p < .005.

Figure 10.2.   Personality and motivation factors at MCS:0, males and females.

desired could be avoided. They also indicated more self-confidence in their projective responses.

Supporting evidence for the women's greater sense of self-confidence comes from their higher scores on the Poise factor. The women had higher average scores on nearly every scale in this factor, although the differences were statistically significant on only three, as shown in Figure 10.3. On the CPI, the women's higher Self-Acceptance scores indicated that they were socially poised and sure of themselves, while their higher scores on Capacity for Status indicated a self-assuredness that they could fit into a position of high status within their own milieu. The Sociability scale of the G-Z portrayed the women as more inclined to have many friends and acquaintances, to seek out social contacts, and to enjoy social activities and conversations. They were similarly rated higher on Affiliation on the projective exercises (in the Submissiveness factor), although the Sociability scale of the CPI and the Affiliation scale of the Edwards did not show significant gender differences.

The women's higher average scores on the Affability factor did not come primarily from either affiliative tendencies or a nurturing attitude toward others. Rather, as shown in Figure 10.4, the higher scores resulted from their greater desire to have their own emotional needs met by others, evidenced by their higher Succorance scores, and their lesser needs to show aggression against others. Other scores also dramatized the women's greater intimacy with others. They scored higher on the Edwards scale of Intraception (in the

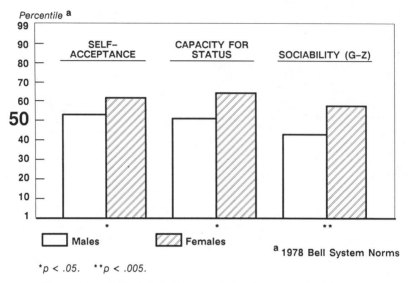

Figure 10.3.   Scales in Poise factor at MCS:0 showing gender differences.

Impulsivity factor), showing an interest in analyzing others' behavior and motives and in understanding how they feel. They were also more willing to reveal their own feelings and motivations on the projective exercises than were the men.

It is worthy of note that in spite of the men's higher scores on the Edwards scale of Aggression, the projective rating of Aggression/Hostility did not show a gender difference; it did not even come close to doing so. This disparity suggests that the men and women may have been giving responses to the Edwards items that were tainted by social desirability. It may have been difficult for the women to admit to feelings of hostility on a questionnaire, even though such tendencies were equally as characteristic of them as of the men in the more subtle discriminations of the projective exercises. In a study of coalitional behavior, Lirtzman and Wahba (1972) found that women were just as capable as men of exhibiting aggressive, competitive, or exploitative behavior when the situation demanded it.

Jackie's positive self-concept was clearly shown by her 93rd-percentile score on the Self-Acceptance scale of the CPI. The projective report also supported this overall impression, based on such responses as "*When I compare myself with others* I like what I see." There were seldom any specifics, though, or indications that she gave much thought to self-appraisal. She tried to dismiss any need for self-evaluations with such superficialities as "*I am one helluva individual.*"

There were many indications on both the written personality tests and the projectives of Jackie's ebullient and outgoing nature. She had extremely high scores on the Sociability scales of both the G-Z and the CPI, as well as the Capacity for Status scale

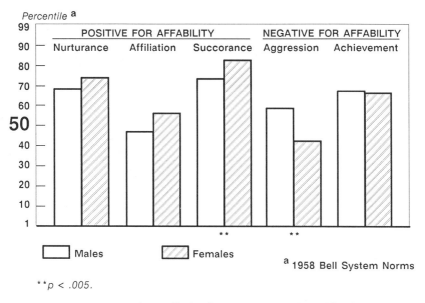

Percentile ^a

| | POSITIVE FOR AFFABILITY | | | NEGATIVE FOR AFFABILITY | |
| Nurturance | Affiliation | Succorance | Aggression | Achievement |

Males   Females   ^a 1958 Bell System Norms

**p < .005.

Figure 10.4.   Scales in Affability factor at MCS:0, males and females.

on the CPI. Her high Exhibition score on the Edwards showed an enjoyment at being in the limelight, supplemented by a Succorance score at the 85th percentile expressing her pleasure at receiving sympathetic attention.

From the projective exercises it was deduced that her interpersonal style was probably outgoing, cheerful, and spontaneous. She showed a strong orientation toward people and was very involved with her relationships with family members and friends. Parties, fun activities, and socializing free of commitments were attractive to her. She responded, "*Getting others to like you* is important," though "*Making close friends at work* can be dangerous."

Flexibility

In addition to being more self-assured and gregarious, the women showed more flexibility. As Figure 10.5 shows, the men were much more likely to take an authoritarian approach. Their higher scores on the Bass showed greater preoccupation with power relationships and insistence on adherence to conventional values. In like manner, the men scored higher on the Edwards Deference scale (from the Impulsivity factor), pointing to a greater acceptance of the leadership of others and inclination to follow instructions and do what is expected. The women's higher scores on the Tolerance scale of the CPI (in the Adjusted Conformity factor) were also consistent with the Bass findings, since the Tolerance scale measures nonauthoritarianism and openness.

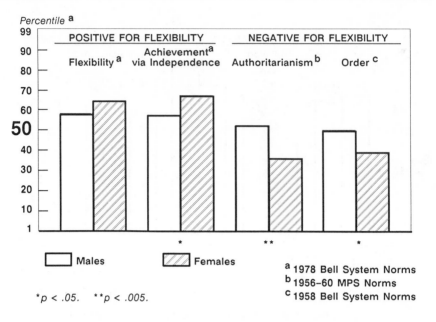

Figure 10.5.   Scales in Flexibility factor at MCS:0, males and females.

The men's higher scores on the Edwards Order scale showed a penchant for organization and precise, well-planned arrangements. These qualities were in some ways opposite to those in the CPI Achievement via Independence scale, where the women's higher scores indicated their rejection of simple dogmatic attitudes or conventional answers. Rather, the women were more attracted to achievement in settings where independence of thought and creativity were rewarded. If their self-descriptions were true, one would expect them to be better able than the men to tolerate ambiguity. Consistent, too, were the women's higher scores on the Edwards Change scale (from the Unconventionality factor), indicating their greater interest in experiencing novelty and change.

Jackie illustrated on the projective exercises that she was attracted to diversions and likely to use self-pleasures and self-indulgences to control her emotions. She was attracted to change, new experiences, and travel, also indicated by her high score on the Change scale of the Edwards and low score on the Endurance scale. She seemed impatient in her projective responses to establish her own way of life, one that allowed for flexibility and personal pleasures.

Jackie believed in dealing with decisions quickly, with the possibility of responding impulsively. Her low score on the Edwards Order scale and high General Activity score on the G-Z, along with her high Intellectual Efficiency score on the CPI, indicated that she would work quickly and efficiently but would probably have a cluttered desk.

Ambition

One final set of gender differences needs to be pointed out. Even though there were no statistically significant differences between the men and women on the Submissiveness and Ambition factors, the men did score higher on two important variables within the Ambition factor. On the Edwards Dominance scale, the men scored on the average at the 34th percentile, while the women were only at the 24th; this indicated a greater interest, although still below average, on the part of the men in being regarded by others as a leader and directing the actions of others. Similarly, Brenner (1982) found males more dominant, although Miner (1974, 1977) found no gender differences in the motivation to manage. The MCS men were also rated higher in the interviews on Need for Advancement (3.2 vs. 2.9), indicating greater concern with moving into higher-level positions.

There was more evidence for this on the Personal History Questionnaire. When asked to rate the importance of being advanced one more level, 75% of the men responded that it was "extremely important," compared to only 58% of the women. Similarly, 62% of the men rated being advanced two more levels as "extremely important," compared to 42% of the women.

Jackie's Sarnoff scores were above average on Motivation for Money but below average on Motivation for Advancement. When asked about her future career plans, Jackie said, "I certainly am not tied into marketing or even to the Bell System in general." She seemed easy-going about advancement, saying that she probably would make the second level within a couple of years and could make third according to the promises of the fast-track program. She was disinclined to predict where she would be in 10 years, saying, "As a woman, I have different kinds of decisions to make, specifically about children. I just don't know where I'll be."

On the projective exercises she indicated she was seeking personal happiness, and career goals were important only to the extent that she felt they were consistent with an immediate sense of contentment. She created the impression that her interest in work was to some extent based on her lack of interest in being relegated to the role of housewife and on her desire for money. For example, she responded, "*The only trouble with having fun is that it doesn't pay well,*" "*I hate doing housework,*" and "*A mother is a tough job to have.*"

In sum, the personality and motivation measures found the usual differences in masculine and feminine interests and fears, as expressed in traditional scales of masculinity and femininity. These scales were still quite effective in differentiating the men and women. In fact, discriminant function analyses that included the Masculinity factor (in analyses of personality and motivation factors alone or in combination with biographical data, life themes involvement, and/or ability factors), tended to be dominated by the Masculinity factor, with its coefficient three or four times larger than those for the other variables.

There were other temperamental differences that could presage different styles of management between the males and females in the study. The men seemed more oriented toward power relationships — toward using existing structures and procedures, pledging their allegiance to higher authority, and aspiring (more than the women) to be in such positions of power and authority themselves.

This orientation among the men was confirmed in a number of their responses to the Rokeach, where they ranked two sets of 18 values, and the Q sort, where they selected from among 70 statements those most to least like them. On the Rokeach, the men gave higher rankings to being obedient and self-controlled than did the women. On the Q sort, the men rated as more like them such items as pleasing supervisors, planning before acting, being well organized, and believing that hard work pays off.

The women took a warmer approach with others, analyzing others' motives and feelings, and revealing their own characteristics in return. They indicated that they more often sought others out and were comfortable and poised in interpersonal situations. This warmth and openness, combined with their greater flexibility and lack of dogmatism, should attract others and make them well liked. Here, too, some Q-sort responses supported the other personality measures, for the women claimed they were more likely to under-stand the needs of others and to express their own feelings.

The women could not necessarily be counted on to perpetuate company traditions. They gave a much higher ranking to being independent on the Rokeach than did the men and rated being independent as more like them on the Q sort. Their orientation was toward doing things differently to please themselves, rather than doing things as expected to please the boss. The boss just did not seem to matter as much to the women as to the men.

ABILITIES

Although some of the MPS ability scores were not available for MCS, a set of exercise scores and dimension ratings, when subjected to a factor analysis, produced the same three ability factors — Administrative, Interpersonal, and Cognitive. Since no separate ratings were made directly from the MCS In-Baskets, the Administrative Ability factor was comprised of dimension ratings on Decision Making, Organizing and Planning, and Creativity. Comprising the Interpersonal Ability factor were observer ratings of depth of understanding and contribution to effective group functioning for the Counseling Center Group Discussion, and observer ratings of oral presentation and overall performance in the competitive group exercise (the City Council Problem or the School Board Problem). Cognitive ability factor scores included the Verbal and Quantitative scales from the SCAT, the total score from the General Information Test, and the rating on the dimension of Written Communication Skills.

The only ability factor producing a statistically significant difference between the sexes was Administrative Ability. The factor score difference was primarily accounted for by the women's higher scores on the Creativity dimension; they were rated 2.2 on the average, compared to 2.0 for the men.

In the In-Basket, Jackie's organizational ability suffered from a lack of attention to detail, but she did do some planning. Her decisions seemed reasonable on the most important items, and she tended to be very people-oriented in deciding what to do. She was rated higher on decisiveness than on the quality of her decisions, for she would not hesitate to take action but frequently did so without in-depth deliberation. She placed a high value on being innovative, and she was able to use personnel and policies in flexible, creative ways.

In the interview about the In-Basket, Jackie was poised, confident, and easily able to explain and justify her management decisions. In those cases where her decision making was weak, she was able to compensate somewhat by trying to sell the interviewer on her rationale for taking certain actions.

Although the Cognitive Ability factor showed no overall difference between the sexes, there were compensating disparities in the separate scores, as shown in Figure 10.6. The women scored notably higher on the Verbal scale of the SCAT, a typical gender difference, but the men did not score significantly higher on the Quantitative subtest. Perhaps the extra recruiting for female math majors served to more nearly equalize the sexes in this particular sample.

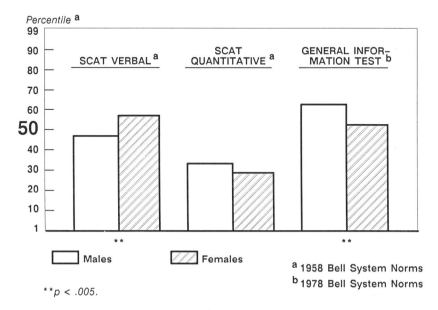

Figure 10.6.   Cognitive ability test scores at MCS:0, males and females.

The men scored higher on the General Information Test, indicating more factual knowledge on a variety of topics. On ratings of their sociocultural attitudes from interviews, the men also showed greater political understanding (the men were rated 2.9, the women 2.5) and greater political conviction (the men were rated 3.2, the women 2.8).

Jackie's Verbal scores on the SCAT were at the 70th percentile, and her interview behavior clearly indicated that she was verbally oriented. Her written responses to the projective exercises, essay questions, and In-Basket items pointed to writing skills that were well above average. She demonstrated a good vocabulary and interesting, well-constructed sentences free of errors.

In spite of greater verbal skills and interpersonal poise, the observers did not rate the women any better than the men in making oral presentations in the competitive group discussion. There was also no gender difference in face-to-face leadership in the group discussions. In neither the Counseling Center Group Discussion nor the competitive group exercise was one gender rated higher than the other in overall contribution to the group, whether the ratings were made by peers or observers. This is consistent with other research showing that males and females are equally likely to emerge as leaders through sociometric choice (Schneier & Bartol, 1980), and that male and female supervisors are seen as similar in leader behaviors and effectiveness (Day & Stogdill, 1972).

Interestingly, the men did rate themselves higher in overall performance in the competitive group exercise. Their self-ratings were more disparate from the observer and peer ratings of them than were the women's, suggesting that the men were unrealistically positive in their self-appraisals.

Both observers and peers rated the women higher than the men in depth of understanding in the Counseling Center. Since the exercise was oriented toward personal problems of living, the women's higher ratings supported their greater interest in the motives and feelings of others as shown on the Edwards questionnaire. Even on depth of understanding, the men were more inclined to overrate their own performance relative to the observers' evaluations.

In the presentation she made for the competitive group exercise, Jackie spoke in a clear and convincing voice but talked rapidly, evidencing energy and some nervousness. Her talk was detailed, but portions were quite repetitious, and she was not as organized as she should have been. Nevertheless, it was an acceptable if not outstanding performance.

In the group discussion that followed, she was an active participant throughout. Her most noteworthy contribution was a strong push to have all the money assigned to one cause. She was not successful in selling this idea, however, and the group never did reach a definite conclusion.

In the Counseling Center Group Discussion she again failed to wield much power, although she was talkative as usual and showed moments of sensitivity for the people in the cases. She was most interested in the case of the dual-career couple, finding it closest to her own situation. She tried to clarify and suggest what should be done with each case, and ended up rated above average by both the observers and her peers for her contribution to the group.

OVERALL ASSESSMENT EVALUATIONS

The MCS assessment center was designed shortly after the initiation of MPS:20. Although it was desirable to keep the research instruments and approach as close to that of the original MPS assessment as possible, in order to promote maximum comparability between the samples, many of the additional assessment dimensions defined for MPS:20 were considered useful for MCS. Ten of the 21 new dimensions created for MPS:20 were added to the original MPS set, producing 36 dimensions on which to rate the MCS participants.

These 36 dimensions were subjected to a new factor analysis to evaluate their underlying structure. With a few deviations, all the MPS dimension factors reappeared, occasionally supplemented by one of the 10 new dimensions. The Nonconformity factor did not emerge again, however, but was replaced by three new factors. A summary of the interpretation of the 10 resulting dimension factors follows, with differences between their components for MCS and MPS indicated for the factors they had in common.

Administrative Skills: In common with MPS, Organizing and Planning, Decision Making; new to MCS, Creativity. In addition to planning and organizing work effectively, making decisions willingly, and making high-quality decisions, the MCS high-potential manager finds creative solutions to business problems.

Interpersonal Skills: In common with MPS, Leadership Skills, Behavior Flexibility, Personal Impact; new to MCS, Oral Communication Skills, Perception of Threshold Social Cues, Self-Objectivity. As in MPS, the high-potential manager makes a forceful and likeable impression on others, leads others to perform, and modifies behavior when necessary to reach a goal. In addition, the MCS high-potential manager makes a good oral presentation, is sensitive to interpersonal cues, and is objective about his or her own characteristics.

Intellectual Ability: In common with MPS, General Mental Ability, Range of Interests; new to MCS, Written Communication Skills. The MCS high-potential manager has good written communication skills, in addition to learning readily and having a wide range of interests, as in MPS.

Advancement Motivation: In common with MPS, Need for Advancement, low Ability to Delay Gratification, low Realism of Expectations; new to MCS, Financial Motivation. As with the MPS high-potential manager, there is a desire to advance more rapidly than one's peers, an unwillingness to delay rewards too long, and a lack of realism about one's own limitations. The

MCS high-potential manager also is motivated toward financial gains. Energy and a low Need for Security are not part of this factor, as they were in MPS.

Work Involvement: In common with MPS, Primacy of Work, Inner Work Standards; new to MCS, Energy. Energy was important in this factor rather than in Advancement Motivation, as for MPS. The high-potential manager in both samples finds satisfaction from work more important than that from other areas of life and wants to do a good job for its own sake.

Stability of Performance: In common with MPS, Tolerance of Uncertainty, Resistance to Stress; new to MCS, Adjustment, Happiness. As in MPS, the high-potential manager maintains effective work performance under uncertain or unstructured conditions and in the face of stress. In addition, the manager changes or adapts to his or her life situation in an emotionally healthy way and finds pleasure in life.

Independence: In common with MPS, low Need for Superior Approval, low Need for Peer Approval; new to MCS, Cynicism, Selfishness. Low Goal Flexibility was not part of this factor for MCS, as it was for MPS. High-potential managers are still not greatly concerned with gaining approval from superiors or peers. In addition, the independent manager refrains from idealizing human nature and is occupied with self-interest, with little or no concern for others.

Company Loyalty: New to MCS, Bell System Value Orientation, low Goal Flexibility, Need for Security. In this new factor, the loyal manager is characterized by identification with the organization and its values, concern with having a secure job, and an unwillingness to change life goals in accordance with reality opportunities.

External Self-Development: New to MCS, Range of Interests, Involvement, Avocational Interest, Self-Development. Those high on this new factor have a broad range of interests, identify with or take an active part in affairs of the world or community, find meaning and satisfaction in a hobby or hobbies, and attempt to expand their skills, knowledge, or personality.

Social Liberalism: New to MCS, Social Objectivity, low Conservatism, low Religiosity. Those high on this new factor are free from prejudices against racial, ethnic, socioeconomic, educational, and other social groups, and they do not tend to oppose social change or refrain from challenging traditions. They are less inclined to practice or abide by a system of religious or humanistic beliefs.

When the MCS men and women were compared on these dimension factors, differences appeared on nearly every factor, as shown in Figure 10.7. The women's superiority on the Administrative Ability factor has already been discussed in the section on abilities; as will be recalled, they were seen as more creative in finding solutions to business problems.

In contrast to the Interpersonal Ability factor, the Interpersonal Skills dimension factor did show a gender difference, in favor of the women. Even though the women were not rated better at face-to-face leadership in the two

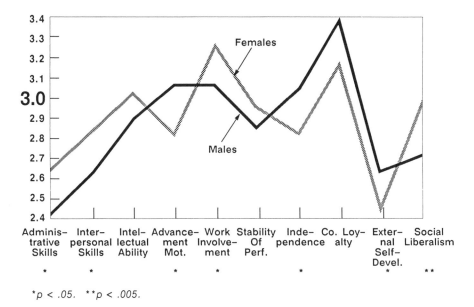

*p < .05.   **p < .005.

Figure 10.7.   Dimension factors at MCS:0, males and females.

group discussions, they were in possession of more of the qualities measured by the Interpersonal Skills dimension factor, as shown in Table 10.4. Their sensitivity (Perception of Threshold Social Cues), Behavior Flexibility, Personal Impact, Likeableness, and Self-Objectivity were rated notably higher than the men's. However, they showed no superiority to the men in Leadership Skills, Oral Communication Skills, or Forcefulness.

The Intellectual Ability factor showed no overall difference between the men and women, with both rating comparably on General Mental Ability and Range of Interests. The women did have better Written Communication Skills; their average dimension rating was 3.1, compared to only 2.8 for the men.

The two motivational factors showed opposite results, with the men scoring higher on Advancement Motivation and the women scoring higher on Work Involvement. The men's higher rating on the Need for Advancement dimension (3.2 vs. 2.9) was just shy of statistical significance, but the sexes were rated much more comparably on Financial Motivation and Ability to Delay Gratification.

The greatest disparity between the sexes with respect to Advancement Motivation was in the dimension of Realism of Expectations. The women were much more realistic about their chances for advancement in the company than were the men (2.8 for the men, 3.3 for the women), but being *un*realistic signaled greater drive for advancement. The women may have expected to suffer from interrupted careers for family reasons, or may have anticipated

Table 10.4   Interpersonal Skills Dimension Factor at MCS:0, Males and Females

	Mean rating		
Dimension	Males		Females
Leadership Skills	2.6		2.7
Oral Communication Skills	2.9		2.9
Behavior Flexibility	2.6	*	2.8
Personal Impact	2.3	*	2.5
Forcefulness	2.9		2.7
Likeableness	2.8	**	3.1
Perception of Threshold Social Cues	2.8	**	3.1
Self-Objectivity	2.7	**	3.0

* $p < .05$.
** $p < .005$.

being discriminated against; the men may have had inflated views of their own chances. Regardless of the source of the women's expectations of future advancement, the fact that they were lower than the men's suggests the possibility of a self-fulfilling prophecy. If the women did not believe they would go as high as the men, they might not be motivated to strive as hard.

This did not mean that the women would not apply themselves to their present jobs. Within the Work Involvement factor, they were rated higher than the men on two of the three dimensions. Both sexes were judged equivalent on Primacy of Work, but the women were rated higher on Inner Work Standards, indicating a concern for the quality of their productive activities regardless of what might be considered adequate by the boss or others (the men were rated 3.1, the women 3.3). The women were also rated higher in Energy (the men were rated 3.1, the women 3.3).

In the personality sphere, there were no differences in Stability of Performance between the two sexes. The sexes were rated as equal in Resistance to Stress and Tolerance of Uncertainty, in spite of the personality test score differences favoring the women. Happiness and Adjustment also seemed to be distributed equally between the sexes.

The women's orientation toward other people meant that they drew lower scores on Independence. They were rated higher on Need for Peer Approval (men 2.8, women 3.1) and lower on Cynicism (men 2.8, women 2.4). Their ratings on Selfishness also tended to be lower than the men's, just missing statistical significance.

Company Loyalty showed higher scores for the men, coming primarily from the Goal Flexibility dimension. The women seemed less intent on having long-term careers in the telephone company. They often were keeping their options open for different turns of events that could result from marriages, two careers, and children. The men were more active in External Self-Development activities, primarily due to their greater interest in hobbies; they were rated 2.9 on Avocational Interest, compared to 2.5 for the women.

The women had higher scores on Social Liberalism. The men were rated higher on Conservatism, as indicated by interview ratings of political philosophy and by biographical inventory responses on political party identification. The women's greater Social Objectivity also disposed them in the liberal direction.

To put the gender differences in perspective, the dimension factors were submitted to a discriminant-function analysis to see which of the factors could most effectively differentiate the men and women. The masculine pole of the function, shown in Table 10.5, gave the most weight to Company Loyalty and External Self-Development, supplemented by, with lesser weight, Advancement Motivation and Independence. At the feminine pole, most weight went to Work Involvement, with Social Liberalism also making an additional secondary contribution.

The function is as important for the factors that were not included as for those that were included. Values, interest, personality, and motivations differentiated the men and women, but they were seen as equal on the major abilities and in psychological adjustment.

Table 10.5   Discriminant Function of Dimension Factors Separating Males from Females at MCS:0

Group	Function evaluated at group centroids	% classified
Males	0.40	68
Females	−0.47	65

Factor	Standardized canonical discriminant-function coefficient
Company Loyalty	0.73
Work Involvement	−0.69
External Self-Development	0.67
Independence	0.41
Advancement Motivation	0.38
Social Liberalism	−0.34

When the assessors faced the job of putting all the information together about the men and women and making predictions about their potential in telephone company management, they clearly had to evaluate some tradeoffs. The women certainly had advantages in terms of interpersonal sensitivity and flexibility, verbal skills and written communications, high work standards, and creativity. But the men were more goal-oriented within the company, attentive to power structures, and upward-striving. In the final analysis, the assessors' judgments called it a standoff on management potential, as shown in Table 10.6.

Regardless of whether the assessors' predictions referred to making middle management in 10 years, having the real potential to do so, or being qualified to go beyond the middle-management entry point, just as many women as men were judged to make the grade. The only differences shown in Table 10.6 have to do with the predictions of leaving the company. Although the predicted turnover for the two sexes was not significantly different overall, more men than women were expected to be asked to leave the company because of getting into difficulties, while more women were expected to leave the company voluntarily. In the last analysis, it came back again to the difficulties for the women of tying together career and family roles. Jackie was a good example of this dilemma.

After rating Jackie on the dimensions, the assessors concluded that she would and should be advanced to the third level of management, but probably no more — the same conclusions they had reached about Jeff. Her friendliness and personableness were likely to make her attractive. Her verbal abilities were also quite good, and she had potentially high creativity if she could harness her energy and build a commitment to self-initiated work. Her administrative skills and face-to-face leadership skills were seen as no more than average, although there was always the possibility that they might develop further with time.

Table 10.6   Predictions at MCS:0, Males and Females

Prediction	Males (%)	Females (%)
Will reach middle management (10 years)	51	53
Should reach middle management (10 years)	39	45
Should go beyond third level	11	13
Will stay with company	63	56
Reason for leaving company *		
Voluntary	65	90
Questionable	13	6
Forced	23	4

* $p < .05$.

The staff was split on whether Jackie would stay with the Bell System. A primary question was whether her boyfriend would move and whether she would follow him to another city. There was also some possibility that she might leave to return to law school. Jackie seemed more naive than her 23 years would usually imply, perhaps because she had not had to deal with many hardships in her life. She was ambivalent about her boyfriend and her career — not sure which was more important to her or which she would choose in a conflict situation. The couple had not really worked out such issues as marriage and children.

It was easy to overlook such things in casual moments with Jackie, however, for she was naturally exuberant, talkative, and friendly. She had a tendency to "put her foot in her mouth" in an innocent way — a quality that might endear her to subordinates but be less popular with superiors. She had little psychological insight into herself, but this was not so surprising at her age.

The effervescent Jackie, verbally skillful and energetic, was an attractive potential addition to the middle-management ranks, if only she could definitely decide that this was what she wanted to do with her life.

THE YOUNG WOMAN'S PERSPECTIVE

If Jackie and the other MCS women had discussed women's issues with older family members, they would recognize what a different world their predecessors lived in. Their mothers were raised with the confining "feminine mystique" of the 1950's; their grandmothers, if they worked, could have been fired during the Depression to provide jobs for men; and their great-grandmothers grew up without the right to vote, which wasn't granted to women in the U.S. until 1919. During the two World Wars, women were brought into the work force to help keep the country moving; there were even equal pay laws for government contractors. But once the wars ended, the women were sent home again to tend to their families and to leave wage-earning primarily to men. Women were thus treated as an elastic labor force.

The women's movement of the 1960s and 1970s, described in Chapter 5, brought major changes in the educational and occupational patterns of women, changes that show no such signs of reversal. On the educational front, 22.7% of the recipients of bachelor's or first professional degrees were women in 1910; this percentage increased to 35.0% in 1960 (U.S. Bureau of the Census, 1975) and to 49.1% by 1983 (U.S. Bureau of the Census, 1986). Master's or second professional degrees showed a similar historical pattern, with degrees evenly divided between men and women in 1983 (U.S. Bureau of the Census, 1986).

Not only have the numbers of women graduating from college increased rapidly in the last two decades, but choices of major curriculum indicate less disparity by gender. For example, among those enrolled in college in 1966, 8.9% of the women majored in business, compared to 18.4% of the men. By 1982, 23.2% of the women and 24.2% of the men were business majors.

Whereas 95% or more of those receiving professional degrees in medicine, dentistry, or law were men in 1960, by 1983 women were awarded 26.7% of the medical degrees, 17.1% of the degrees in dentistry, and 36.2% of the law degrees (U.S. Bureau of the Census, 1986).

Labor force participation has also shown considerable change for women. In 1960, 37.7% of women in the civilian noninstitutional population were in the civilian labor force, compared to 83.3% of men. By 1984 these percentages were 53.6% of women and 76.4% of men, with projections of participation by 60.3% of women by 1995. The most radical change in labor force participation for women has been among those married. Only 16.7% of married women were in the labor force in 1940 compared to 54.7% in 1985. Moreover, over half (53.4%) of the married women with children under the age of 6 years were participating in the labor force in 1985; this percentage had been only 18.6% in 1960 (U.S Bureau of the Census, 1986).

In recent years women have moved away from the traditional secretarial, teaching, and nursing jobs, although these professions are still overwhelmingly female. Traditionally male occupations were increasingly occupied by women during the 1970s, with the most dramatic changes occurring among managerial positions (Beller, 1985). In 1985, the total civilian labor force age 16 or older was 43.7% female, and 33.6% of the managerial jobs were held by women (U.S. Bureau of the Census, 1986). By contrast, in 1960, when the labor force was 32.8% female, only 14.8% of the managers were women (U.S. Bureau of the Census, 1975). Such statistics point to a genuine revolution in progress, and women today, like those in the MCS sample, take for granted the educational and employment privileges that were so hard won less than a generation ago (Moore, 1986).

This attitude has not met with favor among many feminists, who believe young women have become complacent about a war that is not yet won. In later re-evaluations of the women's movement, Betty Friedan (1981, 1985) has noted that many feminist goals have not been achieved; for example, ERA has not been passed even though opinion polls indicate that the majority of the population favors it. At the same time, other measures of freedom for women, thought to have been won, have been challenged or taken away, especially during the Reagan administration, with little of the outcry that would have been heard in the early 1970s. For example, abortion rights were denied to poor women under Medicaid, and the basic Supreme Court decision legalizing such rights is constantly challenged. The Reagan administration has also tried to reopen legal cases that established equal pay for not just the same job but for work of comparable worth.

The problem of pay inequity remains particularly intractable. In spite of dramatic changes in women's educational and occupational status, the ratio of the full-time median earnings of women to those of men in the US has been virtually the same since before World War II — about 60% (Norwood, 1982). Controlling for a variety of economic and demographic factors, such as area, occupation, industry, union membership, part-time status, labor force experience, age, and education reduces the wage gap between men and women but does not come close to eliminating it (Norwood, 1982; Barrett, 1979). A recent report comparing the 24 industrial nations who belong to the Organization for Economic Cooperation and Development showed that a gender-related wage gap persists in spite of equal pay laws in most of the participating countries. However, the earnings differential is narrowing elsewhere, and American women may be singularly disadvantaged in this regard. For example, in 1981 women's earnings were 89.9% of men's in Sweden and 86.2% in Australia (Lewis, 1986).

One of the problems leading to the wage gap is the continuing practice of segregating men and women into different occupations. Sex segregation of jobs has been estimated to explain 40% of the U.S. wage gap, such that for each additional percentage point of women occupying the nearly 500 occupations in the 1970 census, there was $42 less in median annual earnings (Trost, 1986). Between 1900 and 1970, about 66% of women (or men) would have to change their occupation for the genders to be distributed equally across occupations. Even with the occupational changes in the 1970s, the percentage was reduced to only 63% by 1980 (Strober & Arnold, 1984b).

One explanation for this lack of progress is that occupations often become resegregated as women move into them. There seems to be a tipping point at which a formerly male-dominated occupation rapidly becomes a female-dominated occupation. This happened, for example, with bank tellers and insurance examiners and adjusters (Strober & Arnold, 1984a). Another method of keeping women separate occupationally is within-occupation sex segregation. For example, female pharmacists are more likely to work in hospital, with lower wages, and male pharmacists are more likely to work in high status industrial laboratories or to manage retail pharmacies, at much higher wages (Reskin & Phipps, 1987).

Men have typically pre-empted managerial positions, even in predominantly female professions such as those of social worker or librarian. Women have now become a significant portion of the managerial labor force, but they are often concentrated in low-profit or nonprofit industries or segregated into particular departments or nonoperating staff functions, especially those that are service-oriented, such as personnel (Reskin & Phipps, 1987). Among the MCS group there was a small amount of sex segregation by department at hire, and this will bear watching over the ensuing years of the participants' careers.

Wage differentials for men and women within the same occupation widen with time; salaries may be nearly the same at hire, but a gap becomes significant after only a few years. Studies of graduates of MBA programs at both Columbia and Stanford showed comparable starting salaries by gender, but significant wage gaps favoring the men appeared after 5 to 10 years of job experience (Gallese, 1985). Again, it will be important to track the MCS men and women in terms of salary progress as their careers take shape.

The wage gap among managers may show a sharp rise as women hit what has been frequently referred to as the "glass ceiling". That is, women manage to get into middle management, but they cannot seem to break through an invisible barrier to senior management. Although women are now one-third of the management work force, they represent only 2% of top executives (Blumenthal, 1986). There may be several factors contributing to the glass ceiling effect, but many point to a discomfort of senior managers with women in their midst (Hymowitz & Schellhardt, 1986; Kasten, 1986; Moore, 1986). One result of the glass ceiling has been an exodus of successful women from corporations, either to join smaller companies or to start businesses of their own. Women currently own one of every four businesses and are starting them at twice the rate of men (Hellwig, 1986).

Another reason postulated for women's difficulty in crossing this barrier is their less well-developed skills in arenas of power, politics, and competition. Upbringing for girls typically discourages strong competitiveness and fighting as not ladylike and encourages accommodating others, smoothing over conflicts, and depending on others for rewards. Boys are encouraged to "stand up and take it like a man," and to ask for what they want (Kasten, 1986). Boys are brought up to play competitive games with the goal of beating their opponents; gloating over victories is quite permissible. For girls, relationships are emphasized over winning, and they may change the rules of their games to spare feelings (Greenhalgh & Gilkey, 1986). A consequence of these differences in upbringing is an increased emphasis among men on advancement (winning), dominance, and having things depend on their decisions, exactly as found in the MCS results. The MCS men's higher scores on the Bass Authoritarianism scale and the women's higher scores on the CPI Flexibility scale may indicate the men's more hard-nosed approach to negotiation and less willingness to give in.

Other MCS findings can also be related to observations and advice about power and politics in organizations, which get full attention from writers such as Harragan (1977). As Gallese (1985) has pointed out,

> Unlike the professions in which women have always been more likely to enter, the milieu of management rewards not so much excellence at a particular task, but the pursuit of sheer power; not so much the results of any one individual's effort, but an individual's ability to relate to others up and down a chain of command. Indeed, the very point of management becomes not the product but the process, the struggle for that next rung on the ladder. . . . Corporations are not democracies, and in the years ahead, the men who are currently in positions of power will be the single most important determinant of whether or not women are allowed access to the senior positions in the country's institutions. (pp. 17—18)

The MCS men's higher scores on the Edwards Deference scale acknowledge their acceptance of the corporate environment and the need to please the boss to get ahead, while the women's higher scores on the CPI Achievement via Independence scale indicate a focus on the task rather than the power structure. The men's greater interest in forming friendships at work, shown on the Expectations Inventory, may signal their acknowledgment of the importance of finding mentors, champions, and useful contacts.

Not all agree that political maneuvering and gathering mentors is that important. Kanter (1986) claims that these approaches may work well in static organizations, but that the competitive, volatile markets of today will require managers who can lead change productively and positively. Women's greater flexibility and interest in change as well as their lesser authoritarianism could be decided assets in such an environment.

A major problem for young women today, and one certainly anticipated by Jackie and the other MCS women, is the struggle of trying to "have it all" with a family and a career. According to Friedan (1985), the problem arises because jobs are still structured for men who have wives to care for them, and homes are still structured for women who have no other responsibilities than raising children. Women also tend to become isolated with guilt feelings about not being able to handle their dual responsibilities as well as they would like, much like the women of the 1950s became isolated with their lack of fufillment in living the life dictated by the feminine mystique.

It has frequently been observed that women have considerably more difficulty than men in integrating a career with family life. In the MCS data, the women were rated lower on both the Occupational and Marital-Familial life themes, as if they could give their full concentration to neither activity. The difficulty seems to spring from the fact that, in addition to the biological burden of bearing children, women are most likely to take the ultimate responsibility for child care and household management. Although many men today are performing more household tasks than in the past, this change has moved slowly; one study indicated that men increased their proportion of family work from 20% to 30% between 1965 and 1981 (Hellwig, 1986). Thus clichés have arisen such as "What every working woman needs is a wife," and "Women are afraid not of success, but of exhaustion" (Moore, 1986, p. 6).

Recently some successful, ambitious career women in their 30s have made the decision to put their careers on hold and to devote a few years to full-time child-rearing. Although this does not represent the decision of the majority of working mothers, some company representatives have reacted to this phenomenon with anger and a sense of betrayal. This trend does not appear to represent a resurgence of the 1950s feminine role, since these women typically indicate they will be back in the work force within 5 years. However, there is a general uneasiness that their decisions will cause a backlash against developing and promoting women in management and professional positions (Basler, 1986).

Another way women may be avoiding family/career conflicts is by retreating from marriage and the family altogether. There was already a significant difference in marriage rates of the MCS men and women in their early 20's, and this may very well increase in the future. In a study of more than 80 women receiving MBA degrees from Harvard in 1975, Gallese (1985) noted that well into the fourth decade of their lives, fewer than 60% were married. A recent study of census data (Greer, 1986) estimated that 50% of college-educated white women who do not marry by age 25 will never do so; these proportions increase to 80% by age 30 and 95% by age 35. The reasons for this phenomenon have not been fully explained, but many women state that they would rather not marry than be forced into traditional, dependent relationships with men who do not respect their independence or equality.

The desires of women to marry those with equal educational achievements could also be a factor in the lower marriage rate of professional women. The MCS data, which confirm the gender difference in demographic characteristics of spouses, suggest that there will not be enough college-educated men to marry college-educated women as long as large proportions of such men marry women with lesser academic achievements. Not marrying as a solution to the family/career conflict is unlikely to be a constructive one for the emotional satisfaction of the woman or for society as a whole.

On the positive side, there are some indications of social and economic developments that should ease family/career conflicts. A plethora of new businesses have recently emerged that perform a variety of household chores, such as laundry, cleaning, cooking, and running errands. Prepared gourmet meals are becoming readily available, convenience stores are proliferating, and child care has become a $1.6 billion business. In fact, San Francisco has adopted an ordinance requiring developers either to construct on-site child-care facilities in new offices or to contribute to a citywide child-care fund (Hellwig, 1986). Corporations, too, are increasingly sponsoring or paying for child-care facilities and offering benefits packages to accommodate parental responsibilities ("More Employers," 1986).

There is no question that women have made tremendous strides in educational and occupational status, especially in the last decade, and the MCS data presented in this chapter point to management capability that equals that of men. But if women are to achieve true equality with men in organizational life, some additional changes will no doubt need to be made — in the women, in the men who share both their personal and work lives, in the organization, and in society. Some specific recommendations on what organizations can do to further gender equality will be made in the concluding chapter of this volume.

Meanwhile, some variations in gender differences are shown in the next chapter, where we contrast men and women of different race and ethnic backgrounds.

CHAPTER 11

Race and Ethnic Group Differences

The composition of the MCS sample by race and ethnic group as well as by sex has been described in Chapter 1, specifically in Table 1.3. The majority group was white (237 participants), and the largest minority group was black (79 participants). Another minority group, Hispanics, was represented by 22 participants. The remaining persons included six of Asian descent and one American Indian.

In this chapter, comparisons are made of the differences revealed at the initial assessment center among the three largest groups — the whites, blacks, and Hispanics. The data about Hispanics are based on a rather small group, of course, and may be somewhat unreliable. Still, it seems desirable to provide at least some information on how Hispanics might be expected to compare to whites and blacks, given that they represent an increasingly important ethnic group in the United States. Both sexes were well represented within each race and ethnic group, and in some cases there were gender differences within races/ethnic groups. For example, on a particular variable, black males might have one set of characteristics while black females might have another. These, too, are discussed along with the major findings on race and ethnic group differences. First, however, we review what belonging to a minority group has .meant.

THE MINORITY EXPERIENCE IN UNITED STATES HISTORY

America's founders were primarily White Anglo-Saxon Protestants (WASPs) who, though ethnically homogeneous, were dedicated to freedom and self-government rather than to particular ethnicity. However, the arrival of floods of immigrants differing from the WASPs in language, culture, and religion began to pose troublesome questions about the meaning of being an American. Initially there were crises around the subject of religion, while so-called racial qualities became the focus of debate in the late 19th century until the marked reduction of immigration in the 1920s (Gleason, 1980).

A number of identifiable groups have been the victims of prejudice and discrimination in U.S. history. The harshest treatments have been reserved for the indigenous American Indians and the black Afro-Americans. Also subjected to maltreatment have been Asians arriving on the West Coast during the 19th and early 20th centuries; white "ethnics" from Europe who deviated in cultural and social attributes from Anglo-Americans; various Hispanic groups, especially from Mexico, Puerto Rico, and Cuba; and a number of other populations, in both the past and the present. Hispanics and blacks are currently the most populous minorities, comprising 6% and 12% respectively of the U.S. population in the 1980 census (U.S. Bureau of the Census, 1986), and their absolute and relative numbers are expected to increase in the future.

The different Hispanic groups, though united by a common language, have distinct positions in U.S. history as well as different racial compositions and geographical preferences. One segment of the Mexican-American community was annexed to the United States in the mid-1980s and bore the stigma of a people both conquered and racially mixed with low-status Indians (Fredrickson & Knobel, 1980). Mexican immigrants supplemented the native-born Spanish-speaking population of the southwestern United States; this process accelerated in the 20th century due to the instabilities created by the Mexican Revolution and economic pressures. More recently, immigration quotas have produced a large number of illegal Mexican immigrants, who have been simultaneously exploited and resented for supposedly depressing American workers' wages in the Southwest.

Puerto Ricans have not had a problem with illegal immigration, since Puerto Rico became a U.S. possession in 1898. Overpopulation and underemployment have motivated Puerto Ricans to migrate to the mainland, where they have primarily settled in the New York and Chicago metropolitan areas. It has been extremely difficult for the Puerto Ricans to escape from urban poverty, even more so than the blacks, because they have been saddled with few marketable skills, high fertility rates, and language barriers to education and assimilation. Though widely mixed in terms of race, Puerto Ricans have typically been identified as nonwhite or brown, making them vulnerable to accusations of racial inferiority as an explanation of their difficulties in escaping from poverty and cultural insularity (Fredrickson & Knobel, 1980).

The Cubans are more recent Hispanic arrivals in the United States, migrating mainly for political reasons after the 1959 revolution led their country into Communism. Most have settled in the Miami, Florida area and have achieved considerable economic prosperity. Their education and skills, strong entrepreneurial ethic, fierce anti-communism, and concentrated political clout, combined with the mostly white skin of those who immigrated, have helped them escape much of the prejudice and discrimination to which other minority groups have fallen victim (Fredrickson & Knobel, 1980).

By contrast, those of African ancestry were involved in the initial formation of the country. The first African slaves were sold from a Dutch slave ship to English settlers in Jamestown in 1619, a year before the Pilgrims landed at

Plymouth (Holt, 1980). As early as 1640, many blacks were held in slavery for life, a status passed from mother to child. Although the black Africans were originally degraded as heathens, their conversion to Christianity eliminated this distinction, and there was a shift to race and color as justifications for discrimination (Fredrickson & Knobel, 1980).

The first half of the 19th century saw the building of an agricultural economy in the United States, and large planters, primarily in the South, controlled the lives and destinies of most of the slaves. Living conditions for the slaves were usually harsh. Most lived in very small, one-room huts with dirt floors and no windows. Clothing was drab and uncomfortable, and their limited, vitamin-deficient diet led to numerous diseases. Despite these conditions, families were formed and stabilized, with three out of four headed by both a male and a female parent. The family and the slave community performed the important emotional and supportive functions that allowed the slaves to thrive and multiply even within their hostile environment (Holt, 1980).

The first serious attack on the system was begun in the 1830s by abolitionists, who called for the elimination of slavery and denounced the caste barrier in American society. Those favoring slavery reacted by articulating a full-blown racist doctrine of inherent black inferiority. Scientific and pseudo-scientific thought was used to claim that blacks were a distinct and permanently inferior species who were biologically incapable of performing more than the most menial and subservient roles, hence making them natural slaves. Such argumentation posed a threat to the many freed blacks in both North and South, and they began to be treated with a pattern of exclusion and segregation. Free blacks were either denied access to or accommodated separately in most public facilities — theatres, hotels, taverns, steamboats, railroad and street cars, churches, prisons, orphanages, schools, and even cemeteries (Fredrickson & Knobel, 1980).

The Civil War led to liberation of the slaves, and the Thirteenth Amendment to the Constitution provided unconditional emancipation in 1865. But freedom from slavery did not mean equality for blacks. Although free blacks began to agitate for civil and political rights even before the Civil War had ended, successful assaults on southern segregation were generally limited.

The imposition of "Jim Crow" laws, proscribing the rights of black citizens, culminated in their segregation and disenfranchisement by the end of the 19th century (Holt, 1980). This legislation avoided a conflict with blacks' constitutional rights by employing the dubious principle of "separate but equal" public accommodations for the black and white races. Once again racist propaganda was used to justify a system that pronounced the social superiority of any white to any black, no matter how accomplished or prosperous the latter might have been. Blacks were portrayed as subhuman, and miscegenation was considered a crime (Fredrickson & Knobel, 1980).

The massive migration of blacks from the rural South to the urban North, just prior to World War I, brought some relief from poverty in an economically declining South, but it did not bring relief from prejudice and discrimination. Discriminatory practices in housing and trade unions quickly consigned blacks to overcrowded ghettos and deprived them of the best industrial jobs. Still, the move north offered opportunities to vote, to organize, and to make some inroads into skilled and semiskilled occupations in a time of economic expansion (Fredrickson & Knobel, 1980).

Black institutions soon developed to serve a migrating population denied access to accommodations in the larger society. Cultural activities as well as economic and social enterprises began to flourish, and there was a groundswell of black artistic creativity. Perhaps most significant was the expansion of educational opportunities for blacks; between 1916 and 1930 the black illiteracy rate went from 31% to 16%. Still, in 1930 the southern states spent only 30% as much on education for blacks as was spent on that for whites, and black teachers were paid only 61% of white teachers' salaries (Fredrickson & Knobel, 1980).

A major change in race relations was foreseen by the Swedish social scientist, Gunnar Myrdal, in his classic book, *An American Dilemma* (1944). Commissioned by the Carnegie Corporation in 1937 to study the black problem in the United States, Myrdal predicted that World War II would bring a redefinition of the status of blacks. Racial tolerance was inherent in America's stand against Nazism and fascism. The theoretical bases for racial prejudice had broken down, and Myrdal predicted that blacks would organize and fight the caste system. Their cause would be upheld by the ideals of democracy, liberty, and equality to which America was pledged by her Constitution and by the beliefs of her citizens.

Myrdal's understanding of the race situation proved prophetic. The irrationality of racial prejudice and the flagrant discrepancy between America's ideals and racial practices discredited racism among the better-educated and liberal whites. Black assertiveness, supported by liberalized white attitudes, led to a successful attack on the Southern system of segregation and the civil rights movement of the 1950s and 1960s (discussed in Chapter 5), crowned by passage of the Civil Rights Act in 1964, almost a century after the emancipation of the slaves.

By the early 1960s there was a growing ethnic feeling among blacks, both a sense of group conciousness and a restoration of feelings of pride and dignity. "Black" became the designation of the race rather than "Negro," and black pride, black history, black studies, and black consciousness acquired respectability. These developments were based on the insights of such moderates as Martin Luther King, Jr. and Kenneth Clark, who noted that centuries of racism had so damaged blacks' self-esteem that a re-establishment of their feelings of dignity and pride was of paramount importance (Thernstrom, 1980).

Survey data show that since World War II, whites' attitudes have gradually softened toward interracial contacts and political and economic equality for blacks. In fact, prejudice, discrimination, and ethnic stereotyping in the mass media have all declined markedly in the United States over the last three decades (Pettigrew, 1980). As educational and occupational barriers have broken down, interracial contact and acceptance have increased, especially among the younger, better educated, and more urbanized segments of the population (Holt, 1980).

A number of national statistics are testimony to the progress of blacks in the last few decades, although they do not yet show parity of blacks with whites. In 1910 only 45% of blacks aged 5—20 were enrolled in school. By 1940 that rate had climbed to 65% and by 1975 to 87%, equal to that of whites (U.S Bureau of the Census, 1980). Median years of school completed by members of the labor force in 1979 was 12.7 for whites and 12.3 for blacks (Ploski & Williams, 1983). But similar amounts of schooling do not necessarily mean similar quality of schooling; many blacks must cope with inferior inner city schools that are still largely segregated. Blacks are also underrepresented among the college educated. In 1979, among the 25—34 year old population, 24.9% of whites had completed 4 or more years of college compared to 12.8% of blacks (Ploski & Williams, 1983).

On the employment front, blacks still have more difficulty than whites in finding jobs. Unemployment among blacks has been approximately double that of whites since the 1950s (U.S. Bureau of the Census, 1980). At the start of 1982, nearly one of every six black adults and more than two of five teenagers were unemployed. However, blacks have been increasingly gaining entry to the more prestigious and high-paying jobs. In 1940 blacks were 1% of the nonfarm managers and 3% of the professional workers(U.S. Bureau of the Census, 1980); by 1980 these percentages were 5% and 10% respectively (Ploski & Williams, 1983).

Average earnings of employed blacks have also edged closer to those of whites. The earnings ratio of black to white men was 61% in 1969 and 65% in 1978, but among managers progress has been much greater — from 60% to 81% over this same period (Ploski & Williams, 1983). The black to white earnings ratio for women went from 74% in 1969 to 95% in 1978, while among managers black women earned more than white women in 1978 (the ratio was 111%). In dollar terms, annual mean earnings for managers in 1979 were $23,377 for white men, $17,557 for black men, $10,434 for white women and $10,887 for black women. In all occupational categories it is clear that earnings disparities are more a function of gender than of race (Ploski & Williams, 1983).

In retrospect, America has come a long way toward equality for its black citizens, but the process is not yet complete. With this situation in mind, let us turn to the race and ethnic group differences found among the MCS participants.

BACKGROUNDS

Although the MCS men and women did not differ much in family and educational background, disparities abounded when the participants were compared by race and ethnic group. In comparing the families of the three groups, it should be kept in mind that among the whites and blacks, very few mothers or fathers were not of the same race/ethnic classification as the participants. Among the Hispanics, however, three classified their fathers and six classified their mothers as white non-Hispanic, and another had an Asian mother.

Physical appearance differentiated the groups, of course, including skin and hair color and facial features. There were also differences in size. Among the men, the blacks were largest, at 5'11.3" tall and 179 pounds on the average. The whites followed, at 5'10.7" tall and 172 pounds, with the Hispanics the smallest, at 5'9.6" tall and 168 pounds. Among the women, the whites were taller but slimmer than the blacks; the average white woman was 5'5.3" tall and 125 pounds, and the average black woman was 5'4.6" tall and 132 pounds. The Hispanic women were the smallest of all, at 5'3.5" tall and 117 pounds.

Family and Childhood Experiences

The Personal History Questionnaire showed some prominent differences in family backgrounds among the three race and ethnic groups, summarized in Table 11.1. One marked disparity was in the length of time the families had been residing in the United States. The blacks were the residents of longest duration, with 89% indicating that their families had been in the United States for four or more generations. In stark contrast to this were the Hispanics, only 10% of whom had been in the country that long. In fact, among one-third of the Hispanics, either they themselves or their parents were foreign-born. A little over half the white families had been in the United States at least four generations.

The communities in which the participants grew up also varied markedly by race and ethnic group. The blacks were primarily city dwellers, with 61% of them indicating they were from areas of more than 100,000 population. Only one-third of the whites and 40% of the Hispanics came from metropolitan areas of this size. Movement from one dwelling to another in childhood was much more frequent among the Hispanics, but within the race and ethnic groups there were also gender differences. The white men and women had similar experiences in their youth, but among the minority groups the men were considerably more mobile than the women. The Hispanic men were particularly unsettled, moving nearly seven times on the average before they were 16 years of age, while the black women were the most stable of all the race—gender groups, moving two to three times on the average.

Table 11.1   Family and Background Variables Differentiating MCS Race and Ethnic Groups

Variable	Whites	Blacks	Hispanics
Fourth or more generation in United States	53%	89%	10%
Childhood community: City	56%	80%	64%
No. of dwellings before age 16 (mean)			
Males	3.5	3.6	6.8
Females	3.3	2.4	3.6
No. of siblings (mean)			
Males	2.8	4.9	3.1
Females	2.6	2.7	3.5
Birth rank (mean)			
Males	2.2	3.4	1.6
Females	2.2	2.3	2.7
Parents ever separated	11%	35%	50%
Parents divorced	7%	23%	23%
Father's education			
College graduate or more	42%	18%	32%
Less than high school graduate	12%	53%	23%
Mother's education			
College gradate or more			
Males	29%	9%	36%
Females	24%	26%	18%
Less than high school graduate			
Males	10%	34%	36%
Females	5%	14%	73%
Father's occupation			
Business	44%	8%	41%
Professional	13%	8%	18%
Service	2%	9%	14%
Unskilled	4%	29%	9%
Mother's occupation			
Housewife	57%	29%	32%
Professional	14%	22%	23%
Service	1%	15%	14%
Parent disciplining			
Mother	23%	30%	36%
Father	25%	49%	32%
Both	52%	49%	32%

Note. On all variables differences among groups significant at $p < .05$.

The minorities also came from more crowded homes, with the blacks averaging 3.9 brothers and sisters, compared to 3.3 for the Hispanics and a low of 2.7 for the whites. Again there were differences by gender within these groups, with the black males having the largest families (4.9 siblings on the average). They stood in sharp contrast to the black females, who, with an average of 2.7 siblings, did not differ from the whites. Birth rank also varied by race and ethnic group and by gender within those groups. The blacks were more likely to be later-born, but it was really the black males who accounted for this finding rather than the black females. Among the Hispanics, the males were more likely to be earlier-born than were the females.

Family stability was much greater among the whites, with only 11% of them indicating that their parents had ever been separated, compared to more than one-third of the blacks and half of the Hispanics. Similarly, only 7% of the white participants' parents were divorced, compared to nearly one-quarter of the parents in the black and Hispanic groups.

There were large differences in the education of the fathers of the participants in the different race and ethnic groups, with the whites' fathers having the most education and the blacks' fathers the least. More than half the blacks' fathers did not finish high school, compared to about one-quarter of the Hispanics' and only 12% of the whites'. At the other end of the scale, 42% of the whites had fathers with a college education or beyond, compared to 32% of the Hispanics and only 18% of the blacks.

Occupational differences among the fathers mirrored their educational differences to some extent, although the fathers of the Hispanics had somewhat more education than those of the blacks. Business or professional occupations characterized more than half the whites' and the Hispanics' fathers, but only 16% of the blacks'. At the other extreme, 29% of the blacks' fathers were in unskilled jobs, compared to less than 10% of the Hispanics' or whites'.

Education of the mothers did not show an overall difference by race and ethnic group of the participants, but there were sex differences within those groups. Among the males, more than one-third of the minorities' mothers had less than a high school education. Among the females, a startling 73% of the Hispanics' mothers had this limited an education, compared to only 14% of the blacks' mothers. At the other end of the educational scale, the mothers of the black males were least likely to have a college education or more (only 9%).

The most significant difference in occupations among the mothers was the contrast between housewives and those in paying occupations. More than half the white mothers were housewives, compared to between one-quarter and one-third of the minorities' mothers. The minorities' mothers were more likely to be in professional (including semiprofessional) and service occupations than were the whites' mothers. There were some small differences in parental disciplinary practices among the race and ethnic groups, with the blacks' fathers having a less important role than the Hispanics' or whites' fathers.

The parents of the participants also provided different points of view with respect to religion, politics, and other activities, in accordance with the race and ethnic groups of the participants. The mothers and fathers of the blacks were more religious but had more left-of-center political affiliations than those of the other two groups. The whites' fathers were the most likely to be involved in recreational activities in their spare time, and the blacks' mothers were the most likely to be involved with clubs.

Considering the family and childhood experiences as a whole, it is clear that whites had the most advantages and the blacks had the least, with the Hispanics somewhere in between. The gender differences within races/ethnic groups were also revealing. The whites generally showed great homogeneity in family background between the two sexes, so that neither had a clear advantage over the other. Among the blacks, however, the women had considerably more stability in family background, less competition from siblings, and better-educated mothers.

The race and ethnic group differences indicated here, as well as others that emerged in the interviews, are illustrated by three composite characters. Again, each is a blend of six case histories selected to represent the midpoint of the managerial potential and adjustment ratings for the represented group. Joanna, a black female, shows the major ways in which blacks differed from the whites and Hispanics, and Julius, her black male counterpart, is brought in to contrast gender differences within the black group. For Hispanics, there was considerable inconsistency among the females, so six compatible cases could not be found for an illustration. Instead, the Hispanic experience is illustrated by a male, José.

Joanna seemed to come alive in the interview, appearing confident and at ease. She had a pleasant appearance and demeanor and a well-modulated speaking voice.

Joanna was born and raised in New Orleans. She described herself as a young girl as being "sensitive about other people and their feelings. I was concerned about not offending others. I was a neat child and would lay out my clothes for the next school day before going to bed. I was also careful about my academic work; I would rather stay up all night finishing my homework than go to school with it unfinished."

Her mother was an even-tempered woman, proud and hard-working. She was a community leader of sorts who could be depended on to assume responsibilities. She was a high school graduate and worked as a medical secretary.

Joanna's father had not completed high school, but he had been employed for many years by a freight company. Joanna described him as "handsome as anything, but stern-looking even though he's really very nice. He's smart, too, and strong. We are really very close."

She was also close to her sister, who was 3 years older, while they were growing up. Their brother, 5 years younger than Joanna, was thought of as the baby and somewhat of a nuisance.

Julius, at 26, was an attractive black man, neatly groomed and dressed in brown slacks, a brown tweed jacket, brown and blue tie, and a blue business shirt. He remained fairly stiff throughout the interview, with his arms crossed and some hesitancy in his voice.

He grew up in a black ghetto in Detroit, and the family moved many times from rented home to rented home. He considered himself somewhat of a square because he would read or play by himself in order to avoid fights. "It was tough trying to study at home because of all the goings on of my brothers and sisters. So I would look for other places to do my homework. I also spent a lot of time in various jobs trying to earn money to help the family income. I began shining shoes when I was just 8 years old. I also delivered groceries, worked as a stock clerk, and sold shoes."

Julius's mother, a nurse, set a strong example of moral righteousness and self-discipline. She neither drank, smoked, nor swore, and she was extremely religious. Said Julius, "Her father was a Reverend, and she takes the Lord very seriously. She was very picky with us kids and didn't stand for any foolishness. We always had to interact with her in a very serious manner. She was the disciplinarian in the family, and she always pushed us to get educated and to work hard.

"My dad was a truck driver for a bakery, but he left us when I was in high school. My oldest brother was gone by then, so I became the man of the house. Dad was a big guy — I'm built like him — and a natural athlete. He was also smart, but he never finished high school. Our family consisted of six kids: three brothers, two sisters, and me."

José had a good tan and rugged facial characteristics that gave his appearance a strong, masculine quality. He had brown, somewhat curly hair cut medium short and had a brown moustache. He seemed cooperative and likeable in the interview and was mostly candid and open, but a guardedness appeared sometimes when he talked of his personal life. He generally exuded an air of self confidence and appeared to have a more balanced view of the world than many of his peers. A quiet, inner assurance appeared in discussions with him that made it quite pleasurable to engage him in conversation.

José's parents had emigrated from Mexico, and he spent his early childhood in and around San Antonio. During this time his father was a co-op farmer who leased land and worked on it, sharing the profits with the landowner. The family would move from farm to farm, which usually meant little continuity of school or friends for the children. José was closest to a sister who was a year and a half his senior. He said, "We were close growing up, even though we fought at times. We were actually like another set of parents to our brother and sister, who are much younger."

José described his mother as generally old-fashioned and protective of her four children. He said, "She seemed always to be there when we needed her. She was loving and strong. She sometimes got very emotional when we kids acted up, though, and ended up calling in our father to discipline us." When she first entered the United States she could only get a job as a maid, but she later found factory work.

The father of the family was quite strict about disciplining the children when they were out of line. José described him as "a boss and really tough about making me work in school and not goof off. It's really better that he was so strict; lots of guys I went to grammar school with never accomplished anything.

"My parents' marriage almost fell apart a number of times. Once my mother really blew up about it and decided to move to California, where she had relatives. She took us kids to San José first, but she had trouble getting work so we moved down near Los

Angeles, in Orange County, where she found another factory job. We were really poor then, along with all the other Mexicans in the neigborhood, but I still had enough food and clothing, so I didn't quite realize the extent of our problem. Eventually my dad rejoined us and started earning much better money in a sales job. He still has that job now, and he also has his own orange grove, which he loves to work."

Educational Experiences

In the self-reports of the participants about their high school grades, there were no statistically significant race or ethnic group differences. The three groups also had the same average educational level. Yet there were some disparities in their experiences in higher education.

As summarized in Table 11.2, the whites had better undergraduate grades than either of the other two groups, whether indicated by their categorization of grades as "excellent," "good," "fair," or "poor" or by their grade point averages. The whites' grade point average was about 0.1 higher than the Hispanics' and about 0.3 higher than the blacks'.

Graduate grades showed a similar disparity, with whites' grades the highest, Hispanics' grades slightly lower, and blacks doing less well than the other two groups. Undergraduate major showed no great differences by race or ethnic group, but whites were most likely to major in business in graduate school than were the other two groups.

When Joanna was in the ninth grade, she was sent to a small private seminary on a scholarship. It was an all-girls school whose students were cohesive in spite of being racially mixed. She played with the band and was also in a drama group and felt well

Table 11.2   Educational Experiences Differentiating MCS Race and Ethnic Groups

Variable	Whites	Blacks	Hispanics
College grades			
Excellent	53%	30%	23%
Good	39%	53%	64%
Fair or poor	8%	17%	13%
Grade point average (mean)	3.37	3.08	3.29
Graduate school grades			
Excellent	68%	41%	56%
Good	32%	44%	44%
Fair or poor	0%	15%	0%
Graduate major			
Business	71%	33%	33%
Social science	7%	10%	22%
Education	7%	19%	0%

Note. On all variables differences among groups significant at $p < .05$.

accepted. She did think her adolescence was prolonged due to parental sheltering. Her mother wanted her to stay at home most of the time and taught her embroidery, knitting, and crocheting to keep her busy.

Joanna maintained a good academic record at the seminary and was offered several scholarships to college. She selected a small university that offered her the best financial package and was still close to home. She majored in chemistry with a minor in biology. By taking various jobs on campus, such as working in the library and the dean's office, she was able to afford to live on campus, which finally offered her some independence. She began to date a lot and found that she was not quite as good a student as she had been in high school.

Joanna became engaged in her senior year and followed her fiancé after graduation to a job in Richmond, Virginia. She enrolled there in a master's program in science education, which she completed in 2 years. During the course of the program, she decided she did not want to go into teaching because of the low salaries offered.

Julius saw how difficult his home life was, especially after his father left, and he knew he wanted something different for himself. He decided education was a way out and he did as well as he could in high school, even taking extra training in English and speech at the suggestion of his teachers. Still, his big preoccupation was sports, and he did well, "but not as good as my father." He carefully avoided the gangs that often formed in his high school, some of which were violent.

Julius was able to attend a public university in Detroit while living at home. He soon discovered that he wasn't doing nearly as well as he'd like to, and he would really have to work. He failed mathematics in his freshman year but scored successes after that, majoring in economics. He joined the Black Student Alliance, where he enjoyed several new friendships, and played basketball on an intramural team. He maintained a regular work schedule, as a security guard and a department store clerk, to support himself and his education.

José's family moved out of the poor neighborhood when he was about to enter junior high school. He was put in a school with mostly white, non-Hispanic students, and found his grades began to fall as he faced more difficult competition. He said, "My motivation began to flag, but my father took me aside and said I was missing a good opportunity. He said where he spent his young days in Texas, Chicanos were held in very low esteem and it was difficult to put themselves forward. I would have a chance to do that now if I would just shape up and take advantage of it. I tried hard after that and got the grades up."

The urgings of his father directed José's thoughts toward higher education, and his high school grades were strong enough for him to hope for a college scholarship. Yet his first attempts were rather tentative; he entered a California community college primarily to find out whether getting higher education really would broaden his life. He spent the summers during his junior college days as a field worker, picking prunes, apples, and onions. This experience made him decide he'd like to be able to find employment in a job where "I didn't have to get my hands dirty." He earned an AA degree in business and decided to continue in the state university system and get a bachelor's degree.

Various other jobs helped José to support himself in the university program, such as working in a pharmaceutical factory and being a restaurant waiter. He decided to pursue a degree in public administration, which he described as "a combination of business, political science, philosophy, ethics, and other social sciences. I chose this major because it is a more liberal discipline than business administration, yet there is still some overlap with business, especially as it concerns policy analysis and formulations."

José decided to become involved in student politics while at the university, and this led him into several clubs, including the Spanish club, which offered him leadership experience and prestige. He played softball and volleyball in intramural sports. He looked toward an MBA as an additional credential, but for financial reasons decided to pursue employment first and enter such a program on a part-time basis.

LIFESTYLES

Life themes coded from the interviews give some summary information about the most salient areas of current involvement for the race/ethnic groups. As shown in Figure 11.1, there were two themes with strong race and ethnic group differences — Financial-Acquisitive and Religious-Humanism.

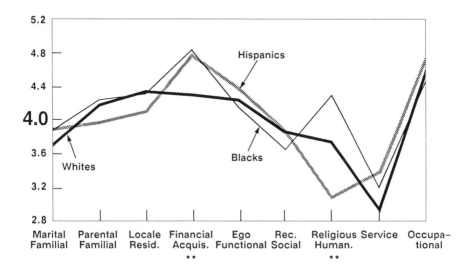

**p < .005.

Figure 11.1.   Current involvement in life themes at MCS:0, race and ethnic groups.

Family, Home, and Finances

Coding of involvement in the Parental-Familial life theme showed gender differences but did not show significant race differences. The white men and women were very similar in the frequency of visitation with parents, according to questionnaire responses, with about one-quarter visiting their parents once a week or more. Among the minorities, however, the women were much more likely to spend a lot of time with their parents than were the men; in fact, more than half saw their parents at least once a week.

The race and ethnic groups did not differ in Marital-Familial involvement and satisfaction or in marital status. Within each race and ethnic group, however, the women were less satisfied with their marriage and family situations than were the men.

Joanna's personal life was not going as well as her work life at the time of the assessment, for she had recently broken off her engagement. She said, "I date some and would like to date more, but it's not really necessary. My family raised me to be an old-fashioned girl, which means I should marry and have kids. But I'm really kind of conflicted about it. I want to be independent and always able to support myself well with a career, but I'm not sure I can have that and a family too."

Julius met his wife when he was a senior in college. He described his wife, who worked in the controller's office of a finance corporation, as "loving and caring." Their daughter was now nearly 3, and he described her as "beautiful, very smart, good memory, and hard-headed like me."

José had met his wife in college, and they felt ready to start a family now, hoping to have two or three children. They agreed that she would stay home a few years while the children were little but would eventually return to her teaching profession. They participated in some marriage counseling before their legal union and were now confident that their marriage would be steady and enduring.

The Financial-Acquisitive life theme pointed to a motivational difference among the race/ethnic groups. Both the minority groups indicated considerably more concerns with making money and acquiring possessions than did the whites. It can readily be assumed that the minority groups had more meager family incomes, given the occupational characteristics of their parents and the sizes of their families. A possible consequence is that they were currently more concerned with financial security than the more well-to-do whites, who may have taken it for granted. Current satisfaction on the Financial-Acquisitive life theme did not show any race or ethnic group differences.

Joanna's salary (in 1979) was $18,000, most of which she spent for her apartment and car repairs. Anything left over went for clothes, books, records, and savings. But her dreams for the future were much bigger. She said, "Ten years from now I'd like to be living in a big house with a two-car garage. I'd like it to be a log house with solar heating and all sorts of electrical time-saving gadgets. And I'd like a Mercedes in the garage."

Julius was currently earning $20,400 (in 1978) but finding it hard to save with a family. He said, "I'd really like to have a three-bedroom house. When I was growing up we had three bedrooms for eight people, so it would be a real luxury to have that for three. I'd also like my wife to have some nice things in life."

Although José was satisfied with his work at Pacific Telephone, his ultimate dream was to be able to start his own company. He said, "Financial independence is my long-term goal. I had to worry about money a lot growing up, and I'm looking forward in the future to not having to worry about it. I'm not all that concerned about acquiring a lot of material possessions; I mostly want the security that money can bring me." And indeed he and his wife were frugal with their money, saving quite a bit and taking modest vacations. His income (in 1982) was $32,000 per year; hers, as a school teacher, was about half that.

Recreation and Self-Development

Although the Recreational-Social life theme did not show differences in level of involvement by the different race and ethnic groups, the groups were distinguished by some off-the-job preferences, as summarized in Table 11.3. The minority groups reported that they did more reading off the job than did the

Table 11.3   Off-the-Job Activities and Interests Differentiating MCS Race and Ethnic Groups

Variable	Whites	Blacks	Hispanics
Hours per week reading (mean)	1.6	1.8	2.1
No. newspapers read daily (mean)			
Males	1.4	1.9	1.9
Females	1.4	1.3	1.5
Hours television daily (mean)			
Males	1.4	1.8	2.0
Females	1.3	2.3	1.4
Interest in current events			
Extremely interested	31%	24%	50%
Moderate or less interest	30%	42%	25%
Informal social activities 2+ nights/week			
Males	44%	47%	11%
Females	64%	28%	73%
Outdoor recreation fairly often or often			
Males	62%	53%	67%
Females	61%	14%	18%
Participation in the arts fairly often or often	14%	28%	21%
Hobbies fairly often or often	23%	31%	16%

Note. On all variables differences among groups significant at $p < .05$.

whites, with the minority males indicating more newspapers read per day. The minority males also did more television watching daily than did the white males; among the females, this was also true for the blacks but not the Hispanics. Yet the black men and women indicated less interest in current events, suggesting that their focus in the newspaper reading and television watching was on different things.

Informal social activities involved the white and Hispanic women in particular, but the black women were not so sociable. Among the men, the Hispanics had fewer social activities than the others. Outdoor recreation was popular among all the men and the white females, but the black and Hispanic women were not captivated by this kind of activity. The minorities exceeded the whites in degree of participation in the arts, and the blacks topped both the other groups in interest in hobbies and more time spent with clubs.

Exercise was a frequent activity for most of the MCS group, although the black females exercised somewhat less than the others. The whites acknowledged more physical strain, suggesting that they might overdo the exercise a bit. The majority in all groups described their overall health as "excellent," although more of the whites (79%) made this claim than the minorities (68%).

Poor eating habits were more likely to dog the whites and blacks than the Hispanics. Eating unhealthy food "often" or "fairly often" was reported by 28% of the whites and 21% of the blacks, but by only 10% of the Hispanics. Overeating also characterized the whites and blacks more than the Hispanics, though few in each group admitted to doing so with any great frequency. The whites were more likely to drink alcohol; 22% said "often" or "fairly often," compared to 11% of the blacks and 5% of the Hispanics. The blacks were the most conservative in this regard, with 23% indicating they "never" drank alcohol, compared to less than 10% of the other two groups.

The overall picture of off-the-job activities and interests again shows great similarity between the white males and females. The only notable difference was that the white women had more informal social activities than the men, possibly because more of them were unmarried. Among the minorities, the sexes were not as much alike. The black women were more likely to stay home and watch television than either the Hispanic women or the black men, while the Hispanic women were more likely to be out socializing with their friends.

On involvement in the Ego-Functional life theme, where both mental and physical self-development activities are considered, there was no overall race/ethnic group difference, but the black females scored lower than the other groups. Based on their questionnaire responses, one might infer that they had too much television and too little exercise.

In her spare time, Joanna enjoyed listening to jazz and classical records while she was crocheting and knitting. She was not an outdoor person and loathed exercising, though she felt guilty about it. "I'm a little on the heavy side," she said. "I keep talking about dieting, like all my friends do, but I never seem to get around to it." She spent a lot of time watching television and going to the movies. Her favorite television program was *The Paper Chase*, because it reminded her of going to school. She would occasionally read, but said she counted on television to keep her up on current affairs.

For self-development, Joanna was interested in taking some French or African history courses, but they would be purely recreational. She was uninterested in either self-help groups or self-help books, saying she didn't trust any of them.

Julius had some vague thoughts of going back to school again, perhaps for a master's degree, although he wasn't sure what kind of focus he would like it to take. He showed some interest in self-development by reading *I'm Okay, You're Okay*. He especially enjoyed reading magazines with a focus on the black experience, such as *Ebony* and *Black Enterprise*. Sports magazines were also of interest. In fact, sports remained a passion for Julius. He played volleyball in his apartment complex, joined in basketball games in a local gym, jogged, and played tennis. His health was very good, and he did little drinking. He watched all the sports he could on television, as well as programs like *The Jeffersons* and *Good Times*.

José's bachelor friends were ceasing to be of interest, he confided, and he and his wife were not big socializers. They did enjoy going out to films together, and backpacking and camping were also favorite activities. José usually played softball on Friday nights with a company team, and he indulged in racquetball and working out with weights for exercise. He also watched a lot of sports on television, admitting, too, that he probably watched more television in general than he should.

José usually read about 2 hours a day, typically before bedtime. The *Los Angeles Times* and the *Wall Street Journal* were on his regular newspaper reading list; in addition, he read *Time, Newsweek, Gentleman's Quarterly* and *Psychology Today*. He subscribed to the last of these magazines because of "a little girl who was selling them door-to-door," but admitted he had come to enjoy it. Recent books he had read included *Ragtime* and *Theory Z*.

Religion

The Religious-Humanism life theme showed the blacks to be the most concerned with religion and the Hispanics the least. Projected developments were similar to current involvement, although race/ethnic group differences in the ratings of current satisfaction on this life theme did not quite reach statistical significance. The lesser involvement of Hispanics is particularly surprising, given the strong messages usually associated with the Catholic Church.

Responses on the Personal History Questionnaire, shown in Table 11.4, indicated that one-third of the blacks "often" or "fairly often" made religion a part of their lives. Only 18% said they never participated in religious activities, compared to two-fifths or more of the whites and Hispanics. Two-thirds of

Table 11.4   Religious and Civic Interests Differentiating MCS Race and Ethnic Groups

Variable	Whites	Blacks	Hispanics
Religious activities			
Often or fairly often	14%	33%	0%
Occasional or seldom	42%	49%	60%
Never	44%	18%	40%
Religious affiliation			
Protestant	40%	66%	14%
Catholic	41%	17%	77%
Other	6%	12%	0%
None	14%	5%	9%
No. civic groups belong to (mean)	0.5	0.8	0.7
Political affiliation			
Republican	44%	2%	20%
Middle-of-the-road	39%	46%	45%
Democrat or liberal	17%	52%	35%

Note. On all variables differences among groups significant at $p < .05$.

the blacks were affiliated with Protestant denominations. The Hispanics were primarily Catholics (77%), while the whites were evenly divided between Protestants and Catholics.

Two additional types of data lend support to the blacks' concern with religion. On the Rokeach terminal values, the blacks assigned a median rank of 9 out of 18 to "salvation," compared to a rank of 13 by the whites and 15.5 for the Hispanics. The blacks were also most likely to describe themselves as "deeply religious" on the Q sort. Many national surveys have found that blacks tend to be more devout than whites, and their religious preferences are fairly heavily concentrated on the Baptist denomination (Wright, Rossi, & Juravich, 1980).

Joanna described herself as religious, and she attended the Methodist church about once a month. She explained, "I see God not as something external but as something internal. God is achievement in striving and thinking for yourself. Life has meaning, and religion motivates me."

Julius was raised as a Baptist and still attended church regularly, including singing in the choir. He said, "My basic understanding of right and wrong are the words of Jesus to do unto others and to love one's neighbor as oneself. I read the Bible and feel the difference between the Old Testament and the New Testament. Now I reflect on how times have changed since the coming of Jesus. I feel a responsibility to provide for my wife. If she wants to work, that's fine, but according to the Bible it's my responsibility to assure that if she doesn't want to work she's taken care of."

José still identified with the Catholic Church but admitted he didn't attend church very often. Expressing some guilt, he said, "I probably should attend more; I guess I'm just lazy." He also confessed that he did not agree with many of the church's rules, especially regarding sexual behavior, and he thought there was a lot of hypocrisy in organized religion. Still, he thought religion was necessary, believed in a Creator, and planned to raise his children in an organized religion to provide necessary structure.

Community and Political Interests

Although there were no group differences in current involvement in the Service life theme, current satisfaction with that theme showed a small difference favoring the blacks. The minorities indicated more civic group memberships, and the blacks belonged to more clubs.

The political views of the three race/ethnic groups were markedly different, as shown in Table 11.4. The whites were the most conservative, with 44% of them lining up in the Republican or conservative camp. The sharpest contrast was provided by the blacks, with more than half citing Democratic or liberal affiliations and only 2% lining up with the Republicans or conservatives. The Hispanics took more of a middle course.

Ratings of sociocultural attitudes from the interviews showed similar results. The blacks were rated 2.4 on a scale of political philosophy (where conservatism was 5 and liberalism 1), compared to 3.2 for whites; there were too few Hispanics to code in this manner. There was also a gender-within-race effect, with the white males the most conservative (3.5), followed by white females (2.9), and then by the black males and females (both at 2.4). On economic issues the disparity between the two races was even greater (whites 3.6, blacks 2.5), while on social issues the difference was less (whites 2.6, blacks 2.1).

Several specific issues showed the differences in point of view between the whites and blacks. The blacks were more supportive of welfare (also noted by Clarke, 1973), being rated 3.3 on a 5-point scale of favorableness in contrast to the whites' 2.5. They also had more favorable views toward ERA (4.0 to the whites' 2.4 ratings), EEO programs (3.6 to the whites' 2.8), and affirmative action within the Bell System (4.1 to the whites' 2.9). The whites were more positive toward the Reagan administration, being rated 3.6, compared to 2.3 for the blacks and 3.0 for the Hispanics. The whites were also less negative to the state of the economy (1.4 to the blacks' 1.2), though neither group was very positive about economic conditions in times when the Carter administration predominated.

The alignment of the MCS blacks with the Democratic party is consistent with national trends, although it was not always so. The Republicans had originally been the anti-slavery party, and following the Civil War the blacks who were permitted to vote remained loyal to the party of Lincoln. However, the Republicans seemed to lose interest in black rights in the ensuing years. Following the Depression, in which blacks were particularly hard hit, they moved almost en masse into the Democratic camp. The Democrats' stance on economic issues and civil rights has kept them there since (Kantowicz, 1980). Recent surveys have found that blacks are consistently the most liberal of the major population subgroups on political issues (Wright *et al.*, 1980).

Joanna was not currently involved in any community activities, although she had previously taught Sunday school. She was a member of the National Council of Negro Women but was not active in it.

Joanna was registered as a Democrat but said, "I'm not a political person and not very interested in politics. I would like to be aware of the political arena so that I can carry on a conversation. But I really think the world is much simpler and more logical than it's made out to be."

Like her white counterpart, Jackie, Joanna was positive toward ERA. She said, "I'm in favor of the amendment because people should have the opportunity to do the job they want to regardless of, not because of, things like race or sex. I don't limit myself to women's rights because I am a black person first and a woman second."

Joanna was much more positive toward affirmative action in the Bell System than Jackie was. Speaking from the standpoint of a white woman, Jackie said, "I think the company has gone too far with affirmative action in terms of minority groups, though they could do more to develop women. I don't think I was hired because I'm a female; I prefer to believe it was because of my earned skills."

As a black woman, Joanna had a different point of view. She said, "I think the company should be doing a lot more with affirmative action. There are a lot of talented people in the company who are not being promoted or developed. They should be in fourth- or fifth-level positions by now, but they're not because they're black. We've come a long way, but we have a long way to go.

"A lot of bosses still have trouble relating to minorities and women. Since they have different backgrounds, their thinking processes and perceptions are different. The majority of middle managers are threatened by black men; if the quota system is filled, it is by white women or black women, because these middle managers are less threatened. But women are only promoted into certain areas in the company.

"The affirmative action program looks good to people at higher levels, but they really have the wool pulled over their eyes. Part of the problem is that there are too many complacent minorities that are afraid to blow the whistle about what's really happening."

On political issues, Julius identified with the Democrats. He generally supported Carter's policies and thought the president was an honest man who was making an earnest effort. He said he was against inflation, but if it meant a tradeoff with unemployment he'd favor employment over lowering inflation. He found then-challenger Ronald Reagan "cold and heartless about social problems and unsympathetic to the little people."

Julius' white counterpart in MCS, Jeff, was more moderate about welfare programs than the MPS standard bearer, Joe, had been, saying it was a "painful necessity" to cut some welfare programs back. But Julius was even more positive toward the idea of welfare. He said, "People who make money have an obligation to help others. Political leaders generally don't know about poverty. We should take care of the masses now or have social upheavals and uprisings later."

There was an even stronger contrast between Julius and Jeff with respect to affirmative action. As a white male, Jeff recognized that he could be a victim of reverse discrimination. "I'm for equal opportunities," he said, "but reverse discrimination is not the answer. You don't put out fires with gasoline! Affirmative action programs are based on a faulty assumption. They are an attempt to right wrongs which occurred in the past. The problem is that promoting some people now does absolutely nothing for the people who were prevented from advancing before. It just hurts qualified people who can't be promoted because they don't fill the slots. People today shouldn't be punished for things their ancestors did. The pendulum has swung in favor of the minorities and women, and the white males are being hurt as a result of it."

Julius had a very different point of view. He said, "These programs exist to make up for past discriminatory practices in private institutions as well as public facilities. The first AT&T study, the Management Progress Study, is a good example; there were no blacks in it at all because they never had a chance. There has to be a mechanism to right the wrongs. There are going to be some qualified people who lose their jobs to minority groups as a result of affirmative action, but that's just the breaks. It should keep going until the complexion of a company accurately represents the community in terms of racial equality.

"I know a lot of people who have suffered because they are minorities — not in terms of salary, but because people have preconceived ideas of minorities' abilities, and this presents a problem. Many whites don't understand that less qualified people are not being brought in as a result of affirmative action programs. I'm sure Bell didn't lower its standards to bring me in."

José's politics could best be described as middle-of-the-road. He claimed to be very interested in current events, and his awareness of world situations seemed strong for his age. He commented, "Actually, I'm less interested in politics per se than in political issues. I support the country and the government, but not the Democrats or the Republicans. It seems as if particular governmental regimes really don't affect much at all. Take the economy, for instance. Each nation and the world go through economic cycles, and there are many variables that just can't be controlled. Sometimes the actions of governments designed to improve conditions actually make them worse. No matter what our leaders do, we will come into another boom time and then the economy will drop again after that."

Meanwhile, José did his best to protect himself. "I've paid off my credit cards and saved some cash so I'm not in debt. This is to protect me against the possibility of losing my job; if it happens, I won't have any debts to pay."

His attitudes toward the Reagan administration were a mixed bag of admiration and scorn. He said, "Reagan is very charismatic, but I question his wisdom. Sometimes I really think he's a dangerous and ignorant man. Maybe I'm prejudiced against an actor becoming president; someone who did Bonzo movies is an insult to the office.

Still, I don't think he's doing that bad a job. He's taking the bull by the horns and trying to get the budget balanced and taxes down, which is essential for this country."

WORK INTERESTS

The occupational experiences of the participants differed somewhat by gender within race/ethnic group. The black females had fewer full-time jobs before joining the telephone company than did the black males. Among whites and Hispanics, the women had slightly more previous jobs than did the men.

Within the Bell System, there were some regional differences by race and ethnic group. The blacks were more often found in the Southeast (20% were in Southern Bell and 15% in South Central Bell), while one-third of the Hispanics came from Pacific Telephone. There were no notable differences in the departments to which the different race and ethnic groups were assigned across the telephone companies.

Job security seemed to have a different meaning for the different race and ethnic groups. When asked what kinds of job conditions prevalent elsewhere might encourage them to leave their Bell System jobs, the minorities were more likely to cite finding greater job security as a reason. However, this difference was really accounted for by the black and Hispanic females, where large proportions acknowledged such a possibility (60% of blacks and 80% of Hispanics). Only 10% of the white males or females indicated that they would be tempted by such an alternative job. On the Q sort, the blacks were more likely to describe themselves as wanting job security, consistent with other research showing similar black—white differences (Alper, 1975; Brenner & Tomkiewicz, 1982; Veroff *et al.*, 1981; Watson & Barone, 1976).

Expectations

The total score on the Expectations Inventory showed a meaningful difference by race and ethnic group, with the minorities less pessimistic than the whites. The level of scores was low for all groups relative to the MPS norms, with the whites scoring at only the 13th percentile, compared to the 25th percentile for the blacks and the 23rd percentile for the Hispanics.

Race and ethnic group differences in responses to some individual items of the Expectations Inventory are shown in Table 11.5. On the most desired items, greater concern by the blacks for financial security was indicated by their greater proportion indicating "earning $35,000 a year or more" as one of the most desirable outcomes 5 years hence. This was consistent with their greater involvement in the Financial-Acquisitive life theme and with other research showing that blacks attach more importance than whites to levels of pay (Alper, 1975; Weaver, 1975).

Few Hispanics responded thus to this Expectations Inventory item, but it may be because of the use of that specific dollar figure; on the average the

Hispanics were assessed in later years than the blacks, and thus inflation had taken some of the glamor out of $35,000. Moreover, they were more likely to be employed on the West Coast, with salaries especially higher than those in the Southern states. This was no doubt also a factor in the Hispanics' greater confidence in achieving that monetary goal.

Other financial concerns are suggested by responses to the least desirable items. The blacks indicated that they would find it more unpalatable if their salary increases lagged behind the cost of living or if they were making less

Table 11.5   Responses to Most Important Items in Expectations Inventory at MCS:0, Race and Ethnic Groups

Most desired items	% citing most desirable			% fairly certain of favorable outcome		
	Wh	Bl	Hp	Wh	Bl	Hp
I have deep friendships with at least two or three work associates.	17	18	36	49	54	64
I have a real chance to follow my basic interests and work at the things I like to do.	50	42	36	45	52	36*
I live in a desirable community with relatively easy access to my job.	25	14	9	50	57	46
I have reached the district level of responsibility.[a]	45	37	55	37	40	55
I am earning $35,000 a year or more.	35	53	14**	65	53	86*
I have gone back to school for additional courses useful in my work.	27	22	27	55	57	68
My job is challenging with many opportunities to learn and do new things.	65	63	64	44	52	55
My family is complete; all the children my spouse and I plan to have have already been born.	4	18	23**	22	33	41*
I have discovered that working for the Bell System has helped me to meet the kind of people I like and to engage in desirable social and community activities.	16	18	27	23	26	32
I am advanced about as rapidly as my interest and ability warrant.	40	37	36	27	24	27
My spouse is happy that I work for the Bell System.	24	22	23	40	42	45
I have a real chance to use my imagination and don't have to be concerned with traditional procedures.	20	14	46*	9	18	18
My associates are intellectually stimulating.	16	14	32	17	25	27**

Table 11.5 (Cont'd)

Least desired items	% citing least desirable			% fairly certain of favorable outcome		
	Wh	Bl	Hp	Wh	Bl	Hp
I am in the department of the company in which I shall stay for the rest of my career.	23	24	32	37	29	41
I have too much invested in the company — both psychologically and materially — to feel free to move to another job.	31	17	46*	22	14	38
I have fewer opportunities for promotion than if I had gone to work for a different company.	31	31	18	42	32	64*
I find the company to be generally "old-fashioned" about its way of doing business and dealing with personnel.	16	23	14	19	30	23
I have to travel and be away from home a lot of the time.	23	18	18	16	13	18*
I don't know what the company thinks of my potentialities.	19	23	36	42	52	55
I feel an increasing amount of conflict between obligations of my job and family.	49	49	46	16	43	41**
The company doesn't provide sufficient opportunity for me to learn new things.	25	26	32	28	52	50*
I am making less money than those in similar jobs in other companies.	17	35	5**	41	52	77
I have found that an open display of ambition or competitive drive is detrimental to a successful career in the company.	10	10	23	33	34	59
I am earning less than $30,000 a year.	24	26	18	77	65	100**
I regret not having gone to work for another company.	29	30	14	47	63	30
My bosses pay very little attention to good human relations.	18	18	23	29	36	32
Our regular salary increments lag behind the cost of living.	10	22	14*	23	33	36
I have not reached as high a level of responsibility as most of those who started in the company when I did.	37	26	41	49	46	68

Note. Group differences in desirability computed from chi-square tests on proportions; expectations from *t* tests on means. Abbreviations: Wh, whites; Bl, blacks; Hp, Hispanics.

[a] The district level is the third of seven levels of management running from foreman to president.

* $p < .05$.   ** $p < .005$.

money than those in similar jobs elsewhere. The Hispanics again indicated little concern with these matters and had high expectations that they would not be the case. All the Hispanics were confident that they would not be earning less than $30,000 annually within 5 years.

The Hispanics gave much greater preference than the other groups to being able to use their imagination without too much concern for traditional procedures, but they were less optimistic than the others about having a chance to follow their basic interests in their work. On the other hand, they were more optimistic than the others that some other company would not have offered them more opportunities for promotion. They, like the blacks, were more optimistic than the whites that the company would provide sufficient opportunities for them to learn new things and that their associates would be intellectually stimulating.

On the personal front, more Hispanics hoped that their families would be complete within 5 years, and more expected that this would be the case. The whites hoped for and expected to delay their families the longest. The minority groups expected far more conflict between the obligations of their jobs and their families than did the whites. In light of the greater number of broken homes among the minorities, they may have predicated their expectations on the experiences of their parents.

Work Preferences and Attitudes

On the questionnaire measure of work conditions, the blacks did not consider work that requires much initiative or that involves a lot of responsibility as desirable as did the whites and Hispanics. This is consistent with Weaver's (1975) finding that more whites than blacks preferred work that is important and gives a feeling of accomplishment. It is also consistent with Watson and Barone's (1976) result that white managers rated risk and change as more important personal goals than did black managers.

The blacks indicated that they would be the most disturbed by being always under supervision or experiencing frequent foul-ups. The whites were the least interested in having intimate personal interviews, or (among the males) having to give advice on personal difficulties. The whites also found it most undesirable to have jobs working only with women.

On the Management Questionnaire administered in years 1 and 2, 9 of the 10 scales showed no significant race/ethnic group difference. Other research has frequently noted lesser job satisfaction among blacks, but recent analyses (Konar, 1981; Weaver, 1977) show that these effects dissipate when mediating variables are taken into account.

The only scale showing a race/ethnic group difference was that of Salary, where the blacks were more dissatisfied. Within geographic regions there were no differences in salary by race or ethnic group, but attitudinal differences persisted. Although neither group differentially expected unfair salary treatment in the future, the blacks more often complained that their salaries were not adequate for the work they were doing or that telephone company salaries did not compare favorably with those for supervisory people in other businesses.

Joanna took her first full-time job as a research technician for the county manpower office. She was involved with allocating federal money to youth programs designed to curb delinquency and keep youngsters in school. Although she enjoyed making contacts in the community, the job was an insecure one built on "soft money" and she left before she had spent a year there.

She contacted a number of businesses in the Richmond area, including the Chesapeake & Potomac Telephone Company. They invited her to come for a visit; she took one short test; and the next day they made her an offer. She was pleased with the salary and benefits in particular and knew that the Bell System had a reputation for job security, so she accepted immediately. She said, "I think I may have been hired for affirmative action reasons. I'm proud of my skills and my education and would like to think I was hired for those, but I know the Bell System has a strong affirmative action program and I may have been hired to fill a slot. I feel somewhat uncomfortable about that, but I needed the money so I took the job anyway."

Her current job was as a group manager in Operator Services. She was trained in several stages, including working as an operator for 2 weeks, working as a service assistant to help with operator problems, and then taking operator instructor's training and teaching operators for 3 weeks. She described the position supervising on-line operator personnel as "very hectic. There's always some new crisis or scheduling problem with too few or too many operators on duty. One day I went to the bathroom and came back and there was a bomb threat! However, I can't complain about the job being dull."

When asked if she planned to stay with the Bell System, Joanna replied, "I sure would leave if some great opportunity with large income hit me over the head, but I'm not looking for another job at this time. I do keep my resumé up to date, because you just can't trust people. Still, I think C&P [Chesapeake & Potomac] is basically a good place to work."

After graduation, Julius decided to try the department store business as a permanent career. He began as an assistant buyer and after a couple of years had advanced to assistant store manager in a suburban mall. He wasn't really happy with his work, however, and switched to another department store. He then found that he was the first black assistant manager in that department of the store, and "racial issues" seemed to develop between him and his supervisor. He finally decided that part of his problem was that he didn't really like retail sales that much.

One day he read an article in the magazine *Black Enterprise* indicating that Bell was a good company for affirmative action. He applied to Michigan Bell and was hired to maintain a switching control center, with the title of assistant manager of equipment. His job was to get needed switching information into the computer when area codes and prefixes were changed. He felt it was a high-pressure job because customers were irate if there was no service, and his department could wipe out whole areas of the city if they made a mistake.

Reporting to Julius were three trained white technicians. He felt they had racist attitudes, but he made a point of talking to them regularly about their views of him in the position, and he felt he had been able to create a reasonably productive and cohesive work group. He resented the fact that he got what he considered was only surface technical training before coming to work on the assignment. He also felt he should have been taught how to manage.

Julius viewed Bell as a gigantic, stable corporation. The advantages he cited were the challenge of the work and its ability to pay high salaries to employees and offer terrific benefits. He said, "We provide a necessary service, and the company won't go out of style — it's secure."

José's working career began with an electronics firm. He said, "I was in charge of one product from the inception until its mailing, so I had to schedule with other shops and try to get them to do my product as quickly as possible. This involved a lot of scheduling hassles, which was a challenge at first but later became a boring routine. I really was little more than a high-paid go-fer, so I decided to leave there and start elsewhere.

"My next job was as an underwriter for an insurance company, where I would review policies and decide to accept them or reject them. I was on a management program there, but I soon realized that the salaries in the insurance industry are really poor and I wouldn't be very well off even if I got several promotions.

"I was attracted to the Bell System by the brochures and advertising they had left at my old university. They indicated it was a forward-looking company that wanted people with good organizational skills and an ability to learn. I got an interview with Pacific Telephone and apparently survived that as well as their mental abilities test. I was really drawn by their special high-risk, high-reward program, because it offered good opportunities for promotion if I did well. The company also looked good for benefits and salary possibilities.

"My first job was as a splicing foreman, where I soon found out that the other foremen who had come up from the ranks were not too sympathetic toward the privileges I was getting for being on the special program. After about 9 months I was transferred to Network Services, where I have to schedule other people who make connections at the central computer. I occasionally take work home and have some overtime, and I do feel a little pressured. But the job is interesting, and I have a lot of latitude to set up my own day."

PERSONALITY AND MOTIVATION

For an overview of group differences in personality and motivation, Figure 11.2 compares the average scores of the whites, blacks, and Hispanics on the personality and motivation factors. There were significant group differences on half of the factors, in each case brought about by low scores on the part of the blacks.

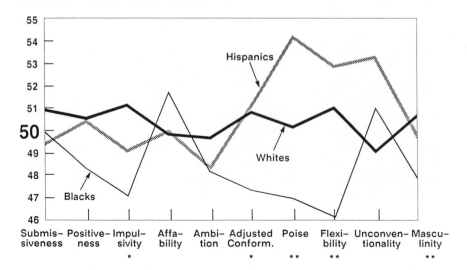

*p < .05.   **p < .005.

Figure 11.2   Personality and motivation factors at MCS:0, race and ethnic groups.

Impulsivity

On the Impulsivity factor, the Hispanics were midway between the blacks and the whites. Gender-within-race differences indicated that the extreme group on the low side was the black males, with a factor score of 45.1. The white and Hispanic males scored slightly higher than the females in their respective groups, while the black females scored much higher than the black males.

The group differences in the Impulsivity factor came from two Edwards scales, Exhibition and Intraception. Low scorers on the Exhibition scale were the black males (at the 44th percentile), and the Hispanic females (at the 47th percentile), indicating their reluctance to be in the limelight, compared to the other groups. The Intraception scale measures interest in analyzing others' motives and feelings, a quality that typically stands in opposition to exhibitionism. Here the minorities were the high scorers and the whites low, with commonality again between the black males and the Hispanic females. The white males were the lowest scorers, at the 34th percentile, while the black males were at the 58th. There is a first glimpse here, then, of a tendency by the black males to stand back, to wait and see, rather than to step forward immediately.

The blacks scored highest (40th percentile) and the Hispanics the lowest (24th percentile) on the Edwards Deference scale, although with the small sample of Hispanics this difference did not reach statistical significance. As corroborating evidence, on the Q sort the Hispanics identified the item "tries hard to please supervisors" as less like them and "frequently criticizes those in authority" as more like them than the other groups.

There were some indications of impulsivity for José. His level of General Activity was quite high on the G-Z, yet he was also low on G-Z Restraint and on the Edwards scale of Order. His projective responses indicated that he was a quick-reacting, spontaneous person who readily became impatient when events did not turn out as he wanted.

His low Deference score on the Edwards indicated that José was not too concerned with or impressed by superiors. The projective exercises indicted that his reactions to superiors were ambivalent. He resented their potential interference and control over him, yet he wanted a mentor and an advisor. He believed that his superiors should be sensitive to his needs, but was easily disappointed by them. He was also critical and questioning about policies and regulations, preferring a free hand in his activities.

Poise and Adjusted Conformity

There is additional evidence of Hispanic forwardness and black reticence within the Poise factor. Figure 11.3 indicates that the relative standing of each race/ethnic group on the five scales showed group differences (three other scales showed no differences). The blacks scored lowest on each of the five scales, while the Hispanics scored the highest. There were no gender-within-race effects, so the findings were as true of the females as the males in each group.

Interpretation of the scales showing these differences (CPI Sociability,

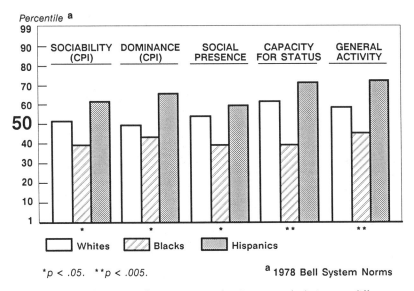

Figure 11.3   Scales in Poise factor at MCS:0 showing race and ethnic group differences.

Dominance, Social Presence, and Capacity for Status; G-Z General Activity) suggests that the Hispanics were the most likely to take the initiative in interpersonal situations and to be quick in action. They acknowledged greater feelings of self-assurance and confidence that they could meet stress and unforeseen circumstances without anxiety or self-doubt. They liked to be in the presence of others, whereas the blacks were more likely to avoid social visibility, to lack self-confidence, and to withhold spontaneity and vitality. Some responses to the Rokeach Values Survey were consistent with this pattern: The Blacks gave lower ranks to "an exciting life," "social recognition," and being "cheerful" than did the other two groups.

There are related findings in the Adjusted Conformity factor, shown in Figure 11.4. Here the blacks still scored low, but the Hispanics and whites were more similar in their responses. Again, the males and females within each race/ethnic group did not differ significantly. The lower scores by the blacks on this factor are consistent with their lower ratings of General Adjustment from the projective exercises; there the blacks' average rating was at 2.6, compared to 2.9 for each of the other two groups (a difference not quite reaching statistical significance).

The blacks' lower scores on the CPI Sense of Well-Being scale indicated some anxieties and conflicts that left them feeling not quite up to demands on their time and energy. This was substantiated by their lower scores on the CPI Intellectual Efficiency scale, showing more difficulty in directing their efforts

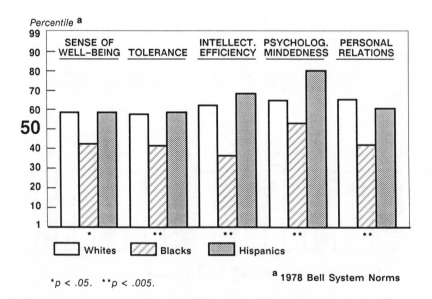

Figure 11.4.   Scales in Adjusted Conformity factor at MCS:0 showing race and ethnic group differences.

and applying their abilities. Christmas (1973) has noted research on elementary and high school students indicating that blacks often develop and retain a negative self-concept early in life, while whites show more progressive identity formation. However, racial and personal self-esteem may be different, and blacks may have a personal sense of self-worth independent of the negative associations ascribed to them by a racist society (Jenkins, 1982).

In light of the blacks' higher scores on Intraception, described for the Impulsivity factor, their lower scores on the CPI Psychological Mindedness scale probably indicated some intolerance of ambiguity and an orientation toward the practical rather than the abstract. The Hispanics scored quite high on this scale, corroborating their interest in the inner needs and experiences of others.

Both the G-Z and the CPI showed a relative absence of high scores for Joanna, suggesting she did not have a well-developed self-concept. The projective reports confirmed this, noting that she seemed unsettled and ambivalent about many aspects of herself and was presently searching for a greater sense of identity and direction.

Low scores on such scales as CPI Social Presence suggested that Joanna did not see herself as very self-confident or poised. She replied on the incomplete sentences, "*I suffer* fits of depression whenever my self-confidence is undermined," and "*I am very* insecure despite my outward bravado."

Joanna scored in the lowest quintile on G-Z Emotional Stability, G-Z Objectivity, and CPI Sense of Well-Being, indicating that she tended to be thin-skinned. Fears prevailed in her thinking, as when she responded, "*My greatest worry* is that my family will forget me," and "*In 20 years from now* I hope this constant worry about the future will have subsided." Some of her reported worries centered around the typical needs and concerns associated with her stage of life. For example, she expressed dissatisfaction with her physical appearance and complained of loneliness. Yet the stories she created to the TAT pictures also appeared to reflect her tendency to feel troubled, tense, and preoccupied with emotionally complex situations and reactions.

Julius showed an undercurrent of concern about his own competence and possible failures. On many projective responses he seemed to be guarded, reluctant to reveal too many feelings and thoughts — a reaction consistent with his low Exhibition score on the Edwards. Although he did not state it directly, Julius appeared to be worried about his career progress and job performance, as well as about the possibility of race discrimination. His concerns with race issues were sometimes poignant; to the blank white card of the TAT, his first response was "There are no black people presented in this picture."

José presented a strong, positive self-image on the personality tests by scoring high on many scales of the G-Z and CPI. He described himself as sociable, poised, and comfortable in a high status and influential position. Yet the projective exercises indicated that there was some ambivalence in his self-concept. He would show high self-esteem in such statements as "*Back home* people think I'm the best thing since peanut butter." But he could also be self-critical, chastising himself for his impatience, procrastination, and other somewhat undesirable traits. It seemed likely that he vacillated in his self-evaluation between overestimation of his assets and major self-doubts and discouragement. He seemed aware of these tendencies, responding, "*I suffer* from an overinflated ego."

His high scores on Psychological Mindedness on the CPI suggested that he was interested in understanding others' motives, but the projective exercises indicated that there was more complexity involved. He appeared to enjoy observing others, was eager to meet new people, and looked forward to "fun" interactions. But he could also be evaluative and indifferent. With respect to his own motives, he seemed to be more introspective than self-disclosing and would only open up on specific matters.

Flexibility

Two other scales in the Adjusted Conformity factor pointed up the blacks' difficulty with uncertainty, suggested by their low scores on the Psychological Mindedness scale. Their low scores on the CPI Tolerance scale indicated some rigidity and lack of permissiveness in social beliefs and attitudes — a concomitant, perhaps, of their religiosity. Cynicism and suspicion are also characteristic of low scorers on the CPI Tolerance scale as well as on the Personal Relations scale of the G-Z, where the blacks were also significantly behind the other two groups.

These same themes of rigidity and lack of permissiveness were picked up in the Flexibility factor, another area of low scores for the blacks, as shown in Figure 11.5. The blacks lagged behind both the whites and Hispanics on the CPI Achievement via Independence scale, where high tolerance of ambiguity, independence of thought, and enjoyment of nonutilitarian activities are valued and simple dogmatic or authoritarian attitudes are rejected. On the other side, the blacks were high scorers on the Order scale of the Edwards, where spontaneity may be sacrificed for the sake of having things organized and under control. The Hispanics were particularly low on this scale.

Race/ethnic group differences did not quite reach statistical significance on the CPI Flexibility and the Bass Authoritarianism scales, but the results followed a similar trend. Other evidence comes from the Rokeach, where the blacks gave higher ranks than the other two groups to being "clean" and "self-controlled."

Joanna's test scores indicated some constriction in her personality. She scored below average on G-Z General Activity and in the lowest quintile on CPI Flexibility, while her scores were quite high on G-Z Restraint, Bass Authoritarianism, and CPI Self-Control. She expressed the wish on the projective exercises that she could be more open, but her independent manner and suspiciousness of others encouraged quiet, self-contained behavior. Still, her stories were quite imaginative and seemed to be symbolic expressions of concerns on her mind. For example, in responding to the blank card, she

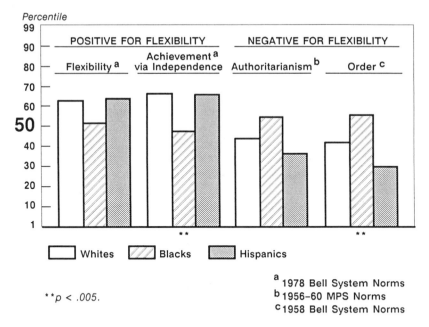

Figure 11.5.   Flexibility factor at MCS:0, race and ethnic groups.

wrote, "The picture is of me. Right now I am so glad to be finished with this test I could scream. I came from an average background with self-doubts and a few weak spots in my self-image. But now after surviving this I can conquer the world. My thoughts are a jumbled mess fading into numbness."

Julius often revealed strongly moralistic values. He scored high on the Bass Authoritarianism scale and the Edwards Order scale, and was low on Flexibility (CPI) and Change (Edwards). He expressed strong feelings of guilt and fear of punishment if he deviated from the values he thought others held. His values derived in great part from his commitment to religion. He stated on an incomplete sentence, "*I need* Christ in my life to make me whole."

His lack of flexibility and authoritarian attitudes were likely to mean that Julius would have difficulty rolling with the punches. The projective exercises indicated that he preferred to work in situations that were well planned and tightly structured, so that he knew exactly what he was expected to do. Decision-making situations made him uneasy, and he tried to deal with decisions slowly and carefully, relying on rules and available structures to guide him. He hoped to gain the support and approval of superiors by being respectful and obedient. A strong desire was to have a mentor who would give him advice and help him to be targeted for advancement.

José's low Authoritarianism scores indicated that he would not be dictatorial and impose rules and regulations on his subordinates. Indeed, his projective responses indicated that he would develop subordinates by allowing them to express their views and by providing them with the help and support they needed.

Masculinity and Affability

The G-Z Masculinity and CPI Femininity scales were quite consistent in their results. Among the men, the blacks showed the least preference for masculine attitudes and interests described in these scales, while the Hispanics showed the most. It might be speculated that the stereotypical "macho" attitudes could be sneaking through in the Hispanic male results. The tendency of the black males to admit to more anxieties on the CPI Sense of Well-Being scale might well have carried over into the admission of fears characterized as feminine on these scales. Among the women, the minorities were more traditionally feminine in their choices than the whites.

Several other scales showed race and ethnic group differences in personality and motivation, even though no remaining factor scores showed significant differences. Within the Affability factor, the blacks scored lowest on the Edwards Affiliation scale (41st percentile), which measures interest in friends, while the Hispanics scored highest (63rd percentile); this again showed the blacks' reluctance to enter into social situations and the Hispanics' relative comfort with others. The Rokeach added more evidence to this: The blacks gave lower ranks than the other groups to "true friendship" and being "loving," while the Hispanics gave higher ranks than the others to being "helpful." The Hispanics also sorted the Q-sort item "goes out of the way to help and support others" as more like them.

Even though the Hispanics were more gregarious with others, they were less inclined than the whites to reveal their underlying motivations and concerns on the projective exercises; this was also true for the blacks. Yet both minority groups showed more underlying aggression in their projective responses than did the whites, in spite of similar scores on the more trans-parent Aggression scale of the Edwards. Dreger (1973) also noted greater aggression shown by blacks than whites among high school students.

It is conceivable that part of the strategy of adaptation for minority groups is to suppress the natural rage that they feel and to be cautious about revealing their true feelings and attitudes. Among Hispanics, this may be managed within an external framework of extraversion and affiliation, while blacks may simply hold back both positive and negative behaviors and emotions in an effort to stay in control. It is also likely that blacks feel the effects of discrimination much more acutely than do Hispanics. Among the 18 Rokeach terminal values, the blacks gave "equality" a median rank of 7, compared to 13 by the Hispanics and 14 by the whites. Fernandez (1981) also found that black managers reported more discrimination than those in other race/ethnic groups and claimed that they had suffered the most historically.

In spite of average scores on the Edwards Aggression scale, Julius used frequent expressions of hostility and annoyance in his incomplete sentences. He used humor as a way of dealing with issues, but his humor often communicated a perception of life as unpredictable, stressful, and difficult to control. He tempered his own feelings to avoid difficulties, saying *"If a supervisor criticizes me* I try to keep my patience and self-control."

Motivations

Although there were no overall differences among the race and ethnic groups on the Ambition factor, a number of scales within the factor did show group differences intertwined in a rather complex pattern. Figure 11.6 illustrates several scales concerned with different aspects of motivation that showed race and ethnic group differences.

The blacks had the strongest Motivation for Money on the Sarnoff, consistent with the importance they gave to financial items on the Expectations Inventory, the Management Questionnaire, and involvement in the Financial-Acquisitive life theme. They also showed greater Motivation for Advancement on the Sarnoff, although they did not bring it up more than the others in the interview, and they gave less importance to advancing at least two more levels in the telephone company hierarchy than did the other two groups on the

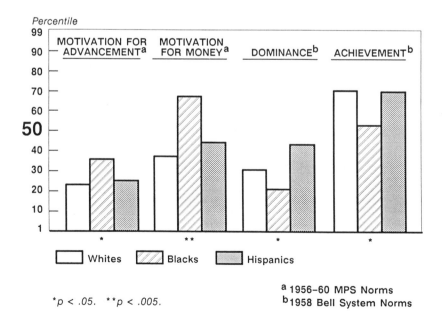

Figure 11.6.   Motivational variables at MCS:0 showing race and ethnic group differences.

Personal History Questionnaire. Yet other research has also indicated higher aspirations by blacks (Fernandez, 1981; Kirkpatrick, 1973; Miner, 1977).

The whites seemed more interested in doing high-quality work, according to the interview rating of Inner Work Standards, which was corroborated by their higher scores on the Edwards Achievement scale. The blacks' low standing on this scale relative to the other two groups was consistent with their scores on the CPI Achievement via Independence scale, shown for the Flexibility factor. Other research has also noted less achievement motivation for blacks (Dreger, 1973; Kirkpatrick, 1973).

The Hispanics scored highest on the Dominance scale of the Edwards, showing interest in leading others; the blacks scored lowest here. This was a repetition, perhaps, of the pattern of Hispanic orientation toward influencing others and black reluctance to do so. Thus the blacks seemed to want the external rewards of success, such as money and advancement, even though they showed less enthusiasm for the functional activities of managerial work, including meeting challenges, solving problems, and leading others.

Although Julius was interested in having supervisory status, his motivation to lead and influence others was not high according to his expressions on the projective exercises and his low Dominance scores on the Edwards and CPI. He seemed somewhat uncomfortable in a leadership role, saying, "When I am in charge of others I stay on my toes." His achievement scores were low average on the Edwards and CPI, especially Achievement via Independence. Yet his career involvement was high, and he wanted advancement and financial rewards, according to the Sarnoff scores and projective responses. He said, "My ambition is to be successful," and "In 20 years from now I want to be financially independent."

José's goals in life included making money, for he also wanted financial independence. There were also indications that he was striving for recognition, status, power, and influence, though in a moment of candor he confessed, "My ambition probably outweighs my ability." The high scores turned in by José on the Dominance scales of the Edwards and CPI and the Ascendance scale of the G-Z consistently pointed to his desire to be in control in group situations. This, too, was revealed on the projective exercises, as he expressed a preference for directing others. He stated, "When working with others I tend to try and dominate."

Overall, the motivation and personality data show that on the average the blacks were concerned with having financial security and equality. Yet they tended to feel that they must conceal their very natures, including some underlying hostility, to achieve their goals. Their approach to others was more likely to be reticent, cautious, and suspicious, with clear signs of discomfort. They more often indicated that they lacked self-confidence and suffered from conflicts and anxieties. They valued order and self-control, but may achieve these by sacrificing flexibility and spontaneity.

By contrast, the data for the small number of Hispanics studied here suggests that they were more likely to exhibit poise, sociability, and friendliness. They were interested in others' motives and wanted to be helpful to them, but were also quite comfortable in leadership roles. Although they, like the blacks, were somewhat reluctant to reveal their inner selves and harbored some hostility, they were likely to employ powers of persuasion to achieve their objectives. They did not feel constrained by rules and order and were more likely than the other groups to challenge authority.

The whites were generally much more like the Hispanics than like the blacks in motivation and personality. On the average they were comfortable in social situations and generally well adjusted and conforming without being inflexible. Compared to the other groups, their motivations were oriented more toward high quality work than toward leadership or financial gains.

ABILITIES

Given the less favorable childhood and educational experiences of the minorities, one might expect that their abilities would not be as well developed as those of the whites. This was true, as shown by the average scores of the race and ethnic groups on the ability factors in Figure 11.7. The blacks were clearly at a disadvantage on the Administrative and Cognitive factors, although there were no significant group differences on the Interpersonal Ability factor.

The group differences on Administrative abilities were evident in all the dimensions that made up the factor — Organizing and Planning, Decision

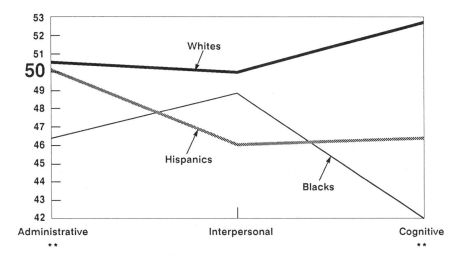

$**p < .005.$

Figure 11.7.   Ability factors at MCS:0, race and ethnic groups.

making, and Creativity. In each case, the whites and Hispanics had nearly identical scores, while the blacks lagged behind. Gender-within-race differences were pronounced for Organizing and Planning, where the black women were rated higher than the black men (2.9 vs. 2.2) and the Hispanic men were rated higher than the Hispanic women (3.3 vs. 2.6).

Race/ethnic group differences were even more pronounced on the Cognitive Ability factor, with the blacks doing most poorly. The Hispanics also had a disadvantage here relative to the whites, although their composite factor score was higher than the blacks'. All the scores that made up the Cognitive Ability factor showed large race/ethnic group differences. On the Written Communication Skills dimension, both minority groups were at a disadvantage; the whites were rated 3.3, compared to 2.6 for the blacks and 2.7 for the Hispanics.

The Hispanics came closer to the higher scores of the whites on the SCAT Verbal subscale and the General Information Test, as shown in Figure 11.8. They did more poorly on the Quantitative subscale of the SCAT, bringing their total SCAT score (at the 28th percentile) somewhat closer to the low score of the blacks (at the 18th percentile) than the high score of the whites (at the 54th percentile). Both the SCAT Quantitative and Total scores had sex-within-race differences, with the black females scoring better than the black males and the Hispanic males scoring better than the Hispanic females.

The black—white difference in total SCAT score paralleled that reported

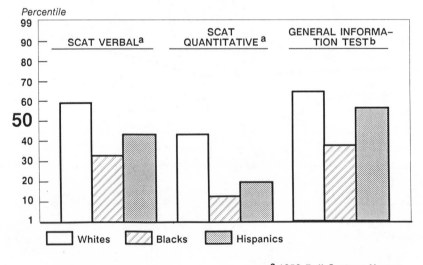

Figure 11.8.   Cognitive ability test scores at MCS:0, race and ethnic groups.

recently by the College Board for the Scholastic Aptitude Tests ("100-Point Lag," 1982), a difference of approximately one standard deviation. Other research has for many years indicated substantial black—white differences on all aptitude and employment tests (Kirkpatrick, 1973), while factor structures of abilities remain the same across the races (Sung & Davis, 1981). Inferior schooling is one obvious explanation for such race differences, but it has also been hypothesized that different cultures may foster different conceptual styles. For example, minority children may not have developed thinking strategies needed for particular task demands or types of problem-solving activities emphasized in the white American culture, or they may not have learned to use language to cue in thinking strategies already developed (Jenkins, 1982).

Although the Interpersonal Ability factor showed no overall group differences, the ratings and ranking by observers, peers, and selves of group members' overall performance in the competitive group exercise did show a differentiation. The whites were always rated and ranked the highest, regardless of who was doing the evaluating. Peers tended to give the Hispanics the lowest ratings, while self-ratings and self-rankings for the blacks were the lowest, reflecting their lower self-esteem. The observers ranked the blacks and Hispanics about the same but lower than the whites.

The low score of the Hispanics was generated exclusively by the women, who were primarily too reticent to speak out; the Hispanic men were rated and ranked similarly to the white men. Among the blacks, the men had the lower scores; the black women were rated and ranked below the white women but higher than the Hispanic women. The lower ratings of the blacks were attributed not to being retiring but to being unyielding. The exercise (the City Council Problem or the School Board Problem) involved allocation of a fixed pool of funds, with each participant to represent a particular cause. The black men in particular showed no lack of competitive drive but tended to adhere rigidly to their own demands, resisting the kinds of compromise necessary to achieve the group goal specified by the exercise. This is consistent with the lack of flexibility they showed on the personality measures.

It is interesting to observe that the Hispanics did no better than the rest in any of the observer or peer ratings or rankings for the two group exercises, in spite of describing themselves on the personality tests as more poised with others and interested in influencing them. At the same time, the blacks did no worse in the Counseling Center Group Discussion or in the oral presentation part of the competitive group exercise, in spite of their lack of confidence in themselves and general reticence. Clearly, the blacks warranted more self-assurance about their performance in such group exercises.

It should be noted that the blacks' lower scores on the SCAT Verbal did not result in correspondingly lower ratings on Oral Communications Skills. While it is true that spoken language does not require the same level of precision as written, oral communications permit cues other than words to express thoughts and feelings. It may be that the black participants could better communicate their reasoning and intent aided by black speech styles, which are "rich in the structured use of nonverbal communications to convey specific social meanings" (Jenkins, 1982, p.101).

When the data on abilities are considered together, it appears that the closer one comes to academic experiences, the greater was the difficulty for the minorities, who were most likely to attend substandard schools. The SCAT showed the most extreme differences among the race/ethnic groups, and the other measures of Cognitive Ability also showed highly disparate results. It was the group with the most impoverished backgrounds, the blacks, who had the most difficulty with these kinds of exercises.

On Administrative Ability, the differences were not as pronounced; in fact, the Hispanics did as well as the whites. The ratings on these dimensions were taken primarily from the In-Basket, which requires some cognitive reasoning but also a good deal of judgment in dealing with others.

On the Interpersonal Ability factor, there were few differences at all. On this factor, which is probably more influenced by the home and neigborhood than the school, the minorities showed development equal to the whites. These results parallel the findings of Huck and Bray (1976) for white and black nonmanagement women assessed for management positions, where whites had the greatest advantage on the assessment factor of Effective Intelligence; were significantly higher, though with a lesser mean difference, on Administrative Skills; and had no advantage on the factor of Interpersonal Effectiveness.

These data also point to the advantage to minorities of being evaluated by a comprehensive procedure such as an assessment center. If only cognitive tests were used for selection and placement, as is frequently the case, there would be more disparate results that would be to the disadvantage of minorities than in a process that looks at a broader range of abilities, where their performance is more competitive.

OVERALL ASSESSMENT EVALUATIONS

When the MCS assessment data were integrated and the dimensions rated by the assessors, three factors showed significant overall race/ethnic group differences, as shown in Figure 11.9. The Administrative Skills dimension factor is the same as the Administrative Ability factor, and showed the differences discussed above. The Intellectual Ability factor covers the dimensions of General Mental Ability, Range of Interests, and Written Communication Skills; all of these showed highly significant group differences, with the blacks at the greatest disadvantage. The Hispanics equaled the whites in Range of Interests, in spite of somewhat lower scores on the General Information Test. This was due to their greater interest in current events, also observed in the

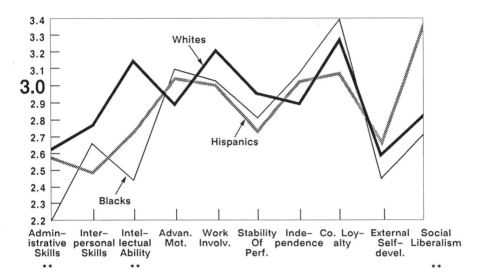

Figure 11.9.   Dimension factors at MCS:0, race and ethnic groups.

Involvement dimension, where the Hispanics were the high scorers and the whites the low scorers.

There were no overall differences between the groups on the motivation factors (Advancement Motivation and Work Involvement), although some dimensions did reflect the different emphasis of the groups mentioned earlier. Within Advancement Motivation, the groups did not differ on Need for Advancement or Ability to Delay Gratification. However, the greater desire of the blacks to have money was reflected in their somewhat higher ratings on Financial Motivation. There were strong group differences in Realism of Expectations, with both the blacks and Hispanics considerably more unrealistic about their chances for promotion within the telephone companies than were the whites.

The personality differences observed among the race/ethnic groups were reflected primarily in the Social Liberalism factor. The differences in ratings of Religiosity could readily be predicted from the data presented so far, with the blacks scoring high and the Hispanics low. The ratings on Conservatism were not quite so obvious. The political conservatism of the whites no doubt explains their high ratings, but the left-leaning political orientation of the blacks was tempered by their more traditional allegiance to rules and authority. This left the more free-wheeling Hispanics as the least conservative of them all.

The final predictions of the assessors are shown in Table 11.6. The ratings

Table 11.6   Predictions at MCS:0, Race and Ethnic Groups

Prediction	Whites (%)	Blacks (%)	Hispanics (%)
Will reach middle management (10 years)*			
Yes	57	42	36
Questionable	8	14	23
No	34	44	41
Should reach middle management (10 years)**			
Yes	48	25	46
Questionable	11	8	0
No	41	67	55
Should go beyond third level**	15	6	5
Will stay with company*			
Males	68	55	46
Females	52	74	36
Reason for leaving company**			
Voluntary	87	53	70
Questionable	9	16	0
Forced	4	32	30

* $p < .05$.
** $p < .005$.

of those qualified for middle management reflect the difficulties of the blacks, where one-quarter were clearly felt to have middle-management potential, compared to nearly half the whites and Hispanics. Those definitely not qualified for middle management included 41% of the whites, 67% of the blacks, and 55% of the Hispanics. Among the whites and blacks 10% more women than men were rated qualified for middle management, but 64% of the Hispanic men and only 27% of the Hispanic women were so rated.

On the predictions of those expected to reach middle management, 9% more of the whites were expected to be promoted this far than should be (the difference between 48% called qualified and 57% expected to be promoted), compared to 17% more of the blacks. This difference indicates the predicted effect of affirmative action programs in the telephone companies. The figures for Hispanics suggested that they would be underpromoted, but an additional 23% were in the "questionable" category on getting promotions; if the "questionables" were included as likely to be promoted, the Hispanics' rate of promotion relative to qualifications would be between the whites' and blacks', as the other data indicate they should be.

Although the overall predictions of termination among the race/ethnic groups did not vary in a meaningful way, there were significant gender-within-race differences, with more Hispanic and white females and more black males expected to leave. The reasons for leaving varied distinctly by race, with more

blacks and Hispanics expected to be forced out for reasons of poor performance. Among the blacks, 46% of the men predicted to leave were expected to
be forced out; this was true for none of the black women. Among Hispanics,
one-third of the women and one-fourth of the men who terminated were
expected to be asked to leave the company. None of the white women and
only 10% of the white men were thought vulnerable to being forced out.

The overall results clearly indicate that the whites had the most favorable
prognosis for the future as managers in the telephone companies. The blacks
faced the most disadvantages in terms of their abilities and personalities,
although they were motivated for financial and job security. The Hispanics fell
somewhere between these two groups in potential. Another clear finding was
that although the white men and women showed great similarities, there were
frequent differences between the men and women of the minority groups. The
black women and Hispanic men had the best overall potential among the
minorities, while the black men and Hispanic women faced a less promising
future.

When the gender differences described in Chapter 10 were considered in
combination in discriminant functions, the men and women were differentiated by personality and motivation and by lifestyles. They were not well
distinguished by abilities or by biographical data. The situation was quite
different for the two race groups, whites and blacks. Table 11.7 shows
discriminant function coefficients for variables from biographical data, life
themes involvement, ability factors, and personality/motivation factors that, in
combination, best differentiated blacks from whites.

The variable carrying the most weight (two or three times that of the other
variables) was the Cognitive Ability factor, scored positively for the whites.
Also scored toward the white pole were level of father's education, better
undergraduate grades, and the Masculinity, Poise, and Submissiveness (lower
aggression) personality factors. Weighted toward the black pole were coming
from a home where families were larger and the parents were separated,
deviating more from conventional norms, being more interested in community
affairs, and being more religious.

There were gender-within-race differences that further complicated the task
of differentiating the two races. Each of the four race—gender groups was
also subjected to a discriminant-function analysis, shown in Table 11.8. The
first function differentiated the males from the females, and focused on
Masculinity and Submissiveness at the male pole and Positiveness and better
high school grades at the female pole.

The second function primarily separated the black males from the other
three groups. They were from the largest families, had the most poorly
educated fathers, and were most likely to deviate from conventional norms.
They were rated positively on self-development interests (the Ego-Functional
life theme) and negatively on Adjusted Conformity, Impulsivity, and involvement in their work (the Occupational life theme).

Table 11.7   Discriminant Function Separating Whites from Blacks at MCS:0: Biographical Data, Life Themes Involvement, Ability Factors, and Personality/Motivation Factors

Group	Function evaluated at group centroids	% classified
Whites	0.47	83
Blacks	−1.48	85

Variable or factor	Standardized discriminant-function coefficients
Cognitive ability	0.68
Masculinity	0.36
Father's education	0.33
No. of siblings	−0.31
Poise	0.30
Service life theme	−0.28
Submissiveness	0.28
Religious-Humanism life theme	−0.28
Undergraduate grades	0.23
Unconventionality	−0.22
Parents separated	−0.22

The third function distinguished the white females from the black males and females. Cognitive ability and good undergraduate grades were positive factors in differentiating the white females, but they were less likely to be interested in community service (the Service life theme).

Race differences, then, were more pervasive throughout the MCS assessment center exercises than were gender differences, including family backgrounds, lifestyles, abilities, personality, and motivation. A further complication was the dissimilarity of the sexes within the race groups.

A question could be raised as to whether the gender-within-race differences would characterize the general population for each group or whether they are a result of the selection process into this study. In the case of the Hispanics, the sample size was simply too small to draw any firm conclusions; all these results must be considered only suggestive. Moreover, there are distinct subsets of the Hispanic population that are dependent on ancestry, which are likely to promote great differences among them; thus, it may be inappropriate to generalize from any mixed Hispanic group.

Table 11.8 Discriminant Functions Separating Race and Sex Groups at MCS:0: Biographical Data, Life Themes Involvement, Ability Factors, and Personality/Motivation Factors

Race—Sex group	Functions evaluated at group centroids			% classified
	Func 1	Func 2	Func 3	
White males	0.89	−0.15	0.08	72
White females	−0.95	−0.29	0.71	72
Black males	0.64	1.54	−1.26	73
Black females	−1.18	−0.38	−1.06	67

Variable or factor	Rotated standardized discriminant-function coefficients		
	Func 1	Func 2	Func 3
Masculinity	1.06	0.15	0.05
Submissiveness	0.39	0.14	0.28
Positiveness	−0.35	0.32	0.26
High school grades	−0.32	−0.09	−0.15
No. of siblings	0.01	0.56	−0.01
Ego-Functional life theme	−0.10	0.54	0.42
Impulsivity	0.10	−0.49	0.07
Occupational life theme	0.19	−0.28	0.06
Father's education	0.11	−0.26	0.22
Adjusted Conformity	−0.17	−0.25	0.21
Unconventionality	−0.23	0.25	0.03
Cognitive Ability	0.29	−0.33	0.62
Service life theme	0.07	0.05	−0.39
Undergraduate grades	0.06	0.08	0.37

Among the blacks, the clear differences in family background between the men and women suggest a disparate selection process for entering the Bell System. One possibility is that the telephone companies were not able to attract as many top quality black men. Because of still prevalent occupational sex segregation, many more jobs and industries are open to men than to women; thus it may be that the telephone companies, traditional employers of women, had less competition in recruiting black women than black men. The lesser differences between white men and white women might seem to contradict this hypothesis; however, the prevalence of affirmative action policies positioned against a relative shortage of black college graduates intensifies the competition among the black group.

In light of the difficult history of blacks, reviewed earlier in this chapter, the data presented here should not be a surprise. It is likely that Julius and Joanna feel as though they have just gotten their feet in the door to occupational equality, and their footsteps are still rather tentative. The pre-eminence of financial gains and security in their values is a natural consequence for members of groups historically deprived of economic opportunities and familiar with the devastations of poverty. The inadequacies of their educational experiences are no doubt reflected in their SCAT scores, and their lower levels of self-esteem signal both uncertainty about competition with more privileged, better-educated whites and assimilation of derogatory allegations about their fundamental nature. Their behavioral reserve and lower level of poise reflect their tentativeness about being accepted by a majority that is only recently giving up its prejudices. The data in this chapter should be interpreted not to show the inadequacies of the minority group members but to show the inadequacies of a nation that claims to stand for equal treatment for all its citizens.

In presenting the data for this chapter, we have focused on a statistical average as representative of each race/ethnic group and a composite case history to represent the average. This should not suggest that all blacks or all Hispanics or all whites were like those portrayed here. Each race/ethnic group displayed a full spectrum of individual differences, ranging from those very competent and well-adjusted to those with severe problems. Some of this diversity is addressed and illustrated in the next chapter. Also considered in Chapter 12 is how the various participant characteristics evaluated in the assessment centers — including those that differed by race and gender — varied in importance for judgments of managerial potential and adjustment.

CHAPTER 12

Managerial Potential and Personal Adjustment in the New Generation

We have seen in Chapters 3 and 4 how characteristics of the MPS managers at the initial assessment were related to later advancement and adjustment after 20 years of work and personal life. A question to be raised is whether the MCS sample showed similar indicators of their futures.

In this chapter, comparisons are made between the MPS and MCS samples (and between race and gender groups within MCS) on the variables that led the assessors to their ratings of managerial potential and current personal adjustment. The assessors in MCS were instructed to use the same standards in making their dimension ratings and predictions as had been used in MPS, so that fair comparisons could be made across generations. Yet the weighting of different dimensions used to make the predictions was unspecified, and there were some new exercises in MCS for which no precedent had been set by MPS. Consequently, it becomes useful to see whether the additional data contribute to our understanding of the constructs of managerial potential and adjustment, and whether changing times resulted in different emphases by the assessors in coming to their conclusions.

For MPS, managerial potential was indicated by the average (modal) assessor judgment on the question, "Should this person be advanced to the third level of management within 10 years?" Responses were coded as "no," "questionable" if there was substantial disagreement among assessors, "yes," or "above" if the participant had more than third-level potential.

Unfortunately, there was no dimension rating of Adjustment at the first MPS assessment center; this dimension was added only at MPS:20. Further analyses showed that there were two important variables contributing in an independent way to the Adjustment rating at MPS:20: the General Adjustment rating from the projective exercises, and the assessor rating of the dimension Resistance to Stress. Consequently, a predicted Adjustment rating for the original assessment was computed, using these two variables from MPS:0 in a regression equation derived with MPS:20 data. For the sake of tabular summaries, the Adjustment ratings were categorized into "low," "moderate," and "high," such that the proportion of the college group in

349

those categories at MPS:0 matched their distribution in the MPS:20 categories as closely as possible.

For MCS, managerial potential was indicated by the average (modal) assessor judgment on the question, "What level of management should this person reach?" Responses were given as "low potential for the third level," "marginal potential for the third level," "third level," or "above third level." Adjustment was rated as a dimension by the assessors on the usual 5-point scale, with ratings from 1 to 2 considered low, from 2.5 to 3.5 considered moderate, and from 4 to 5 considered high.

A comparison of the numbers of persons falling into each category is shown in Table 12.1. Both samples showed the effects of a relationship between the ratings of managerial potential and Adjustment; in MPS the correlation between the two variables was .34, while in MCS it was .42. This is a stronger relationship than that between Adjustment and management level attained by MPS:20. In both samples at the original assessment, the majority of those rated highest in management potential were also rated high in

Table 12.1   Ratings of Management Potential and Adjustment, MPS:0 and MCS:0

Management potential rating	Adjustment rating			Total
	Low	Moderate	High	
MPS:0				
Should be third level				
Above third	3 (9%)	14 (41%)	17 (50%)	34 (100%)
Yes	15 (27%)	19 (35%)	21 (38%)	55 (100%)
Questionable	8 (19%)	20 (47%)	15 (35%)	43 (100%)
No	60 (50%)	38 (32%)	21 (18%)	119 (100%)
Total	86 (34%)	91 (36%)	74 (29%)	251 (100%)
MCS:0				
Level should be:				
Above third	6 (15%)	13 (32%)	22 (54%)	41 (100%)
Third	27 (23%)	59 (49%)	34 (28%)	120 (100%)
Marginal for third	63 (51%)	43 (35%)	18 (15%)	124 (100%)
Low for third	36 (61%)	20 (34%)	3 (5%)	59 (100%)
Total	132 (38%)	135 (39%)	77 (22%)	344 (100%)

Note. MPS:0 Adjustment was predicted from the projective rating of General Adjustment and the dimension rating of Resistance to Stress. MCS:0 Adjustment was rated as an assessment dimension.

Adjustment, while the majority of those rated low in Adjustment were felt to have the lowest potential for management. This trend was even more pronounced in the black sample of MCS.

A total of ten composite case studies will be used to illustrate this chapter, and the reader is referred to Figure 1.1 for a review of the criteria used to select the A, B, C, and D types and the names assigned to them. It will be recalled that white males have been given one-syllable names, white females two-syllable names, and black males and females three-syllable names.

CORRELATES OF MANAGEMENT POTENTIAL

The MCS:0 assessment improved on that of MPS:0 by adding a more complete biographical inventory, the CPI and G-Z personality measures, and 10 of the dimensions developed for MPS:20 to measure personal satisfaction and functioning. As will be seen, all of these contributed in some way to the ratings of managerial potential.

Backgrounds

The relationship of family experiences to ratings of management potential were better established in MCS than in MPS, as shown in Table 12.2. It appears that intellectual stimulation was probably more prevalent in the homes of the higher-potential candidates, who had better-educated parents and well-read mothers. The lower-potential candidates were more likely to have fathers in skilled or unskilled occupations and less likely to have fathers in business or professional jobs. Among blacks and males, coming from large families and being one of the younger children in the family had a strong negative relationship to potential for management. The higher-potential candidates had also established their independence by the time of initial assessment and saw their parents less frequently than did the lower-potential assessees.

To illustrate various kinds of data in this section on management potential, composite case examples of type A are contrasted with those of type C. Different race and sex groups are brought in to exemplify relevant points. First, family backgrounds are illustrated for Art, a high-potential, well-adjusted white man, and Adrian, his black male counterpart.

Art was born and raised in a small town in Missouri. His accounts of his childhood brought mental images of Tom Sawyer venturing into the wilderness. As a youngster, Art filled the house with frogs, birds, snakes, and other small creatures. He spent a lot of time exploring on his own, since his sister and brother were, respectively, 5 and 7 years younger than he.

Art had a very close relationship with his father, who read to him when he was a child. His father, a college graduate, was in the life insurance business and for several years led the state in sales. He was a role model for Art, who found his father intel-

Table 12.2 Family and Educational Variables Significantly Correlated with Ratings of Management Potential, MPS:0 College Group and MCS:0 by Sex and Race

Variable	MPS college (n = 274)	MCS total (n = 344)	MCS males (n = 186)	MCS females (n = 158)	MCS whites (n = 237)	MCS blacks (n = 79)
Family						
No. of siblings	.07	-.09	-.15*	.02	.12	-.34**
Birth rank	.04	-.09	-.16*	.01	.10	-.26*
How often see parents	N/A	-.24**	-.20*	-.30**	-.25**	-.18
Father's education	.01 †	.17**	.12	.24**	.05	.19
Mother's education	.11	.17**	.17*	.16*	.10	.22*
Well-read mother	N/A	.16*	.13	.18*	.16*	.02
Education						
Level of education	N/A	.14*	.07	.24**	.12	.33**
High school grades	.20**	.07	.12	-.08	.05	.06
Undergraduate grades	.18**	.16*	.10	.24*	.02 †	.39*
College extracurricular activities	.02	.13*	.11	.18*	.11	.12

Note. N/A = Data not available.

† Significant difference between correlations at $p < .05$.

* $p < .05$.

** $p < .005$.

352

lectually inspiring and tough when pushed. However, he was also generally compassionate and understanding.

Art's mother had forsaken her college education in her sophomore year for marriage, a situation she was later to regret. She had been an excellent student in both high school and college, and she continued her own educational development after leaving school by reading extensively. She was active in politics, the community, and church affairs.

Adrian had had a less idyllic childhood than Art but one that provided important intellectual stimulation. He grew up in Chicago and was the oldest of two boys. His parents were divorced when he was quite young, and he was raised by his grandmother until his mother remarried.

Adrian's stepfather insisted that he get the best possible education, so he joined a small group of blacks integrating a junior high school by being bussed to a distant suburb. Although Adrian had a difficult time with some white bullies at first, things soon settled down and he was accepted. He was resourceful and popular as a young man and participated in a number of extracurricular activities while in high school, which was also integrated.

Adrian's stepfather was a high school graduate who was employed by the U.S. Post Office. Adrian described him as "kind to my mother and devoted to her sons. He was always trying to help people and teach them to do things, even if he wasn't asked." Adrian's mother was trained as a licensed practical nurse. He saw her as "a kind, generous, and sensitive person. She was always looking for the best way to handle problems and situations."

The family backgrounds of Art and Adrian, both high-potential, well-adjusted managers, differ from that of Craig, a white man who represents the C type — high in Adjustment but low in management potential. Craig's parents provided a loving and emotionally healthy environment but their values were not oriented toward exceptional achievement.

Craig was third in a family of four, having two older sisters and one younger brother. His father was a high school graduate employed as an electrician. He described him as "loving and fair." He never pushed Craig either in school or in sports but seemed primarily concerned that he behave properly and follow religious teachings.

Craig's mother was a housewife who enjoyed floral designing when she was not caring for the household or the children. She was light-hearted and sentimental, and she tended to be somewhat overprotective of her children.

Educational experiences were related to management potential in both samples, as has been documented in more detail elsewhere (Howard, 1986). The most potent predictor among them was college major (not shown in Table 12.2 since it was a qualitative variable), with the humanities and social science majors generally performing best at initial assessment and the engineers and other technical majors being rated much more poorly.

Although postgraduate training was rare for the MPS generation, a large proportion of MCS participants had gone on to graduate school, and the higher-potential managers tended to have more education, especially among women and blacks. Undergraduate grades were correlated with management potential for both the MPS and MCS samples, with high school grades also predictive for MPS but not MCS. The number of extracurricular activities was also related to managerial potential in the MCS sample.

The educational backgrounds of high-potential MCS participants are well illustrated by the case of Amy, a white female of type A, and Alison, her black female counterpart.

Amy never had academic problems in the early grades and was, in fact, skipped from the third grade to the fifth. Her academic excellence continued into high school, where she always scored high on national tests. She was very active in student government and played basketball and softball, since these were the only sports open to women.

Amy had numerous scholarship offers, and she accepted one in a private university with a strong emphasis on the liberal arts. She majored in biology and sociology, earned excellent grades, and considered going on to medical school. She worked in a drug store for spending money but still had time for an active campus life, including the chorus, the yearbook, and a little theatre group.

An early marriage changed Amy's mind about pursuing medicine, and she enrolled in an MBA program. She completed the degree in record time, earning mostly A's.

Alison grew up in a southern city where the urban schools enrolled only black students. She was very popular among her classmates, being both physically attractive and academically outstanding. She said, "I met whites for the first time in junior high school while I was travelling with the girls' basketball team. I noticed that the books used at the white school were new and up-to-date, while those at my black school were worn and second-hand, having been used previously by white students. It was the first time I really felt the effects of discrimination, and it made me angry."

Alison was on the college preparatory track in high school and was in the national honor society. She still had time to pursue many extracurricular activities, including a modern dance club and the student government, of which she was elected president.

College was a rewarding experience for Alison, who commented, "It gave me a chance to develop a sense of responsibility. I learned how to schedule my time and balance my academic load and my social life." Her parents couldn't afford to send her to a private school, so she went to a state university, living at home her first two years. She majored in psychology and earned money for tuition and other expenses by doing peer counseling that was related to the psychology curriculum and by providing support at the university counseling center. She became a minority recruiter for the university and was an advocate for the Black Student League. The psychology club and the drama club also stirred her interest and participation.

Alison applied to several graduate schools but decided not to attend. She said, "I was afraid I couldn't afford it, and I was tired of not having enough money. Also, I feared graduate school might lead me into teaching, which I was set dead against, because I wanted to avoid the stereotype of the educated black woman." She liked the image of a corporate executive and decided to pursue a business career instead. After settling into her Bell System job, she enrolled in some business classes at night to re-orient her career.

Cathy, a white woman of type C (high in Adjustment, low in management potential), provides a contrast to Amy and Alison. Although as emotionally stable as her high-potential peers, Cathy did not pursue academic life with the same kind of vigor.

In her elementary and high school years, Cathy was able to get good grades without working very hard, and she felt this made her somewhat lazy. She was a cheerleader and pom-pom girl in high school, where she particularly enjoyed the excitement associated with sports.

Cathy majored in math in college, primarily because she did well in such courses. This left her free for a lot of dating, and she admitted, "I had a terrific social life in college; that was one of the best things about it." She participated in musical variety shows and was a dance coordinator for her sorority but had no extracurricular activities that weren't primarily entertainment-oriented.

Lifestyles

In addition to early background, current lifestyles also differentiated those rated higher versus lower in management potential. Table 12.3 shows correlations of involvement in the nine life themes with rated management potential.

Table 12.3   Correlations of Current Involvement in Life Themes with Management Potential, MPS:0 and MCS:0

Life theme	MPS ($n = 220$)		MCS ($n = 344$)
Marital-Familial	.05		.01
Parental-Familial	−.11		−.10
Locale-Residential	.01		.02
Financial-Acquisitive	.20**	†	−.03
Ego-Functional	.27**		.22**
Recreational-Social	.02		.01
Religious-Humanism	−.01		.00
Service	−.02	†	.17**
Occupational	.29**		.13*

† Significant difference between MPS and MCS correlations at $p <$ .05.
* $p < .05$.
** $p < .005$.

In each sample, three themes showed a relationship to rated potential, although one of the three was inconsistent across the two generation groups.

Involvement in the Marital-Familial life theme was not related to managerial potential, although within MCS there was a tendency for those with higher potential to be married at assessment. As shown in Table 12.4, the older MPS and MCS black assessees were also rated somewhat higher in potential, suggesting that maturity may have been an advantage. Among the married in MCS, the educational level of the spouse was highly related to the participant's rated potential, especially among blacks. Higher-potential men more often had wives who were not housewives. Perhaps intellectual stimulation in the marital home was a characteristic of high-potential managers, just as it had been in the parental home.

Art married his girlfriend during his junior year of college, but their marriage was to last only 2 years. Their relationship did not become hostile or unfriendly, but seemed to peter out due to a lack of mutual interests. There were no children, and they agreed to divorce.

Art felt he was more mature in selecting his second wife, and he fully expected this marriage to last. He said, "She's a special-education teacher for autistic children and very career-minded. We're able to discuss current events and music and other things with similar interests and perspectives. She generally likes the same things that I do. She's very sensitive and accepting of me, and I respect her and love her very much."

Table 12.4   Marital and Lifestyle Variables Significantly Correlated with Ratings of Management Potential, MPS:0 College Group and MCS:0 by Sex and Race

Variable	MPS college	MCS total	MCS males	MCS females	MCS whites	MCS blacks
Married at assessment	.08	.12*	.13	.15	.14*	.02
Spouse's education	N/A	.34**	.35**	.29*	.28**	.51**
Age at assessment	.22** †	.05	.08	.04	.03	.26*
Read more newspapers	N/A	.15*	.12	.22*	.23**	.04
Read more magazines	−.03	.12*	.08	.17*	.07	.24*
Read more books	.17*	.24*	.16*	.29**	.24**	.22
More interested in current events	N/A	.20**	.20*	.24*	.19*	.06
Make more public speeches	.16*	.19**	.11	.28*	.17*	.37**
Better public speaker	.13	.20**	.09	.33**	.17*	.30*
Drink alcohol more often	N/A	.16*	.20*	.10	.03	.27*
Frequency of exercise	N/A	.09	.10	.09	.17* †	−.30

Note. N/A = Data not available. n's for all groups as in Table 12.2.
† Significant difference between correlations at $p < .05$.
* $p < .05$.
** $p < .005$.

Adrian was 33 years old, married, and the father of one child when he appeared at the assessment center. His maturity was evident, as well as his self-confidence.

Adrian's wife was a high school English teacher, a profession that provided her with optimal working hours for raising their son. He described her as "Fantastic! She's very talented and smart. She attends classes at night in pursuit of a master's degree in guidance and counseling. She really likes having an impact on young people."

In contrast to Art and Adrian, Craig, a low-potential manager, was not married. He was officially engaged, however, to a woman who worked as a dental assistant. He did not anticipate any career conflicts with her, saying, "Our main goal is to raise a family, so I don't expect her to be working very long after we're married. We both want a large family, and she won't think of returning to work until they are all in school."

Across both the MPS and the MCS samples, the managers rated higher in potential were more involved in the Ego-Functional life theme (see Table 12.3). Table 12.4 elaborates this finding, in that high-potential participants read more newspapers, magazines, and books, and had a greater interest in current events. Frequency of public speaking was also a correlate of potential for both the MPS and MCS samples. The meaning of exercise is more difficult to interpret, since high-potential whites exercised more often, while high-potential blacks exercised less often. Both males and blacks in the high-potential category drank alcohol more often than those rated lower — an interesting finding about which we will avoid conclusions of cause and effect!

Having greater Financial-Acquisitive interests was related to high potential in MPS but not in MCS. Instead, those rated highest in MCS were more interested in service to the community, although in general these interests were not very prevalent in the MCS sample. The high-potential managers were rated from their interviews as having more political understanding and stronger political conviction. Political philosophy was unrelated to management potential within each race group.

Reading was a favorite pastime for Amy. While studying so hard for her master's degree, she had promised herself a year of reading nothing but novels. She had generally kept that promise but had begun to read self-development books again, such as *Dress for Success*. She tried to improve her vocabulary by reading and volunteered as often as she could for public speaking to improve her rhetorical abilities.

Politics was of more than a passing interest to Amy, and she intended to run for the school board. She always voted in elections, typically Democratic, and had worked for McGovern when he ran for president.

In keeping with her college career, Cathy's primary interests outside of work were recreational. She had many friends with whom she enjoyed parties, plays, movies, and travel. For exercise as well as pleasure she went to dance classes twice a week, studying modern jazz. When asked about developmental activities, Cathy replied, "I'm happy with myself, and I see no reason to go out seeking self-development experiences or to read a lot of books."

Cathy kept up with current events "by accident—word of mouth or television." She was obviously not well informed when questioned about recent news stories. Moreover, she seldom had a firm opinion on an issue, stating, "I could never take a public position on something like welfare because I can see both the positive and negative sides of it." For example, when asked about affirmative action, she was both for and against. "I think it's necessary, but I'm opposed to hiring people because they're black or female."

Work Interests

For both the MPS and MCS samples, the higher-potential managers were differentiated by greater interest and involvement in work, as shown by the Occupational life theme in Table 12.3. This was also true for projected developments on that theme, in spite of the fact that they did not show any higher expectations on the Expectations Inventory about what life as a manager would be like. There was no indication at original assessment in either MPS or MCS that the high-potential candidates were any more satisfied with work; current satisfaction on the Occupational life theme was unrelated to potential ratings. Likewise, in both samples, scores on the attitude scales of the Management Questionnaire administered in year 1 or 2 after the original assessment showed no relationship to rated potential.

The high-potential managers did have different work preferences from those of their less promising cohorts. There were several items differentiating the management potential groups on the Work Conditions Survey, and these were consistent in direction across the MPS sample and each MCS race and sex group. The higher-potential managers gave more desirable ratings to work that involved a lot of responsibility, required much initiative, was dependent on their decisions, and required practical intelligence and quick decisions. They were more put off by very routine work than those rated lower in management potential.

Before coming to the Bell System, Amy worked for about 9 months with a consulting firm. There she encountered evident sex discrimination, in the form of lower salary levels for women doing essentially the same jobs as men and a lack of women in positions of real responsibility. At group meetings a woman was always made to act as the secretary, and it was clear that the head of the firm had little respect for women. Realizing that she had no future there, she sought out a firm with a reputation for fair treatment of women and won a job at the telephone company.

Her job at the time of assessment was as a group manager in Operator Services, supervising 25 operators and 2 junior supervisors. She rotated with five other group supervisors to assure that force requirements were met on the boards, with a total staff of 115. She was also responsible for training and development, including assuring monthly remote observations and feedback interviews with each operator.

Amy was very well organized and found it easy to get her work done within the regular day. She began to become bored with too little to do and took up various pet projects on her own responsibility and initiative. One of her seminars gained wide approval and dissemination throughout the company, but she soon discovered that her peers bridled at her quick success. After she realized their feelings, Amy made special efforts to include them in her projects and to be friendly, and she thought matters had improved. She hoped she would soon be promoted to a more challenging position.

Cathy worked in a standards group, solving problems for computer programmers. She performed classroom instruction for new trainees, taught the essentials of new releases to the floor staff, and solved physical problems on the terminal, such as troubleshooting malfunctions and switching cables.

Cathy enjoyed her job and her co-workers, although she did not share the same values with many of her colleagues. She commented, "I've never worked with people who take their jobs as seriously as some of these computer jocks. They spend their lunch hours playing with the computer instead of relaxing! I could never do this. When people don't take vacations, that's not a creditable event to me; that's a flaw. The job does not come first with me. I'm a person before I'm a Bell System employee."

Personality and Motivation

A number of personality and motivation scales were related to ratings of management potential. Table 12.5 shows the results arranged in terms of factors, both those from the MPS factor analyses and those derived using the MCS scores. The results were very consistent for MPS and MCS, with Leadership Motivation, Positiveness, Impulsivity, and Ambition all related to potential. The Edwards Achievement scale, a negative contributor to the MCS-derived Affability factor, also was weighted positively in considering promise for future management roles.

The higher-potential managers, then, were characterized by stronger desires to achieve as leaders and professionals. They had greater ambition to advance in the organization and perform in settings where they could be in charge, while the lower-potential managers indicated in their interviews that job security was most valued. Making themselves seen and heard loomed large for the higher-potential managers, and they became restless with the kind of routine that required plodding dependence on rules and regulations or overemphasis of a subordinate role.

Art was highly motivated and was committed to succeeding in his business career. He believed he had an aptitude for selling but an even greater aptitude for managing other personnel in sales. "I want to succeed in this company," he said to his interviewer, "but I'll leave if I'm not evaluated well or moved ahead. I can find another corporation that will reward my skills and motivation."

Art had high scores on both the Edwards Achievement scale and the Sarnoff Motivation for Advancement scale, and his projective responses indicated he was experiencing inner pressure to be successful. "*I secretly* believe I can reach top manage-

Table 12.5   Correlations of Personality and Motivation Factors
with Management Potential, MPS:0 and MCS:0

Factor	MPS college ($n = 274$)	MPS total ($n = 344$)
Factors derived from MPS sample		
Leadership Motivation	.24**	.28**
Positiveness	.15*	.26**
Impulsivity	.14*	.20**
Affability	−.09	−.06
Ambition	.25**	.27**
Factors derived from MCS sample		
Submissiveness		−.11*
Positiveness		.26**
Impulsivity		.04
Affability		−.14*
Ambition		.33**
Adjusted Conformity		.18**
Poise		.36**
Flexibility		.24**
Unconventionality		.02
Masculinity		−.02

* $p < .05$.
** $p < .005$.

ment," he wrote, and, "*In 20 years from now* I could be running a large portion of this show."

Craig scored at only the 10th percentile on the Sarnoff Motivation for Advancement scale, and showed a similar lack of drive on the projective exercises. He noted, "*I regret* not working harder in college," and "*Sometimes* I get lazy." His career goals were vague, illustrated by the response, "*I feel* not pressured at all to decide a career path in the next few years."

When asked about his career goals in the interview, Craig said he had no burning desire to be promoted to high levels in the company. He and his fiancée did not want to relocate out of the Midwest, where they were raised, and he said he was happy doing what he was doing now. Rather than striving for wealth and prestige, he preferred a secure home and involvement in non-work-related activities like golf. Although he thought it might be nice to advance to the third level and be part of middle management, he said he would certainly not be crushed if it didn't happen.

The new MCS factors at the bottom of Table 12.5 provide additional insights about the characteristics of higher- versus lower-potential managers. The relationship of the Adjusted Conformity and Poise factors to potential was very consistent with the relationship of potential to the Positiveness factor. The Positiveness factor indicated that the higher-potential managers had higher General Adjustment, Optimism, and Self-Confidence as rated from the projective exercises. A rating of self-confidence on the Personal History Questionnaire was also strongly related to managerial potential.

All the scales on the Poise factor were significantly related to management potential, indicating that the higher-level managers were more sociable and willing to take the initiative in social situations. They were comfortable and secure with themselves and with others. There was a negative correlation between the Edwards Succorance scale (on the Affability factor) and management potential, indicating that even though the high-potential managers were more at ease in social situations, they were not dependent on others for emotional support.

The Adjusted Conformity factor contained a number of scales pertaining to presenting oneself in a favorable light and being responsible and under control. Of the 13 scales in the factor, 6 related to management potential for the total MCS group, but there were strong race differences, as shown in Table 12.6. Many scales were much more predictive of management potential

Table 12.6 Correlations of Scores in Adjusted Conformity Factor with Management Potential at MCS:0 Showing Race Differences

Score	Whites ($n = 237$)		Blacks ($n = 79$)
Total factor	.05		.34**
CPI scales			
Sense of Well-Being	.00	†	.26*
Self-Control	−.13*	†	.25*
Tolerance	.08		.31*
Good Impression	.03		.13
Achievement via Conformance	.16*		.30*
Intellectual Efficiency	.18*	†	.40**
Psychological Mindedness	−.02	†	.38**
Socialization	−.05		.12
Responsibility	.22**		.34**
G-Z scales			
Emotional Stability	.03		.13
Objectivity	.01	†	.23*
Personal Relations	.07		.17
Friendliness	−.10	†	.23*

† Significant difference between white and black samples at $p < .05$.
* $p < .05$.
** $p < .005$.

in the black group than in the white group. Higher-potential blacks were better distinguished from lower-potential blacks on the CPI scales of Sense of Well-Being, Intellectual Efficiency, Psychological Mindedness, and Self-Control, as well as on the G-Z scales of Objectivity (being thick-skinned) and Friendliness (lacking hostility). In contrast, high-potential whites were more impulsive and indicated less self-control than did low-potential whites.

Amy's high standards and tendency to feel guilty if she didn't meet them constituted a potential source of stress for her, but her firm belief in self-worth and her confidence level counteracted the likelihood of any major difficulties. She presented a very positive self-concept, saying, "I like myself." Her mostly high scores on the CPI and G-Z measures confirmed these positive attitudes toward herself. She was above the 85th percentile on such scales as CPI Capacity for Status (showing the ambition and self-assurance that lead to status), CPI Social Presence (self-confidence and verve in social interactions), CPI Self-Acceptance (social poise and sureness of self), and G-Z Ascendance (persuasiveness and ability to defend self).

Alison was just as positive about herself as Amy but had a stronger sense of deliberateness, patience, and self-control. On the projective exercises she indicated the belief that women should be assertive and that men value a strong woman. Hence she expected success from being self-directed, determined, and expressive. Yet she was sensitive to uncooperative interactions that she felt might result from assertiveness, and she rejected behavior likely to promote conflict, ill will, or aggression. Her attitude toward subordinates was accepting, and she avoided developing and acknowledging critical feelings toward others.

Alison displayed a great deal of faith in her own capabilities. She wrote, "*My best qualities* are my motivation and strength to do whatever I want," and, "*The things I want out of life* I believe I can get." She indicated her self-assurance more specifically by responding, "*When faced with a decision which involves others I* can take care of it."

Cathy's responses to the projective exercises seemed natural, unpretentious, and relaxed. She was a daydreamer, and she conjured up fantasies of success, freedom, friends, and lovers. While Alison had held a positive image of female strength, Cathy associated strength with men and was very receptive to being helped by and receiving emotional support from men. She wrote, "*Most women* want to be treated like women."

Cathy's projective responses gave the impression of a compassionate person who never gave offense. She seemed the sort of person to whom others would go for a sympathetic audience, kind words, and a little nonthreatening advice. It was likely that she had difficulty maintaining a proper balance between empathizing with subordinates and maintaining her authority over them, and it would be difficult for her not to get involved in their personal problems.

One final personality and motivation factor distinguishing higher- from lower-potential managers within the total MCS group was Flexibility. The higher-potential managers showed more interest in achieving in unstructured situations (CPI Achievement via Independence) and scored lower on Authoritarianism on the Bass version of the California F Scale.

By scoring high on Flexibility and low on Authoritarianism, Art described himself as adaptable, open-minded, and able to cope with uncertainties. His projective responses indicated that he was attracted to new assignments and to the challenge of the unfamiliar and unstructured tasks. He wrote, "*I like* to struggle with a new job." He adopted an accepting and tolerant attitude toward other people, stating, "*My best qualities* are flexibility and the ability to understand and motivate people."

While Craig was likely to avoid hostile or aggressive actions toward others, he could be critical of others when they deviated from his values. As might be expected from his high Authoritarianism score, he had conservative views toward such groups as women and migrant workers. He stated, "*Migrant workers* should be sent back to their own country," and "*Most women* should be happy being housewives." He further stereotyped women with "*Men* are the superior sex," and "*The only trouble* with women is that they complain too much." Though he harbored these prejudices, his desire for harmony would probably result in his being seen as a likeable and not very forceful manager.

Abilities

Although there were significant differences between the management potential groups on background, personality, and motivation factors, the exercises that differentiated them to the greatest degree were those that revealed abilities. Table 12.7 shows the relationship of the three ability factors as well as some other individual exercise scores to ratings of management potential. Results were very much the same across the MCS race and sex groups.

All three ability factors weighed heavily in the ratings of management potential in both the MPS and MCS samples. The Administrative Ability factor correlated with potential to a significantly greater degree for MCS than for MPS, but it should be remembered that the scores making up this factor were not derived in the same way in the MPS and MCS samples. The MCS factor was based on dimensions, rather than post hoc coding, and the assessors were of course influenced by their own dimension ratings in making their final predictions of management potential. The Organizing and Planning and the Decision Making dimensions were equally important in determining ratings of potential.

Art made extensive use of the calendar in his In-Basket to organize his time and to plan meetings to be held on his return. He requested specific reports from different individuals and outlined his expectations for subordinates. He was comfortable with delegating and provided clear-cut instructions while refusing to be drawn into making all the decisions himself.

Art solved problems quickly but not before considering various alternatives. He then

Table 12.7   Correlations of Ability Factors and Selected Ability Scores with Management Potential, MPS:0 and MCS:0

Factor/score	MPS college		MCS total
Ability factors			
Administrative	.42*	†	.72*
Interpersonal	.55*		.64*
Cognitive	.57*		.46*
SCAT			
Verbal	.56*		.42*
Quantitative	.21*		.20*
Total	.50*		.38*
Competitive discussion			
Oral rating — observer	.35*	†	.54*
Overall rating — observer	.49*		.53*

Note. n's as in Table 12.5
† Significant difference between MPS and MCS samples at $p < .05$.
* $p < .005$.

selected the best solution in accordance with company policy and his own guiding philosophies. He was willing to bite the bullet in refusing a vacation request, but he did so in such a tactful and sensitive manner that the recipient would likely be favorably disposed to him. His decisions generally reflected a smooth blend of assertiveness and sensitivity. In his response to a complaint, he was particularly creative in devising a technique for solving minority issues.

Craig's decisions on the In-Basket were of mixed quality; some were perceptive and sound, while others were decidedly off the mark. He was particularly at fault for delegating issues to some of his more reckless subordinates without sufficient guidance and provision for following up on them. He seemed to see himself as a shirtsleeves manager who expected to win the support of his subordinates by working alongside of them.

He was often unorganized in his approach to the In-Basket and failed to complete a required letter, saying that it "got lost in the shuffle." Although Craig claimed to have ranked the items in order of priority, it was clear that he did not vary much the order in which they appeared. He seemed uncomfortable with the lack of structure and the limited information provided. He continually sought reassurance from the interviewer and apologized for his deficiencies.

The SCAT was relied on somewhat more heavily in MPS than in MCS, although the difference between the correlations was not statistically significant. For both samples, the Verbal scale was given notably more weight than the Quantitative scale. Thus this trend persisted in spite of the fact that both scales were equally predictive of later success in MPS.

The General Information Test also showed a strong relationship to potential in MCS, even though the Contemporary Affairs Test used with MPS was unrelated to predictions of future management level. The General Information Test was a measure of cumulative learning across a variety of fields rather than just current events, so it was more related to academic performance and the SCAT test. In both samples the Written Communication Skills dimension was also a strong predictor of management potential.

Amy scored at the 81st percentile on the Verbal scale of the SCAT and at the 72nd on the Quantitative. Both of these skills served her well on the In-Basket, as she prepared clear, crisp memos and readily sized up the meaning of quantitative materials. The projective stories and sentences also showed her writing to be clear, with a good vocabulary and excellent grammar, spelling, and punctuation.

Cathy scored at the 60th percentile on the Quantitative scale of the SCAT, a strong score that might be expected of a math major, but her Verbal score was only at the 25th percentile. Her writing ability was no more than fair and included grammatical errors, spelling mistakes, and awkward constructions. She was in the lowest quintile on the General Information Test, no doubt reflecting both her narrrow range of interests and her lack of concern with self-development.

Within the Interpersonal Ability factor, the rating of the oral presentation in the competitive group exercise was more closely tied to overall ratings of potential for MCS than for MPS. The average rating on oral presentations was lower for the MCS group, and it may have been that those doing well in this exercise made a particularly good impression on the assessors relative to their peers.

Within MCS, ratings of depth of understanding and contribution to the group functioning in the Counseling Center Group Discussion were equally related to overall potential. The ratings by the staff observers were most predictive, with correlations in the .40s and .50s across the race and sex groups. Self-ratings had much weaker relationships to potential, with correlations ranging from .09 to .34.

Art made a well-organized and effective presentation in the competitive group discussion. He used a great deal of the reference material, and he backed up his arguments with details and specific budget figures.

During the group discussion, Art used the easel to formulate a complete package, listing in detail the various proposals with their cost and benefits. He assumed leadership of the group because of his ability to listen to others and to work out compromises.

In the Counseling Center Group Discussion, Art seemed to be the only one who understood and expressed the complexity of issues involved in the different cases. He also made certain that the other participants attended to each of the points raised in the handout. Art took on a variety of roles in the discussion including those involved in clarifying ideas, formulating recommendations, and hammering out issues. His own ideas were invariably included in the final recommendations.

Craig read his presentation for the competitive group exercise word for word from his notes and delivered it in an unenthusiastic monotone. He spoke much too rapidly, with few gestures and little eye contact. Moreover, his story was disjointed and difficult to follow.

In the group discussion part of the exercise, he made occasional statements and asked questions that were perceptive and analytical, but he failed to follow up on them. He did not try to convince the group that his suggestions were good ones, and he never defended his own proposal directly. He continually tried to compromise on the issues and attempted to diffuse conflict and confrontation at all costs. He ended up with very little money for his own proposal.

Craig also seemed overly anxious to avoid conflict in the Counseling Center Group Discussion. He was easily swayed by others' arguments and frequently just restated their ideas. He seemed not to recognize the fact that he reversed himself on issues at times. The ambiguities of the cases also appeared to leave him at a loss.

Overall Assessment Evaluations

The dimensions created for the original MPS assessment were developed with the intention of their relating to success as a manager. It is no surprise, then, that nearly all of them correlated significantly with ratings of management potential in both MPS and MCS. Only the dimension of Bell System Value Orientation, or identification with the organization, had no relationship to predictions of management success in either sample.

The 10 new dimensions added to MCS were taken from the MPS:20 assessment, where management potential was no longer the dominant concern. Still, three of these had strong positive relationships with ratings of potential in MCS. One of these was Self-Development, and its relationship to managerial potential was consistent with that shown by involvement in the Ego-Functional life theme. The other two, Adjustment and Happiness, were in line with the Adjusted Conformity and Positiveness personality factors, also shown to be related to managerial potential. Modest relationships with potential were shown for the dimensions of Involvement (in affairs of the world and the community) and (lack of) Cynicism. No significant relationships with management potential were shown for Financial Motivation, Conservatism, Religiosity, Avocational Interest, or Selfishness.

The relative contributions of the various dimension factors to ratings of management potential are shown in Table 12.8. Three factors showed a significant difference in correlations between the MPS and MCS samples. Both Interpersonal Skills and Stability of Performance carried more weight in the

Table 12.8   Correlations of Dimension Factors with Management Potential, MPS:0 and MCS:0

Factor	MPS college		MCS total
Factors derived from MPS dimensions			
Administrative Skills	.62**		.69**
Interpersonal Skills	.57**	†	.74**
Intellectual Ability	.61**		.47**
Advancement Motivation	.29**		.40**
Work Involvement	.47**		.54**
Stability of Performance	.44**	†	.65**
Independence	.27**	†	.06
Nonconformity	.46**		.32**
Factors derived from MCS dimensions			
Administrative Skills			.71**
Interpersonal Skills			.75**
Intellectual Ability			.50**
Advancement Motivation			.07
Work Involvement			.61**
Stability of Performance			.58**
Independence			.04
Company Loyalty			−.14*
External Self-Development			.31**
Social Liberalism			.12*

Note. n's as in Table 12.5
† Significant difference between MPS and MCS correlations at $p <$ .05.
* $p < .05$.
** $p < .005$.

assessors' ratings for MCS than for MPS. On the other hand, Independence was related to management potential for MPS but not for MCS.

The dimensions involved in the three factors showing generational differences are shown in Table 12.9, along with their correlations with management potential. In every case except Need for Peer Approval, all the dimensions in each factor played a role in producing the different magnitudes of correlations within the two samples.

The assessors evaluating management potential among the MCS participants were more influenced than the MPS assessors had been by the assessees' performance on Leadership Skills, Behavior Flexibility, Personal Impact, Tolerance of Uncertainty, and Resistance to Stress. Thus forceful leadership qualities and the ability to deal flexibly with unstructured and stressful conditions took on an added importance in evaluating the relative success of the new generation.

Table 12.9   Correlations of Dimensions with Management Potential for Factors Showing Generational Differences, MPS:0 and MCS:0

Factor	MPS college		MCS total
Interpersonal Skills			
Leadership Skills	.51**	†	.70**
Behavior Flexibility	.41**	†	.63**
Personal Impact	.48**	†	.65**
Stability of Performance			
Tolerance of Uncertainty	.37**	†	.60**
Resistance to Stress	.40**	†	.57**
Independence			
Need for Superior Approval	−.34**	†	−.11*
Need for Peer Approval	−.22**		−.14*
Goal Flexibility	−.11	†	.14*

Note. n's as in Table 12.5.
† Significant difference between MPS and MCS samples at $p < .05$.
* $p < .05$.
** $p < .005$.

This new generation would be dealing with an environment that was considerably less predictable and stable than had been true in the past, and one probably requiring greater skills of communication and persuasion.

By the time of MCS, the assessors were much less impressed by low Need for Superior Approval in evaluating management potential, perhaps because the MCS group as a whole was so much more independent than the MPS group had been. Goal Flexibility, showing the likelihood of reorienting oneself toward a different life goal, had a mildly negative relationship with ratings of potential for MPS and a mildly positive one for MCS. Combined with the results on the Stability of Performance factor, it appears that in the 1950s the assessors were impressed when the MPS men showed signs of independence, but in the 1970s and early 1980s the assessors were impressed when the MCS participants showed signs of flexibility.

The factors derived from the 36 MCS dimensions added little to the prediction of management potential. External Self-Development was characteristic of the high-potential candidates, although being deeply involved in a hobby (Avocational Interest) was not a significant dimension. The very small though statistically significant relationship between management potential and Social Liberalism came from the Social Objectivity dimension; Conservativism and Religiosity showed no relationships with potential. The small negative relationship between potential and Company Loyalty was due primarily to the lesser need for job security among the high-potential candidates.

Race Differences Among High-Potential Participants

In light of the many race differences shown in this chapter and in Chapter 11, an additional question to pose of the data is whether blacks and whites within each management potential category have essentially the same strengths. This is of particular importance in viewing those in the high-potential category, or those for whom the assessors estimated that their ultimate level should be middle management or higher. To answer this question, t-tests were computed between the 23 high-potential blacks and the 127 high-potential whites on all the essential variables relating to management success.

Three dimension factors showed significant differences between the two groups. On one of the factors the high-potential whites were higher, but on the other two factors the high-potential blacks had higher ratings. The differences suggest that relative weaknesses among the blacks in one area were compensated for by superior performance in other areas.

Table 12.10 shows the three dimension factors involved and some critical dimensions and scores that comprised these factors. The high-potential whites scored higher than the high-potential blacks on the Intellectual Ability factor. There were no significant differences between the groups in Written Communication Skills or Range of Interests, but General Mental Ability did show an

Table 12.10 Dimension Factors and Key Variables Differentiating MCS High-Potential Whites and Blacks

	Mean		
Factor	Whites ($n = 127$)		Blacks ($n = 23$)
Intellectual Ability	3.4	**	2.8
General Mental Ability	3.6	**	2.5
SCAT Verbal	69 %ile	**	45 %ile
SCAT Quantitative	47 %ile	**	12 %ile
Interpersonal Skills	3.1	*	3.4
Oral Communication Skills	3.4	**	4.2
Personal Impact	2.8	**	3.4
Forcefulness	3.2	*	3.7
Likeableness	3.3	*	3.6
G-Z Ascendance	75 %ile	*	88 %ile
Stability of Performance	3.5	*	3.8
Resistance to Stress	3.6	*	3.9
Tolerance of Uncertainty	3.4		3.8

* $p < .05$.
** $p < .005$.

advantage for the whites. Both the Verbal and Quantitative scales of the SCAT pointed to this difference.

In spite of having lower measured mental ability than the high-potential whites, the high-potential blacks earned comparable grades in high school and college. Nor was there a significant difference in the quality of the colleges attended by the high-potential whites and blacks, according to ratings published either in the Gourman report (1983) or in Barrons' listings of college competitiveness (1984). More of the high-potential blacks had received master's degrees (47.8% of blacks and 28.4% of whites), although among the master's degree holders, more whites majored in business (70.3% of whites and 37.5% of blacks).

The high-potential blacks were rated higher than their white counterparts on the Interpersonal Skills factor. The assessors gave the blacks higher dimension ratings on Oral Communication Skills and on both the Forcefulness and Likeableness ratings of Personal Impact. Stability of Performance was also an area where the blacks outperformed the whites. The difference was statistically significant for Resistance to Stress and nearly so for Tolerance of Uncertainty. Thus even with lesser measured verbal skills, the high-potential blacks were able to communicate orally better than the high-potential whites, and their overall interpersonal impact was definitely superior.

It should be noted that the high-potential blacks performed better than the high-potential whites on the two dimension factors that were given increased importance by the MCS staff in evaluating overall potential for management. The assessors were using the same standards for both the white and black groups, since correlations of Interpersonal Skills and Stability of Performance with overall potential did not differ significantly by race.

The high-potential blacks achieved these high levels of performance in spite of background factors that put them at a definite disadvantage compared to the high-potential whites. Over half the blacks in this category had parents who had been separated (52.2% of the blacks compared to 10.2% of the whites) and one-third had parents who were divorced (33.3% of blacks and 6.4% of the whites). The fathers of the blacks were less likely to be college graduates (18.0% of the blacks compared to 43.3% of the whites), less likely to have managerial occupations (8.7% of the blacks compared to 42.5% of the whites), and more likely to have skilled or unskilled jobs (39.1% of the blacks and 18.9% of the whites). That the high-potential blacks could achieve so much without the favorable environments enjoyed by the whites is indeed testimony to their outstanding potential for taking on the challenges of management.

Adrian provides an example of the kinds of interpersonal skills that the high-potential blacks exhibited.

Adrian's presentation for the competitive group discussion was exceptional. He spoke at length, and he knew his facts well. He was forceful and enthusiastic and quite dramatic in his examples. In the ensuing discussion he was the clear leader as he questioned each participant in sequence and coordinated the group in the task of listing priority requests and deleting secondary requests. He made the difficult tasks of negotiation and compromise look simple, and all rated him extremely well.

In the Counseling Center discussion, Adrian was not as controlling but was highly effective in encouraging individuals to present opinions and in helping the group members to come to a consensus. He had many clearly stated opinions, but he was able to incorporate others' ideas into his own and to create compromises.

The assessment staff commented favorably on Adrian's commanding presence and ability to withstand stress. His strong interpersonal and administrative skills as well as his clear commitment to his career and to advancement made him an exceptionally fine candidate for management. The assessors unanimously rated him as having potential above the third level of management.

CORRELATES OF ADJUSTMENT

Since the assessors' ratings of management potential and Adjustment were significantly correlated, many of the variables just discussed also related to current ratings of Adjustment. Yet there were many other characteristics differentiating those well adjusted from those poorly adjusted.

Backgrounds

A number of questions about family background and childhood experiences were asked of MCS in a questionnaire that was more extensive than that administered to the MPS men. Significant relationships between responses to these questions and ratings of Adjustment are shown for the primary race and sex groups of MCS in Table 12.11.

There was a strong negative relationship between family size and Adjustment among the blacks but not among the other groups. The black males in particular showed wide variation in family size, ranging from no brothers and sisters to 13. In general, those from the largest families had more difficulties adjusting to their current life circumstances.

Parental separation and divorce took a bigger toll in terms of Adjustment ratings on the whites and males; relationships were not significant for the blacks or females. A strong indicator of maladjustment was mental illness in the family. There was a trend in the direction of physical illnesses in the family to be related to maladjustment among the participants, but this trend did not reach the level of statistical significance.

There were several parental characteristics that related to Adjustment ratings in the females but not the males. The well-adjusted women had mothers who worked a lot around the house and participated more frequently in religious activities, had greater spiritual interests, and were more likely to

Table 12.11   Family Background Variables Significantly Correlated with Adjustment at MCS:0 by Race and Sex

Variable	Males ($n = 186$)		Females ($n = 158$)		Whites ($n = 237$)		Blacks ($n = 79$)
No. of siblings	−.10		.04		.04	†	−.24*
Parents separated	−.17*		−.06		−.18**		−.06
Parents divorced	−.18*		−.07		−.21**		−.10
Severe physical illness in family	−.15		−.11		−.11		−.23
Mental illness in family	−.14		−.28**		−.20**		−.21
Father's participation in arts	−.04	†	.21*		.06		.13
Mother works a lot around house	.09		.21*		.21**	†	−.14
Father's religious participation	.04	†	.25**		.15*		.11
Father's spiritual interest	.05		.21*		.20**		.11
Mother's religious participation	−.01		.18*		.15*	†	−.30*
Mother's spiritual interest	.03		.07		.14*	†	−.31*
No. athletic teams in high school	.19*		.08		.15*		.04

† Significant difference between correlations of sexes or races at $p < .05$.
* $p < .05$.
** $p < .005$.

participate in the arts. A factor relating to Adjustment ratings in white males was participating in more athletic teams in high school.

The parental characteristics associated with well-adjusted women applied predominantly to the white women, for the same relationships did not hold for blacks. In fact, mothers' spiritual involvement and religious participation was a negative factor relating to the Adjustment ratings of blacks. It may be that in the families with the greatest adjustment problems, the mothers turned to religion for some solace.

Some other family background information on the MCS questionnaires was qualitative in nature and not subject to the correlational analyses shown in Table 12.11. Among these was the influence of different parents on the participants. The poorly adjusted were more influenced by their mothers (44% gave their mothers as the primary influence, compared to 35% of the moderately adjusted group and 30% of the well-adjusted group), perhaps because fathers were often no longer with these families. Among the whites, the moderately adjusted and well-adjusted groups were more likely to cite influence by both parents (59% of the well-adjusted, 54% of the moderately adjusted) than were the poorly adjusted (36%).

There was a distinct race difference in the influence of the childhood community. Among blacks, 84% of the poorly adjusted grew up in cities, compared to 78% of the moderately adjusted and 73% of the well-adjusted. Among whites, only 53% of the poorly adjusted grew up in cities, compared to 48% of the moderately adjusted and 71% of the well-adjusted. Thus city life seemed to signal high coping skills among whites but low coping skills among blacks.

Both Alison's and Cathy's upbringings were examples of the solid family backgrounds that characterized the well-adjusted participants.

Alison was raised in a black neighborhood that was a suburb of a southern city. She had one brother, 5 years younger. Her mother was a teaching assistant for kindergarten children and was very loving and caring. Alison felt they had a close relationship and considered her mother a friend and confidante.

Alison's father was a foreman for a utility company, of whom she said, "He's very intelligent; he can fix almost anything. He was very supportive of me when I was growing up and was also a buddy — we'd play ball in the yard, and he took me to football and baseball games with him." Both her parents stressed academic excellence, but they did not apply undue pressure.

Cathy was raised in Chicago and had both a happy and stable childhood; her family never moved. Her parents were equally influential in her upbringing and got along very well together. She attributed the latter to their marrying later in life after they were confident of what they wanted in a mate. They both attended church regularly and tried to encourage Christian values of love and charity in their three children.

Cathy's father was a salesman, and he filled their home with his warm, radiating personality. Her mother mixed a healthy dose of tolerance and liberalism with her childrearing principles and was "spontaneous and fun. She's a neat lady," said Cathy.

In contrast to the close family environments described by Alison and Cathy were the more difficult childhood experiences of Becky, a high-potential, poorly adjusted participant.

Becky's father was with a large corporation that relocated him every 2 years; as a result she lived in ten different places before she was 16 and never felt that she had a real home town. She described herself in childhood as "spoiled, bratty, and strong-willed; I wouldn't give in. One thing I did do was study a lot, but it was more because I was afraid of doing poorly than because I loved to study."

Becky claimed that her parents got along well with each other but never seemed to have time for Becky or her brother and sister. "They were rotten parents," she said. "I think that parents have to sacrifice something for their children. Mine never did. They provided for us well materially, but they would never give up any of their time for us or sacrifice personally. I had an emotionally tense childhood, primarily due to the lack of love from my parents. We were always competing for their attention, but it never did any good."

Lifestyles

As might be expected from the previous information about the parental families, the well-adjusted MCS participants showed greater Parental-Familial

Table 12.12   Correlations of Involvement in and Satisfaction with Life Themes with Adjustment, MPS:0 and MCS:0

Life theme	Involvement		Satisfaction	
	MPS ($n = 220$)	MCS ($n = 344$)	MPS ($n = 220$)	MCS ($n = 344$)
Marital-Familial	.09	.22**	.07 †	.29**
Parental-Familial	−.03	.02	.00	.12*
Locale-Residential	.04	.01	.13	.01
Financial-Acquisitive	.15* †	−.04	.03	.07
Ego-Functional	.12	−.04	.19*	.26**
Recreational-Social	.07	.05	.09	.02
Religious-Humanism	.03	.13*	.07	.06
Service	.04 †	.22**	.08	.11*
Occupational	.20**	.12*	.18*	.32**

† Significant difference between MPS and MCS correlations at $p < .05$.
* $p < .05$.
** $p < .005$.

satisfaction at the time of the assessment. This is evidenced by the coding of the life themes from the interviews, shown in Table 12.12. Such a relationship was not established for the MPS sample, however.

Also evident for MCS but not for MPS were greater Marital-Familial involvement and satisfaction among the better adjusted. One might surmise that more rewarding experiences with their parental families inspired the well-adjusted participants to repeat the experience with their own marriages and families.

Further evidence about the participants' marital families comes from several items on the Personal History Questionnaire, shown in Table 12.13. The well-adjusted whites and males were, first of all, more inclined to be married by the time of the original assessment center, and all except the blacks showed that more importance was given to family activities. Among the married women, the best-adjusted had husbands who were apparently more intellectually active; they were better educated, spent more time on job activities, and had greater interest in current events. Their husbands were also more likely to participate in the arts and to have more interest in spiritual matters.

Another important point about the husbands of the well-adjusted women is that they were very positive about the participants' work activities, in terms of both supporting their careers in general and valuing their job advancement. This was much more true for the blacks than for the whites. The husbands of well-adjusted blacks were also the ones likely to be better educated and more interested in the arts. In general the pattern of relationships suggests that a

Table 12.13 Marital Variables Significantly Correlated with Adjustment at MCS:0 by Sex and Race

Variable	Males		Females	Whites		Blacks
High importance to family activities	.24**		.23*	.29**		.04**
Married at assessment	.20*		.09	.20**		.08
Spouse better educated	.24*		.31*	.15		.60**
Spouse participates in arts	−.02	†	.33*	−.03	†	.45*
Spouse time spent on job activities	.20		.45**	.29*		.35
Spouse interested in current events	.04	†	.40**	.11		.09
Spouse interested in spiritual matters	.00	†	.43**	.11		.16
Spouse positive about participant's career	.12	†	.46**	.16	†	.41*
Spouse values participant's job advancement	.07	†	.37*	.15	†	.41*

Note. Total n's as in Table 12.10. Married n's as follows: males, 83; females, 48; whites, 94; blacks, 27.

† Significant difference between correlations of races and sexes at $p < .05$.

* $p < .05$.

** $p < .005$.

well-rounded, supportive husband was even more significant for a well-adjusted black woman than a well-adjusted white woman.

Amy's husband was very involved in his own career as a university professor, but he was also interested in her work experiences and supported her career ambitions.

Alison met her husband in college, where he stayed to complete his MBA. He was employed by a large corporation and had urged Alison to apply for a job there as well. However, they were discouraged by the company's nepotism rules, and she decided to come to the telephone company instead.

Alison described her husband as "lovable, with a good sense of humor, and maybe not quite grown up! We do everything together except sports activities. He likes the fact that I'm working and is very proud of me. He has always supported me in my endeavors and seeks to help in any way he can."

Becky, a poorly adjusted participant, was much less positive about her marriage.

"I'm afraid I use my marriage as an excuse for not being able to have a more successful career, and I use my career as an excuse for not having a successful marriage. My marriage is disappointing. My husband was a psychology major, and he's always trying to psychoanalyze me. He plays games with my mind and makes me feel rotten and unimportant.

"He is convinced that my job will not evolve into a career. He can't support a family now, but he figures that he'll be able to someday and that I'll just quit working. Men seem to want women to stay home and cook but don't offer anything in return.

Working wives create male ego problems. I've done very well at school and at my job, and he feels threatened by that. He really sends me conflicting messages about it — in public he praises me, but in private he derides me. He also won't lift a finger to help raise our daughter; sometimes I think he doesn't even like her."

Both low-potential white female participants illustrated here were single, but Cathy, the well-adjusted one, had a very different outlook on marriage than her poorly adjusted counterpart, Debbie.

Cathy, at age 23, was clearly not ready for marriage yet. "I'm just enjoying dating around right now," she said. "But I'm sure I will get married some day. Sometimes I wish I had two lives — on the one hand I'd like to keep on working, but on the other hand I'd like to stay home and raise about eight children. I'll probably give up the job, but maybe I can do some kind of work at home."

Debbie complained about not being able to meet acceptable, eligible men. "All the men I meet now are either married or gay. If there's one thing I can't stand, it's married men cheating on their wives. I don't think I've met any man that I really thought I could trust. I suppose the higher up I go in my career, the harder it's going to be. Money seems to be related to cheating in husbands — the more money they make, the more likely it is to happen. I can tell you one thing: Even though I'm a good Catholic, if I found out my husband was cheating, I'd get a divorce."

Debbie's attitude toward men was partly brought on by her own experience. She had been seriously involved with a man a short time before the assessment and considered their relationship somewhat permanent. However, he had been offered a transfer and accepted it without even asking her if she would like to join him. This hurt her deeply, and she was not sure she wanted to make that much of a commitment to a man again.

The projective exercises revealed some deep-seated suspicions and resentments in Debbie's attitude toward men. She indicated that they made her uneasy, "confused" her, and were "aggressive, unfaithful, and not to be trusted." Yet she also did not want to exclude men from her life, stating, "*Men* are a necessary evil."

Several other life themes shown in Table 12.12 differentiated the well-adjusted participants from the poorly adjusted. Satisfaction with the Ego-Functional life theme, but not involvement in it, was characteristic of the well-adjusted among both the MPS and MCS groups. This suggests that the well-adjusted were more content with their physical, intellectual, and spiritual self-development, even though they were not necessarily making more such efforts than their poorly adjusted counterparts. The only indicator of greater involvement in self-development activities on the part of the well-adjusted was in questionnaire responses, where the whites but not the blacks said they got more exercise.

Art tried to keep up an active exercise program, especially with tennis and jogging, to stay in shape. He was also oriented toward improving his intellectual and managerial abilities, saying "I believe you should re-assess yourself every 2 months and use your strengths to upgrade your weaknesses." He used reading as an avenue to self-development, preferring books that revealed "human nature in a real-world setting rather than heavy subjects." He also read to get information on "how to handle people and paperwork."

Art was quite interested in national politics and had been since high school. He was an active Republican and defended the party in its recent controversies. "Watergate was really a media event," said Art in his interview, "It had little to do with Nixon as a person. The only thing that has given me real doubts about this country was the Vietnam War." Art participated in the political scene with financial contributions and by writing letters to legislators.

Craig, who was low in potential compared to Art, did not share his intellectual interests, but as one equally well-adjusted, he was quite content with his self-development efforts.

Craig occasionally pursued the active sports he had enjoyed in college. He followed professional and college ball avidly, but his personal participation was redirected toward golf, which he played at a local country club. He did little reading outside of work, other than the local newspaper, and *Consumer Reports* was the only magazine he subscribed to. Yet he indicated satisfaction with these aspects of his life as with other aspects.

Craig's interest in politics could be described as mild at best. He called himself "middle-of-the-road," sometimes voting for Republicans and sometimes for Democrats. He voted against Carter in 1976 partly because he admired Ford's involvement in golf.

Craig's maladjusted counterpart, Drake, got no systematic exercise. He was uninterested in politics and did not vote, saying, "I don't see any reason to support one political party over the other." His long list of favorite television shows (*M*A*S*H*, *Barney Miller, Taxi, Archie Bunker's Place*, and *Dukes of Hazzard*) suggested that he spent many hours in front of his television set. He also frequented the night spots with his buddies, although he indicated some dissatisfactions with this life. "The bar scene is boring," he said. "I wish I could develop the rap [become a better conversationalist] so I'd be more comfortable in that situation."

There was some tendency for the well-adjusted participants in MCS (though not MPS) to be more involved in the Religious-Humanism and Service life themes. The well-adjusted also indicated more religious participation in their Personal History Questionnaires.

An active Protestant, Art had a strong belief in God and felt that his faith gave him a great deal of inner strength. He said, "Religion has played a major role in American life — it has had a positive influence on the family and on the way we live as individuals. I feel I have gained a deep sense of self-worth and security from religion. I live by principles that were taught in a religious context."

Brad, high in potential but low in Adjustment, seemed unable to support religious practices to the same degree that Art, his better-adjusted counterpart, was able to. He said, "I'd love to believe there is an afterlife, but deep down I really don't think so. I think individual choice in religion is very important. For that reason, sects and cults disgust and infuriate me. People are lining their pockets at the expense of the free choice of others. I also can't stand people who are self-righteous in their attitude toward religion. I'll challenge any individuals with that attitude and insist that they justify their opinions."

Among the low-potential men, the well-adjusted Craig and his fiancée were fairly regular churchgoers. He said, "I pray a lot; my faith calms me down and carries me over the rough spots."

Drake, who showed many signs of maladjustment, had become disenchanted with formalized religion and looked to other sources of personal growth. He claimed to have benefitted from training in EST. "That experience empowered me to take control of myself," said Drake. "I have learned to meditate and to find my center, where I can handle things in my mind."

Work Interests

The Occupational life theme showed that the well-adjusted MPS and MCS assessees had both greater involvement in work and more satisfaction from it. A number of questionnaire items reflected their more positive attitudes toward work, as shown in Table 12.14.

Among all gender and race groups in MCS, the well-adjusted had more favorable scores on the Expectations Inventory. This meant that they were more positive in their views of what a manager's career would be like in the telephone companies, in areas ranging from promotion opportunities to the quality and congeniality of peers. This had not been true for the MPS men, most of whom were considerably more positive than the MCS group as a whole, regardless of their Adjustment ratings. On the Management Questionnaire administered in years 1 and 2 of the study, however, Adjustment correlated with General Management Attitude, Job Satisfaction, and Pride (in working for the company) in both samples. Personal Satisfaction, Identification (with management), and Authority also correlated with Adjustment in the MCS group.

The well-adjusted MCS participants were less likely to have considered leaving the company and thought it more improbable that they would leave the company within the next few years. When asked more specifically why they would or would not leave the company, results varied by race and gender. The well-adjusted women indicated they might leave for better salaries, and the well-adjusted whites considered leaving for more education.

In terms of what would discourage them from leaving the company, which was another way of indicating their satisfaction with the telephone company, the well-adjusted in all the race and gender groups pointed to interest in the

Table 12.14   Company Attitude Variables Significantly Correlated with Adjustment at MCS:0 by Sex and Race

Variable	Males		Females	Whites		Blacks
Expectations Inventory	.28**		.25**	.34**		.23*
Willing to take courses for career	.18*		.26**	.25**		.17
Have considered leaving company	−.37**		−.26**	−.32**		−.31**
Probability of leaving company in next few years	−.24**		−.07	−.17*		−.24
Might leave company for more salary	.02	†	.31**	.20		−.17
Might leave company for higher education	.21		.15	.33**	†	−.21
Discouraged from leaving company by:						
Advancement	.19*		.00	.12		.20
Job responsibility	.23*		.13	.20*		.20
Salary	.16*		.08	.08		.14
Fringe benefits	−.06		.22*	.01		.02
Job security	−.19*	†	.15	−.11		.00
Interest in work	.37**		.23*	.31**		.38**
Job challenge	.24*		.18	.22**		.09
Job location	.02	†	.27**	.11		.09
Coworkers	.16		.28**	.16*		.25
Supervision	.15		.20*	.19*		.17

Note. n's as in Table 12.10.
† Significant difference between correlations of sexes or races at $p < .05$.
* $p < .05$.
** $p < .005$.

work. The well-adjusted men also mentioned advancement, while the well-adjusted women were well satisfied with their job location and job security. Differences between blacks and whites on these measures were not significant.

Amy spoke in glowing terms about the Bell System as an employer. "If it's not the best corporate employer in the country, it's probably one of the best. It's hard to beat in terms of opportunity for internal advancement and the money that they pay at each level. I'd like very much to stay with the Bell System, although I could leave my specific company if I changed geographic locations."

Amy's poorly adjusted counterpart, Becky, had just as promising a future in terms of management potential but found various things not to her liking at work.

Becky was a service supervisor whose responsibility was to monitor and analyze the efficiency of customer repair services and to troubleshoot the logistics of repair work. She looked for such indicators as how quickly customer complaints were processed and how many repeated complaints were necessary. Though challenged by her work, she had a rather negative view of the company. "This company is so large and bureaucratic, it's unwieldy," said Becky. "They seem a lot more concerned about documentation than about problem solving. Having to deal with middle management is the biggest pain. They're not quick or on top of things and are very uninspiring. The jobs may be interesting but the people aren't."

When asked if she had ever thought of leaving the company, Becky replied, "About twice a week. I've heard it said that the only people who succeed in my department don't have any backbone — they're like jellyfish. Rather than have my backbone removed, I'd leave."

One of the things keeping Becky on the job was her salary. She said, "When I was hired, I learned that I was in the top 15% of earnings of women in this country — at the age of 22. That's really a disgusting state of affairs, but it makes me think twice about leaving here."

As with MPS, the low-potential, poorly adjusted managers seemed to deliver a steady barrage of complaints, perhaps because they often had their own job performance to be concerned about. Both Debbie and Drake provide good illustrations of this.

Debbie's job was in the Network Switch Services Department, where she supervised circuit layout records. Reporting to her were 13 clerks who primarily input data.

In describing her job, Debbie commented, "I hated it the first 3 months because I wasn't given any decent training. I don't mind learning something new, but they gave me absolutely no structure. Now that I've learned it, I find it boring. Actually boring isn't quite the right word since I have so much to do. But the structure is rigid, and there is no room for innovation. If they don't find me something more interesting to do soon, I'll probably leave."

Debbie had other complaints. "It seems to me that people are just too hung up on the class system within the Bell companies," she remarked. "It's just not possible to cross over lines of authority and attempt to straighten out a problem. My present boss is so uptight about dealing with his boss, the district man, that he quivers and can't even talk in his presence. There are a lot of people around here who are willing to kiss behinds to get what they want, and I won't lower myself to do that."

Drake was a manager in a test center, which he described as "a glorified repair bureau." His job was to determine the types of communications systems that would best fit the needs of individual small businesses. He had undergone technical training at Bell to prepare him for the job, which he stated was "an absolute waste of time for an engineer."

Drake felt his job was quite easy and said he really worked only a few hours a day. He said, "This company doesn't take advantage of the special talents that employees possess. It misuses its employees and then discards them. The formal appraisals aren't really accurate assessments; they're just cattle prods to motivate you."

One of Drake's biggest gripes was with the craft people. "They are overpaid and inefficient — babies who cry about every little thing and run to the union because they don't want to work. They're lazy, low-mentality people who want to stay home and collect a paycheck without working." Nor were his comments about middle-management personnel favorable. "The third-levels have the good life," said Drake. "They come in late, spend a couple of hours reading the paper, have lunch at the Rotary Club, do their in-basket, and leave about 4:00 in the afternoon."

Apparently Drake was trying to project his own lack of motivation and hard work onto everyone else in his environment. It was clear that he did not enjoy work and longed to escape. "Eventually I'd like to have a ranch in the wide open spaces where I can have some animals and my freedom." Unfortunately for Drake, he also had expensive interests, and his work at Bell was his only current source of income.

Personality and Motivation

Abilities carried the heavy weight in determining management potential, but it was personality and motivation that offered the best glimpse of personal adjustment, as shown in Table 12.15. A most influential personality and motivation factor in both the MPS and MCS samples was Positiveness, incorporating projective ratings of General Adjustment, Optimism, and Self-Confidence. There was, of course, an artifact in the MPS data, in that General Adjustment was used to generate the predicted Adjustment score, but the

Table 12.15   Correlations of Personality and Motivation Factors with Adjustment, MPS:0 and MCS:0

Factor	MPS college ($n = 274$)		MCS total ($n = 344$)
Factors derived from MPS sample			
Leadership Motivation	.24*	†	.04
Positiveness	.75*		.62*
Impulsivity	.11		.00
Affability	−.04		.08
Ambition	.41*	†	.24*
Factors derived from MCS sample			
Submissiveness			.21*
Positiveness			.61*
Impulsivity			−.07
Affability			−.08
Ambition			.31*
Adjusted Conformity			.52*
Poise			.36*
Flexibility			.08
Unconventionality			−.09
Masculinity			.04

† Significant difference between MPS and MCS correlations at $p < .05$.
* $p < .005$.

MCS data confirmed that a strong relationship probably would have existed anyway.

An MCS Personal History Questionnaire item measuring level of self-confidence also correlated significantly with Adjustment, but it was not nearly as strongly related as the projective ratings. For blacks, the higher level of self-confidence on the part of the well-adjusted was clearly manifested in their tendency to rate themselves higher on their own performance in the two group discussions. For whites and women, there was a negative relationship between Adjustment and having had individual psychotherapy.

Adrian had a definite image of what he should be, and he presented himself in accord with this image. His responses to the projective exercises indicated that he was goal- and action-oriented, and he expressed confidence that he could accomplish whatever he set out to do. He also had a sense of self-satisfaction about his accomplishments and development to date, replying, "*I have impressed* a lot of people I have met."

Adrian had a clear impression of his strengths and weaknesses and used that information to set goals. He responded to the incomplete sentences "*My best qualities* are planning, persuading, and leading," and "*My weakest qualities* are analysis and mathematics." He had laid out realistic paths for his career ("*The job I am best fit for is* in personnel, public relations, government affairs, or marketing") and seemed quite sure that he would achieve his goals ("*In 20 years from now* I will be a Vice President").

Art's positive thinking and reality orientation allowed him to make resourceful responses to his experiences and to tolerate disappointments and problems without becoming upset. He could even attribute benefits to anxiety reactions, answering "*My nerves* help me to accomplish much — the nervous energy is good."

Although Brad realistically had as much reason as Art and Adrian to expect a career of high achievements and progress, his maladjustments clouded his vision of his future.

Low scores on the G-Z and CPI scales were typical for Brad, indicating his low self-esteem, his detachment, and his lack of concern for what others thought of him. He was very self-revealing on the projective exercises, reporting his own "lack of self-confidence and self-esteem," his tendency toward pessimism and fears concerning the future, and his expectation of feelings of depression. He gave the impression that he was longing for something more than he now had and that he was experiencing inner doubts in his search for greater self-acceptance and self-confidence. He expressed many criticisms of himself, writing, for example, "*I wish* I could open up more with people."

An interesting twist on the optimism and self-confidence themes was provided by Drake, a poorly adjusted, low-potential participant. Drake tried to project a positive, self-assured air, but other aspects of his personality picture, particularly evident in the projective exercises, showed this projection to be indeed air rather than substance.

Some of the paper-and-pencil test scores of personality showed Drake's need to think positively; for example, he scored extremely high on most of the G-Z and CPI scales. His responses to the projective exercises also contained many positive statements, but they seemed forced and defensively self-generated rather than being based on objective evaluations of himself and the requirements of others. His self-concept focused on his potential and self-determination, but he avoided specifics and showed little self-awareness. For example, he wrote, "*My weakest qualities* are none," and "*My best qualities* are all my qualities."

Many of Drake's responses were also simplistic and naive generalities. He wrote, "*The happiest time* is all the time," and "*I failed* at nothing, but I learned from everything." His coping strategies were largely repressive — he avoided planning, denied disappointments, and intentionally disengaged from problems. He wrote, "*I secretly* withhold items from myself which I need to handle." He tried to maintain control over his thoughts and feelings, as with "*Sometimes* I notice myself thinking things with bad intention, but I correct it immediately."

Because of the correlation between management potential and Adjustment, several of the significant relationships in Table 12.15 are also in evidence in Table 12.5, which shows the relation of personality and motivation factors to management potential. Ambition and Poise seemed equally related to management potential and Adjustment, while Positiveness and Adjusted Conformity were predominantly related to Adjustment. Similarly, the MPS Self-Esteem factor correlated significantly with Adjustment but not with management potential.

All 13 G-Z and CPI scales within the MCS Adjusted Conformity factor were highly related to the assessors' ratings of Adjustment, with correlations ranging from .21 to .50. The highest two correlations were with Achievement via Conformance and Sense of Well-Being. Thus the well-adjusted participants coupled a strong need for achievement with a deep appreciation for organization and structure and an acceptance of rules and regulations. They also had a sense of good health, energy, and verve, and were generally lacking in tensions, anxieties, and fears. Questionnaire responses indicated that the well-adjusted gave higher ratings to their physical health and said they were less often worried or bored with life's routine.

Among the low-management-potential MCS participants, the well-adjusted Cathy was very accepting, respectful, and deferent toward supervisors. She acknowledged, "*When I talk with someone in authority* I recognize them as Sir or Ms." She also had a rather childlike respect for rules and authority, as in the response "*Rules and regulations* should never be forgotten."

Cathy tended to portray herself as a Pollyanna who was sure that problematic situations would turn out all right. In fact, it would be difficult to insult her, for she gave others the benefit of the doubt and assumed they were trying to help her in a well-intentioned way. She was eager to avoid conflict, writing, "*When I disagree with others* it usually turns into an enjoyable argument."

Debbie, who was poorly adjusted compared to Cathy, was apt to become overly involved with fears and frustrations. She wrote, "*I am dissatisfied* often." One of the stories she wrote to a TAT picture featured a young woman daydreaming at her job, "just relaxing a few moments before starting back into her dull routine." Another character thinks, "Life is a drudge." She thought back to the "easier" life she had as a child and to the "shelter from the real world" while in school, and she longed to return to less demanding times.

Debbie was subject to worries and self-doubts. She responded, "*Depressed feelings* pervade my mind often," and "*Most of my thoughts* are sad ones." She complained of headaches, said her nerves were "on edge," and seemed to have a generalized fear of failure. She wrote, "*My greatest worry* is that I will disappoint my parents so much that they will feel they wasted the best years of their lives." She tended to be an obsessive worrier who expended considerable energy thinking about possible courses of action and their potential pitfalls. She stated, "*My mind* tends to analyze events too intensively." Her tendency to dwell on the negative was indicated by the responses, "*I can't forget*," and "*I suffer* to be a martyr."

Factors relating to management potential but not related to Adjustment for MCS included Flexibility, Impulsivity, and Leadership Motivation (although Leadership Motivation was related to Adjustment in MPS). An explanation of this difference is given in Table 12.16. Among the MPS men, the well-adjusted were clearly oriented toward leadership and advancement and away from dependent relationships in their projective responses. The positive rela-

Table 12.16   Correlations of Scores in Leadership Motivation Factor with Adjustment, MPS:0 and MCS:0

Score	MPS college		MCS total
Positive for Leadership Motivation			
Leadership Role	.40*		.26*
Achievement/Advancement Motivation	.23*		.27*
Negative for Leadership Motivation			
Subordinate Role	−.08	†	.20*
Dependence	−.28*	†	.00
Affiliation	.07		.21*

Note. *n*'s as in Table 12.14.
† Significant difference between MPS and MCS correlations at *p* < .05.
* *p* < .005.

tionships of Adjustment with leadership and advancement were also true for the MCS participants, but the well-adjusted MCS managers were also more comfortable with a subordinate role and were more affiliative.

The well-adjusted MCS participants were rated higher on the MCS Submissiveness factor, derived from the projective exercises, and comparable (in reverse) to the MPS Leadership Motivation factor. However, the high-potential MCS participants were rated lower on Submissiveness. It should be noted that Aggression, rated from the projective reports, did not show this oppositional tendency; Aggression was negatively correlated with Adjustment but unrelated to management potential.

Further analyses indicated an interaction between management potential and Adjustment on the factors of Submissiveness and Ambition. Among those rated low or marginal in management potential, the well-adjusted (those like Craig or Cathy) had higher Nurturance scores on the Edwards, while among those rated as having middle-management potential or above, the well-adjusted (those like Amy, Art, Adrian, or Alison) had lower Nurturance scores. This appears to be a precursor of the "cool at the top" syndrome described in Chapter 7. The C types, with high Adjustment ratings and low or marginal management potential, were also the least ambitious of the groups, as measured by the Sarnoff scale of Motivation for Advancement and by Q-sort items of determination to get ahead and caring about promotions.

Amy was not particularly people-oriented, in spite of her ability to socialize with comfort. She described team projects as "a pain," showed impatience with "slow-moving people," and criticized those she regarded as "inconsiderate or stupid." Her low scores on the Edwards scales of Endurance and Succorance reiterated her impatience with having to spend too long in any one activity and her lack of need for the encouragement of others. Although she enjoyed her friends, affiliation was not a major goal for her. She placed more importance on respect and trust between people than on being liked.

Relative to her peers, Amy scored high on the Sarnoff scale of Motivation for Advancement, indicating her interest in moving up the Bell System hierarchy. In the interview, she stated that she aspired to the fifth (department head) or sixth (vice president) level. Her ambitions were also revealed on the projective exercises, as when she responded, "*I want to know* how to get ahead in business," and "*My greatest worry* is not succeeding in business." She attached high importance to her career and expected great satisfaction from work. Yet she expressed some concern about sex-role differences, stating, "*Most women* don't understand my motivation for wanting a career."

Craig showed the same positiveness and confidence as Amy but was less driven to succeed and had a warmer approach to others.

Craig indicated on the projective exercises that he preferred to keep his life uncomplicated and oriented toward harmony with others and personal happiness. He was interested in other people and derived considerable satisfaction from interactions with friends. He was an even-tempered, open, and direct person whose response to life was accepting, undemanding, calm, and stable.

Craig framed his ambition in terms of being "happy and comfortable." His aspirations did not seem pressing, as in the response, "*I have impressed* some people, but to me, it doesn't matter a whole lot."

Unlike Amy and Craig, the poorly adjusted managers had an edge of aggression in their interpersonal relationships and a distaste for affiliation.

Like other high-potential candidates, Brad was low on the Affability factor, but his 20th-percentile score on the G-Z Personal Relations scale indicated that he was, in addition, hypercritical and suspicious of others. The projective exercises presented him as a distant observer of others, which was probably his way of avoiding emotional complexities. He was uncomfortable with others and experienced strong emotional reactions toward them; several of his TAT stories involved emotional interactions between family members. He completed the sentence, "*Other people* are the trigger to my impatience shotgun."

Brad was cautious about making close friends at work and wondered whether any attempts to try to get others to like him would result in a compromise of his personal integrity. He could be very critical and rejecting of others in his attempts to maintain emotional distance. For example, he said, "*The average person* is not particularly intelligent and can oftentimes bore me." There were also indications that his lack of confidence concerning the opposite sex discouraged him from thinking about marriage, since he clearly feared being rejected and hurt.

Drake came across at the assessment center as fast-reacting, free-swinging, and blunt. He had strong reactions to his experiences, which he readily expressed and punctuated at times with profanity. With a focus on himself and his frustrations, Drake used anger, cynicism, and diversions as important outlets and sources of expression.

The paper-and-pencil personality measures indicated that Drake had little concern for the norms of society or the expectations of others (scoring at the 10th percentile on the CPI Communality scale and at the 94th percentile on Edwards Autonomy) and was not particularly comfortable around others (low CPI Sociability and Edwards Affiliation scales). He was thick-skinned in response to criticism (scoring at the 99th percentile on the G-Z Objectivity scale) and little inclined to accept blame readily (20th percentile on the Edwards Abasement scale). He enjoyed getting attention (80th percentile on the Edwards Exhibition scale) and was unperturbed if others were aggressive towards him, perhaps because he could readily retaliate in kind (95th percentile on Edwards Aggression and 15th percentile on G-Z Friendliness scales).

The projective exercises indicated that Drake was attracted to nonconformity and rebellion. His goals in his interactions with others were self-centered and consisted of getting others to comply with his wishes or to provide him with recognition. He wrote, "*When I first meet someone* I like to listen more than talk as I feel this knowledge leads to control." He prided himself on his ability to get along without needing help or encouragement from others, stating, "*Advice and guidance* are bull — that doesn't help anyone, they must decide."

Abilities

Although the personality and motivation factors were the most influential determinants of the assessors' ratings of Adjustment, there was also a tendency for the better-adjusted participants in both MPS and MCS to perform better on some ability measures at the original assessment center. The correlations of Adjustment ratings with the ability factors are shown in Table 12.17. Also presented are the Interpersonal Ability exercise scores that were common across both the MPS and MCS samples.

Both Administrative and Interpersonal abilities showed a positive relationship to Adjustment. Within Interpersonal Ability, oral communications as well as overall leadership and facilitative behavior in the competitive exercise related to Adjustment. Perhaps because of their greater self-confidence, the well-adjusted individuals had an edge in these kinds of exercises. In the Counseling Center Group Discussion, administered only to MCS at the original assessment, greater depth of understanding and better contributions to group functioning were similarly related to ratings of Adjustment.

Although Becky was rated as having high potential in management, there were some indications that her maladjustment had a negative effect on her performance in the simulations.

Becky tended to treat the In-Basket exercise as if it were an opportunity to test her subordinates. She formed initial impressions of them while working on the exercise, and she held to these impressions strongly during the interview. Her relationship with

Table 12.17   Correlations of Ability Factors and Selected Ability Scores with Adjustment, MPS:0 and MCS:0

Factor/score	MPS college	MCS total
Ability factors		
Administrative	.31*	.21*
Interpersonal	.37*	.28*
Cognitive	.13	.05
Competitive discussion		
Oral rating — observer	.22*	.22*
Overall rating — observer	.34*	.23*

Note. *n*'s as in Table 12.14. Ability factors had different components in MPS and MCS samples; see Appendix.
* $p < .005$.

the interviewer began to deteriorate toward the end of the hour as she showed obvious signs of impatience and loss of interest.

Debbie performed much more poorly on the simulations, but even for her it was clear that her maladjustment was causing her to operate at a disadvantage.

During the Counseling Center Group Discussion, Debbie was active in short spurts but then retreated into a quiet posture with a displeased look on her face. This seemed to be caused by others' disagreeing with her opinionated statements and by her inability to persuade them to her views. Her comments often brimmed with sarcasm and disdain, so that she appeared to impede rather than to facilitate the group's progress.

There was no overall relationship between Cognitive Ability and Adjustment in either sample, whether the former was measured by the SCAT test or by the General Information (MCS) or Contemporary Affairs (MPS) Tests. Yet for MCS, within each category of management potential, there was a tendency for the poorly adjusted to have higher verbal abilities, as illustrated in Figure 12.1. This relationship is reminiscent of the low but significant correlation between managerial level at MPS:20 and low scores on the SCAT Verbal scale at the MPS:0 assessment. Among the MCS participants with potential above the third level of management, for example, the well adjusted scored on the average at the 64th percentile on the SCAT Verbal while the poorly adjusted scored at the 82nd percentile. Similarly, among those rated as low in potential,

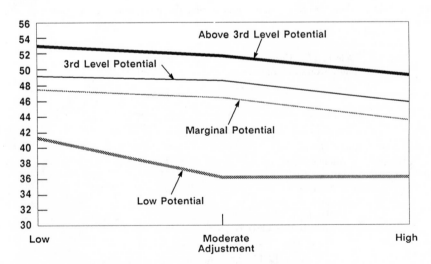

Figure 12.1.   Average SCAT Verbal scores by Adjustment and management potential at MCS:0.

the well-adjusted scored at the 16th percentile while the poorly adjusted were at the 31st.

As has been suggested in connection with the MPS participants, the most intelligent managers in MCS may have found more issues to worry about and may have been more inclined to verbalize their concerns. Brad provides an example.

The stories written by Brad to the TAT pictures tended to be imaginative, abstract, and intentionally enigmatic. He gave the impression of being a highly intellectualized, curious, introverted person who was full of inner complexity. He wrote, "*People* are a paradox: They form your threat, but to a great extent determine you."

Brad was both introspective and self-evaluative. He sized up himself with "*My weakest qualities* are stubbornness, impatience, and insensitivity to others," and "*My best qualities* are reflectiveness, honesty, independence, and enthusiasm.

Overall Assessment Evaluations

Most of the MPS-derived dimension factors were correlated with Adjustment in MCS, but to a lesser degree than with management potential. As shown in Table 12.18, Adjustment had the strongest relationships with Interpersonal Skills and Stability of Performance. The MCS-derived factor of Stability of Performance showed a higher correlation than that derived by using the MPS dimensions, but this is because the MCS-derived factor included the rating of Adjustment as well as a rating of Happiness.

Among the new MCS-derived factors, External Self-Development related to Adjustment as it had to management potential. However, Company Loyalty had a positive correlation with Adjustment but a negative correlation with management potential. The high-potential candidates apparently looked beyond the company in terms of furthering their careers, while the well-adjusted persons were more concerned with loyalty to and identification with their current employer.

Among the old MPS dimensions, the highest correlations with Adjustment for the MCS sample (all over .40) were Resistance to Stress, Personal Impact, Likeability (a subset of Personal Impact), Behavior Flexibility, Energy, and Bell System Value Orientation. Added to this list from the 10 new dimensions were Happiness and (lack of) Cynicism. Low Selfishness was also a characteristic of the best-adjusted persons ($r = .34$).

The primary predictions of both management potential and Adjustment at the initial MCS assessment are summarized in Table 12.19. The table has a format similar to that of Table 4.5, where the predictors from MPS:0 of advancement and Adjustment at MPS:20 are presented. Table 12.19 has many more entries than Table 4.5, due both to the concurrent nature of the relationships and the fact that there were more measures developed for MCS than MPS. Yet the similarities between the two are still evident.

Table 12.18   Correlations of Dimension Factors with Adjustment, MPS:0 and MCS:0

Factor	MPS college		MCS total
Factors derived from MPS dimensions			
Administrative Skills	.42**	†	.18**
Interpersonal Skills	.44**		.43**
Intellectual Ability	.11		.12*
Advancement Motivation	.25**		.15*
Work Involvement	.39**		.30**
Stability of Performance	.73**	†	.53**
Independence	.27**	†	−.09
Nonconformity	.22**	†	−.01
Factors derived from MCS dimensions			
Administrative Skills			.21**
Interpersonal Skills			.43**
Intellectual Ability			.14*
Advancement Motivation			.00
Work Involvement			.38**
Stability of Performance			.86**
Independence			−.34**
Company Loyalty			.19**
External Self-Development			.20**
Social Liberalism			.03

† Significant difference between MPS and MCS correlations at $p <$ .05.
* $p < .05$.
** $p < .005$.

The MCS data showed a stronger relationship between predictions of management potential and ratings of Adjustment, so more variables were predictive of both criteria. These included more involvement in work and the community, better Administrative and Interpersonal Skills, a better-educated spouse, more involvement in External Self-Development, and high scores on the personality and motivation variables of Positiveness, Ambition, Adjusted Conformity, and Poise.

Predictive of management potential but unrelated to Adjustment were several variables relating to intellectual stimulation and individual development. These included advanced parental education, high undergraduate grades, strong Ego-Functional involvement, and high Cognitive Ability. The high-potential managers had strong Leadership Motivation but were low in Affability. There was an openness to their personalities, suggested by high scores on Flexibility, Social Objectivity, Nonconformity, and Impulsivity.

The well-adjusted participants showed many indications of satisfaction,

Table 12.19   Predictors of Management Potential and Adjustment at MCS:0

	Potential	Adjustment
Predictive of one criterion	Advanced parental education	Parental family stability
	High undergraduate grades	Good family mental health
	Strong Ego-Functional involvement	High Parental-Familial satisfaction
	Strong Leadership Motivation	High Ego-Functional satisfaction
	High Impulsivity	High Marital-Familial involvement
	Low Affability	High Marital-Familial satisfaction
	High Flexibility	Strong Religious-Humanism involvement
	High Cognitive Ability	High Occupational satisfaction
	High Nonconformity	High Expectations
	High Social Objectivity	Low Independence
Predictive of both criteria		Strong Service involvement
		Strong Work Involvement
		High Occupational involvement
		Spouse better educated
		High Positiveness
		Strong Ambition
		High Adjusted Conformity
		High Poise
		High Stability of Performance
		Good Administrative Skills
		Good Interpersonal Skills
		High External Self-Development
Predictive of criteria oppositely	Low Submissiveness	High Submissiveness
	Low Company Loyalty	High Company Loyalty

including that with their parental families, their marital families, and their own self-development activities. They were also well satisfied with their work situations and had high expectations of what their managerial careers would be like. They came from stable homes with little mental illness and were themselves involved in their marital families. Religion was important to them, and they tended to be dependent on others for emotional support.

There were only two variables that clearly related to the two criteria in opposite directions. The high-potential managers were low on Submissiveness and would consider moving to other companies. The well-adjusted managers were high on Submissiveness and remained loyal to the telephone company. Although tested mental ability did not show a negative relationship with Adjustment for the total group as it had with MPS over a 20-year interval, the better-adjusted within each group defined by management potential in MCS had lower verbal ability scores. Some oppositional tendencies still existed, then, between high Adjustment ratings and high management potential.

To eliminate redundancies among the predictors of managerial potential and Adjustment while viewing them in combination, multiple correlations were computed using both the dimension factors and a combination of life themes involvement, ability factors, and personality and motivation factors. Results for managerial potential are shown in Table 12.20.

For both the MPS and MCS groups, the ability factors and corresponding ability dimensions were the most significant predictors of managerial potential, and each made an independent contribution to the prediction. These basic abilities were supplemented by factors related to personality and motivation, though none carried a very high regression weight. In both samples Work Involvement was important, while Independence also contributed to ratings of management potential for MPS. In MCS, Positiveness and Stability of Performance were among the more important nonability characteristics.

In both samples, Positiveness and Stability of Performance were much more important in ratings of Adjustment than of managerial potential, as shown in Table 12.21. In fact, the regression weights for these variables were two or three times larger than those for other variables in the same equations. Adjusted Conformity added to the prediction independently of Positiveness for the MCS group, and Interpersonal Ability made an additional contribution in

Table 12.20 Multiple Correlations of Assessment Variables with Management Potential, MPS:0 and MCS:0

MPS variable	R	Beta	MCS variable	R	Beta
Life themes involvement, ability factors, and personality/motivation factors					
Cognitive Ability	.57	.57	Administrative Ability	.70	.70
Interpersonal Ability	.70	.42	Interpersonal Ability	.78	.39
Administrative Ability	.74	.25	Positiveness	.80	.18
Occupational life theme	.75	.12	Cognitive Ability	.81	.17
			Poise	.82	.11
			Ambition	.82	.08
Dimension factors					
Administrative Skills	.62	.62	Interpersonal Skills	.75	.75
Intellectual Ability	.72	.42	Administrative Skills	.83	.41
Interpersonal Skills	.76	.27	Stability of Performance	.84	.19
Independence	.78	.17	Intellectual Ability	.85	.14
Work Involvement	.78	.15	Work Involvement	.86	.16
			Social Liberalism	.86	−.06

Table 12.21   Multiple Correlations of Assessment Variables with Adjustment, MPS:0 and MCS:0

MPS variable	R	Beta	MCS variable	R	Beta
Life themes involvement, ability factors, and personality/motivation factors					
Positiveness	.72	.72	Positiveness	.62	.62
Administrative Ability	.77	.27	Adjusted Conformity	.67	.30
Interpersonal Ability	.79	.21	Interpersonal Ability	.70	.21
			Parental-Familial life theme	.72	.15
			Submissiveness	.72	.10
Dimension factors					
Stability of performance	.72	.72	Stability of Performance	.85	.85
Work Involvement	.74	.16	Independence	.80	−.26
Intellectual Ability	.75	−.13	Administrative Skills	.81	−.09
Independence	.75	.10	Company Loyalty	.81	.07

both samples. Independence was a positive indicator of Adjustment for MPS but a negative indicator for MCS in the combined equation.

To maximize one's chances of selecting such well-adjusted high-potential candidates as the A types, emphasis should be put on the key abilities — Administrative, Interpersonal, and Cognitive. These abilities should be combined with a healthy dose of Work Involvement, Stability of Performance, and Positiveness.

The data presented in this chapter are, of course, only predictions about what will happen in the future. The appropriateness of the weight given to the different kinds of data in making the predictions can only be demonstrated later, as the MCS participants move through their lives and careers and take their places in the company and in society.

There are many more possible illustrations of individual differences among the MCS participants, but our major points have been made. It is now time to bring together all our findings and to draw some conclusions, which we do in the next and final chapter.

CHAPTER 13

The Studies in Perspective

The research reported in this volume was undertaken because of a conviction that it would lead to the improved selection and development of managers. As the years went on, it became clear that, in addition to that practical concern, the data being amassed were increasingly relevant to the study of adult human development. Not only were we learning about the characteristics essential to effective performance as a manager, but we were discovering changes and stabilities in these and other characteristics through time. Stability and change were evident within individuals as careers and lives unfolded, and across individuals as the young replaced the older in beginning management jobs.

The two cohorts of managers, in MPS and MCS, have different contributions to make at this writing to knowledge of change and stability. MPS has provided developmental data from early adulthood into middle age; MCS has more to say about generational differences and cultural change. In time, MCS will, we hope, yield longitudinal data that will deepen understanding of what has been learned from MPS.

The data from MPS, tracing the course of abilities, motives, personality, attitudes, and lifestyles through a substantial portion of adulthood, lead inevitably to a consideration of the current conflicting points of view relative to the course of adult life. These are the questions of continuity-discontinuity over time in individuals; whether there are significant group changes over time; and, if so, to what extent these changes can be described as normative.

CONTINUITY-DISCONTINUITY

Continuity-discontinuity of personality is the longitudinal counterpart of consistency-inconsistency in the cross-sectional study of the individual, to paraphrase Block (1981). The question of consistency has been hotly debated, particularly since Mischel's (1968) conclusion that "highly generalized behavior consistencies have not been demonstrated, and the concept of personality traits as broad response dispositions is thus untenable" (p. 146). McClelland

(1981, 1985) has sharply criticized such conclusions as being based on superficial and inadequate measures of personality dispositions and inattention to criterion situations.

Those who hold that consistency has not been and perhaps cannot be demonstrated cannot logically, it would seem, accept the notion of continuity across time. It is, however, possible to hold the converse position: One can believe that there is consistency in personality at any point in time, but that personality may change due to life experiences, resulting in at least some apparent discontinuity.

This last position would be implied by those who have found significant personality changes over time, particularly those who have found significant group changes. A significant average change (e.g, in motivation for autonomy) points to some discontinuity, if continuity is narrowly defined. It might turn out, of course, that those who have become more driven for independence possessed predispositions to such a change, so that continuity might be established.

There does seem to be an accumulating body of evidence that at least some aspects of personality do change for many individuals (cf. Thomae, 1979). Otherwise there would not be much point in the study of lives; one comprehensive look at the individual would be enough. Yet the interpretation of such data still avoids consensus. Costa and McCrae (1986) have recently concluded that "[o]ver the past decade, a series of longitudinal studies have demonstrated that personality traits are stable in adulthood: there are no age-related shifts in mean levels, and individuals maintain very similar rank ordering on traits after intervals of up to 30 years" (p. 2).

If age-related changes are observed in adult life, there is the question of whether they should be considered normative. Are they changes that all or nearly all persons experience? Do they appear in a certain sequence? This is, of course, the question of whether the personality progresses through life by stages (Erikson, 1950), particularly when it is asserted that changes take place at particular ages (Levinson *cum al.*, 1978). Stage theories have come under considerable attack. Giele (1980) notes that Erikson and Gould worked primarily with a privileged upper-middle-class and professional elite, and points out that Fiske has found no clear pattern of stages among lower-middle-class or blue-collar people. Certainly there is little evidence of precisely defined stages in the MPS data.

Even if clear stages were to be found, there are those who believe the findings would be mostly of historical importance. Looft (1973) declares, "No longer should developmental psychologists focus so exclusively on ontogenetic age functions; each new generation will manifest age trends that are different from those that preceded it" (p. 51).

Those who find a continuous sequence of change in adulthood also note a high degree of interindividual variability in the degree of change, as well as in its onset, direction, and quality (Thomae, 1979). In this regard, Block (1981) has concluded that there is great variation in individual predictability: "[S]ome individuals [are] impressively predictable thirty to thirty-five years later from their character structures in early adolescence while other individuals are unrecognizable in later years from their junior high school descriptions" (p. 36).

So the findings of the studies reported in this volume must find their place in a confused research area. Smelser (1980) notes the "diversity and noncomparability of many of the intellectual frameworks that inform the study of the adult years" (p. 4) and the limited number of established empirical findings. Baltes and Schaie (1973) observe that lifespan developmental theory has not reached a level of maturity permitting enunciation of its conceptual and empirical network. We will, nevertheless, review the highlights of our results in terms of the issues outlined above.

To begin with the question of continuity versus discontinuity, the data provide substantial evidence for a solid core of stability in the MPS participants over the 20-year period. The 20-year consistency correlation for General Effectiveness, the primary higher-order factor to emerge from the factor analysis of the assessment center dimensions, was .40. The rated dimensions themselves had 20-year test-retest correlations ranging from a low of .09 (Resistance to Stress) to .78 (General Mental Ability), but typical correlations were in the .20s and .30s. Tested mental ability (SCAT total score) had the highest test-retest reliability, with a correlation of .89 across the 20 years.

On the personality measures, test-retest correlations over the 20 years usually reached the level of statistical significance, although they varied somewhat by test instrument. High correlations were demonstrated by the GAMIN, ranging from .45 to .61 with a median of .57. On the Edwards, 11 of the 15 scales had test-retest correlations in the .40s. Deference and Affiliation were at the low end, each at .31, while both Aggression and Dominance showed greater stability, both in the low .50s. Lower test-retest correlations prevailed for the Bass version of the California F Scale (.39) and the Sarnoff scales (.26—.29).

These rating and test results are not far different from those reported by Block (1981). For example, for ratings made on the basis of evidence at high school age as compared to those made at middle age for such characteristics as "self-defeating," "high aspiration level," and "fluctuating moods," the results were .46, .45, and .40, respectively. The Edwards test-retest correlations are roughly comparable to those found by Stevens and Truss (1985) for a sample tested in 1965 and retested 12 years later, but higher than those produced with a sample from the 1950s retested 20 years later. The GAMIN coefficients found in MPS are somewhat lower than those reported by Costa and McCrae (1986) for the G-Z over a 12 year period, in the .72—.75 range.

Additional evidence of stability is provided by a count of those whose score on the Edwards scales changed appreciably from MPS:0 to MPS:20. The standard used was whether the MPS:20 score was different by half a standard deviation or more from the MPS:0 score. On none of the 15 scales did as many as half the participants change their responses to that degree. Using this measure, most change was seen on the Affiliation scale, where 46% did change more than half a standard deviation. At the other extreme, only 32% changed the required amount on the Order scale.

The MPS data, then, show considerable continuity in the characteristics of the participants over the 20 years under consideration. The great preponderance of all test-retest and rating-rerating correlations over the years were significantly different from 0, and many were substantial. None of these correlations were corrected for unreliability of the measures used. Had this been done, the evidence for continuity would be stronger. We must cast our vote with those who reject the proposition that the individual is simply the reactive victim of the situation.

Additional evidence on the side of continuity is the fact that it was possible to predict management level 20 years later from evaluations made at the MPS:0 assessment center. For example, of those college graduates predicted to reach fourth level or higher, 60% did so as compared to only 24% of the rest of the group. This highly significant difference was found in spite of the many influences that may well have diluted the relationship, such as assignment to departments with varying opportunities for promotion, working for supervisors with different management styles and performance standards, family and societal influences, and changes that took place in many of the participants. If individuals were not generally continuous, such a level of predictability could not be achieved.

The prediction of ascendance into higher management levels was highly dependent on the abilities demonstrated at the initial assessment center — Administrative, Interpersonal, and Cognitive — as well as a healthy dose of Ambition. Personality structures characterized by high Self-Esteem and Positiveness were related to later success, as they were to later Adjustment ratings. Strong Work Involvement also characterized the young men who would be both highly successful and well adjusted. The well-adjusted were high in affability and indicated good mental and physical health in their youth.

Some other stable traits indicated a trade-off between being successful and well adjusted. Those who advanced the furthest were, as young men, a rather restless lot — bright (high Cognitive Ability), interested in developing themselves further (high Ego-Functional involvement), and somewhat high on Impulsivity. They had low Need for Security, remaining ready to explore greener pastures. Their marital life may have been taken somewhat for granted; at least, it did not have top priority among the things in life that could interest them. By contrast, those rated as especially well adjusted in midlife were, as young men, more complacent. Marital-Familial satisfaction was high among them, and they were quite interested in secure jobs. They were low in Impulsivity; they did not show the same depth of Cognitive development as the high-potential managers; and their motivation for enhancing themselves further was unimpressive (low Ego-Functional involvement).

The MPS evidence for stability of individual characteristics over time by no means indicates, however, that change was not apparent. On the contrary, change was widespread in a great many of the motivations, personality characteristics, and management skills evaluated.

Whether or not the mean changes observed in the total group of participants can be considered to be normative changes depends on the rigor of the definition of the word "normative." If it refers to an almost completely general change, then the increase in verbal intelligence is the only one of our measures that would qualify. If the definition is less strict, one is still left with the question of what percentage of a group must move in the direction of the trend, how many may move counter to the trend, and to what extent sub-samples can move with or against the trend and still have the change be called "normative." If a relaxed standard is adopted, then a fair number of the changes observed here, summarized in the next section, can be said to be normative.

With these reservations, we come down on the side of those who claim that adult personality changes, but not totally (Kimmel, 1974; Stevens & Truss, 1985). The latter authors have said, "Apparently, adult personality retains a degree of flexibility and adaptability in meeting new life situations, roles, and cultural expectations" (p. 582). If adult life is a sequence of challenges and risks that require such adjustment, then "change in personality during middle age is not only possible, but it may be required in order to survive" (Thomae, 1979, p. 296).

CAUSAL ATTRIBUTIONS FOR CHANGE: ADVANCING AGE OR CHANGING TIMES?

The ways in which the combined group of MPS men changed over time have been documented in Chapters 5 and 6. These changes may have been due to maturation and common experiences related to aging. On the other hand, they could have been due to an absorption of different attitudes, values, and points of view related to developments in the external cultural environment, also documented at the beginning of Chapter 5. Examining where the new generation scored on a number of measures permits us to make hypotheses about the causes of the changes observed in MPS.

Models that form the basis of such hypothesizing are illustrated in Figure 13.1. Model 1 depicts the following possibility: There is a notable increase (Model 1a) or decrease (Model 1b) for the MPS men on some characteristic, but when that same characteristic is measured for the MCS participants, they score about the same as the MPS men had scored when they were young. The uniformity, then, would be between both groups in their youth, while the divergence would come from the MPS group in middle age. One could hypothesize, then, that the reason for the difference in scores at MPS:20 was that the MPS men had undergone a change due to aging or the common experiences that accompany aging.

The model is presented as a hypothesis rather than a fact, for more data are needed before a final conclusion can be drawn. In particular, it would be desirable to see how the MCS group progresses with age for confirmation. If the MPS group went up in a certain characteristic over a 20-year period (Model 1a) and it were due to maturation, then one would expect the MCS group to increase on that same characteristic by a comparable amount over a comparable period of time. The same would be expected for the decrease modeled in 1b.

Model 2 illustrates this hypothesis: The MPS group shows the same types of changes as depicted in Model 1, but this time the MCS group scores unlike MPS:0 but not as extremely as MPS:20. In statistical terms, MCS is significantly different from both MPS groups. Since the MPS group does not score as extremely as the MPS:20 group in middle age, one would be led to believe that there is still an aging effect. However, there would also appear to be an effect due to a culture change, for the MCS group is not exactly like their predecessors when young, either. This model is considered a mixed model, then, which assumes some changes in the culture but also assumes some effects of aging.

Model 3 points more directly to a change in the culture that would seem to affect its members generally, regardless of the generation to which they belong. The following scenario is suggested: The MPS group changes in the same way as illustrated in Models 1 and 2, but this time the MCS group scores the same as the MPS:20 group and quite differently from the MPS group when they were young. The two points in common here would be measurements taken in the late 1970s and early 1980s, regardless of cohort; consequently, what would be shown is that the 1970s and 1980s were different from the 1950s. If this is true, we would not expect the MCS group to change in the future, unless, of course, there was another culture change, which would be demonstrated with still a third cohort.

It should be noted that Model 3 is not as definitive as the two preceding models. It is quite possible that there could be both a maturation effect and a generational effect that happened to be of the same magnitude. This would make the model just another variation on the mixed case presented in Model 2. In such a case, the MCS group should change further in the same direction over time.

The final model posits stability rather than change within the MPS group over time. In the hypothesis suggested here, the MCS group scores differently from the MPS group, regardless of when the MPS group was measured. This model thus illustrates a generation or cohort difference. This would undoubtedly be due also to a culture change, but one that primarily affects the younger generation rather than all generations experiencing the culture. Such a finding would suggest that growing up in the 1960s and 1970s was uniquely

MODEL 1: Aging/Experience

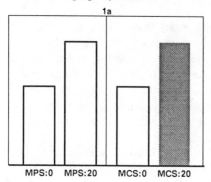

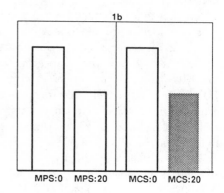

MODEL 2: Mixed

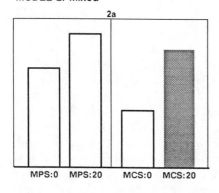

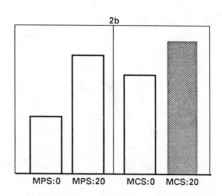

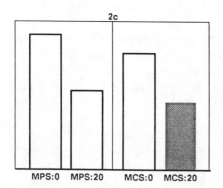

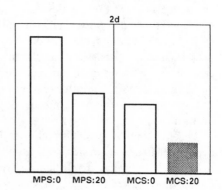

MODEL 3: Culture Change

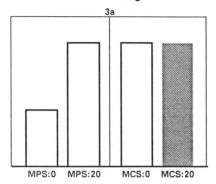

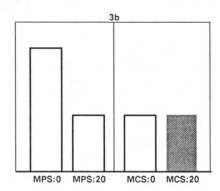

MODEL 4: Generation Difference

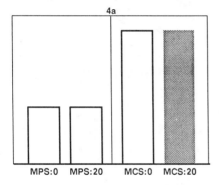

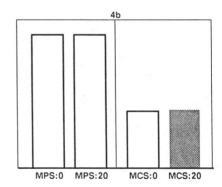

Figure 13.1.   Models for hypothesized causes of differences across time.

different from growing up in the 1940s and 1950s, making the young adults of those two periods different from each other.

The various kinds of data on changes in the MPS college group over time (presented in Chapters 5 and 6) and the data on ways in which the MCS group was different from the young MPS men (in Chapter 9) were analyzed according to the four models presented in Figure 13.1. Only data that rather clearly fit the models for the total MCS group as well as the MCS white males were included. These data are presented, categorized by appropriate model, in Table 13.1. The MPS:0 scores are those of the entire 274 men at the original assessment, although scores for those remaining until MPS:20 were used for the comparisons over time in Chapters 5 and 6. Differences between the MPS:0 average scores of the entire 274 men and the 137 who stayed for 20 years were usually negligible.

Table 13.1   Hypothesized Causes of Differences across Time

Scale or score	Data source	MPS:0	MPS:20	MCS:0 (total)	MCS:0 (white males)
				Average scores	
Aging/experience					
Verbal ability	SCAT Verbal	47 %ile	69 %ile	51 %ile	55 %ile
Inner Work Standards	Interview	3.6	4.0	3.6	3.6
Inner Work Standards	Dimension	3.2	3.5	3.1	3.6
Achievement	Edwards	62 %ile	82 %ile	68 %ile	70 %ile
Ability to Delay Gratification	Dimension	3.3	3.8	3.3	3.3
Realism of Expectations	Dimension	3.2	4.1	3.0	3.0
Resistance to Stress	Dimension	3.0	3.3	3.1	3.0
Aggression	Edwards	55 %ile	68 %ile	51 %ile	61 %ile
Abasement	Edwards	50 %ile	35 %ile	47 %ile	49 %ile
Affiliation	Edwards	55 %ile	36 %ile	51 %ile	49 %ile
Intraception	Edwards	43 %ile	28 %ile	45 %ile	34 %ile
Marital-Familial life theme	Interview	4.2	4.9	3.9	4.1
Recreational-Social life theme	Interview	4.0	4.2	3.9	4.0
Mixed					
Autonomy	Edwards	57 %ile	85 %ile	64 %ile	65 %ile
Independence	Dimension factor	2.6	3.3	3.0	3.1
Need for Peer Approval	Dimension	3.3	2.5	2.9	2.9
Parental-Familial life theme	Interview	4.6	3.4	4.2	4.0
Service life theme	Interview	4.0	3.1	3.5	3.5
Motivation for Advancement	Sarnoff	50 %ile	8 %ile	25 %ile	21 %ile
Need for Advancement	Interview	3.5	2.3	3.1	3.2

Table 13.1 (Cont'd)

Scale or score	Data source	Average scores			
		MPS:0	MPS:20	MCS:0 (total)	MCS:0 (white males)
Need for Advancement	Dimension	3.3	2.8	3.1	3.1
Forward Striving	Sarnoff	55 %ile	25 %ile	50 %ile	47 %ile
Need for Security	Interview	3.4	3.9	3.1	3.1
Career expectations	Expect. Inv.	51 %ile	6 %ile	17 %ile	13 %ile
Personal Satisfaction	Mgt. Quest.	1.01	0.88	0.74	0.75
Impersonal Communication	Mgt. Quest.	0.67	0.54	0.42	0.40
Authority	Mgt. Quest.	1.02	0.86	0.72	0.73
Salary	Mgt. Quest.	1.12	1.07	1.32	1.25
General Management Attitude	Mgt. Quest.	1.19	0.85	0.79	0.78
Supervision	Mgt. Quest.	1.29	0.80	0.86	0.89
Job Satisfaction	Mgt. Quest.	1.27	1.01	1.05	1.02
Pride	Mgt. Quest.	1.41	1.06	1.01	1.00
Personal Communication	Mgt. Quest.	1.36	1.05	1.04	1.09
Interpersonal Skills	Dimension factor	2.8	2.5	2.6	2.5
Behavior Flexibility	Dimension	3.0	2.6	2.7	2.6

Culture change

Deference	Edwards	43 %ile	36 %ile	35 %ile	35 %ile
Need for Superior Approval	Dimension	3.7	3.2	3.1	3.2
Religious-Humanism life theme	Interview	4.2	3.7	4.0	4.0
Masculinity	GAMIN/G-Z	12.5	11.9	11.8 (Males)	11.9

Generation differences

Dominance	Edwards	49 %ile	53 %ile	29 %ile	34 %ile
Nurturance	Edwards	49 %ile	49 %ile	71 %ile	69 %ile
Succorance	Edwards	66 %ile	65 %ile	79 %ile	74 %ile
General Activity	GAMIN/G-Z	7.2	7.6	8.1	8.0
Oral Communication Skills	Dimension	3.1	3.0	2.9	2.9
Identification	Mgt. Quest.	0.99	0.90	0.60	0.63
Nonconformity	Dimension factor	2.6	2.6	2.8	2.8

Note. Abbreviations: Expect. Inv., Expectations Inventory; Mgt. Quest. Management Questionnaire.

Among the characteristics hypothesized to be related primarily to aging was the increase in verbal ability measured by the SCAT, which other longitudinal studies have confirmed (Eichorn *et al.*, 1981). The fact that the MCS white male group scored higher than the MPS:20 group suggests that this characteristic might have been better placed under the mixed model, assuming that the culture has continued to progress in wisdom and mental capabilities. The data are confounded somewhat in these studies, however, by the fact that some of the telephone companies began using mental ability tests to screen management candidates between the time of MPS and that of MCS.

On the other hand, Scholastic Aptitude Test scores have been declining for some time, indicating that the culture of late has been progressing toward lesser rather than greater mental powers on the average. The culture influence is not at all clear with respect to verbal abilities, then, but the aging effect seems solidly demonstrated.

The next five items under the aging model illustrate motivational changes. The MPS men became more concerned with having high standards of quality for their work (Inner Work Standards) and with appreciating challenging work with problems to solve (the Edwards Achievement scale). Yet the issue of upward movement lost salience, with the men growing more patient about promotional opportunities (Ability to Delay Gratification) and more realistic about attaining them (Realism of Expectations).

Personality changes reflected greater resistance to stress with maturity, including a growing disinclination to take the blame when things go wrong (Edwards Abasement). At the same time, there was less restraint on the expression of hostility (Edwards Aggression).

Maturity also brought a decline in the role of friends (Edwards Affiliation) and subdued youthful preoccupations with analyzing the motives of others (Edwards Intraception). At the same time that friends decreased in importance, marriage and family increased in importance, as did recreational activities. It should be remembered that about half the MPS men were not married at the time of the original assessment, and friends were still a strong source of interpersonal satisfaction. But as work and marriage took hold, and children came along, the marital family became the dominant source of such satisfaction. Friends moved away (or the men moved away from them) and entered into similar pursuits of their own.

Additional changes are shown in the mixed models, with the added influence of a culture moving generally in the same direction. For example, scores on the Edwards Autonomy scale were sharply up for the MPS men at MPS:20 — one of the most pronounced changes in the study. This same type of change was shown in the Independence dimension factor. Maturity and experience prompted the men to want to exert more control over their lives and to escape from the domination of father and mother (the Parental-Familial life theme) as well as peer influences (Need for Peer Approval). At the same time the culture was encouraging people to "do your own thing," so that young people were also relatively more independent-minded, though not so much as the more mature, established, middle-aged people. The MCS group's lower Need for Security was probably a symptom of desires for independence, helped by the economic advantages of dual-career families.

Also in the mixed model is the declining Need for Advancement on the part of the MPS men; certainly, after either a number of achievements at work and/or a realization that the pyramid was narrowing and chances for progression were lessening, youthful ambitions should have subsided. A secure job became a more important consideration in middle age than one with a plethora of advancement opportunities. There was generally less emphasis on the future (lower Forward Striving), consistent with the Veroff *et al.* (1981) finding that young people are more optimistic about the future than older people. Interest in performing services for the community (the Service life theme) also declined, perhaps because they had served as an aid to promotion in the early years, or perhaps just because the men had achieved all that was desired in that area.

Other changes with experience were less positive attitudes toward various company experiences. The initial youthful enthusiasm shown on the Expectations Inventory and Management Questionnaire receded over time as the men got more realistic about the company's operations. They declined in attitudes toward their supervisors and higher management, job satisfaction, pride in working with the company, personal and impersonal communications, personal satisfaction, and satisfaction with their salaries and degree of authority.

While these changes in motivation and attitude seem sensibly related to aging and experience, the younger group was also less interested in advancement and forward striving, had lower career expectations, had poorer job attitudes (except for salary), and was less inspired toward community service. There is a cultural force at work here also, probably born of a slowing economy, competition within the baby boom generation, and the pessimistic malaise cited by President Carter in the 1970s.

The last four attitude scales in the mixed model, as well as Interpersonal Skills and Behavior Flexibility, could fall under the culture change model. However, since the criteria for this model are somewhat ambiguous, our best judgment is that they make more sense in the mixed model. The drop in Interpersonal Skills over the 20-year period is surprising, since it is difficult to conceive of such skills actually declining. It may be more exact to say that the effectiveness of interpersonal behavior declined. This is what the assessors were rating. It seems that some of the motivational and attitudinal changes indicating less concern with others that took place between assessments led the participants to care less about being smooth and cooperative than they had as new, and possibly less confident, managers. Nevertheless, it is disheartening to see that the MCS group did not demonstrate better skills in this area at their young age.

Other reverberations from the 1960s and 1970s are shown in the characteristics related to the model of general culture change. In the later 1970s and early 1980s, both middle-aged and young alike showed a decline in respect for society's institutions. This was reflected in less inclination to defer to those in authority (lower Edwards Deference scores) and lower Need for Superior

Approval, in contrast to the conformist 1950s. The decline in the influence of religion is also apparent in the Religious-Humanism life theme. It is likely that none of society's institutions escaped untouched from the growing suspicion and alienation of the 1960s and 1970s culture.

Another interesting change, presumed to derive from cultural shifts, is the decline among men in identification with those qualities traditionally thought of as manly or masculine. The exact items on the common Masculinity scales did not necessarily show commonality between the MPS:20 middle-aged men and the MCS young men. The MPS men reported less inhibition about showing tears and more interest in literary and artistic pursuits than did the MCS men; for their part, the MCS men were less oriented toward hunting, killing, and outdoor occupations — interests held by the MPS men that they did not drop over the 20 years of the study. Nevertheless, the direction of the change was clearly toward softening of the traditional macho qualities for both generations.

Interpretations of the cultural change model may, of course, be open to revision when the MCS reassessment data are obtained. It is possible that such things as diminished Deference and Masculinity reflect both maturational and cohort effects, in which case the MCS group is likely to decline further with time.

A few characteristics defined the MCS group as a generation apart from its predecessors, regardless of when the predecessors were measured. The MCS group's decline in interest in leading others (lower Edwards Dominance scores) posed a possible threat for organizations searching for strong leaders. Miner and Smith (1982) reported a similar decline in the motivation to manage among a series of college students tested across a number of years with the Miner Sentence Completion Scale. Declines continued through the 1960s and have plateaued at a lower level since the 1970s. The lower Oral Communication Skills, less Identification (with management), and increasing Nonconformity for the MCS group were no doubt related to their greater indifference to the management role. On the positive side, this was a generation more aware of its state of physical health and with an abundance of energy (high G-Z General Activity). But the direction of that energy into the acceptance of responsibilities necessary for the future of organizations might prove to be a particularly difficult challenge for those organizations.

The emphasis on giving and receiving emotional support (higher Edwards Nurturance and Succorance scores) suggests that the younger generation might be more compassionate. Another interpretation comes from the findings of Veroff *et al.* (1981), who noted that seeking informal support had become the primary coping style of the new generation. In reconciling this finding with the tilt toward greater self-sufficiency, found in their data as well as ours, they noted decreased dependence on specific individuals and greater orientation toward seeking more support from a variety of individuals. This approach is more self-protective in the event of losing any single source of support.

It may be argued that we are somewhat bold even to hypothesize about aging and culture changes based on samples from the same organization. Perhaps the changes shown only represent characteristics fostered or restrained or attracted by the Bell System over this period of time. Consideration of these hypotheses prompted us in 1981 and 1982 to initiate the Inter-Organizational Testing Study (ITS), a cross-sectional study of 10 organizations outside the Bell System. The organizations differed in size from a few thousand employees to over 25,000 and varied from a railroad and a bank to an architectural and engineering consulting firm, a news organization, and two government agencies. Samples included nearly 400 middle-aged managers (comparable to the MPS:20 group in age) and about the same number of young managers (comparable to the MCS group).

The managers in ITS went through a half day of testing on many of the measures reported here, including the Edwards, the Sarnoff, the SCAT, some attitude scales, the Expectations Inventory, and a biographical questionnaire. Although full details of this research are too voluminous to report here and will be published elsewhere, on almost every score the differences between the middle-aged and young samples in the other 10 organizations directly paralleled the findings reported here and pointed toward the same hypothesized explanatory models. We conclude that the Bell System results do indeed appear generalizable to managers in other types of organizations, and we offer them on that basis. Whether they are representative of those who start their own businesses, or of those who never reach management at all, or of other groups in completely different professions awaits confirmation by other research.

Results in the psychological literature on age-related changes in personality have not, however, been very consistent. Part of this problem has been due to reliance on either longitudinal or cross-sectional data with no attempts to differentiate maturational changes from those born of cultural influences. One study that did attempt to make such differentiations provides a significant confirmation of many of the trends reported here (Stevens & Truss, 1985). Working with three cohorts of students taking the Edwards, two of whom were administered repeated measures 12 and 20 years later, the authors identified increases in Achievement and Aggression and decreased Affiliation, Abasement, and Intraception as maturational changes, as shown here. Increased Autonomy was identified as a maturational change for men but a mixed result for women.

The maturational increase in Dominance found by Stevens and Truss appeared to only a mild degree in our research. Their data did show a notable mean difference on this scale between men in the 1950s and 1970s generations, with the new generation scoring lower, although this apparently did not reach statistical significance. The younger generation of men was higher on Nurturance, as found here, but also lower on Achievement and Affiliation, as not found here but consistent with some of the other trends.

A significant finding that overrode many maturational and generational comparisons in our data was increased heterogeneity. As time went on, the MPS men grew more different from one another in a diverse group of characteristics. Moreover, the MCS group was more heterogeneous than the MPS group at the start, and this could not be attributed solely to the different ethnic and sex groups in the newer sample.

Increased heterogeneity is best interpreted in the framework of a mixed model. The cultural changes of the 1960s and 1970s toppled traditional attitudes and values and encouraged development of the self in individual-istically determined ways. Yet maturation also involves the establishment of one's own unique identity, a constant differentiation of oneself from the crowd. The prophecies of *The Organization Man* in the 1950s — that those opting for organizational life were doomed to mass conformity — were con-tradicted by the course of adult development toward greater differentiation.

The notion of differentiation and integration as the core of lifespan development was postulated by Werner and elaborated by Whitbourne and Weinstock (1979). The latter authors have said, "Probably the one thing that can be said with any assurance about age in adulthood is that people become more different, more multifaceted, more complex, and more individual as they grow older. The range of possible experiences to which people can be exposed increases dramatically with each passing year of adulthood" (p. 6).

Whitbourne and Weinstock (1979) propose their own model of identity change in adulthood, which includes using one's own identity for the inter-pretation of experience (deductive differentiation) and using one's experience to stimulate a change in one's identity (inductive differentiation). An example is a man highly motivated toward advancement who interprets interactions with coworkers and supervisors in light of his own drive (deductive differ-entiation), but who scales down his ambitions upon increasing awareness of limitations (inductive differentiation). The representation of this example as a general trend in the MPS data is clear, as most of the men declined in ambition over time. Only the highest-level men, whose limitations were still somewhat ambiguous, held onto their original advancement goals.

The addition of the MCS data suggests that superimposed on this model of differentiation should be the declining influence of the external culture as people age. As Table 13.1 indicates, there were few changes experienced by the MPS men that can be hypothesized as due to cultural changes alone. Yet the MCS group showed a wide range of differences from the MPS group, as identified in Models 2, 3, or 4. The major impact of the turbulent 1960s and 1970s fell much more on the younger generation, who experienced them in their formative years, than on the MPS generation, who were settling into adulthood when the changes took place.

Baltes has hypothesized that different conditions of change have differential potency during successive periods of development (Kagan, 1984). Genetically programmed changes are most evident in early childhood; normative regimens (e.g., sending a child to school at age 5 or 6) impinge on childhood and early adulthood; historical events have their greatest effect on adolescents and young adults; and unpredictable events (e.g., divorce or illness) are more significant after age 30, when the other factors wane in significance and when behavior, beliefs, and moods are relatively fixed. As an example of the effect of historical events, during the Vietnam war Americans 15 to 25 were believed to be most influenced by antiwar demonstrations. Kagan states that the influence of the culture overlaps that of the family and looms largest between the ages of 6 and 16 (Sanoff, 1985).

Although adults can and do change in their values and attitudes, the cultural influences on them in their youth leave a basic core that is less susceptible to adaptation in light of further cultural changes as time goes on. Children and adolescents, still in the process of forming their identities, readily absorb cultural messages, but those whose identities are already basically formed when new messages arrive are more difficult to influence. Illustrating this message is a remark by former California Governor Edmund G. Brown: "Like it or not, the pill, the bomb, and the world population explosion have changed our nation. The role of women, the role of war, and the role of America are simply not what they were when Ronald Reagan locked into his basic assumptions about life" (quoted by Reston, 1984, p. A23).

A model of adult development that focuses on both differentiation in adulthood and the declining role of cultural change is presented in Figure 13.2. The periods of time and their concomitant cultural messages are represented as rings on the trunk of a tree. The formative years for the individual are represented at the core of the trunk. For the MPS group, this period was the 1940s and 1950s; for MCS, it was the 1960s and 1970s. The circumference of the trunk is smallest there, indicating less interindividual difference; not all infants are alike, but they are much more alike than 10-year-olds, and 10-year-olds are much more alike than 30-year-olds, and so on. The slice of the trunk selected to represent MCS is wider than that for MPS, signifying the greater heterogeneity in the younger generation spawned by cultural developments.

As individuals age, they may be affected by the cultural events represented by the additional concentric circles. However, their identities reach back into the central core, and they are likely to interpret events in that light. In the earlier years, the boundaries of the self are more permeable, represented by the lighter lines on the individual circles; later in life it is more difficult for the culture to penetrate, indicated by darker circumferences on the outer circles.

There are, of course, wide individual differences in this progression: Those with more diffuse identities will be more easily influenced by the culture, while those with a stronger sense of self will be more resistant. For example, Bruce in the MPS sample was more questioning and unsure of himself than was Al, and he thought more readily about the meaning of the various culture changes. Permeability is not necessarily a concomitant of maladjustment,

MPS

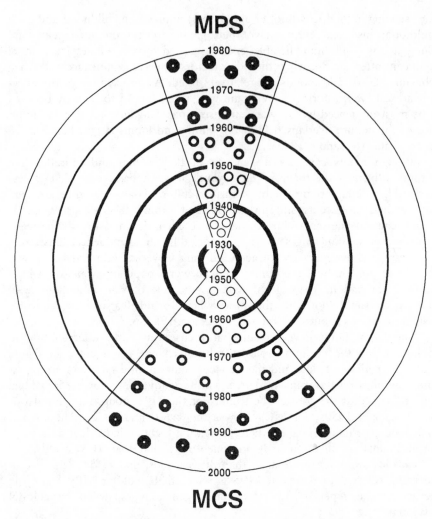

MCS

Figure 13.2.   Expansion model of individual development.

however; some, like Danny in MPS, rigidify and are resistant to the most basic kinds of feedback.

From the start, the men in MPS seemed oriented to a particular route, or prediction of their futures would not have been possible. To characterize only the routes explored in this book, one might say the men early boarded the A, B, C, D, or J trains (the A train was, of course, the fast track). A problem is, once a train is on a particular route, how to change the trajectory. This is why therapy is such a difficult process and why so many corporate training programs have limited effectiveness. A critical element for change is the permeability of the boundaries of self-identity, which are related to age as well as to individual differences.

To shift metaphors somewhat, the 1960s and 1970s were like rough seas, with a fearsome surf and undertow. The MPS men traveled over them as if in a secure boat, moving inexorably toward the safe harbor of middle-class prosperity and respectability. They were not in the middle of the churning, like the students, Vietnam soldiers, or blacks and women, especially the younger ones. The changes witnessed in the MPS men were primarily due to their own maturation and assumption of their various roles in life.

The strong increase in the MPS men's desire for autonomy was an indicator of their push toward differentiation. As they matured, they wearied of being told what to do and were oriented more and more to striking out on their own. For these corporate managers, part of the differentiation process was a move away from other people and toward productive achievements. The declines in their Affiliation and Intraception scores and Need for Peer Approval ratings symbolized a pushing away from others, concomitant with the satisfaction of intimacy needs within the marital family. Veroff *et al.* (1981) similarly found that older people were less likely than younger ones to turn to others in times of difficulty or unhappiness.

The MPS men's approach to life became tougher with time as they increased in hostile impulses and lost a sense of guilt over transgressions. Challenging work took on added importance. At the same time, their identities adjusted to declining opportunities for promotions as they subdued their advancement drives and redefined their expectations about the rewards of a managerial career. If Erikson's (1950) conceptualization of generativity as the primary task of this life stage were to be applied, it would more likely be realized in productive work than in nurturing the young.

CRITERION SUBGROUP CHANGES

With so many change data at hand, it would have been possible to perform analyses exploring their correlates in great detail. Almost every one of the many characteristics evaluated in MPS could have been used as a dependent variable in MPS:20 against each of the others in MPS:0 as predictors. Instead of plunging into this statistical sea, we have limited ourselves to the two major variables around which this volume has been organized — advancement in management and personal adjustment.

A number of the changes observed in the data were related to management level, Adjustment ratings, or both. In addition, there were cases of no mean change over time that still showed differential changes by the criterion variables of interest. In evaluating these differential changes, it should be remembered that other characteristics differentiated the advancement and Adjustment subgroups from the time of the initial assessment, and these differences often remained at a fairly constant level over time.

A summary of the variables that differentiated the advancement and Adjustment subgroups over the 20-year period is shown in Table 13.2. Those indicating differential development (i.e., changes that varied by subgroup) are indicated by superscript letters. Variables without superscript letters differentiated the subgroups rather consistently over time, with no statistical evidence that the subgroups changed over time in different ways.

Table 13.2   Summary of Variables Differentiating MPS Advancement and Adjustment Subgroups across Time

	Advancement	Adjustment
Relating to one criterion	Lower Locale-Residential involvement	Higher Religious-Humanism involvement and satisfaction[b]
	Higher Service involvement	Higher Supervision score (MQ)[b]
	Higher Salary score (MQ)	Higher Job Satisfaction score (MQ)
	Higher Leadership Motivation[a]	Higher Personal Communications score (MQ)
	Higher Ego-Functional involvement	Higher Self-Esteem[b]
		Less Independence
Relating to both criteria	Higher Ego-Functional satisfaction	
	Higher Occupational involvement and satisfaction[a]	
	Higher Pride score (MQ)	
	Better General Management Attitude (MQ)[b]	
	Higher Personal Satisfaction score (MQ)[b]	
	Higher Impersonal Communications score (MQ)[b]	
	Higher Identification score (MQ)[a, b]	
	Higher Authority score (MQ)[b]	
	Greater Positiveness[b]	
	Greater Ambition[a, b]	
	Better General Effectiveness[a, b]	
	Better Administrative Skills[a, b]	
	Better Interpersonal Skills[a, b]	
	Better Stability of Performance[a, b]	
Relating to criteria oppositely	Lower Marital-Familial involvement	Higher Marital-Familial satisfaction
	Lower Parental-Familial involvement	Higher Parental-Familial satisfaction
	Higher Impulsivity	Lower Impulsivity
	Lower Affability[a]	Higher Affability
	Higher verbal ability	Lower verbal ability

Note. Abbreviation: MQ, Management Questionnaire. All variables not marked by superscript letters showed a consistent relationship over time.
[a]   Developed over time for advancement.
[b]   Developed over time for Adjustment.

A large number of variables in the table relate in similar ways to both criteria. A primary reason is that those advanced the most and those best adjusted were more involved in and satisfied with their work. They responded more positively on such Management Questionnaire scales as General Management Attitude, Pride, Personal Satisfaction, Impersonal Communications, Authority, and Identification. The management level groups were rather consistently differentiated on these attitude scales over time, while the Adjustment groups showed increasing dissimilarity as the maladjusted men rapidly declined in favorableness. Greater general Positiveness (the personality factor) was consistently characteristic of both the higher-level managers and the better-adjusted ones.

Rapidly deteriorating attitudes for the maladjusted men also took place on scales that did not differentiate the level groups, including Supervision, Job Satisfaction, and Personal Communications on the Management Questionnaire. The higher-level men showed more satisfaction with their salaries, which would be expected since they were paid more.

Some important management abilities also differentiated the advancement and Adjustment groups. The "rich get richer and the poor get poorer" phenomenon was prevalent for the groups by management level on the dimension factors of General Effectiveness, Administrative Skills, and Stability of Performance. The higher-level groups held their own and the lower-level groups declined in Interpersonal Skills. In the case of the Adjustment groups, there was no particular increase in these important managerial qualities on the part of either the well-adjusted or the moderately adjusted, but the poorly adjusted declined markedly. The higher-level men and the best-adjusted also showed less decline in ambition over time, while the lower-level men and the maladjusted experienced sharp drops.

The relationship between these changes, all important in management, and management level attained was often not regular (i.e. did not show a regular stepwise progression through the five levels). The Ambition factor, for example, showed a large and essentially equal drop over time for all levels except the fifth and sixth. This high-level group showed negligible change. Although all groups advanced on the Edwards Achievement scale, the first-level managers moved up only from the 51st to the 58th percentile, while those at the fifth and sixth levels went from the 61st to the 90th!

The general decline in Interpersonal Skills was strongly related to management level eventually attained. Decreases were very large for those who remained at the lower levels of management. Those who had reached the fifth and sixth levels remained essentially unchanged. On Administrative Skills, the lower-level managers dropped over the 20-year period, while the fifth and sixth level managers rose a full point on a 5-point scale (from 3 to 4!) This great gain was not because of experience in top-level assignments, since somewhat more than half of it had been achieved by the time of reassessment at MPS:8.

We thus get a picture of those who failed to advance very far in management deteriorating in management skills along with, or at least partly due to, a loss of managerial motivation. At the same time, those who wound up at the highest levels held onto their motivation and increased in job involvement as they improved their management skills.

Some personality and motivation characteristics pointed in different directions for the advancement and Adjustment subgroups, sometimes because they related to the different criteria in opposite directions. The higher-level men showed an increase in Leadership and Motivation while the well-adjusted men had greater Self-Esteem and somewhat less Independence. While the higher-level men demonstrated more Impulsivity and less Affability, the well-adjusted men showed just the opposite pattern.

There was a striking difference in the evolution of personality between the highest- and lowest-level men, in that those at the higher levels, though nonauthoritarian and (one hopes) objective, became more uninvolved in personal relationships — "cool at the top" (Howard, 1984). The lower-level men retained their need for friendships and increased in interest in helping and sympathizing with others. This is the group, then, that was most likely to show the kind of generativity (Erikson, 1950) that was involved in developing others, while the majority of men were more concerned with productive outputs.

Lifestyles also showed some disparate results for the advancement and Adjustment subgroups. The high-level men were generally more involved in the Service and Ego-Functional life themes and less involved with their marital or parental families. The well-adjusted expressed more satisfaction with their marital and parental families. The best-adjusted men were also more involved in and satisfied with the Religious-Humanism life theme, especially since the maladjusted declined in this interest with time.

A final variable showing opposite relationships to advancement and Adjustment was verbal ability. Although strong verbal skills characterized the highest-level men throughout their careers, the well-adjusted tended, on the average, to be less verbally accomplished than their maladjusted counterparts.

In many ways, the poorly adjusted managers were similar to the lowest-level managers, so that it might be thought that a common cause was at work. Two types of evidence appear to disprove this possibility. One is that the correlation between Adjustment rating and management level was only .15. The other is that first-level managers made up only about one-sixth of those rated low in Adjustment. It thus appears that a midcareer decline in managerial motivation and managerial skills was taking place among both those who had not advanced and those who were not well adjusted, and a man could fall victim to the trend by being part of either subgroup. There was no evidence that failure to advance pushed one into maladjustment, or that some degree of maladjustment was necessary in forging one's way to the top. Those in high places did not appear to have had to pay emotionally for their success, and those at the bottom of the heap were often satisfied and happy.

This outcome essentially denies the conflict often believed to exist between achievement and personal adjustment. Even if adjustment and achievement were more incompatible than they have been shown to be here, it would still be possible to value achievement highly. What would life be like if there were no great books, art, or music, no outstanding scientists, and no great leaders of the institutions that make modern society possible?

On the other side, if the maladjustment that accompanied Bruce's continual quest for the meaning of life is endemic to the creative achieving person, it may be that the best general models for management are the well-adjusted but less profound practical problem solvers. Bruce may have made for more interesting reading, but Al was probably better able to sustain the business. Still, one would hope for some creative visionaries to provide the insight and zest to meet an unknown future.

MacKinnon (1978) has presented strong evidence that adult effectiveness is not reserved for those who have developed in warm nurturant environments. He reported that the staff of the OSS assessment center in World War II "discovered again and again that persons of the most extraordinary effectiveness had life histories marked by severe frustrations, deprivations, and traumatic experiences" (p. 9). Later in his research into creativity at the Institute for Personality Assessment and Research, he commented on early relationships with parents. The most creative architects, for example, often had had "a lack of intense closeness with one or both of the parents" (p. 67). On the average, in MacKinnon's studies, creative people described their early family lives as less harmonious and happy than those of their peers. Bland, uneventful early childhoods were frequent among those of mediocre creativity.

The ability of a parent to influence a child's personality is far from settled. Kagan (1984) concludes that "scientists have been unable to discover many profound principles that relate the actions of mothers, fathers, or siblings to psychological characteristics in the child" (p. 275). However and to what degree parental behavior does affect the child's future, our data showed only a small relationship between managerial achievements and personal adjustment. It appears that these two parameters of a person may well develop quite independently of each other. That is why numerous cases could be found in which various combinations of achievement level and Adjustment rating coexisted. In spite of this outcome in MPS, the MCS assessors' ratings of managerial potential and Adjustment indicated that they had little faith that the maladjusted would, in general, be very successful. This may indicate an unnecessarily high value placed on the importance of personal adjustment.

In evaluating the normative changes averaged across all participants, it should be noted that the MPS cohort was made up of those who were promising while young in management and does not represent numerically all telephone company managers. At MPS:20 there were 15 managers at the fifth and sixth levels and 31 at the first level — roughly a 2:1 ratio. In the Bell System, before divestiture, there were about 1,500 male managers at the fifth level or above and 500,000 at the first, or 33 times as many at the lowest level. Although the Bell System first-level group contained young as well as middle-aged managers, it may be that the trends we observed for the MPS first-level men are more normative than those observed for the average men in our study.

Those who lead organizations with large numbers of middle-aged managers may, considering the findings described above, be faced with a group different from what they expect. From third-level management on down, and from less well-adjusted managers at various levels, they cannot rely on much ambition (in the conventional sense) to motivate the carrying out of organizational goals. Nearly all managers will continue to perform their assignments in a satisfactory manner, but they will not do such things as seek to improve their skills, modify their management style constructively, or sing the praises of the organization. Many who are above the lowest level of the organization and who are adequately adjusted are, however, motivated for achievement and leadership, and it will be up to the organization to tap these positive motivations.

DEMOGRAPHIC GROUP DIFFERENCES

Some other groups within the samples were distinguishable by demographic variables. In MPS the college and noncollege participants could be treated separately, while in MCS there were gender and race/ethnic groups.

In terms of advancement within the organization, there was a sharp dichotomy within MPS between the college and noncollege participants. Discrepancies in management potential were evident between the two groups from the start, particularly in Cognitive Ability, Ambition, Impulsivity, and the Ego-Functional life theme, in all of which the college men scored or were rated higher. Family and educational backgrounds were also clearly different: The college men's parents had done considerably better occupationally and educationally, and the men themselves had better grades in high school. The noncollege men's ancestors were more likely to have been recent immigrants to the United States.

The discrepancies between the two groups in managerial qualities grew greater with time, although it was declines on the part of the noncollege men rather than increases on the part of the college men that accounted for the difference. Motivational differences seemed primarily at fault, especially since the college men grew in interest in their work over the years while the noncollege men declined. Certainly the lower promotion rates for the noncollege group, in addition to their realization that the college men were favored for advancement, could have contributed to lower motivation.

On the other hand, the motivational levels of the noncollege men were clearly lower at the start, and they did not have the self-development interests that would encourage them to expand their horizons. Although cognitive development characterized the two educational groups similarly, the college men developed their knowledge of contemporary affairs more than the non-college and demonstrated greater political understanding. Veroff *et al.* (1981) similarly found that college-educated people were more concerned with community, national, and international affairs than those with less education; the authors attributed this to more attention to fulfilling their moral and civic duties.

In terms of issues relevant to adult development, especially personality and lifestyles, the similarities far outweighed the differences. For both groups the Marital-Familial life theme grew in importance, while involvement in the Parental-Familial and Service themes decined. The most significant lifestyle difference was the greater involvement in the Occupational theme on the part of the college men; this finding has been supported by cross-sectional surveys (Jurgensen, 1978; Lacy *et al.*, 1983; Veroff *et al.*, 1981). Most of the personality changes were as relevant to one group as the other, such as increases on the Edwards Autonomy, Aggression, and Achievement scales and decreases on the Edwards Affiliation, Intraception, Abasement, and Endurance scales, as well as on the Sarnoff Motivation for Advancement.

When men and women were compared in MCS, the results provided strong support for the qualifications of women for management jobs. On no important dimensions did they come up short, and in many ways they were superior, such as in greater verbal ability, Written Communication Skills, Creativity, Perception of Threshold-Social Cues, interpersonal sensitivity, and Behavior Flexibility. The men showed better general knowledge of the world around them and more political understanding, consistent with the survey observation (Veroff *et al.*, 1981) that men more often reported feeling unhappy about the community, the nation, or world affairs.

A number of personality and motivation scales showed gender differences, although except for the traditional scales of masculine and feminine attitudes and interests, differences were not large and usually favored the women. Greater flexibility and poise were more characteristic of the women, while the men were more power- and authority-oriented. The women were somewhat lower on the Edwards Dominance and Aggression scales than the men, though even here aggressive inclinations showed no gender difference when measured by the projective exercises rather than by the paper-and-pencil questionnaires. The women were higher on Achievement via Independence (CPI) and Change (Edwards).

Confirmation of the MCS results is found in the ITS data, which showed the men scoring higher on the Edwards Dominance, Aggression, and Deference scales and ranking being self-controlled and obedient higher on the Rokeach. The ITS women scored higher on Succorance and Change and gave higher ranks on the Rokeach to being independent. The MCS results are also consistent with survey findings (Veroff *et al.*, 1981) showing that women are more intrinsically involved in achievement and men are more oriented to the social-competitive aspects of work. Even though such personality differences between the sexes were small, they may prophesy less favorable chances for advancement beyond middle management for the women. At higher levels, where job roles place less emphasis on individual production and more on exerting power and influence over others, the women may be at a definite disadvantage.

The fact that the differences between the men and women on personality measures was small is a reflection of the fact that men's and women's scores have been growing increasingly alike over the years. Mean scores for men and women college students in the 1959 Edwards Personal Preference Schedule manual show many more differences than those appearing in MCS. Stevens and Truss (1985) found a similar trend on the Edwards toward greater homogeneity between the sexes in their newer versus earlier cohorts. Likewise, Miner and Smith (1982) noted that past differences between men and women in the motivation to manage on the Miner Sentence Completion Scale have since disappeared.

Other researchers have also concluded that gender differences have declined in the business community, not just in personality and motivation but in attitudes, behaviors, abilities, and job preference (Brenner & Tomkiewicz, 1982; Brief & Oliver, 1976; Terborg, 1977). When factors such as education, age, occupation, and organizational level are taken into account, differences usually recede or disappear. Thus, when women in managerial or executive positions are compared to those in more traditional roles, the managerial women are distinguished by characteristics like those of male managers (Moore & Rickel, 1980; Morrison & Sebald, 1974). Some have postulated that the most effective managers will be androgynous, incorporating both masculine and feminine behaviors (Sargent, 1983), but others argue that women must act in a masculine manner if they are to succeed in competitive, corporate life (Lifton, 1986).

In spite of the MCS women's strong performance in the assessment center, they must still face three major problems. First, family/career conflicts may make strong demands on their time and energy and interrupt their careers. Second, their attachment to individual achievements may come at the expense of developing their political and competitive skills. Last but not least is the spectre of sexism, seemingly receding in the lower levels of management, but still untested in the most important corporate positions.

Assessed abilities among race and ethnic groups were much larger than those between the men and women in MCS, especially comparisons between blacks and whites. The data on Hispanics were provocative but await confirmation with a larger sample. Some attitude research suggests that they do fall between the position of whites and blacks, but a more definitive statement could be provided if the Hispanics were divided by particular ancestry (Fernandez, 1981).

Gender-within-race differences were prominent for the minorities, even though men and women among the whites were much alike. The black men more often came from very deprived homes with many children; perhaps as a consequence, they were more likely to be deficient in some abilities and to be reticent — qualities shared somewhat by the Hispanic females. The blacks generally exerted more self-control, in comparison to the more relaxed and sociable whites and Hispanics.

Even among a group of college-educated young people like those in MCS, many of whom had advanced degrees, early family and educational backgrounds showed sharp differences between the races, with the whites, as would be expected, having been more advantaged. These differences no doubt account, at least in part, for the disparity in the average level of assessment center performance between the two groups. Black—white differences in abilities have been frequently reported elsewhere, but various aspects of managerial ability were differentiated by the MCS assessment center. Cognitive tests showed the most discrepancies between blacks and whites, while measures of interpersonal skills showed very few differences. It appeared that the closer an assessment exercise was to academic situations, the less well the blacks performed.

A particular problem for the blacks was the juxtaposition of a lower level of some abilities against their higher level of aspirations. Probably because of the lower socioeconomic status of their families relative to the whites', they drew particular motivational strength from the appeal of financial gain, job security, and other extrinsic rewards that advancement would bring; results were nearly identical in the ITS data. In addition, average blacks were seen as overly optimistic about their future advancements. Many blacks were also understandably suspicious that they would not be treated fairly, and these feelings, unfortunately, could intensify if they overestimated their potential for promotions that were not forthcoming.

In spite of high expectations about future advancements, the average black was not as self-confident as the average white or Hispanic. In addition, the average black showed signs of adjusting less easily to disappointments, having less flexibility and resilience. The greater tension and unhappiness shown among blacks in MCS was supported in the survey data of Veroff *et al.* (1981). These same authors comment on blacks' greater involvement in religion, also shown in MCS, as a help in coping with frustration in an all too frequently hostile world.

The fact that blacks had lower average scores and ratings on a variety of measures does not mean that all blacks had less management ability than all whites. On the contrary, a large proportion of blacks scored the same or higher than the average white, and the high-potential blacks were quite exceptional — more so than the high-potential whites — on Interpersonal Skills and Stability of Performance. The danger of prejudicial overgeneralizations about blacks' abilities underscores the need to recognize and reward the many blacks who do have high potential for management.

IMPLICATIONS FOR ORGANIZATIONS

The data presented in this volume, particularly in Chapter 3, demonstrate clearly that organizations can greatly improve the quality of their managerial pools by more rigorous selection methods. This applies not merely to initial selection for employment, but to advancement in management. The road to the improvement of the total management of an organization is a long one, however, since some years have to elapse before the impact of improved selection is widely felt. Organizations must be far-sighted enough to invest in the future.

Many organizations are loath to make such an investment, both because of immediate budgetary concerns and because of a lack of conviction that selection really can be improved. Top executives can usually think of several exceptions — people who turned out well, even though they were not impressive at the time of employment. Such observations may be germane, but they ignore the fact that false positives, those who look good initially but peter out, greatly outnumber the false negatives that executives recall. In MPS, 40% of the participants who were rated as having at least fourth-level potential at the original assessment center did not reach such levels (false positives), while only 21% of those who were rated as having less than third-level potential rose to this level (false negatives). This number is exacerbated by the fact that the number who were expected to do poorly far exceeded those who were expected to go to high levels.

Care in initial screening can pay big dividends, but it should be supplemented by an even more careful look at those still on the payroll after a few years. Our data show that prediction of future success made at the MPS:8 reassessment was even more accurate than that made at the MPS:0 assessment. Of those predicted at MPS:8 to eventually reach fourth level or higher, 73% did so, compared to only 12% of those who were rated to reach lower levels. This enhanced predictability was due, in part, to the strong gain in Administrative Skills and Work Involvement registered during the first 8 years by those on their way to the top.

These recommendations should be considered in light of the fact that the predictive power cited above was derived from a 3-day assessment center utilizing a variety of evaluation methods. This would not be practicable in all selection situations, but the general approach of the assessment center can always be applied. For example, there should be general agreement on the important dimensions to be evaluated. Multiple judges are preferable to one, and behavioral simulations will add greatly to the predictive power of selection measures. Much has been written about the assessment center method (cf. Thornton & Byham, 1982), and this can provide guidance for those interested in the process.

Although assessment centers have established their reliability and validity for evaluating managerial competence when matched against criteria of advancement and performance ratings, they have rarely been used to predict terminations (Thornton & Byham, 1982). The MPS data presented in Chapter 3 illustrate that this, too, can be done with accuracy considerably better than chance. It may have been expected that the assessment center could predict forced terminations, which are highly related to ability. However, an important additional finding was that the MPS forced terminators demonstrated not just lower ability but less resilience, evidenced by low Endurance, poor Resistance to Stress, and low Realism of Expectations.

The ability of the assessment center to predict voluntary terminations is less intuitively obvious, but the depth of information produced by the MPS assessment process was able to differentiate this group even better than the group of forced terminators. Although just as capable as the men who stayed with the company, the voluntary terminators had a rather insistent urge to advance, with less loyalty to the organization and less involvement in work in general. It was as if they wanted the extrinsic rewards of a high-level management job but were unwilling to put in the time or the effort to achieve on their own merits. Organizations who capitalize on this information as part of their initial selection process could save untold dollars in reduced attrition.

Various measures used in this research showed the ability to predict later personal adjustment. Whether or not an employer can make use of this type of information in selecting its work force is more open to question. There was certainly enough of a negative relationship demonstrated between maladjustment and work performance to justify selecting out some of the more extreme cases. But this must be done with caution. Danny's contribution to the company may not have been worth all the supervisory time spent trying to improve his performance, and his chronically negative attitudes certainly did not help morale in his group. Yet Bruce was clearly making a good contribution to the company, in spite of his ruminations and worries. Thus, it would be difficult to justify using potential adjustment as a selection criterion into many jobs, and doing so might result in the loss of some very bright and creative people.

An organization is faced not only with yet-to-be-hired managers, but with its staff of current managers. These are the people who will determine the viability and the vitality of the enterprise in the present and the near future. This volume has laid out in numerous ways the great variation among these existing managers in abilities, motivations, values, attitudes, and personality characteristics. Understanding and addressing these variations is the key to the successful management of the enterprise and the well-being of the managers themselves.

Executives at the top of organizations are faced today with a host of problems in the turbulent economic world that now surrounds them. In addressing these problems, they often seek to change their organizations so as to make them more competitive in spirit, more concerned with quality and productivity, more participative and concerned with the quality of work life.

They usually find such changes difficult to accomplish and often fail, in spite of ringing announcements from the executive suite and inspirational articles in employee publications.

One suspects that at least some of their difficulties spring from failing to consider what the managers who must carry out these changes are really like. They may imagine that their typical manager is striving for advancement, or is at least highly work-involved, and identifies strongly with the organization. As has been seen, this is often not the case. The typical manager is not likely to make a great effort to change, which compounds the difficulty raised by the usual failure to set forth specifically what new behavior is desired. It is hard to translate abstract concepts like "competitiveness" into actions.

Perhaps the first injunction for upper echelons of management is that they pay more careful attention to the motivations of the managers below them. The central message of the research reported here is not, however, to act as though all managers are typical. Executives should understand that the motives and values of importance to the organization vary widely according to the age of the managers and the level in the organization they have attained. Developmental programs, whether aimed at change or merely at enhancement of management skills, need to build on the motivations that are salient for the particular subgroup addressed.

For middle-aged middle managers, a most important group, it is unlikely that advancement motivation will be strong; in any case, openings for these individuals may be few and far between. Our data indicate that autonomy and achievement are important to this group. This suggests that changes the organization has decided it wants should be shown to lead to greater independence of action and a greater sense of achievement. This, in itself, will require change *above* the target level of management. Some organizations will have to change quite fundamentally in order to capitalize on motivations for autonomy and achievement.

Top executives should be concerned, of course, not only with motivation to change, but with the feasibility of developing managers' abilities. Our data convince us that there are three main areas of ability of critical importance in successful management: general mental ability, interpersonal skills, and administrative skills. What can be expected to happen to these skills as managers go through their careers, in the absence of interventions to change them? What implications does this have for both selection and development?

As far as mental ability is concerned, a small general increase can be expected, but the relative standing of individuals will change little. Nor will any known intervention significantly alter basic mental ability in adults. It is strongly related to advancement in management, and it determines how readily individuals will gain the technical knowledge needed for their jobs and how skillful they will be in solving the problems that will confront them. Mental ability is, therefore, a key dimension in the selection of managers, but probably not a good target for a planned intervention for developmental purposes.

The level of interpersonal skills at the beginning of a management career is predictive of success in management, making it a target for selection. This takes on added importance with the new generation of managers, who were notably poorer on interpersonal skills than the MPS men had been at the same young age. This problem may loom even larger in the future if the number of liberal arts majors brought into business continues to decline in favor of technical majors, who were the least accomplished in interpersonal skills in both the MPS and MCS samples.

No increase in interpersonal skills can generally be expected with years of management experience, even for those on their way to high places. In fact, such abilities are highly likely to decline among those who remain in the lower-management ranks. This suggests that many who will be employed could profit from specific training. It will also be important to have a reward system in the organization that encourages skillful interpersonal behavior, lest declining motivation inhibit its demonstration.

Administrative skills show the most varied picture. Once again, no general increase from on-the-job experience can be expected. Those with high potential, however, can be expected to show an early and sharp improvement. This is evidence that administrative skills can be strengthened, but it will not happen in most cases without direct intervention.

In prescribing training in management skills, attention must be given to motivation to improve. A disturbing finding in the MPS research was the general decline in demonstrated abilities, especially by the noncollege men who remained at the lower levels of management. Many of these men commented on their inability to compete with the college recruits — not just because the college men had better skills, which they often didn't recognize, but because they felt the company favored the college men when it came to promotions.

Although there were certainly ability differences that would have militated against the noncollege men's generally rising as far in the hierarchy as the college men, there was also evidence that the most astute noncollege men could have been better used by the company. As another analysis has reported in detail (Howard, 1986), the noncollege men who later earned their baccalaureates at night performed just as well as the college men (those without graduate training) at the MPS:20 assessment, but they experienced fewer promotions. Companies would do well to look carefully at this underused resource and to provide mechanisms, such as assessment centers, for such individuals to get on the "fast track" and compete more equitably with those who come into the company with college degrees.

A special problem appears to be presented by today's young managers. Although as young people they are more advancement-oriented than middle-aged, middle managers, they are nowhere nearly as motivated for advancement as those of the previous generation, relatively speaking. Even though that motivation declined with age in the MPS group, it was a powerful force for achievement early in their careers. In addition, the motivation to exert leadership is notably weaker in the college graduates now entering management positions. Organizations can no longer count on these once-reliable motives to drive performance.

Because of the impact of the 1970s culture, the baby boom generation has absorbed the philosophy of self-actualization and self-involvement. From an organizational standpoint, Joe, the typical MPS college recruit, was a more welcome middle-management candidate; he was committed to the company, unquestioning about doing what was expected of him, and motivated by his strong drive for advancement and yen for leadership. Jeff, his MCS counterpart, was considerably less willing to be imposed upon, although his values could influence the organization toward greater responsiveness to individual, human needs. Unfortunately, by devaluing leadership roles, he might be denying himself the pleasure obviously derived by Joe and others of his generation in leading others toward accomplishments.

Yet the younger generation shows no less interest in doing a good job or achieving satisfaction from successfully completing a difficult assignment. They thus have adequate motivation for individual accomplishments in management. The problem for organizations is how to arrange the early experiences of new managers so as to tap this motivation. There is an understandable tendency to give new recruits routine jobs until they learn more about the organization and to give them little latitude to make mistakes. This obviously imparts little sense of achievement.

The needs of both younger and older managers will require changes in traditional management style in the direction of more delegation — pushing tasks and responsibility downward, instead of pushing decision making upward. In addition, beginning managers need to be given a sense of career and reliable information on the positives as well as the negatives of higher-level positions. Liberal feedback and frequent interactions with supervisors are also advised for a generation that, more than the preceding one, turns to others for succorance. The need for good feedback is particularly acute for the blacks, whose self-esteem is on more tenuous grounds.

The MCS generation had a more pessimistic view of what life as a manager would be like and were less willing to offer their loyalty and emotional involvement to the company than their MPS predecessors. At the same time, current business developments have put many organizations in a mode of paring down their management forces, thus violating the psychological contract of lifetime security proffered to employees in past decades. The MCS generation would be expected to suffer less from such a contract violation than those in the MPS age group, since the newer managers are less concerned with security and already have less trust in organizations. Yet the phenomenon of paring down, especially if carried out insensitively, is likely to increase the feelings of cynicism, pessimism, and self-concern among these younger managers and to undermine whatever organizational loyalty has been cultivated.

The women in management show considerable talent, and as they move into higher-level jobs, organizations are likely to discover that they are facing a considerable loss if steps are not taken to make it easier for women to raise families and have careers at the same time. Relocation policies should accommodate the movement of dual-career spouses by offering such things as professional counseling, financial incentives, and assisting spouses in finding jobs. Variable starting and quitting times and shared jobs can provide some relief for overburdened mothers.

The child-care problem needs some resolution by either corporate or societal programs. A recent report (Hellwig, 1986) claimed that in spite of corporate reluctance to be in the business of child care, 2,500 companies (up from 600 in 1982) offer some kind of assistance with such problems. This may include referral services; subsidies, vouchers, or discounts at public child-care centers; funding of community day-care centers; or in some cases establishment of an on-site child-care center. Cafeteria benefit plans can offer parents some child-care options, and parental leaves may be offered to parents of both sexes.

For both women and minorities, affirmative action programs have been one of the best stimuli to their advancement and better utilization. The original implementation of the program in the Bell System, as a test case, was controversial and at times required extreme measures, but the outcome offered new hopes to a previously underutilized work force. Although "quotas" are no longer in place at AT&T, affirmative action policies continue strongly, primarily because the top management is convinced that these policies should be in place.

Affirmative action policies were instigated by government policies and lawsuits, yet attempts by the Reagan administration to dismantle or roll back such programs have met with great resistance from corporations. A recent survey of federal contractors found that affirmative action is seen as an essential management tool that serves to capitalize on the talents of the entire work force and to reinforce accountability. Moreover, results have been impressive. Between 1974 and 1980, female employment increased 15% and minority employment 20% among federal contractors, but among comparable companies without federal contracts, women's jobs grew by 2% and minorities' jobs by 12%. This record was particularly impressive in light of the fact that overall job growth during this period was considerably greater for the noncontractors (8%) than the contractors (2%) (Simpson, 1986).

A critical challenge for organizations now is to assure that affirmative action policies apply up to the top of the management hierarchy. If women and minorities feel there is an inpenetrable glass ceiling impeding their progress up the corporate ladder, they are likely to turn to smaller businesses or entrepreneurial activities.

One thing that should not be overlooked in the push toward the most effective use of affirmative action is the importance of using proper personnel selection methods and standards. At the time of MCS, in their zeal to meet affirmative action goals, some of the telephone companies had not been as rigorous in their selection methods as they might have been, which could have depressed the average level of minorities' performance in some of the assessment center exercises. Since the first challenges to personnel selection and testing were mounted as part of equal employment concerns, a great deal of professional work has been accomplished to validate selection methods and to assure that they do not discriminate unfairly against protected groups. This body of work has shown that tests that are valid for one demographic group are usually valid for another, and proper use of such tests should result in the best candidates being selected from each demographic group.

A problem does arise from the common finding that minorities on the average typically do not perform as well on cognitive tests as whites, resulting in a smaller proportion of them being selected. To overcome this problem, organizations need to recruit more heavily among the minority population. In the Bell System companies, not only was more recruiting done for the minorities but more hiring was done as well, since their representation as one-third of the MCS sample was considerably higher than their representation in the college graduate population. If all race and ethnic groups were to be promoted strictly on their merits identified in the MCS assessment center ("yes" or "questionable" on "Should be third level"), with neither an affirmative action push for the minorities nor unfair discrimination against them, the college graduate segment of the middle-management work force in a few years would be 8% black and 3% Hispanic (and 46% female), not far from their representation in the college graduate population. But these proportions of minorities are definitely below their representation among the Bell System college hires, indicating a further selection process at each promotional hurdle.

If affirmative action were to provide some extra impetus for minorities who come close to the usual standards ("yes" or "questionable" on "Will be third level"), the proportions at middle management would be 13% black and 4% Hispanic, with a negligible loss of management quality. Such numbers are close to the proportions of such groups in the general population. The MCS assessors rated more minorities as "Will be third level" than as "Should be third level," under the assumption that affirmative action would have a positive effect on their careers. However, in spite of the best intentions of the company and individual managers, it is still possible that inadvertent or unconscious discrimination could occur and have a negative effect on minority careers. It will be important to monitor the progress of minorities at each level as part of the affirmative action effort.

Considerations of personnel policies quickly bump into the reality that organizations do not exist in a vacuum. They are inextricably intertwined with the society in which they are embedded. The fundamental nature of employees is shaped before they enter the organization's ranks; organizations add to those experiences, but as the expansion model (Figure 13.2) shows, their impact is unlikely to be as great as that of individuals' preceding experiences.

Women's personalities, motivations, experiences, and opportunities are molded by social sex roles; it is unlikely that they will be able to claim equal status in organizations as long as their rights are abridged and their needs not met in the larger society. Minorities have been consistently denied equal education and status; until society can freely open its arms to them, organizations will have to struggle with the uneven outcomes. Colleges and universities are under increasing criticism for losing the goal of developing leaders and citizens with a high-quality liberal education; if their input into management ranks is weak, organizations will suffer. Work organizations should do everything in their power to select and develop a work force in a way that capitalizes on America's multicultural resources and maximizes its competitive position in the global marketplace. But they should also use what influence they have to help society resolve its problems, which so directly affect the organization's survival.

WHAT NEXT?

Notwithstanding all the data presented in this volume, there is still much to learn from the AT&T longitudinal studies. If present plans are carried out, several more volumes will be forthcoming.

Since the MCS assessment, bi-annual interviews have been conducted with participants and their bosses to learn more about how they are treated and how they fare in the early years of their careers. What happens to the attitudes, motivation, and performance of a group that began with lower expectations and ambitions about a management career? How will the minorities be treated? As noted in Chapter 11, prejudices die hard; moreover, even if supervisors and peers are well intentioned, they may lack insight into the most effective way to make minorities feel at home and to help them develop their competencies. Will women be promoted according to their abilities, or according to preconceived notions of their roles in the organization? What will be the effects of training programs, performance appraisal processes, job characteristics, and sequences of job assignments? How will different bosses, peers, and subordinates impact on the participants? All these questions and more are currently being addressed to the interview data.

A top priority is to reassess the MCS cohort to determine the ways in which their abilities, motivations, and personalities changed after a few years of work experience. This measure of change will permit a determination of the impact of the organizational influences documented from the earlier interviews. For example, does having a good role model lead to better skill development than having a more informative appraisal from a less admirable boss? Are some approaches better for developing minorities or women than for white males? Another issue to be resolved by the reassessment is whether the MCS participants will change in ways that are similar to the ways in which the MPS group changed. This will be an initial check on the hypotheses relating to developmental versus generational changes that have been set forth in this chapter. For example, will they continue to increase in motivation for autonomy? Will their affiliation needs decline?

Some data already collected with the MPS group await further exploration. For example, extensive medical data were collected at each of the three assessment periods. These findings will be integrated with information on personality, lifestyles, and experiences of stress throughout the career and with the midlife and midcareer findings from new exercises developed for MPS:20.

Additional follow-up interviews were conducted at the 25th year of MPS, and the hope is to follow the MPS men into retirement. As of this writing, more than 100 men have retired and are being asked to participate in a retirement interview and to complete relevant questionnaires. Some of the questions we hope to answer are which types of men retire first, what kinds of experiences precipitate retirement, how the retirees feel about the company at the ends of their careers, and how different men adjust to retirement.

In the meantime, the participants in these studies have faced a strong break with their past. Since the divestiture of January 1, 1984, the parent company as well as the seven regional Bell operating companies face new competitive arenas in an environment that has become increasingly turbulent and unpredictable. What skills will managers need to face such a future? It seems unlikely that the old characteristics measured by our dimensions will become obsolete, though additional ones might be added, such as risk taking. More likely, higher levels of traditional skills will be demanded than ever before. In Chapter 12 we have observed that the MCS assessors gave added importance to dimensions in the Interpersonal Skills factor, such as Leadership Skills and Behavior Flexibility, and to the Stability of Performance Factor. To see if the assessors' bets were correctly placed, the MPS and MCS managers will be observed as they move with their organizations into an unknown future.

And now we join our participants in saying goodbye to the Bell System, an imposing giant of 1 million employees and 3 million stockholders, a Goliath stoned by the Davids of microwave transmission and terminal equipment.

Appendix

Measures Used in the Research

THE ASSESSMENT CENTER METHOD

The assessment center is a method of evaluating the characteristics of an individual on the basis of performance in behavioral simulations, often supplemented by one or more of the following: interviews, cognitive tests, personality/motivation inventories, attitude and value questionnaires, and projective techniques. Evidence from the several sources is combined in consensus judgments during the integration session, a meeting of the assessors to review and integrate observations. Judgments take the form of ratings of the assessment dimensions — the ability, motivational, personality, and attitudinal characteristics around which the particular center is organized.

Although the method can be applied to a single individual, participants usually attend the center in groups of 6 or 12. This is not only for reasons of efficiency, but because group simulations are almost always among the assessment techniques. The amount of assessee time required depends on the goals and complexity of the assessment; 1—3 days is the range. Again depending on the purposes and methods of assessment, assessors may be professional psychologists, trained laypersons, or a combination of these. The modal ratio of assessors to assessees is 1:2. Assessor time required, including report writing and integration sessions, may total 50% to 150% more than assessee time.

Although there were slight variations over the years, the assessment centers in MPS and MCS generally evaluated 12 participants a week, with the participants under observation for 3 days. There were eight assessors — either all psychologists, or six psychologists and two middle-level managers. Descriptions of the assessment dimensions and techniques, and the various scores derived from them, make up the remainder of this appendix.

ASSESSMENT DIMENSIONS AND PREDICTIONS

The assessment dimensions were rated on scales from 1 to 5 with 5 as the high point. The following basic set of 26 dimensions was used for all the MPS and MCS assessment centers described in this book. (MPS:0, MPS:8, MPS:20, and MCS:0).

Administrative Skills

- *Organizing and Planning*: How effectively can this person organize, and how well does he or she plan ahead?
- *Decision Making*: How ready is this person to make decisions, and how good are the decisions that are made?
- *Creativity*: How likely is this person to solve a management problem in a novel way?

Interpersonal Skills

- *Leadership Skills*: How effectively can this person lead a group to accomplish a task without arousing hostility?
- *Oral Communication Skills*: How well can this person present an oral report to a small conference group on a subject he or she knows well?
- *Behavior Flexibility*: How readily can this person, when motivated, modify his or her behavior to reach a goal? How able is this person to change roles or style of behavior to accomplish objectives?
- *Personal Impact*: How forceful and likeable an early impression does this person make? (Note: Forcefulness and Likeableness were rated separately, and the lower of the two ratings was used for the Personal Impact rating.)
- *Social Objectivity*: How free is this person from prejudices against racial, ethnic, socioeconomic, educational, and other social groups?
- *Perception of Threshold Social Cues*: How readily does this person perceive minimal cues in the behavior of others?

Intellectual Ability

- *General Mental Ability*: How able is this person in terms of the functions measured by tests of intelligence, scholastic aptitude, and/or learning ability?
- *Range of Interests*: To what extent is this person interested in a variety of fields of activity such as science, politics, sports, music, art, and so on?
- *Written Communication Skills*: How well can this person compose a communicative and formally correct memorandum on a subject he or she knows well? How well written are his or her memos and reports likely to be?

Stability of Performance

- *Tolerance of Uncertainty*: To what extent will this person's work performance stand up under uncertain or unstructured conditions?
- *Resistance to Stress*: To what extent will this person's work performance stand up in the face of personal stress?

Work Involvement

- *Primacy of Work*: To what extent does this person find satisfaction from work more important than satisfactions from other areas of life?
- *Inner Work Standards*: To what extent will this person want to do a good job even if a less good one is acceptable to the boss and others?

- *Energy*: How continuously can this person sustain a high level of work activity?
- *Self-Objectivity*: How realistic a view does this person have of his or her own assets and liabilities, and how much insight into his or her own motives?

Advancement Motivation

- *Need for Advancement*: To what extent does this person need to be promoted significantly earlier than his or her peers? To what extent are further promotions needed for career satisfaction?
- *Need for Security*: How strongly does this person want a secure job?
- *Ability to Delay Gratification*: To what extent will this person be willing to wait patiently for advancement if he or she is confident that advancement will come?
- *Realism of Expectations*: To what extent do this person's expectations about his or her work life with the company conform to what is likely to be true? (Convention: If *under*estimates, rate 5).
- *Bell System Value Orientation*: To what extent has this person incorporated Bell System values, such as service, friendliness, justice of company position on earnings, rates, wages, and so forth?

Independence

- *Need for Superior Approval*: To what extent does this person need warmth and nurturant support from immediate supervisors?
- *Need for Peer Approval*: To what extent does this person need warmth and acceptance from peers and subordinates?
- *Goal Flexibility*: To what extent is this person likely to reorient his or her life toward a different goal?

An additional 21 dimensions were added at MPS:20, only one of which is reported in this volume (Adjustment). Ten of these 21 were also used at the MCS:0 assessment (including Adjustment), as follows:

Financial Concerns

- *Financial Motivation*: To what extent does this person want a significantly higher income than currently provided from Bell System employment?

Philosophical Attitudes

- *Conservatism*: To what extent does this person tend to oppose social change and refrain from challenging traditions?
- *Cynicism*: To what extent does this person disbelieve in human goodness and refrain from idealizing human nature?
- *Involvement*: To what extent does this person identify with, relate to, become concerned about, and/or take an active part in affairs of the world or the community?
- *Religiosity*: To what extent does this person practice or abide by a system of religious or humanistic beliefs or ethical values?

Self Concerns

- *Avocational Interest*: To what extent does this person find meaning and satisfaction in a hobby or hobbies? (Considers depth and intensity of interest, not breadth. Includes work if not Bell System work.)
- *Self-Development*: To what extent does this person attempt to expand his or her skills, knowledge, or personality?
- *Adjustment*: To what extent has this person changed or adapted to his or her life situation in an emotionally healthy way?
- *Happiness*: To what extent does this person find pleasure in life at the present time?
- *Selfishness*: To what extent is this person occupied with self-interest, with little or no concern for others?

After the rating of the dimensions, the assessors made predictions about the future careers of the participants. At MPS:0, these were as follows:

- *Will*: Will this person be advanced to middle management (third level) within 10 years? The modal assessor rating was used for each participant, either "yes," "no," or "questionable" (if there was substantial disagreement).
- *Should*: Should this person be advanced to middle management (third level) within 10 years? The modal assessor rating was coded as above. In addition, those with potential for positions higher than the third level were coded as "should be above third level."
- *Stay*: Will this person stay with the Bell System for the rest of his or her career? The modal assessor ratings were coded as in "Will."

At the MCS assessment, the same predictions were made as in MPS:0, with a few alterations. With the "Should" rating, there was no additional code for those with potential higher than the third level. Instead, another prediction was made:

- *Level Should Be*: What level should this person attain in the Bell System? Responses were "above third level," "third level," "marginal potential for third level," and "low potential for third level." Modal assessor ratings indicated the final prediction code used for each participant.

In addition to rating whether or not the participant would stay with the Bell System, the assessors indicated reasons for termination among those predicted to leave. These were coded "voluntary," "forced" (for those expected to be asked or encouraged to leave because of poor performance), or "questionable" (when the assessors had substantial disagreement).

ASSESSMENT TECHNIQUES

Once dimensions are decided upon, the next step in building an assessment center is the selection or development of techniques that will provide the information necessary for evaluating the dimensions. In this research, these techniques fell into four broad categories: managerial simulations, interviews, projective tests, and paper-and-pencil tests and inventories. The specific techniques are described below. (This list does not include each and every paper-and-pencil instrument. Some administered during the first few years of the research were judged not to be helpful and were not used later.)

Managerial Simulations

Business Game

The business game at the MPS:0 assessment center was called the "Manufacturing Problem." This simulation, in which six subjects at a time participated together, involved purchasing Tinker Toy parts, using them to manufacture simple toys (models of which were provided), and selling them back to the member of the assessment staff designated as the buyer/supplier. The problem was divided into six periods for a total of approximately 2 hours. Prices for products and amounts for which assembled toys could be sold changed sharply from period to period, and good organization was necessary to show a profit. Group action was necessary; no one could buy or sell as an individual. The group was given a small amount of money to start with and was allowed to keep any profit made.

The business game used at MPS:8 was the "Investment Problem." This simulation, in which six subjects at a time participated together, involved a miniature stock market (listing 15 fictitious issues). The participants played the roles of managing partners of a mutual fund. Their task was to invest the fund's money (bogus) to make a profit for the shareholders. Stock prices fluctuated during the several trading periods in accordance with general market trends and factors affecting particular issues. Group action was necessary; no one could buy or sell as an individual.

No business game was included in the MCS assessment exercises.

Group Discussion

At MPS:0, the group discussion exercise was the "Promotion Problem." Again in groups of six, the participants were instructed to assume that they were second-level managers meeting to decide which of their subordinates should be promoted to fill a current vacancy. Each participant was told that he had a strong candidate from among his own subordinates and was given a 300-word summary of this person's strengths and weaknesses. Each participant was required to make a short formal presentation of his candidate. The group then was given 1 hour for free discussion to select one of the six foremen to receive the promotion and to rank-order the others.

The group discussion problem used in the MPS:8 centers was the "Organization Problem." In this, groups of six participants were asked to assume they were a task force preparing recommendations for top management on how the telephone company might be reorganized for greater efficiency. As background, they were each given a copy of a recent interviewing study on possible reorganization and allowed 1 hour for preparation. Each participant was then allowed up to 10 minutes to present his recommendations orally. A 1-hour discussion followed in which the participants were required to agree on proposals for top management.

There were two group discussions in MCS assessment. One of these paralleled the original MPS Promotion Problem in that it was structured to produce competition. The "City Council Problem" (made available gratis by Development Dimensions International, the copyright owner) had each group of six participants play the roles of members of the city council of a small Midwestern city. They were told that they were about to attend a meeting of the council in which they would have to decide how to spend a $1,000,000 windfall from the federal government. Each participant was given the same background data on the fictitious city and its budget. Each participant was told that he or she would represent a different city department (such as the Fire or Police Department) and that he or she should attempt to secure at least a major share of the money for that department. The participants were given 30 minutes to prepare and 10 minutes to present their proposals at the council meeting. A 1-hour discussion followed, with the requirement that the group agree on the distribution of $1,000,000 before time elapsed.

The 119 participants assessed during the first 2 MCS years experienced a different but highly comparable exercise, the "School Board Problem." Here the task was also the distribution of a budget windfall, this time to particular aspects of school district functioning. This exercise was discontinued due to its adoption in an operational assessment center program that some of the participants might later attend.

The second MCS group discussion exercise, used throughout MCS assessment, was the "Counseling Center Group Discussion," originally developed for MPS:20. In this, six assessees were asked to assume that they were senior members of a community counseling center meeting to discuss guidance for junior counselors dealing with five different clients, each with a different "problem of living." They were given brief descriptions of each case and required to develop a consensus on guidance to be given the junior counselors.

At the conclusion of each group exercise, overall ratings and rankings of individual performance were made by the observers and by the participants themselves.

In-Basket

The In-Basket was an individual rather than a group simulation. In it, each participant faced a range of managerial problems presented through the medium of materials that might well come across a manager's desk. These materials could include letters, interoffice memos, reports, records of telephone calls, specific requests from the boss, and so on. The participants were usually told that they were entering a new job in a new location on an emergency basis because of the death or unexpected departure of the previous incumbent. They were further instructed that the job had been empty for a while, that they had come into their new office for the first time on a Sunday afternoon, and that they had to be away for the next several working days. This setting tended to explain why considerable material had accumulated and why it had to be dealt with by written memos and instructions rather than by immediate meetings and telephone calls.

Following this individual work, 3 hours of it in the MPS and MCS assessment centers, each participant met with an assessor who sought to learn exactly how the assessee tackled the work in terms of such areas as overall organization, priorities, and interrelationships among the items. In addition, the interviewer attempted to discover what perception the assessee had of the general situation of the new work group. Finally, and most importantly, the assessor tried to dig into the reasoning the assessee followed in each action or lack of action in response to each item. In some In-Baskets the assessor operated merely as an interviewer, not involved in the fictitious organization. In others, the assessor played the role of the assessee's new boss.

The In-Basket at the original MPS assessment center (MPS:0) called upon the participants to assume the role of a third-level manager in the Plant Department of a telephone company. At MPS:8 the simulated job was that of a division operations manager, also in a telephone company.

In MCS, for the first 119 participants, the role to be assumed was that of a division operations manager in the Imports Ltd. Co. For the remainder, the new position was personnel manager in the Woolex Manufacturing Company (also provided gratis by Development Dimensions International). The change was due to adoption of the Imports Ltd. In-Basket in an operational assessment program.

Interview

Each participant underwent a private interview lasting from $1\frac{1}{2}$ to 2 hours. The session was loosely structured, with the interviewer free to vary the approach according to his or her own style and perceptions of what would work best with a specific participant. Subjects covered usually included educational background, extracurricular activities, career aspirations and expectations, marital and family situations and prospects, religious and political interests, and hobbies.

Projective Tests

The participants took three different projective exercises, which were given in group administration rather than individual fashion. One of these was the Thematic Apperception Test (TAT), developed by the same Henry Murray who later directed the OSS assessment centers. Only six pictures were administered in MPS, but up to nine were given in MCS, since pictures with female figures in prominent roles were added for the sample of women.

The other projective exercises were incomplete sentences, in which the participant was given the stem of a sentence and asked to finish it. One of these was the Rotter Incomplete Sentences Blank; the other, devised especially for the present research, was the Management Incomplete Sentences Test developed by Dr. Walter Katkovsky.

Personal History Questionnaire

A biographical questionnaire about each participant's education, parents, spouse, interests, and so forth.

Paper-and-Pencil Tests and Inventories

Cognitive Tests

- *School and College Ability Test (SCAT)*: A multiple-choice test composed of Verbal and Quantitative subscales measuring intellectual ability.
- *Critical Thinking in Social Science Test*: A multiple-choice test requiring the subject to make inferences from verbal, tabular, and graphical material. (This test was not administered in MCS.)
- *Contemporary Affairs Test*: A multiple-choice test measuring each participant's knowledge of recent events in national and international affairs, science and medicine, the arts, and sports. In MCS this test was replaced by a General Information

Test, measuring general knowledge, since the annual construction and norming of the Contemporary Affairs Test had been discontinued.

Work Expectations and Preferences Questionnaires

· *Expectations Inventory*: An inventory containing 56 statements describing various aspects of life as a manager both on and off the job. The participant was asked to look ahead 5 years and to mark each item in terms of how likely it was to turn out to be true. In addition, the participant was to indicate which five of the items would be of most positive importance personally and which five would indicate the most negative outcomes.
· *Work Conditions Survey*: A list of 30 job characteristics, such as "irregular hours," which the participant was asked to rate as to desirability.

Personality/Motivation Inventories

Definitions of the characteristics in the personality and motivation inventories are often phrased in terms of behavior. The statements are to be read, however, as conveying the essence of what the scales are intended to evaluate, with no implication of a necessary correlation with overt behavior.

· *Edwards Personal Preference Schedule*: A forced-choice inventory designed to measure 15 motivational needs:
  · *Achievement*: To do a difficult job well. Persons scoring high on this scale have a need to do their best and seek to solve difficult problems.
  · *Deference*: To conform to authority and regulations. Those who score high tend to seek opinions from others, follow instructions, and do what is expected.
  · *Order*: To have things planned and systematized. Individuals scoring high tend to organize their work neatly and in detail, to have definite schedules, and to plan ahead.
  · *Exhibition*: To attract attention to oneself. Individuals scoring high like to talk about their achievements and enjoy being the center of attention.
  · *Autonomy*: To be free and independent. Persons scoring high want to be able to come and go freely, express their views openly, and be able to make decisions independently.
  · *Affiliation*: To make and enjoy friends. Individuals scoring high form new friendships readily and would rather do things in friendly groups than alone.
  · *Intraception*: To understand motives and feelings. Those scoring high tend to analyze the motives, feelings, and behavior of others.
  · *Succorance*: To receive understanding and help. Persons scoring high seek help from others when in trouble and look for encouragement and support from others.
  · *Dominance*: To lead and direct others. Individuals scoring high seek positions of leadership and want recognition as leaders.
  · *Abasement*: To feel guilty for errors and wrongdoing. Individuals scoring high accept blame readily when things go wrong and feel a need to confess their errors.
  · *Nurturance*: To be sympathetic and helpful. Those scoring high assist friends in difficulty, show sympathy and consideration for others, and enjoy receiving personal confidences.

- *Change*: To have new and different experiences. Persons scoring high like to seek variety and novelty in their day-to-day experiences.
- *Endurance*: To stick to a task until it is finished. Individuals scoring high work hard at problems until they are completed and would rather work on one job at a time.
- *Heterosexuality*: To have erotic relationships with the opposite sex. Persons scoring high like activities that include the opposite sex and like to talk and read about sex.
- *Aggression*: To be hostile to others. Individuals who score high tend to attack opposing viewpoints and will criticize others publicly.
- *Guilford-Martin Inventory (GAMIN)*: A questionnaire designed to measure five personality characteristics:
  - *G — General Activity* (pressure for energetic rapid action). Persons scoring high prefer a fast pace, enjoy excitement, and show enthusiasm and energy.
  - *A — Ascendance* (in social situations). High scorers are eager to voice their own opinions, even if others disagree, and risk confrontation to protect their rights.
  - *M — Masculinity* (of interests and attitudes). High scorers prefer science, math, and outdoor activities over music, art, literature, and quiet indoor hobbies; they are not fearful of such things as deep water, burglars, snakes, and bugs.
  - *I — Lack of Inferiority Feelings* (self-confidence). Those scoring high indicate feelings of self-worth independent of the approval of others.
  - *N — Lack of Nervousness*. High scorers are calm and easily able to relax and resist distraction.
- *Guilford—Zimmerman Temperament Survey (G-Z)*: Used in MCS assessment instead of GAMIN; a questionnaire designed to measure 10 personality characteristics. Three of these overlap with GAMIN (General Activity, Ascendance, and Masculinity). The other seven are as follows:
  - *R — Restraint*. High scorers are deliberate, serious-minded, persistent, and self-controlled.
  - *S — Sociability*. High scorers like social activities, seek social contacts, and enjoy friends and acquaintances.
  - *E — Emotional Stability*. High scorers show evenness of moods and energy, are optimistic and cheerful, and seldom worry.
  - *O — Objectivity*. High scorers are thick-skinned, not suspicious, and unlikely to take things personally.
  - *F — Friendliness*. High scorers tolerate hostility, are not belligerent or resentful, and can accept domination.
  - *T — Thoughtfulness*. High scorers are reflective, meditative, introspective, and interested in thinking as opposed to overt activity.
  - *P — Personal Relations*. High scorers are tolerant of people and have faith in social institutions.
- *California Psychological Inventory (CPI)*: Used in MCS assessment only. A questionnaire designed to measure 18 characteristics:
  - *Do — Dominance*: Tendency to behave in a dominant, ascendant manner; capable of influencing others and exercising leadership.
  - *Cs — Capacity for Status*: Self-confidence and self-assurance underlying anticipation of success and high status.

- *Sy — Sociability*: Motivation to be outgoing and participative; liking of people and their company.
- *Sp — Social Presence*: Interest in displaying poised, broad-minded spontaneity in social interactions.
- *Sa—Self Acceptance*: Sense of personal worth and independence.
- *Wb — Sense of Well-Being*: Feeling of good health, sufficient energy, and absence of problems.
- *Re — Responsibility:* Concern with being conscientious and dependable; avoidance of impulsivity or rebelliousness.
- *So — Socialization*: A positive and optimistic view of the world; adjustment to one's situation.
- *Sc — Self Control*: Freedom from impulsive, self-centered, and irrational behavior.
- *To — Tolerance*: Possession of permissive, accepting, and nonjudgmental attitudes towards others; freedom from rigidity or dogmatism.
- *Gi — Good Impression*: Tendency to give overly favorable impressions of self; denial of negative behavioral tendencies.
- *Cm — Communality*: Possession of conventional behavior and attitudes, conformity, and optimism.
- *Ac — Achievement via Conformance*: Need for achievement coupled with responsiveness to structure, organization, and rules and regulations.
- *Ai — Achievement via Independence*: Need for achievement coupled with responsiveness to ambiguous, independent, and nonauthoritarian settings.
- *Ie — Intellectual Efficiency*: Ease and efficiency in applying abilities.
- *Py — Psychological Mindedness*: Interest in the psychological workings of others; extraspection.
- *Fx — Flexibility*: Impulsive and changeable with high tolerance for uncertainty and ambiguity.
- *Fe — Femininity*: Preference for conventional female roles and interests.
- *Sarnoff Survey of Attitudes Toward Life*: A short questionnaire intended to evaluate the strength of conventional ambition for upward mobility and financial rewards. (This questionnaire was contributed to the study by Dr. Irving Sarnoff.) Three subscales were later defined by two independent raters as Motivation for Advancement, Motivation for Money, and general Forward Striving.
- *Q Sort*: Seventy statements were each printed on small individual filing cards. The participants were asked to sort the cards evenly into seven piles according to how characteristic they thought each statement was of themselves. The original MPS Q sort was modified for MCS.
- *California F Scale (Bass)*: A questionnaire designed to measure adherence to conservative values and their rigid enforcement (here called "Authoritarianism"). The version used followed the recommendation of Bass (1955) that each statement in the questionnaire be phrased in both its positive and negative form to avoid acquiescence bias.
- *Rokeach Value Survey*: A set of 18 "terminal" values, such as happiness, wisdom, and self-respect, and a set of 18 "instrumental" values, such as responsibility, ability to forgive, and capability, to be rank ordered separately. No AT&T norms were developed for this survey; median rankings of the values for different groups were simply compared. Administered only at MPS:20 and MCS:0.

Norms

The norms for the tests and inventories described above were not all based on the same population. Some of them had been administered to large representative Bell System samples; in other cases, the MPS participants themselves provided the norms. There were basically four norm groups:

A. A random sample of 585 college graduates employed by the Bell System telephone companies in 1958.
B. A random sample of 300 third-level telephone company managers, 1958-1968 (annual norming of updated test).
C. The 274 college graduate participants assessed in MPS:0.
C-2. The 191 college graduate participants in MPS interviewed in year 1 of the study.
D. A random sampling of 589 college graduates employed by the Bell System telephone companies in 1978.

The following list identifies the norm group for each test and inventory.

Cognitive
Contemporary Affairs   B
Critical Thinking   C
General Information   D
SCAT   A

Personality and Motivation
California F Scale (Bass)   C
California Psychological Inventory (CPI)   D
Edwards Personal Preference Schedule   A
Guilford—Martin (GAMIN)   C
Guilford—Zimmerman (G-Z)   D
Sarnoff   C

Expectations and Attitudes
Expectations Inventory   C
Management Questionnaire   C-2

POSTASSESSMENT CODING

At the conclusion of each assessment center, the following materials were available:

1. Biographical data responses.
2. Test and inventory item responses.
3. Test and inventory scores.
4. Q-sort item categories.
5. Overall observer and participant ratings and rankings in group simulations.
6. Behavioral simulation reports.
7. Interpretive interview reports.
8. Interpretive projective test reports.
9. Ratings of assessment dimensions.
10. Predictions of termination and progress.

In the years following the assessment centers at both MPS:0 and MPS:8, the narrative reports on the assessment center exercises were coded to produce much additional quantitative data. The reports on the group simulations, the In-Basket, and the interview were coded for all relevant dimensions from the list given above.

Interviews conducted at the assessment centers were content-analyzed from two additional points of view. One such coding was for nine life themes, developed and applied by Dr. Joseph F. Rychlak.

· *Marital-Familial*: Spouse, children, in-laws; premarital relationships such as dating and engagement.
· *Parental-Familial*: Parents, siblings, relatives on the parents' side, activities deriving from parents' home.
· *Locale-Residential*: Kind of housing and its location.
· *Financial-Acquisitive*: Wealth and material possessions, including savings, investments, conspicuous consumption, concern with making ends meet.
· *Ego-Functional*: Conditioning and development of the mind and body, including reading, educational pursuits, exercise, self-help efforts, therapeutic activities; concern with disease or disability.
· *Recreational-Social*: Leisure-time pursuits, including hobbies, sports, partying, and socializing.
· *Religious-Humanism*: Ethical and humanistic involvement, not necessarily part of an organized religion; concern with a philosophy of life that acts as an ethic.
· *Service*: Community activities such as the Chamber of Commerce, Boy Scouts, and political parties; excluding church activities (scored under Religious-Humanism).
· *Occupational*: Work life, including job content, supervisors, promotions, raises, attitudes toward the company, and the like.

Each theme was rated in respect to current involvement, current satisfaction, retrospective developments, and projected developments. For an overall impression of the life theme, the four ratings were averaged.

The other content analysis of the interviews was for sociocultural attitudes, developed and applied by Donald D. Gallo and Walter G. Jordan of New York University. Each interview was coded for responses to questions in the interview about the most critical current events the participants believed were facing the country and the company. Each issue mentioned was rated in terms of the participant's position, degree of understanding, and degree of conviction. In addition, the material in each interview was rated from liberal to conservative in respect to political philosophy, social issues, and economic issues, and from dovish to hawkish in military matters.

The projective test interpretive reports were also coded for a special set of nine categories, developed and implemented by Dr. Walter Katkovsky.

· *Achievement/Advancement Motivation*: Extent to which the person is ambitious, motivated, and interested in advancement and success.
· *Self-Confidence*: Confidence of success at work and lack of self-doubts and anxieties concerning success.
· *Work Orientation*: Importance of work in the person's life compared to other things (such as family and recreation), and degree of satisfaction gained from the job compared to other things in life.

- *Dependence*: Extent to which the person needs or seeks help, advice, direction, and encouragement from others.
- *Affiliation*: Interest in being liked and accepted by others, being a part of groups, helping others, and avoiding arguments and friction with others. Extent of participation in group situations and outgoing nature.
- *Optimism*: Degree of optimism about and satisfaction with life in general; degree of positiveness in reaction to most experiences.
- *Leadership Role*: Willingness to make decisions and accept leadership or supervisory responsibilities; strength of dominance or leadership needs.
- *Subordinate Role*: Willingness to act as a follower or subordinate in relationships with others; degree of suggestibility or submissiveness.
- *General Adjustment*: Extent of good adjustment, characterized by high self-confidence and ability to adapt to difficult situations and accept frustrations; lack of feelings of insecurity, stress or anxiety reactions, and emotional conflicts and problems.

Two additional categories were added at MPS:20 and MCS:0:
- *Aggression/Hostility*: Extent to which the person is critical and hostile toward others and has aggressive and negative feelings and reactions to them; readiness to experience and express anger, annoyances, resentments, impatience, and differences with others.
- *Willingness to Reveal Self*: Extent to which the person's responses indicate openness, candor, and a readiness to report specifics about experiences and feelings, especially of a socially undesirable nature; lack of guarded, evasive, or defensive responses.

DATA FROM FOLLOW-UP INTERVIEWS

The participants in MPS were interviewed annually in each of the 7 years between MPS:0 and MPS:8, and again in years 10, 13, 16, and 19 of the study. These interviews, usually referred to as "Personal Follow-Up Interviews," were conducted by a psychologist in an off-the-job location. Like the assessment interviews, they were wide-ranging, covering not only job and career matters but family matters, recreational pursuits, political attitudes, and so forth.

These interviews produced interpretive interview reports and some immediate quantitative material as well. In advance of each tri-annual interview, the participant was asked to complete a biographical form bringing the facts of his life up to date. He also filled out at the times of each of the first seven interviews the Expectations Inventory described above.

An additional questionnaire was also part of the interview procedure for these 7 years. This was the Management Questionnaire, an attitude survey form used widely in the Bell System during the 1950s, which yielded scores on 10 scales reflecting feelings about one's job situation and the organization as a whole. These scales were as follows:

- *Supervision*: Attitudes towards one's immediate boss, including fairness and appreciation of and interest in the participant.
- *Personal Satisfaction*: Satisfaction with various aspects of the job, including responsibility, freedom, variety, challenge, and promotional opportunities.

· *Job Satisfaction*: Global measure of satisfaction with working for the telephone company.
· *Pride*: Pride in working for the company as shown in relating to outsiders.
· *Impersonal Communications*: Satisfaction with information about company policies and the workings of the business.
· *Personal Communications*: Information and freedom of expression between participant and supervisor.
· *Identification*: Feeling of being consulted and appreciated as a member of management.
· *Authority*: Satisfaction with freedom to make own decisions.
· *Salary*: Satisfaction with fairness of salary treatment.
· *General Management Attitude*: Selected items from the other nine scales, somewhat weighted toward attitudes toward supervision; one additional item on confidence in higher management.

All of the interviews were later coded on the life themes and sociocultural scales described earlier. The Personal Follow-Up Interviews eventually yielded the following material:

1. Biographical data responses.
2. Inventory item responses.
3. Inventory scores.
4. Interpretive interview reports.
5. Life theme interview ratings.
6. Sociocultural interview ratings.

At approximately the same time as the participants were being interviewed, someone in each participant's company who was knowledgeable about him was also being interviewed. During the early years of MPS, the interviews were done with someone in the personnel department for fear of influencing careers by approaching bosses. By year 6, however, bosses were being interviewed. These interviews, usually called "In-Company Interviews," were done by telephone company managers borrowed from a company other than the one in which the participant worked. No extensive analysis of these individual interviews has been made as yet, although those through MPS:8 in combination were rated on such aspects as job stimulation and supervisory assignments. Later the interviewers made similar ratings as they wrote up or dictated their interviews. The In-Company Interviews, therefore, have provided the following:

1. Facts about each participant's job and career.
2. Interpretive interview reports.
3. Ratings on job dimensions.

The MCS participants have been interviewed every 2 years since their original assessment, as have their bosses. Because of their wide geographical dispersion, these interviews have been conducted by telephone rather than face-to-face. The participants have also filled out a biographical data form, the Expectations Inventory, and the Management Questionnaire prior to each interview.

MEASURES DERIVED THROUGH FACTOR ANALYSIS

In addition to all the measures described so far, groups of measures were produced by factor analyses of the assessment center dimensions and assessment center tests and ratings. The following list presents those derived from the ratings of the assessment center dimensions at the initial assessment of the MPS and MCS participants. These analyses were done separately for the two groups.

The following list, which shows the assessment dimensions making up each factor, shows MPS and MCS in parallel for easy comparison. It will be recalled that the MCS assessment included 10 dimensions not rated for MPS.

Dimension Factors

MPS	MCS
General Effectiveness	*General Effectiveness*

A higher order factor, additional to those below, made up of all but a few of the dimensions; it appeared to reflect the assessors' overall model of the high potential manager.

MPS	MCS
Administrative Skills	*Administrative Skills*
Organizing and Planning	Organizing and Planning
Decision Making	Decision Making
	Creativity
Interpersonal Skills	*Interpersonal Skills*
Leadership Skills	Leadership Skills
Behavior Flexibility	Behavior Flexibility
Personal Impact	Personal Impact
	Oral Communication Skills
	Perception of Threshold Social Cues
	Self-Objectivity
Intellectual Ability	*Intellectual Ability*
General Mental Ability	General Mental Ability
Range of Interests	Range of Interests
	Written Communication Skills
Advancement Motivation	*Advancement Motivation*
Need for Advancement	Need for Advancement
(−) Ability to Delay Gratification	(−) Ability to Delay Gratification
(−) Realism of Expectations	(−) Realism of Expectations
(−) Need for Security	(−) Need for Security
Energy	Financial Motivation
Work Involvement	*Work Involvement*
Primacy of Work	Primacy of Work
Inner Work Standards	Inner Work Standards
	Energy
Stability of Performance	*Stability of Performance*
Tolerance of Uncertainty	Tolerance of Uncertainty
Resistance to Stress	Resistance to Stress
	Adjustment
	Happiness

Independence
(−) Need for Superior Approval
(−) Need for Peer Approval
(−) Goal Flexibility

Nonconformity
Social Objectivity
Range of Interests
(−) Need for Security
(−) Bell System Value Orientation
(−) Need for Superior Approval

Independence
(−) Need for Superior Approval
(−) Need for Peer Approval
Cynicism
Selfishness

Company Loyalty
Bell System Value Orientation
Need for Security
(−) Goal Flexibility

External Self-Develoment
Range of Interests
Involvement
Avocational Interest
Self-Development

Social Liberalism
Social Objectivity
(−) Conservatism
(−) Religiosity

Additional factor analyses were performed to extract sets of ability factors and personality/motivation factors from the assessment exercises themselves. Included were all the test scores, behavioral ratings given during particular assessment center simulations, and postassessment codings of the projective exercise reports. Dimension ratings made at integration sessions were included in only those very few cases where no other evaluation of a particular exercise was available.

The first of the following lists presents the ability factors; the second gives the personality and motivation factors. Once again, MPS and MCS results are shown in parallel fashion. Asterisks indicate postassessment ratings.

Ability Factors

MPS	MCS
Administrative Ability	*Administrative Ability*
In-Basket overall rating	
In-Basket Organizing and Planning*	Organizing and Planning dimension
In-Basket Decision Making*	Decision Making dimension
	Creativity dimension
Interpersonal Ability	*Interpersonal Ability*
Competitive group overall rating	Competitive group overall rating
Competitive group oral rating	Competitive group oral rating
Competitive group Oral Communication Skills*	

Competitive group Leadership Skills*
Business game overall rating
Business game Forcefulness*
Interview Oral Communications Skills*

Noncompetitive group overall rating
Noncompetitive group oral rating

Cognitive Ability
SCAT Verbal score
SCAT Quantitative score
Critical Thinking Test score
Contemporary Affairs Test score

Cognitive Ability
SCAT Verbal score
SCAT Quantitative score

General Information Test score
Written Communication Skills dimension

Personality and Motivation Factors

MPS

Affability
(+) Affiliation (Edwards)
(−) Aggression (Edwards)
(+) Nurturance (Edwards)
(−) Autonomy (Edwards)

MCS

Affability
(+) Affiliation (Edwards)
(−) Aggression (Edwards)
(+) Nurturance (Edwards)

(+) Succorance (Edwards)
(+) Achievement (Edwards)

Ambition
(+) Motivation for Advancement
  (Sarnoff)
(+) Need for Advancement (interview)
(+) Primacy of Work (interview)
(+) Inner Work Standards (interview)
(+) Forward Striving (Sarnoff)
(+) Dominance (Edwards)

Ambition
(+) Motivation for Advancement
  (Sarnoff)
(+) Need for Advancement (interview)
(+) Primacy of Work (interview)
(+) Inner Work Standards (interview)
(+) Forward Striving (Sarnoff)
(+) Dominance (Edwards)
(+) Achievement/Advancement
  Motivation (projectives)
(+) Work Orientation (projectives)
(+) Leadership Role (projectives)

Impulsivity
(+) Exhibition (Edwards)
(−) Endurance (Edwards)
(−) Deference (Edwards)
(+) Heterosexuality (Edwards)
(−) Abasement (Edwards)
(−) Order (Edwards)
(−) Need for Security (interview)

Impulsivity
(+) Exhibition (Edwards)
(−) Endurance (Edwards)
(−) Deference (Edwards)
(+) Heterosexuality (Edwards)

(−) Intraception (Edwards)
(−) Restraint (G-Z)
(−) Thoughtfulness (G-Z)

Positiveness
(+) Optimism (projectives)
(+) Self-Confidence (projectives)
(+) General Adjustment (projectives)

Leadership Motivation
(+) Leadership Role (projectives)
(+) Achievement/Advancement
   Motivation (projectives)
(−) Subordinate Role (projectives)
(−) Dependence (projectives)
(−) Affiliation (projectives)

Self-Esteem
(+) Ascendance (GAMIN)
(+) Masculinity (GAMIN)
(+) Lack of Inferiority Feelings (GAMIN)
(+) Lack of Nervousness (GAMIN)
(−) Succorance (Edwards)

Positiveness
(+) Optimism (projectives)
(+) Self-Confidence (Projectives)
(+) General Adjustment (projectives)

Submissiveness

(+) Subordinate Role (projectives)
(+) Dependence (projectives)
(+) Affiliation (projectives)
(−) Aggression (projectives)

Adjusted Conformity
(+) Achievement via Conformance (CPI)
(+) Good Impression (CPI)
(+) Intellectual Efficiency (CPI)
(+) Psychological Mindedness (CPI)
(+) Responsibility (CPI)
(+) Self-Control (CPI)
(+) Socialization (CPI)
(+) Tolerance (CPI)
(+) Sense of Well-Being (CPI)
(+) Emotional Stability (G-Z)
(+) Objectivity (G-Z)
(+) Personal Relations (G-Z)
(+) Friendliness (G-Z)

Flexibility
(+) Achievement via Independence (CPI)
(+) Flexibility (CPI)
(−) Authoritarianism (Bass)
(−) Order (Edwards)

Masculinity
(+) Masculinity (G-Z)
(−) Femininity (CPI)

Poise
(+) Dominance (CPI)
(+) Capacity for Status (CPI)
(+) Self-Acceptance (CPI)
(+) Sociability (CPI)
(+) Social Presence (CPI)

(+) Ascendance (G-Z)
(+) General Activity (G-Z)
(+) Sociability (G-Z)

Unconventionality
(+) Autonomy (Edwards)
(+) Change (Edwards)
(−) Communality (CPI)

References

Adelman, C. (1985). *The standardized test scores of college graduates, 1964—1982.* Washington, DC: National Institute of Education.

A good man is hard to find. (1946, March). *Fortune*, pp. 92, 95, 217, 221.

Alper, W. S. (1975). Racial differences in job and work environment priorities among newly hired college graduates. *Journal of Applied Psychology, 60*, 132—134.

Bachman, J., & Johnston, L. D. (1979, April). The freshman, 1979. *Psychology Today*, pp. 79—87.

Baltes, P. B., & Schaie, K. W. (1973). On life-span developmental research paradigma: Retrospects and prospects. In P. B. Baltes & K. W. Schaie (Eds.), *Life-span developmental psychology: Personality and socialization* (pp. 365—395). New York: Academic Press.

Barrett, N. S. (1979). Women in the job market: Occupations, earnings, and career opportunities. In R. E. Smith (Ed.), *The subtle revolution: Women at work* (pp. 31—61). Washington, DC: The Urban Institute.

Barron's profiles of American colleges (14th ed.). (1984). Woodbury, NY: Barron's Educational Series, Inc.

Basler, B. (1986, December 7). Putting a career on hold. *The New York Times Magazine*, pp. 152—153, 158, 160.

Bass, B. M. (1955). Authoritarianism or acquiescence? *Journal of Abnormal and Social Psychology, 51*, 616—623.

Bayley, N. (1955). On the growth of intelligence. *American Psychologist, 10*, 805—818.

Beller, A. H. (1985). Changes in the sex composition of U.S. occupations, 1960—1981. *The Journal of Human Resources, XX*, 235—250.

Block, J. (1971). *Lives through time.* Berkeley, CA: Bancroft Books.

Block, J. (1981). Some enduring and consequential structures of personality. In A. I. Rabin, J. Aronoff, A. M. Barclay, & R. A. Zucker (Eds.), *Further explorations in personality* (pp. 27—43). New York: Wiley.

Blumenthal, K. (1986, March 24). Room at the top. *The Wall Street Journal*, Section 4, A special report: The corporate woman, pp. 7, 9.

Boettinger, H. M. (1977). *The telephone book.* Croton-on-Hudson, NY: Riverwood.

Bray, D. W., Campbell, R. J., & Grant, D. L. (1974). *Formative years in business: A long-term AT&T study of managerial lives.* New York: Wiley.

Bray, D. W., & Grant, D. L. (1966). The assessment center in the measurement of potential for business management. *Psychological Monographs, 80* (17, Whole No. 625).

Brenner, O. C. (1982). Relationship of education to sex, managerial status, and the management stereotype. *Journal of Applied Psychology, 67*, 380—383.

Brenner, O. C., & Tomkiewicz, J. (1982). Job orientation of black and white college graduates in business. *Personnel Psychology, 35*, 89—103.

Bridgman, D. S. (1930). Success in college and business. *Personnel Journal*, *9*, 1—19.

Brief, A. P., & Oliver, R. L. (1976). Male—female differences in work attitudes among retail sales managers. *Journal of Applied Psychology*, *61*, 526—528.

Brooks, J. (1975). *Telephone: The first hundred years*. New York: Harper & Row.

Carroll, P. W. (1982). *It seemed like nothing happened: The tragedy and promise of America in the 1970s*. New York: Holt, Rinehart & Winston.

Christmas, J. J. (1973). Self-concept and attitudes. In K. S. Miller & R. M. Dreger (Eds.), *Comparative studies of blacks and whites in the United States* (pp. 249—272). New York: Seminar Press.

Clarke, J. W. (1973). Race and political behavior. In K. S. Miller & R. M. Dreger (Eds.), *Comparative studies of blacks and whites in the United States* (pp. 517—541). New York: Seminar Press.

Costa, P.T., Jr., & McCrae, R. R. (1986). Personality stability and its implication for clinical psychology. *Clinical Psychology Review*, *6*, 407—423.

Day, D. R., & Stogdill, R. M. (1972). Leader behavior of male and female supervisors: A comparative study. *Personnel Psychology*, *25*, 353—360.

Dickstein, M. (1977). *Gates of Eden: American culture in the sixties*. New York: Basic Books.

Doctorow, E. L. (1984). *Lives of the poets*. New York: Random House.

Dreger, R. M. (1973). Temperament. In K. S. Miller & R. H. Dreger (Eds.), *Comparative studies of blacks and whites in the United States* (pp. 231—248). New York: Seminar Press.

Eichorn, D. H., Hunt, J. V., & Honzik, M. P. (1981). Experience, personality, and IQ: Adolescence to middle age. In D. H. Eichorn, J. A. Clausen, N. Haan, M. P. Honzik, & P. H. Mussen (Eds.), *Present and past in middle life* (pp. 89—116). New York: Academic Press.

Erikson, E. H. (1950). *Childhood and society*. New York: Norton.

Fernandez, J. P. (1981). *Racism and sexism in corporate life*. Lexington, MA: Lexington Books.

Fredrickson, G. M., & Knobel, D. T. (1980). History of prejudice and discrimination. In S. Thernstrom (Ed.), *Harvard encyclopedia of American ethnic groups* (pp. 829—847). Cambridge, MA: Harvard University Press.

Friedan, B. (1963). *The feminine mystique*. New York: Norton.

Friedan, B. (1981). *The second stage*. New York: Summit Books.

Friedan, B. (1985, November 3). How to get the women's movement moving again. *The New York Times Magazine*, pp. 26—28, 66—67, 84—85, 89, 98, 106.

Galbraith, J. K. (1958). *The affluent society*. Boston: Houghton Mifflin.

Gallese, L. R. (1985). *Women like us*. New York: William Morrow.

Giele, J. Z. (1980). Adulthood as transcendence of age and sex. In N. J. Smelser & E. H. Erikson (Eds.), *Themes of work and love in adulthood* (pp. 151—173). Cambridge, MA: Harvard University Press.

Gleason, P. (1980). American identity and Americanization. In S. Thernstrom (Ed.), *Harvard encyclopedia of American ethnic groups* (pp. 31—58). Cambridge, MA: Harvard University Press.

Goldberger, P. (1981, November 8). The new American skyscraper. *The New York Times Magazine*, pp. 69—96.

Goldman, E. F. (1960). *The crucial decade—and after: America 1945—1960*. New York: Vintage Books.

Gourman, J. (1983). *The Gourman report: A rating of undergraduate programs in American and international universities*. Los Angeles: National Education Standards.

Greenhalgh, L., & Gilkey, R. W. (1986). Our game, your rules: Developing effective negotiating approaches. In L. L. Moore (Ed.), *Not as far as you think: The realities of working women* (pp. 135—148), Lexington, MA: Lexington Books.

Greenstein, F. I. (1982). *The hidden-hand presidency: Eisenhower as leader*. New York: Basic Books.

Greer, W. R. (1986, February 22). The changing women's marriage market. *The New York Times*, p. A48.

Harragan, B. L. (1977). *Games mother never taught you*. New York: Warner Books.

Heller, J. (1961). *Catch-22*. New York: Simon & Schuster.

Hellwig, B. (1986, November). How working women have changed America. *Working Woman*, pp. 129—134, 137—139, 142—144, 146, 150—151.

Holt, T. C. (1980). Afro-Americans. In S. Thernstrom (Ed.), *Harvard encyclopedia of American ethnic groups* (pp. 5—23). Cambridge, MA: Harvard University Press.

Howard, A. (1984, August). Cool at the top: Personality characteristics of successful executives. In P. D. Lifton (Chair), *Industrial assessment and personality psychology*. Symposium conducted at the meeting of the American Psychological Association, Toronto.

Howard, A. (1985, August). Assessment center validity after 25 years. In R. F. Silzer (Chair), *Assessment center validity: Recent data and current status*. Symposium conducted at the meeting of the American Psychological Association, Los Angeles.

Howard, A. (1986). College experiences and managerial performance (Monograph). *Journal of Applied Psychology, 71,* 530—552.

Howard, A., & Bray, D. W. (1980, August). Continuities and discontinuities between two generations of Bell System managers. In D. W. Bray (Chair), *Today's college recruits: Managerial timber or deadwood?* Symposium conducted at the meeting of the American Psychological Association, Montreal.

Huck, J. R., & Bray, D. W. (1976). Management assessment center evaluations and subsequent job performance of white and black females. *Personnel Psychology, 29,* 13—30.

Hymowitz, C., & Schellhardt, T. D. (1986, March 24). The glass ceiling. *The Wall Street Journal*, Section 4, A special report: The corporate woman, pp. 1, 4—5.

Jenkins, A. H. (1982). *The psychology of the Afro-American: A humanistic approach*. New York: Pergamon Press.

Johnson, P. (1983). *Modern times: The world from the twenties to the eighties*. New York: Harper & Row.

Jones, L. Y. (1980). *Great expectations: America and the baby boom generation*. New York: Coward, McCann & Geoghegan.

Jurgensen, C. E. (1978). Job preferences (What makes a job good or bad?). *Journal of Applied Psychology, 63,* 267—276.

Kagan, J. (1984). *The nature of the child*. New York: Basic Books.

Kanter, R. M. (1986). Mastering change: The skills we need. In L. L. Moore (Ed.), *Not as far as you think: The realities of working women* (pp. 181—194). Lexington, MA: Lexington Books.

Kantowicz, E. R. (1980). Politics. In S. Thernstrom (Ed.), *Harvard encyclopedia of American ethnic groups* (pp. 803—813). Cambridge, MA: Harvard University Press.

Kasten, B. R. (1986). Separate strengths: How men and women manage conflict and cooperation. In L. L. Moore (Ed.), *Not as far as you think: The realities of working women* (pp. 121—134). Lexington, MA: Lexington Books.

Kennedy, E. (1979, December 2). The booming 80s. *The New York Times Magazine*, pp. 68, 116, 118, 119, 120.

Kerouac, J. (1957). *On the road*. New York: Viking.

Kimmel, D. C. (1974). *Adulthood and aging: An interdisciplinary view*. New York: Wiley.

Kirkpatrick, J. J. (1973). Occupational aspirations, opportunities, and barriers. In K. S. Miller & R. M. Dreger (Eds.), *Comparative studies of blacks and whites in the United States* (pp. 355—373). New York: Seminar Press.

Konar, E. (1981). Explaining racial differences in job satisfaction: A reexamination of the data. *Journal of Applied Psychology, 66,* 522—524.

Lacy, W. B., Bokemeier, J. L., & Shepard, J. M. (1983). Job attribute preferences and work commitment of men and women in the United States. *Personnel Psychology, 36,* 315—329.

Lamm, R. D. (1982, November 28). The economic pie isn't growing, but more Americans need slices. *The New York Times*, p. E15.

Lasch, C. (1978). *The culture of narcissism: American life in an age of diminishing expectations.* New York: Norton.

Leuchtenberg, W. E. (1973). *A troubled feast: American society since 1945.* Boston: Little, Brown.

Levine, A. (1980). *When dreams and heroes died: A portrait of today's college student.* San Francisco: Jossey-Bass.

Levinson, D. J., with Darrow, C. N., Klein, E. B., Levinson, M. H., & McKee, B. (1978). *The seasons of a man's life.* New York: Knopf.

Lewis, P. (1978). *The fifties.* Philadelphia: J. B. Lippincott.

Lewis, P. (1986, December 21). In wages, sexes may be forever unequal. *The New York Times*, p. E20.

Lipton, M. (1986). Successful women in a man's world: The myth of managerial androgyny. In L. L. Moore (Ed.), *Not as far as you think: The realities of working women* (pp. 163—180). Lexington, MA: Lexington Books.

Lindsey, E. H., Holmes, V., & McCall, M. W., Jr. (1986). *Key events in executives' lives.* Greensboro, NC: Center for Creative Leadership.

Lirtzman, S. I., & Wahba, M. A. (1972). Determinants of coalitional behavior of men and women: Sex roles or situational requirements? *Journal of Applied Psychology, 56*, 406—411.

Looft, W. R. (1973). Socialization and personality throughout the life span: An examination of contemporary psychological approaches. In P. B. Baltes & K. W. Schaie (Eds.), *Life-span developmental psychology: Personality and socialization* (pp. 25—52). New York: Academic Press.

Maccoby, M. (1976). *The gamesman: The new corporate leaders.* New York: Simon & Schuster.

MacKinnon, D. W. (1978). *In search of human effectiveness: Identifying and developing creativity.* Buffalo, NY: Creative Education Foundation.

Married couples show more decline in nation. (1981, November 16). *The New York Times*, p. A16.

Maslow, A. H. (1954). *Motivation and personality.* New York: Harper & Row.

Matusow, A. J. (1984). *The unraveling of America: A history of liberalism in the 1960s.* New York: Harper & Row.

McClelland, D. C. (1981). Is personality consistent? In A. I. Robin, J. Aronoff, A. M. Barclay, & R. A. Zucker (Eds.), *Further explorations in personality* (pp. 87—113). New York: Wiley.

McClelland, D. C. (1985). How motives, skills, and values determine what people do. *American Psychologist, 40*, 812—825.

Miner, J. B. (1974). Motivation to manage among women: Studies of business managers and educational administrators. *Journal of Vocational Behavior, 5*, 197—208.

Miner, J. B. (1977). Motivational potential for upgrading among minority and female managers. *Journal of Applied Psychology, 62*, 691—697.

Miner, J. B., & Smith, N. R. (1982). Decline and stabilization of managerial motivation over a 20-year period. *Journal of Applied Psychology, 67*, 297—305.

Mischel, W. (1968). *Personality and assessment.* New York: Wiley.

Moore, L. L. (1986). Introduction. In L. L. Moore (Ed.), *Not as far as you think: The realities of working women* (pp. 1—12). Lexington, MA: Lexington Books.

Moore, L. M., & Rickel, A. U. (1980). Characteristics of women in traditional and non-traditional roles. *Personnel Psychology, 33*, 317—333.

More employers offer child care benefits (1968, December 7). *The New York Times*, p. A33.

Morris, C. R. (1984). *A time of passion: America 1960—80.* New York: Harper & Row.

Morrison, R. F., & Sebald, M. (1974). Personal characteristics differentiating female executive from female nonexecutive personnel. *Journal of Applied Psychology, 59*, 656—659.

Myrdal, G. (1944). *An American dilemma: The Negro problem and modern democracy*. New York: Harper & Row.

Nobile, P. (Ed.). (1971). *The Con III controversy: The critics look at the greening of America*. New York: Simon & Schuster.

Northrup, H. R., & Larson, J. A. (1979). *The impact of the AT&T-EEO consent decree*. Philadelphia: Trustees of the University of Pennsylvania.

Norwood, J. L. (1982). Earnings gap. *Monthly Labor Review, 105* (11), 2.

Office of Strategic Services (OSS). (1948). *Assessment of men: Selection of personnel for the Office of Strategic Services*. New York: Rinehart.

100-point lag found in blacks' S.A.T. scores. (1982, October 5). *The New York Times*, p. A21.

Pettigrew, T. F. (1980). Prejudice. In S. Thernstrom (Ed.), *Harvard encyclopedia of American ethnic groups* (pp. 820—829). Cambridge, MA: Harvard University Press.

Ploski, H. A., & Williams, J. (1983). *The Negro almanac: A reference work on the Afro-American*. New York: Wiley.

Reich, C. (1970). *The greening of America: How the youth organization is trying to make America livable*. New York: Random House.

Reskin, B. F., & Phipps, P. A. (1987). Women in male-dominated professional and managerial occupations. In A. H. Stromberg & S. Harkess (Eds.), *Women Working* (pp. 190—205). Palo Alto, CA: Mayfield.

Reston, J. (1984, July 25). The battle for the dropouts. *The New York Times*, p. A23.

Riesman, D. (1950). *The lonely crowd*. New Haven, CT: Yale University Press.

Rossner, J. (1975). *Looking for Mr Goodbar*. New York: Simon & Schuster.

Rychlak, J. F. (1982). *Personality and life-style of young male managers: A logical learning theory analysis*. New York: Academic Press.

Salinger, J. D. (1951). *The catcher in the rye*. Boston: Little, Brown.

Sanoff, A. F. (1985, March 25). "Your mother did it to you" is an excuse Americans overuse. *U.S. News & World Report*, pp. 63—64.

Sargent, A. G. (1983). *The androgynous manager*. New York: Amacom.

Schaie, K. W. (1965). A general model for the study of developmental change. *Psychological Bulletin, 64*, 92—107.

Schaie, K. W. (Ed.). (1983). *Longitudinal studies of adult psychological development*. New York: Guilford Press.

Schaie, K. W., & Baltes, P. B. (1975). On sequential strategies and developmental research. *Human Development, 18*, 384—390.

Schnall, M. (1981). *Limits: A search for new values*. New York: Clarkson N. Potter.

Schneier, C. E., & Bartol, K. M. (1980). Sex effects in emergent leadership. *Journal of Applied Psychology, 65*, 341—345.

Siegfried, W. D., Macfarlane, I., Graham, D. B., Moore, N. A., & Young, P. L. (1981). A reexamination of sex differences in job preferences. *Journal of Vocational Behavior, 18*, 30—42.

Simpson, P. (1986, November). Why the big backlash is a big bust. *Working Woman*, pp. 164—168, 264—265.

Smelser, N. J. (1980). Issues in the study of work and love in adulthood. In N. J. Smelser & E. H. Erikson (Eds.), *Themes of work and love in adulthood* (pp. 1—26). Cambridge, MA: Harvard University Press.

Stevens, D. P., & Truss, L. V. (1985). Stability and change in adult personality over 12 and 20 years. *Developmental Psychology, 21*, 568—584.

Strober, M. H., & Arnold, C. L. (1984a). *The dynamics of occupational segregation by gender: Bank tellers (1950—1980)*. Paper prepared for the Conference on Gender in the Work Place, sponsored by the Brookings Institution and the Committee on the Status of Women in the Economics Profession, Washington, DC.

Strober, M. H., & Arnold, C. L. (1984b). *Integrated circuits/segregated labor: Women in computer-related occupations*. Paper presented at the annual meeting of the American Educational Research Association, New Orleans.

Sung, Y. H., & Davis, R. V. (1981). Level and factor structure differences in selected abilities across race and sex groups. *Journal of Applied Psychology, 66*, 613—624.

Terborg, J. R. (1977). Women in management: A research review. *Journal of Applied Psychology, 62*, 647—664.

Thernstrom, A. M. (1980). Language: Issues and legislation. In S. Thernstrom (Ed.), *Harvard encyclopedia of American ethnic groups* (pp. 619—629). Cambridge, MA: Harvard University Press.

Thomae, H. (1979). The concept of development and life-span developmental psychology. In P. B. Baltes & O. G. Brim, Jr. (Eds.), *Life-span development and behavior* (Vol. 2, pp. 281—312). New York: Academic Press.

Thornton, G. C., III, & Byham, W. C. (1982). *Assessment centers and managerial performance*. New York: Academic Press.

Time-Life. (1970). *This fabulous century: 1950—60*. New York: Author.

Trost, C. (1986, March 24). The new majorities. *The Wall Street Journal*, p. 15D.

U.S. Bureau of the Census (1975). *Historical statistics of the United States: Colonial times to 1970*, Part 1. Washington, DC: U.S. Government Printing Office.

U.S. Bureau of the Census (1980). *The social and economic status of the black population: An historical view, 1790-1978*. Washington, DC: U.S. Government Printing Office.

U.S. Bureau of the Census (1986). *Statistical abstract of the United States* (106th ed.). Washington, DC: U.S. Government Printing Office.

Veroff, J., Douvan, E., & Kulka, R. A. (1981). *The inner American: A self-portrait from 1957 to 1976*. New York: Basic Books.

Walker, J. E., Tausky, C., & Oliver, D. (1982). Men and women at work: Similarities and differences in work values within occupational groupings. *Journal of Vocational Behavior, 21*, 17—36.

Watson, J. G., & Barone, S. (1976). The self-concept, personal values, and motivational orientations of black and white managers. *Academy of Management Journal, 19*(1), 36—48.

Weaver, C. N. (1975). Black—white differences in attitudes toward job characteristics. *Journal of Applied Psychology, 60*, 438—441.

Weaver, C. N. (1977). Relationships among pay, race, sex, occupational prestige, supervision, work autonomy, and job satisfaction in a national sample. *Personnel Psychology, 30*, 437—445.

Whitbourne, S. K., & Weinstock, C. S. (1979). *Adult development: The differentiation of experience*. New York: Holt, Rinehart & Winston.

White, T. H. (1982). *America in search of itself: The making of the president 1956—1980*. New York: Harper & Row.

Whyte, W. H., Jr. (1956). *The organization man*. New York: Simon & Schuster.

Williams, D., & Peterfreund, S. (1958). *Bell System management men at midcareer*. New York: American Telephone and Telegraph.

Wright, J. D., Rossi, P. H., & Juravich, T. F. (1980). Survey research. In S. Thernstrom (Ed.), *Harvard encyclopedia of American ethnic groups* (pp. 954—971). Cambridge, MA: Harvard University Press.

Yankelovich, D. (1979). Work, values, and the new breed. In C. Kerr & M. Rosow (Eds.), *Work in America: The decade ahead* (pp. 3—26). New York: Van Nostrand Reinhold.

Yankelovich, D. (1981). *New rules: Searching for self-fulfillment in a world turned upside down*. New York: Random House.

INDEX